4357

The Cross in the Dark Valley
The Canadian Protestant Missionary Movement in the Japanese Empire, 1931-1945

The Cross in the Dark Valley
The Canadian Protestant Missionary Movement in the Japanese Empire, 1931-1945

A. Hamish Ion

Wilfrid Laurier University Press

This book has been published with the help of a grant from the Humanities and Social Sciences Federation of Canada, using funds provided by the Social Sciences and Humanities Research Council of Canada.

We acknowledge the financial support of the Government of Canada through the Book Publishing Industry Development Program for our publishing activities.

Canadian Cataloguing in Publication Data

Ion, A. Hamish.
 The cross and the rising sun

Includes bibliographical references and index.
Vol. 3 has title: The cross in the dark valley.
Partial contents: v. 3. The cross in the dark valley : the Canadian Protestant missionary movement in the Japanese Empire, 1931-1945.
ISBN 0-88920-977-4 (v. 1)   ISBN 0-88920-218-4 (v. 2)
ISBN 0-88920-294-X (v. 3)

1. Protestant churches – Missions – Japan – History. 2. Protestant churches – Missions – Korea – History. 3. Protestant churches – Missions – Taiwan – History. I. Title.

BV3445.2.I65 1990   266'.00952'09   C90-093683-5

© 1999

WILFRID LAURIER UNIVERSITY PRESS
Waterloo, Ontario, Canada   N2L 3C5

Cover design by Leslie Macredie, using a 1927 photograph of the social service staff at Aiseiken, Kameido, Tokyo. Reproduced by permission of the Archives of The United Church of Canada, Victoria University, Toronto, Ontario.

Printed in Canada

The Cross in the Dark Valley has been produced from camera-ready copy supplied by the author.

All rights reserved. No part of this work covered by the copyrights hereon may be reproduced or used in any form or by any means—graphic, electronic or mechanical—without the prior written permission of the publisher. Any request for photocopying, recording, taping or reproducing in information storage and retrieval systems of any part of this book shall be directed in writing to the Canadian Reprography Collective, 214 King Street West, Suite 312, Toronto, Ontario M5H 3S6.

TO

STEVE JONES AND UJIHARA KOSAKU

Contents

Acknowledgments	x
Abbreviations	xi
Illustrations	xii
Introduction	1

CHAPTER ONE
Undertones of the Past	9
The Early Development of the Japanese Protestant Movement	10
Canadian Missions in Japan	22
Progress in North Korea	28
Foothold in North Taiwan	31

CHAPTER TWO
Toward the Kingdom of God: Evangelism and Social Concern in Japan	35
The Depression, Christian Revival, and Kagawa	36
The Evangelistic and Social Work of the United Church Mission	39
Canadian Anglicans and the Revival	48
Canadian Presbyterians and Koreans in Japan	53

CHAPTER THREE
On the Colonial Frontier	57
On the Border	58
The Manchurian Crisis	62
With Goforth in Manchuria	68
Financial Cuts in Korea	72
Staying On in North Taiwan	75

CHAPTER FOUR
The Shrine Question 81
    The Shrine Question in Japan 82
    Conflict in North Korea 92
    Tensions in North Taiwan 100

CHAPTER FIVE
Educational Work in Japan 113
    Girls' Schools in Japan 113
    The Kwansei Gakuin 127

CHAPTER SIX
Specialized Educational and Medical Work 142
    The Canadian Academy 143
    The Canadian Anglican Kindergarten Training School 147
    The New Life Sanatorium at Obuse 151
    Educational Work among Koreans in Japan 155

CHAPTER SEVEN
Contrast in the Colonies: Educational and Medical Work in Korea, Manchukuo, and Taiwan 158
    Budgetary Challenges and Educational Work in Korea 159
    Boys' and Girls' Schools in Korea and Manchukuo 160
    Dealing with the Colonial Authorities 166
    Training Evangelists in Manchukuo 171
    Medical Work in Korea 173
    Difficulties in Taiwan 178
    The Happy Mount Leprosy Colony 182

CHAPTER EIGHT
Missionary Life in Japan and Its Empire 186
    Growing Up in Japan 187
    Young and Old Missionaries in Japan 193
    Living and Working in Rural Japan 200
    Contrast in the Japanese Empire 202

CHAPTER NINE
Canadian Missionary Attitudes to Politics in Japan 210
    Darkening Clouds of Ultranationalism 212
    The 26 February 1936 Incident and Its Aftermath 214
    The Marco Polo Bridge Incident
        and War in North China 215
    The Nanking Atrocities and the Continuing War 222

Changkufeng, Nomonhan, and Fear of the Soviet Union ..	224
Chiang Kai-shek and the China Crisis	228
Typhoon Weather	230

CHAPTER TEN
Growing Pressure for Church Union in Japan 238
    The Twists and Turns on the Road to Church Union 240
    The Marco Polo Bridge Incident and Its Aftermath 243
    Nipponteki Kirisutokyo and Overseas Evangelism 247
    Growing Pressure for Union 256
    The Salvation Army Crisis 260
    United Church Missionaries and the Impending Union..... 261
    The Predicament of the NSKK 266

CHAPTER ELEVEN
Union and Withdrawal 272
    Making Missionary Adjustments 273
    Withdrawal from Mid-Japan 281
    Canadian Presbyterian Evacuation from Taiwan,
        Manchukuo, and Japan 291

CHAPTER TWELVE
Into the Fires of War 296
    The Japanese Christian Deputation 297
    Working on in Japan and Korea 300
    The Nippon Kirisutokyodan and the NSKK 304
    Internment 312
    Hoping for the Best 316

Conclusion 325
Notes 343
Select Bibliography 399
Index 418

Acknowledgements

Many people have been kind enough to lend me their support and encouragement while I wrote this book, and it is my pleasure to thank them publicly. I am especially grateful to Professor Matsuzawa Hiroaki of the International Christian University, Tokyo, for his help and kindness over many years. I owe a debt of gratitude to Professor Sugii Mutsuro of Doshisha University, Kyoto, for his help during the initial stages of my research into the Japanese Christian movement during the 1930s. Likewise, Professor Sumiya Mikio was unstintingly generous during a later stage of my research with his advice and assistance, not the least of which was access to his magnificent personal collection of materials and rare books relating to the Japanese Christian movement now housed in the Hikaku Bunka Kenkyujo of Tokyo Joshi Daigaku. Nakamura Naoko and other staff members of the Hikaku Bunka Kenkyujo and at the library of Tokyo Joshi Daigaku have always been extremely kind in facilitating my research. Professor Takahashi Masao and other members of the Nihon Purotestanto Shi Kenkyukai in Tokyo have also been most encouraging over the years. Dr. William F. Honaman and Paul R. Sakata at the Provincial Office of the Nippon Seikokai made available to me the collected historical materials in the Provincial Archives and introduced me to other holdings at Neeza campus of Rikkyo University, Tokyo.

I must thank Professor John Howes of Oberin University, Tokyo, and the University of British Columbia, Vancouver, for his sharing his vast knowledge about the early Japanese Protestant movement with me. Dr. Ian M. Gow, director of the Centre for East Asian Studies, University of Sheffield, England, was as ever most encouraging and helpful with his advice.

I owe a particular debt to John Holmes, who provided me with his written reminiscences and tape recordings of his boyhood days in Japan. The archivists at the United Church of Canada Archives, Victoria College, University of Toronto, at the General Synod Archives, The Anglican Church of Canada, Jarvis Street, Toronto, and at the Archives of the Presbyterian Church of Canada, recently moved from Knox College, University of Toronto, were extremely helpful. I hope that this book helps to underline the value of the archives of Canadian missionary societies as a source of information about Japan, Korea, and Taiwan.

A. Hamish Ion

Abbreviations

APCC	Archives of the Presbyterian Church in Canada
APPC	*Acts and Proceedings of the General Assembly of the Presbyterian Church in Canada*
BDFA	*British Documents on Foreign Affairs: Reports and Papers From the Foreign Office Confidential Print*
CC	*Christian Century*
CR	*Chinese Recorder*
FS	*Fukuin Shimpo*
JCQ	*Japan Christian Quarterly*
KS	*Kirisutokyo Sekai*
KSMK	*Kirisutokyo Shakai Mondai Kenkyu*
KS (NSKK)	*Kirisutokyo Shuho*
MSCEC	Missionary Society of the Church of England in Canada
NAC	National Archives of Canada
NCC	National Council of Churches
NKRDJ	*Nihon Kirisutokyo Rekishi Dai Jiten*
NMJ	*Nippon Mesojisuto Jiho*
NSKK	Nippon Seikokai
PR	*Presbyterian Record*
RJ	*Renmei Jipo*
UCC BFM	The United Church of Canada Board of Foreign Missions
UCCYB	*The United Church of Canada Year Book*

Illustrations

PLATE

1. Quiet before the storm of the Depression...................................... xiii

2. Bishop and the missionary staff of Mid-Japan diocese, 1936...... xiii

3. The NSKK Church at Takata... xiv

4. The Sanatorium at Obuse.. xiv

5. The missionary residences at Hamheung, Korea.......................... xv

6. Missionary, staff and kindergarten class....................................... xv

7. Missionary group at Lungchingtsun, Manchuria, 1933................. xvi

8. Sewing for the war effort.. xvi

PLATE 1.—Quiet before the storm of the Depression. A rare photograph of the social service staff at the Aiseiken, Kameido, Tokyo, taken in the late 1920s, including Annie Allen and Evelyn Lackner, seated in the first row third and fifth from the left, respectively. (The Archives of The United Church of Canada, Victoria University, Toronto)

PLATE 2.—Bishop and the missionary staff of Mid-Japan diocese, 1936. Seated in the second row at the extreme left is P. S. C. Powles. Bishop Sasaki Shinji is in the centre and Victor Spencer is on the extreme right. Horace Watts is standing in the third row, third from the right. (Anglican Church of Canada, General Synod Archives)

PLATE 3.—The NSKK Church at Takata. (Anglican Church of Canada, General Synod Archives)

PLATE 4.—The Sanatorium at Obuse. (Anglican Church of Canada, General Synod Archives)

PLATE 5.—The missionary residences at Hamheung, Korea. (The Archives of the United Church of Canada, Victoria University, Toronto)

PLATE 6.—Missionary, staff and kindergarten class. Nora Bowman is in the centre of the back row of this group taken in the late 1930s in Mid-Japan diocese. (Anglican Church of Canada, General Synod Archives)

PLATE 7.—Missionary group at Lungchingtsun, Manchuria, 1933. *First row, left to right*: Billy Ross, Rita Black, Jean Ross, David Black, Frank Black, Bobby Ross. *Second row, left to right*: Beulah Bourns, Mrs. Black, Helen McLellan, Ann Armstrong, Pearl Bacon, Hugh Bacon, Mrs. A. Ross. *Third row, left to right*: George Bruce, Emma Palethorpe, Dr. Donald Black, A. R. Ross, Alice Ross, Roland Bacon. (MacRae Collection, The Archives of the United Church of Canada, Victoria University, Toronto)

PLATE 8.—Sewing for the war effort. Sewing class for kindergarten teacher trainees in the late 1930s. (Anglican Church of Canada, General Synod Archives)

Introduction

The foreign missionary movement was a significant aspect of the history of Japan's international relations with the West during the early twentieth century. This book studies the end of the missionary age in the history of Japanese-Canadian international relations.[1] Because Japan was an imperial power, this study also investigates the end of the missionary age in Canada's relations with Japan's two major colonies, Korea and Taiwan, and with Japan's client state of Manchukuo. It focusses on the experience of the Canadian Protestant missionary movement between 1931 and 1945 to shed further light on the challenges to, and the responses of, both the broader Western missionary movement and the Japanese Christian movements during years of unprecedented crisis, turmoil, and challenge. It is about the end of an era in Japanese relations with the West, an era that began with the appearance of Commodore Perry's squadron in Tokyo Bay in 1853 and finished with war and occupation. By looking at the example of a small group of Western residents, this study investigates the tensions, misunderstandings, and sympathies that contributed to the breakdown of international informal and personal relations.

The Canadian Protestant missionary experience was exemplified by the activities of missionaries belonging to the United Church of Canada, the Anglican Church of Canada, and the Presbyterian Church in Canada. This work concentrates on the experiences of the United Church missionaries because their numbers were larger and their activities more extensive than those of their Anglican and Presbyterian colleagues. The purpose is not to provide a detailed history of these missions and their theologies but to tell a worthwhile story about a group of Canadian men and women and their Japanese, Korean, and Taiwanese counterparts who still strove to remain open to the reciprocal influences of cultural interaction despite the approaching roar of war and the harangues of xenophobes. Even so, no Christian phoenix would rise out of the ashes once the fires of war were spent. The missionary age died in failure.

The fifteen years from the Manchurian incident of September 1931, which led to the Japanese military occupation of, and political control over, that Chinese province, to Japan's surrender in August 1945 at the end of the Pacific War, form a watershed in Canadian-Japanese relations. Since 1945, a new era in Canadian-Japanese relations has emerged, but it has as yet failed to fix in the minds of most ordinary Japanese a sense of Canada as a distinct cultural and national entity separate from the United States of America. This failure stems in part from a growing provincialism within Canada itself, which increasingly makes it difficult for the Canadian abroad to project cultural and societal values that are representative of the country as a whole rather than of a particular region. However, the end of the missionary age is the concern of this book, not what has followed it.

This age in Canadian-Japanese relations extended some eighty years between 1872 and 1945. During this time, the missionary movement was the predominant link between the peoples of Canada and Japan. Its beginning was marked by the arrival of the Canadian Presbyterian George Leslie Mackay, the first Canadian missionary in East Asia, in Taiwan in 1872. The memory of Mackay is still revered by Taiwanese Christians.

Certainly from 1872 until the opening of the Canadian Legation in Tokyo in May 1929, the Canadian Protestant missionary movement was the chief vehicle of contact between the peoples of the Japanese Empire and Canada. Because initially there was a lack of Canadians proficient in Japanese at the new legation in Tokyo, the Department of External Affairs still had to rely on the British Foreign Office for much of its information about Japan.[2] Because the prime concerns of the legation were bilateral issues of trade and immigration, the missionary movement remained an important link between peoples, especially given the low-keyed nature of Canadian-Japanese diplomatic relations throughout the 1930s.

Indeed, Robert Wright, in his recent study of Canadian Protestantism and the quest for a new international order in the interwar years, has stressed not only that English-Canadian views of the non-Western world in general were shaped to a large extent by missionaries but also that Canadian churches "laid much of the groundwork in the interwar period for Canada's postwar approach to foreign aid and development."[3] Clearly, the international role that Canadian churches played through the overseas missionary movement provided a reason for church and missionary leaders in Canada to carry on a debate concerning those overseas affairs.

With the exception of the Japanese military, the Japanese Christian movement received the most publicity of all things Japanese in the West in the years prior to Pearl Harbor. This movement was a mirror in which the characteristics of the broader Japanese society were reflected to Canadian Christian audiences. Yet this image of Japan was modified as it reached this transpacific audience because Japan could not be divorced from its empire. Reports from Korea alphabetically followed those from Japan in United Church of Canada missionary publications. The same was true of the work of Canadian Presbyterians in Formosa (Taiwan), among the Koreans in Japan, and in Manchukuo (Manchuria). Whereas the Cold War in East Asia drew closed the Bamboo Curtain after 1949, isolating Japan, its culture, people, and politics from continental Asia, imperial responsibilities prior to 1945 joined Japan to the continent with the mailed links of military power and the will to rule. However, caution has to be exercised in order not to exaggerate the degree of missionary influence on Canadian public opinion and on Canadian foreign policy.

Although there was some Canadian academic and journalistic interest in Japan, expressed most clearly through the conferences of the Institute of Pacific Relations and the Canadian Institute of International Affairs, there was generally little specialized knowledge of Japanese culture and language in Canada.[4] A. R. Lower, for instance, a specialist in Canadian history and a Canadian nationalist, was interested in East Asian problems more by the hope of creating a Canadian place in Pacific affairs than by a concern for East Asia per se. In investigating Canadian-Japanese diplomatic relations during the 1930s, Gregory A. Johnson has argued that, for fear of upsetting the equilibrium of the North Atlantic triangle, timidity characterized the Canadian approach to East Asia. Johnson is highly critical of the Canadian government for surrendering the initiative in Far Eastern affairs to the United States and Britain.[5] However, given the lack of a Canadian military presence on either side of the Pacific, it is difficult to see how Canada could have had a significant influence in international response to the political events in East Asia during this time. In fact, there is every indication that Canadian diplomats, despite their limited resources, served Canadian interests in Japan remarkably well.

Nevertheless, the presence of Canadian diplomats in Tokyo after 1929, did not bring an immediate and profound change in Canadian-Japanese relations. And the missionary age limped on until a second and clear period began in Canadian-Japanese relations following the end of the Pacific War. But the turmoil of the old period between 1931 and 1945 casts a long shadow on the achievements of the Canadian missionary movement in the Japanese Empire during its first sixty years.

Despite its failure to convert many people to Christianity, the Canadian missionary movement in Japan, Korea, and Taiwan, the major constituents of the Japanese Empire between 1872 and 1931, achieved considerable success. From small beginnings, the missionary endeavour grew to include hundreds of Canadian workers in metropolitan Japan and its two colonies. Canadian missionaries founded churches, schools, hospitals, and other specialized institutions. And the social work of Canadians drew the attention of Japanese authorities to hitherto neglected areas such as the plight of impoverished industrial workers living in slum areas. Even in their leisure activities, Canadian missionaries had significant influence on Japanese society; they introduced the idea of the summer cottage to the Japanese and focussed interest in outdoor activities such as hiking, mountain climbing, and tennis. The translation of *Anne of Green Gables* into Japanese made a story of childhood in Prince Edward Island a favourite for generations of Japanese girls. Missionaries themselves wrote books, which are still being read, about Netsuke, Japanese Buddhism, and the history of the Korean people.[6]

The men and women who made up the Canadian missionary movement worked to achieve a common Christian aim in the mission field. There is a danger in overemphasizing the differences and exaggerating the antagonisms between the men's and the women's missionary movements. During the 1930s, relations between male and female missionaries were cordial and free from controversy. Foreign missionary work traditionally gave Canadian single women a respected and envied occupation in which neither their unmarried status nor their gender was a barrier to their success.[7] This remained true in the 1930s, but the demands of modernization, often enforced by government regulations, meant that the opportunity for female missionaries without specialized skills or linguistic ability became increasingly limited in the Japanese Empire. Furthermore, the separate-spheres approach to missionary work summed up in the slogan "women's work for women," which had characterized their late-nineteenth-century endeavours, had begun to disappear. Especially in medical work, female missionaries had adopted modern standards of professionalism that transcended notions of gendered work.[8]

Even though, by the 1930s, single women provided the numerical backbone of the Canadian missionary endeavour in the Japanese Empire, their voices often remain silent in its history. There is a wealth of information concerning the Christian work that female missionaries undertook, but the broader political, social, and economic trends in Japan and its empire normally elicited little comment. In contrast, leading figures among male missionaries, often at the behest of the missionary society authorities in Toronto, commented at length on such matters. In the last months before the Pacific War, there were differences in attitude between male and female missionaries in regard to the wisdom and the need of missionary withdrawal from Japan, differences that can be attributed to the emphasis that each put on changes taking place both inside and outside the Christian movement. Inevitably, the opinions of male missionaries dominated the discussion of events and trends beyond the Christian sphere. It is not possible to create a balance of views between male and female missionaries. This imbalance in no way detracts from the crucial importance of female missionaries in the Canadian missionary endeavour in the Japanese Empire, for it was they, and not their male counterparts, who bore the brunt of evangelistic work in rural areas and carried on the bulk of educational work. However, in an era of dramatic and rapid political, social, economic, and religious change, neither male or female missionaries could remain immune to internal and external pressures that threatened the very existence of the missionary movement and its Western connections.

Although Canadian-Japanese relations since the signing of the surrender document on board USS *Missouri* have become increasingly complex and diverse, the legacy of contact between Canadians and Japanese prior to 1931 remains potent and positive. Both Canadians and Japanese can point to the missionary age as a time when individual Canadians made lasting impressions upon Japanese society. The history of Canadian-Japanese relations since 1945 must take into account the cold realities of trade, and it lacks much of the warmth of individual contact that characterized the earlier years of the missionary age. Indeed, though it might be a manifestation of their lack of knowledge of the broader Canadian society, the Japanese, like their East Asian neighbours in China and Korea, see certain individuals as representing the essence of what they wished to believe are broad Canadian characteristics. Thus the fascination of the Chinese for Norman Bethune, of the South Koreans with Frank Schofield, and of the Japanese with E. H. Norman. Two of these three figures, of course, were closely connected with the Protestant missionary movement in the prewar Japanese Empire: Schofield was a missionary in Korea between 1916 and 1920, and Norman, the diplomat-historian, was the son and brother of Canadian missionaries in Japan, with Bethune, the medical doctor and communist sympathizer, the odd man out.[9] However, Bethune was a harbinger of a secular Canadian commitment to China and East Asia, which has characterized Canadian connections to that region since the end of the Pacific War.

The exigencies of the East Asian situation after 1931 caused most of the Canadian missionaries in the Japanese Empire to withdraw before the beginning of the hostilities in the Pacific in December 1941. However, the 1930s also saw the coming together of various trends both in the Christian movement and in government policies toward Christianity. The policies of the Japanese government, aimed at bringing Christianity and other religions in Japan and its colonies under its control, were an aspect of the emperor system, or *tennosei*, the name given to the prewar political system by which imperial authority was used to promote national unity and to maintain it in the face of rapid societal change.[10] The *tennosei* system, as it developed from its beginnings in the Meiji era, sought to bring all facets of Japanese life under government control. It particularly affected the Christian and missionary movements in the areas of Christian education and religious organization. In order to achieve its ends, the government used legislation or imperial rescripts to regulate Christianity in Japan and its colonies. Because freedom of religion had been guaranteed in the Meiji Constitution (although its meaning was open to interpretation), the government often resorted to the excuse that its demands were suprareligious. For example, during the 1930s, this explanation was used by the government and widely accepted by Christians and missionaries in Japan over the shrine question. This crucial issue, which confronted Japanese Christians as well as those in Korea and Taiwan in the mid-1930s, was over the attendance of Christians at ceremonies at state Shinto shrines (ultimately, most Christians did attend).

The shrine question of the 1930s can be taken as a watershed, because government authorities would allow no interpretation of *tennosei* other than their own. The interest of national security, against which there was no recourse, was another gambit used by the government in order to ensure compliance to its directives. By the beginning of the 1940s, the persecution of new religions such as Omotokyo and of Christian groups such as the Salvation Army revealed to the Japanese Christian movement the serious consequences of noncompliance.

Government pressure in the form of legislation, the implied threat of punishment by the thought-control police, or the social ostracization of Japanese Christians on the grounds of disloyalty also contributed to the creation of a single Protestant denomination (the Nippon Kirisutokyodan) in June 1941. But it is doubtful whether the Nippon Kirisutokyodan (*Kyodan*) could have come into being so swiftly and easily without the existence of opinion within the Japanese Christian movement itself in favour of a similar goal. A precondition of the success of the government-forced amalgamation of Protestant denominations was the strong movement for church union led by the Japanese National Council of Churches (NCC). Indeed, one of the major themes in the history of the Japanese Christian movement in the 1930s was this cooperative search for ecclesiastical unity led by the NCC. Yet in the decade that preceded the formation of the Kyodan, the government had an almost uncanny ability to strike responsive chords within the Christian movement, of which the internal desire for church union was only one. By its policies, the government freed the church in Japan from real or imagined vestiges of Western control, and it gave the Kyodan the hope of a vital role in the expansion of Christianity in East Asia. Distaste for any form of foreign control, as well as desire for a special role in leading the Christian movement in East Asia, were powerful forces in the Christian movement. Coupled with these forces was Japanese Christian bewilderment at the negative response of missionaries in Japan, especially American ones, to the Manchurian incident of 1931, which gave further impetus to the Japanese desire to become independent of outside control.

Since the 1880s, the Western missionary movement had been separated from the Japanese Christian movement. For their part, Canadian missionaries had refused to give up control over money received from Canada. They had retained the principalships and deanships of the schools and colleges that Canadians had founded. For over half a century, missionaries had maintained a privileged position free from Japanese control. In the 1930s, the Western missionary movement, including Canadian missionaries, paid the price for its separation from the Christian movement. Faced with pressure from the government to rid the Christian movement of Western influence, Japanese Christian leaders were loath to defend the need for a missionary presence in Japan. They believed that the missionary movement was no longer essential to the continuation of the Christian movement in Japan and its empire.

Missionaries nonetheless remained loyal to the Japanese Christian leadership and sympathetic to the Japanese people. During the 1930s, Canadian missionary attitudes toward Japan were sharply at variance with those of the majority of Canadians at home. This variance was a manifestation of the decline of the influence of the missionary movement, which had historically served as a trusted and important interpreter of Japan to the Canadian people. Naturally, this decline was not simply restricted to Canadian missionaries in Japan.[11] Nevertheless, regardless of their prewar views, the Canadian government was not adverse to using missionaries in Japan for expertise, especially in language training for the military and in military intelligence in the Pacific theatre.

The question of how missionaries and Japanese Christians alike were changed by their contact with each other is a fascinating one, especially during years when stereotypical and racist views of Japanese and Westerners were hardening in both Japan and Canada. Reports of Japanese mistreatment of Koreans and Chinese were a significant factor in the growth of anti-Japanese feeling in North America. The fate of the Christian movements in Korea and China was intimately connected to what happened to the Christian movement in metropolitan Japan. Likewise, as the Japanese Empire expanded into Manchuria, north China, and Southeast Asia as a result of military conquest, the Christian movements in those areas came under the aegis of Japan. Any consideration of the Japanese Christian movement has to take into account its overseas implications and the responsibility of missionaries for what occurred. Indeed, the overseas activities of the Japanese Christian movement must be regarded as one of its most important facets during the Pacific War, for large numbers of Christians in the Japanese Empire and occupied territories came under its jurisdiction.

The vacuum left by the withdrawal of missionaries from the mission field of colonial Korea in the late 1930s was filled by Japanese Christian leaders. Without missionary protection, the Korean Christian movement was defenceless against persecution by the Japanese colonial authorities. The Christian leaders in charge of the Korean Church were viewed by the Japanese government general with the greatest suspicion. This was especially true after the spirited stand of Korean Christians over Shinto shrine worship. Furthermore, given the acquiescence of Japanese Christian leaders to the demands of their government at home, it was extremely doubtful whether they would have had the courage to challenge any government regulations in order to protect Korean Christians.

During the halcyon days of the Independence Movement of 1 March 1919, Frank Schofield and other Canadian missionaries had stood up against the Japanese military and had readily sympathized with their Korean and Chinese converts, who sought to avoid Japanese suzerainty. In the mid-1930s, American missionary opposition to participation in the Shinto shrine ceremonies precipitated a crisis that led to the withdrawal of many American missionaries from educational work in protest to government general policies. Misjudging the resolve of colonial officials to achieve their goals, the protest did not bring about change in Japanese colonial policies. It did, however, leave the missionary movement in disarray and much weakened to face the severe challenges from the Japanese authorities at the end of the decade. The response of Canadian missionaries in northern Korea to the shrine issue was different from that of many of their American colleagues. They were not prepared to sacrifice their educational endeavour (and forfeit a considerable investment in plant, property, and history) on a controversial matter of principle that would leave their Korean Christian constituents unprotected against the whims of Japanese colonial officialdom.

But nothing could have prepared missionaries in the Japanese Empire for the grave challenges of the 1930s. Few had been struck from Cromwellian flint or possessed the iron ardour for their faith of a Richard Baxter. Yet they became the first Canadian casualties in a war that the Japanese waged to prevent Western ideas from infiltrating their cultural traditions.

The Pacific War tore apart the Japanese Empire forever. Before it ended, the picture world of convert, hospital, and mission station—which had brought northern Korea and the borderlands of Manchuria as close as the next town to thousands of Canadian Sunday school children—had vanished. A close bond between ordinary folks in town and country Canada and those far beyond the western shore of the wide Pacific had dissolved. The destruction of the missionary age coincided with the shrinking of the known world.

CHAPTER ONE
Undertones of the Past

The Protestant movement in Japan has always been small. During the 1930s, it numbered some 300,000 people.[1] Yet, despite its size, an impressive nationwide network of Christian churches, schools, and organizations for social welfare gave the movement a visible presence in Japanese cities that belied its few members. Although they came from all walks of life and all social classes, the majority of Protestants belonged to the middle class and lived in the major urban centres. Likewise, though there were some forty different denominations representing a broad spectrum of Christian views, most belonged to one of the four major denominations: the Nihon Kirisuto Kyokai (Presbyterian), the Kumiai (Congregationalist), the Japan Methodist, and the Nippon Seikokai (NSKK, Anglican).

By the 1930s, the Protestant movement in Japan had a history that stretched back over sixty years. Although Japanese Christians could look back with considerable pride on their achievements, the Protestant movement was clearly at an important crossroads in its development, partially because of the emergence of new leaders of the Protestant movement as elder leaders passed away.[2] However, long-standing issues both theological and secular often confronted the movement as it entered the 1930s. Some of these issues were of considerable importance to the future relations of the Canadian missionary movement with the Japanese Protestant movement. Of concern were Japanese Christian attitudes to Japanese nationalism, the unique attributes of Japanese Christianity, the place of Western missionaries in the development of Japanese Protestantism, the overseas role of the Japanese Protestant missionary movement (especially in Korea), and the ecumenical movement.

The prime themes of Christian reflection were enunciated by influential Meiji or Taisho Japanese Christian leaders or opinion makers whose ideas served as antecedents to the arguments of Japanese Christian leaders during the late 1930s. As far as Canadian missionaries were concerned, the legacy of the early development of the missionary movement in Japan—with its burden of mission interest in educational and social welfare institutions—restricted their responses to the concerns of the Japanese Protestant movement. The development of Protestantism in Japan before the 1930s points to the gradual divergence of the Western missionary movement and the Japanese Protestant movement into two solitudes largely independent of each other. In the past, strong personal ties between the older Japanese Christian leadership converted in the early Meiji period and Canadian missionaries had helped to bond the Canadian missionary endeavour and the Japanese Protestant movement together. These ties became weaker as the older generation of Japanese Christian leaders passed away. Another meeting point between Canadian missionaries and the Japanese Christian leadership was in the various national evangelistic campaigns, such as that conducted by the Continuation Committee of the Edinburgh Conference during World War I or the Kingdom of God Movement during the early 1930s.

The responses of Korea and Taiwan were different than that of Japan. The political conditions in, and the geographical circumstances of, the northern Korea-Manchuria borderlands, where Canadian Presbyterian missionary work was concentrated, brought missionaries and Korean Christians together.

THE EARLY DEVELOPMENT OF THE JAPANESE PROTESTANT MOVEMENT

Christianity was introduced into Japan in the mid-sixteenth century when St. Francis Xavier landed in southern Kyushu. For nearly a century, Jesuit and later Franciscan and Dominican missionaries propagated the Gospel in Kyushu and southern Honshu. Yet, by the early seventeenth century, all missionaries had been driven out of Japan and Christianity had been proscribed, more for political reasons than religious ones.[3] Indeed, it was not until after the signing of the treaties between Japan and the Western powers in 1857 and 1858 that missionaries were able to reside in Japan again. Even so, it was only after diplomatic pressure upon the Japanese government in 1873 that missionaries were allowed to proselytize among the Japanese, and the official proscription of Christianity was not removed until the promulgation of the Meiji Constitution in 1889.

During the 1870s, Protestant development was characterized by the emergence of groups of young converts, often referred to as bands, who had been first attracted to Christianity by Western lay people or missionary teachers at new Western studies schools.[4] Unlike in the sixteenth century, when mass conversions were typical, conversion to Protestantism in the late nineteenth century took place on an individual basis.[5] Kenneth and Helen Ballhatchet have noted that "the most notable feature of early Protestant Christianity in Japan was the conversion of a significant group of educated Japanese *ex-samurai* who emphasized the importance of self-support and independence."[6] Many of these ex-samurai had been adherents of the defeated Tokugawa side at the time of the Meiji Restoration, and it has been argued that their loss of status and their suffering caused by the Meiji Restoration, as well as their lack of hope in finding success in the secular world were among the reasons for their conversion to Christianity.[7] At the same time, patriotism for the new Japan motivated many of the young converts, because they believed that Christianity was the essence of Western civilization and that their conversion would enable Christianity to become the religion of the spiritual restoration aimed at the creation of a new Japan.[8] Missionaries did little to contradict this view. Certainly, early Japanese-language Christian journals such as *Shichi Ichi Zappo* (1875–83) skilfully combined explanations of the latest Western scientific inventions, descriptions of world travel, and Christianity.[9] Likewise, many converts were attracted to Christianity because they thought that Christian ethics were superior to the Confucian ethics with which they were familiar.[10] Furthermore, it was often through reading Chinese-language Christian texts that Japanese converts acquired their first knowledge of Christianity.

Matsuzawa Hiroaki has pointed out that many converts, as they became more familiar with Western ideas, also picked up prejudices against both Chinese and Japanese traditional culture.[11] With the introduction of scientific scepticism and Darwinian ideas into Japan in the late 1870s, the link between Christianity and Western civilization and progress was seriously challenged.[12] Japanese Christians responded to the threat posed by scientific scepticism, most notably by taking up the pen and founding the *Rikugo Zasshi* (1880–1921), a journal published by the Tokyo Seinenkai (YMCA) that contained articles and commentary on a broad range of philosophical, political, social, and economic subjects, as well as on Christianity.[13] During the late 1870s and early 1880s, moreover, some leading intellectuals also criticized Christianity because of its Westernization.[14]

The proper relationship between Japanese Christians and their society bedevilled Japanese Christianity from its beginnings. In this, Japanese Christians were the victims of two factors: first, the historical perception of Christians held by both the authorities and many of their fellow Japanese as a result of the Japanese experience with Christianity in the early seventeenth century; and second, the historical method of dealing with Christians, which was persecution. The imprisonment and exile of the Urakami crypto-Christians by the Japanese government after the Meiji Restoration showed that Christianity, even as late as 1872, was regarded as a danger to the state. Many of the early Protestants encountered hostility from family members and acquaintances as well as from Buddhists and Shintoists. The arguments put forward in the anti-Christian treatise *Bemmo* by the Confucian scholar Yasui Sokken in 1873 not only summed up the traditional Japanese criticism of Christianity but also pointed to the crux of opposition, which was that the Western religion threatened to disturb Japanese society and its form of government.[15] That form of government was presided over by the emperor, to whom loyalty at all levels was expected. Although the Meiji Constitution of

1889 granted religious freedom to Japanese Christians, the Imperial Rescript on Education of 1890 brought further problems for Christians in Japan.

A collision between religion and education was brought to the fore with the accusations of disloyalty levelled in 1891 at Uchimura Kanzo, the founder of the Mukyokai (Non-Church Movement), who was then a teacher at the Tokyo First Higher Middle School, for lowering his head rather than bowing to the Imperial Rescript on Education during a school assembly.[16] As Janet Hunter has perceptively pointed out, this incident was "a clear indication of the perceived incompatibility of Christian belief with loyalty to the Japanese state."[17] Despite religious freedom for Christians, the perception that Christianity was not adaptable to Japan and could not be harmonized with the Imperial Rescript on Education had not changed.[18] A fierce controversy broke out as Christians strove to show that Christianity was not incompatible with traditional Japanese customs and public morals.[19]

The opportunity for Christians to show their loyalty to the Japanese state came with the outbreak of the Sino-Japanese War in 1894.[20] The few pacifists were outnumbered by those who strove to demonstrate their support for Japan's cause by providing comfort for bereaved families, disseminating information that justified the war, and performing other useful activities in their neighbourhoods. War became the medium through which Japanese Christians could most visibly show that they were as patriotic and nationalistic as their non-Christian fellow citizens. As war broke out three times for Japan in the twenty years from 1894, Japanese Christians had ample chances to prove their loyalty to emperor and country. During the Russo-Japanese War, the Japanese Seinenkai (YMCA) was active in providing comforts for troops overseas.

As well as patriotically supporting Japan's war efforts against China and Russia, Japanese Christians searched for a suitable relationship between Protestantism and the Japanese intellectual tradition. Many were influenced by liberal theological views. Of particular attraction to them was the fact that theological liberalism sought to divorce Christianity from its cultural association with the West.[21] Liberal Protestants did not have the strong belief in the superiority of Christianity to other Japanese religions that had generally been held in the late nineteenth century. Some liberal Protestants believed that a creative rapprochement between Buddhism and Christianity was both possible and necessary.[22] Others thought when it came to the evangelization of Japan, that Christians should study the national spirit of Japan and do nothing either to offend it, particularly the relation of the Japanese to the emperor, or to condemn the Japanese veneration of imperial ancestors and their own ancestors.[23]

One of the most interesting features of Japanese Christianity was its syncretism. Uchimura Kanzo, influenced by orthodox Christian views, held that the best Christian converts had never given up the essence of Buddhism or Confucianism but had welcomed Christianity because it helped them to become more like their own ideals.²⁴ Even a Quaker, Nitobe Inazo, claimed that bushido—the warrior code of feudal Japan—was the soul of the country. As late as 1931, Nitobe continued to believe that "before very long the Christian faith, enriched by the intellectual treasures of centuries and deepened by Oriental mysticism, will be a part of the forces which will drive the nation towards its destiny."²⁵ By the intellectual treasures of centuries, Nitobe was clearly referring to the positive influence of Confucianism, Buddhism, and bushido. Yet, though bushido could serve as a bridge between the warrior tradition and Christian ethics, Professor Notehelfer has pointed out that it could "also be internalized as an ethical construction intended to serve only the Japanese state as the Ministry of Education confirmed in the 1930s."²⁶ Although critical of bushido, Imai Judo, a leading Japanese High Anglican, believed that "Yamato damashii—the spirit of Japan—cannot suffice but must be purified, renewed and perfected in its union with Christ."²⁷ Here Imai enunciated a widely held High Anglican view that there was much good in Japanese culture but that it needed Christianity to perfect it. The affirmation of traditional Japanese concepts was also clearly designed to identify Japanese Christians with their cultural heritage, from which they had been distanced by their acceptance of Christianity.

During the Meiji and Taisho periods, Protestantism had exerted a significant influence on emerging popular movements for social and political change.²⁸ Some early Japanese Christians had been active in the Popular Rights Movement of the 1880s. In the following decade, Christians had been among the leaders of the first major environmental protest over the pollution caused by the Ashio Copper Mine. A number of the early leaders of the Japanese socialist and labour movements were Christians or influenced by Christianity.²⁹ The importance of Christianity and Japanese Christians in these two movements was largely in heightening social awareness of certain problems and in providing the initial leadership for new organizations. Sumiya Mikio has pointed out that the working-class and socialist movements had individual freedom and social reform as their main objectives, ideals shared by Christianity. However, social reform was not as strong an element in Christianity as in socialism, with the result that Christian influence on the socialist movement declined.³⁰ By the early 1920s, the role of Christians in the leadership of mass social and political movements had greatly declined and these movements became increasingly radical in the face of the hardening resistance of the ruling elite to fundamental change in the structure of Japanese politics and society.

Christian influence was important in the early development of rural as well as urban movements. Christians Kagawa Toyohiko and Sugiyama Motojiro were important in the initial organization of the tenant-farmer associations and in the Zenkoku Suiheisha, an organization for the outcaste class. Kagawa was a proponent of social Christianity, but his theology retained most of the basic beliefs of orthodox Christianity.[31] He stressed the active participation of Christians in the problems of society, especially in helping to improve the conditions of the poor and the underprivileged. Within the Protestant movement itself, however, these activities had to contend with considerable hostility from Church leaders who did not wish Christianity to be seen as opposing the status quo. As Cyril Powles has indicated, if socialists who were Christians wished to be fully accepted by the Church, then it meant "forsaking socialism."[32] As a result, many Christian political and social activists either abandoned their Christian beliefs or so moderated their political and social views that they did not challenge the existing system.

For some Christians, however, their religion was the foundation of the political doctrine of democracy and the fundamental principle behind their pursuit of the goal of universal suffrage.[33] Yoshino Sakuzo, a Tokyo Imperial University professor, was one of the foremost opinion leaders in the movement for parliamentary democracy during the Taisho period. His conception of democracy was based on the Christian belief in universal brotherhood, which for him was the banner for the worldwide endeavour to create a new world. He was thus unable to compromise with Marxism, which consented to the necessity of class struggle to raise the working class to a level where their worth as human beings would be affirmed. For Yoshino, there was an intimate relationship between democracy and Christianity because they both emphasized personalism.[34]

Even at the height of their influence, however, political and social activists made up only a small minority of Christians. As it failed to attract politically and socially concerned young people, the Protestant movement began to lose much of its earlier dynamism as a force actively supporting the liberalization of politics and the amelioration of social conditions. This does not imply that Christian interest in social welfare work among the slum dwellers of Tokyo and Osaka, lepers, prostitutes, and those stricken with tuberculosis disappeared. However, such work was largely palliative and did not attack the root causes of social distress. By the end of the 1920s, theologically orthodox views that eschewed political and social activism in favour of inward-looking spiritual concerns had come to dominate the thinking of most Japanese Christians.

Yet, if there was controversy about the role of Japanese Christians in social and political movements at home, there was much less debate about Japanese Christianity's overseas role. The identification of Japanese Christianity with Japanese national aspirations is clearly seen in its support of Japanese expansion abroad. Indeed, missionary work overseas became a major vehicle for the Japanese Christian movement to show that its patriotic interests coincided with those of the state. The importance of the overseas activities of the Japanese Christian movement within the context of patriotism should not be underestimated. Japanese missionary work in Taiwan followed in the path of Japanese colonialization. However, nowhere was the importance of Japanese missionary work to the Japanese Church at home made clearer than in Korea. Furthermore, overseas missionary work, with the possibility of reforming the spiritual and physical lot of Koreans and other colonial subjects in the cause of Japan, served as an outlet for the energies of a Japanese Christian movement whose early influence on the new political and social movements at home was declining.

Although the Japanese Christian movement had been interested in mission work in Korea since the signing of the unequal Treaty of Kangwha between Japan and Korea in 1876, the establishment of the Japanese residency generalcy in Korea in 1905 increased this interest dramatically. At first, this activity was only among Japanese residents, but it quickly extended to include Koreans. The Kumiai (Congregationalist) Church was the most active Japanese Church in Korea, and its mission work there has been described as the "religious spearhead of Japanese imperialism."[35] This is an overstatement, for the extent of Japanese missionary work in Korea was always small, and its role cannot be equated with that of British missions, for instance, in India and Africa. In an essay on "Japan's New Responsibilities" published in October 1905, Nitobe, the Japanese Quaker and colonial expert, stressed that the world meaning of the Russo-Japanese War was the liberation of Asia from Europe through Japanese leadership, and he urged that Japanese colonialization take over the management of Korea.[36] Implicit in this view was also a missionary responsibility for Japanese Christians. The attitudes of the Chosen Mondai Kenkyukai (Korean Problems Study Group) in the Hongo Church in Tokyo, among whose members was Yoshino, revealed that Japanese Christians supported the idea of a benevolent Japanese colonization of Korea and viewed the Russo-Japanese War in terms of a civilized Japan fighting a tyrannical Russia.[37] At this stage, it was clear that many Japanese Christians sympathized with Japanese policies toward Korea.

Behind this support was the belief of many Japanese Christians that their fellow citizens would hold adverse opinions of Christianity if the Protestant movement did not participate in the colonization of Korea. Indeed, some Christians considered that the fate of Christianity in Japan was linked to the ability of the Japanese to evangelize the Koreans.[38] It was thought that the same anti-Christian sentiment existed in both Korea and Japan and that failure in Korea would mean a similar failure in Japan. Some Japanese Christians thought that missionary work was needed in the peninsula because Koreans had become completely Japanese after the annexation of their country in 1910, but others simply saw Korea's colonization as having been God given.[39]

In Japan itself, certain influential non-Christians, such as the leading politician Okuma Shigenobu, willingly supported the Japanese missionary movement. Some zaibatsu, notably Mitsui, also contributed funds. In the years immediately after 1910, however, the Japanese government general in Korea gave the most financial support to missionaries. The Japanese gendarmerie told Koreans that if they were Christians they had to attend Kumiai churches. Likewise, if a Korean Christian belonged to a Japanese church, he or she was able to obtain special tax relief and received favourable treatment from the gendarmerie. The government general also helped to finance Christian activity in Korea by funding an increase in the number of Japanese churches and mission schools.[40]

The provision of public funds for the support of Japanese missionary work abroad was the rule rather than the exception. In 1920, the South Sea Island Missionary Association, founded shortly after Japan had received the League of Nations mandate over the former German possessions in the Pacific, was given a sizable grant by the navy department.[41] This level of support was later continued by the Japanese government itself. Clearly, through their support of Japanese missionary work in Korea and the South Sea islands, the Japanese colonial authorities were attempting to utilize Japanese Christianity as a means of controlling their colonial subjects.

As well as in Korea and the South Seas, the Nippon Kirisutokyo Kyokai had begun missionary work as early as 1903 in Manchuria among the Japanese residents of Mukden. By 1912, the Japanese Presbyterians had also established a church for Manchurian Chinese. Likewise, by 1914 they had three churches for Korean Chinese. This missionary work had grown by 1930 to include nine churches for Manchurian Chinese and sixteen for Korean Chinese.[42] After the Manchurian incident in 1931, Japanese missionary effort quickly expanded as Japanese responsibilities for Manchukuo became apparent.

There were opponents to Japanese missionary work in Korea and elsewhere, but they were a minority. However, especially after the independence demonstrations in Korea on 1 March 1919, some Japanese Christians began to criticize their government's colonial policies, including Yoshino Sakuzo, who had given up his earlier idea that Korea could be ruled through a benevolent Japanese government general. Yoshino came to agree with a small number of critics who thought that the central Japanese colonial policy of assimilation was impossible and therefore that Korean independence was inevitable.[43]

While still a junior professor at Tokyo Imperial University, Yanaihara Tadao, a disciple of Uchimura Kanzo and a specialist in the economics of colonization, was sharply critical of Japanese colonialism.[44] Yanaihara, who had also been a pupil of Nitobe Inazo, continued through the 1930s to espouse ideas that had their intellectual roots in the thinking of Uchimura and Nitobe. After the Manchurian incident in 1931, Yanaihara came to believe that, unless the Japanese state was fundamentally reorientated, its military expansion into China and beyond would ultimately lead to national destruction.[45] One of the crucial issues for Yanaihara was "how to reinterpret *kokutai*, especially its relationship with Christianity and Christians' responsibility in this task, and how Japan's old tradition could be transformed into a new one without destroying the past heritage. His unique interpretation of *kokutai* constituted the foundation of his evangelistic campaign for peace."[46] About Yanaihara, Fujita Wakao has stressed that "his patriotism and love of the imperial family was inspired by Christianity. In this regard, he was very different from ordinary patriots, who hoped to promote the national polity based upon Shinto. It was on precisely this point that he clashed headlong with the dominant tides in prewar Japan."[47]

Whereas Yanaihara held clear opinions about Japanese colonial policies, many Japanese Christians faced a dilemma concerning Japanese colonial rule. Because the Japanese missionary movement was effectively assisting the colonial administration and being subsidized by it, it was difficult or impossible for Christians to support missionary work and to criticize colonial policy. Furthermore, Japanese Christian leaders felt a sense of responsibility to take over missionary work in Japanese colonies and occupied territories from Western missionaries. There remained, however, the widespread belief among Japanese that the loyalty of the Christian movement was less than that of non-Christians. The criticisms of Yasui Sokken concerning Christianity had still not been put to rest, nor would they be before 1945.

Yet the difficulties that the Japanese Christian movement faced within Japan were partially obscured to outsiders by the wide swath that its leaders cut in international Christian circles. By the turn of the century, Japanese Christian leaders had already gained a respected position abroad and were represented at all major missionary conferences, including the Pan-Anglican Conference at Lambeth in 1907 and the World Missionary Conference in Edinburgh in 1910. Likewise, Japanese Christian representatives attended the Jerusalem Conference in 1928 and the Madras Conference in 1938.

Visiting Western missionary plenipotentiaries at the World's Student Christian Federation Conference in 1907 and at the Conference of the World Sunday School Association in 1920 were dazzled by Japanese hospitality, interpreted as a sign of the high esteem in which Christianity was regarded in Japan. Western delegates were impressed by the many receptions held for them by leading Japanese political figures. Although the Japanese government was not an advocate of Christianity, it extended hospitality to visiting overseas delegates at international Christian conferences as part of the general desire of Japan to gain international esteem.

The recognition given to Japanese Christian leaders and the Christian movement in Japan by Western Christians was based in part on the hopeful assumption that if Japan was Christianized then much of East Asia would also become Christian.[48] In 1913, the ever-optimistic John R. Mott, a leading figure in the American YMCA movement, writing about Christian prospects in Japan, noted that "this field, like China, is dead-ripe unto harvest."[49] Clearly, he thought that the prospects for future growth in Japan were excellent. Between 1913 and 1916, the Continuation Committee of the Edinburgh Conference— made up of missionaries and Japanese Christians—mounted a significant interdenominational evangelistic campaign throughout Japan.[50] Although the campaign failed, despite Mott's hope, to increase Church membership significantly, it did bring most Protestant denominations into close cooperation in evangelistic work. The NSKK was the only major denomination that did not whole-heartedly enter into the evangelistic campaign.

In 1922, the ecumenical movement in Japan came to a climax with the formation of the NCC (National Council of Churches, which superseded the Japan Federation of Churches). The NCC included not only most Protestant denominations, with the major exception of the NSKK (which eventually joined in 1929), but also Christian schools, social institutions, the YMCA, the YWCA, and the WCTU (Women's Christian Temperance Union). Although its actual power over individual denominations was limited to moral persuasion, the NCC did play an important role in coordinating the cooperative endeavours of the Protestant movement. Increasingly, the NCC also assumed the duty of representing the Protestant movement in its dealings with the Japanese government.[51]

The NCC was also deeply involved in supporting evangelistic initiatives. The most important of them was the Kingdom of God movement, discussed by the NCC as early as 1928. The importance of this movement and its impact on the direction of evangelistic efforts of both Japanese Christians and Western missionaries during the first half of the 1930s cannot be overestimated. Simply, under the leadership of Kagawa Toyohiko, it was the largest interdenominational evangelistic endeavour in the history of Japanese Christianity.[52] It had the support of all the major Protestant groups in Japan. Furthermore, the connection between this united evangelistic effort and the growing movement toward church union in the early 1930s needs to be stressed.[53]

The international missionary movement also strongly supported the Kingdom of God movement. Indeed, this foreign support for Kagawa's evangelistic movement was illustrative of the close ties between the NCC and the Western missionary movement. In April 1929, the IMC (International Missionary Conference), headed by Mott, held a special cooperative meeting at which Kagawa's proposal for the Kingdom of God movement was heard and approved.[54] The first phase of the movement lasted for three years, from April 1929 to November 1932. Central to the endeavour was Kagawa, who had been deeply involved for twenty years in the labour, the farmers, and the union movements. In November 1932, the first phase of the Kingdom of God movement came to an end with a conference of the groups involved. It was decided, and subsequently approved by the All Japan Christian Cooperative Conference and at the Tenth Renmei (Union) General Conference, to continue the Kingdom of God movement for a further two years, until December 1934. Unlike the first three years, directed toward mass evangelism, the second phase focussed on rural evangelism, factory evangelism, and the spread of Christian ideas in schools. In rural evangelism, the development of Farmers Gospels Schools was advocated; in factory evangelism, better coordination between groups through conferences was proposed. Support remained strong from Japanese Christian and missionary organizations, including the NCC, which continued to provide publicity for the movement through helping to publish its evangelistic newspaper. The emphasis of the second phase of the Kingdom of God movement parallelled the interests of United Church of Canada missionaries in rural and urban evangelistic work.

The focus of the second phase also owed much to the NCC's interest in rural evangelism. This interest had been stimulated by a resolution supporting rural evangelistic efforts at the IMC Jerusalem Conference. In July 1931, a Rural Evangelistic Cooperation Conference, the first of its kind in Japan, established an organization for rural evangelism under NCC auspices. The NCC also established and supported until 1935 a research centre for rural culture. However, in addition to interest in rural evangelism, the NCC arranged a cooperative conference on factory evangelism in Tokyo in May 1932 and a second conference in Osaka the following year. As with rural evangelism, there was cooperation between the NCC and the Kingdom of God movement in factory evangelism.

The NCC was also deeply concerned with Christian education in Japan. Again, some of its interest in this issue stemmed from outside influence. In April 1929, Mott addressed conferences in Kamakura and Nara and raised the question of Christian education. In September 1931, a twelve-person Commission on Christian Education in Japan was made up of four American Christian educators and eight Japanese connected with Christian education. The report of this commission was published in New York in 1932[55] and called for the establishment of one union theological college in the Kansai and another in Tokyo, as well as for the creation of a union university. Charles Bates, a United Church missionary, who served on the committee, gave the impression privately that this was not a good time for the idea of a new university to be raised and that even if it were established, its practical value would be somewhat problematic.[56] The problem for Bates, who was the president of Kwansei Gakuin University, was that an extensive Christian university system, albeit along denominational lines, already existed in Japan. However, the NCC made no commitment toward the creation of such a university before the opening of the Pacific War.

Clearly, the NCC was influenced in its endeavours in Christian education and in rural and factory evangelism by the ideas of Mott and others in the international missionary movement. The NCC saw cooperation between Japanese and Western Christian leaders as important in helping to solve the problems of evangelism and Christian education in Japan.[57] Nevertheless, despite this cooperation, the second phase of the Kingdom of God movement was not as successful as the first phase. Dohi Akio has pointed out that the second phase was hindered by the liberal movement within the Christian community and "the advance of Fascist control" in secular politics.[58]

Although the Kingdom of God movement saw close cooperation between Japanese Christians and Western missionaries, political events in East Asia caused the relations between the two groups to become increasingly strained. The Manchurian incident of 1931 was a crucial watershed, for during it Japanese Christian opinion of missionaries, especially American ones, dramatically changed midstream. In early 1932, the NCC stood out against the Manchurian incident by appealing to the government to make it clear both at home and abroad that the Japanese people held in regard the League of Nations, the Nine-Power Treaty, and the Kellogg Pact. At the same time, the NCC used its international connections to appeal to Christians overseas to implore governments to help in bringing about a peaceful settlement between China and Japan.[59] By doing this, the NCC hoped for a quick solution to the Sino-Japanese question. Among those who came out strongly against the actions of the Japanese military and government was Kashiwagi Gien, one of the most famous elder pastors in the Kumiai Church.[60] However, few Christians appeared to support Kashiwagi's outspoken condemnation of Japan's actions.

The critical point was the decision of the League of Nations to condemn Japanese actions. Inside Japan, Japanese Christians were confronted with the severe protests of Western Christians against Japanese machinations in Manchuria. The attitude of the United States seemed particularly unyielding, and American missionaries in Japan appeared to support this position. The Japanese Protestant Church was bewildered by this missionary stance.[61] Clearly, Japanese Christians felt let down by American missionaries in Japan. By their hostility toward Japanese policies during the Manchurian crisis, missionaries themselves contributed to the Japanese Christian desire to be independent of them. By the time of the Shanghai incident of 1932, many Japanese Christians had accepted the Japanese army's position.[62]

Although the NCC was careful not to alienate missionary support, it was at the forefront of encouraging church union, which would help to give the Japanese Protestant movement greater independence from foreign control. As early as 1928, the NCC set up a special committee of members representing a wide range of churches to look at the problem of church union.[63] The chairman was Presbyterian minister and historian of Japanese Christianity Yamamoto Hideteru, and its secretary was Ebisawa Akira, a Congregationalist pastor. Support for ecumenicalism during the 1920s was clearly reflected in Yamamoto's obviously biased but still important history of Japanese Christianity published in 1929.[64] Yamamoto emphasized the various attempts to break down denominational barriers and to develop church union from the formation of the Yokohama Band onward.[65] It was apparent by the end of the 1920s that the Japanese Christian movement, with the NCC at its head, was eager to bring about church union among Protestant denominations.

The movement toward church union was clearly welcomed by such an influential Japanese Christian as Nitobe Inazo. In October 1929, in an article in the *Japan Christian Quarterly* on the penetration of the life and thought of Japan by Christianity, Nitobe suggested that union was imminent despite the great number of different Christian groups.[66] He saw the union not only of churches but also of educational institutions as important to exerting better Christian influence on Japan. Even though Nitobe suggested that "we are in a very hopeful stage in our task of Christianizing this country,"[67] it was clear that without unified endeavour in the future the Christian movement would remain weak.

The beginning of the 1930s saw the movement gain momentum and important support. In 1930, the American "Laymen's Mission," which visited Japan that year, was seen as a spur to amalgamation.[68] In the same year, the Nippon Kirisuchan Kyokai amalgamated with the Kumiai Church.[69] Whereas Nitobe might have seen union as a means of overcoming the weakness of the Christian movement at the end of the 1920s, Ebina Danjo, one of the most influential Japanese Congregationalist pastors, saw the need for a revitalized Christianity. In July 1931, Ebina argued that Japan needed "a philosophical Christianity which will satisfy the longing of the philosophical mind of the Japanese; secondly, it needs a social gospel capable of meeting the present difficult situation; finally, it needs a cosmopolitan Christianity which is capable of giving a basis for a commonwealth of nations."[70] Ebina did not want a Christianity bound by time-worn doctrines, but, in emphasizing the need for a living Christianity, he was much more positive in terms of the possibilities for Christianity than Nitobe had been two years earlier. At the same time, his call for a "cosmopolitan Christianity," laudable as that concept might be, shows much wishful thinking, for these views were expressed only a few months before the Manchurian incident and at the beginning of a decade characterized by nationalistic thought both inside and outside the Japanese Christian movement.

In the aftermath of the Manchurian incident, Kozaki Michio,[71] the son of famous Congregationalist Kozaki Hiromichi and a rising leader in the Japanese Christian movement in his own right, strongly urged church union. In December 1932, Kozaki, in an article in the Congregationalist magazine *Kirisutokyo Sekai*, made a number of important points concerning church union that were commonly shared by other Japanese advocates of union. He argued that there was no history in Japan that could serve as a reason for the continued existence of church denominations. Kozaki thought that the intellectual challenges that confronted Christianity from both the left and the right made it necessary for Japanese Protestants to have a union agreement in order to respond effectively to these threats. And he believed that, as the amount of aid from overseas lessened over time, it was necessary to concentrate the strength of Japanese Protestants in one church. It was argued that a cooperative evangelistic effort such as the Kingdom of God movement could be used to bring the various denominations together, and in this way progress could be made toward church union.[72] The clear test of Protestant will to create a united church came in 1933 with the negotiations between the Kumiai and Presbyterian Churches, two of the three major Protestant denominations. However, their respective representatives, meeting in Kyoto, failed to reach agreement because of theological differences. Following this attempt, the Presbyterian appetite for union particularly slackened. Indeed, after the Marco Polo Bridge incident in 1937, which helped to revitalize the church union movement, it was the Methodists who were at the forefront. Even though church union was not immediately achieved, Kozaki remained committed to this goal through the 1930s. Indeed, he became one of the most influential figures in the Kyodan when it was eventually formed in 1941.

The sophistication of the Japanese Christian movement was in keeping with the highly developed society in which it worked. However, despite its complex organization, the chief challenge for the movement at the beginning of the 1930s was to increase its membership. There was also a desire among missionaries and Japanese Christians alike to make their work relevant to the needs of Japanese in both urban and rural areas.

CANADIAN MISSIONS IN JAPAN

In the summer of 1873, two pioneer missionaries of the Wesleyan Methodist Church in Canada landed at Yokohama to begin the first Canadian mission in Japan.[73] The Canadian Anglicans began their work in Japan some years later. In 1887, the autonomous NSKK (Nippon Seikokai) was formed in Osaka by one American and two British Anglican missions.[74] In response to their appeal for missionary reinforcements, the first Canadian Anglican missionary was sent to Japan.[75] Quickly, female missionaries also extended their work into the mission field. The Woman's Missionary Society (WMS) of the Methodist Church of Canada owed its genesis in 1880 to the needs of the mission field in Japan.

Although independent of the male missionary society, especially in financial matters, the WMS was to work in harmony with the male authorities of the Methodist Church of Canada—or so it was hoped. Tensions did arise, particularly when the women found their male colleagues inclined to disregard the autonomy of the WMS. Rosemary Gagan has described the relationship between male and female Canadian missionaries between 1881 and 1895 as "two sexes warring in the bosom of a single mission station,"[76] but by and large in Japan the WMS and its male counterpart did cooperate successfully.

Coming later into mission work than the Canadian Methodists, the

Canadian Anglicans saw from the start the need for single female missionaries.[77] The major areas of endeavour for the female Anglican missionaries, as for their Methodist counterparts, were women's education and evangelistic work among women. Although some of the women missionaries had excellent academic credentials, they were prohibited because of their sex from becoming priests. Furthermore, because most, especially those engaged in evangelistic work, were single, they were expected to endure a degree of isolation and even physical hardship that their married counterparts refused to accept. Although male missionaries most often received the kudos for missionary success, most missionaries were female. Without the backbone of self-sacrificing single female missionaries, the Canadian missionary endeavour in Japan would have had little impact beyond the successes of its first years.

The intention of the first missionaries in Japan was to establish a Methodist Church patterned on the Canadian model. In their determination to duplicate Western church organization as well as that denomination's theology and discipline, they made few concessions to the sensibilities of Japanese culture and society, and it is somewhat surprising that they were able to make any headway at all. Happily, they began their work in Japan at a propitious time, for the Japanese government had just ceased its prohibition of Christianity, and forward-looking Japanese desired instruction from Westerners. The pioneer Canadian missionaries shared what would come to characterize early Canadian work in Japan: an ability to serve as a catalyst for changes desired by respected Japanese colleagues.

Although missionaries saw evangelism as the central task, with education looked upon as an adjunct, changing attitudes toward Christianity during the late 1870s led the missionary movement away from teaching in Japanese-owned schools and toward establishing their own mission schools. Indeed, Sumiya Mikio has even suggested that it was the Canadian Methodists who set the standard for mission schools.[78]

The opening of mission schools marked the beginning of a change in the relationship of the missionary movement to the indigenous Christian movement and to Japanese society at large. By founding schools, missionaries hoped to eliminate their dependency on the whims of Japanese individuals and to dissipate the impact of temporary currents within society on mission development. The continued existence of the missionary movement after the 1880s was linked more closely than before to the Japanese acceptance of Westerners in their midst. Missionaries could no longer be removed by the cancellation of individual contracts, only by the wholesale rejection of things Western. Missionary investment and commitment in Japan were concrete and integral parts of Western relations with Japan. And, because of its physical investment in Japan, the missionary movement was cushioned against all but the most extreme reaction of the Japanese against the West.

Female education was a particularly important and successful area of missionary endeavour. During the Meiji era, Japanese authorities did much less for female education than for male education. The rise of mission schools for girls also coincided with the arrival of female missionaries in Japan. In 1884, the Canadian Methodist WMS opened its first school for girls, the Toyo Eiwa Jo Gakko in Azabu, Tokyo.[79] From the start, this school was a resounding success. The Toyo Eiwa Jo Gakko offered to teach Japanese girls all the Western graces and could compete with the best girls' schools in Tokyo.

The success of the Toyo Eiwa Jo Gakko led to the opening of two other schools, both located outside the capital. In 1887, the WMS opened the Shizuoka Eiwa Jo Gakko,[80] and two years later a third girls' school was opened in Kofu in Yamanashi Prefecture.[81] The three Canadian Methodist schools eventually offered education from kindergarten to high school, following a curriculum similar to that of government or other state-recognized schools. The schools offered more hours of English tuition and morals classes than did government girls' high schools. The syllabus of the morals classes extended from the Imperial Rescript on Education to Bible study, the latter receiving particular stress. As well as providing high school education for girls, the WMS wanted to increase women's opportunities for higher education. To meet this goal, the Canadian Methodists cooperated with three American missions to found, in 1918, the Tokyo Woman's Christian College (Tokyo Joshi Daigaku). If Tokyo Joshi Daigaku represented the pinnacle of the WMS's educational endeavours, then at the bottom were kindergartens run by WMS missionaries in virtually all the Canadian Methodist mission stations. Although far from glamorous, the rural kindergartens especially had a lasting local influence and created an abiding link between hundreds of ordinary Japanese and WMS missionaries.

The WMS effort in education was marked by growth and sustained success, but the results of the Canadian Methodist educational endeavour on behalf of boys were less impressive. The authorities considered male education vital; thus, the government was prepared to regulate the curriculum of private boys' schools. The government's attitude did much to undercut mission schools' potential as an evangelistic agency. The girls' schools faced serious competition from only a handful of government schools; boys' schools, by contrast, had to compete with an impressive range of both state and private schools. Whereas government financing provided state schools with excellent facilities, mission schools lacked such resources and largely came to be second-class institutions that attracted second-class students.

This problem was not initially clear when the Toyo Eiwa Gakko opened in Azabu, Tokyo in 1884. For fifteen years or so, the Toyo Eiwa Gakko met with some success as a mission school. In 1899, the Ministry of Education prohibited religious teaching in any school approved to grant government diplomas. The Canadian Methodists thought that to obey the new regulations would be disloyal to their Christian supporters at home. They decided, therefore, to sever their formal connection with the Toyo Eiwa Gakko, which became the independent Azabu Middle School.

For some time afterward, the Canadian Methodists were loath to engage in educational work. In 1907, however, with the formation of the Japan Methodist Church, through the union of the American Episcopal Methodist North mission, the American Episcopal Methodist South mission, and the Canadian Methodist mission, an opportunity for cooperation in educational work with the other two Methodist missions reappeared. In 1909, the Methodist Episcopal South mission invited the Canadian Methodists to join them in the educational project that they had begun in Nishinomiya, near Kobe. By 1910, this school, the Kwansei Gakuin, consisted of a middle school and a theological seminary, with a total of more than 400 students.

The aim of the proposed united educational endeavour was to build a college of higher learning, and a college department that gave courses in literature and commercial science was added to the existing school. This was the first time that Canadian Methodists had embarked on a major endeavour not completely under their control and outside their established Tokyo-Shizuoka-Kofu triangle. But, though the Canadian Methodists did assist the Methodist Episcopal North mission in Tokyo with the development of Aoyama Gakuin, opportunities for extensive educational cooperation did not exist there. It was, instead, the Methodist Episcopal South mission in Kobe that needed financial help from the Canadian Methodists. The Kwansei Gakuin was to be jointly managed by the Canadian Methodists and the Methodist Episcopal South mission. Even with the Methodist Episcopal South mission paying half the expenses, the Kwansei Gakuin proved very costly to develop. This was especially true after 1919, when it was decided to circumvent even more stringent restrictions on religious education in government-recognized schools by attempting to take advantage of other new government regulations allowing a few leading private schools and government colleges outside Tokyo and Kyoto to become universities. The Christian character of the Kwansei Gakuin could be guaranteed by a university constitution. This was not an impossible dream. The Methodist Episcopal South mission quickly raised its share of the endowment required by the government for granting university status, but the Canadians were unable to raise their half until 1932. Only then did Kwansei Gakuin finally attain university status.

Whereas the Canadian Methodists largely concentrated on education for the Japanese, one of the most successful Canadian missionary educational endeavours was the Canadian Methodist Academy, which opened its doors in Kobe in 1913 to educate the children of Canadian missionaries. The lack of educational facilities for Western children had hampered the Canadian mission in stationing missionaries with families in rural areas, where facilities for their children were unavailable. The creation of the Canadian Academy allowed missionaries who preferred to keep their children with them during the crucial years of adolescence to have them educated in Japan, rather than in Canada, up to university age.

The Canadian Academy almost immediately found itself serving a much wider community, instructing students from the Kobe business community as well as from other missions. As a result, by the 1920s the academy had become a union school supported financially by other missions as well as by the Canadian Methodists. But the school always remained the preserve of Western children, and it followed the curricula prescribed by the Department of Education of Ontario. The Canadian Academy quickly expanded to offer high school-level courses, which enabled its graduates to enter the University of Toronto.

Despite the success of the Canadian Academy and the mission schools for the Japanese, educational endeavour was still an adjunct to the central task of evangelism for Canadian missionaries. However, because evangelism did not go as well as expected in Japan and competition with government education became difficult, the social gospel came to the rescue by providing a humanitarian motive for social work. Canadian missionaries never engaged in social work on a large scale; what they did undertake usually reflected personal social concern and interest. The most famous of all Western missionaries in Japan during the 1920s was Caroline Macdonald, the "White Angel of Tokyo," a Canadian who was instrumental in establishing the YWCA in Japan and whose name is associated with the rehabilitation of prisoners.[82] Although another Canadian, Arthur Lea, had pioneered penal rehabilitation in Gifu in the 1890s, the activities of female missionaries tended to attract more publicity. However, the Canadian Anglican Blind School (the Kunmoin) in Gifu exemplified a Christian work ethic that pointed the way for further Japanese government effort in a necessary field of social work. This school began after the great Mino-Hide earthquake in 1891 as a blind men's club. At the time, only one other school for the blind existed in Japan. Until the late 1920s, when the Kunmoin passed from Canadian Anglican hands into the control of the Japanese government, the Canadian Anglican missionaries provided an extremely valuable service to the community.

Another area that engaged missionaries was health care. Canadian Anglicans maintained a sanatorium for those suffering from tuberculosis and by World War I social work in the slums of the larger cities had attracted the attention of many missionaries. Canadian Methodists were especially active in social work in the slums of East Tokyo, which had been created by the large-scale migration of young people from rural areas seeking work in the capital's developing industry. Canadian Methodists began their work by preaching in Kameido ward and by developing a hostel originally founded by Annie Allen of the WMS in the 1910s for factory women.

Slum work represented a clear response to the changing conditions of Japanese society brought about by industrialization. Rosemary Gagan has suggested that a few WMS missionaries, such as Allen, were prepared "to strike out on their own in social-work, where they thought they could be helpful as harbingers of the social gospel's message of universal brotherhood," but the majority of their colleagues "were more comfortable with the traditional modes of teaching, conducting women's meetings, itinerating."[83] The conservatism of missionary societies often stifled innovation, and shortages of personnel and revenue often prevented the inauguration of new projects. Furthermore, because established areas of work were rarely closed down, new projects were merely added to existing work. As a result, a good deal of missionary effort was expended in specialized work, thus diverting effort from the expansion of orthodox evangelism.

Although education and social work had served missionaries well in the past, by the 1930s it was apparent that new methods were needed to meet the challenge of the future. The findings of the Laymen's Commission on Christian Missions, which investigated the Japanese mission field in 1931, concluded that missionaries lacked understanding of the effects of industrialization and urbanization. They were seemingly not keeping up with the times. The commission laid part of the problem at the feet of the churches at home.[84]

Yet the Laymen's Commission argued for an approach to missionary work that was in keeping with the pronouncement of the 1928 Jerusalem Conference that "man is a unity, and his spiritual life is indivisibly rooted in all his conditions, physical, mental and social."[85] The commission believed that missionary work had to be sufficiently comprehensive to serve every aspect of a person's life. Because it emphasized on the importance of evangelism as well as social uplift, the commission implicitly approved of the Kingdom of God movement in Japan. Yet, if more attention should have been placed on coupling social work with evangelism, the commission also pointed out that more should have been done to minister to Japan's moral and intellectual life. In this, the commission was suggesting nothing new, for Japanese Christian leaders had long been aware of this need. Yet the missionary movement, given its limited personnel and circumscribed financial resources, was unlikely to meet fully the recommendations of the commission.

For his part, Charles Bates, one of the senior United Church missionaries, thought that the Commission was "very good, but very American," and more concerned with "the 'spirit of the age' than the 'spirit of the ages.'"[86] Despite this criticism, outsiders did see a need for the modernization of missionary work.

PROGRESS IN NORTH KOREA

The Korean response to Christianity and to the missionary movement was different from that of the Japanese.[87] There were many cultural and religious reasons for this difference, not the least of which was the place that Christianity played in the Korean political milieu. From the late eighteenth century, when Christian ideas first entered Korea by way of tribute missions returning from China, Christianity was associated with factional opposition to the ruling group within the Yi court. In the early twentieth century, the Protestant movement became associated with opposition to Japanese colonial rule and defence of Korean cultural independence. Although Canadian missionaries felt called to preach the Gospel, and all that they did stemmed from this basic motivation, their somewhat naïve humanitarianism and concern for Korean Christians produced results that were interpreted as political actions by their Korean associates and by Japanese colonial officials. As in Japan and Taiwan, the work and actions of missionaries often produced results of which the missionaries were largely unconscious.

The first resident Protestant missionaries began work in Korea in the early 1880s following the opening of Korea to Western penetration. Prior to the 1900s, however, few converts were made. It was in northern Korea that the missionary movement made its greatest early gains. Although the capital city of Seoul became a major centre for Christian education and church administration, Korean Christianity maintained, until the end of the Pacific War, its strong northern bias, and P'yongyang remained a key Christian stronghold. Unlike in Japan, where the Christian movement was largely an urban phenomenon, in Korea derived much of its strength from rural constituencies. Furthermore, also different from Japan, Korea, following the great revival of the mid-1900s, captured the imagination of the world missionary movement as a country that might be Christianized. Indeed, the missionary movement was more successful in Korea than in any other part of East Asia in converting a significant percentage of the local population to Christianity.

The first Canadian missionaries to work in Korea arrived in the late 1880s or early 1890s. They were drawn to mission work and to Korea through the influence of the recently formed Student Volunteer Movement and through speeches by American missionaries on furlough from the peninsula.[88] In the fall of 1898, the first three official Canadian Presbyterian missionaries, all Nova Scotians and all Dalhousie University graduates, left for Korea.[89] When they arrived in Seoul, they were asked by the American Presbyterian societies already in the peninsula to undertake work in northeastern Korea, with their base in Wonsan. By 1913, their territory had been extended into the adjacent

Manchurian borderland and beyond to Siberia. By that time, the Canadian Presbyterians maintained mission centres at Sungjin, Hoiryung, Hamheung, and at Lunchingtsun in Manchuria. They developed their work along evangelistic, educational, and medical lines.

In their evangelistic work among the rural communities, Canadian Presbyterians experienced considerable success through their utilization of the Nevius Method, an evangelistic technique first developed in China. In many ways, Korea was an easier field than either Japan or Taiwan. One reason was the relative lack of religious opposition. Unlike in Japan and Taiwan, where, Shintoism, Confucianism, and Taoism within the Chinese tradition prevented the rapid growth of Christianity, religious opposition in Korea was not as powerful a deterrent to Christian growth. Shamanism, and new religions such as Chondokyo, did not have an important impact on organized religious life,[90] and Buddhism was not a vital force in Korea. Christianity helped to fill a religious vacuum in Korean life left after the long decline of Korean Buddhism during the Yi dynasty. Moreover, missionaries in rural areas did not face the rigorous intellectual opposition that confronted them in Japan. Owing to the lower educational level of many rural Koreans in comparison to their urban Japanese counterparts, missionaries in Korea could propagate a much simpler Christian message than was generally possible in Japan. By the end of the 1920s, the missionaries could boast of some 10,000 converts.

Their educational endeavours proved less successful. In all their mission centres, the Canadian Presbyterians tried to maintain mission schools of a "higher level" for boys and girls in order to provide an apex to a local church system of Christian primary schools. Most of the latter were primitive. By 1915, the Canadian Presbyterians claimed to be operating some forty-one day schools. This might seem more impressive than the Canadian Methodist endeavour in Japan, with its three girls' schools and half a college, but the difference was in the quality.

The issue of quality in educational institutions became increasingly important after the Japanese annexation of Korea in 1910. The new Japanese government-general actively began to develop a government educational system and to regulate standards in private schools. Mission schools in Korea had to meet Japanese standards, which demanded a Japanese curriculum and teachers who had passed Japanese teacher-training courses. The government general's educational policies were directed at replacing Korean with Japanese cultural values. The Christian movement in Korea, which by 1910 had reached every corner of the peninsula, found itself as one of the mainstays for the continued existence of Korean culture and, as such, operated contrary to Japanese policy. As far as the Canadian Presbyterians were concerned, they did not have the financial resources to raise the educational standards of their many rural schools to comply with Japanese regulations. Thus, the Canadian Presbyterians gradually came to see their main educational contribution stemming from their cooperation with wealthier and larger American missions in support of three higher educational union institutions: Chosen Christian College (now Yonsei University), founded in 1917; Severance Union Medical College, established in 1900; Union Christian College (now Soonjun University), founded in P'yongyang in 1906. With the union colleges in Korea, the Canadian Presbyterians hoped, as the Canadian Methodists did in Japan with the Kwansei Gakuin, that the development of institutions of higher learning would give them greater freedom from government regulations concerning religious instruction of the sort that had hamstrung their educational efforts among boys at the secondary level.

If the Canadians thought that their educational work was hampered by Japanese regulations, their modest medical work was faced with both competition from government general hospitals and increasingly strict qualifications for Korean nurses, doctors, and surgical assistants. In their main mission centres, the Canadian Presbyterians could only afford to maintain small cottage hospitals with limited if not primitive facilities served by a single missionary doctor. As in education, by far the most acceptable standards were achieved through union medical work. The Canadian Presbyterians cooperated with other missions in medical work and helped to found the Severance Union Medical College in Seoul. This teaching college proved able to compete with government-general institutions in terms of quality.

One way to overcome Japanese government-general regulations was to develop missionary work outside their jurisdiction. Manchuria was one such place, and the weak Chinese authorities there did not insist on the same stringent regulations in regard to educational and medical work as the Japanese. Furthermore, foreign rights in Manchuria, as a part of China, were protected under extraterritoriality laws. In 1911, following the path of northward Korean emigration, the Canadian Presbyterians opened a mission centre at Lungchingtsun (Ryuseison) in Chientao (Kanto) province of Manchuria. By the 1920s, Canadian Presbyterians in Lungchingtsun were maintaining a middle school for boys and a higher school for girls, as well as a hospital, in their extensive missionary compound. A large network of churches and Christian primary schools also stretched out from the mission centre into the surrounding rural districts. In 1925, mission work in Chientao was taken over by the United Church of Canada, as was all work in Korea. By that time, such was the extent of work in Chientao that it had become the largest single mission centre for the Canadian missionary endeavour among Koreans.

Largely populated by Koreans, but outside Japanese control, the Chientao region was a hotbed of anti-Japanese resistance and agitation in the years following the annexation of Korea.[91] Among the most active in the Korean nationalist movement in Chientao were Korean Christians. The intensity of anti-Japanese resistance increased as a result of the Siberian intervention of 1918, which Korean nationalists opposed, and came to a head with the

Independence Movement demonstrations on 1 March 1919 in the major towns of the Chientao region as well as in metropolitan Korea itself.[92]

Canadian missionaries in Korea were among the most vociferous of the foreign missionary community in their protests at the brutality of the Japanese military toward innocent Koreans at the time of the Independence Movement demonstrations. After the movement's suppression in metropolitan Korea, Koreans in Manchuria and Siberia continued to wage armed struggle against Japanese colonialism. In October 1920, the Japanese army, in response to "bandit" attacks on Japanese residents in Chientao, dispatched a punitive expedition into Chientao that resulted in many deaths and much damage to property. Canadian Presbyterian missionaries in Lungchingtsun protested against Japanese military actions in this part of Manchuria, and the Japanese in turn, responded by accusing missionaries of supporting anti-Japanese elements. The result was an international diplomatic incident that ultimately cleared missionaries of any wrongdoing and stopped any Japanese desire to occupy that part of Manchuria (at least for the time).

The missionary response to the Chientao punitive expedition was an early example of the missionaries' power to influence events in remote areas by publicizing their views in the international press and by pressing the British Foreign Office. In protesting against Japanese actions, the Canadians were motivated by humanitarian feeling. Even though both Japanese and Koreans interpreted missionary actions in defence of Koreans as being politically motivated, Canadian missionaries were not outright supporters of Korean political aims. As the 1930s would show, missionaries were primarily concerned with protecting Korean Christians against whoever—either Japanese or Korean—threatened them. The identification of Christianity with Korean nationalism that was so important to the development of Christianity in the peninsula from the 1900s onward remained true only so long as the aspirations of Korean Christians coincided with the secular aims of the nationalist movement. By the 1930s, the identification of Christianity and nationalism had started to disappear. It was also a time when the growth of Christianity in Korea stalled.

FOOTHOLD IN NORTH TAIWAN

There was never a question of identification of Christianity and nationalism as far as Taiwan was concerned. Furthermore, there was little antipathy to Japanese colonialism in Taiwan among the Canadian Presbyterian missionaries who worked there. Although the Canadian Presbyterian mission schools and hospital in north Taiwan, like those in north Korea, had to contend with stringent Japanese regulations, the Canadian presence in Taiwan was very small. The missionary movement in Taiwan did not have the same impact upon Taiwanese life and society as it did in Korea or even in Japan. In Taiwan, the Canadian missionaries faced the adamantine resistance of traditional Chinese culture and the obdurate indifference of the mass of Chinese Taiwanese to their Christian message. Christian work was no easy matter in Taiwan.

Taiwan was the first mission field for Canadian missionaries in East Asia. In 1872, a year before the Canadian Methodists opened their mission in Japan, George Leslie Mackay arrived to commence Canadian Presbyterian missionary work in north Taiwan.[93] For over fifty years, the Canadian and English Presbyterians[94] would be the only Western Protestant missionaries working on the island, and, up to the time of the Pacific War, the Presbyterians remained the most important missionary group. From the earliest days, there was cooperation between Canadian and English Presbyterians (they were further knitted together because nearly all were Scots by blood, background, or inclination). Yet there were differences between the two missions, not the least being that the English Presbyterians in the south had more money than the Canadian Presbyterians in the north.

Nonetheless, the Canadian Presbyterian Church was willing to send Mackay missionary reinforcements. Until 1892, when William Gauld, the fourth reinforcement and a man who preferred administration to direct evangelism, arrived, Mackay seemed to be unable to get on with the missionaries sent out from Canada to help him. There was good reason for this. Mackay chose not to develop the Canadian Presbyterian mission along the standard lines adopted by the English Presbyterians in south Taiwan; rather, he devoted his considerable energies to itinerant evangelistic work in order to establish quickly Taiwanese Christian groups led by Taiwanese evangelists. Producing far greater and quicker results in terms of baptisms and Christian congregations in comparison to the orthodox but more methodical approach to mission development of the English Presbyterians (which expanded painfully slowly), Mackay, James Rohrer has suggested, unwittingly created a distinct religious cult in which his personality and direction played central roles.[95] The involvement of other Canadian evangelists, especially those who held more orthodox views in regard to missionary work, could have jeopardized Mackay's effort to create quickly an indigenous Christian movement in Taiwan. So Mackay actively discouraged missionary reinforcements from being sent out. As it was, many of the more than 3,000 Taiwanese whom he had led to Christianity dropped away from the Church after his death in 1901. There has been a suggestion that Mackay suffered from mental illness,[96] but that is an unfair allegation that cannot be substantiated.

Mackay was rightly regarded as a Canadian missionary hero, and truly he was hewn out of the same spiritual granite as Chalmers Burns, the English Presbyterian missionary who was his boyhood hero. But like Burns or David Livingstone of Africa fame, Mackay had his human failings. One of his failings was his attitude toward female missionaries. Whereas the English Presbyterians welcomed female missionaries in all aspects of their work, Mackay refused to have them in north Taiwan on the grounds that they were constitutionally too weak to withstand the rigours of the tropical climate and that they were unsuited for evangelistic work among the Chinese.[97] This was patent nonsense, as the success of the female missionaries in south Taiwan clearly illustrated. Obviously, Mackay felt that female missionaries might threaten his authority. He married a Taiwanese woman whom he loved deeply. In missionary terms, this was an unusual step, for he was one of only three nineteenth-century missionaries in China to have an interracial marriage. Mackay died of cancer in 1901, before his herculean efforts developing the mission had come to fruition.

After Mackay's death, the Canadian Presbyterian mission continued to grow along evangelistic, educational, and medical lines similar to those followed by the English Presbyterians in the south. Two middle schools, one for boys and the other for girls, were developed in Tamsui. George W. Mackay, the only son of George Leslie Mackay, was principal after 1914 of the boys' school in Tamsui. As the years went by, G. W. Mackay increasingly became an influential figure in the Canadian Presbyterian mission. He was a bridge between Taiwanese and Canadians, but as a result the Japanese educational authorities looked at him with suspicion. He was seen as being too close to the Taiwanese, and, unfortunately for an educator, he did not speak Japanese. As well as undertaking educational work, the Canadians maintained the Mackay Memorial Hospital. In 1912, it was transferred to a new building in Taipeh, the capital of the Japanese government-general, which became the second major centre of Canadian Presbyterian activity. For a small mission, progress was slow. Medical work was closed down during the World War I for lack of a missionary doctor, and it was only opened again in 1924.

The next year, 1925, brought the formation of the United Church of Canada through the union of the Methodist, Congregationalist, and Presbyterian Churches. The formation of the United Church of Canada did not have a significant impact on the development of the missions in Korea and Japan, for they retained their affiliations with Presbyterian missions in the peninsula and with Methodist missions in Japan. The same missionary society leadership—the Methodist James Endicott and the Presbyterian A. E. Armstrong—continued after the union to supervise the work in Japan or Korea, which they had guided for their separate missionary societies for a decade or more before 1925. The creation of the United Church of Canada brought no new leadership or change of personnel to the work in those two mission fields. The greatest change for those working in Japan or Korea was the new name of their supporting denomination. For Canadian work in Taiwan, however, the creation of the United Church of Canada had a debilitating impact.

A rump of the Canadian Presbyterian Church decided not to join the United Church of Canada but to continue as a separate Presbyterian Church in

Canada. As the first Canadian mission field in East Asia, the small mission in Taiwan was retained by the Canadian Presbyterians. Apart from a lone Canadian Anglican missionary, N. P. Yates, who worked from 1915 among the aborigines at Taite, the Canadian Presbyterian mission remained the only Western Protestant mission in the northern half of Taiwan until the Nationalist government moved to the island in 1949. Although the Canadian Presbyterian mission continued, missionaries themselves remained divided in their loyalties. Some decided to join the English Presbyterians in south Taiwan. In terms of the loss of personnel, the creation of the United Church of Canada further weakened in Taiwan what had always been a shoestring mission. The future of the Canadian presence in Taiwan seemed even less secure as the storm clouds of the 1930s appeared on the horizon. Moreover, as well as maintaining their mission in Taiwan, the Canadian Presbyterians found themselves engaged in new work among Koreans in Japan and in supporting the small mission to the Chinese in Manchuria associated with Johnathan Goforth, which after 1931 came within the Japanese sphere of influence.

By the beginning of the 1930s, Canadian missionaries had maintained missions in Taiwan and Japan for close to sixty years and that in Korea for over thirty years. Over those years, it had become clear that Christian growth was achieved only slowly and through hard work. The seasoned United Church leadership in Toronto and the veteran missionaries in Tokyo, Tamsui, and Lungchingtsun could take heart that every crisis had eventually been weathered and that seemingly nothing could stop Christian growth in the mission field. There was still, and there always would be, a need for missionaries from Canada to help the development of Christianity in Japan, Korea, and Taiwan.

CHAPTER TWO
Toward the Kingdom of God: Evangelism and Social Concern in Japan

It was against a changing background within the Japanese Protestant movement that the direct evangelistic work of Canadian missionaries in Japan was undertaken during the late 1920s and early 1930s. A major feature of these years was the union of evangelism and social concern that clearly manifested itself in the Kingdom of God movement, which was based upon a social creed adopted by the NCC in 1928. The movement was led by Kagawa Toyohiko, whose concern with social problems was coupled with an evangelistic desire to win a million souls for Christ.

Many United Church missionaries viewed Kagawa's Kingdom of God movement as being central to their own missionary efforts. This reliance on a single Japanese Christian leader to stimulate interest in Christianity was a new phenomenon for Canadian missionaries, who had previously taken the lead in evangelistic work. Despite the new campaign, however, there was little apparent change from the ways in which missionaries had conducted evangelistic work in the past. This was especially true of work in the interior of Japan. Canadian Anglicans working in the rural NSKK diocese of Mid-Japan in central Honshu were in a good position to take advantage of the Christian revival stemming out of the Depression. The larger United Church of Canada mission conducted both rural and urban evangelistic work. There was a division between missionaries, with those in rural districts emphasizing well-tried evangelistic methods and those in Tokyo eagerly applying the latest approaches of social science to their work in the slums of east Tokyo.

In 1927, new Canadian work began in Japan with the opening of a small Presbyterian mission among Koreans in Japan, who responded more positively to the Christian message than either the Japanese or colonial Koreans. Direct evangelistic work in Japan in the late 1920s and early 1930s was not affected by political considerations (though economic factors stemming from the Depression did have an impact). On the colonial frontier in north Korea, Manchuria, and even north Taiwan, political undertones affected everything.

For both Japanese Christians and Canadian missionaries, however, the late 1920s and early 1930s held the promise of revival and expansion for the

Christian movement in Japan.

THE DEPRESSION, CHRISTIAN REVIVAL, AND KAGAWA

During the Depression, Christian work benefited from its emphasis on individual spirituality and its lack of overriding concern with Japan's immediate social malaise. Between 1929 and 1933, pietistic and fundamentalist groups (especially the Holiness, Free Methodist, and Nazarene Churches) experienced significant revivals. Revivalists viewed the social state of Japan as apocalyptic and looked for the imminent Second Coming of Christ, which would release people from every kind of suffering.[1]

This message of hope, albeit otherworldly, expounded by the Holiness Church, for instance, struck a responsive chord in many people suffering as a result of the Depression. In five years from 1929, the Holiness Church more than doubled its membership to reach over 19,000.[2] Furthermore, like other Japanese Churches, the Holiness Church extended its work beyond metropolitan Japan to Karafuto, Korea, the South Sea Islands, and Manchuria.[3]

More other orthodox denominations also undertook evangelistic campaigning. The largest was the interdenominational Kingdom of God movement led by Kagawa.[4] One of the most enthusiastic supporters of Kagawa among Canadian missionaries was Charles Bates, the president of Kwansei Gakuin in Nishinomiya. For Bates, one of the attractive things about the movement's evangelistic endeavours was that Kagawa looked to missionaries for support. In November 1928, Bates stated that, "to us missionaries, Mr. Kagawa has brought a new message. He has told us that our work is not done in Japan, that our presence is necessary for the very life and well being of the church, and he asks for our cooperation. Shall we withhold it. God forbid."[5] Bates saw Kagawa's campaign as a great challenge for missionaries and Japanese Christians and Kagawa himself as "a prophet" and "a man on fire" with evangelistic zeal and devotion. He believed that Kagawa was crucial to a religious revival in Japan, and he placed him in the same evangelistic company as Wesley and Moody.[6] Later, in 1936, Bates went so far as to consider Kagawa a world figure to be grouped with Albert Schweitzer, Stanley Jones, and Mahatma Gandhi.[7]

Kagawa stood for the organized church and the need for expansion of Christian numbers. Although the organized church in Japan might want to achieve the ideal of self-support, Bates thought that what the church really needed was more members.[8] Many missionaries and Japanese Christians would have agreed with him. Bates believed that one of the weaknesses of the church in Japan was that the church institutions, by which he meant Christian schools and other organizations, had grown faster in numbers and size than the church itself. However, a more important weakness for Bates was the lack of evangelistic fervour within the church, which he considered stemmed from either "an excessive toleration of other religions, or a hesitancy to interfere in the private affairs of others, or the magnitude of the difficulties that are inevitable in so fully organized a social, industrial and political life as is found in Japan today."[9] Yet Bates was attracted to Kagawa because he saw "a process of social crystallization" taking place in Japanese society and feared that Christianity, without some strong stimulus, would become

> the spiritual culture of the elect few, a fine class of people, fairly well educated, of moderate means who will not, however, be large enough in numbers or of sufficient strength of influence to affect the life of the nation very deeply, a place similar to that held by Confucianism in feudal Japan, by Zoroastrianism in India, or by Coptic Christianity in Egypt."[10]

Bates was not alone among Canadian missionaries in his admiration of Kagawa. P. G. Price was another United Church missionary struck by Kagawa's amazing personality, tremendous energy, and great oratorical skill. He was impressed both by the straightforward approach that Kagawa adopted in his evangelistic meetings and by the plain "Kagawa-fuku"[11] (working clothes) that he wore. Price understood that, whereas the first part of Kagawa's career had been more political than religious, Kagawa had come to realize that "the religious foundation is the first essential. Hence his tremendous energy is now turned upon preaching and cooperation with the churches."[12] In 1931, it was reported that "central to the success of all our work in Japan is the progress of the Kingdom of God Movement, under the inspiring leadership of Dr. T. Kagawa."[13] Through his meetings, Kagawa was able to provide excellent advertising for the local congregations, who were left with the task of exploiting any interest in Christianity among those who heard him speak and bought his book. An important aspect of the Kingdom of God movement, which United Church missionaries obviously appreciated, was the cooperation that it engendered with other missions.

Importantly, Kagawa, appealed not only to country folk and foreign missionaries but also to students and their teachers. In 1933, he made a strong impression on teachers and students at the Kwansei Gakuin during a visit in which "he outlined an apologetic for religious faith by a masterly study of modern scientific movements in the spheres of physics, astronomy, biology, sociology, economics and psychology."[14] Kagawa could also draw large audiences into that rarely filled church, the Central Tabernacle in Tokyo. In 1934, it was reported from the Central Tabernacle that Kagawa had done outstanding work during its fall evangelistic meetings, bringing crowds of 1,000 to each of two evening meetings, with the result that on both occasions over 300 people signed cards as being "desirous of entering the religious life."[15] New converts entered the Japan Methodist Church as a result of Kagawa's work. Writing about the evangelistic work at the Kwansei Gakuin in 1935, Bates reported that "the most significant of the special religious meetings held during the year were Dr. Kagawa's lectures, and the Oxford Group House party, the latter attended by nearly one hundred men and women."[16] The United Church missionaries seemed to consider their own efforts secondary to those of Kagawa, he visited Canada in the early 1930s, so United Church members at home were familiar with his name, and this familiarity might account for the emphasis that Canadian missionaries in Japan put on him. Indeed, Kagawa was more famous overseas than he was in Japan itself.

The Kingdom of God movement was a highly organized effort directed by a central committee and by regional committees. It had its own fund-raising network in Japan and North America and its own newspaper. Kagawa's efforts in Japan were supported by the Kagawa Cooperators, an international body that provided Kagawa with nearly $1,000 a month in the spring of 1932 from its two main support groups in New York and California.[17] Among the five members of the Japan Committee of the Kagawa Cooperators were Bates and Price.[18] Kagawa responded to this help in a way that emphasized the important role of the missionary movement. He stated that he himself was "a result of a Christian Mission. If a missionary had not come to Japan, I would never have seen the fact of God."[19] Furthermore, he was sensitive enough to North American views to strike the proper note as far as political events in East Asia were concerned. In May 1932, Kagawa wrote to Arnup in Toronto that:

> I am so ashamed of the actions of our militarists. I anticipated some such movement and tried to forestall it by starting the Kingdom of God Movement. And I am glad to say that this religious movement is not interrupted by the fascist explosion, which cannot capture the sympathy of numbers of our people.[20]

Kagawa went on to say that his work for peace was a long-term undertaking that required "both the transformation of men's inner souls through a religious awakening, and also the gradual changing of the economic system under which they must live from a competitive to a cooperative one."[21] This desire for economic transformation would undoubtedly have appealed to many in Canada, caught up as they were in the Depression.

Kagawa's appeal to Canadians was that his example gave impetus and hope for revival within their own Christian movements.[22] Indeed, an effort was made to create a Canadian Kingdom of God movement that Kagawa himself saw as part of a worldwide movement "to bring into active operation the Christian Cooperative Internationale."[23] Although this might have been a pipe dream, Canadian Christian leaders were grateful for any help that his name might give to their revival efforts in Canada. Even though his trip to Canada in 1931 was a packed three-day visit to Toronto following a much longer tour of the United States, his popularity in North America was enhanced by other evangelistic tours there in the years to 1936.

With the exception of absences abroad, Kagawa, between 1930 and 1934, devoted all his time to the Kingdom of God movement. During the course of the campaign, he reportedly spoke before 1.5 million people, of whom some 25,000 were said to have accepted his appeal to become Christians.[24] The Kingdom of God campaign was relatively successful in publicizing the Christian message and drawing in new converts. However, the Holiness Church, with much less fanfare and far fewer resources, was able to increase its membership by 7,000. Kagawa was not the only one who could gain converts. Nevertheless, it was his involvement in the Kingdom of God movement that attracted widespread foreign missionary interest to him. Although missionaries were content to see a role for themselves in evangelistic work, they did not look to their own efforts either in the slums of Tokyo or in the provinces to achieve the Christianization of Japan. They looked to Kagawa. This deference was to be vital to the future of the Japanese Protestant movement.

Although the missionaries in the United Church mission could look back on the grand history of Canadian Methodist missionary endeavour in Japan dating from 1873, they were still adjusting in the late 1920s to the fact that they were from 1925 part of a new United Church of Canada. Clearly, they were not in such a good position to capitalize on the new interest in Christianity that the Depression brought.

THE EVANGELISTIC AND SOCIAL WORK OF THE UNITED CHURCH MISSION

Optimism for the future had characterized the response of missionaries in Japan to the formation of the United Church of Canada.[25] They anticipated great things from the new United Church, but there was still plenty of work for the missionary in Japan for years to come.

The flagship of Canadian evangelistic work in Tokyo was the Central Tabernacle Church. Originally built in 1891 as an evangelistic agency directed toward the student population of the nearby Tokyo Imperial University, this large church had never fulfilled its potential in that regard. Partly, this failure due to competition from more dynamic Japanese Christian churches such as the Kumiai (Congregationalist) Church's Hongo church. However, it was mainly due to the lack of interest of university students in religion, particularly of the foreign variety. From the beginning, the Canadians had a white elephant with a seating capacity of 1,000. The Central Tabernacle also housed a small but self-supporting Japan Methodist congregation, among whose members was Kobayashi Yataro (Yashichi), a wealthy businessman who was married to the granddaughter of the Christian founder of the famous Lion company of dentifrice products. Kobayashi's generous donations were important to the maintenance of the Japanese church, but his relations with the Japanese congregation were not always good.[26] Nevertheless, money was found to rebuild the Central Tabernacle.

As well as its evangelistic work among students undertaken at the Central Tabernacle, the United Church mission carried on work in the slum areas of east Tokyo. The WMS maintained the Aiseikan (later named the Kyoaikan),[27] a social settlement for factory women in Kameido ward that consisted of a dormitory and other facilities. This work, begun in 1916, was identified with Annie Allen, who was in charge of the WMS work there until her departure for Canada in 1940. Not only did Allen pioneer Canadian Methodist evangelistic work among factory women in the Tokyo slums, but she pioneered missionary residence in the slum areas.[28] Using the Aiseikan as the centre, Allen and her Japanese colleagues would go to different factories in the neighbourhood to hold meetings. Because most factory women worked long hours and lived in company dormitories, it was usually necessary for the Aiseikan staff to go to them, for most factory women did not have the free time to attend regular meetings at the Aiseikan itself.

The work of the Aiseikan, however, was not restricted to factory women, for there were many other classes of female wage earners, such as switchboard operators, bus drivers, typists, typesetters, railway ticket collectors, and saleswomen, who also lived in Kameido.[29] By the early 1920s, the pattern of work at the Aiseikan had been established, with English-language classes given at night and an English club organized; there were also opportunities for women to receive personal counselling. Together with this night school work, much effort was put into helping children, and a day nursery, children's library, and children's club had been started. An important turning point for the work of the Aiseikan was reached with its relief efforts in the wake of the great Kanto earthquake in 1923. Help was given not only to unemployed women, to whom the Aiseikan opened the doors of its dormitory, but also to the children of victims. Temporary accommodation was arranged for well over 200 children in the local Japan Methodist church.[30] The work of Allen and her colleagues did much to win the trust of the Tokyo metropolitan government concerning their activities. Without the approval and support of the Tokyo authorities, it would have been difficult during the late 1920s and early 1930s to expand the work of the Aiseikan by opening children's clubs in Tokyo metropolitan government welfare institutions and in government schools in the neighbourhood and by starting its own nursery schools and Sunday schools in conjunction with the local Japan Methodist church.

A special effort was made to reach out to women who lived and worked on boats on the canal close to the Aiseikan. The living and working conditions of the canal women were often dire, but they were preferable, at least to missionary eyes, to those of the thousands of unlicensed prostitutes who inhabited the vicinity of the Aiseikan. The Aiseikan tried to help the purity and prostitution-abolition movements in Kameido ward. So widespread was prostitution in this east Tokyo slum, however, that the efforts of the Aiseikan were directed mainly at trying to prevent women, particularly factory workers, from entering into prostitution rather than at trying to stamp out the existing trade.

Another expression of WMS concern for the well-being of Japanese women was the Nagasaka Homu, a small orphanage for girls, that had been opened as early as 1893 close to the Toyo Eiwa Jo Gakko in Azabu, Tokyo, and continued to operate into the 1930s.[31] The main work of the WMS in Tokyo was its educational program associated with the Toyo Eiwa Jo Gakko, and the school remained the anchor from which other work—such as the Aiseikan—could develop as opportunities arose. Outside their school responsibilities, missionary teachers superintended the Nagasaka Homu, helped with the Aiseikan, and worked with local congregations. Before moving to Kameido, Allen, for instance, taught at the Toyo Eiwa Jo Gakko, and of course much of the activity at the Aiseikan revolved around teaching.

The example of the Aiseikan led the male mission board to become also involved in slum work. In 1919, the East Tokyo Mission was begun by J. W. Saunby and later continued on by P. G. Price and G. E. Bott. The centrepiece of this work was in Nippori, where a free clinic, dispensary, and small industrial school were maintained along with a primary school for poor children. Kobayashi, so important to the financial well-being of the Central Tabernacle, was initially responsible for donating property and contributing money for this school. From Nippori, the East Tokyo Mission undertook work in Negishi in conjunction with the local Japan Methodist church and at Kameido and Ukeji. At Ukeji, following the great Kanto earthquake, the Tokyo metropolitan government provided the Canadians with a grant of ¥30,000 to build and manage a boarding house for ninety workers on mission-owned property.[32] This aid showed that the Japanese authorities were prepared to utilize foreign missionaries in their own efforts to improve the lot of workers in the east Tokyo slums. And the Canadians had no qualms about taking government money to build their dormitory.

Yet United Church mission work was not concentrated only in Tokyo. The influence of the Canadian missionary effort remained strong and largely unchanged in that region of central Honshu that had been associated with Canadian activity since the late nineteenth century. Work was carried on in the provincial cities of Kofu and Shizuoka, with their respective girls' schools run by the WMS and in Nagano, Hamamatsu, Toyama, Kanazawa, and Fukui, each of which had a seasoned Canadian missionary in place. Nagoya and Matsumoto were newer stations added to Canadian missionary jurisdiction after World War I. Whereas Kofu, Shizuoka, Fukui, and Nagoya could boast self-supporting Japan Methodist churches, the term "aided" applied to most of the churches in central Honshu in the late 1920s.

Perhaps it was because some of these congregations had been in existence up to forty years and still had not become self-supporting that Canadian missionaries were loath to withdraw from their long-standing work in the small cities of central Honshu in favour of a strictly Japanese Christian presence. In September 1927, C. P. Holmes, the chairman of the Japan Mission Council, argued that he had seen only adverse consequences of missionary withdrawal from central Honshu. He believed that the history of the Canadian Methodist missionary endeavour in Japan had resulted in a special relationship between the missionaries and Japanese Christian workers based on a policy from the beginning of absolute equality between Japanese Christians and Canadian missionaries. And "that policy saved us from a thousand Miseries," and "there never was an anti Missionary spirit among the Christians in our work here."[33] In the light of this relationship, Holmes and his colleagues thought that Canadian missionary presence in Japan should continue and increase. He argued that Christian progress was slow because there were tremendous forces, especially from Buddhism, opposed to Christianity, and "nothing but patience and good hard work will ever get Jesus his place here."[34] The challenges to Christianity in central Honshu were clearly different from those confronting Price and Bott in the East Tokyo Mission.

There were two distinct Japans of evangelistic work: rural and urban. Nevertheless, the direction of missionary work was driven by urban imperatives, in part, because the problems of modern Tokyo were more understandable to the missionary authorities in Canada, who commuted every day to their desks in Toronto. The dramatic changes in Japan since the turn of the century had occurred in Tokyo and the major cities. The industrialization and urbanization of the largest Japanese cities created slums and sweatshops that bore a resemblance to problems that had beset Toronto or Montreal as they had developed into industrialized cities. To remain up-to-date and thus appeal to modern Japan, authorities were tempted to change mission thinking. Yet Holmes was pointing out that the old-fashioned methods of missionary work were still applicable in the rural areas of central Japan, where change had been less rapid than in the cities.

In his report of the East Tokyo Mission for 1928, Price pointed out the different challenges faced by evangelistic missionaries in the industrialized city, noting that "We have them in Tokyo as elsewhere. The downtown problem. The suburban problem. The problem of the working man. The slum problem. The student problem."[35] In leading to the inevitable solution to these problems—more money—Price applied suitably modern jargon. At different places in his report, he contended that "the modern social worker knows that poverty can be overcome" (that is, according to Price, with large appropriations of public money and large amounts of private charity) and that "It [slum work] is a laboratory for the study of society and its workings." He added that "if it [slum work] is to accomplish anything permanent it should be thoroughly scientific in its approach."[36] At the same time, however, he called for a change in the direction of evangelistic work in Tokyo. He wrote that in the past the Christian movement had concentrated much of its energy on students, but now they were in a new age very conscious of social inequalities and eager to find solutions to them. He thought that the Church had to demonstrate that it was concerned with helping the worker and finding a solution to the slum problem because it could not hope to keep, let alone increase, its influence with Japanese students. As a result, he believed that "our success or failure with the working men and with the slum will have far reaching effects on all our church work."[37] Perhaps this was wishful thinking given the limited resources of the United Church for this work.

Whereas Price was concerned with the east Tokyo slum, his colleague, Hennigar, was active in a more general movement calling for the abolition of prostitution. Previously, the movement had largely directed its attention to influencing the Japanese Diet, but during the mid-1920s Hennigar had achieved some success by mobilizing public opinion at the prefectural level. Writing in the *Japan Christian Quarterly* in early 1929, he was optimistic that the abolition movement, despite its relatively short history, was gaining the support of public opinion.[38] Part of the reason for his optimism was the support of Christian members in the National Diet. Hennigar's hopes for abolition, however, proved to be premature. In the late 1930s, the movement ran into trouble with the pressure to cooperate with the Japanese war effort.[39] It was not until 1947, during the Allied occupation of Japan, that the National Diet abolished the practice throughout Japan.

Hennigar was also a passionate advocate of temperance, an issue that struck a responsive chord in some Japanese Christians. Their temperance activity was most clearly seen in the Women's Christian Temperance Union (WCTU), founded as early as 1886. In fact, the WCTU was numerically only a small element in the broader secular movement for temperance, for the Japan Temperance League in 1934 had 3,300 branches and a total membership of 300,000.[40] Hennigar cooperated with the WCTU and the Purity Society. In 1934, he noted that Japanese drinking habits had changed. He pointed out that in the past most liquor had been consumed at mealtime in the home, but now more was being drunk in bars and cafés, many of which were sponsored by brewers.[41] In one sense, the relatively recent change in drinking habits made it easier for the authorities to control liquor consumption. Yet bar and café owners, together with breweries, represented a large vested interest opposed to the temperance movement. As with prostitution, Hennigar's efforts were directed at the local level and were most successful in the poorer villages in the countryside, where the economic benefits of temperance could quickly be gauged.

Newspaper evangelism was one method through which temperance ideas reached people in rural districts. Perhaps a more important medium was the Farmers Institute. In 1930, for instance, a Farmers Institute meeting was held in the Toyoshina church in Matsumoto. It lasted for three days, during which the subjects treated included the best methods of rice cultivation, supplementary employment for farmers, the general rural situation, and health matters. Only one hour a day was devoted to a Christian lecture. Yet the results of the Farmers Institute in Matsumoto were considered excellent, and it was reported that "Our pastor gets a fresh welcome as he goes among the villages. These young men have helped him in the Purity [antiprostitution] campaign, several have become active Temperance workers."[42] Abstinence was introduced into the mix of practical advice for farmers. Without being part of such a mix, temperance propaganda would not have been readily accepted. After all, abstinence was rare among Japanese adults, and the idea of temperance ran against the grain of Japanese society and traditional culture.

As much as Hennigar and other missionaries wished that Japanese become teetotallers, they also clearly saw that the living conditions in rural Japan were difficult. In 1929, Dan Norman, a long-serving missionary in Nagano and an advocate of rural evangelism, wrote in the *Japan Christian Quarterly* about a ten-day-long school for young men and women interested in rural problems from a Christian standpoint. According to Norman, the Nomin Fukuin Gakko, as this school in Nagano was named, was "a Gospel institution but the aim was instruction and culture of a practical nature that the students might be led to face real situations in life honestly, reverently, and, above all truthfully following in the path that leads to the ideal as best we can see it."[43] The school in Nagano owed much to Norman, but it was also much a part of the Farmers Gospel School movement associated with Sugiyama Motojiro, the friend of Kagawa.[44]

Whereas the ten days of the school were devoted to lectures on Christianity, the evenings saw papers given on topics of agricultural and rural interest. Norman wrote that the school helped to train young men for leadership in their rural hamlets, and in such work both "churches and missions can unite and be richly blest in doing so. All distinction as between Japanese pastor and foreign missionary was lost sight of and it was for the good of all that it was so."[45] Norman was obviously pleased that the Nomin Fukuin Gakko served to bring Japanese and Western workers together in a united evangelistic effort. He also clearly thought that it helped to dispel interest in some unwelcome ideas, such as Russian communism. He saw a danger for rural Japan from Marxism unless Christianity stepped in.

The problems of rural life and their challenges to Christianity comprised a recurring subject of missionary discussion. The Christianization of village life might have been the aim of rural work, but the first priority was often practical help in the amelioration of social and economic conditions. Indeed, it was the practical advice in regard to sericulture or rice cultivation that brought farmers into the Farmers Gospel Schools. To bring farmers into the schools was not enough. In 1934, A. R. Stone, who had taken charge of the Nomin Fukuin Gakko in Nagano, wrote that "young men have gone home from our central Rural Gospel Schools full of visions and Christian faith, only to find themselves alone in a community which laughed at them."[46] Stone believed that the Farmers Gospel Schools should be localized, with a single village becoming the unit of Christian endeavour. Influenced by the ideas of Sugiyama on the nature of Japanese rural villages, Stone argued that "Christian rural technique will need to take cognizance of community solidarity and the various types of communities with their respective backgrounds and psychologies."[47] He thought that there was no program of Christian rural reconstruction applicable to all parts of Japan and that adjustments had to be made to meet the varying conditions in different areas of the country. He believed that one of the difficulties in the Christian movement was the lack of trained leadership for rural evangelism. He also believed that rural evangelists must understand farmers' problems from their point of view, and this understanding could not be achieved merely by "studying Rural Economics and Sociology in a city seminary; for the real rural leader must know the *feel* of rural life and problems."[48] This goal was difficult to achieve in the short term because most of the Japanese pastors and evangelists came from urban backgrounds.

Stone saw a further problem in the inelasticity of the methods and the message of the Christian movement in Japan. He believed that both missionaries and Japanese ministers found it difficult to broaden their vision to include a program that was "necessary if the rural people of Japan are to be able to enjoy the fullness of life in Christ."[49] What Stone did see, however, like Norman before him, was that the missionary could play a positive role. Stone argued that, despite problems posed by nationality and language, some missionaries—through newspaper evangelism, tent evangelism, rural gospel schools, temperance and purity education, and seasonal day nurseries—were making a difference in rural evangelistic work. One of the advantages that Canadian missionaries had was that they had come from rural backgrounds; Norman had been brought up on a farm near Aurora, Ontario, and Stone himself came from Highgate, Ontario. They thus had an affinity for rural work that many of their Japanese colleagues coming from urban backgrounds did not possess. At the same time, Stone saw that any headway in rural evangelistic work would require a tremendous effort. Even though he was still young, he did not possess the optimism for rural evangelistic work that the much older and seasoned Norman exuded. Yet, though both saw a role for Canadians in rural evangelistic work, missionaries could not avoid the financial impact of the Depression on their evangelistic endeavours.

Canadian missionaries tended to put a positive face on trying to obtain funds during to the Depression. In 1934, one missionary even suggested that the general effect of the Depression would be helpful because it would force missionaries to adopt more efficient methods in their work and bring about "a fresh evaluation of the various forms of missionary effort; a new emphasis upon the value of personal evangelism; a stronger realization of the worthlessness of material things; and, I believe, a fresh faith in those spiritual resources without which all our efforts will be in vain."[50] Although the Depression might have brought fresh faith to the missionaries in Japan, by 1935 the Board of Foreign Missions in Toronto was clearly worried about money and the level of giving for foreign missions, which had declined from what it had been before Canadian Church union. It was openly wondered: "Is the 'depression' accountable for all this decline in giving? Has Union been detrimental to Foreign Missions? Is an average of two cents a week for each family for the great business of carrying out the Lord's *Great Commission* the measure of the foreign missionary interest of United Church people?"[51] In 1928, $163,388.95 was disbursed to Japan from a Foreign Missions Board total of $693,590.54 for all foreign missions.[52] In 1935, only $88,368.94 was given to Japan from a Foreign Missions Board fund that disbursed a total of $543,972.86.[53]

With money or without, with the help of Kagawa or not, in the east Tokyo slums or in the rural interior, evangelistic work remained frustrating. Writing from Tokyo in March 1934 to his parents-in-law, Howard Norman expressed the muted disappointment—forever, missionaries were grasping optimistically for light rays among the shadows—that was clearly under the surface of much evangelistic work. Declining attendance at his Bible study class had led him to wonder whether or not he was an inspired teacher.[54]

It was obviously hard graft being a young missionary. Yet Howard Norman was not alone in being disillusioned by not achieving marked results from his evangelistic activity, for the young Stone in Nagano also expressed frustration with the challenges of rural evangelism. But individual disappointment had little place in the summaries of work that were published at home. The Oxford Group Movement (Moral Re-Armament) offered some spiritual solace to Howard Norman and other young missionaries. Among the most enthusiastic supporters of the Oxford Group Movement was Price, who hosted in early 1934 "house parties" characteristic of this movement. Despite missionary interest in it, most Japanese Christians, according to Howard Norman, were quite critical of the Oxford Group Movement.[55]

In contrast to the disappointment of young Norman in Tokyo, 1934 for those in Nagano, where his father, Dan Norman, had been a missionary for some thirty years, sparkled with hope. In Nagano the senior Norman wrote that

> we see rural parishes breaking out here and there over this extensive field. The call and guidance that is clear to me is that we go on the way as led that will

establish the Kingdom of God in Japan. I have had more invitations to speak in rural villages where no Christian work is done than I have been able to accept.[56]

Although the public face of the missionary effort might have revealed itself as determined as ever to convert the Japanese to Christianity, it was equally as clear by 1935 that the Kingdom of God would not be established in Japan in the near future. The publicity associated with Kagawa and his movement, on which missionaries had pinned so much hope, had not led to any great increase in conversions for United Church missionaries. The work of Canadian Anglicans suggested that patient work—without the hubbub of the grand evangelistic campaign—could yield results as good as those achieved by missionaries with the help of Kagawa. Indeed, the United Church missionaries might be criticized for their apparent reliance on Kagawa to generate interest in Christianity. Yet Kagawa was seen in the early 1930s to be the modern representative of the future for Christianity in Japan.

The United Church missionaries were caught on the horns of an evangelistic dilemma that the high stature of Kagawa as a Christian evangelist in both Japanese and Canadian circles helped to obscure. Missionaries conducted evangelistic work that was deemed necessary for the expansion of the Japan Methodist Church but that was too expensive for the Church itself to support without missionary aid. This was particularly true for the specialized work in the east Tokyo slums, but it was also clear that missionaries provided much of the energy that went into rural and newspaper evangelism. However, though Canadians were left with providing money for evangelistic work, it was the Japan Methodist Church that saw more converts from this effort.

At the same time, many of the Japanese congregations of the Japan Methodist Church were self-supporting only on paper and were still in need of missionary dollars, directly by grant or indirectly by missionary donations. Kagawa's evangelistic campaigning showed to the outside world that the Japanese Christian movement took a leading role in drawing Japanese to Christianity. Furthermore, the Kingdom of God movement directed attention away from the lacklustre performance of missionaries themselves in bringing in many new converts. A danger, of course, was the attractiveness of Kagawa and other Japanese Christian leaders, and overseas belief in their evangelistic effectiveness could jeopardize Canadian support for the missionary movement in Japan.

Certainly, this was a factor in the response to events after 1935, when the National Christian Council of Japan emerged as the dominant body in giving direction to the Japanese Christian movement. However, during the early 1930s, it was the impact of the Depression in Canada more than any other reason that saw the dollar value of the appropriations for the mission in Japan drop so dramatically by 1935 from the levels it had reached prior to the world recession.

Nonetheless, the United Church mission and the Japan Methodist Church during the early 1930s failed to achieve the same growth or to exude the same confidence in their work as their Canadian Anglican colleagues in the diocese of Mid-Japan. In part, this failure was the result of the United Church mission being larger and involved in a broader array of evangelistic projects. Evidence suggests, however, that evangelistic work in rural Japan, away from the modernity of urban Tokyo and Osaka, offered greater opportunities for Christian conversion. Yet the Kingdom of God in both rural and urban Japan was far off. In sharp contrast to the Japan Methodist Church (with its Canadian and American missionaries), the Holiness Church (without any missionary help) achieved remarkable growth during this period. The workers of the Holiness Church were consumed with evangelistic enthusiasm and directed their attention to the underprivileged in urban society. Even those Canadian missionaries at work in east Tokyo looked out at the surrounding slums from the building of their model settlement and went home at night to the mission compound in a more salubrious suburb.

The main evangelistic effort of both Japanese Christians and missionaries was directed toward the cities. Despite Kagawa's desire to open up rural Japan to the Christian message, his main evangelistic effort was in the metropolitan centres. The NSKK, however, did conduct extensive work outside the major urban areas. Of the major orthodox denominations, the NSKK grew significantly up to 1937. Not the least of the work undertaken by the NSKK was that carried on in the smaller cities and towns of central Honshu within the Canadian Anglican-supported diocese of Mid-Japan since its creation in 1912.

CANADIAN ANGLICANS AND THE REVIVAL

At the top of the Canadian Anglican endeavour in Japan, Heber J. Hamilton, the bishop of Mid-Japan, remained optimistic. After some thirty-five years as a missionary in Japan, of which the last fifteen were as bishop, his dedication to and hope for ongoing missionary work in the mountains of central Honshu remained undimmed. In early 1927, Hamilton wrote glowingly to Canon Gould in Toronto that "Japan with its stability, ability and strength is the out-standing nation of the Orient, one of the keys to open other doors and with its steady progress in Occidental ways, the buffer state between East and West," and that "Christianity, which already is influencing Japan out of all proportion to the number of Japanese Christians is what Japan needs to do its great work and Canada, its neighbour, ought to help more than ever, by precept and by practise, to give her that."[57] Hamilton's opinions about Japan's special position as a buffer state between East and West and its continued need for Christianity are important because they enunciate (with an appropriate Canadian twist) a widely held missionary attitude toward progressive Japan and Christianity. However, it is not surprising that Hamilton expressed such sentiments at the end of a letter asking for more Canadian as well as Japanese workers and appealing for financial support for a new project.

That project was a sanatorium. For many years, Hamilton had watched with concern the rising incidence of tuberculosis within the diocese of Mid-Japan, and he believed that the opening of a small sanatorium would show to the Japanese "a Christian Mission in sympathy with the material as well as with the spiritual needs of those among whom it is working."[58] It was this sympathy for both the material and the spiritual needs of the Japanese that was the hallmark of Canadian Anglican work under Bishop Hamilton.

Although Hamilton did not know it at the time, this Canadian Anglican sanatorium, opened in 1932 at Obuse (near Matsumoto), would provide through the 1930s a cohesive collegiate focus for the Canadian missionary staff and their Christian work in Mid-Japan. For Hamilton, the opening of the sanatorium was the last major achievement of his long tenure as bishop, for he would retire in 1934. In his last years, he also had to deal with serious problems within his mission. By the late 1920s, there was only one other Canadian Anglican missionary, John Waller, apart from Hamilton who had been in Japan from the first years of Canadian Anglican work. Waller had no desire to leave Japan (there was no mission regulation that frowned on missionaries staying on in Japan after retiring), but Hamilton clearly thought that he himself should be replaced as bishop and return to Canada.

Despite the fact that in 1923 the first two Japanese bishops within the NSKK had been consecrated, Hamilton saw that there would be problems in having a Japanese succeed him, because Mid-Japan was not a self-supporting diocese. The only way out, Hamilton thought, was for the missionary society in Toronto to provide the stipend for the Japanese bishop. Money from Canada was important. The question of paying a Japanese bishop's salary only added to a costly policy of supporting Japanese workers. Hamilton hoped that in the future the missionary authorities in Toronto would provide him with $14,000 a year to help support the salaries of 30 Japanese clergy and Catechists (in 1930, there were 24 Japanese clergy and Catechists in the diocese). Beyond this, he envisaged the Japanese providing $4,000 toward the support of salaries.[59]

As well as an increase in Japanese clergy, Hamilton wanted in 1930 at least two more Canadian men to be sent out for evangelistic work. He believed that "we need capable earnest young men, able to lead and yet willing to work, if need be, under Japanese priests of more years and longer experience. Canadian energy, resourcefulness and initiative, will be needed for some time yet."[60] Moreover, he wanted an additional four Canadian women on his staff.

Yet, over the crucial issue of his successor as bishop, Hamilton vacillated, swinging from advocating a Japanese to a Canadian and back to a Japanese. If the successor was to be a Canadian, then the choice for Hamilton boiled down to a member of his own missionary staff because he thought that it would be disastrous to post a new man who was utterly ignorant of Japan. Among the six clerical missionaries who were possible candidates for the position, though, there was little choice. Two were too young, one was too old, and another was "too erratic and moveable although a most whole-souled and spiritually minded worker. His executive and business ability would not be on a par with his zeal."[61] That left the last two, Victor Spencer and P. S. C. Powles. Hamilton wrote:

> I would vote for Powles myself. He has more elasticity than Spencer, is freer in his use of the language, is, I think, more approved of by the Japanese and has an invaluable asset in the person of his wife. No Bishop could ask for more faithful devout and able clergy than these two are. It is only in the matter of physical health that Spencer has the advantage over Powles. Both of them are B.D. and both have good business ability.[62]

Although Hamilton clearly preferred one over the other, both missionaries were out of the running by the next year. They continued to provide leadership within the Canadian Anglican mission through the remaining years of the 1930s.

In September 1932, Hamilton informed Canon Gould in Toronto that the conference of the Canadian Anglican mission had discussed the question of his successor and unanimously decided that the person should be Japanese.[63] Even though Hamilton thought that the time had come for a Japanese bishop for Mid-Japan, he added that "there is still good work to be done in Japan by Canadian Missionaries. It may be so also with Canadian Bishops, and that their day is not yet past."[64] Indeed, the day of Canadian bishops within the NSKK was not past, but it was not until after the end of the Pacific War that another Canadian was consecrated bishop in Japan.

When Hamilton left Japan in July 1934, Bishop Samuel Heaslett, the bishop of South Tokyo and the primate of the NSKK, temporarily took charge of Mid-Japan. The search for a suitable successor to Hamilton ended in May 1935 when the eight bishops of the NSKK attending the general synod of the Church, after considerable lobbying, unanimously elected Paul Shinji Sasaki.[65] His appointment was clearly welcomed by Anglicans in Canada, who quickly invited him to visit Canada. According to Waller, the most senior Canadian Anglican missionary, "work is a disease with Bishop Sasaki,"[66] and, in January 1938 Sasaki did suffer a bad breakdown as a result of overworking himself.

During his first years as bishop, he maintained fairly good relations with his missionary colleagues, in part because until 1939 he was never faced with making difficult decisions. By 1941, when Canadian Anglican missionaries left Japan, many of them questioned Sasaki's ability and judgment, and many likely regretted that he had been appointed bishop of Mid-Japan. In contrast, Anglicans in Canada remained convinced that Sasaki was an outstanding

Christian leader with an untarnished reputation. Even though he became bishop of Mid-Japan in 1935, financial control of the diocese remained in Canadian hands. Canon Gould was quick to write to Sasaki, stressing that "we [Canadian Anglicans] all desire to sustain the hands and support the activities, of *our first Japanese bishop*, by every means in our power" but, naming Spencer as the secretary-treasurer of the mission in Mid-Japan.[67]

The question of a successor to Hamilton absorbed a great deal of time and energy in the early 1930s, yet the work of the Canadian Anglicans continued to develop. Hamilton was a strong believer in evangelistic work, and he extolled the virtues of tent missions. Tents would be set up in vacant town lots and meetings held for children in the afternoon and for adults at night. A great deal of Christian literature was given out at these meetings. In 1929, he reported that the mission had recently bought not only 100,000 copies of a series of tracts written by Kagawa at a cost of $1.25 per 1,000 but also several thousand copies of Kagawa's book "New Life in God," which cost five cents a copy.[68] This literature would either be given away or sold at cost. Given the cheapness of his pamphlets and the volume of their sales, no wonder Kagawa was the best-known Christian worker in Japan. Newspaper evangelism was another area in which Hamilton saw great opportunities. And in regard to evangelistic campaigns, he reported that the NCC was exhorting Canadian Anglicans to take part in the Kingdom of God movement, but he noted that the NSKK had already begun its own "special three years campaign, its 'Uniting Strength Campaign', commemorating thereby the 70th anniversary of the beginning of modern Christian missionary work in Japan. It was in 1859 that Messrs Liggins and Williams, two of the Priests of the American Church, landed in Japan at Nagasaki and began that work."[69] Hamilton, despite buying Kagawa's pamphlets by the thousands, seems to have been more enthusiastic about the NSKK's own campaign than about the interdenominational Kingdom of God movement.

The evangelistic campaigns seemingly did have some impact. In May 1933, Hamilton noted—concerning the growth of the NSKK as a whole—that "progress year by year is very slow but the twenty years growth is quite substantial, especially in the matter of contributions both in the total and per head."[70] As a bishop, Hamilton was deeply concerned with money and contributions. Mission work in Japan had taught him patience and the ability to view Christian expansion from a long-term perspective.

In 1934, Hamilton suggested that the societal atmosphere in Japan was not conducive to Christianity, stating that social unrest and anxiety had not

> provided the best field for the things of the spirit and nationalism and militarism are apt to look askance at a religion not only essentially one of peace but also, in profession at all events, the religion of the nations which are looking at Japan to-day with a none too sympathetic eye.[71]

Yet this was not the only cause for concern. Some years earlier, Hamilton had expressed the hope that the serious business depression and increasing unemployment then beginning to affect Japan would mean that people would have "more inclination for religious thinking. Man is not the grateful creature he ought to be or prosperity would turn his thoughts to God, the giver of all. Adversity is more likely to lead men to seek for Him, so now is one of our special opportunities."[72] This optimism was not borne out by major increases in church membership or congregational giving. Indeed, as the economic difficulties in Japan deepened, the congregational contributions to the diocese of Mid-Japan, much of which was rural, went down. Yet more important was the impact of the world depression on monies from Canada.

In October 1931, Hamilton wrote to Toronto that the Canadian gold embargo had caused the Japanese mission considerable difficulty and that it lost thirteen percent its income from Canada because of the poor exchange rate.[73] Belt-tightening took place, with the Japanese workers voluntarily agreeing to a five percent reduction of their salaries to prevent a reduction of personnel. Likewise, the Canadian missionaries found that their own salaries dropped by seven percent because the missionary authorities in Toronto could not make up completely the loss in exchange.[74]

The reduction of missionary salaries posed a difficult problem. It had long been understood that missionaries should be paid enough to maintain a standard of living in Japan at least equivalent to that which they could have expected had they remained in Canada. They were not expected to live on the edge of poverty, which seemingly was the lot of many married Japanese clergymen and catechists. Missionaries and their families lived as best they could as Westerners in Japan (putting up with the lack of lamb, mutton, or veal and the high cost of cheese and breakfast foods, but also benefiting from the low wages, twenty-five dollars per month, for servants). Missionaries with school-age children were obviously faced with considerable expense, and the fees for boarding schools in Japan were not much cheaper than the fees for similar schools in Canada.[75] The suggested budget for the diocese of Mid-Japan for 1935 incorporated a reduction of twenty percent. Among the items subject to this paper clawback were missionary salaries and children's allowances.[76] The line between missionary children having and not having meat for months was getting dangerously thin.

Over the years, Hamilton strove to maintain a balance between missionary costs and salaries and support for Japanese agencies and field expenses. Likewise, the Woman's Auxiliary (WA), which supported the salaries and work of the female missionaries, attempted to keep a balance. This was sound policy and predicated on the belief that the status quo in Japan, which allowed Canadians to support Christian work in the diocese of Mid-Japan, would remain unchanged. Although self-support for Japanese churches was an eventual goal, and Hamilton did harp on Japanese contributions, Mid-Japan was a largely rural diocese and unlikely to become self-supporting financially. Simply put, with or without Canadian missionaries, the diocese was dependent on the constant inflow of Canadian money. Without Canadian money for rents, rates, and taxes—for travelling, schools, and miscellaneous needs—the diocese would be devastated.

The United Church of Canada missionaries in Japan worked under different conditions, for they belonged to the Japan Methodist Church, in which Japanization of key positions in that Church's hierarchy had long since taken place. Even though the United Church mission undertook extensive work in the provincial cities of central Honshu, much of its energy was directed toward specialized social and educational work in Tokyo. Owing to the greater extent of work undertaken by United Church missionaries in comparison to that of Canadian Anglicans, the position of United Church missionaries in Japan was more complex and open to critical questioning than that of its small Canadian Anglican counterpart. Whereas the Canadian Anglican mission operated at the diocesan level in close contact with its provincial Japanese constituency, the United Church mission functioned at a higher level, for it was a major Protestant mission and played that part in the community of Protestant missions in Japan.

CANADIAN PRESBYTERIANS AND KOREANS IN JAPAN

The Presbyterian Church in Canada could not claim any long historical connection with Japan. During the late 1920s, however, the Women's Missionary Society (Western Division) (WMSWD) of the Presbyterian Church in Canada began to give a yearly grant of $2,000 to support partially the settlement of Japanese factory girls and the night school that Caroline Macdonald, whose name is associated with the beginning of the Japanese YWCA, had established in Tokyo.[77] The WMSWD gave a grant for work in Japan—to which it had no previous connection—simply because Macdonald was a well-known missionary figure from a well-connected family in London, Ontario, who was in need of financial help. Moreover, in 1925 her work in Japan had been recognized by her alma mater when the University of Toronto awarded her an LLD.[78] In 1929, it was reported about Macdonald's activities that "her splendid work has so many aspects that it is impossible to do more than pay tribute to her unselfish devotion to the betterment of the conditions among factory workers."[79] It was with some pride that WMSWD could state that Macdonald had also served in 1929 as the interpreter for the Japanese labour delegate to the International Labour Conference in Geneva.

One of the attractive things about Macdonald for Presbyterians in

Canada was that despite her recognition she remained fervently committed to her Christian work. Her pioneer work among prisoners and her efforts to better the lot of factory workers certainly placed her as a leader among Christian workers who combined evangelism with social work.[80] Unfortunately, Caroline Macdonald suddenly fell sick in the summer of 1931 and returned home to Canada to die. This tragedy brought an end to Canadian Presbyterian support for work in Tokyo.

Earlier, in 1927, Canadian Presbyterians had begun to work in the port city of Kobe among Koreans in Japan. The Presbyterian Church of Korea had begun Christian work among Koreans in Japan as early as 1912, when it had sent its first pastor to minister to the needs of Koreans in Tokyo. By 1926, this endeavour had come under the supervision of the Federal Council of Churches and Missions in Korea.[81] It was in consultation with this organization that the Canadian Presbyterian Church decided to send Reverend L. L. Young, a veteran of nineteen years of missionary work in northern Korea, together with his wife to begin work in Kobe. Korean work in Japan allowed Young and other Canadian Presbyterians to retain their Presbyterian affiliation, which would not have been possible had they continued to work in the Korean peninsula itself, which was now under the auspices of the new United Church of Canada. The work in Japan was supported by the male Board of Missions and by the two divisions, east and west, of the WMS. In that respect, it represented a missionary effort of the whole Canadian Presbyterian Church. But the mission remained small, having a staff of two male clerical and five female missionaries in 1934.

Nevertheless, there was great scope for work among the Koreans in Japan. In 1927, the Korean population in Japan was given at 400,000, but seven years later in 1934, it had risen as a result of immigration to well over 500,000.[82] Writing in January 1930, J. A. Foote, in charge of the Canadian Presbyterian work among Koreans in Japan, noted:

> The plight of the Korean in Japan is not a happy one. He is exploited by labour "bosses," he is excluded from residence in the better localities, he is the ditch-digger, the coal miner, the railway construction coolie, the scavenger in the cities. The strong physique of the Korean woman, for she appears very erect and strong beside her Japanese sister, makes her wanted in the factories where she can endure long hours of tedious work. The wage paid the Korean is always less than that paid the Japanese labourer. When retrenchment sets in business circles he is the first to be "given the sack." Out of work, away from his homeland and the patriarchal system, he is alone and hungry.[83]

Foote believed that the Koreans, despite their shocking exploitation, needed above all a friend. He thought that it was not money, work, or a meeting place for Christian services that a Korean in Japan required from a missionary; rather, the Korean did need "a friend, someone to smile with him, someone to pray with him, someone to stand with him before the police and the government officials. This people needs a go-between, an interpreter. The missionary among the Japanese has a wonderful opportunity to be this to the Korean."[84] Canadian missionaries in Korea had often acted as defenders of Korean Christians against the Japanese colonial authorities, and Foote saw a similar role for missionaries in Japan. The Canadian Presbyterian missionary would serve as an interpreter of the Korean to the Japanese.

The work of the Canadian Presbyterians was centred in the Kobe-Osaka area, but churches were also established under Korean pastors in Nagoya, Kyoto, Wakayama, and Fukui. In 1933, evangelistic methods were described thus: "among the young people the work in the Sunday Schools, Christian Endeavour Societies, Night Schools, Daily Vacation Bible Schools and in the Kindergartens was stressed. . . . Tent meetings were held during the summer months and always drew large crowds of people who might not otherwise have heard the Gospel."[85] The Canadian Presbyterian mission was seemingly carrying on an extensive and sophisticated program of evangelistic activity for a mission that had only been in existence for some six years. However, the Presbyterians had a couple of advantages. First, they could rely upon the Korean Presbyterian Church for trained pastors and Christian workers. Second, some of the Koreans in Japan were already Christians, so the Canadians were not creating a new church from scratch. Their missionary presence, however, helped to bring definition and order to the Korean Christian community in Japan.

Unlike many Japanese, Koreans in Japan were open to the Christian message. In 1930, it was reported that "the Koreans are despised and rejected in Japan and for this reason they are very friendly toward the missionary and grateful for the message of salvation he brings."[86] Yet the same report noted that "one of the discouraging features is the opium habit. There is little restriction put upon this traffic with the result that the Koreans in their loneliness and poverty fall easy victims."[87] The problem of opium addiction illustrates the gulf between Koreans in Japan and Japanese, for opium was never mentioned as a barrier to evangelistic work among Japanese (unlike alcohol consumption or prostitution, with which missionaries took issue). Perhaps it was simply that Canadian Presbyterian work was situated in the port of Kobe, where opium might be more easily available than in the interior of Japan. However, there is a suspicion (given the low opinion of Koreans held by Japanese) that Japanese authorities condoned the use of opium among Koreans and other colonial subjects (as a manifestation of both their moral laxity and their inferiority) whereas societal values prevented its widespread consumption among Japanese.

Despite this problem, there was a marked sense of optimism that was not seen among the United Church missionaries working among the Japanese. In 1934, the Canadian Presbyterians reported that there was still great opportunity for Christian work among Koreans and that they had had "the privilege of seeing growth and advancement and of seeing men and women become new creatures in Christ Jesus."[88] This small mission exuded energy and a spirit of accomplishment. Just as Japan had its Kagawa, so Korea had its famous evangelists. In 1933, one of them, the Reverend Kim Iktoo, spent October holding special meetings in Japan and was enthusiastically received: "during these meetings over five hundred Koreans expressed their desire to study the Word of God and become Christians. Like the famous evangelist Bill Sunday, whom in his methods, he is said to resemble, he preaches the simple Gospel in great power and effectiveness."[89] By 1934, the Canadian Presbyterians were looking after a Korean Church that had 2,351 members (768 communicants), some forty-five churches (most of them in rented premises), nine Korean pastors, and fourteen Bible women.[90] Just as with the United Church and its Japanese work, the Canadian Presbyterians placed an emphasis upon self-support and self-propaganda for the Korean Church. The Canadian Presbyterians did "find in Japan that they [Koreans] carry a burden for the salvation of their people living there, and they frankly tell us that without Christ their people living in the crowded slum districts in the big cities there are doomed."[91] Regardless of their Christian zealousness, many Korean Christians did live in poverty, and self-support for their churches was as remote as it was for most of their Japanese Christian counterparts.

    The energy and Christian spirit of the Korean Church in Japan were also seen in metropolitan Korea itself. However, the work of Canadian missionaries on the Japanese colonial frontier in north Korea and Manchuria was conducted under very different circumstances than the work in Japan, be it among the Japanese or the Koreans. The activities of the small Canadian Presbyterian mission in north Taiwan provide a different example of the response to Japanese colonialism.

CHAPTER THREE
On the Colonial Frontier

"The United Church has in this strategic centre of the Orient one of her greatest opportunities for service."[1] So thought the United Church of Canada in 1928 of its mission field in Korea, which constituted "an area of one-fourth of Korea and a population of 2,000,000 in that and adjoining areas." The geographical position of the territory served by the United Church of Canada (pre-1925, Canadian Presbyterian) mission in Korea, straddling northern Korea and the Manchurian borderland along the Tumen River, created circumstances different from those experienced by other missions in metropolitan colonial Korea. Situated on the disputed frontier of the Japanese empire, and catering partly to the needs of the Korean community exiled in Manchuria, the Canadian mission faced questions of security that did not exist in metropolitan Korea after the independence demonstrations of 1919. Furthermore, a new dimension was added after 1931. As a result of the Mukden incident, the Manchurian mission of the Presbyterian Church in Canada was brought into the Japanese fold. Consequently, the interests of Canadian missionaries did not always correspond with those of their American colleagues in P'yongyang or Seoul, who operated within a stable metropolitan Korea where opposition remained focussed on Japanese colonial rule. Certainly, the Canadian position in regard to Japanese rule brought little solace to Korean nationalists struggling against it.

Indeed, independence protests would come and go, but missionaries believed that they would always remain. Throughout the 1920s and 1930s, they stayed on as trustees of physical plant built with Canadian money and as protectors of a Korean Christian community. Their sense of responsibility meant that, by the beginning of the 1930s, in contrast to their opinions of some ten years before but consistent with their self-appointed role as protector, Canadian missionaries looked to the Japanese army to ensure law and order.

Whereas the United Church missionaries worked in north Korea and Chientao province of Manchuria, the Canadian Presbyterians led by Johnathan Goforth began new missionary work in central and western Manchuria among the ethnic Chinese. Despite banditry and the turbulent political conditions that sometimes made Christian work difficult, Goforth and his missionary colleagues proved to be determined evangelists. But Canadian evangelistic efforts in the Japanese Empire were not confined to the Asian mainland. The

Canadian Presbyterian mission in Manchuria provides an interesting comparison to that in Taiwan. The dynamism of Goforth as an evangelist focussed Canadian Presbyterian attention on Manchuria and the changed circumstances there. By the 1930s, the Canadian Presbyterian mission in north Taiwan was a small missionary backwater but one that continued its traditional role of service to the ethnic Chinese in colonial Taiwan.

ON THE BORDER

Much of the appeal of Christianity to Koreans during the 1910s had been the link between it and Korean nationalism. Korean Christians had been closely identified with the Independence Movement of 1 March 1919 and had suffered the consequences.[2] However, during the 1920s, the relationship of Christianity to Korean nationalism underwent a subtle but definite change. In part, this was a response to political changes taking place in metropolitan Japan, where the spirit of Taisho liberal democracy was gaining influence in domestic politics and auguring a more tolerant attitude to imperial possessions overseas. It was also a response to a changed international system following the Paris Peace Conference, which saw the emergence of a new order in the Pacific region with the abrogation of the Anglo-Japanese Alliance and the signing of broader agreements stemming from the Washington Conference. There was hope, albeit ultimately proven forlorn, that the international community would be more sympathetic to Korean aspirations for independence.

As far as the leadership of the Korean Christian movement itself was concerned, a parallel might be made between its increasing maturity and that of the Japanese Christian leadership twenty years before, when social and political activism began to be subordinated to a desire for respectability. Certainly, for many of the Korean Christian leaders imprisoned for their support of the 1919 independence demonstrations, their confinement resulted in a strengthening of their spiritual faith. It also impressed upon them the futility and the danger of open opposition to Japanese rule. Following their release from incarceration, many Christian leaders adopted a more moderate and gradual approach to the question of Korean independence by supporting movements for cultural and social revival[3] and by eschewing open political activism.

The adoption of a gradual approach was matched by a more open and reform-minded approach to the problems of colonial administration, personified by the appointment of Saito Makoto as governor general following the independence demonstrations in 1919.[4] The Japanese colonial authorities reiterated that the government general stood for freedom of religion and stressed the positive contributions made in educational and medical fields by the Christian movement in Korea.[5] The new atmosphere created during Saito's two terms as governor general was conducive to the development of the nonviolent cultural and social movements supported by moderate leaders within the Korean Christian movement. These movements created discussion about culture, education, and the encouragement of religion. Under Saito, the government general began to move slowly away from assimilation, theoretically a fundamental tenet of Japan's colonial policy, and toward transferring limited political powers to Koreans. Although enthusiasm for the independence movement continued among Korean Christians, there was also a desire for religious catharsis that stemmed from a feeling of hopelessness. As a result, the majority of Christians were prepared to follow the moderate approach of the leadership elite.[6]

However, other Koreans still held a more active attitude toward social and political problems within Korea. Just as in Japan, the conservatism of the Korean Christian leadership in the late Meiji and Taisho periods lessened the appeal of Christianity for political or social activists. As a result, many young Koreans looked to the socialist, communist, or anarchist movements rather than to the Christian movement for leadership in the continuing struggle to gain independence from Japan. From 1920 onward, socialists, together with Marxists, were active in organizing the labour movement and the agricultural workers movement in metropolitan Korea. In April 1925, three major communist organizations formed the First Korean Communist Party. Clearly, it was difficult, because of the vigour and success of the colonial police and security forces in tracking down communists, for a viable communist party to exist in the peninsula. Korean communist groups in Japan, Shanghai, and Manchuria, therefore, became most important in continuing to keep the Korean communist movement alive and active. Of particular interest to both Korean communists and the Japanese security forces was the Chientao (Kanto) region, which ran along the Manchurian side of the Tumen River.

The population of Chientao in 1932 was over 500,000 people, most of them Korean. Lungchingtsun, the centre of United Church missionary work, was a small city with a population of slightly fewer than 20,000, of whom thirty-two were foreign residents.[7] It was at the heart of an agriculturally rich and extensively forested region. It was a place of considerable commercial activity as well as the administrative centre for the surrounding countryside, with government schools and hospitals. The city, with its Christian schools and Canadian mission hospital, was also the main Christian centre for the district. Among Koreans registered as religious believers in the Chientao region, Christians were the most numerous, and Christian churches had an overwhelming presence as far as houses of worship were concerned.[8] However, it was not Korean Christians per se who worried the Japanese in their attempt to combat the threat from communist partisans in Chientao to colonial Korea across the Tumen River.

Japanese authorities in Korea were especially concerned that communist ideas were widespread in the schools associated with the Canadian missionary endeavour and in their German Roman Catholic counterparts.[9] At Lungchingtsun, the Canadian Presbyterians operated a middle school for boys and a girls' school. The Christian schools in Chientao offered an alternative for Koreans to those of the Japanese in terms of Western-style education, an alternative that was beyond Japanese control and shielded by the extraterritorial privileges that Canadians enjoyed in Manchuria as part of China.

The position of the Canadian missionaries was linked to the world of international relations. As British diplomatic and consular figures had done in the past, they looked after Canadian interests in Chientao and in Korea. Japanese actions in Chientao before 1931 were monitored by the Western diplomatic community because they served as one measuring stick by which to gauge Japanese ambitions concerning Manchuria as a whole. Furthermore, British diplomats were much concerned with the maintenance of their extraterritorial privileges in Manchuria, which were contravened whenever Japanese police or military trespassed onto British or Canadian property or questioned British subjects. Moreover, although the effective administration of Chientao was of direct concern to the government general of Korea, it was the Japanese Foreign Ministry that conducted any negotiations over Chientao with the Chinese authorities. As it turned out, Chientao proved to be of little value in predicting Japanese intentions for Manchuria, for it was Kwantung army officers rather than Japanese diplomats who precipitated the Manchurian crisis in September 1931. Once this had happened, diplomatic interest in Chientao quickly disappeared.

In 1930, the British consul general in Seoul admitted in his annual report on affairs in Korea that "the situation in Chientao is a curious one."[10] The Japanese claimed that their powers in Chientao came from extraterritorial rights secured by treaty with China. Chientao was often lawless and turbulent, and the Japanese consequently acted as a police force despite the dubious legality of it. One of the problems for the Japanese security forces was that they could not guarantee complete security for Korean farmers. In the spring of 1930, the Chinese Communist Party called upon its Korean comrades to launch a major uprising in Chientao.[11]

Christians were not always able to escape this trouble. Clearly, some Korean Christians were communist sympathizers, especially at the mission school in Lungchingtsun. In January 1931, G. F. Bruce, who taught at the boys' school in Lungchingtsun, reported that he was being asked by his Sunday school pupils difficult leading questions about killing "those who are killing our national spirit."[12] Not surprisingly, Bruce argued for a better way. Interestingly, as one way to change his students' anti-Japanese views, he suggested the development of cooperation and scholarships between his school in Lungchingtsun and the Kwansei Gakuin in Nishinomiya so that Korean Christians could meet good Christian Japanese and find out what they were like.

However, Korean students were very sensitive to any apparent backsliding on Korean nationalism, and they had gone so far as to accuse one of their Korean Sunday school teachers (who had taught at the Kwansei Gakuin) of being pro-Japanese. This was unfortunate, for Bruce thought that the Koreans would be in for a difficult time if they did not cooperate with the Japanese. Although he believed that the Koreans were not ready to govern themselves, he also believed that the actions of the Korean communists in Chientao only reinforced similar views held by foreigners. Nevertheless, Bruce remained optimistic that the Japanese were moving toward granting Korea more autonomy as a result of the initiatives of Governor General Saito in regard to local Korean government.

While Canadian missionaries had to contend with the political situation and its impact on Korean Christians in Chientao, across the border in Sungjin they had to face a less political but still serious incident involving relations between a missionary and Korean Christians. This incident resulted after Dr. Grierson, pioneer medical missionary in Sungjin and principal of the mission school for boys, struck a former teacher of the school during a heated encounter.[13] In April 1931, D. A. MacDonald reported that a Korean being struck by a missionary "caused a regular upheaval in the community and for a while it looked as though the nationalist psychology would work up an anti-foreign case."[14] One group within the Sungjin church demanded the removal of Dr. Grierson from his missionary duties. Indeed, feelings among Koreans ran so high that a gang of them beat up the doctor in his own hospital. This attack gained Grierson some sympathy, but even among the missionaries in Sungjin opinions differed about the wrongs and rights of the two sides. It was hoped that the formation of a new church, to which the anti-Grierson party would go, would solve the problem. This solution might have satisfied some Koreans, but disagreements between missionaries persisted. Indeed, at a special meeting of the Executive Council of the Presbytery held in April, not only Grierson but all the missionaries in Sungjin handed in their resignations. Fortunately, after discussion they were withdrawn.

One of those accused as a leader of the party that "trying to 'Drive Dr. Grierson away' " was Maud Rogers, a WMS missionary.[15] Rogers was not trying to drive Grierson out of Sungjin, but she did realize that young Koreans had legitimate grievances about the way in which Grierson managed the boys' school and the hospital. Grierson had worked in Korea for over thirty years, and he was probably less accepting of new ways and less aware of the views of young Koreans than was a younger WMS missionary. Rogers was conciliatory, and the crisis between WMS missionaries and their male counterparts was defused.

The summer of 1931 was marred by serious anti-Chinese rioting in many Korean cities in reaction to reports of the ill treatment of Koreans by Chinese in Manchuria. In P'yongyang, some ninety Chinese were killed, and this violence prompted questions why Japanese police did not intervene.[16] Yet, for missionaries vacationing at Wonsan Beach, there was little expectation that the end of summer would bring so serious an event that it would lead to the shattering of their world within ten years. The end of that summer saw the Mukden incident take place and the Manchurian crisis begin.

THE MANCHURIAN CRISIS

The Manchurian (Mukden) incident of 18 September 1931[17] and the subsequent occupation of strategic cities in Manchuria by the Kwantung army created a storm of international protest against Japan. The initial reaction of Canadian missionaries was cautious optimism. In October 1931, MacDonald in Wonsan hoped that war between China and Japan could be avoided. He believed that the avoidance of war "ought to prove the worth of the League of Nations. If the League cannot function effectively in such a case as this then what good is it? It is for just such cases as this that the League machinery has been set up." He added that "Japan has everything to gain and nothing to lose by standing in well with the League, so let us hope for the best."[18] Even so, he was pessimistic that the League of Nations could solve the problem. Armstrong at the United Church Missionary Society headquarters in Toronto took some comfort from the view of Fraser in Lungchingtsun that the crisis should not affect Chientao, but he was concerned with Japan's attitude to the League and its opposition to the League's invitation to the United States to sit in on the deliberations over Manchuria. Armstrong sincerely hoped that "Japan will not be so foolish as to further irritate China and alienate the good-will of practically all the nations."[19]

But the crisis did continue, and Japan started to alienate international good will toward it. However, in Korea, MacDonald, sceptical as he was of the League of Nations, took up Japan's case, arguing that "there is much to be said for the Japanese point of view. Japan is really only trying to get what she wanted and what she won in fair fight twice in the two wars she fought with China and Russia."[20] MacDonald's pro-Japanese stance undoubtedly reflected the fact that Canadian work in Chientao was made easier by Japanese intervention.

In January 1932, Fraser wrote from Lungchingtsun that

> Japan is suppressing the bandits all right, and Manchuria will be the better for it. The Chinese officials have been replaced by other Chinese who are favourable to the real rulers, and there are Japanese advisers with them, so things will smooth down, and trade will be much advanced in Manchuria.[21]

According to Fraser, the border country was now much quieter than it had been in 1930, when it had been much disturbed by Korean communists.

Fraser's view that communist activity had been reduced was echoed in February 1932 by Ross in Lungchingtsun. Although Harbin had recently been the scene of fighting between Chinese and Japanese, Manchuria was quiet: "interest in the Japan-China trouble seems largely to have swung away from Manchuria to Shanghai."[22] However, one result of the political upheaval, coupled with the Depression, was the large number of destitute Koreans coming into Lungchingtsun and causing a refugee problem.[23] On a more positive note, the Japanese had begun to survey for a new railway line that would connect Lungchingtsun to Fukjaga, a large Chinese town thirteen miles away. It was hoped that within a year a line between Kirin and Korea would be completed on which both Lungchingtsun and Hoiryung would have stations.[24] This new railway would not only facilitate travel between the two Canadian mission centres but also bring prosperity to this agriculturally rich but underdeveloped region of Chientao.

The lessening of communist disturbances augured well for Christian work. In April 1932, Fraser saw evidence of a spiritual movement in the Korean Church that he thought connected to the disturbances caused by communist activities. One Korean evangelist had told him that he had been able to bring eighty new people into regular worship in his district in one month because some "see the evils of communistic teaching and wish to get their families away from its contamination. Others feel that communism is not a satisfying thing and wish to get the satisfaction they feel that Christianity can offer."[25] The hope for rapid growth in the number of Korean Christians was short lived, though, for the political situation took a turn for the worse. The fighting was brought home to the missionaries in Lungchingtsun when Father Rapp, one of the German Roman Catholic missionaries, was killed outside the town. Chinese bandits were conveniently blamed for his murder.[26] Conditions had deteriorated so much in Manchuria that the British minister suggested evacuation, and, indeed, the wives and children of Canadian missionaries in Lungchingtsun took the precaution of crossing over the border to the safety of Hoiryung.[27]

Yet the resurgence of banditry and the activities of communist partisans were not the only difficulties that the Canadian missionaries faced. They and Korean Christians in north Korea had to deal with immediate practical difficulties in their work, often a result of communist activity. Kim Kwan Sik, the principal of the United Church of Canada Hamheung Boys Academy, wrote that "there was a communistic trouble among all the middle schools in North Korea" and that a number of students had been expelled as a result.[28] The expulsion apparently put the rest of the student body in a much better spirit. Just as important as the arrest of students was the arrest of a Korean English-language teacher whom the police thought was the leader of the student trouble. Principal Kim insisted that the teacher was "an earnest Christian and a good student of the socialism, but certainly, not a communist."[29] Because communists had been known to use teaching positions in Christian schools as a cover for their political and national activities, the Japanese authorities were naturally concerned more about the teacher's socialism than about his earnest Christian faith, especially in a school where so many students had been arrested.

Despite putting students in prison, the Japanese still had difficulty with communist partisans. In November 1932, Robb, teaching at the Presbyterian Seminary College in P'yongyang and physically more distant from the security problems on the border, put the onus for the troubles on the Japanese. The farther removed from the border and personal involvement in the crisis, the more likely people were to be critical of the Japanese. Robb noted that "the eyes of the world are on Manchuria now. Conditions there are worse than ever before. Japanese intervention turned Chinese soldiers into bandits. War and banditry have reduced many Chinese & Koreans to the verge of starvation."[30] He added that "the Japanese militarists are in the saddle and foolishly & short-sightedly are doing their best to make great China a militaristic nation and Japan's life-long enemy."[31] Robb was perceptive about the short-sightedness of Japanese militarists in regard to their impact on China.

Fraser—stationed close to the border at Hoiryung—disagreed with Robb. In December 1932, Fraser noted that the country west of Lungchingtsun was largely deserted because of the continuing troubles as communists and Japanese police played cat and mouse while Korean farms and crops burnt. This guerrilla warfare was not new, and he felt

> a great deal of sympathy for the Japanese in this matter, as we can see no other way for the Manchurian land to reach a state of peace and quiet. . . . I certainly hope the League will not take action that will bring about a worse state in Manchuria than has existed for the past generation.[32]

Even though he disapproved of some of the methods that the Japanese employed, Fraser believed that only Japan could bring peace to Manchuria. The Lytton Commission, when it visited Manchuria in the course of its enquiries into the Manchurian crisis on behalf of the League of Nations, had travelled from Dairen north along the line of the South Manchurian Railway. Lord Lytton and his colleagues had not visited Chientao, so they had not seen first-hand the problems there, which had been going on for many years. Whether or not a visit to Chientao would have altered the commission's views of the overall crisis is a moot point, but it might have helped the Japanese case.

Despite the unsettled state of Chientao, the Canadian missionaries in Lungchingtsun were in no danger, because the Japanese maintained a garrison in the town. Furthermore, the Japanese controlled the main roads and the railway line into Korea. Having failed to establish solid links with local Chinese patriotic groups, the Korean communists in Chientao suffered setbacks during 1932 that led to their being forced out of the cities and towns. Desperate for food because of pressure from the Japanese military, the communists had no alternative but to raid villages for supplies. As a result of this activity, many ordinary folk came to see the communists as indistinguishable from bandits. However, despite the best efforts of the Japanese military, the Korean communists continued to survive in Chientao.[33] But the immediate result of the sustained Japanese campaign against the communists was a marked lessening of trouble in the countryside.

As well as wanting peace to return to Chientao, missionaries were also interested in the broader consequences of the Manchurian crisis on Japan's international standing, especially in regard to the League of Nations. In a letter written at the end of January 1933, Armstrong mentioned to Duncan McRae, one of the three pioneers of the Canadian mission in Korea, that he believed Japan's sense of loneliness in international affairs would be intensified "should Japan commit the folly of withdrawing from the League. I say folly though it would be quite logical if the Japanese Government intends to follow the program of the militarists and thus violate all the principles subscribed to by the more than fifty nations in the League."[34] In early February 1933, Robb wrote from P'yongyang wondering what would be the outcome of the situation in Geneva, which pitted Japan against the League. He believed that "there was not so much unanimity in Japan as the papers would like one to understand, but anything else is very risky at present."[35] He was correct that there was Japanese opposition to Japan's actions in Manchuria and that it took courage for Japanese to protest those actions. Despite this opposition, Japan gave notice of its withdrawal from the League of Nations on 27 March 1933. The hope of MacDonald, expressed seventeen months earlier, that the League might find a solution to the Manchurian crisis proved illusory. The Japanese had committed the folly that Armstrong had feared.

Indeed, Armstrong had begun to believe that the Japanese were now thinking of world conquest. In a letter to Black, who was about to return to his medical work in Lungchingtsun after furlough in Canada, Armstrong noted that a postcard showing the new Manchukuo flag crossed with the Japanese flag over a representation of the world had made him recall the famous Tanaka Memorial. This memorial, Armstrong informed Black, "indicated the Japanese plan for gradual conquest of Asia and ultimate domination of the world—a wild dream that did not come true even for Germany, and if pursued will mean national hari-kiri for Japan."[36] Although the Tanaka Memorial was proven a fake, Armstrong probably did not imagine that both Germany and Japan would commit national suicide within twelve years in attempts to gain world domination.

To those in Lungchingtsun, the threat was not the Japanese. Indeed, Bruce had hoped to draw Japanese guards from the local prison and the consular police into his English-language night classes. However, he had been thwarted because, though there was a real language spirit, it was not for English but for

Japanese and Manchu. Yet Bruce saw the Japanese as a positive element in Chientao, building railways that promised future prosperity for the region. In October 1933, he was not surprised when his article on "Communism in Manchuria" was rejected by the United Church of Canada's *New Outlook*, "for there are different ideas of what communism really is."[37] Nevertheless, he added—regarding communism as it was known to Korean Christians and to him in Chientao—that "it is terrible; but it nevertheless is active propaganda, and is terrible in its torture. I am thankful to say that it seems to be checked considerably. The Japanese armed Koreans to defend themselves against the communist groups—these might be either Manchu or Korean."[38] Black, whom Armstrong had asked to keep him informed of political developments in Manchuria, also took a positive view of the efforts of the Japanese in the past year. Although Black noted that much of the expensive railway and road building that the Japanese had undertaken was for military purposes, monetary reform had been a great benefit for ordinary people.[39] He believed that Japan was in Manchuria to stay, and he welcomed this. He thought that Japanese withdrawal would lead to nothing but anarchy and that the common people had much to gain from the law and order that the Japanese brought. He noted that the Koreans had much to gain by the change to Japanese rule because in the past they had been used "as innocent agents of Japanese penetration and, as such, were disliked and persecuted by the Chinese. Now they will have equal citizenship. Further, the Japanese have created employment for a good many educated Koreans in connection with the new government offices which have been set up."[40] Regardless of the international consequences of the Manchurian crisis for Japan and the world beyond Manchuria, Black and his fellow workers in Lungchingtsun clearly believed that the creation of a Japanese-dominated Manchukuo would benefit the Koreans. They thought that the Japanese had the best chance of any group to bring law and order and prosperity to their part of Manchuria, which had suffered for a generation from disturbances and guerrilla warfare. It was bandits and communist partisans, in their opinion, who posed a greater threat to the well-being of Korean Christians in the Chientao region than the Japanese with their armoured cars and railways. Their view was parochial, for their concern was the safety of the Korean Christians whom they served. They were virulently anticommunist at a time when many Canadians at home were sympathetic to communist ideas. Similarly, they were anticommunist when many in Korea, including some Christians, saw the very Korean partisans in Chientao, whom the Canadian missionaries so abhorred, as the vanguard of the movement to liberate Korea from Japanese colonial rule. In order to achieve their nationalistic goal, communist groups burnt crops and buildings and terrorized and slaughtered innocent farmers, including Christian ones. What Canadian missionaries saw in Chientao were the violent and destructive results of their actions.

    As might be expected, Canadian missionaries in Japan held strong views on the crisis in Manchuria. Among Canadian Anglicans, Loretta L. Shaw came out strongly in favour of the Japanese actions in Manchuria, which were designed both to provide stability to a region fraught with problems and to protect Japan's economic well-being in its confrontation with American and Australian exclusionist legislation and threat of economic boycott.[41] Shaw was not alone in her support of the Japanese. In August 1932, Melvin Whiting, a United Church missionary in Japan, visited first Korea, then Manchuria, and finally metropolitan China. He wrote that "poor old China is in an awful state however. Going from Japan where everything is order, progress, safety and peace, it is very depressing. Poverty, ruin, and dirt seem to sum up largely what one sees in China."[42] It was this contrast between a progressive and safe Japan, setting out to bring law and order to Manchuria, and the "awful state" of China that reinforced in the minds of missionaries in Japan that the Japanese held out the best chance for the future for Manchuria. In the fall of 1932, H. F. Woodsworth, who taught at the Kwansei Gakuin, echoed Whiting's views when—after a visit to Korea—he came back to Japan impressed by the beneficial effects of Japanese rule: the "country seemed much prosperous and the people are apparently happy and quietly contented. One wonders whether Japan can repeal [sic] Manchuria. The nearer I came to Manchuria the more my sympathies turned towards Japan."[43] Woodsworth went on to argue that the United Church should immediately take advantage of the situation in Manchuria and send missionaries to work among the Japanese there.

Canadian missionaries in Japan were troubled when others did not agree with their pro-Japanese point of view. Holmes in Fukui attacked *New Outlook* for having taken the Chinese side in its editorial position on the Manchurian crisis. Professor Robert Wright has suggested that some observers in Canada, including W. B. Creighton, the editor of *New Outlook*, attempted to see both sides of the issue but found themselves torn "between their realistic understanding of political and diplomatic circumstances at the local level and their 'idealistic' hopes for a new international order based on the tenets of liberal internationalism."[44] Indeed, this was the last major crisis in East Asia during the 1930s for which there was some sympathy in Canada for the Japanese government's point of view.

But there was also opposition in Japan itself to Japanese actions. In early 1932, the National Christian Council (NCC) stood out against the Manchurian situation. At the same time, the NCC used its international connections to appeal to Christians abroad to implore their governments to help bring about a peaceful settlement between China and Japan.[45] This proved to be the last time that the NCC came out against Japanese actions. Bates at the Kwansei Gakuin captured the atmosphere within the Japanese Church when he wrote in July 1932 that

> They are having a very difficult time, not only or mostly financially although

that is very hard, but also intellectually, and spiritually and politically. They are between the upper and the nether millstones of Fascism and Communism. And at the same time are being weakened by the decreasing support to the financial and personnel of the Mission.[46]

There was so much change within the Japanese Church as a result of the Depression that it was difficult to deal with political and international developments. Yet some prominent Japanese Christians did come out against the actions of the Japanese military, including Yoshino Sakuzo and Yanaihara Tadao.[47]

However, there were Japanese Christians who supported the Japanese actions. Hayashi Mikiotaro, a priest in charge of a Mukden church and thus more familiar with local conditions than many Japanese Christian critics in Japan, defended the Japanese. Hayashi put the blame for the incident on the ambitions of the Chinese warlords and on anti-Japanese sentiment among the Chinese, which had caused Japanese to suffer political and economic persecution in Manchuria. He believed that Japanese and Chinese had agreed to cooperate in the development of Manchuria and that Japanese rights had to be protected. He portrayed the incident as a natural occurrence that the Chinese, who had held the Japanese in contempt since the Sino-Japanese War and the later Twenty-One Demands, had brought upon themselves. In other words, Hayashi, and other Japanese involved in missionary work in Manchuria,[48] saw the root of the incident in the long-standing anti-Japanese feelings of the Chinese and not in any aggressive actions by the Kwantung army. Among other Japanese Christians, Nitobe Inazo, the director of the Japan Council of the Institute of Pacific Relations during the crisis, defended the Japanese actions.[49] Although the Japanese members of the Institute of Pacific Relations tried to defend Japan, diplomatic and military events outside their control discredited their position. By the spring of 1933, Japan had withdrawn from the League of Nations and was internationally isolated.

WITH GOFORTH IN MANCHURIA

Among those affected most by the Manchurian crisis were Canadian missionaries who worked among the Chinese population in Manchuria. In 1925, when the Canadian Presbyterian North Honan Mission decided to join the new United Church, veteran missionary Johnathan Goforth decided to remain within the Presbyterian Church in Canada.[50] As a result of this decision, in 1927 Goforth, no longer welcome in North Honan, began work at Szepingkai, an important junction on the South Manchurian Railway north of Mukden, with the blessing of the Irish Presbyterian mission.[51]

This was not completely new ground for Goforth. He had been in Manchuria during the great revival of 1908 and had achieved remarkable evangelistic success in Mukden that year.[52] Going back to Manchuria in the late 1920s, Goforth and his wife, Rosalind, followed the stream of Chinese immigrants looking for new opportunities. In 1927, Goforth wrote about his new field:

> Our location is on the South Manchuria Railway about half way between Dalney and Harbin. We are at the South end of the Taonan Tsitsihar railway. The area of our field is much larger than that of the old Honan field with a population about as great as that of Ontario. This North East of China is the counter part of the North West of Canada. It has vast areas for colonization. Almost a million settlers from Honan, Chihli and Shantung provinces poured in this spring. In working the field we can take advantage of the railways for five hundred miles. In the western part of our field lives one of the most noted and powerful of the Mongol tribes. It will be our privilege and duty to carry the gospel to them also.[53]

In December 1927, Allan Reoch, who together with his wife went to Manchuria to work with Goforth, noted that "we were surprised at the vast stretch of territory which will be the battle ground of our Church in the struggle against the darkness of heathen unbelief and sin."[54] Reoch's language bespoke an evangelistic fire that had long since disappeared from the vocabulary of United Church missionaries in Japan or Korea. In calling for the Presbyterian Church in Canada to send out more workers (he himself had just arrived), Reoch exclaimed: "the people are so friendly and receive the Gospel gladly, not having been poisoned by the soul-destroying doctrines of the Bolsheviks. Souls are perishing for lack of preachers. We must possess the land before it is too late. Now is the time to strike while the iron is hot."[55]

This was an evangelistic enterprise in Manchuria; the Canadian Presbyterians there were unencumbered by the physical plant and the responsibilities of mission schools or hospitals. They had the train or the bus to take them over their large field. Manchuria had been called by one clerical visitor "the greatest missionary opportunity of the present generation."[56] This view had echoes of Student Volunteer Movement hopes for Korea a quarter century before, but Goforth and his colleagues sincerely believed that Manchuria offered a grand Christian opportunity. The story of the Manchurian mission could always be summed up in the one word "PROGRESS," and even in the hardest times "the outlook here is most hopeful."[57] By 1933, there were twelve Canadian Presbyterian missionaries with two mission stations at Szepingkai and Taonan (on the Tsitsihar railway) at the centre of a large number of outstations. It was reported in 1933 that "there ought to be more," but not "until after the financial stringency in the homeland is more relieved."[58]

Aside from the shortage of money, there were other problems. One was the ill health of Goforth and his wife, both of whom were old to be working as missionaries. Yet it was his reputation and the letter-writing energy of his wife (who wrote close to 700 letters to supporters in 1929) that kept the Manchurian mission at the fore among supporters in Canada. Partially as a result of her extensive correspondence, $12,123.61 Mexican was raised in 1932 through unsolicited donations from friends in the United States and Canada. This was enough to support fifty Chinese evangelists.[59]

An equally significant problem was the unsettled nature of the countryside. The work of the Canadian Presbyterians, like that of their United Church colleagues in Chientao was bothered by bandits. Ta Tze Cheng, one of the farthest northern outstations, was cut off by army operations and bandit activities. So bad were bandit conditions around the outstation at Pa Mien San Chao near Taonan that the Chinese preacher sensibly took his family to the safety of Taonan. In 1932, the bandit forces in western Manchuria were so powerful that they gained control of Tung Liao, a small city on the railway 140 miles west of Szepingkai. This action put Christian work by Chinese evangelists in one of the most hopeful outstations in jeopardy. Despite all the difficulties in Tung Liao, the Chinese evangelists in charge believed that their troubles in fact strengthened their faith. Goforth remained optimistic, stating that, "in spite of disturbances and alarms the work goes steadily on and is really encouraging. God is with us and nothing else matters."[60] The next year, it was reported that the bandits had been driven out by Japanese troops, but the seriousness of the situation was underlined by the fact that, "as protection from the bandits and Volunteers [Mongols], T'ungliao [sic] is now surrounded by electrically charged wire."[61] To go to the expense of ringing a large city with an electric fence meant that the Japanese, at least, considered the bandit problem serious. There is no indication in Canadian Presbyterian records of just who the bandits were. The majority were likely former Chinese soldiers and not Communists.

Other places were affected by fighting between Japanese and Chinese forces following the Mukden incident. There was a major battle at the Nonni River near Tai Lai, an outstation, that brought Christian work there temporarily to a halt. At Pai Cheng Tze, an outstation at the railway junction for a new road leading into the Great Khing An Mountain Range, where the murder of Japanese officers in 1931 was one of the precipitating causes of the Mukden incident, evangelistic work was disrupted at bayonet point by overzealous Chinese police.

Yet these troubles were seen by Goforth and his Canadian Presbyterian missionary colleagues as bringing fresh evangelistic opportunities. Indeed, the Irish Presbyterians in Manchuria drew parallels between the religious climate in 1932 and that during the revival movement of 1908.[62] National disasters and social insecurity marked both years. Goforth must have been aware of the similarities between 1908 and 1932, because he had achieved considerable evangelistic success in Manchuria in the wake of the earlier revival. Perhaps it was simply that he was so single-mindedly concerned with the possibilities of a new revival or so inured to unsettled times as a result of his long years in Honan that he did not find the disturbed state of Manchuria exceptional.

However, it is more probable that the Canadian Presbyterians simply attempted to avoid political involvement in Manchuria. Austin Fulton, an Irish Presbyterian missionary in Manchuria, pointed out that Irish Presbyterian missionaries discouraged political involvement before the Japanese took over Manchuria. Because of the confusion of Chinese politics, they were wary of direct political involvement and thought that politically minded Christians became less useful to the Church. There was a feeling among Chinese Christians in Manchuria, according to Dr. Fulton, that "the willow which bends with the storm will outlast the oak (or the pine) which withstands it seemed to apply."[63] All available evidence points to the fact that the Canadian Presbyterians, like their Irish counterparts, eschewed political involvement during the Manchurian crisis and in the years following it. Given the fluidity of the political situation, this approach was wise. There was the danger of arrest and imprisonment if the Japanese authorities had even a suspicion of a Manchurian's anti-Japanese sympathies. This was dramatically illustrated in early October 1935, when some forty Christians were among those arrested in Mukden during a dragnet against anti-Japanese sympathizers by the Japanese security forces.[64]

In early 1935, Fulton noted that it was rumoured among missionaries that "the Japanese Army had made up its mind not to repeat what it now considered to have been a major blunder, made when Korea had been occupied over twenty years earlier. Their mistake, they now believed, was that they had not done away with the Christian Church in that land."[65] The arrests in October 1935 were obviously an attempt to break the spirit of the Christian movement in Manchuria. Those Christians arrested were found to be members of The One Cent Society, a group formed to support the educational costs of a theological student in training; the Japanese authorities misconstrued it to be a communist organization.[66] In reporting this incident in January 1936, the *Chinese Recorder* pointed out that there was another and pertinent reason for the arrests:

> all arrested were connected with organizations related to countries other than Japan. The attempts of the British consul to register a protest on behalf of those connected with British firms met with the reply that Manchukuo is not Japan hence the negotiations, that had to be carried on through Tokyo as Great Britain does not recognize Manchukuo.[67]

The Japanese authorities were particularly interested in finding out who had given information to the Lytton Commission.[68] There was obviously a close connection between the persecution of Chinese Christians with links to British missionaries and outstanding diplomatic issues between Japan and Britain relating to Manchukuo or later to the Sino-Japanese War. Naturally, Canadian Presbyterian missionaries, because of their close identification with Britain, were considered by the authorities as part of the British missionary group.

Fulton made the point that Manchuria knew what had happened in Korea and tried to take no risks.[69] Missionary relations with the Japanese were by no means acrimonious. Fulton noted that Irish Presbyterian missionary relations with Japanese ministers of various Japanese churches in Manchukuo were always cordial and characterized by mutual trust. In times of trouble, as in October 1935, the Irish Presbyterians in Mukden would often turn to Japanese ministers to intercede with the authorities on behalf of Chinese Christians. Indeed, "some of these men [Japanese ministers] took considerable risks, we thought, in their readiness to help missionaries and Chinese christians when there was trouble with the authorities."[70] Fulton also noted that missionary relations with Japanese officials in the civilian government "were correct and sometimes cordial. We found that those in the higher ranks tried to understand our position and point of view and to deal with us as generously as their regulations allowed.... Contacts with the army were few and avoided as far as they possibly could be."[71] Missionary relations with the civilian Japanese authorities in Manchukuo were thus similar to those of United Church missionaries in northern Korea. Clearly, though, missionaries wanted to keep contact between themselves and the Japanese military to a minimum. This sentiment was shared by Canadians in both Korea and Manchukuo as well as by the Irish and Scots Presbyterians. After October 1935, Chinese Christians and missionaries alike knew that it was physically dangerous for them to run afoul of the Japanese military authorities. However, Fulton also wrote that in a territory in the east, where Korea and Manchuria came near to Siberia, a communist group reportedly existed in defiance of the Japanese, and "such news was welcome to Manchurian christians, not necessarily because it was communists who so resisted Japanese domination but because there was some group, no matter what their ideology, which was able to do so."[72] Clearly, the area referred to was Chientao. It was resistance to the Japanese, and not necessarily ideology, that evoked support.

FINANCIAL CUTS IN KOREA

Armstrong, who supervised the Korean mission from United Church headquarters in Toronto, visited Korea in the wake of the 1 March 1919 independence demonstrations. In 1934, he went to Korea for the third time and spent some six weeks visiting all the major centres of Canadian work in the peninsula and in Chientao.[73] The Canadian missionaries believed that the week Armstrong spent at Wonsan Beach, where nearly all of them came together, was particularly beneficial. Indeed, his visit to Korea deepened his understanding of the challenges confronting the missionary and Korean Christian movements and would later help him to come to grips with the different sides of the shrine question.

Armstrong also visited Seoul, where he took on the role of the visiting Canadian missionary statesman, calling on the governor general of Chosen and on the heads of the government general's Departments of Education and Foreign Affairs as well as inspecting the Chosen Christian College, Ewha College (the leading Christian school for women), and Severance Union Hospital and College. From Seoul, he went to Sorai, where William MacKenzie, the famous Nova Scotian missionary, had died tragically in 1894, to dedicate a memorial church there. Armstrong spoke at the meeting of the General Assembly of the Korean Presbyterian Church at P'yongyang. He also addressed an open-air meeting of up to 20,000 Christians gathered in P'yongyang to celebrate the fiftieth anniversary of the beginnings of Protestant missions in Korea. The huge size of this meeting demonstrated the strength of the Korean Christian movement in P'yongyang prior to the confrontation over the shrine ceremonies.

Before his trip to Korea, Armstrong had been enthusiastic about the merits of the Oxford Group Movement in helping "to quicken thousands of Christians in the Churches of Canada and send them out radiant and eager to share Christ with others."[74] However, Canadian missionaries in Korea apparently did not share the same enthusiasm for the Oxford Group Movement. Armstrong also put great stock in the work of Kagawa. Armstrong's experiences in Korea, and elsewhere in East and South Asia, seemingly reinforced his support for Kagawa. Indeed, in April 1935, in a public address in Toronto about his visit to the mission fields of Japan, Korea, Honan, South China, and India, he reported "a new day in the friendliness of peoples and officials, in the change in their attitude toward the missionaries and their work, and closed with a strong appeal to harken to the question of Kagawa, 'Can we at home go further until we go deeper?'"[75] It was soon apparent, however, that the Church in Canada could not go further because of the financial shortfall caused by the continuing Depression.

In April 1935, the same month that Armstrong gave his address in Toronto about "a new day" in the mission field, he broke the bad news to those in Korea. Perhaps the size of the Christian gatherings in P'yongyang, or his trust in the efficacy of the evangelistic methods of Kagawa, had worked to the disadvantage of the Korean mission. Perhaps the visible success of Christianity in Korea in the steeples of P'yongyang and Seoul had been too impressive. In any case, Armstrong wrote to Fraser that the Policy Committee of the Foreign Mission Board had recommended that the budget of the board should be reduced by $100,000. It had been determined that in the upcoming 1936 budget $40,000 would be taken from the Korean mission—a sixty percent reduction—

for it.⁷⁶ There would have to be a reduction in the number of missionaries. Some such as Grierson and MacRae, who had been with the Korean mission from its start, were at retirement age, but cuts would have to go deeper than that.

There was considerable protest, not only from missionaries but also from Korean Christians. One Korean pastor reacted to the news by saying that "Japan is an important country with influence so they would not cut the work there in that way but Korea not having that influence must bear the heavy cut."⁷⁷ More important was the opinion of another Korean minister, who noted that "today when the Korean Church is facing so many problems both internal and external . . . it would be fatal to withdraw the support of the Canadian Mission."⁷⁸ For missionaries, the financial crisis at home was perceived as a real threat to the continued existence of the mission. In August 1935, in an open letter to friends of the Korean mission in Canada, it was pointed out that the cut would leave the Korean mission with "not more than a quarter of the maximum grant received before Union."⁷⁹ There is a hint here that the United Church was not living up to its obligations in taking over the Korean mission from the Canadian Presbyterians in 1925. Yet the main argument against the cuts was that members of the Korean Church were too poor to support the level of work that the Canadian missionaries had done. Perhaps there was a feeling that the success of the mission work in Korea, which had helped to create a dynamic Korean Church, had resulted in the Korean mission being penalized with greater reductions in its budget than any other mission of the United Church of Canada. It was contended that the United Church of Canada, unless it declared itself bankrupt, had responsibilities to maintain its evangelistic, educational, and medical work in Korea. The Parthian shot was to quote the moderator of the United Church of Canada, Dr. Roberts, who had stated that "The Church that ceases to be Missionary ceases to be Christian."⁸⁰

Some missionaries in Japan also rallied to the support of the Korean mission. One of the most notable supporters was Bates in Nishinomiya. He expressed a commonly held view of the role of the Korean Christian movement in East Asia when he urged that the Canadian mission in north Korea be spared from damaging cuts because Christianity meant so much to the spiritual life of the Korean people, whom he thought were destined to be spiritual leaders in East Asia. Bates argued that "God has not maintained the identity and integrity of the Korean people between the upper and nether millstones of Japan and China for nothing. They have a mission to fulfill. They have lost their independence but they have not lost their soul."⁸¹ Nevertheless, though Bates believed that the Korean Christian movement had a special mission to fulfil, it is doubtful that he would have been willing to see money taken from the Kwansei Gakuin, of which he was president, to lessen the cuts to the Korean mission.

The protests against the proposed cuts led the Foreign Mission Board to reconsider its decision. It halved its demands, but even this reduction meant that three missionaries and one doctor had to be withdrawn, the hospital in Sungjin closed, and Foreign Mission Board work in the Sungjin station discontinued.[82] The end of Sungjin as a major mission centre can also be seen as one of the enduring results of the earlier controversy over the conduct of Dr. Grierson.

STAYING ON IN NORTH TAIWAN

Although 1925 saw the creation of the United Church of Canada, those who remained within the Presbyterian Church in Canada wished to see the continuation of Presbyterian missionary work in both Korea and Taiwan. It was argued that, "to introduce a new denomination in such fields for instance as Formosa and Korea that are Presbyterian in polity and doctrine and have been so from the beginning, we believe to be a great mistake."[83] The mission in Korea did join the United Church of Canada, but the mission in north Taiwan remained within the Presbyterian Church in Canada. During the late nineteenth century, the Taiwan mission had been largely associated with its founder, George Leslie Mackay, and during the early twentieth century the Mackay family remained the backbone of this small mission. The founder's son, George W. Mackay, a layman whose life work was in Christian education in Taiwan, was the dominant figure in the mission during the 1920s and 1930s. Mackay and his wife decided to remain Presbyterians, and so the mission did.[84] A few missionaries joined the United Church of Canada but decided to remain at work in Taiwan. Although some missionaries did leave at the time of Church union in Canada, the Taiwan mission was kept functioning until a "new crew" went to take over.[85] This meant that, throughout the late 1920s and early 1930s, the mission was short of missionaries, especially Chinese-speaking evangelistic ones. But it also meant that the Taiwan mission possessed a number of younger missionaries at a time when the Japan and Korea missions of the United Church were made up of veterans.

Remaining within the Presbyterian Church in Canada did make sense for another reason, for apart from N. P. Yates, a lone Canadian Anglican missionary working from 1915 among the aborigines at Taite,[86] the Canadian Presbyterian and its English counterpart in south Taiwan were the only Western Protestant missions in Taiwan. Moreover, although joining the new United Church of Canada might have been tempting because of greater financial security, this lure would prove illusory, as those in Korea found out to their chagrin in 1935.

Despite the lack of missionaries, the Presbyterians in Taiwan remained optimistic about their future prospects. In 1929, it was reported that missionaries did not face the same difficulties that confronted their counterparts in China:

Everywhere the Gospel is welcomed and the foreigner is received as an ambassador from the "mysterious and wonderful western world." The present problem for us is that although almost everyone is ready to stand and praise the Gospel with his lips and make promises to do this and that, yet to actually do something about it is a different matter. This is "heathenism" as it is found here. Were this attitude of the Formosan people to be analyzed further, no doubt most of the familiar forms of heathenism would be discovered beneath the surface. However, to make progress for the Kingdom among these people is our problem, our challenge, and our fascinating opportunity.[87]

Taiwan was a Japanese colony with a relatively efficient colonial bureaucracy that ensured law and order. It was pointed out in 1930 that "it is generally recognized that were it not for the strong arm of Japan conditions here would be as bad or worse than they are on the mainland of China to-day."[88] Yet, though evangelistic workers in Taiwan encountered much the same scepticism from ethnic Chinese islanders as that which frustrated missionaries in Fukien province across the strait, the major challenge to educational and medical work came from the colonial authorities.

As in Korea, it was the relationship between missionaries and Japanese authorities that ultimately determined the success or failure of Presbyterian mission work in Taiwan. Just as in the peninsula, the political and military policies of the government general in Taiwan impinged upon the Christian work undertaken by Western missionaries. In both colonies, the concern of Japanese officials was to ensure that Japanese values and ideas were inculcated into their colonial subjects and that conflicting views were rooted out. This goal became all the more important as Japanese politicians became sensitive to what was happening in Taiwan. Any untoward event in Taiwan provided opposition parties with ammunition to use against the government in the Imperial Diet in Tokyo. Between 1923 and 1930, there were frequent changes in the highest officials in the island, including six changes of governor general.[89] This rapid turnover, often caused by political considerations in Tokyo rather than by any negligence on the part of the administration of the governor general, meant that important decisions were left untaken. One question not tackled by the government general was meeting Taiwanese aspirations for greater political power. A further grievance of the Taiwanese was the failure of the colonial authorities to provide adequate higher education for Taiwanese.[90]

Accessibility to higher education was an important question for the Canadian Presbyterian mission in north Taiwan that maintained the Tamsui Middle School and the Tamsui Girls' School. One appeal of these schools was that they offered an alternative, albeit a limited one, to the Japanese educational system in the island. However, for the vast majority of Taiwanese, who depended upon the colonial educational system for their elementary education, there would be no immediate liberalization of educational policies.

An event with immediate and serious political consequences for the governor general of Taiwan, as well as an acute embarrassment for the metropolitan government in Japan, was the aboriginal uprising in the Musha region in late October 1930.[91] The reasons for the uprising, which resulted in some 150 Japanese casualties, were that the aborigines were used as forced labour, were underpaid, and had to deal with police graft.[92] The uprising was quickly put down, but many of the Taiyal aborigines committed suicide rather than submit to the Japanese.[93] Perhaps as a result of their suffering at the hands of the Japanese military, many of the aborigines who survived became open to the Christian message.

For missionaries, a key problem in Christianizing the aborigines was that foreigners were not allowed to enter the remote aboriginal areas in east Taiwan except with special permission. Before Japanese rule, both Canadian and English Presbyterians had made some attempts to convert the Pepo-hoans. Canadians likened the aborigines in Taiwan to the Native peoples in Canada and saw their evangelization as an endeavour separate from their main constituency, the ethnic Chinese in Taiwan. Certainly, after the beginning of Japanese rule in 1895, limitations of personnel and money meant that virtually all resources were directed toward the evangelization of the latter. Although Western missionaries were not allowed into restricted aboriginal areas, other aborigines were. It was reported in 1930 that "this year a woman from a head hunting tribe, who was educated at our Women's School, has volunteered to go back to her people, and now Chi-oang, for that is her name, is leading a trail that we hope many will follow."[94] In March 1931, Douglas Wilkie admitted that little was being done among the aborigines, "who are scattered and in some parts formidable. There was an outbreak a short time ago and two Japanese in a nearby village were killed," but "among the headhunters on the east coast we have one Biblewoman, a native, who preaches to her own people."[95] The extent of the Musha uprising was not well known, for it was obviously the "outbreak" to which Wilkie was referring.

Chi-oang felt optimistic and pleased with the welcome given to her Christian message by the Taiyal aborigines. During a visit in early 1931 to Horasshi, a small village, where some forty people came to hear her,

> the [Japanese] police were very glad to have me speak and after I had spoken they asked the people whether they understood or not. "What do you ask us that for?" they said. "Doesn't she speak in our own language, what do you mean by asking us whether we understand?" The police went on to tell the people that if they paid attention to the teaching they would be helped.[96]

In part, her positive reception might well have been because she was "the daughter of a Sediq chief, and she inherited all the Sediq spirit of resistance against the Japanese masters."[97] Even more than that, Chi-oang, who spoke both

Chinese and Japanese as well as her own native language, had acted as a mediator between Sediq rebels and the Japanese, and had thus become an adviser to her tribe. In speaking to the villagers at Horasshi, the Japanese police were sympathetic to Chi-oang's Christian message. However, the police watched the aborigines closely, and any Christian success among them could only be achieved if the police allowed it. Indeed, the Japanese did try to stop Chi-oang and attempted to arrest her.

A second aboriginal worker, Do-wai, a Taiyal, who had been attracted to Christianity after attending an evangelistic meeting at a Chinese church in 1928 and had subsequently been trained as a preacher, went to work in the early 1930s among the Taiyal in the central mountains. Like Chi-oang, Do-wai ran afoul of the Japanese authorities because they wanted to convert the aborigines to Shintoism.[98] He later suffered persecution and imprisonment as a result of continuing his Christian work.

Circumstances were such that these two aboriginal workers could not convert many aborigines to Christianity. But their efforts and heroism created a link between Christianity and the Taiyal and Sediq aborigines that was exploited with significant results once the Japanese police were removed at the end of the Pacific War.

The Canadian Presbyterians had greater success in converting the ethnic Chinese in Taiwan. Much emphasis was placed on evangelistic work, especially in 1932, the diamond jubilee of the mission.[99] Despite the enthusiasm of Church members, the evangelistic element of the celebrations was not fully successful. It was reported in 1933 that the policy of the Church that year was one of concentration rather than expansion and that, with less than one percent of the population associated with the Church, it was difficult for Christian influence to permeate the community. Furthermore, "the effort of trying to maintain struggling groups of twenty-five or thirty Christians widely scattered is not only pathetic but ineffective. For the present, therefore, concentration on the work already established would seem to be the better policy."[100] This statement is surprising coming from a mission that had just celebrated its sixtieth anniversary, for it depicted disappointing results and low spirits, which stand in sharp contrast to the ever-optimistic, misguided though it might have been, spirit of the Canadian Presbyterians in Manchuria. The Canadian Presbyterians served a total Christian community in north Taiwan of some 8,000, even though only 250 new members had been added in 1932.[101] The Presbyterian Church in north Taiwan had apparently reached a plateau beyond which it could not be expected to grow. Given that the number of Canadian missionaries was fewer than twenty, and that the total Taiwanese ministry was only fifty-eight, of whom only ten were ordained pastors, it is unreasonable to believe that the Church would have been able to expand much further.

Yet missionaries remained optimistic that their evangelistic work would be successful. In 1934, it was reported that evangelistic work during 1933 had met with encouraging responses in most parts of the mission field, and that "large crowds of people have greeted the evangelistic message and there has been a notable lack of opposition from the non-Christians. While there have been no spectacular in-gatherings, the church has experienced a quiet, steady growth."[102] Year in and year out, similar reports were made.

Despite yearly fluctuations in the number of converts, the Canadian Presbyterians remained committed to achieving their goal. In 1935, it was reported that "our constant aim in Formosa has been to produce a Church which will be in every sense of the word an indigenous one; self-governing, self-supporting, and self-propagating."[103] Yet the Church in north Taiwan was far from being able to dispense with the help of missionaries. Even though complete self-support was a long way off for the Taiwanese Church, it was reported that "the Formosans, nevertheless, realize the lethargic effect of too much money from Canada and are determined that the amount of opiate (as they themselves have called it) must gradually be decreased."[104] This was wishful thinking, for there were only twelve self-supporting congregations out of a total of seventy-six congregations. Although the number of self-supporting congregations had doubled since 1924, it was still discouragingly low after over fifty years of missionary work in north Taiwan. As far as self-propagation was concerned, beyond work within the established congregations, the Taiwanese Church had only been able to fund two men to go and preach to the Ami tribe. It is clear that self-government, self-support, and self-propagation comprised a long-term goal, if one attainable at all. Indeed, no Canadian mission in Japan, Korea, Manchuria, or Taiwan was able to achieve its goal of self-support before the outbreak of the Pacific War.

While evangelistic work ticked over, the Canadian Presbyterians had some success with their medical work. The Mackay Memorial Hospital in Taipeh had a somewhat chequered career owing to the shortage of missionary doctors and money. However, it had been in continuous operation since 1925, and in 1934 it treated some 143,000 out-patients and 8,000 in-patients.[105] The figures show that this was a large and active hospital that dealt with all types of operations and illnesses. In 1935, it had two Canadian doctors on staff. Of the two, Dr. G. Gushue-Taylor, a Newfoundlander, was much involved with the Happy Mount Leprosy Colony, which he had been instrumental in founding and developing. Prior to working for the Canadian Presbyterian mission, Gushue-Taylor was active in leprosy work in Japan and should be regarded as an important and energetic figure in helping the plight of lepers. The many medical demands upon missionary doctors meant that they had little time to try to convert their patients to Christianity. The press of work there might have been one reason the Canadian Presbyterians always had difficulty finding missionary doctors for Mackay Memorial.

The hospital had less difficulty finding Canadian nurses, even though the work conditions for them were often harder than for their male doctor counterparts. The training of Taiwanese nurses was one of the responsibilities of the Canadian nurses at the hospital. In the years after 1925, only some twenty-five nurses graduated, and the majority of these graduates either married and left nursing or went to work at Mackay Memorial or the English Presbyterian hospital in Tainan. The nursing school at the Mackay Memorial was small beer, but it supplied enough nurses to meet the needs of Presbyterian medical work in Taiwan. One of the difficulties encountered in training nurses was the low educational standard of the candidates. Nevertheless, those who gained admittance could look forward to a career within the hospitals of the Christian movement. Wider nursing opportunities existed, but greater educational qualifications were required for Taiwanese who went to a government general institution for nursing training.

The shortage of funds also meant that the Canadian Presbyterian hospital lacked the modern facilities that the government general hospital system, with its greater financial resources, could provide. Where the Canadian Presbyterians could make a real difference was in the direction of their medical work. The Happy Mount Leprosy Colony was one example of Canadian Presbyterian work making a significant contribution to the betterment of Taiwanese society. Mackay Memorial Hospital itself received from the government general a small subsidy for "serving the poor of the neighbourhood."[106] Likewise, once or twice a year, free evening clinics were held at the suggestion of the Department of Social Services of the government general. Medical work was regulated by the government general, which set rigorous guidelines in regard to the qualifications of doctors and nurses as well as the services that could be offered. In that respect, Canadian Presbyterian medical work continued as long as the government general saw that it was useful and met the required standards. Mackay Memorial Hospital enjoyed a good name in the community and served the foreign community and the British consulate. Through their medical work, the Canadian Presbyterians provided a service that the Japanese thought worthwhile or, at least, not threatening to their control of the Taiwanese.

CHAPTER FOUR
The Shrine Question

The participation of Christians in state-sponsored Shinto ceremonies was a long-standing issue in Japan. The shrine question touched on sensitive topics for Japanese Christians such as their loyalty, patriotism, and attitude toward the emperor. During the 1930s, the Japanese government moved to increase its control over religious organizations as part of the increasing emphasis on *tennosei*, the emperor system. The shrine question brought about the collision between the freedom of religion and the national Shinto system.

Immediately following the Meiji Restoration, the policy of the government was to make Shinto the state religion in order to obstruct the surging demand for religious freedom.[1] Yet, in order to allow national Shinto and the freedom of religion to coexist, the government decided to separate Shinto ceremonies and religion. The result was that the ceremonies at the state Shinto shrines became suprareligious and beyond the control of religious sects.[2] The government then moved to ensure that the activities of religious sects did not infringe on the prerogatives of the national Shinto system. Beginning in 1899, when the Yamagata cabinet first introduced a Religious Organizations Bill, and continuing for some forty years until the successful passage of the Religious Organizations Law of 1939, there was a constant struggle between the government wanting to enforce its control over religion and those wanting to maintain religious freedom.

For Christians, taking part in state Shinto rites was bedevilled by the uncertainty of whether or not participation in them was a religious act. And there were denominational nuances. This was especially true for Japanese Anglicans. The case of the NSKK is important, for it not only provides a denominational example of the subtlety of the problem of *tennosei* for Japanese Christians but also reveals that the transfer of structural forms and ideas across cultural boundaries can create unforeseen difficulties. The shrine question also required a missionary response. A major desire of missionaries, including Canadians, was to see that the freedom of religion guaranteed by the Meiji Constitution was upheld so that a Christian atmosphere could be maintained at their mission schools. The Japanese authorities, for their part, wanted to exclude foreign ideas that might pollute the values of loyalty and patriotism which they hoped to inculcate into the young. The 1930s saw an intensification of the efforts of the Department of Education to ensure that the pupils at private Christian schools took part in the national rites at state Shinto shrines.

There was an imperial dimension to this issue. The export to Korea and Taiwan of similar regulations regarding the attendance of school children at shrines, or at Confucian rites in Manchukuo, created grave problems for mission schools. Canadian missionaries in north Korea, in contrast to their American counterparts in Korea and Scottish and Irish Presbyterian ones in Manchukuo, were generally prepared to accept the government general's explanation that participation in state Shinto or Confucian rites was merely a patriotic act without religious significance. Furthermore, the Canadians saw this as an educational issue separate from the later problem of the attendance of churches at state Shinto rites, which was considered a matter for the Korean Church itself to decide.

The case of the Canadian Presbyterians in Taiwan shows that the shrine question was exploited by the Japanese colonial authorities to bring about the end of Canadian missionary educational endeavours in north Taiwan. What happened in Taiwan underlines the fact that it was in the colonies where the full implications for the Christian and missionary movements of Japanese nationalistic policies in regard to religion were first played out.

THE SHRINE QUESTION IN JAPAN

Whereas sectarian Shinto had its origins in the earliest days of Japanese history, state Shinto emerged with the Meiji Restoration in 1868.[3] The new Japanese leaders hoped that Shinto would provide "a symbolic legitimation" for the Meiji regime, and as a result they established the Department of Divinity, which was briefly the highest organ of government.[4] Faced with serious opposition to its rule, the Meiji government needed to use every means, even religious ones, to ensure that it was not overthrown by a counterrevolution. Caught amid a deluge of new Western ideas in Japan after 1868, the new regime emphasized the development of state Shinto partly as an attempt to maintain traditional Japanese values in a time of uncertain but great change in society. Most important for the future was the publicity now given to the performance of Shinto ceremonies by the emperor at his palace in Tokyo and at the imperial shrines at Ise. The shrines at Ise were the principal place for the worship of Amaterasu Omikami, the Sun Goddess, who symbolized the unity between the emperor and his imperial ancestors. It was this unity that gave the emperor derived his religious authority and allowed for the claim of state Shinto that he belonged to an "imperial line unbroken for ages eternal." The ceremonies at the imperial palace conducted by the emperor and the rites of the Ise shrines were carried out in tandem.[5]

Lesser shrines were also required to bring their rites in line with those of Ise. The ordinary person was thus brought into the state cult. Importantly, Buddhist priests were also obliged to participate in the Shinto ceremonies. The coordination of ceremonies by the emperor and his people were duplicated at the Yasukuni shrine, which became a great centre of state Shinto in Tokyo after the Russo-Japanese War because it enshrined the war dead. It was at the Yasukuni shrine and its prefectural branches, the nation-protecting shrines (*gokoku jinja*), that the emperor, government officials, military figures, and general public simultaneously performed ceremonies. This was a nationwide attempt "at the most daring social engineering. Here was a plan to use religion to unify the people in a single cult, headed by the emperor as head priest, focussed upon his ancestors (and later the war dead), who had also been declared national deities."[6] Although the government and the emperor provided the centre, local organizations, especially ex-servicemen groups, played a significant role in the proliferation of shrines and memorials to the war dead in the provinces.

Yet initially the Japanese government's efforts to develop state Shinto had little impact upon missionary work in Japan. Shinto as a barrier to Christianity does not appear to have merited much missionary attention in the years before mission schools became well established. The precursor to the shrine question of the 1930s was the clash between government officials and Christian educators over the continued effort of the government to control educational content through the separation of nongovernmental religious ideas from education. This was clear in the 1899 ordinance of the Ministry of Education that prohibited the teaching of religion in government-recognized schools. This policy was directed primarily toward Buddhist schools, but it had a severe impact on mission schools.[7] Because the Bureau of Religions came under the jurisdiction of the Ministry of Education, there was a clear bureaucratic connection between schools and government policy toward religions.

The attempts to control and to standardize the activities of religious groups, especially Buddhist groups, were seen again in 1899 when the Yamagata cabinet introduced a Religious Organizations Bill. In introducing this legislation, Yamagata accepted religious freedom "only to the extent that it was harnessed to the goal of strengthening imperial authority, not as an inherent right of Japanese subjects."[8] Yamagata's bill was defeated in the House of Peers in 1899 and again in 1900, when a revised bill was rejected. The question of infringing on the autonomy of religious organizations caused parliamentarians to defeat the passage of this legislation. Importantly, it was not voted down on the meaning of religious freedom. Most government officials agreed with Yamagata's view that there was only religious freedom so long as it was "strengthening imperial authority." This remained the official view until the end of the Pacific War.

Although the Diet rejected the Religious Organizations Bill, it did pass the Peace Police Law in 1900; this law gave the police stronger surveillance powers over religious activities as well as broader discretion in suspending undesirable religious ceremonies without the need for legislation.[9] These increased police powers could have had an impact upon Christian endeavours, but they were primarily intended to give the authorities tighter control over the practices of new Japanese religions.

Japan's military victories in the Sino-Japanese War of 1894-95 and, more importantly, in the Russo-Japanese War of 1904-05, led to an intensification of government activities to project state Shinto as a major force in Japanese society. The activities of the Japanese government in promoting state Shinto attracted the scorn of a few well-informed Westerners, such as Basil Hall Chamberlain,[10] but the Japanese were undeterred by outside criticism of their efforts. Indeed, most Westerners, missionary or otherwise, were either indifferent to the Japanese activities in developing a new state cult or simply too good mannered to ridicule it.

Missionaries and Japanese Christians were willing to participate in the Three Religions Conference in 1912. This government-sponsored conference brought together representatives from sectarian Shinto (some thirteen sects sent delegates), Buddhism, and Christianity.[11] The attraction of the Three Religions Conference for Japanese Christians was that it confirmed that the Japanese government recognized Christianity as one of the three major religions in Japan. This recognition signalled that the persecution of Christianity by the Meiji government was a thing of the distant past and that the authorities stood by the guarantee of religious freedom in the Meiji Constitution.[12] The participation of Japanese Christian leaders in the conference also gave them the stamp of respectability that they so fervently wanted. But they had to recognize that not only Buddhism but also sectarian Shinto were religions equivalent to Christianity.

Although missionaries were prepared to recognize sectarian Shinto, some viewed the emerging state Shinto as a threat to Christianity. In 1918, J. Cooper Robinson, a Canadian Anglican missionary in Nagoya, expressed a concern that "Mikadoism" was a serious threat to Christianity and that it was being used by the authorities to restrain the rougher elements in Japanese society.[13] He might have been correct in his assertion, but the relationship of the NSKK to "Mikadoism" or *tennosei* was complex.

The complexity of this relationship had its roots in the two major founding Churches of the NSKK. Although the American Protestant Episcopalian Church was independent, until 1789 it had been the Church of England in America. The idea, inherited from the English Church, that it served nation and people remained strong.[14] The Church of England was the established (state) church, with the British monarch as its head and defender of the faith. In the *Book of Common Prayer*, there was a prayer for the monarch.

In the early Meiji period, British Anglican missionaries, without any deep thought on the matter, came to regard the position of the British monarch and the Japanese emperor as the same. As early as 1879, the Japanese Anglican prayer book contained a prayer for the ruler and the ruled that asked for the emperor and government officials to be heeded. The NSKK was loyal to the ruler;[15] indeed, it was fulfilling what Yamagata Aritomo believed to be the function of religious freedom: that of "strengthening the imperial authority." However, the process of praying for the emperor and his officials helped to make Japanese Anglicans susceptible to the demands of *tennosei*. Furthermore, the search for the establishment of a Japanese Christianity led by Imai Judo, an influential Japanese Anglican clergyman,[16] only increased this susceptibility.

One obvious time when government policies were supported by Japanese Anglicans was during the Sino-Japanese and Russo-Japanese Wars. For Imai Judo, underpinning his support for Japan in the Sino-Japanese War was his belief that Japan's vocation was to bring the light of civilization to East Asia.[17] He also strongly believed that it was the responsibility of Japanese Christians to undertake evangelistic work in China, Korea, and Taiwan. When it came to the Russo-Japanese War, he used a different rationale to justify Japan's actions against Russia, arguing that it was a just war. Although Imai believed that Japan had a special calling to bring enlightenment and Christianity to East Asia, he did not understand that this very belief was an important cause of Japan's aggression overseas.

It was not only during the wars with imperial China and imperial Russia that the Japanese authorities received loyal support from Japanese Anglicans. The wholesale transference of doctrinal ideas across cultural boundaries was not without consequences within metropolitan Japan. Whereas most American, British, or Canadian Anglicans saw individual liberty and rights as being of primary importance, it was difficult for many Japanese to separate love of one's self and family from love of one's people and nation. Indeed, the nation was seen as an extension of the family. Yet Japanese Anglicans were merely continuing Church of England custom by offering prayers for the well-being of Japanese imperial family members in time of sickness. During the 1920s, like courtesies were extended to the British monarch. For instance, Bishop Motoda of Tokyo would preside over a special service on King George V's birthday for the benefit of British Embassy staff. Perhaps this practice did contribute to undue respect for those in political authority and a willingness to accept their judgments without much questioning. Certainly, as early as 1911, in regard to the attendance of Christians at state Shinto ceremonies, Motoda had accepted the government's position that they were not religious in nature.[18]

Similarly, even though it could be regarded as having a religious meaning, there was little Japanese Anglican opposition to the building of a shrine in the Yoyogi district of Tokyo to commemorate the Meiji emperor; this shrine was actively promoted by the government but was only made possible by donations and tremendous support from the public.¹⁹ The Meiji jinja (shrine), begun during World War I, was completed in 1920. During the 1920s and after, the Meiji shrine served as a focal point for the cult of emperor worship.

Despite widespread popular support for the Meiji shrine, the government in the mid-1920s still thought it necessary to introduce legislation concerning religious organization patterned on that of the Yamagata cabinet more than twenty years before. In 1926, the Wakatsuki cabinet announced a Religions Bill and established a Religious Systems Investigation Board. Although the legislation was rejected by the Diet in 1927, the Tanaka cabinet in 1929 introduced a Religious Bodies Bill. It was soon withdrawn. However, the fact that two cabinets brought forward legislation showed that the passage of a religious organization law was becoming a priority.

The Christian movement saw that it was a priority to prevent this from happening. In December 1926, the Japanese Christian movement presented a united front against the Wakatsuki cabinet's bill, as it did in 1929 against the Tanaka cabinet bill. To the Christian movement, both bills infringed upon the right of religious freedom that was guaranteed by the Meiji Constitution and interfered with the autonomy of self-governing churches. In opposing these bills, the Christian movement organized many public meetings, lobbied individual Diet members, and received strong support from Buddhists. The secular press also came out strongly in support of the opposition movement.²⁰ Despite the fact that some influential Christian leaders, including P. Y. Matsui of the NSKK, thought that the wording of the 1929 bill did not offend religious belief or the self-governing churches, other Christian leaders were able to stage an impressively large rally at the Aoyama Kaikan against the proposed legislation of the Tanaka cabinet.

This Christian opposition obviously played a part in forcing the withdrawal of the 1929 Religious Organizations Bill. The government was sufficiently chastened by this experience that it was not until the end of the 1930s that it again pursued this legislative approach to controlling religious bodies. However, as the Religious Organizations Bill crisis passed, the shrine question became more acute. It was no coincidence that the government, having failed to gain control over religious bodies by legislative means, adopted a different approach. In 1930, the government established the Shrine System Investigation Committee, which argued that the shrines were suprareligious in nature but institutionally represented the national religious character.²¹ Although it emphasized that state Shinto had the attributes of a national religion, the Ministry of Education held that worship at state Shinto shrines was suprareligious. This claim was supported by Shinto priests, who also held that shrine worship was above religion and that all people should give reverence at the shrines. It was accepted at face value by the Buddhists, especially the Shinshu Sect, which came out in support of the shrines.

At first, the Christian movement was completely united in its opposition to this challenge, which aimed at creating a state religion based on the excuse that its tenets were above religion. Many Christians held the view that the majority of Japanese believed that state Shinto was a real religion and that state Shinto priests performed ceremonies that were religious in character. This position changed as the Far Eastern crisis deepened in the 1930s. Even though the *tennosei* ideology underpinned state Shinto, Japanese Christians thought that they belonged to the same body Japanese as the emperor. It was explained that the Japanization of Christianity allowed for participation in state Shinto ceremonies and that Christians should give their lives for the emperor. Acceptance of this viewpoint by Japanese Christians meant that they were able to cooperate with the wartime effort.[22]

One of the difficulties for missionaries concerning Shinto was to differentiate between traditional sectarian Shinto, which they had a tendency to view as a creed similar to Western religions, and the new state Shinto. A clearer understanding of state Shinto was achieved in 1930 when D. C. Holtom, an American missionary authority on Shinto, published an important article on the nature of modern Shinto. Holtom stated his belief that "on the basis of content it is appropriate to classify modern State Shinto as a religion exactly as we classify the Shinto of Old Japan as a religion."[23] Thus, he came out decisively in favour of those who opposed attendance at state Shinto ceremonies on the grounds that they were religious.

The issue of state Shinto involved all Christians, but its most obvious effect was on Christian education. This impact was illustrated in 1932 in an incident at a Roman Catholic school, Jochi University (Sophia University), in Tokyo, when a student demurred to visit the Yasukuni shrine with the rest of the school on the grounds that doing so was contrary to his religious convictions. The extensive network of Roman Catholic schools in Japan was put in jeopardy if the Roman Catholics did not obey government guidelines requiring them to send their students as a body to pay their respects at shrines. The Roman Catholic archbishop of Tokyo asked the Ministry of Education to clarify its position on whether or not going to a shrine was considered a religious obligation. The ministry's reply was that the student visits to a shrine were based on educational considerations and that the statements the children were required to make on these occasions were simply meant to indicate their patriotism and loyalty.[24] Furthermore, the ministry reinforced its argument by pointing out that it would contravene its own 1899 instruction on keeping religion outside the scope of general education if students were asked to take part in a religious exercise.

The position taken by the Ministry of Education satisfied the Roman Catholic authorities. Indeed, it was thought that the Roman Catholic Archdiocese could congratulate itself for having reached with comparative ease a satisfactory solution to an important question of principle.[25] Clearly, the Ministry of Education had been placed in a quandary by the Ministry of War when the military seemingly attached so much importance to the absence of one student. This was one reason, it was believed, that a solution was so easily reached. Possibly, without the goading of the military, which was eager in the light of the growing seriousness of the situation in Manchuria to stimulate the patriotism of the rising generation, the educational authorities would not have pressed Jochi students to pay their respects at the Yasukuni shrine. It was to the advantage of the Ministry of Education to placate the Roman Catholics and other Christian groups involved in education because mission schools did not encourage the spread of communist ideas, which had caused trouble at some secular Japanese schools. Whereas the military wanted to stimulate patriotism, educational authorities were concerned with curtailing the influence of communism on Japanese youth.

Even though the situation at Jochi University was resolved, there was reason for concern for the future. One of those particularly concerned about Canadian missionaries and their work in Japan, Korea, Manchuria, and Taiwan was Sir Herbert Marler, the Canadian ambassador to Japan. Marler was clearly worried about the long-term impact of Japanese policies—of which the shrine question was only one manifestation—toward Canadian missionaries and their Christian work. In Japan, Marler's concerns came to a head in late 1935 and early 1936 with the persecution of Canadian Roman Catholic missionaries on the island of Oshima and in Kagoshima in southern Kyushu. Marler was also aware of the difficulties that Canadian Protestant missionaries were experiencing with the Japanese authorities in northern Korea and in Taiwan. In January 1936, as a response to the persecution encountered by Canadian Roman Catholic missionaries, Marler was asked by O. D. Skelton, the deputy minister of the Department of External Affairs in Ottawa, to "request the Japanese Government to make a full investigation with a view to determining the action that should be taken to prevent the recurrence of incidents of this nature and to preserve the security and safety of Canadian nationals exercising their peaceful and legitimate calling in Japan."[26] The Canadian government was willing to make diplomatic efforts to protect Canadian nationals engaged in missionary work. In asking Marler to bring the matter to the attention of the Japanese government, Skelton told him "to indicate that the Catholic Missionaries, who wish to keep their religious work free of political or official complications, did not request that representations be made."[27] It is not clear whether this request was made out of fear of reprisal against the missionaries or simply out of tact. What is apparent was that the attacks on Canadian Roman Catholic missionaries in south Japan did not stop immediately.

In the light of continued difficulties in south Japan between the missionaries and the authorities, in late May 1936 Marler wrote a significant dispatch to Ottawa in which he mentioned some of his concerns for the Canadian missionary movement in Japan, and urged the Canadian government to act. He noted that there had been "a new outbreak against the Franciscan

THE SHRINE QUESTION 89

Mission at Tanegashima resulting in the expulsion of several Canadian missionaries and the closing of the Mission Church there on the pretext that the 'heretical religion' was subversive of the requirements of national defence and national polity."[28] Marler clearly showed that the Japanese authorities could level a number of different accusations against Christianity in order to stop missionary work. Invoking "the requirements of national defence" was obviously enough to override any Japanese objection to the authorities' actions. What is not explained was why Christianity was seen as "subversive" to Japanese national defence. Unstated was the belief that the Japanese military thought Canadian missionaries to be spies whom they did not want close to the Japanese military installations in the Ryukyu Islands and in southern Kyushu. Marler wrote that it was his increasing conviction that "under the present so-called patriotic national mentality of Japan, the work of foreign Christian missions and missionaries is faced with a growing opposition by Japanese official, unofficial and especially military circles."[29] In his mind, there was no question of appeasement. He urged that

> unless some notice is taken diplomatically of the serious handicaps being offered to the work of foreign missionaries in this Empire—work which is constitutionally and by treaty nominally guaranteed and safeguarded—the continuance of these enterprises (including not only propagation of the Christian faith but extremely valuable medical, educational and social activities) will be frustrated.[30]

His call for diplomatic action was not simply out of concern for the 450 or more Canadians then engaged in Christian work in Japan, Korea, and Taiwan, even though he thought they constituted "numerically a majority of all the foreign missionary work carried on here."[31] Marler believed that the difficulties Canadian missionaries faced could be the harbinger of problems for Canadian business interests.

Marler repeated his pessimism about the future of missionary work not only due to the obstacles put in the way of missionaries

> by Japanese authorities or so-called patriotic organizations, but also due to the fact that the Japanese Christian leaders themselves are now able to carry on the work of propagation of the faith and related missionary activities on their own account—so far as this religion is permitted by the Japanese patriots themselves.[32]

He went on to argue that

> the present trend of Japanese self-sufficiency, cultural as well as political isolation, and opposition to foreign institutions, except when they are merely subservient to Japanese policies, would seem to bear out the opinion of Dr.

Batchelor and confirms me in my own disquietude over the future of Canadian mission work in Japan.[33]

Marler was one of the first Canadians in Japan to see that the future for Canadian missions in that country was bleak. Few Canadian Protestant missionaries in May 1936 shared his disquiet over their future.

Marler's opinions stemmed from a broad perspective, for his diplomatic responsibilities encompassed the Japanese Empire and crossed denominational lines in that both Canadian Roman Catholic and Protestant missionaries fell under his purview. Part of his pessimistic view of the future came undoubtedly from an assumption that what happened in Korea and Taiwan could have an adverse impact on the missionary movement in metropolitan Japan. Most Canadian Protestant missionaries in Japan, being Nipponocentric, held the opposite position that what happened in Japan would have a beneficial impact in the overseas colonies. Canadian missionaries in Japan, for instance, were critical of their counterparts in Korea when they did not take their lead over the shrine question. Unlike Marler, who saw various political and cultural trends in Japan dovetailing into a broad opposition against foreigners and their institutions, the missionaries apparently compartmentalized their difficulties. There was a tendency among them to see problems such as the shrine question in isolation from other issues. Despite their own limited perception of the shrine question, missionary authorities in Toronto thought that Canadian missionary interests were well served by Marler at the legation in Tokyo. In March 1936, Arnup expressed his approval of Marler in a letter to Hennigar in Tokyo. Arnup wrote, on hearing a rumour that Marler was going to be posted to Washington, that

> I am fearful lest some Frenchman should get the call for the post in Japan. I wrote the Premier complimenting him upon the services rendered by Sir Herbert Marler and expressing the hope that he might be retained and if not that someone of similar spirit and outlook should be sent.[34]

Arnup's fear was probably grounded in the thought that a Roman Catholic Frenchman would be less sympathetic to Canadian Protestant missions in Japan and its empire than was the Anglican Marler, but it proved to be unfounded. Marler's successor was Robert Randolph Bruce, a prominent Liberal like Marler and a former lieutenant-governor of British Columbia.[35]

As had been the case for Roman Catholics, the issue of Shinto as a religion caused some friction in Protestant schools. One of the most significant incidents occurred in 1935 when right-wing students at Doshisha Higher Commercial School in Kyoto criticized their headmaster for removing Shinto god shelves from the school.[36] The incident was only one of a series of annoying student disturbances that rocked Doshisha University and its affiliated schools in the mid-1930s. In early 1937, there was a student siege of the university chapel. In the same year, silly accusations that Yuasa Hachiro, the president of Doshisha University, had misread the Imperial Rescript on Education led to his resignation.[37] Yuasa realized that Doshisha, because of its American and Christian connections, and he personally as university president, were the targets of Japanese nationalists.[38] Yet his resignation did not bring peace to the Doshisha campus; it only removed one champion of resistance to extreme nationalistic policies.

The incidents at Doshisha were the most dramatic at a Protestant institution, but others occurred. At Rikkyo University, the president was forced to resign in 1936 over allegations of disrespect concerning the reading of the imperial rescript marking the emperor's birthday.[39] Two years later, the Ministry of Education took action against Meiji Gakuin University because the school authorities had not set aside a special place for the imperial portrait. From the mid-1930s on, the issue of whether an institution reverently accepted the meaning of the Imperial Rescript on Education became a factor for Christian schools raising endowments that would allow them to regulate the educational basis. In 1938, Meiji Gakuin revised its constitution to make it clear that the purpose of the university's legal corporation (*hojin*) was to conduct Christian education so that the meaning of the Imperial Rescript on Education was reverently accepted.[40]

There was a tendency, however, for Christian educators to see problems within individual schools, such as Meiji Gakuin or Doshisha, as being particular to those institutions. The United Church of Canada had a significant investment in physical plant and personnel at Kwansei Gakuin in Nishinomiya. Because Bates served as its president, Kwansei Gakuin was much more vulnerable to the charge of being under the influence of foreigners than was Doshisha. After all, Doshisha had a Japanese president and a long tradition of independence from Western missionaries. However, anti-American feeling might have been a factor in why Kimura of Rikkyo and Yuasa of Doshisha, who were Japanese scholars with strong ties to the United States, were singled out for criticism. Undoubtedly more important, though, were the military officers attached to the faculties of Rikkyo and Doshisha, for they egged on students to complain or brought charges forward themselves.[41] Nevertheless, Canadian missionaries seemed to have little sympathy for the problems of other Christian educators.

In April 1937, Outerbridge wrote from Kwansei Gakuin a stinging criticism of the American Presbyterians in Korea for closing their mission schools over the shrine question. He wrote that tens of thousands of Japanese Christians went to the shrines without any twinge of conscience about disloyalty or worship, and he thought that Korean Christians also had no difficulty in doing the same thing, "but because some American missionaries think the meaning is not clear, this great evangelistic opportunity must be thrown up. I am glad that our Can. Mission has seen things differently."[42] Outerbridge was correct about the attitude toward the shrine question of the Canadian mission in northern Korea. In regard to the American Presbyterian attitude to the shrine question in Korea, he wrote that "the greatest need on the Mission Field as elsewhere is a little more consecrated common sense."[43]

Yet it was not only the Korean case in which Outerbridge was interested. In looking at the relationship between Christian education and the national spirit of Japan, he also pointed out that Kwansei Gakuin enjoyed complete freedom in its religious teaching and that the things students and staff were required to do to engender patriotism were comparatively only a small factor in the whole educational situation.[44] This point of view illustrates how wholeheartedly Outerbridge and his fellow United Church missionaries in Japan had come to accept the Japanese government's position that the shrine question was not religious.

The United Church missionary acceptance of the government's position can also be taken as a manifestation of the basic trust held by many missionaries for the Japanese government. Missionaries might have disagreed with some of the actions of the government, but they believed that there was nothing malevolent behind these actions.

CONFLICT IN NORTH KOREA

One characteristic of Western missionaries in Korea was their willingness to stand up to the Japanese government general (except during the Manchurian crisis, when their sympathies lay with the Japanese). This was especially true when it came to the religious and educational policies of the Japanese colonial authorities. Although both missionaries and Christians in Japan tended to acquiesce to Japanese government policies, their counterparts in Korea almost invariably chose to fight for their principles against the government general, which was often merely applying to Korea policies already in place and accepted in Japan. Was it that missionaries in Korea were more radical in their political and social views than their counterparts in Japan?

Denominational affiliations did make some difference, for it was the Presbyterians in Korea who stood in the forefront of protest against the government general on the shrine question. Other factors also played a part, however. As long as Japan was sensitive to international opinion on its colonial policies in Korea, the government general was chary about enforcing laws that might cause an international outcry. Missionaries realized that adverse international publicity could embarrass the Japanese authorities into giving them concessions. Just as importantly, however, missionaries and Korean Christians also realized that resistance to Japan helped to garner support from the broader Korean society. In January 1934, Bruce, writing from

Lungchingtsun after a trip to Japan, noted that he thought that some missionaries—including himself—were "sliding along, afraid it seems to take a stand on some issues."[45] Even though Bruce himself was "beginning to see that we are in danger of making mountains of mole-hills"[46] over the issue of "Shrine worship," it proved to be one issue over which Korean Christians and missionaries could join together in resisting the Japanese.

With the communists gaining the upper hand as the vanguard of Korean nationalism, the shrine question offered one way in which the Christian movement could reestablish its identification with the nationalist aspirations of Koreans. Although missionaries and Christians based their challenge to the Japanese authorities on religious principles, their resistance could have been interpreted as being politically motivated. Indeed, in the context of colonial Korea, it was unlikely that the government general would have interpreted it any other way. In looking at the question of Korean Christians and the Shinto shrine issue, Spencer J. Palmer has pointed out that "it was precisely the dynamic influence of Christianity in Korean life that convinced Japanese government officials of the need to insist upon Christian obeisance at Shinto shrines in Korea after 1919."[47] The Japanese authorities used the school system to inculcate in Koreans values of loyalty and patriotism to the Japanese Empire. The participation of Koreans, especially schoolchildren, was seen by the government general as part of this process and a visible demonstration to them of Korean loyalty to the Japanese emperor.

Shinto shrines had first been built in Korea by Japanese merchants as early as 1609. However, it was not until 1875, with the Treaty of Kangwha Island, that Japanese residents built small shrines at Wonsan and at Inchon. By the time of the annexation of Korea, there were some forty-two Shinto shrines in Korea.[48] Although the residency generalcy supported the building of Shinto shrines in the years after the Russo-Japanese War, it did so for the benefit of Japanese residents. Indeed, this support extended into the Chientao region as well as into metropolitan Korea, for the Kanto *jinja* was begun in 1909 with the assistance of the Chinese and completed in 1912.[49] This Japanese-only policy began to change with the creation of the government general. As early as August 1915, regulations were issued governing worship in Shinto shrines in Korea. In 1919, the Imperial Diet in Tokyo directed that a state Shinto shrine be built in Seoul to serve as the official shrine of the government general. This proved to be a long and very expensive undertaking, for the shrine took seven years to build at a cost of ¥1,600,000.[50] The building of this shrine can be seen both to parallel the building of the Meiji *jinja* in Tokyo in honour of the Meiji emperor and to serve as a Japanese expression of pride in their achievements in Korea. Achievements that needed to be crowned by a splendid Japanese religious monument equivalent to the Christian cathedrals that the British built in the capitals of their colonies. However, the Japanese authorities were not prepared to leave it at that. Like Japanese, Koreans were expected to attend ceremonies at the Chosen *jinja* or other state Shinto shrines. One of the lessons for the Japanese of the Independence Movement in 1919 was the need to intensify their efforts to inculcate loyalty to Japan in Koreans, and promotion of state Shinto was one means to try to do this.

In 1925, the year that the Chosen *jinja* was completed, there were the first serious Korean Christian protests against state Shinto in the name of religious freedom. The Korean Christian point of view was that there was a religious aspect to ceremonies at the state shrines and that to coerce Christian students and teachers to attend such ceremonies ran counter to their right of religious freedom.[51]

The shrine question quickly became associated in 1925 with protests by students in mission schools, but it was the Manchurian crisis that deepened the conflict between missionary educators and their Korean Christian supporters and the Japanese authorities. In September 1932, a memorial service for the Japanese officers and men killed in the fighting in Manchuria was held in P'yongyang, but Christian schools refused to take part. This type of nonparticipation showed that people refused to give their loyalty to the Japanese.[52]

P'yongyang was an important Christian stronghold in north Korea, and it was in P'yongyang that the shrine question was most deeply felt. In November 1935, a critical situation was created when two American Northern Presbyterian missionaries in P'yongyang, George S. McCune, president of the Union Christian College (Soong Sill Academy), and Miss V. L. Snook, principal of the Soong Sill Girls' High School, refused to take part in the opening ceremonies at the state Shinto shrine in P'yongyang at a conference of educators in South Heian province presided over by the Japanese provincial governor. The action of the two missionaries led the Japanese authorities to threaten to take away their educational qualifications if they did not change their minds within sixty days.[53] McCune and Snook received the almost complete support of the Korean Presbyterian ministers in P'yongyang as well as that of their missionary colleagues in taking this stand against state Shinto. The government general warned McCune that it was prepared to take all the necessary steps to ensure that he and his students complied with the colonial government's wishes over shrine attendance.[54] At the same time, the Japanese stressed the official line that the shrine ceremonies were not religious but a display of students' patriotism and loyalty. It was not a matter of freedom of religion, which was assured by the Meiji Constitution: rather, attendance at the shrine had to do with instilling reverence and respect for ancestors, and these values were "most important from the point of view of national education as the essentials of our national moral virtue."[55] It is not clear if McCune completely understood that the government general would make no compromise over the shrine question, and that resistance to its wishes would be in vain. However, McCune did not waver in his views, even though doing so meant trouble not only for him but also for Korean Christians. Among those who supported him was MacRae, the veteran Canadian missionary, for he believed that Watanabe and other Japanese officials of his ilk were deliberately trying to deceive those who were ready to be deceived over the shrine issue.[56]

There was no middle ground between McCune's position and that of the Japanese authorities, who might not have taken his opposition too seriously had he not included his students in the confrontation with the colonial government. He indicated that he could not ask them to perform an act of obeisance before the shrine that he himself refused to do.[57] McCune had tendered his resignation to his school's board of directors, but they had refused it "because they felt that he had done nothing."[58] The Northern Presbyterians were apparently prepared to force the governor's hand over the shrine question.

This was a serious matter. The Japanese authorities were prepared to use strong-arm methods to get their way. Their patience had been tried to the limit, and the petty officials who carried out the directives from above were not always burdened with the polished and gentlemanly manners of their superiors. In February 1936, the police in P'yongyang attempted to cancel a meeting of the Presbytery and harassed Christians attending it. Such activities by the police apparently only stiffened the Korean resolve to resist the Japanese.[59] The two offending missionaries had their educational qualifications revoked, and McCune was shadowed by the police.[60]

In their defiance of the wishes of the Japanese authorities, it is plain that McCune and the Korean Presbyterians in P'yongyang believed that the Presbyterians would not be able to preach the Gospel if they gave in to the Japanese. They thought that no one would consider them sincere if, after fifty years of teaching that the worship of any spirit other than God was wrong, they were now willing to condone state Shinto. For McCune and his Korean supporters, state Shinto was the worship of deified ancestors.[61] McCune soon returned home to the United States (he left on his own free will; he was not deported), but others paid dearly for their resistance. The American Presbyterians' stand ultimately led to the closure of their mission schools, first in P'yongyang and then throughout the peninsula in 1938.[62]

Moreover, the Presbyterian stand led to widespread persecution of Christians and to the forced closure of many Christian churches. In September 1938, the Korean Presbyterian General Assembly was forced by the Japanese authorities to pass a resolution declaring that shrine worship was not religious in nature and that all Christians should participate in the state Shinto ceremonies.[63] Already the Roman Catholics in Korea, like their counterparts in Japan, had come to terms with the shrine question.[64] It is important to realize that the shrine question for Korean Protestants was not simply about mission schools, Christian education, and Shinto, the issue that confronted McCune and his fellow educators. For Korean Protestants, participation in the state Shinto ceremonies was seen to threaten the evangelistic nature of the Korean Church.[65]

Yet, from a Japanese point of view, once the Marco Polo bridge incident (that marked the beginning of the Sino-Japanese War in 1937) had taken place, the shrine question became vital within the government effort to control religion as part of its wartime system.[66] The colonial authorities were thus quick and ruthless in bringing to heel Christians and other religionists who showed disrespect by not participating in state Shinto ceremonies.

McCune cannot be blamed for everything that followed his stand in 1936. Where he can be criticized is for not realizing that the Japanese would get their way and that many ordinary Korean Christians would get hurt in the process. Although his views were influential, there were other opinions, even among Presbyterians. This was particularly true of United Church of Canada missionaries. In February 1936, Armstrong in Toronto, who had acquired since 1919 a great deal of experience dealing with religious and other crises in Korea and had fairly recently visited Korea, wrote to one of his American counterparts in New York that he was, with some misgivings, prepared to accept the government's view of the nature of the shrine ceremonies.[67] Armstrong thought that "the Japanese are tiring of it and that the Government is finding it difficult to keep up interest in it; and that the Buddhists were lukewarm about it, seeing that it is a Shinto matter and not religious as the Buddhists would like to make it."[68] If this was the case, then McCune and those in P'yongyang misjudged the political atmosphere when they precipitated this crisis. However, Armstrong did note variations in different parts of Korea in how local authorities looked upon the shrine ceremonies: "the authorities in the Pyengyang area are inclined to make it more of a religious affair than in other parts just because your Mission is so strong in that district and has always adopted a non-compromising attitude."[69] If he was correct in assuming that local Japanese authorities had some leeway in interpreting the religiosity of the state Shinto ceremonies, then the authorities in P'yongyang were going out of their way to antagonize the Korean Christian community there.

However, Armstrong's attitude was little help to the American Northern Presbyterians, who complained that their stand on the shrine question was greatly weakened because the government general could argue that other Christian missions were willing to attend the ceremonies.[70] Whereas the American Southern Presbyterians felt obliged to follow the Northern Presbyterian lead, the American Methodist missions did not. For their part, the Canadian Presbyterians could provide moral support to their American counterparts because the Canadian Presbyterians in north Taiwan were facing similar pressures on their schoolchildren to attend state Shinto ceremonies. One missionary leader who was not prepared to offer an opinion on the shrine question was Canon S. Gould, the general secretary of the Missionary Society of the Church of England in Canada, because Canadian Anglicans left "immediate consideration and, if possible, the solution of all such problems as the 'Shrine question' to the Bishop and his diocesan advisers in the field."[71] By this time, the Canadian Anglicans in Japan, along with the majority of other denominations, had accepted the government's position on state Shinto. By the beginning of 1936, the Christian and missionary movements in Japan had largely resolved the shrine question.

So had the United Church missionaries in Korea. In March 1936, Burbridge wrote to Armstrong in Toronto that "we are taking the Government at its word and consider the shrine attendance as a matter of national ritual."[72] Even so, the Japanese could be quite threatening if it appeared to them that missionaries were not toeing the line. But what line was to be toed was unclear at times. In October 1936, Black reported from Lungchingtsun that a missionary in Manchuria had been asked by a Japanese military official "to state whether he considered the Emperor of Manchukuo or God to be more divine. It was further indicated that any one who taught in Manchukuo that any one was superior to the Emperor was guilty of treason. I am not just sure where Confucius comes in on the scale."[73] That a Japanese military officer should be trumpeting the superiority of Henry Pu Yi, the emperor of Manchukuo, and not his own Japanese emperor showed that the Japanese army took the task of supporting the Manchukuo government seriously. It also clearly indicated that the issue was control over education and ideas and not a matter of religion. Furthermore, that there was a crisis of observance in Manchukuo underlines the fact that this was an imperial question and not one restricted to Korea and Taiwan. A little curious to Black was the place of Confucius in the hierarchy, because the Manchukuo government in early 1936 had started to make Confucian worship compulsory in schools. This issue had led to confrontation between the Irish Presbyterian mission school in Kirin and the Manchukuo authorities. Missionaries and Chinese Christians in Kirin believed that "participation in Confucian sacrifices," as required by the authorities, was idolatrous.[74] The authorities in Manchukuo were substituting Confucian ceremonies for the shrine ceremonies in Korea, Taiwan, and Japan, and sometimes, as in the case of the Japanese military official, they got mixed up about what was the correct line where.

It was pointed out about the situation in Manchukuo that "the real power is the Japanese army, anti-foreign and anti-Christian, although the ostensible power is the Manchukuo Government."[75] There was a suspicion among missionaries that the authorities in Manchukuo were deliberately using the persecution of the Chinese Christian community, with its close ties to Scottish and Irish Presbyterians, as a way to pressure the British government to recognize the state of Manchukuo.[76] Already the Japanese security forces had acted against Chinese Christians with the arrests in October 1935 of members of The One Cent Society. The insistence on Confucian worship was clearly another aspect of the attempt to bring the ideas of religious bodies, including Buddhist sects and Christian groups, under the control of the central government.

In order to protect the Christian movement from too close scrutiny by the Japanese authorities, the Scottish and Irish Presbyterians attempted "to make use of the mediation of influential Japanese Christians" and formed a united Manchurian Christian Council, which represented all the Protestant missions and included a few Japanese members.[77] The Scottish and Irish missionaries saw that Japanese Christian leaders might play a role in protecting the Manchurian Christian movement against pressure from government and military officials. Although using influential Japanese Christians as mediators was a missionary initiative, the Japanese Christian movement increasingly saw itself as the 1930s progressed as the protector of indigenous Christian movements in Japanese colonies and occupied territories. If Japanese Christian intervention failed, then the Presbyterian missions were prepared to withdraw gradually. Naturally, as the Canadian Presbyterians in Manchuria did not have schools, the question of Confucian rites did not directly affect them. However, the writing was on the wall, for local Japanese officials were making conditions for both foreign missionaries and Chinese Christians in Manchukuo far from pleasant.

In Korea, by the end of 1936, Canadian missionaries had reached the conclusion that the Japanese authorities were not going to retreat from their position and that Christians would be required to participate in the shrine ceremonies. Scott in Hamheung, whose views clearly influenced those of Armstrong in Toronto, noted in December 1936 that his appreciation of the shrine question had not changed from earlier in the year. Scott argued that more harm would be done by refusing to participate in shrine ceremonies, because nonparticipation would lead to the closure of Christian schools and complete government control over education in Korea. He pointed out that

> How long this emphasis upon extreme nationalism will continue no one knows. I prefer to maintain my place, do my bit for the Kingdom—which by the way is not so limited as it is in most non-Christian countries—and hope for the time when the Japanese themselves, will see the folly of super-nationalism, and seek a truer internationalism. My own impression is that the change will come sooner than we usually expect.[78]

Scott held that the Japanese were quickly tiring of an ultranationalism that was producing only disappointing results. In these circumstances, he believed that the task of Christians was "all the more imperative—to teach the law of love, the benefit of mutual goodwill, the interdependence of all people, and their final dependence upon God. And how shall they learn without a preacher, and the Christian teacher?"[79] Moreover, Scott had gone to a shrine ceremony at Hamheung along with students from the United Church-supported mission school there, and he reported that it had been a simple and unobjectionable service. He noted that "there is no idol on the altar, no incense is burned, a simple prayer is said, the hands clapped twice, all bow reverently; and the ceremony ends."[80]

One Canadian missionary disagreed with Scott and continued to object to Christian attendance at the shrine ceremonies. MacRae still maintained that the Shinto ceremony was religious in context. He thought that spirit worship did not necessarily entail an idol or incense being burnt, as was the case in Buddhist temples. The wine, fish, and bread offerings on the altar reminded him of the food offerings that Koreans took to their ancestral graves to appease the spirits.[81] In early 1936, MacRae delivered a sermon at a mission service on the subject of the Shinto shrine and the Canadian mission in which he put the question to his fellow missionaries: "have we substituted the Sun Goddess for Jesus, the Light of the World?"[82] He went on to ask his audience: "Have we compromised with idolatry? What has happened to our conscience toward God? There is but one answer. We are guilty! What punishment will God bring us? Leave us to die? or call our sin to judgement?"[83] In February 1936, Armstrong wrote to MacRae that he thought that they should accept the government general's view and not read into the ceremonies at the shrines things that the authorities had not intended.[84] At 299 Queen Street, the missionary society's headquarters in Toronto, Scott's view held sway. Indeed, once MacRae was home in Canada, not only Armstrong but also some of those interested in missions in MacRae's hometown of Baddeck, Cape Breton Island, got tired of his public attacks on the Korean mission over the shrine and school questions.[85]

In Korea itself, Scott maintained that the Southern Presbyterians had become extremist in their opposition to attendance at Shinto shrine ceremonies and had closed many of their schools. Likewise, the Northern Presbyterians had announced their intention to close their college in P'yongyang as well as their high schools there. However, other Northern Presbyterian schools, in Seoul, Taiku, and other centres, continued to function. Scott even suggested that there might have been a split in Northern Presbyterian ranks over the shrine question, not the least because in Seoul the authorities had not pressed the Seoul mission schoolchildren to attend the last shrine ceremony that had been held.[86]

With the closing of Union Christian College in P'yongyang, Chosen Christian College in Seoul (also a union institution) remained the only Christian college in Korea offering a general education at an advanced level. In September 1938, Armstrong expressed his alarm when he heard that the Northern Presbyterians were planning to withdraw their support from Chosen Christian College in Seoul, the premier union college in Korea.[87] Armstrong thought that missionaries must not desert Korean Christians, because "they need us all the more because of the hardships and persecutions which they are enduring and which I fear will become increasingly severe as the Japanese become more desperate with reference to the conflict in China."[88] Armstrong was able to influence the Northern Presbyterians to reconsider their decision. In March 1939, Horace Underwood, the president of Chosen Christian College, thanked Armstrong for helping to convince the Northern Presbyterians to postpone their decision to withdraw from the college until 1941. Underwood noted that "the Korean Christians cling almost tearfully to their hope and faith in this institution."[89] That statement does ring true. Armstrong and Scott obviously believed that the continued existence of mission schools was more important than fighting with the Japanese authorities over the shrine question.

Canadians were not always thinking about the shrine question, for there were other concerns and issues that directly affected Canadian work in north Korea during the mid-1930s. One concern was the constitutional crisis in the royal family brought on by King Edward VIII's proposal of marriage to Mrs. Simpson. This crisis worried Scott and his wife. He admitted to Armstrong that

> it is at times of great national crises like these that we feel our exile most. We could picture you all getting radio news, and talking things over. Here we had to wait for the five minutes English broadcast every night and the brief reports in the Seoul press the following day.[90]

Happily, King Edward did the right thing and abdicated, which Scott thought "was a great vindication of the Christian moral standard, and of the British constitutional form of government."[91] Indeed, he believed that Edward's renunciation of the throne in favour of the Duke of York "made a great appeal to the Korean mind."[92] There was a Christian twist in the drama taking place on the other side of the world that had meaning in the Korean mission field.

TENSIONS IN NORTH TAIWAN

In a memorandum on education in Taiwan prepared for the British Consulate in Tamsui in 1932, it was noted that the girls' school operated by the Dominican Sisters in Taipeh and three secondary schools supported by the Canadian or English Presbyterians "may be said to be the only up-to-date and thoroughly efficient schools for Formosans which, while imparting a modern education (in Japanese) have not forced attention to the superiority of an alien language."[93] The government general in Taiwan was attempting to transfer to the island a replica of the educational system used in Japan, and Japanese was therefore the obligatory language of instruction. According to the British consul in Tamsui, language was used as a means of restricting education for Taiwanese to the elementary level, thus ensuring that practically all administrative posts on the island would be reserved for the Japanese. The consul added that "the desire to keep the Formosans as a race of labourers is largely responsible for the reluctance to grant equal educational opportunities, and it is therefore not surprising that the native sees little attraction in what his rulers offer him."[94]

Because they represented an alternative to the Japanese system, the mission schools had some attraction for the Taiwanese. But the Presbyterian schools had not received government recognition because they did not observe "Shinto rituals" (that is, the in-school ceremonies revolving around the Imperial Rescript on Education). Hence, their students were barred from taking entrance examinations to higher government educational institutions. Even so, government inspectors kept a close watch on the mission schools, and, though missionaries were respected, there was some suspicion about their activities. This suspicion was only natural because all missionary work was conducted in Chinese and because missionaries were known to be sympathetic to the Taiwanese. As far as education was concerned, the Japanese realized that even though mission school work was limited "it commands the highest admiration of those Formosans who, were it not for these facilities, would be deprived of a chance of more than elementary education."[95] The Presbyterian schools could be seen to pose a challenge to government educational policies on language, but the fact that they were highly admired by some Taiwanese was probably more important to the Japanese authorities. Nevertheless, the small number of mission schools meant that they had little impact on overall education in Taiwan. However, together with Western businesses and residents, the mission schools and missionaries were visible enough to be targets of "spy-fever," which seemed to reach disturbing proportions in the summer of 1936.[96]

Despite its nonrecognized status, the Tamsui Middle School had an average enrolment in the early 1930s of some 220 boys, of whom 160 were boarders, and a teaching staff of seven Taiwanese and three Japanese in addition to missionaries. By 1933, the course of study at the middle school was the same as that of a government middle school, except that Bible study was required in all years. All the boys went through a five-year course in Japanese, Chinese, English, history, geography, drawing, arithmetic, algebra, geometry, trigonometry, physics, chemistry, botany, geology, ethics, music, and the Bible. The boys also played sports, including baseball, tennis, English rugby, and basketball. In basketball, the school team was able to defeat that of Taihoku (Taipeh) Imperial University in 1933.[97] However, the real powerhouse of school sports was the rugger team. In 1933, it had not lost a game since its inception many years before; it always beat the sides from other comparable schools, the university, and even the sportsmen of the Imperial Railroad Team. Among its many victories was a surprising one in October 1932 against a visiting team from H. M. S. *Cumberland*, the famous cruiser that would gain renown seven years later at the Battle of the River Plate.[98] The school needed all the victories that it could manage, because the government general was one team that would not play fair in the matches over language and the shrine question.

In April 1934, following a thorough inspection of both the Tamsui Girls' School and the Tamsui Middle School by government inspectors, the government general requested changes in the curricula of both schools. In future, Bible classes would be conducted in Japanese instead of Chinese, and students would no longer be allowed to speak to each other in Chinese or Formosan dialect. Teaching would be conducted in Japanese, and all teaching in Chinese language (that is, Amoy Romanized or Formosan dialect) would be stopped. Furthermore, all teachers who did not speak Japanese would learn the language or be retired.[99] Some of the older staff, who did not speak Japanese, thus decided to sever their connection with the school.

The new regulations put the principal of the Tamsui Middle School, G. W. Mackay, who spoke no Japanese, in a difficult position. However, the Japanese authorities appeared satisfied for the moment, for an inspection by the government general's minister of education in the fall of 1934 passed without incident. Indeed, the next year it was reported that the students seemed "to take to Japanese quite naturally" in their dormitories and on the sports field and enforced the rule that no Taiwanese language would be allowed.[100] The policy to create ersatz Japanese out of young Taiwanese appeared to be working.

This change was recognized by the Tamsui Middle School itself, for it was reported in 1936 that "one of the great needs of young people at the present time in Formosa is to find themselves in the new environment of the Japanese language and culture. Creative religious experience through the medium of Japanese will help them find themselves."[101] Despite the hope that the school might continue to prepare its pupils for their place in Taiwanese society, the Japanese authorities demanded more change.

The Canadian Presbyterians understood the nature of the pressures that they faced. In 1935, the Tamsui Middle School had been in the limelight more than usual. Moreover,

> Rapidly changing conditions in a period when the currents of Nationalism blow so strong make for difficulties in the carrying on of a Christian institution, particularly like that of a Middle School. In a country like Japan, where the Government puts so much stress on education, and has made such strides in making education universal for all people, it is to be expected that the desire to do the job themselves will be increasingly evident. In a colony like Formosa, we can understand how this desire becomes heightened, particularly during these "crisis" years.[102]

The chief difficulty was that the government general required the school to participate in shrine ceremonies. This requirement created a great deal of trouble for the Canadian Presbyterians.

In fact, the shrine question was only one in a growing list of disagreements with the government general. Indeed, one can only assume that the Japanese aim was to see the Tamsui Middle School closed. If this was so, then they went about it in a devious way. By the middle of 1935, Mackay had come to the conclusion that "there is not the slightest doubt that the

Government means to make radical changes in our institutions. Formerly our schools were regarded as Mission Schools, but that is no longer to be so. We are to be treated as private schools, under Government regulations for private schools."[103] To the government general, a mission school was an institution that taught religion and must be constituted as a theological college: the Tamsui Girls' School and the Tamsui Middle School definitely did not meet that criterion. Thus, they came under the jurisdiction of the Department of Education.[104] Despite the lack of government recognition of the Canadian Presbyterian schools, they had to comply with all government general regulations or close.

C. H. Archer, the British consul in Tamsui, whose residence was next to the Canadian missionary property, was acutely aware of the problems in the Tamsui Middle School. In June 1935, he wrote a perceptive memorandum, which went into detail about these problems, on the position and prospects of the Canadian and English Presbyterian missions in Taiwan. Archer reported that the school was a chronic source of trouble that sometimes took on serious proportions. He noted:

> There is much friction between different elements in the personnel, which are exceedingly difficult for an outsider to follow. Racial differences are complicated by personal differences, and one of the Japanese teachers with a grievance recently enlisted the support of a scurrilous weekly paper of "patriotic" tendencies known as the "Taiwan Keisei Shimpo," which accused the school of being a centre of disloyal teaching, and even tried to excite ill-feeling by raking up the perpetual lease controversy. The charge of disloyal activities had its ostensible foundation in a slight misunderstanding over the flying of the Manchukuo flag on the occasion of the Manchurian Emperor's recent visit to Japan.[105]

Archer believed that Mackay was not the best person to deal with the current situation because the latter did not have the personality to deal with such a delicate situation. This was especially so, Archer thought, because "at present officials are in and out of the schools at all hours, and the Tamsui Mission affords rather an unhappy picture of frayed nerves and obscure quarrels, which are interpreted by different persons in widely different ways;" he added that "the mission as a whole strikes one at present as being deficient in leadership."[106] Certainly, he was pessimistic about the future of the Canadian and English missions in Taiwan:

> With the difficulties presented by the dual language and the ever more delicate political background, one is compelled to wonder how long the foreign missions can survive. One may indeed hope that conditions will perceptibly improve when all the organisations are headed by men who can converse freely with the higher officials in their own language. Many of these officials are not

unsympathetic, and some are known to feel much admiration for the great linguistic effort now being made.[107]

One of the problems for the Canadian mission was that Mackay did not speak Japanese. The English Presbyterians in south Taiwan were in a much better position than their Canadian counterparts in the north because Edward Band, the principal of the Tainan Middle School, was fluent in Japanese as well as in the local Chinese dialect. Seeing great difficulties for mission schools in Taiwan, Archer still thought that "the more thoughtful officials are not likely to wish to close the schools until their own educational projects are very much further advanced; but patriotic agitations place them in a very difficult position, and might compel action which they are loth to take."[108] Unfortunately, neither the Canadian nor the English Presbyterians had any means of countering patriotic agitations on the part of Japanese residents on the island.

Archer clearly believed that Mackay was partially responsible for the difficulties between the Canadian mission and the Japanese authorities. In his own explanation of the troubles, Mackay, of course, did not see himself as part of the problem. Such was the pressure put on him by both Japanese and Taiwanese during this crisis that nerves were bound to get frayed. What is apparent, however, is that Mackay did the best he could under very difficult circumstances. Mackay thought that the beginning of the trouble for his school came in 1933 when racial differences were complicated by a strike by Japanese teachers at the English Presbyterian Middle School in Tainan caused by the dismissal of its Japanese head teacher. The missionaries and Taiwanese staff at the school were suspected of being disloyal and were criticized in the press. The trouble in south Taiwan had an immediate impact on the Canadian Presbyterian schools in the north. Government inspectors visited the schools in Tamsui and asked the pupils stock questions such as, "Which is more to be respected, the Imperial Rescript or the Bible?"[109] The authorities also demanded a suitable place for a copy of the Imperial Rescript on Education. This place turned out to be Mackay's office, which the principal had to vacate in order to accommodate a screen behind which was a safe that held the Imperial Rescript. This episode could be considered high comedy except for the unsmiling seriousness of the Japanese.

In the spring of 1935, the government general requested further changes to the curriculum of the Tamsui Middle School. Some of them, such as increased hours for Japanese language and decreased hours for English instruction, posed no real difficulty. Other requests did:

> the word "yohai" meaning "worshipping at a distance or bowing at a distance" [sic] must be inserted in our curriculum instead of "paying respect to" as we had in our old school prospectus. According to our prospectus we had to "pay respect to," in other words "bow" toward the Soldiers' Mausoleum, the Meiji

Shrine, the Ise Shrine and the Taiwan Shrine in Taihoku [Taipeh], once each year.[110]

The request to change the wording in the prospectus was first made to the Tamsui Girls' School, and it allowed for discussion between Mackay and Phyllis Argall, his counterpart at the girls' school. Mackay wrote that there was a division between those who wanted the wording changed and those who advocated that the missionaries make a stand. Indeed, one of the Japanese teachers at the Tamsui Girls' School was even prepared to approach the government authorities in Japan itself on behalf of the missionaries if they chose to resist.[111] Despite different opinions, the mission council decided that the words *pay respect to* would be maintained in the prospectus of each schools.

Argall and Mackay were given the job of explaining the Canadian Presbyterian position to the Department of Education's Taihoku Prefecture inspector and to the chief inspector of Formosa. These latter two gave the two missionaries a lesson in Japanese by explaining that *yohai* ("bowing at a distance") and *sampai* ("bowing in front of the shrine") had no religious significance and that the act of bowing simply showed respect. Demonstrating surprising reasonableness, the chief inspector went so far as to suggest that if the missionaries still had reservations "we might insert a clause after the word 'yohai,' to say that it was not a religious act."[112] This proved enough to convince the mission council to change the words *pay respect to* to *yohai*. The incident was not quite over, because the day after the interview one of the newspapers in Taipeh, in reporting the meeting, insisted that "we missionaries and our schools had failed to understand the Japanese Spirit etc. The write-up was calculated to stir up anti-foreign and anti-christian spirit."[113] Fortunately, the government general authorities countered this newspaper report with a fair presentation of the interview.

The damage was not easily repaired. Before the government general's statement appeared in the press, Mrs. Jean Ross Mackay reported that when she had taken a boat to Japan she had been discourteously treated by customs officials because she was the wife of Mackay of the Tamsui Middle School and accused of being an "anti-god." Although such an incident was disturbing, Mrs. Mackay believed that the Japanese authorities had Christian educators in a vise over the shrine question. She wrote:

> Do we say, "We cannot go, as we believe it to be worship." They reply with a statement and a question. The statement is, "We do not demand an act of worship." The question is, "If it is wrong for a Christian to go, why do so many Christian schools in Japan proper go?" Do we delay, and put off? There is a rising tide of insinuation, "You are opposing Japanese subjects, your students, from performing a patriotic act which is required by law."[114]

The Canadian Presbyterians did obey the law, and Mackay took the Tamsui

Middle School boys to the Taiwan shrine in June 1935. For several weeks before, Mrs. Mackay noted,

> we had had almost daily urgings from our christian teachers, from lower officials whom our failure to obey was involving in possible or actual reproach from forces higher up, or from the military party . . . say the dread name under ones breath . . . that we should go and save all the misunderstanding and suspicion that was steadily being engendered by our delay.[115]

However, she realized that this action on the part of the school was perhaps only a temporary reprieve. She believed that "the day of religious liberty may be passing. There is a new Religions Bill in process of preparation which, while still granting religious liberty, qualifies that term. Anything unpatriotic or seditious may be allowed to masquerade under the name of religion, and go unchecked."[116] Moreover, there was a genuine fear that charges of *lèse-majesté* could be brought against the Church for openly discussing a matter that concerned the imperial family. Apparently, this was a reason why the English Presbyterian missionaries did not place the shrine question before their southern presbytery. Interestingly, Mrs. Mackay wondered whether the trial of Minobe Tatsukichi, a Tokyo Imperial University professor, which was an example of what could happen to even a prominent individual if he openly discussed the imperial family, had been featured in Canadian papers. Clearly, missionaries in Taiwan had to be careful or Taiwanese Christians could suffer.

Missionaries themselves came under attack from a group of people made up of war veterans, businessmen, and lawyers. G. W. Mackay believed that the enemies of the missionaries were gathering forces. In April 1935, there was a meeting of some military men in Taipeh at which speakers attacked the Canadian Presbyterian mission, the missionaries, and the mission schools, especially the Tamsui Middle School. Posters calling for the destruction of the school were distributed about Taipeh. Whether missionaries could ever convince such "enemies" that the missionary movement and its schools should be left in peace was highly doubtful. Nevertheless, the Canadians agreed to allow their students to go to the Taiwan shrine "in the hope that in yielding to this demand as so many other Mission schools have done, we are not sinning against God."[117]

Other missionaries, like Mrs. Mackay, had grave reservations about allowing the schoolchildren to take part in shrine ceremonies. Hildur K. Hermanson, who taught at the Tamsui Girls' School, believed that these ceremonies had a religious significance and that to go and bow at the Taiwan shrine went against her personal convictions. However, she was hesitant about standing up for her convictions. She wrote in June 1935:

> But if on the other hand, the Government should demand that our schools bow

at the Shrine or be closed, I am unable to decide what steps would be wise to take. Closing the schools on the grounds of objecting to Shrine attendance may lead to persecution of the Native Formosan Church by the ultra-patriotic Japanese, thus making things very difficult for the Formosans.[118]

Hermanson's colleague, Alma M. Burdick, was also very concerned about the possible closing of the Canadian Presbyterian schools and the repercussions for the Taiwanese Church. However, Burdick did believe that "the clear witness a mission School should give is in my opinion, greatly marred by such an act [participating in shrine ceremonies]."[119] Argall took a strong stand against taking part in shrine services:

> I feel that though I might, as a private individual accept the word of the Minister of Education to the effect that the bow to the shrine required of the school pupils is not religious, but patriotic, it would be against my conscience and convictions to take, or permit to be taken, the members of any of our Christian Institutions to the shrine.[120]

She argued that "to many the shrine is religious, a place for the performance of religious acts and ceremonies. I feel it might stumble such if we, as teachers of the religion of the One and true God, who is a Spirit, were to attend one of these shrines."[121] Unlike Hermanson and Burdick, Argall skirted the question of whether or not she would take schoolchildren to the shrine if the alternative was closure of the girls' school.

Despite Argall's stand, teachers at the Tamsui Girls' School learned something about the way in which the Japanese authorities pursued their objectives. In a statement in regard to the shrine question as it concerned the Tamsui Girls' School, it was pointed out: "the Japanese touched on the point of loyalty is oblivious to all other obligations and impervious to argument. To quote a missionary of many years service—'The Japanese do not think with their intellect—they move with their emotions.'"[122] This statement was undoubtedly correct, but the missionaries did not go out of their way to curry favour by indulging the Japanese. The girls' school refused a piece of wood from the imperial shrine at Ise because it would have to be housed in a small structure similar in shape to a *jinja* and treated with the utmost respect and reverence. It is understandable that the Presbyterians would reject this offer; it is also equally clear that there were people who wanted any excuse to do them harm. The teachers at the girls' school realized that

> The military and patriotic and nationalist party is exceedingly strong, and is rapidly gaining strength. . . .The slightest suspicion of attitude of anything less than worship of the Emperor and of Japan would be sufficient cause for this party to launch an attack. Formosa used to be under Military Government, and the military party at present, being disgusted with the policy of gentleness and

tolerance displayed by the Civil Government now in power is doing its best to gain control of the Island once more. A convenient weapon of attack is the Christian Church.[123]

More frank in their assessment than Mackay perhaps was in his, the female missionary teachers at the girls' school saw that their own crisis was part of a more general attack against the Church in Taiwan.

No sooner was the shrine question settled than another crisis occurred. This one involved flags and showed how sensitive the Japanese were to perceived slights. On the occasion of the visit of Emperor Kangte (Henry Pu Yi) of Manchukuo to Japan on 6 April 1935, all public institutions in Taiwan were ordered to put up both the Japanese and the Manchukuo flags. Unfortunately, the government instruction to fly the Manchukuo flag was issued too late to arrive at the two Canadian Presbyterian schools in Tamsui before the designated day. The Canadian schools were reported by the police for failing to put up the appropriate flags. This failure led to a newspaper attack against the schools, for "word travelled far and wide that the Mission, following the League of Nations, refused to 'recognize' Manchukuo as a nation."[124] Even though this incident was defused, it was noted by those at the girls' school that "the incident did serve to give the patriotic party yet one more excuse for attacking the schools, and through them, the Christian Church."[125] This was true.

New requests were made of the Tamsui Middle School. Following the flag incident, Mackay wrote that the minister of the interior sent new instructions demanding that the school do its utmost to foster national spirit and that Japanese had to be used by both teachers and students in school. Moreover, strict minutes were to be kept of all meetings, and more than half the staff had to be Japanese.[126] Clearly, whatever concessions the missionaries made, the Japanese authorities would demand more. In order to placate the Japanese, Hugh MacMillan, who had undergone Japanese-language study in Japan, took over as principal of the Tamsui Middle School from Mackay. However, the end was near.

In March 1936, a Japanese teacher left the school to return to Japan. His leaving sparked an outbreak of new criticism, and it did not pass quickly, because for the next three months the school was continuously in the press. The activities of the "Annihilation Society" became increasingly open, and, as if to add fuel to the fire, "in April a minute inspection was made of the school by government officials. The standing of the school was declared low, particularly with regard to the cultivation of the national spirit."[127] The coup de grâce to the school was delivered at the end of May 1936. It was reported that "on May 30th the 'Aeroplane incident' took place. Two teachers were accused of lacking the proper patriotic attitude toward the visit of a squadron of hydroplanes. Following this 'incident' all but two of the staff resigned."[128] Archer, the British consul, reported that "during the term Government officials, police and military

THE SHRINE QUESTION 109

police were in and out of the schools at all hours, teachers were subjected to prolonged interrogations, and the discipline of the students became more and more difficult to maintain."[129] The Canadian Presbyterians had had enough.

Through the summer of 1936, negotiations took place with government authorities in regard to the future management of the two schools. Archer reported that at the beginning of May the provincial governor had proposed that the two schools in Tamsui be handed over to him

> on the ground that while a religious flavour in education was good, schools which used the national education primarily as a means of propagating a particular religion could no longer be allowed, and that the conditions obtaining in Formosa demanded that all schools catering for general education must, in future, be kept exclusively under Japanese control.[130]

The theological college escaped because it gave a special course to a few selected students who had already finished their general education. In any case, it was generally understood that, once the middle school and its sister institution passed into Japanese hands, the missionary staff and the theological college would move to Taipeh. Sir Robert Clive, the British ambassador in Tokyo, thought that the arrangement between the Japanese and the Canadians was very reasonable "in contrast to the intolerant treatment to which missions throughout the Japanese Empire are . . . at present being subjected."[131] However, some in London did not take such a charitable view. It was minuted on a Foreign Office report that

> The Mission authorities are to have seats on the governing board, but may not govern, they have handed over all the school buildings & equipment. In other words the teaching of the Mission (which is its reason for being there) is to be altered to suit nationalistic ideas and their property has been confiscated. But because they have been paid for the site & treated with less abruptness than usual it is an unexpectedly conciliatory treatment. It all depends on the standard.[132]

The "conciliatory treatment" was perhaps only due to the fact that money was exchanged. In such an appropriation, there was no opportunity to bargain or to appeal, for the government general set the agenda. The middle school's buildings were handed over as a gift to a management committee headed by the governor of Taihoku province, and the grounds, the women's school, and the teachers' residence were sold to the government for ¥90,000.[133] Surprisingly, the sites of the theological college and the missionary residences, including the whole frontage of the property on the estuary, remained in Canadian Presbyterian hands.[134]

In a businesslike fashion, the Japanese authorities agreed that classes at the Tamsui Girls' School would continue more or less as before until the end of 1936, because it was only in the middle of November. Before the final transfer was complete, the Japanese catalogued all records and equipment at the school and required the missionaries to sign off the catalogued articles, and so "ended a tragic chapter in the history of Christian Educational work in Formosa."[135]

The Japanese had achieved their aim in destroying the two Canadian Presbyterian schools. As the British consul in Tamsui noted in his report for 1936, "with the aim of education so narrowly nationalistic, it was inevitable that any foreign control in this field should be more and more actively resented."[136] There was little that the British or Canadian government could do immediately to alter the policies of the government general in this matter. The loss of the educational work was a crippling blow both to the Presbyterian Church in north Taiwan and to the prestige of the Christian movement. Unfortunately, there was no silver lining to what had happened:

> While the giving up of this educational work removes a most heavy responsibility from the mission and the home church in these difficult times it places us under new obligations. Obligations to the Native Church and to the yet unevangelized millions as well. How shall we provide educated leadership for the growing church now that the schools have gone? How shall we again build up the Church's impaired prestige? These are questions many are asking.[137]

One way for the Canadian Presbyterians was to emphasize evangelistic work. In1936, Dr. John Sung, a well-known Chinese evangelist, visited Taiwan, and his preaching contributed to high attendances at evangelistic meetings held in conjunction with the opening of The Three-Year Movement, an evangelistic campaign that lasted until the end of 1938. However, evangelistic success could not alter the fact that the physical core of the Canadian Presbyterian mission had been cut out, not only by the closure of the schools but also with the disappearance of the safe green of the mission compound in Tamsui where Canadians had lived since the early 1870s.

The swiftness of events might well have caught the missionaries by surprise. Certainly, there was little hint of coming difficulties with the government general at the beginning of the 1930s. Apparently, many Japanese Christian friends criticized the Canadian Presbyterians for failing to adjust their educational methods to new conditions.[138] This criticism was unfair. Even though they initially baulked at the requests regarding participation in shrine ceremonies, Mackay and his colleagues did accommodate the Japanese in this matter. Indeed, the shrine question was settled in only few months. However, more and more demands were made on them by the Japanese authorities until the two schools were closed.

The Canadian Presbyterians were not as astute or simply as lucky as their English Presbyterian colleagues in south Taiwan in the matter of schools. In 1934, the English Presbyterians appointed Kato Chotaro, an ex-commander in the imperial Japanese navy, to be principal of the Tainan Middle School, with Edward Band, an experienced educational missionary who spoke Japanese, as honorary principal with responsibilities for teaching the scriptures and English.[139] The Canadian Presbyterians lacked a Japanese-speaking missionary of the same experience as Band. This was one of the results of the change in missionary personnel in north Taiwan brought about by Church Union in 1925. Just as important, however, was the fact that the Canadian Presbyterian mission was so closely identified with the Chinese community in Taiwan as a result of the founder George Leslie Mackay's marriage to a Chinese woman. This close connection with the Chinese community made the Canadian Presbyterian mission suspect in Japanese eyes. Even though they worked in the seat of colonial government, the Canadian Presbyterians were slow to realize the importance of Japanese language and the need to understand the official colonial mind. In contrast, the English Presbyterians in south Taiwan had always tried to maintain good relations with the Japanese. In 1895, the English Presbyterians, acting as mediators between Chinese and Japanese, had arranged the capitulation of Tainan to Japanese military forces. Overall, the English Presbyterians seemed more adept at dealing with the Japanese than were their Canadian counterparts and more aware of the necessity of having a missionary who was fluent in Japanese.

Yet what neither Canadian nor English Presbyterian missionaries in Taiwan could combat was a deliberate campaign to bring an end to their educational work and eventually to their missionary work. In hindsight, it is clear that the shrine question was the opening salvo of a campaign to close the Tamsui Middle School and the Tamsui Girls' School. The goal of the government general was to have complete control over education on the island. Because relations between Japanese and missionaries in Taiwan had generally been good since 1895, the tenacity of the Japanese campaign must have caught most of the missionaries by surprise.

The shrine question and its consequences for missionary educational work in north Taiwan showed a clearer pattern of colonial government pressure than in Korea. The difference in Korea was the strength of the missionary movement and the size and place of the Korean Christian movement within Korean society. Korea was a much harder nut to crack. Although the stand of the American Northern Presbyterians McCune and Snook in P'yongyang can be commended in terms of their religious principles, they were also clearly politically naïve in their dealings with the Japanese authorities. Their personal security was never in doubt, but they should have recognized that a major crisis with the Japanese authorities could result in great suffering for many Korean Christians. To precipitate a crisis that could split opinion within the missionary movement in Korea and weaken the Korean Christian movement was to play into the hands of the government general in Korea, the more so because the missionary and Christian movements in Japan had already come to terms with the shrine question. In that sense, the cautious approach of Armstrong in Toronto and the United Church missionaries in north Korea toward the shrine ceremonies appears to have been wise. Clearly, also, the attitude of Canadian missionaries to this problem was influenced by their liberal theological views, which were different from those of many of their American missionary colleagues, who were more theologically conservative. Yet, as the case in Taiwan illustrated, the policy of riding out a crisis would ultimately prove impossible if more and more demands were being made.

Despite the difficulties posed to the Canadian missionary movement by the shrine question, there were areas of missionary work, especially in Japan, that remained largely untroubled through most of the 1930s. Although the decade saw the transfer of educational leadership from missionary to Japanese Christian, the campuses of the girls' schools that Canadian missionaries supported remained oases of tranquillity. Likewise, Kwansei Gakuin in Nishinomiya continued to operate largely without major difficulties despite the waves of nationalism ebbing and flowing outside its gates. Even though the American Presbyterians and Methodists were ambivalent toward continuing educational work because of the shrine question, the United Church of Canada missionaries decided to keep their schools open. They strongly believed that there was still a need for mission schools and for missionaries to stay on.

CHAPTER FIVE
Educational Work in Japan

Although Canadian missionaries in Japan came to grips with the problem of shrine attendance, they still faced challenges over their educational work. Mission schools in Japan were under pressure from the government to change from institutions dependent on Western support to Japanese Christian schools free from foreign influence. Furthermore, mission schools were obliged to change their curricula in order to meet the strict regulations laid down by the Ministry of Education.

    Missionary educators also had to deal with the ordinary budgetary and administrative problems involved in running a school during years of economic depression. Money was short, even for the most basic repairs in some of the small kindergartens. Despite that shortage, some schools were able to afford to erect buildings and enjoyed increasing enrolments. In a period of dramatic change, one constant problem brought on by government policy with which missionary teachers had to grapple was to maintain their schools as Christian institutions. In the face of rising nationalism in Japan, with its xenophobic undertones, this was by no means an easy task. For so long the campus walls had shut out the unknown and had allowed missionaries to fulfil themselves doing worthwhile work in an understandable environment. The 1930s saw this pleasant existence change as missionary educators found themselves confronted with unprecedented challenges both academic and financial.

GIRLS' SCHOOLS IN JAPAN

Throughout the 1920s and 1930s, the WMS missionaries working at the three girls' schools in Tokyo, Shizuoka, and Kofu attempted with some success to maintain the high standards that they had inherited from Martha Cartmel and other pioneer Canadian Methodist educational missionaries. There was a strong demand for missionary education for girls. Despite overcrowding, the Toyo Eiwa Jo Gakko was able to maintain its *haikara*, that is, its smart and fashionable image, into the late 1920s.[1] However, the rising generation of students was seemingly less docile in its acceptance of authority than its predecessors had been, and there were tensions at the school.

Challenges to the strict way in which Canadian missionaries ran the Toyo Eiwa Jo Gakko began to appear in the wake of the 1923 great Kanto earthquake. Although the school buildings were not badly damaged in that catastrophe, the earthquake served to disrupt the life of the school long after its tremors had dissipated. In 1924, for instance, the strict rule that prohibited students from bringing candy to eat as dessert at school lunch was challenged by the pupils themselves. Picayune though this matter might appear, it does reveal a restiveness among the students over the close supervision and tight regulations that the Canadian missionary teachers imposed. There was also a hint of cultural unease among the students, who found themselves in a garden of Western freedoms rather than Japanese ones. The formation of the United Church of Canada allowed the WMS to show that it was prepared to turn over a new leaf at the Toyo Eiwa Jo Gakko. In 1925, a new principal was appointed, Gertrude Hamilton,[2] who would remain principal until 1938 and so provide continuity in guidance for the school through most of the 1930s. Although Hamilton's Japanese was not good enough for her to chat freely, she was able to understand people, and her lack of fluency in Japanese did not prevent her from being a successful administrator during a period of change. One of her first acts, and an important step in the progress toward moving the management of the school out of missionary hands into those of the Japanese, was the appointment in 1926 of Fujita Shizuo to be in charge of school affairs in the high school. Fujita went to the Toyo Eiwa from Kumamoto Prefecture where he had been a teacher in the Prefectural Middle School and Teachers' School.[3] Importantly, Fujita had experience in government schools and knew their educational standards, and this experience was undoubtedly a help to Toyo Eiwa to come when curriculum change had to be made in order to conform to government guidelines.

In 1925, the Toyo Eiwa Jo Gakko had a total student body of 522, with 240 in the high school, 195 in the primary school, 55 in the kindergarten, and 32 training to be kindergarten teachers.[4] As a result of continued expansion, one of the immediate tasks that Hamilton faced was to increase the physical size of the school. As the fiftieth anniversary of the Canadian Methodist mission in Japan approached, the completion of new buildings for the Toyo Eiwa was seen as fitting way to celebrate the first half century of Canadian work.

Despite the gathering Depression in North America, in 1930 sufficient funds became available to reconstruct the school completely. The news that construction funds had been granted came as a delightful surprise to those "who felt that the Toyo Eiwa must have a new habitation or cease to be."[5] Because adjoining land was not available, it was decided to separate the kindergarten, dormitory, and foreign residence from the main school, and a new property was purchased close by along Toriizaka.[6] The cost of this new property was shared by the WMS and by the Alumnae and Patrons Associations. Work began on the new site in January 1931, and the buildings were ready for occupancy early in February 1932. With the earthquake danger in mind, the new dormitory was built with reinforced concrete. It had a capacity for sixty residents and was finished and furnished in Western style. The two smaller buildings on the new property were wood framed and stuccoed in a buff colour. A central oil-fired hot water heating system provided heat for the new buildings. Once the new dormitory was completed, work began on demolishing the old dormitories and school buildings on the main campus. This was done in a way that allowed classes to go on despite the work. The new school building was occupied in June 1933. It was an impressive building, that formed three sides of a rectangle, with its main classroom wing facing Toriizaka. It was designed to provide classrooms and up-to-date facilities, including special-purpose rooms, a gymnasium, cafeteria for 650 students, as well as administrative offices.

Fortunately for the WMS, the exchange rate during most of the construction period was favourable; according to Hamilton, the rate "made it a very much easier proposition for our friends in Canada than was anticipated at the time the [building] grant was made."[7] The architects, W. M. Vories and Company, who supervised every detail of the building and equipping, charged ¥421,867 for the main school building, and, with the buying of the new property and the construction of the three buildings on it, the total cost came to ¥842,306. Of this *amount*, the WMS paid some eighty-seven percent or ¥738,000,[8] and the remainder came from the alumnae.

Even though the WMS paid for most of the construction and land, it did not own the school. In the past, the property of the Toyo Eiwa and its two sister schools had been held by the Zai Nippon Kanada Godo Senkyoshi Shadan, the corporate juridical association of the United Church mission in Japan. This was to change. As Howard Norman has pointed out, "as nationalism grew more raucous it was felt advisable that the WMS schools should be incorporated as separate bodies, as was done later with the two FMB orphanages."[9] Although discussions in the Business Committee of the Toyo Eiwa about separate incorporation had begun as early as 1929, the requirement of the Ministry of Education that a reserve sum of money be held in Japan before incorporation could be granted slowed the school's application. It was not until 1934 that the financial requirements could be met. The minster of education then gave permission for the formation of a *zaidan hojin*, a property-holding association, with Bishop Akazawa Motozo of the Japan Methodist Church as president of its board of directors.[10] The other two schools followed suit in forming their own *zaidan hojin*, with the Shizuoka Eiwa Jo Gakko gaining permission in 1937 and the Yamanashi Eiwa Jo Gakko in 1939. Although the creation of the *zaidan hojin* was another step in taking the control of mission schools out of foreign hands, it also meant that the WMS could no longer look to the Canadian or British governments to safeguard their considerable investment in these three schools. The WMS had to rely solely on the wisdom of its board of directors and the dubious goodwill of the Ministry of Education to protect its interests.

While the discussions leading to the formation of the *zaidan hojin* and the construction of the new school buildings were going on, Hamilton also had to restructure the curriculum in order to meet the changing regulations of the Ministry of Education. One of the strengths of the Toyo Eiwa was its music department, and piano had been taught as a high school subject. In 1927, the music department offered a sophisticated course of six progressive levels. In 1932, however, Mombusho regulations, which took piano out of the regular curriculum, led to the closure of the music department.[11] Although piano lessons continued to be given outside school hours, the closure of the department also meant that teaching opportunities for WMS missionaries were reduced, for a good number of them, like Hamilton herself, had come from Canada to teach music.

The loss of music was compensated for in part by the creation in 1933 of a special program that played to the linguistic capabilities of the teaching staff of the Toyo Eiwa. This was a class for the daughters of diplomats or businesspeople who had been born or brought up abroad and who did not have the necessary Japanese-language skills or other requirements to enter the regular primary or high school courses. According to their particular needs, girls in this class would receive individual coaching, lasting from one up to three years, until they reached the standards of the regular courses. Although the class for returned pupils began as an experiment with twenty-one students, the demand was such that the special program continued until 1943. From beginning to end, it was directed by Akiyama Shunko, a teacher who spoke good English.

This special program was outside the mainstream of the primary and high school departments. During the late 1920s and early 1930s, however, important changes took place in both primary and high school courses. In 1929, the high school course was extended from four to five years, for without the extra year graduates would not have been able to go on to Tokyo Joshi Daigaku or to other institutions of higher learning. Although the Ministry of Education issued new regulations in 1932, once the five-year system had been set up the essential elements in the high school course remained the same until the end of the decade. At the Toyo Eiwa, there was a strong emphasis on English, with six hours of English classes within the thirty hours of class time per school week in all five years. Indeed, English rivalled Japanese as the class with the most contact hours in high school.[12] Other subjects included history, science, mathematics, geography, morals, home economics, gymnastics, music, sewing, educational psychology, law, and economics. It was a packed program of different subjects in the fourth and fifth years.

Outside of the classroom, there were other demands on high school students at the Toyo Eiwa. In 1935, the minister of education invited the fourth and fifth high school years to ceremonies at the Meiji shrine in Tokyo.[13] In 1938, the Ministry of Education directed that pupils in the fourth and fifth years break their summer vacation to spend a week at school at the beginning of September to cut and sew white robes (*byakui*), and pupils in the third year and below were to spend three days on a great clean-up. In July 1939, the high school students were made responsible by the Tokyo government for 3,000 *tsubo* (one *tsubo* is an area of about thirty-six square feet) of barley fields, which became the school farm.[14] Similarly, the primary school students were required to do agricultural work. The students in the kindergarten-teachers training course were lectured to by none other than Kagawa on things agricultural.[15] The demands put on the students to do agricultural work during their summer vacation were, of course, part of the mobilization of resources due to the ongoing Sino-Japanese War.

Whereas the high school curriculum survived without major change through the 1930s, the same was not true of the primary school curriculum. One of the special characteristics of the Toyo Eiwa's Primary School course was its English-language component. However, in 1933 educational reforms caused English to be dropped from the curriculum. This cancellation can be taken as proof of the growing strength of the Japanese military character. The major subject in the six-year course was Japanese, taught at least eight hours a week in every year. Arithmetic followed, with at least four hours a week in all six years. Pupils in the final year took classes in morals, Japanese language, arithmetic, Japanese history, geography, science, drawing, singing, gymnastics, sewing, and handicrafts during a twenty-nine-hour school week.[16]

The majority of the trainee teachers in the kindergarten-teachers training course were Christian boarders from the provinces. They provided much of the leadership for the school's YWCA students, and many became Sunday school teachers in churches near the Toyo Eiwa . During the 1920s, the trainee teachers came under the strong influence of the WMS missionaries, partially because the boarders shared accommodations with four Canadian women. The missionaries, of course, saw the connection between evangelism and kindergarten education and wanted to encourage it. Indeed, it was from the ranks of the graduates of the kindergarten-teachers course that the teachers in the WMS kindergartens in Shizuoka Prefecture and elsewhere came.[17] In an undated report written in the late 1930s, Sybil Courtice, then the secretary-treasurer of the WMS in Japan, noted:

> Our two nursery schools and more than forty kindergartens are located in about thirty different towns and cities, each missionary in charge being responsible for the superintendence of from one to six kindergartens. In each kindergarten, wherever practicable, an advisory committee is set up of which the church pastor is a member. The kindergartens are greatly valued as part of the church activities, being in many cases housed in the church building. With a yearly enrollment of 1800 little pupils . . . with Sunday attendance an accepted part of the program, with clubs and meetings for graduates, and with the opportunities

for parent education and direct evangelistic effort through mothers' meetings and calling in the home, it would be difficult to estimate what this type of educational work alone has meant and will mean in the life of the church and community and the growth of the family of God.[18]

In training kindergarten teachers at the Toyo Eiwa, the WMS was fortunate in having a succession of talented and educationally qualified women to run the course. From the end of World War I until 1928, Katherine Drake, who had received kindergarten training in Michigan, directed the course.[19] She was succeeded by Marie Melissa Staples, in charge of the course until 1932.[20] In that year, Lois Lehman, an American from Mississippi and a graduate of Northwestern University, transferred from the Shizuoka Eiwa Jo Gakko to direct the kindergarten-teachers program at the Tokyo school.[21] In 1933, legislation was introduced in Tokyo to alter the curriculum for training kindergarten teachers. New subjects, including physiology, hygiene, and dietetics, were added to the course, and increased emphasis was given to child research.[22] Lehman had the educational qualifications to teach the new subjects, and so the changes to the curriculum posed no insurmountable challenge to the program at the Toyo Eiwa.

Despite this, there was an effort to strengthen Christian kindergarten-teacher training through union with other missionary bodies. As early as 1933, there was talk about the amalgamation of Christian kindergarten teaching in Japan. In 1934, the United Church mission was approached by the Evangelical Church of North America mission (Amerika Fukuin Kyokai Senkyoshi Dan) to form a union training course at the Toyo Eiwa. The Canadian missionaries reacted with some caution, but they did allow five students from this American mission to enrol in their course in 1935. Two years later, a union was agreed upon, and Gertrud Kuechlich, a German-born member of the Evangelical Church mission, joined the faculty of the Toyo Eiwa.[23] The few students brought in by this union had little effect on the nature of the course offered by the WMS.

The changes that took place in virtually all the departments of the school during the early 1930s limited the role of missionary teachers. Even as early as 1927, only the veteran missionary Minnie Robertson was serving as a home room teacher in the high school.[24] This reduction might reflect the fact that younger missionaries, such as Hamilton, did not have the fluency in Japanese required to meet the demands of a class of over thirty girls. More important, though, was the fact that the younger generation of missionaries was much more specialized than predecessors such as Robertson or Blackmore. Indeed, it was the missionary specialities—such as piano teaching or English-language teaching—at which the reforms in both the high school and primary School curricula cut away. The kindergarten-teachers training course remained an exception. Even here, however, both Drake and Staples left teaching to undertake kindergarten and evangelistic work outside Tokyo. As teaching opportunities declined, the trend was for WMS missionaries to turn from educational to direct evangelistic work. This was a reversal of the trend in the late nineteenth century, when educational work was seen as a refuge from the rigours of direct evangelistic work.

Despite the educational reforms, Hamilton remained the principal of the Toyo Eiwa, and WMS control over the school seemed secure. Soon after the fiftieth-anniversary celebrations in 1934, however, it became increasingly clear that the Ministry of Education wanted to break the foreign control of mission schools. In 1935, the ministry turned its attention to the question of fostering religious sentiment in schools and established a committee to make recommendations and to submit a written report.[25] Even though the report was not ready until July 1937, one immediate result of the ministry's action was the demand for conformity with the Imperial Rescript on Education.[26] For the Toyo Eiwa, this was a life-or-death matter, because it struck at the concept of Christian education. It raised the issues of Sunday attendance at school and Sunday school, attendance at church, and the teaching of Christian values at the primary school level.[27] There was support in the press for change; for instance, the Tokyo *Nichi Nichi Shimbun* in 1936 came out against religious teaching in Buddhist and Christian schools. In December 1937, at a time when the government was looking for national support in the face of the crisis in China, the Ministry of Education established a deliberative assembly on education that attacked as heretical the basic foundations of Western thought, such as individualism, liberalism, and intellectualism. This can be seen as a step toward the complete control of culture, thought, and education by the government.[28]

It was obvious that there would be grave consequences for Christian education and foreign-controlled private schools in Japan. During 1937, in this atmosphere of impending educational crisis, the board of directors of the Toyo Eiwa Jo Gakko decided to replace Hamilton, away on furlough, with a Japanese principal. Ono Naoichi, who had been the principal of the Tokuyama Girls' High school in Yamaguchi Prefecture, was appointed and took charge at the beginning of 1938. Hamilton remained on staff, and it was clear that she and the WMS welcomed the appointment, for Ono was a Methodist with connections to the Kwansei Gakuin and was known as a friend of the mission. Courtice later reported to WMS headquarters in Toronto that "change from missionary to Japanese principals, although a matter of policy for some years, has during the past two years been carried out and all three schools are now under the principalship of fine Christian gentlemen who are tried and proved educationalists."[29] It might have been a matter of policy for some years to appoint a Japanese principal, but without outside pressure it seems unlikely that Ono's appointment would have been made at that time.

Despite all the difficulties at the Toyo Eiwa Jo Gakko, the number of students continued to climb through the 1930s. In 1938, there were 236 students in the primary school, 22 in the special course, 467 in the high school, 48 in the kindergarten-teachers training course, and 68 in the kindergarten. There were over sixty more students in the high school than there had been in 1934.[30]

Although the Toyo Eiwa Jo Gakko was the largest of WMS schools for girls, the Shizuoka Eiwa Jo Gakko in Shizuoka and the Yamanashi Eiwa Jo Gakko in Kofu also enjoyed growth during the 1930s. Like their counterpart in Tokyo, both schools had to bring their curricula and organizational structures into line with government requirements. Similarly, they had to venture away from the comfortable rut of being mission schools and toward the goal of becoming independent private schools under Japanese leadership. One of the major difficulties that confronted all three schools, but most severely the two provincial schools, was their dependence on the WMS for funding.

Tuition fees did not keep pace with costs. In Shizuoka, the monthly fee for the Shizuoka Eiwa stayed at four yen from 1925 until 1936.[31] The school had to remain competitive in fees with prefectural high schools for girls in order to attract students. As a provincial town, Shizuoka did not have a broad middle-class base from which rich students could be drawn. By keeping its fees competitive with those of prefectural high schools, however, the Shizuoka Eiwa Jo Gakko continued to attract a rising number of applicants for entry into its high school. During the early 1930s, between twenty and thirty new students entered the high school, but after 1935 the number increased significantly. In 1938, 55 of 102 applicants entered, bringing the total number of students in the five-year program to 210. As was the case with the Toyo Eiwa Jo Gakko in Tokyo, the number of applicants and students mushroomed during the Pacific War. In 1941, the high school grew to 353 students, and it reached a maximum of 515 in 1944.[32] Increasing the number of students was one way of making up for the shortfall in donations from the WMS.

As late as 1932, the WMS was still providing for up to half the running costs of the Shizuoka school.[33] In that year, the WMS informed the school that, as a result of the financial conditions in Canada, it would have to reduce its contribution the next year by some fifteen percent. Between 1937 and 1941, though the annual contribution of the WMS, with the single exception of 1938, remained at some ¥6,300, this led to the fall of its percentage of total receipts for the school from 36.4 percent to 21.9 percent.[34] Canadian money was needed not only for the running costs of the school but also for capital expenses. In 1937, for instance, ¥30,000 were asked for to help in the building of a new gymnasium.[35] Moreover, the creation of a *zaidan hojin*, first mooted in 1934, required a reserve fund of ¥20,000, half of which had to come from the WMS. It took three years for the WMS to raise its share, but it managed to do so in time for the fiftieth anniversary of the Shizuoka school.[36]

The WMS also had to press ahead with the policy, agreed upon in 1937, that the three Canadian mission schools appoint Japanese principals.[37] In May 1938, Murota Tamotsu was inaugurated as the fourteenth principal and the first

Japanese one of the school.[38] Prior to his appointment, Murota was principal of the Taihoku No. 2 Girls' High school in Taipeh, a Taiwan government-general school. Clearly, the fact that Murota had been a government-school principal, and perhaps understood better than most the way in which the government bureaucracy worked, was a factor in his appointment. Murota himself thought that, though Westerners came to Japan to teach, they did not thoroughly understand the situation of Japan and made insufficient efforts to understand it.[39] He thought that he himself understood this situation, and he was prepared to tackle broader questions about educational policy, the educational system, and the content of education. Unlike the WMS missionaries, whose experience was limited to their own schools, and the world of mission schools in Japan, Murota had taught long years in government schools.

The missionaries believed that they had made a good choice in Murota as principal. He was a defender of Christian values. It was reported in June 1938 that he had given a speech to teachers at the Shizuoka school in response to an address by General Araki, the minister of education, in which he had stated:

> It is not enough to have knowledge and fine ideals, we must put them into practice in living. . . . What the world needs is not narrow nationalism but great nations, so let us strive to make our nation great in the best sense of the word. . . . Although teachers may change, the standard by which the school is judged is that of Christ and so let us teachers seek to measure up to Christ's standards of living that by our fine example as teachers the girls may be helped to grow in fine character.[40]

This was exactly what the WMS missionaries liked to hear. Courtice noted that "Miss Govenlock says that she is more and more thankful day by day that God has provided us with such a fine Christian gentleman."[41]

Isabel Govenlock, whom Murota replaced, had been principal since 1931, and after 1938 she remained at the school as honorary principal until she returned to Canada in early 1941. She was known for her friendliness and kind concern for the students. The high regard in which she was held locally was underscored by the fact that the mayor of Shizuoka took part in her farewell ceremony her when she left the city in December 1940.[42] Perhaps Govenlock was not suited to be principal during trying times when personal relationships alone could not overcome the pressures of change from outside the school gates.

The approach of WMS missionaries in Shizuoka to the principalship at the Shizuoka school was slightly different from that of their colleagues at the larger Tokyo school. At the Toyo Eiwa Jo Gakko the missionary principal tended to hold the position for a long time. In Shizuoka, it was traditional to rotate the principalship among the WMS missionaries in Shizuoka. Mary Cunningham, the first principal of the Shizuoka school, was principal three times during the course of nineteen years.⁴³ During the 1920s, Govenlock was replaced by and then in turn replaced Olivia Lindsay.⁴⁴

During the 1930s, there were three WMS missionaries working and living together in Shizuoka. All three had demanding jobs, often made even more so because one or another of them could be away on furlough. They were familiar with each other's work and could fill in or exchange jobs as needed. One missionary served as the principal of the Shizuoka school and its associated Primary School, and another supervised the kindergarten and the two other kindergartens run by the WMS in the city. As well as setting policy and providing leadership for the Japanese teachers in the three kindergartens, the missionary in charge was also responsible for administering the finances of the kindergartens. A third missionary looked after women's evangelistic work. This missionary was responsible for supervising the work of at least four Japanese Bible women who lived in outlying districts. Furthermore, the evangelistic missionary took care of evangelistic work among the graduates of the Shizuoka school as well as the students in the school's dormitories. On top of this, the missionary worked in conjunction with the Shizuoka Methodist church, which had its own women's group, Sunday school, and children's group.⁴⁵

The evangelistic system was effective. From 1913 until 1936, a sample of twelve graduating classes showed that ninety-six percent of the students had become Christians, and seven of those classes were entirely Christian. In 1929-30, it was reported that fifty-six percent of the girls in the Shizuoka middle school were Christian, a number significantly higher than those of other mission schools.⁴⁶ The high percentage who became Christian resulted not from one or two missionaries but from a commitment by the whole staff, Japanese and Canadian, to the Christian purpose of the school.⁴⁷ Among the students themselves there was strong support for the YWCA and for the Koyukai, a group made up of Christian alumnae, founded in 1936, that published a bulletin. Significantly, the percentage of girls who were baptized did not decline appreciably during the mid-1930s as Japanese nationalism increased.

Shizuoka was a provincial backwater, so the students of the school were not exposed to the diversity of Japanese and Western cultural influences that the pupils at the school in Tokyo were. Perhaps, therefore, the girls at the Shizuoka school were less cynical toward the Christian message of their teachers or simply more open to persuasion than were their counterparts in Tokyo. Be that as it may, the Methodist church in Shizuoka was long established and its presence tolerated.⁴⁸ The church had historical links with the development of Western-style education and medicine in Shizuoka Prefecture. Most importantly, however, over the years it had been seen that its existence did not threaten Shizuoka society. Likewise, the school had long been a fixture in Shizuoka and, in the Meiji period, a pioneering force in Western-style women's education in the city. By the 1930s, parents understood that Christian baptism did not spell the end of future prospects for their daughters. The expansion of the school through the 1930s showed this acceptance.

The Shizuoka school rarely attracted adverse outside attention. When newspapers did take exception to what was going on in the school, as happened during the so-called disrespect problem (*fukei mondai*) of 1923, the result was often embarrassing. Olivia Lindsay, the principal at the time, had to issue a public statement denying allegations of disrespect to the emperor after the school had been attacked by the *Shizuoka Shinpo* and other local newspapers for devoting too much time to Bible study and not enough time to the Imperial Rescript on Education.[49] Yet this crisis did not have any long-term negative impact on the school. No similar problem occurred through the 1930s.

Like the school in Shizuoka, the Yamanashi Eiwa Jo Gakko in Kofu was located in a city and a prefecture that had ties with the Canadian Methodist mission dating from the 1870s. It was the smallest of the three Canadian schools for girls, having an average student body of 170, of whom 30 to 40 graduated from the high school every year through most of the 1930s. As in the Shizuoka school, the number of students rose dramatically during the Pacific War, reaching a peak of 721 in 1945. However, again like the Shizuoka school, the Yamanashi school buildings were destroyed in the 6 July 1945 air raid on Kofu.[50] As might be expected because of its size, throughout the 1930s the Yamanashi school was even more dependent on financial support from the WMS than were the other two schools. From 1933 to 1939, the WMS provided just over forty-nine percent of funds in four of those seven years, with 42.2 percent in 1933 being the lowest contribution.[51]

As with the other two schools, the Kofu school was well served by dedicated and hard-working WMS missionaries who taught in both the main school and its associated kindergarten. Many of them, in fact, divided their teaching careers between the Tokyo, Shizuoka, and Kofu schools. Katherine Greenbank, the principal of the Yamanashi school from 1926 to 1939, for instance, had taught for five years in the kindergarten of the Shizuoka school.[52]

During the late 1920s and 1930s, Greenbank was the heart and soul of the school. Only thirty-four when she became principal, much younger than was usual, she was approachable and caring. Central to her approach to education was the idea of service.[53] When she became principal at the end of the Taisho period, Japanese society was still open to new ideas from abroad. Indeed, her very appointment as principal was a sign of the openness to foreign influences. However, as far as the broader society was concerned, modern ideas were bringing about change even in provincial Kofu. Young people, including the girls at the Yamanashi school, were being influenced by new trends in clothing and hairstyles, many of them coming from North America, to become "moga" and "mobo," that is, modern girls and boys. Greenbank, because she was younger, was more attuned, if not also more sympathetic than her older predecessors as principal, to the students' desire to have smart Western-style school uniforms and less rigid rules on hairstyles. She was also conscious of the need for good health, and she introduced an emphasis on physical education.[54]

As far as the school and its community were concerned, Greenbank had a genuinely positive impact as principal. However, the 1930s brought challenges from outside the school property. Her tenure as principal coincided with the demise of liberal education under nationalistic pressure. Following the Manchurian incident in 1931, the connection between religion and education once again became an important issue. The question of the enforcement of the 1899 regulation 12 by the Ministry of Education raised its head. Even though it had never been rigorously applied to girls' schools, the regulation prohibited the teaching of religion within the curricula of government-recognized schools. Worry that it might be enforced could well have been a contributing factor in the Yamanashi school's decision to close its dormitories in 1934. It was thought that the school dormitories did not offer the same opportunities for the evangelization of the student occupants as in the past. The early 1930s also saw the problem of compulsory attendance of Christian schoolchildren at Shinto shrine ceremonies come to the fore. In Kofu, as elsewhere, this issue brought Christian educators and the authorities into conflict and focussed more attention on the relationship between religion and education. The decision in 1935 by the Ministry of Education that participation in ceremonies at state Shinto shrines was not a religious act ensured that this issue did not contravene its own regulation 12. Yet, for the Yamanashi school and the other Canadian girls' schools, the 26 February 1936 incident marked the beginning of a second and more intense phase of pressure to develop educational policy in conformity with Japanese national polity and in support of the Japanese national spirit.[55]

Once the Sino-Japanese War broke into full fury after the Marco Polo bridge incident in the summer of 1937, pupils at the Kofu school found themselves ordered to bid farewell at the Kofu railway station to troops going out to the front. At this time, some students at the school advocated peace.[56] Greenbank was always conscious of the safety of her students, and did not openly adopt a position that would annoy the authorities, but she was a target of suspicion because she was a foreigner. Her Christian faith put her into the peace camp. It was in a very changed societal atmosphere from when she had first come to the school that Greenbank, at the fiftieth anniversary celebrations of the school's founding in 1939, passed the baton to Amemiya Keisaku, the long-time head teacher.[57] The WMS had waited until 1939 to make the change from missionary to Japanese principal (a year later than at the other two schools) because of the special anniversary. Nevertheless, just as was the case with Hamilton in Tokyo or Govenlock in Shizuoka, Greenbank in Kofu was a victim of outside pressure. Without Japanese government pressure, which strove by legislation and threat to force mission schools to break their ties with the West, it is unlikely that Greenbank would have stepped down when she did.

During the early 1930s, the Yamanashi school and its Canadian principal were shielded, at least from local criticism, by Shinkai Eitaro, the legal owner of the school, who died in 1935. Shinkai Eitaro, closely connected with Canadian Methodist work in Yamanashi Prefecture from its beginning, was a prominent and wealthy local figure.[58] He was succeeded as legal owner by his son Shinkai Yuroku, who in 1935 received the daunting task of raising the ¥20,000 necessary to establish a *zaidan hojin* in time for the school's fiftieth anniversary in 1939. The WMS was already hard pressed raising endowment funds for the *zaidan hojin* of the other two schools. However, it did manage to provide ¥10,000, and Shinkai Yuroku's committee was able to raise slightly more than the other ¥10,000, with some 381 people making donations toward it.[59] It was an indication of keen support for the school among graduates and local people that so many of them did contribute to the *zaidan hojin* endowment.

One of the key members of the fund-raising committee was Amemiya Keisaku, the future principal, obviously a hard-working and popular figure within the school community. Unlike the other two schools, which chose outsiders to be their principals, the Kofu school appointed Amemiya to succeed Greenbank. Amemiya had been head teacher for nearly twenty years and had the great advantage of being aware of the problems that the school faced. As head teacher during the late 1920s and 1930s, Amemiya had been involved in the curricula changes that the Kofu school, like its counterparts in Tokyo and Shizuoka, had to make at the instigation of the Ministry of Education. The school was also fortunate to have among its Japanese staff Ogata Kiyo, who had studied in the United States following graduation from the Tokyo Woman's Christian College and who had come to the school in 1934. An active member of the Kofu Methodist church,[60] Ogata was the type of well-educated Christian woman whom Canadian WMS missionaries hoped to produce by their educational efforts in Japan. Her presence at the Kofu school was also a sign that the network of Christian girls' schools in Japan was producing well-qualified Japanese teachers for those schools.

The Kofu school needed all the talent and courage of its staff to survive the next few years. In 1940, at the instigation of the Ministry of Education, the name of the school was changed to divest it of any foreign connotation.[61] In March 1941, the proclamation of the National School Order brought the entire school system under the control of the government in support of the war effort. As early as 1935, and continuing through the Pacific War, the Kirisutokyo Kyoiku Domei Kai (the Christian Education Alliance) had organized summer schools on themes relating to Christian education and international or national spiritual issues, with appropriate speeches emphasizing the government's line.[62] In 1940, a special resting place was built to house an imperial portrait, and, on the emperor's birthday on 29 April 1941, a special ceremony was performed at the school to welcome the portrait. No other school observance took priority over the imperial portrait. The symbolism of the portrait showed that nationalism took priority over Christianity.[63] After the Pacific War began, increasing demands were made on the students to help in both agricultural work and factory work. Indeed, the graduation exercises for fourth- and fifth-year students in March 1945 took place away from Kofu, in Aichi Prefecture, where most of the students were working. It was fortunate that so many of the students were dispersed doing war work, because in a two-hour air raid on the night of 6 July 1945 seventy-four percent of the Kofu area was reduced to ash and sixty-nine percent of its houses burnt.[64] Even though the school buildings were destroyed, luckily there were no casualties at the school.

Although the Yamanashi school and its sister schools in Tokyo and Shizuoka made up the main educational work of the WMS during the 1920s and 1930s, the WMS was also involved in supporting important union educational work with other missionary groups. The trend toward the development of union institutions was clearly seen when the WMS decided to support both financially and with staff, Tokyo Union Woman's College (later Tokyo Woman's Christian University [Tokyo Joshi Daigaku]) rather than to develop its own postsecondary educational work. This union institution, supported by some six different missions, had been established in 1918, with Nitobe Inazo, the well-known Japanese Quaker, as its first president. Among the founders of the college were Isabella Blackmore of the Toyo Eiwa Jo Gakko and Ebara Soroku, the most influential of Japanese laymen associated with the Canadian Methodist mission and the past principal of Azabu Middle School.[65] As a college of higher learning (*Senmon Gakko*), Tokyo Union Woman's College was also freer from Ministry of Education regulations concerning its curriculum than was its feeder high schools such as the Toyo Eiwa Jo Gakko.

In 1927, Constance Chappell, who taught at the college for many years before and after the Pacific War, noted about Tokyo Union Woman's College that it was making "a definite contribution to those forces which are working toward the Christianization of this country."[66] The college was an oasis of tranquillity where "the spirit seemed splendid, and lots of good hard work seems to be going on all the time. Our foreign faculty is very congenial this year, and we have very satisfactory servants in the house."[67] Situated on the rural outskirts of Tokyo near Nishiogikubo on the Chuo suburban line, the campus, with its new buildings and missionary residences, was one of the most beautiful in Japan. Provided that the foreign faculty remained congenial and the servants satisfactory, life as a missionary teacher of English at the college was both fulfilling and highly pleasant. It was a world apart from the hurly-burly of ordinary Japanese urban life.

Although Chappell and other Canadian women, including Caroline Macdonald, the famous YWCA and sometime Canadian Presbyterian worker, taught at Tokyo Union Woman's College during the 1920s and 1930s, it was A. K. Reischauer, the American Presbyterian missionary and the father of distinguished Japanologist E. O. Reischauer, whose name was most closely associated with the prewar development of this institution.[68] The college's transpacific intellectual links were not with Chappell's alma mater, Mount Allison University, or other Canadian institutions but with exclusive women's colleges in New England. The close connection between Tokyo Union Woman's College and Canadian missionary work, however, can be seen during the Pacific War, when Yasui Tetsu, the long-time principal of the college, came out of retirement in 1942 to become principal of the Toyo Eiwa Jo Gakko.[69]

The WMS also participated in union training of Bible women. The Canadians joined with the WMS of the Methodist Episcopal Church of the United States in a union training school for Bible women in Tokyo. However, union educational work was not without its disadvantages. One was the loss of immediate identification with that work. This was not only restricted to educational institutions but also applied to the work in Tokyo in general. Despite the relatively large scale of Canadian missionary endeavour in Tokyo, and the many Japanese churches within the capital that owed their foundations to Canadian missionaries, the Japanese bishop of the Japan Methodist Church had his offices and residence in Aoyama, Tokyo, where the Methodist Episcopalians maintained their large Aoyama Gakuin. This naturally led to a clearer identification between the Japanese Methodist Church and the American missionary movement than between the former and the Canadian endeavour. This identification was further reinforced by the fact that, throughout the late 1920s and 1930s, the bishop of the Japan Methodist Church invariably came from the American side of the Church. Sometimes, of course, union did work in favour of Canadian prominence, as in the Canadian endeavour in boys' education at the Kwansei Gakuin.

THE KWANSEI GAKUIN

During the 1920s and 1930s, Charles Bates was the president of the union Kwansei Gakuin in Nishinomiya, supported by the Methodist Episcopal South Church and the United Church of Canada. Bates was cut from the same cloth as his famous contemporary in Peking, John Leighton Stuart of Yenching University, but possessed more charm and much less money.[70] For twenty years, Bates was at the centre of the gradual development of the Kwansei Gakuin from school to university. Yet Canadian support for the Kwansei Gakuin was controversial because of the school's financial and personnel costs as well as doubts about its value as an evangelistic agency. However, the mission authorities in Toronto and Nashville (the headquarters of the Methodist Episcopal South mission) never wavered in their support for the college, partly because of the high regard in which they held Bates. He and his colleagues at the Kwansei Gakuin were able to convince those in Canada and the United States who held the purse strings that the college was fulfilling an important

Christian role.

During the early 1920s, the number of baptisms at the school ran to about fifty each year (only a few more than at the Shizuoka Eiwa Jo Gakko), even though five Canadian and five American missionaries worked at the institution. Nevertheless, it was believed that "the majority of our students are Christian in spirit and conduct" and that the college "was progressively becoming a tremendous power for good in this part of Japan."[71] The theme that the Kwansei Gakuin offered "an unsurpassed evangelistic opportunity and evangelistic agency" was repeated in annual reports.[72] Such hopeful statements helped to sustain Canadian support for this educational endeavour.

The Kwansei Gakuin was a union school, and its overall, if remote, supervision was in the hands of the Joint Educational Commission made up of representatives in Toronto and Nashville. The desire to continue good interdenominational relations between the United Church and the American Church might well have been a factor behind continuing Canadian support for the Kwansei Gakuin.

It was an expensive school to run. In 1926, Howard Outerbridge, the college bursar, reported disbursements of ¥243,384, of which ¥50,000 came from the United Church and a similar sum from the Methodist Episcopal South Church.[73] In light of the cost, Bishop Ainsworth of the Methodist Episcopal South Church suggested that each mission's annual contribution be reduced to $20,000 (¥40,000), which it was in 1928.[74]

In 1926, it was decided, to reduce costs as well as to improve its location, to move the school from the east end of Kobe to Nigawa, a village north of Nishinomiya midway between Kobe and Osaka. As 1929 was the fortieth anniversary of the founding of the college by the Methodist Episcopal South mission, it was hoped that the college could be installed on its new campus by that time. The sale of the old site fetched ¥2,200,000, and sixty acres at Nigawa were bought for ¥550,000.[75] The old site was bought by Kobayashi Ichizo, the general manager of the Hankyu Company and a supporter of the United Church mission, to facilitate the expansion of Hankyu's land and rail holdings in Kobe.[76] The move to a new location also gave impetus to the creation of a *zaidan hojin* for the Kwansei Gakuin, which gave it greater independence from the two North American missions. The Church-related property and housing were placed in a separate holding corporation, a *shadan hojin*, which kept them in mission hands.

In 1928, it was trumpeted of the Kwansei Gakuin, with its 1,800 students:

> a more stupendous opportunity for life service never faced a group of missionaries, and the present move to a new and larger site, away from the daily distractions of the city, will open the doors to greater and more wonderful opportunities to lead this great army of young men to enlist definitely and

wholeheartedly under the banner of Christ.[77]

The move to the new campus also meant that the college could build new facilities strong enough to resist a major earthquake. Since the great Kanto earthquake of 1923, the safety of school buildings was of concern to Canadian missionary educators and one reason why they were so interested in building new schools in the late 1920s and early 1930s. The profit from the sale of the old property allowed them to build strong buildings for the new school. In 1930, it was reported that

> with the money at our disposal we have erected forty buildings of various sorts, shapes and sizes, twelve being of ferro-concrete or truscon steel construction, with ample accommodation for two thousand students in class rooms, and one hundred and thirty students in residences. We have also been able to provide sixteen teachers' residences, ten foreign and six Japanese.[78]

As was the case with the Shizuoka and Tokyo schools, W. M. Vories was the architect responsible for the design of the buildings. To help beautify the new campus, some 150 cherry and seventy-seven camphor trees were brought from the old location.[79]

Although the missionaries gave priority to the School of Theology because of its importance in training priests for the Japan Methodist Church, it was the smallest department, with sixty-seven students in 1930. The College of Commerce and Economics had 745 students, and the College of Literature had 375 students. The middle school was the single largest part of the school, with 809 pupils.[80] If the Kwansei Gakuin was to attract students beyond middle school level, it had to show that it could train people for worthwhile jobs. To do so, it needed to obtain Ministry of Education recognition. As early as 1923, the College of Literature had been given ministry recognition as a school for training teachers of English. In 1932, it was reported that twenty-four out of a total of the forty-four graduates of the English course had received licences as English teachers in middle schools.[81] This showed that graduates could receive professional licences to teach after leaving the Kwansei Gakuin and find employment during the gathering Depression. University status was also considered vital in attracting students to the school and in helping them to obtain employment after graduation.

In 1932, the Kwansei Gakuin was granted a university charter by the Ministry of Education and 200 students were admitted to its new university preparatory course.[82] The Kwansei Gakuin had three departments (theology, literature, and higher commercial) that qualified as specialist departments under the revised *senmon gakko myo* (specialist school order) of 1928. As *senmon gakko*, the literature and higher commercial departments offered four-year specialized courses. The achievement of university status brought change. The *senmon gakko* courses in literature and commerce were reduced to three years. The new university program was five years (two years in the preparatory course and three years in the faculty course).[83] The university faculty was under the direction of Dean Kikuchi Shichiro, with a teaching staff drawn from the existing members in the Departments of Literature and Commerce and Economics.[84] It was exuberantly reported about the Kwansei Gakuin that, "if Tokyo can be compared to the head of this great organism of the Japanese nation, the Osaka-Kobe region is its heart and vital organs. And the Kwansei Gakuin is the one great Christian institution of higher grade in this pulsating centre of the nation's life."[85] As president, Bates gave the university its motto, "Mastery for Service," in keeping with its Christian roots.[86]

Although grand claims were made for Kwansei Gakuin's potential to become an important Christian university, there was another Christian university already famous, Doshisha University in Kyoto, just outside the Osaka-Kobe region. Doshisha could lay claim to being an even greater Christian institution of higher grade than could the Kwansei Gakuin. Doshisha was associated with the Kumiai (Congregational) Church, but it remains a moot point whether the Methodists needed to create a rival institution in the Kansai.

One requirement for university status that the Kwansei Gakuin still had to meet was an endowment fund. In 1933, it was reported that the results of the university fund campaign had been encouraging and that ¥110,000 had been raised, of which almost ¥50,000 had been paid. It was confidently predicted that ¥150,000 could be raised before March 1934.[87] One result of this fund-raising was that the university division was reorganized, with the creation of a Faculty of Commerce and Economics and a Faculty of Law and Literature. Although the Canadian missionary H. F. Woodsworth, who had long been in charge of the literature department in the *senmon gakko*, was made dean of the Faculty of Law and Literature, a Japanese professor, Kanazaki Kiichi, became dean of the Faculty of Commerce and Economics.[88] Apart from Woodsworth as dean, there were only two Westerners, S. M. Hilburn in theology and J. J. Mickle in accountancy, both of whom were Methodist Episcopal South missionaries, designated as university teachers. Notable among the Japanese staff in the Faculty of Law and Literature was Imada Megumi in the psychology department, who became a postwar president of the university.[89] The first classes in the new faculties graduated in 1937. In 1935, the *senmon gakko* was also reorganized, with the higher commercial department becoming a *senmon gakko* separate from that which contained the literature and theology departments.

Despite the impact of the Depression, the university fund campaign was completed in 1935 after ¥197,000 had been subscribed and ¥170,000 actually paid.[90] Indeed, in 1934 Outerbridge, the secretary-treasurer of the mission, went so far as to hazard that the general effect of the Depression would be beneficial to the mission because it would force the mission to be more efficient.[91]

Economies could be made in the direct evangelistic side of the work of the United Church mission, but the demands for support at the Kwansei Gakuin were unending if the university was going meet its responsibilities.

The missionary teaching staff certainly appeared to work long hours in order to meet their responsibilities. In 1934, Arthur P. McKenzie taught a typewriting class, lectured in ethics and psychology, and taught twelve hours a week of oral English. In 1939, he was teaching eighteen hours of classes a week, including a course in industrial psychology. He also taught two hours a week at Kyoto Imperial University. As the son of a missionary, McKenzie, brought up in Japan prior to going to university in Toronto, had the advantage of early and long exposure to Japanese language. He was fluent in spoken Japanese and lectured in both Japanese and English. In 1939, five of the six new courses that he offered were given in Japanese, and he kept two Japanese assistants busy preparing lecture outlines and mimeographing materials.[92] As well as teaching, McKenzie and other staff members were deeply involved in extracurricular activities at the Kwansei Gakuin. In 1940, it was reported that McKenzie and his colleague Leland Albright had helped in "an English-speaking Society, where ideas and ideals are exchanged in English conversation and speeches; a Foreign Language Club, an Automobile Club, a Ski Club and a Yacht Club."[93]

Although missionaries and other staff devoted a great deal of their time to the Kwansei Gakuin, there were still weaknesses on the academic side. In 1934, Melvin Whiting, who taught in the middle school, reported that "teaching English is often rather strenuous work, but it is also very interesting sometimes," and he went on to admit that "our first desire and ambition is not the teaching of English, but the building up of strong Christian characters in the lives of these red-blooded boys."[94] Nonetheless, in 1937 Whiting complained that he was teaching English conversation twice a week to second-year classes ranging in size from fifty to sixty-four pupils, and he thought that he was wasting time unless the classes could be made smaller. During the 1930s, English conversation was not a priority subject in the eyes of the Ministry of Education whose curriculum the middle school had to follow. As institutions of higher learning, the *senmon gakko* and the university division had much more flexibility in their course offerings than had middle schools. This greater freedom was, of course, a major incentive for mission schools to develop into *senmon gakko* or universities. Furthermore, a problem for the Kwansei Gakuin Middle School and other private institutions that had to rely heavily on student fees was that the student-teacher ratio had to be kept high in order for the school to remain sound financially. Naturally, courses such as second-year English conversation, not regarded as very important within the curriculum, would have the largest classes. However, the size of classes did not seem to deter student enrolment, for the Kwansei Gakuin continued to grow. In 1939, for instance, there were 3,000 students in all departments.

One side of college and university life, away from the worries of finances, stood out. This side was sports and extra-curricular activities. In 1929, the soccer team was the national champion. In 1931, the sumo team also won a national meet. The university had a full range of sports teams, including baseball, track, fencing, judo, archery, swimming, mountain climbing, table tennis, basketball, and rugby. In 1937, softball, tennis, and volleyball were introduced. The sports clubs at the Kwansei Gakuin and other universities were important in popularizing Western sports among young people in Japan. And the emphasis on sports at the Kwansei Gakuin reflected a genuine concern among Canadian missionaries to promote good physical health among young Japanese.

Sports also helped to develop healthy competition between schools, such as the tennis rivalry between Kwansei Gakuin and Kobe Commercial College that dated back to the 1910s. The term "noble stubbornness" was coined to describe the tenacious approach of Kwansei Gakuin students to the pursuit of sports victories against other schools.[95] Among the staff, Hata Kanzo, who taught English in various departments for over thirty years, was a keen tennis player and supporter of the tennis club.[96]

For the adventurous and technically minded, there was the aviation club, founded in 1931. The same year, the *Gyomeikan*, a social service institution, was established by Kwansei Gakuin students and members of the staff. The *Gyomeikan*, which first leased and then bought property in the slums of Osaka, attempted to relieve the suffering of those made destitute by the Depression.[97] There were also other clubs that students could participate in, such as the orchestra and mandolin ensemble, the drama club, and the student newspaper. In 1933, the glee club won first place in a national competition. The 1930s were the first golden age of student club activity at the Kwansei Gakuin.[98]

In 1936, Bates noted that the growth in popularity of the Kwansei Gakuin imposed an increased responsibility on the missionary and teaching staff, and he argued that "we need more than ever the sympathetic support of the missions and mission boards, if we are to keep Kwansei Gakuin Christian and make of it, a strong educational and evangelizing agency in this part of Japan."[99] For all his optimism, few students had been baptized during the past year in spite of chapel services and curriculum Bible studies.

This lack of success in converting students came at a time when the United Church mission as a whole was being reduced in size. The mission in Japan was receiving only slightly more than a third of what it had received a few years before. However, the one place seemingly not harmed by missionary-staff reductions was the Kwansei Gakuin, with its five missionary families and a sixth close by at the Canadian Academy in Kobe. A third of the General Board missionaries were teaching at the Kwansei Gakuin. The balance between educational, social, and direct evangelistic work had become skewed in favour of the boys' school.[100]

Although the school was not proving to be an effective evangelistic agency, in the mid-1930s the missionary staff remained optimistic about the influence of Christianity upon the students. In 1936, McKenzie reported that among his students, "despite the prevailing spirit of nationalism, which is accompanied by a critical attitude toward Christianity and Christian nations, some of the best minds are in whole-hearted accord with the ideals of the Kingdom, and find peace and freedom of spirit amidst the bonds with which they are beset."[101] In 1937, Bates, who received much of his inspiration and suggestion from the Kagawa Fellowship and the Oxford Group Movement, stated that

> in these activities I have found a stronger motivation in a challenge to a closer walk with God, and a social programme that is in harmony with the teachings of the New Testament. In these movements, which so effectively supplement each other, I believe we have a programme of evangelization and social service that is needed to supplement the excellent work of the religious education and the service of worship that so largely exhaust the energies of the Church to-day.[102]

Bates was clearly looking for ways to overcome the failure of traditional evangelistic methods to convince students to become Christians. He was also implying that he was striving to find something new and relevant not only for the Church in Japan but also for the deepening of his own faith. In 1939, his long-time colleague at the Kwansei Gakuin, Woodsworth, stressed the strategic importance of training Christian leaders in what he perceived was an age of transition. Woodsworth believed that "we cannot control the political changes that are taking place in Japan and North China; we dare not ignore them."[103] Whether Bates and Woodsworth approved or not, the future Christian leaders in training at the Kwansei Gakuin's theological department and other institutions were being attracted by new theological trends. Outerbridge wrote in 1939 that there was a general tendency among Japanese theological students to turn to European apocalyptic thought due not only to the strong influence of the theologians Barth and Brunner but also "to a very large degree to the general atmosphere of the country. This tendency is accompanied by a loss of interest in practical Christianity and reform work, etc."[104] Canadian missionary work in Japan had long emphasized practical Christianity and social work, and now, amid all the other changes taking place in Japan, there was this tendency among theological students to move away from this type of Christianity. Outerbridge did think that "there is still room for a contribution from a balanced Canadian theology!"[105] Time for that contribution was running out, even though it might not have seemed like it on the campus of Kwansei Gakuin.

In 1939, it was reported that "the most remarkable thing about the reports from the several stations of the Japan Mission is that they almost unanimously testify that the Christian work has gone on normally in an abnormal world."[106] The Kwansei Gakuin continued to maintain its tradition of freedom from serious trouble, and its classes were overflowing with students. Indeed, Whiting reported that over 1,000 students at the middle school continued to attend the daily chapel services. As if not already realized at home in Canada, it was pointed out that "at this time in the history of Eastern Asia the significance of our Kwansei Gakuin contribution to future Christian leadership is very great indeed."[107] Despite the ongoing crisis in East Asia, little appeared to be changing at the Kwansei Gakuin. The next year, 1940, it was reported that, "on the whole, our missionaries have been able to pursue the even tenor of their way, and to complete a year of solid uninterrupted work."[108] It was noted that the Kwansei Gakuin had celebrated its fiftieth anniversary in October 1939 in a simple manner, as befitted the wartime conditions. Because of the war, it had been decided to postpone the anniversary campaign for endowment funds. Nevertheless, it was stated that "the University continues to grow in numbers and influence and to enjoy the confidence of Church, State and Community."[109] Only the absence of a sense of crisis at the Kwansei Gakuin could account for the claim, as late as 1940, that "all the work of the Japan mission is evangelistic in the larger sense of the word. The educational work aims at the production of Christian character and leadership."[110]

Even in 1941, it was reported only that "work in Kwansei Gakuin has been affected by political events and national currents to some extent."[111] The reference was to the previous year, one so full of change caused by the self-support and union movements for missionaries outside the Kwansei Gakuin that one noted: "it has been somewhat of a problem for the missionary to keep abreast of the times, and it is not to be wondered at if sometimes we have found ourselves living in a past age, so hurriedly has the future become the past on not a few occasions."[112] Despite the changes off campus, the attitude of the students continued to be excellent, and that of the Japanese teaching staff had become increasingly cordial. One missionary thought that many students had "become increasingly conscious of the peculiar quality of our corporate life at Kwansei Gakuin—the fact that we stand for something different—something of supreme value."[113] That might well have been true, but it was not necessarily comforting for the students in a time of Japanese national crisis brought on by the war in China. A more sanguine Canadian member of the staff thought that:

> this is a turning point in Japan and that the students are conscious of it. However, they realize that "compared with the young men of the Meiji Restoration (1868) they were not taking their places in the so-called Showa Restoration." Moreover, they realize that they themselves do not possess the clear conceptions, strong convictions, and force of character required to make their influence felt, but are forfeiting leadership to men of strong convictions but narrower outlook and sympathies.[114]

The same missionary believed that this feeling among students "provides an opportunity to challenge them with Christian truth and the personality of Jesus—whether through class-room courses in Bible Study or extramural discussion groups."[115] There was little time left to challenge the students. By the end of April 1941, all the Canadian missionaries had left the Kwansei Gakuin.

The optimism of the missionary staff at the Kwansei Gakuin obscured some of the serious challenges that faced the university during the late 1930s. Bates was one who seemed to have a sunny disposition and who found good regardless of the situation. He wrote in 1941:

> The past year has been a strange one indeed, full of bewilderments and disappointments, of humiliations and kaleidoscopic changes, through which we have been led to the present denouement—I have been and am being treated with embarrassing courtesy and generosity such as I can never forget—Teachers, students and graduates have demonstrated in word and deed their gratitude and affection in ways that can never be forgotten.[116]

About his life in Japan as a missionary, Bates wrote that "we have had a wonderful time in Japan and in the mission these past 38 years" and that "it will be a joyous memory so long as we live."[117] He had experienced such a wonderful time in Japan that he found it difficult to think other than good about the Japanese. Throughout most of his long career as president of the Kwansei Gakuin, he had devoted his energies to developing and expanding the institution. To do this successfully, he had always put the best face on what was going on at the university. Faced with no alternative but resignation when Ministry of Education regulations prohibited foreigners from holding university presidentship, Bates was concerned only about preserving and protecting the Kwansei Gakuin. At the time of his resignation as president in 1939, Outerbridge wrote of Bates that "there was not a word for himself—he was concerned only for the university, the church and Japan."[118] Clearly, Bates thought that any criticism of the Japanese might harm the Kwansei Gakuin and its staff and students. Yet he admonished the staff and students at the time of his departure at the end of 1940 to "keep this holy fire burning."[119] He and his wife were given a tremendous send-off by a throng of students and faculty members when they sailed from Kobe aboard the *Empress of Asia*. It was reported:

> someone remarked that the occasion marked the end of an age. Whatever else might be implied by that remark, the event certainly marked the end of an age of missionary leadership in Christian education—not so much the cessation of missionary services in education as the end of missionary administration and the control of policies from beyond the seas.[120]

This comment, of course, proved to be true. Bates left with mixed feelings. However, even at the end, he retained an unquenchable element of optimism.

Throughout his tenure as president, but particularly, during the 1930s, he was lucky to have avoided the serious confrontations between nationalistic students and Christian faculty such as occurred at Doshisha University in Kyoto or Rikkyo University in Tokyo. Part of the reason for this avoidance was an attempt by the missionaries on staff not to spark controversy. Bates was obviously concerned about the possibility of student or staff disruptions. With transparent relief, he reported in 1934 that

> negatively our life at Kwansei Gakuin has flowed on with unruffled surface, and so far as I know with no serious counter currents. We have had no disaffection among our teachers nor strikes among our students. We are deeply grateful for the spirit of good will and co-operation that pervades the whole institution.[121]

During the early 1930s, Bates was likely worried that Marxism might cause disaffection among the students. Indeed, many Christians both inside and outside Japan saw Marxism as a threat to Christianity. In 1932, the authorities made clear to Protestant leaders the responsibility of Christians in helping to control "extreme ideas with Red tendencies."[122] Kagawa Toyohiko, Bates's friend, was among those who spoke out against Marxism,[123] but Bates was diplomatically silent. Marxism was not alone in having an impact on student thinking in the early 1930s, for militant Japanese nationalism also began to influence students.

As early as 1932, McKenzie, teaching in the commercial college, noted that it was "futile to oppose nationalism in Japan or nationalism in our schools with anything that savours of Western criticism or westernized Christianity."[124] So McKenzie and his missionary colleagues at the Kwansei Gakuin remained publicly mum on that subject. In October 1937, Whiting wrote in the wake of the Marco Polo bridge incident that

> we are living in the midst of a people who are ready to sacrifice everything in order to win a war, which they have been led to believe has been forced upon them. Every Wednesday morning the 1,000 students of our Middle School meet for an early service at ten to eight, to pray for the success of the army. Every Wednesday all students and teachers eat only a Hino-Maru lunch—plain boiled rice with a red pickled plum in the center, which makes the Japanese flag.[125]

All students in Japan made similar sacrifices. Knowing the depth of feeling involved, Canadian missionary teachers did not want to criticize their pupils. In 1939, it was reported that the "waves of nationalism have not interfered with the happy and intimate fellowship between our missionaries and their Japanese co-workers."[126] One main reason why the Kwansei Gakuin escaped major problems was the restraint of the military officers attached to the faculties of the college and middle school.

Since 1925, the government had required middle schools and higher institutions of education recognized by the Ministry of Education to accept military officers on their staffs to offer military training as a required course. This military training at school was in place of having students conscripted for military service. The military officers had a high degree of influence on the overall life of the school, especially in the middle school, where they gradually gained control of all student discipline. However, many of the officers were not antagonistic to the Christian activities at the middle school, and those attached to the *senmon gakko* and university were apparently mostly indifferent to religious practices going on there.[127]

There was, nevertheless, outside interest in the views of the Japanese Christian staff at the Kwansei Gakuin. In March 1938 the *tokko kacho* of the Osaka gendarmerie sent a questionnaire to twenty-four Christian organizations and individuals in the Kansei region.[128] A Mr. Hori, a teacher at the Kwansei Gakuin, was one of the individuals asked to respond. He was to write replies to questions on points such as the relation of the Japanese emperor to the Christian God, the Christian attitude toward ancestor worship, the relation of Christianity to the Japanese spirit, the Christian conception of the spirits of the imperial ancestors, and why Christianity regarded Shintoism and Buddhism as idolatrous superstitions. Because it was the special branch of the military police that was responsible for the suppression of dangerous thoughts in the Christian as well as other movements, Hori had to take some care with his answers, for they would indicate how Japanese Christians at the Kwansei Gakuin came to terms with respect for national symbols. It is useful to look at his answers in some detail.

Hori saw no conflict between Christian ideals and those of imperial Japan. In dealing with the question about the Japanese *tenno* (emperor) and the Christian God, he responded:

> In the "Kokutai no Hongi" published by the Dept. of Education there is the following: "Tenno is a visible 'Kami' who rules the country in accordance with the great will of our Imperial Ancestors. This visible or manifest 'Kami' revealed as man is entirely different from 'Kami' with the meaning of Absolute God, the All-wise and Almighty God. It means that the Imperial Ancestors are revealed in Tenno, who is their descendant, and is one with the Imperial Ancestors, and that he is eternally the source of the growth and development of the land, and is a supremely high and respectable personality." I think this clearly explains the question.[129]

Hori showed some ingenuity in his use of the *Kokutai no Hongi* in determining the place of the emperor as a visible god. Yet the emperor was not the only Japanese god that Hori had to deal with, for he was asked for his view about the *yaoyorozu no kamigami* (8,000,000 gods) of Japan. His response:

> In our country the souls of our Imperial Ancestors and the "Mikoto" who took

> part in the great work of establishing the country, as well as those who were meritorious throughout the generations in contributing to the progress and development of the Imperial Destiny, are from ancient times held in reverence as "Kami," and so I think we, the Japanese, must revere them with a great spirit of reverence, as our Ancestors. Also in our language "Kami" means anything *above*, everything invisible, everything mysterious or worthy of respect and admiration. We must therefore have always respect to those "Kami" which are the objects of such reverence and admiration.[130]

Hori was able to deflect criticism about any lack of respect for the *Kami*. He thought it his duty to show the utmost respect to the spirits of the imperial ancestors and to inherit their spirit of loyalty. His attitude, of course, made it possible for him to attend ceremonies at the state Shinto shrines.

Furthermore, in recognition of the sensitivity of the authorities on this issue, Hori was emphatic in his answer to the question of whether Christianity considered Japanese Shintoism and Buddhism as superstitious idol worship. He insisted that, "in Christianity, State Shinto and Buddhism are not regarded as superstitious idol-worship."[131]

In regard to education, Hori saw no difference or contradiction between the educational policy of the Imperial Rescript on Education and Christian educational principles. In regard to the relation between the Imperial Rescript on Education (*chokugo*) and the Bible, Hori stated: "the Chokugo reveals the great will of Tenno, and must be reverently obeyed by us, his subjects. The Bible is the revelation of the will of our Heavenly Father, relating to the salvation of our souls."[132]

In answer to the question concerning the relation between Christianity and the Japanese spirit (*Nippon seishin*), Hori wrote:

> Christianity is not contradictory to the Japanese Spirit. I believe that the beauty of the Japanese spirit would increase its radiance through Christianity, and also that Christianity lived in accordance with the noble spirit of Yamato Damashii would like its own peculiar contribution to the development of Christian truth such as is not to be found in England, America, Germany, France or any other country.[133]

Clearly, Hori saw Japanese Christianity as distinct from that in North America and Europe. This was a commonly held opinion among Japanese Christians. So was the idea that "the beauty of the Japanese spirit" would be increased by Christianity, an idea that harks back to similar ideas held by Uchimura, Nitobe, and other early Japanese Protestants concerning bushido and Christianity. A danger, however, perhaps more obvious in hindsight, was that the universal characteristics of Christianity might be lost under the pressure of Japanese nationalism.

As to his own Christian faith, Hori wrote that he had been a Christian for fifty years but had always been thankful that he was Japanese, for he had "never felt any contradiction to exist between the Japanese Spirit and Christianity. My urgent prayer is that I may live as a loyal Japanese, and as a faithful Christian throughout my life."[134] The *tokko kacho* of the Osaka gendarmerie could see from this response that his Christianity was not going to lead him to resist Japan's nationalist policies. In that respect, Hori was no Yuasa Hachiro of Doshisha. Hori could see no contradiction between the Japanese spirit and his Christianity. It is apparent from their questions that the special branch of the military police did not have a clear understanding of Christianity. The questionnaire could be interpreted simply as a benign attempt to obtain basic information. No one was arrested for giving the wrong answers. Outerbridge thought that Hori's answers were thoroughly Christian yet entirely loyal to Japan.[135] However, the questionnaire had come from those responsible for stamping out dangerous thoughts. It should be taken, therefore, as a sign of the increasing suspicion in which the authorities held Christians. Indeed, the questionnaire typified the difficulties that helped to engender a widespread feeling of anxiety within the Protestant movement in the late 1930s.[136]

By the beginning of 1940, some of this uncertainty manifested itself in passing hostility of Japanese staff toward the missionaries. In January 1941, it was reported that "in the spring [1940] German propaganda had reached its acme of effect and many members of the faculty were openly sympathetic to the Axis powers and hostile to the so-called grasping imperialism of the Anglo-world."[137] Yet, by the end of that year, the mood had changed, "due to local sentiment and a feeling of chagrin at the excesses of the summer months which seemed to lack in grace and in recognition of the long and faithful services of our missionary staff."[138] Two other reasons, more persuasive ones, were also given for this change of attitude: "a growing fear of the ultimate aims of the Axis powers" and "a reaction, due to the voluntary withdrawal of the missionary staff from all positions of authority."[139] Although the August 1939 signing of a nonaggression treaty between Germany and the Soviet Union was undoubtedly more unnerving for most Japanese, and the opening of the Burma Road by the British in early 1940 certainly contributed to Anglo-Japanese tensions, the Tripartite Alliance with Germany and Italy in September 1940 could conceivably have added to a growing fear among Japanese staff at the Kwansei Gakuin about the ramifications for Japan of this alliance. The voluntary withdrawal of missionary staff was evidence of the concrete consequences of Japanese foreign policies on relations with Britain, Canada, and the United States. Despite the fluctuating feelings of their Japanese Christian colleagues, Canadian missionaries at the Kwansei Gakuin remained, as late as January 1941, remarkably positive about future possibilities. It was reported that there was a sense of tremendous opportunity for work and personal leadership and the initiation of new missionary projects:

And best of all, there is a feeling of expectancy—a strong sense of hope that the aptitude for compromise, which has so often saved Japan at the very brink of destruction, might once more save her from the ultimate disaster, on the one hand of a Pacific war, or on the other of a slavish subservience to the policies of the axis powers: which would equally spell the end of missionary effort in this country, at least for a decade. There is a great sense of a great Christian opportunity whose inner meaning has never been adequately grasped by the Home Church, and a strong belief that new doors are again about to open to us in this eleventh hour.[140]

The great Christian opportunity proved as wishful as the thinking about Japan's aptitude for compromise at the eleventh hour, but that such unfounded opinions were held shows how deeply ingrained was the belief that the ultimate disaster of the Pacific War could be avoided.

Even at the Kwansei Gakuin, there was more subservience to the policies of the government than any expectancy of change as the pace of military activity on campus quickened following the Marco Polo bridge incident in July 1937 and the subsequent call for national spiritual mobilization. In December 1937, a memorial service was held for six alumni killed in the fighting in China. In May 1940, Bates reported that a stone of remembrance, with forty-six names on it of graduates who had given their lives in military service, had been erected.[141] In the summer of 1941, the Kwansei Gakuin National Service Corps was formed. As the war continued and intensified, the Ministry of Education made demands on students to work in factories and in the countryside in support of the war effort.[142] In 1943, many of the Kwansei Gakuin buildings were taken over by the military for use as either military training or munitions manufacturing centres. In December of the same year, the exemption from conscription was withdrawn from students in colleges and universities except for those enrolled in medicine or science. All this military endeavour came at a price. During the war, many students served in the armed forces, and 218 made the supreme sacrifice for their country.[143] Fortunately, though, despite the heavy bombing of Osaka and Kobe during the spring and summer of 1945, the school buildings escaped major damage. War blackened, they stood waiting for the return of Canadian missionary teachers to their halls.

The 1930s saw the age of missionary leadership in Christian education in Japan come to an end. There was a remarkable lack of rancour in the United Church WMS and male clerical missionaries over the changes imposed upon them. Bates and his missionary colleagues at the Kwansei Gakuin obviously thought that they should salvage what they could of Christian education in the wake of Ministry of Education policies. The United Church educational missionaries looked to the Japan Methodist Church and Japanese Christians to keep the holy fires burning. At Doshisha, in nearby Kyoto, Yuasa Hachiro resisted militant students and staff and lost. Clearly, Bates and his missionary colleagues at the Kwansei Gakuin did not share Yuasa's fear that Christian education in Japan was being so fundamentally challenged that a stand had to be taken. However, Bates was fortunate in never having to face the student hostility that Yuasa encountered. If Hori's example can be taken as characteristic of Japanese Christians at the Kwansei Gakuin, then the desire to be both loyal Japanese and faithful Christians meant that they would accommodate themselves to government demands without any resistance. Both Japanese Christians and Canadian educational missionaries in Japan were *attendistes*.

This does not denigrate the achievement of Bates in any way, for he left the Kwansei Gakuin a Christian institution that managed to survive the Pacific War as such. Indeed, it is a testament to his Christian spirit and the charm of his personality that for twenty years as president he led the Kwansei Gakuin through a dramatic expansion to university status without serious challenge to his leadership from inside or outside the institution.

The solid achievements of Hamilton at the Toyo Eiwa Jo Gakko, which also enjoyed great expansion under her principalship, should not be overlooked. Likewise, Govenlock at the Shizuoka Eiwa Jo Gakko and Greenbank at the Yamanashi Eiwa Jo Gakko continued to develop those schools under difficult and changing circumstances. Not the least of their achievements was to pass their schools successfully on to Japanese principals without serious disruption to their students. It perhaps required more skill to be the headmistress of the provincial Shizuoka school or the Yamanashi school than to be the president of an expanding Christian union university, like the Kwansei Gakuin, with its large missionary staff and large grants from overseas. The girls' schools in Shizuoka and Kofu played an important educational role in their local Christian communities but were definitely not in the limelight of missionary endeavour.

CHAPTER SIX
Specialized Educational and Medical Work

In addition to mission schools, Canadian missionaries developed more specialized institutions. Just as raising the status of the Kwansei Gakuin to a university circumvented government regulations that restricted the teaching of Christianity at the middle school level, specialized educational work offered missionaries an evangelistic tool relatively free of government rules. The extent of specialized work was limited, but during the 1930s it took on added importance because it was in this type of activity that the role and the presence of the missionary were least challenged by the authorities. Most of the specialized educational work was established to meet specific needs arising from the Christian work, but the most prominent part of the United Church mission's specialized educational work was a school for foreign children.

The Canadian Academy, founded by the United Church mission, was a private school catering to the needs of English-speaking children in Kobe. Although children of any nationality or race could attend the academy, it was not intended as an evangelistic agency for the conversion of Japanese. It existed to provide a service to the missionary and foreign business communities in Japan and thus provided a link between these communities, which otherwise had little to do with each other. It also helped to raise awareness about the United Church mission in Japan and its activities among the foreign community in the Kansai region. In contrast to the Japanese work of the United Church, the Canadian Academy never suffered from any dramatic shortage of funds, especially because foreign businesspeople could afford to pay much higher fees for the education of their children than the Japanese salaried workers whose children went to the *eiwa* schools or the Kwansei Gakuin.

Whereas the United Church missionaries trained kindergarten teachers within the structure of its *eiwa* schools, the smaller Anglican mission maintained its own kindergarten-training school in Nagoya. Many of the graduates of this school went on to become teachers in the kindergartens supported by the Canadian Anglicans in the Diocese of Mid-Japan. The Canadian Anglican kindergarten work provides a good example of the challenges that confronted missionary teachers working at the parish level away from the major metropolitan areas. The Canadian Anglicans also ran a sanatorium for the treatment of people with tuberculosis at Obuse, close to Nagano. This sanatorium underlined an Anglican commitment to heal the sick, a commitment also seen in the medical work of the American Church Mission in Tokyo and the leper work of British Anglican missionaries such as Helen Riddell and Mary Cornwell Legh. Importantly, the development of the work at Obuse, be it medical or spiritual, also provided an outlet for individual Canadian missionaries different from the routine cares of parish work or diocesan administration. Furthermore, Obuse testified to continued Canadian Anglican endeavour and presence after Bishop Hamilton's departure signalled the change within the diocese from Canadian missionary to Japanese leadership. One Canadian mission, the Canadian Presbyterian mission to the Koreans in Japan, undertook kindergarten work among the important Korean minority group in the Osaka-Kobe area. Kindergarten was also the first level at that students could enter the Canadian Academy.

THE CANADIAN ACADEMY

It might be wondered why the United Church mission, whose rationale was the evangelization of the Japanese, continued to devote resources to the Canadian Academy, when, by the 1930s, there were adequate secular private schools in Japan for the education of Western children. However, it is doubtful that the school took money directly away from the Japanese work. Yet there was never any question during the height of budgetary cutbacks that United Church support for the Canadian Academy should be sacrificed in order to provide more funds for the Japanese work. The United Church mission's predecessors, the Canadian Methodists, had purchased the school's property, and the fees paid by the English-speaking students covered much of its running costs. Furthermore, even though the United Church mission remained intimately connected with the running of the school, other missions had become involved in financially supporting it. It would have been difficult to give up an established institution even though the Japanese side of the United Church mission's work was shrinking because of budgetary restraints.

The Canadian Academy was a union institution that had nothing to do with evangelization of the Japanese. It was an English-language boarding and day school that prepared not only the children of missionaries but also those of businesspeople for adult life in Canada or elsewhere. As a result, the successful report from the matriculation examination for the University of Toronto was a bright spot for the school.[1] In 1936, Kenneth Parker, one of the Canadian missionary staff, emphasized another cherished aspect of the school: it was a "very practical experiment in international co-operation, and the graduates have gone out to universities in England, United States, China and Canada."[2]

The Canadian Academy was a private school without, perhaps, the moneyed snobbery of Trinity College School in Port Hope, Ontario, but with all its close-knittedness and lifelong friendships. The Canadian Academy, moreover, did have strong links to the central Canadian religious, academic, and diplomatic elites through its Methodist connections to Victoria College at the University of Toronto. Even though there were other English-speaking Western schools in Kobe, in other urban centres in Japan, and farther afield in Shanghai and Hong Kong, the Canadian Academy swiftly established itself as a popular school.

One reason for this popularity was its location in Kobe, within easy reach of the Chinese and Korean coasts, that allowed the school to attract students from the Canadian mission fields in China, Korea, and Taiwan. The school took pride in the fact that its students came from so many places and contained so many nationalities. In 1935 it was reported that among the 226 students (eighty in the high school and 146 in the public school), they "come to us not only from Japan proper, Formosa and Korea, but from Amoy, Shanghai, Foochow and Honan in China, and also from homes in Canada. Twenty-two nationalities, including different nations within the British Empire, are represented."[3] In the same year, the school was also pleased that "the gleam had not been 'quenched' at the Academy" and that twenty-four graduates were working either in the mission fields in Japan, Taiwan, and Korea or in the ministry at home. A further twenty-five were in the teaching, medical, or nursing professions in East Asia or at home.[4] This was, after all, a church school, and it was important to stress that some graduates joined the clergy. Nevertheless, the vast majority of pupils were children of fee-paying businesspeople who had no prior connection to the United Church of Canada.

The Canadian Academy possessed good facilities during the 1930s. The school was built close to the summit of a steep mountain with a spectacular view of the port of Kobe and Osaka Bay. It was away from the dense press of the city below. It was so suitably isolated that at the beginning of the Pacific War Japanese authorities converted it into an internment camp for foreigners. One limitation of the site was its lack of flat ground for extensive sports fields. Yet there was a small baseball diamond and basketball courts. The annual classic of the school's sporting year was the basketball games with the American school in Tokyo.

When the main school buildings were built during the early 1920s there was no shortage of money for good Canadian-style classroom buildings and dormitories because rich benefactors, such as Senator Lorne Webster of Montreal, made large donations to supplement grants from the Canadian Methodist missionary society. Royal interest, always useful in attracting the attention of parents of prospective students, was also present. In 1933, King George V gave his permission for a new dormitory to be named Gloucester

House in honour of his youngest son, the Duke of Gloucester.[5] One of the Canadian Academy's friendly competitors was the Windsor House School in Kobe. Perhaps these connections helped the school with its budget. There is a suspicion that it was easier for the Church authorities in Toronto to elicit funds for the Canadian Academy than for its Japanese schools. Even though it remained under the control of the United Church mission, the Canadian Academy had become a union school that received annual grants from five American missions as well as from the Canadians.

It was the policy of the Canadian mission to have a missionary as full-time principal. Because the Kwansei Gakuin was relatively close, the Canadian Academy was able to draw on the part-time services of Canadian staff there. There were also individuals in the foreign community in Kobe who could teach piano or French. The school did not have to search far for staff. As a result of the financial retrenchment of the early 1930s, G. R. Tench and his wife were forced to withdraw from the Japan mission. Melvin Whiting, whose return to Japan after furlough in Canada was delayed in the mid-1930s because of cuts in the Japan-mission budget, was asked in 1936 to live on the Canadian Academy campus in order to look after its real estate. At the same time, he was required to teach in the Kwansei Gakuin Middle School. Only in 1938, when the financial situation at the Canadian Academy through the sale of land and in the Japan mission in general had improved, was Whiting able to move to the Kwansei Gakuin campus.

As late as 1941, it was reported that the Canadian Academy was "one of the most important pieces of work being conducted by our Mission in Japan."[6] Although hundreds of thousands of dollars had been invested by Canadians in schools for Japanese children, it was asked why there was not more recognition given, "both in personnel and finances, to the needs of white children who, by force of tragic circumstances, are compelled to face the future in an alien land? The task of building Christian character was never so great or the need so poignant."[7] The teaching staff at the school thought that, "although the Anglo-Saxon element has been depleted, there yet remains a very considerable group of children and homes, for that we feel a deep sense of responsibility."[8] In February 1941, Eulalie H. Willson, the acting principal, pointed out that she and her staff were "very busy and really happy" and enthusiastic because, even though only a few missionary children remained at the school, "there was still a real need of the school's services in the community. Where would all these kiddies receive their elementary and secondary education if not at our hands?"[9]

From September 1940, when the academic year had opened with great promise, to the time that the acting principal wrote her February 1941 report, the Canadian Academy had been in turmoil. Classes had begun with an enrolment of 200 students and a full complement of teachers, but the growing East Asian crisis had led to an exodus of both students and teachers. At one time, the number of students had dipped to 128. Yet, as the original students and teachers had left, others had arrived.

The closing of the Windsor House School in Kobe saw the transfer of students, as well as Dr. Turner, its headmaster, who possessed a neutral Irish passport, to the Canadian Academy, bringing enrolment up to 163. Willson recognized that "it has been, and is, a difficult time for these young people—seeing so many of their friends sail away and having their little world crumble about their ears."[10] Other schools, such as the Yokohama International School, the American school in P'yongyang, were also closing, and the American school in Shanghai was on the verge of shutting its doors. Some students from those schools could be expected to arrive at the Canadian Academy. As chaos reached into the treaty ports and foreign communities of continental East Asia, many foreigners stopped first at Kobe or at other ports in tranquil Japan before fleeing farther. Some, like twelve Dutch children who sailed one Saturday for the Netherlands East Indies when the women and children of the Dutch community in Kobe were evacuated at twenty-eight hours' notice, left suddenly. Yet others, the eight Russian boys or girls, stayed on, and the school remained open.

As late as September 1941, the Japanese educational authorities in Kobe had no objection to the Canadian Academy operating as before and even hoped that the school would continue. A positive note was similarly struck by a visiting gendarmerie official, who thought that every effort should be made "to continue the school as the education of children of the foreign community was necessary and essential."[11] The policeman did make some suggestions for the future that revealed a complete lack of any sense of international crisis or impending war. One recommendation was simply that no anti-Japanese ideas be taught, and another was that both spoken and written Japanese be taught because "the Roman letters will be discontinued more and more by the government and therefore the children so educated will be able to read the signs at stations and tram cars without any trouble."[12] The policeman further suggested that the principal of the school be a Japanese, for he was not convinced that the new principal, Dr. Turner, even though he was a neutral Irishman, should be allowed to stay at his post on the ground of his nonbelligerent nationality.[13] Clearly, the visit of the gendarme illustrated not only that local officials had wide discretionary powers but also that they did not always understand government policies or their consequences. Despite the goodwill of the local authorities, the Canadian Academy closed.

THE CANADIAN ANGLICAN KINDERGARTEN TRAINING SCHOOL

Unlike the United Church mission, the Canadian Anglicans in the Diocese of Mid-Japan made no attempt in conjunction with their churches to conduct schoolwork beyond Sunday schools and kindergartens. However, they did continue to support the *kunmoin*, a school for the blind in Gifu, founded by A. F. Chappell, an English missionary, and his Japanese assistant, Mori Kenji, in 1894. This was a significant example of Christian work in an important and neglected field, and it pointed the way for further Japanese government effort in a necessary field of social work.[14] However, more important in terms of personnel costs and financial support for the Canadian Anglican mission was its kindergarten work. The Kindergarten Training School in Nagoya, that the Canadian Anglican WA maintained, faced many pressures in common with the larger institutions operated by the United Church WMS.

As early as the late 1890s, Canadian Anglicans began opening kindergartens in Nagoya and other centres of their work.[15] The need for trained kindergarten teachers led the Canadians to operate their own training school to supply the needs of the Diocese of Mid-Japan. As was the case with the training work of the United Church, the late 1930s saw the issue of the appointment of a Japanese as principal of the Kindergarten Training School. In November 1937, this question was raised at the annual Canadian Anglican mission conference. The feeling of the missionaries, though, was that there was no rush. Indeed, they appeared oblivious to the pressures of Japanization, and it was decided that the principalship remain in missionary hands provided that no emergency occurred. However, they did relent somewhat by agreeing that a Japanese principal be appointed at the first suitable opportunity, but they left the matter in the hands of Bishop Sasaki Shinji to study.[16] Similarly, a motion was passed to allow Japanese to become kindergarten principals, but with important restrictions, such as that Japanese principals remain under missionary supervision, indicating that the mission was in no hurry to see this policy implemented.

The same sense of not wanting to rush into things was apparent when the transfer of the *kunmoin* to the supervision of Gifu Prefecture was discussed at the end of the second day of the conference. It was moved that "the Conference recommend to the Board of Trustees that the School be administered in the present manner as long as possible if the transfer to the Prefecture becomes necessary then the endowment and the property be withheld, and the money used for other social work for the blind within the Diocese."[17] Presumably, the missionaries were opposed to the prefectural authorities taking over the school on the ground that it would limit their opportunities for Christian evangelism. Furthermore, the prefecture wanted to take over teaching at the school, thus leaving the mission holding the building and property. For the moment, the Canadians were able to hold off the prefecture. In April 1940, however, it did take over the school department, but the welfare department was allowed to remain in Anglican hands. In May 1941, by that time the Canadian Anglican mission had already withdrawn from Japan, the *zaidan hojin* became the Gifu Blind Association.

The Canadian Anglicans, even at the end of the 1930s, believed that there was considerable opportunity for Christian evangelism in their kindergarten work. Nora Bowman, the principal of the Ryujo Kindergarten Teachers Training School and Kindergarten in Nagoya, was particularly optimistic because of the success of the training school, that celebrated its fortieth anniversary in 1939. She thought that the "influence of Ryujo graduates is like a stream of pure water flowing through a thirsty land."[18]

The support given by parents and the steady enrolment of children in the Anglican kindergartens showed that they were providing a valuable service. Despite its past success, however, Bowman thought that the kindergarten teaching work must expand "or else it will fail to meet the needs of the society that it seeks to serve."[19] Because the war conditions in Japan had opened many good positions for girls as soon as they graduated from high school, comparatively few wanted to devote their lives to kindergarten work. Becoming a kindergarten teacher was unattractive partly because the opportunities for promotion and pension were small given that the Ministry of Education failed to put kindergarten work on the level of primary school teaching. Nevertheless, Bowman thought that "those who do go in for Kindergarten work are really much interested in child welfare and enjoy their profession," suggesting that they would put up with poor salaries and pensions.[20] Moreover, there was a suggestion that teaching in kindergarten often meant delaying marriage if not foregoing it. Yet Victor Spencer, the Canadian Anglican missionary stationed in Nagoya, saw that teaching at the school had a benefit for the staff. Spencer, who taught the Old Testament and sometimes the New Testament, noted that, "although this teaching at the Training School takes a good many hours a week, in preparation and delivery, I feel it is a valuable opportunity for spiritual teaching, for that we all come to Japan. So I am glad to do it."[21]

By September 1939, five Japanese teachers with ten or more years of service had been appointed kindergarten principals. Bowman noted that "we consider this a progressive step in the work. Eventually all leadership should be Japanese if the Church and Christian educational and social work is to grow. The fact that these young women have so far given up marriage for the sake of the work speaks of their consecrated service."[22] In Nagoya, Spencer also saw the appointment of Japanese principals as "a step in preparation for the time when kindergartens will be handed over entirely to Japanese management."[23]

There were opportunities for kindergarten teachers in the Anglican system. In Takata, according to Percy Powles, the year 1938 had been, "a banner one in our lives here. After over 22 years, in my time, and some 15 years before me, of worshipping in an ordinary house we have at last been able to build a small chapel and kindergarten."[24] However, when Powles was away on furlough in Canada, the enthusiasm for the new kindergarten, that had come into being after twenty years of saving, dampened somewhat. In 1939, Adelaide Moss, the WA missionary in Takata, reported that the chief difficulty at the kindergarten, which had forty-five pupils, was the constant change of teachers.[25] For some time, apparently, the school in Nagoya had been unable to provide a graduate to teach in Takata. But part of the problem at the Takata kindergarten might well have been Moss herself. She regarded kindergarten work with a somewhat jaundiced eye: "I am not a kindergartener either by profession or inclination,–and the present method of putting unqualified missionaries into supervisors' jobs, seems to me a poor one."[26] She thought that better evangelistic results could be achieved if more effort was put into Sunday school work rather than into kindergartens.

Despite Moss's reservations, most Canadian Anglican missionaries supported kindergarten work. The problem with Sunday schools was that the number of students attending them was declining. In 1939, Marie Foerstel, the WA missionary in Nagano, noted: "as in all places, the work of the Sunday School gives cause for great anxiety and need of much prayer, for the numbers are very small."[27] She saw the chief reasons for the poor attendance as "the trend of the times, and the pressure of activities centering in the public schools on Sunday."[28] Nevertheless, she believed that a concerted effort should be made to start children's meetings in those parts of Nagano too far away for youngsters to attend the Sunday school regularly. It was not an ideal time to start new work, but Foerstel thought that "it is a time when the church is called on to advance against all odds, and we hope to be faithful in doing our part."[29] This was perhaps wishful thinking.

The advantage of kindergarten work was that the children came on school days, not just on Sundays. One supporter of kindergarten work was Spencer in Nagoya, who wrote in 1939: "work among children is a hopeful effort, especially in Ichinomiya [near Nagoya] where we have a kindergarten. The kindergarten Mothers' Meeting has been well attended, bringing a large number of well educated women in touch with the Church."[30] Yet there were difficulties. Spencer admitted that the kindergarten at Ichinomiya "has not yet got a government license, because the buildings are not up to the government's present high requirements. We are considering how we can improve the equipment so as to secure a license. The question of the cost of improvement is the greatest difficulty."[31] He lamented that "it is too bad the excellent work that has been done in this kindergarten under Bowman's supervision has not been able to receive government recognition yet, because the buildings are not up to the required standard."[32]

In March 1939, Miss Clench, who had recently moved to Toyohashi, wrote to Spencer begging him to help the kindergarten replace the dilapidated *karakami* (paper screens) and to provide a stove for winter. Clench felt cold every time she visited the kindergarten and claimed that the hibachi in use gave no real heat.[33] The Toyohashi kindergarten building was obviously spartan and deficient in the most basic items. Fortunately, Spencer was able to help in finding money to repair the *karakami*.[34]

The case of the Toyohashi kindergarten was not an isolated one. In 1939, Helen Bailey, working in Okaya, wrote that "the work of the kindergarten is hampered by lack of suitable rooms, as the rooms in this house [her residence] used for it, are dark and entirely unsuitable in every way," and she added that "we hope before long to be able to build a kindergarten and expect that then the numbers will increase and its usefulness be much greater."[35] In early 1940, Spencer, pressured by Bowman, suggested that Bailey give up the Okaya kindergarten and take over a "good going" kindergarten in Kami Suwa, closer to Nagoya. Here the Japanese owner and managers might be willing to allow the Canadians to take over.[36]

Spencer obviously thought that this was a good idea. Yet the case of the Kami Suwa kindergarten also illustrates that self-interest and denominational politics sometimes lay under the surface of what appeared to be a good opportunity for the Canadians. In asking Bailey to move to Kami Suwa, Spencer downplayed the fact that a major reason for her presence in Okaya was to conduct evangelistic work among the factory girls in the numerous silk-spinning mills. It is not clear why Spencer acted in this way, although his motive was apparently to increase the number of missionaries in the Nagoya area. Bailey's days might be given to helping in the kindergarten, but her evenings were full with teaching the factory girls. In 1939, Bailey had stated that "this work goes on steadily and very encouragingly, with no very large numbers, but with a good number of inquirers and Baptisms. Naturally the teaching of these inquirers is our most important work."[37] To move away from Okaya would mean an end to this work.

However, there were other reasons why Bailey did not want to take over the kindergarten at Kami Suwa. Having chatted to the property owner over lunch some weeks before, she realized that Mr. Fujimori wanted to get his money out of the kindergarten. Furthermore, the Higuchis, who actually ran the school, wanted to bail out before their competition forced them to close. According to Bailey, "it is *not* a good going kindergarten at all, and they have been having very few children and financial troubles."[38] Apparently, the local authorities were going to open a free kindergarten a block away from the Kami Suwa school. In explaining Fujimori's desire to saddle the Canadian Anglican mission with his property, Bailey wrote that Fujimori believed that the mission had "plenty of money to keep it going!!"[39] The Kami Suwa kindergarten had been running for some twenty years with a strong connection to the Holiness

Church, and it was now going down. Despite Fujimori's opinion about the wealth of the mission, Bailey thought that the chances of the kindergarten were poor if the Canadian Anglicans were gulled into taking it over. However, denominational politics were also involved, for Fujimori apparently interviewed Bishop Sasaki as well as Spencer and Bowman. Although Bailey was as firm as ever in her opinion that the Kami Suwa kindergarten would be impossible to run, in April 1940 she wrote to Spencer: "I hope nobody told Mr. Fujimori that I was opposed—we have to work there so he shouldn't know that, but *we* know the *people* and the conditions and it wouldn't do at all. 'No money' is a good and true reply."[40]

Despite no money, there remained a need for kindergarten teachers. Even so, there was a lack of students enrolled in the teachers-training course at the Ryujo school. In the fall of 1939, there were only sixteen students, nine short of the twenty-five-student capacity. In order to make up the number, Bowman advocated the creation of a short course in household science at the Ryujo school, that would be attractive to those high school graduates who did not want to enter the job market.[41] Unfortunately, this scheme ran into trouble because the prefectural educational authorities would give permission for such a venture only if the mission applied to run a school for household science.[42] Sometimes the best-laid plans were felled by the need to meet prefectural regulations.

THE NEW LIFE SANATORIUM AT OBUSE

Health care was an important aspect of the overall Anglican missionary endeavour in Japan. The American Church Mission (Protestant Episcopalians) maintained the large St. Luke's Hospital in Tokyo. The British Anglicans established leprosia at Kumamoto in Kyushu and at Kusatsu in Honshu.[43] They also tried to help those stricken with tuberculosis. Miss A. M. Henty of the Church Missionary Society (CMS) was responsible for founding the Kujukuri Home for Tuberculosis in Chiba Prefecture. Another CMS missionary, Miss A. M. Tapson, established the Garden Home in Tokyo for tuberculosis sufferers. However, her Garden Home was burnt during the great Kanto earthquake. It was against this background that Bishop Hamilton decided to open the New Life Sanatorium at Obuse, some seven miles outside Nagano, in 1932.[44] Once started, the sanatorium caught the imaginations of the Canadian Anglicans of Mid-Japan.

In October 1935, John Waller wrote enthusiastically that "the San. is a great agent for evangelisation, not only in Japan generally, throughout that it is getting to be well known, and from every part of that we have patients but especially in the diocese, and this district," and he pointed out that there was only one church in the diocese that had more communicants than the one at Obuse.⁴⁵

The medical work at the sanatorium was under the supervision of Dr. Richard K. Start. He was helped by a team of Japanese doctors and assistants led by Dr. "Canada" Ito and by nurses supervised by Miss Powell, a Canadian registered nurse. Start thought highly of Ito, who "proved himself very keen professionally and as a Christian also, and one could not wish for a more faithful and loyal and cooperative colleague, or a finer friend."⁴⁶ This is an important statement; though missionaries often spoke highly of Japanese fellow workers, few expressed this praise in terms of friendship.

In 1936, Start reported that there were 110 in-patients, of whom 74 were new admissions, and 211 out-patients, of whom 85 were new patients. It was calculated that the average cost per patient per day was ¥2.27. In his estimates for the sanatorium's 1937 budget, Start put down its total operating cost as ¥64,000. Most of this amount, some ¥53,450, would be recouped through patient fees, and the part of the shortfall that would have to come from Canadian grants was estimated at ¥9,450.⁴⁷ For a relatively small grant, the Canadian Anglicans were operating an active and practical sanatorium.

In early 1937, Start gave credit to Powles, the Canadian Anglican missionary in Takata, who was by then doubling as the missionary chaplain and honorary treasurer for Obuse, for systematizing the sanatorium's bookkeeping.⁴⁸ Powles was at times anxious about the financial state of Obuse. In early 1938, he reported that there had been a steady increase in the cost of living and that materials had gone up in price by twenty to thirty percent. He thus had to raise the fees for paying patients and cut back on the number of free patients.⁴⁹ In late 1939, Powles, wearing his cap as treasurer, stated that he wanted "to reduce costs and open up beds to revenue of a more profitable kind."⁵⁰ He was expressing a sentiment common to financial administrators of hospitals in Japan and elsewhere. However, in the case of Obuse, reducing costs was important, for Powles believed that "our institution is far above the average running cost of most Japanese sanatoriums, and instead of having this gap widen I would rather like to see it reduced so that there may not be too ready criticism of unnecessarily high costs."⁵¹ Furthermore, he held that, "where our methods are not endangered, it is highly desirable that we should align ourselves wherever possible with other Japanese institutions of similar nature."⁵² One reason for the high cost of the sanatorium was the free patients. In order to reduce expenses, Powles had long thought, Obuse should acquire a low-cost convalescent home so that patients, after receiving treatment, could be stepped down from the high-cost modern wards of the sanatorium. Understandably, there were social and economic complications with this idea. He wrote that many free patients "come from homes to that they are not ready and glad to return and they seek every opportunity to remain under the happy conditions of the Christian Sanatorium," and he added that "sometimes the very mention of possible discharge from the hospital brings on a relapse."⁵³ The problem of a patient being too comfortable in hospital, particularly one such as Obuse, with its fine views and grounds, and loath to go home was undoubtedly faced by many hospital administrators concerned with curbing costs.

Because Powles looked after the financial side of the sanatorium, Start could concentrate on the medical side. Start, who had all the markings of being a highly conscientious individual as well as a competent and confident doctor, occasionally expressed pessimism about what he and his staff could achieve. In December 1939, he wrote: "Since return from furlough, one has noted marked personal dissatisfaction with the work we are able to accomplish here, after seeing what is being done for tuberculous patients in Canada and the United States."⁵⁴ Although he was open to learning new techniques in treatment and surgery, he lacked the equipment budget that many of his colleagues in the United States and Canada enjoyed. As it was, Japanese government regulations meant that such equipment as the sanatorium possessed had to meet strict safety standards. In 1939, Start noted that "next year we are obliged to abandon the Westinghouse X-ray apparatus for a shock-proof assembly of Japanese make, owing to a new law."⁵⁵ It was a sign of the sophistication of the Japanese medical instrument industry that it was able to produce a safer X-ray machine than a well-known American firm. Some small missionary general medical and surgical hospitals found it difficult to meet Japanese government standards, but Obuse encountered no such difficulties, perhaps partly because of the specialized work conducted at the sanatorium.

Start was always concerned with improving standards. He was keen that his Japanese assistant, Ito, upgrade his qualifications by pursuing postgraduate study leading to a *hakase* (doctorate) degree at Osaka Imperial University. He also wanted Ito to study in Canada so that he could "come back prepared to tackle the more major surgery of the chest."⁵⁶

At the end of 1939, Start also worried that the waiting list for in-patient entry was getting longer. This fact might also explain why Powles, likewise at the end of December, stressed to Canon Dixon in Toronto, albeit on the ground of economy, the need for a low-cost convalescent home to help shorten the stays of free patients at Obuse. Start was distressed that a number of patients had to be turned away because of lack of beds or, in the case of poor people, because all the funds set aside for charity had been exhausted. Part of the problem was that the number of in-patient applications had distinctly increased over past years. Yet the reasons for this increase were not immediately clear. Start noted that it was expected that tuberculosis would increase in wartime, but it seemed to him that the majority of new patients were referrals from St. Luke's Hospital in Tokyo or from the tuberculosis clinic run by Osaka Imperial University rather than from families affected by the war. The referrals from Tokyo and especially from the Osaka Imperial University clinic show that some Japanese medical quarters believed that the team at Obuse was doing competent work.

In 1939, Start noted that "six students came from Osaka Imperial University as is customary during the past few years. Professor Imamura appears to think quite highly of the Sanatorium and to take considerable interest in its progress."[57] Dr. Florence Murray, in charge of the United Church mission hospital in Hamheung, was responsible for getting two doctors from Korea sent to Obuse for up to a year in order to get experience in tuberculosis treatment. In a symbolic sense, though, most important for the reputation of the sanatorium was that in 1939 it was honoured with a special imperial gift, that Start considered very generous. He was summoned to receive the gift of money from the hands of the prefectural governor, and he returned to Obuse to find "all the staff and some of the patients . . . lined up on the drive . . . to welcome and acknowledge this favour of the Emperor."[58] The gift offered Start the possibility that a new out-patient clinic could be opened. He wrote: "as this gift reflects the efforts launched this year to combat Tuberculosis throughout Japan, we feel that our appreciation of the honour can best be shown by using the gift to carry out a long-cherished scheme of an Out-patient Clinic in Nagano."[59]

Despite the bright ending to 1939, the end for Start at the prewar sanatorium came within a year. The Canadian Anglican decision of October 1940 to withdraw from Japan led Start and his wife to return home precipitously. Writing to Canon Dixon from Vancouver in November 1940, he stated: "as late as Oct. 22nd I had no idea of leaving but during Conference in that week it was decided that it would be advisable for Savary and me to leave, as we are both of military age."[60] The probability of imminent war between Japan and the British Empire, in the opinion of Canadian Anglicans in Japan, was underlined by the haste of the Starts' departure. The international and shipping news was becoming increasingly serious, so on 5 November Start took what he thought might be the last ship calling at Canadian ports, the NYK Line's *Hikawa Maru*. Despite his belief that the war would start, he was prepared to remain in Japan, if there was any point in doing so. He wrote: "if conditions had promised to be as in the last war I would like to have taken the chance of staying but there was no likelihood of being interned at place of work, only concentration camp, where one could help neither Japanese Christians or Canada."[61]

With Start's departure, Powles had to make the arrangements for the complete withdrawal of Canadian Anglicans from the sanatorium. Although Bishop Sasaki was prepared to see the evangelistic missionaries leave, Powles noted at the beginning of November 1940:

> I doubt if the Bishop or Diocese wanted the staff to withdraw from Obuse or the grant to cease in 1941. He seemed to think it might carry on with both foreign staff & grant, being of special service & no promise having complicated things. However, now the international situation makes it inevitable.[62]

There was little Japanese objection to an institution, albeit a Christian one, that performed a valuable service to the community at large. Except for the immediate international situation, the bishop and others in the diocese might have thought Start'' departure unwarranted and premature. Powles could take comfort in the fact that the Japanese surgical and nursing staff remained in excellent spirits, and the wards were nearly full. Furthermore, he had time to find a suitable and dependable chaplain and a competent treasurer. Were Start to return to Japan, Powles wanted to ensure that the new men would

> uphold the good tradition that has been built up in this institution so that he will come back and find it much the same as when he went away. I know that I am saying a lot when I state it that way, but we must strive to uphold what we have fought to establish.[63]

It was with that hopeful sentiment that Obuse was left by the Canadian Anglicans to face the future on its own. With the end of the Pacific War, Start did return to work in Japan, and the bonds with the Canadian Church reformed.

EDUCATIONAL WORK AMONG KOREANS IN JAPAN

During the late 1920s, when the Canadian Presbyterian mission to the Koreans in Japan was formed, hundreds of Koreans were coming daily to Japan. Ten years later, the number of Koreans immigrating to Japan had greatly declined.[64] Nevertheless, the Canadian Presbyterians, like their colleagues in Manchuria, remained optimistic about their work. In 1937, the mission, served by two male ordained missionaries and five female missionaries, and with two mission centres in Nagoya and Osaka, comprised some 3,500 adherents, thirteen organized congregations, and a further forty-two churches without elders.

The mission had made some strides toward being able to manage its own affairs, but it was noted that "it should not be forgotten that the church is young, and many of its members poor, and because of this it will need outside financial support for some time. Self-support is increasing but necessarily not very rapidly."[65] One problem that the mission faced was the difficulty in finding suitable places for worship, because rents were often prohibitively high and the congregations poor. And, though the missionaries never reported it, Japanese landlords or property sellers may have been loath to rent or sell to Koreans. In any case, purchase or rental costs meant that Korean Christians continued to rely on Canadian Presbyterian support. Indeed, ten of the thirteen ordained Korean ministers still got a large part of their support from the mission. Furthermore, the Presbyterian churches in Korea supported a Korean minister in Tokyo, and the National Council of Churches in Japan partially supported another two ministers. However, by 1937 the Canadians were able to hire ordained Korean graduates of the Japanese Presbyterian seminaries in Tokyo and Kobe instead of having to rely on Korean ministers who had been ordained in their home presbyteries in Korea. The advantage was that the graduates of the Japanese Presbyterian seminaries would be familiar with both Japanese language and Japanese conditions, with which ministers brought directly from Korea might not be familiar.

A continuing problem for the Canadians was finding teachers for the daily vacation Bible schools, some thirty-one of which were run over the summer of 1938. Many of the Sunday school teachers, who would have made suitable teachers for the daily vacation Bible schools, were college students who returned home to Korea for the summer vacation.[66] As a result, there was not much opportunity to hold training classes for Bible school teachers during the summer months. The Canadian Presbyterian missionaries in Japan exuded continued optimism about expansion of their work, but they saw the lack of qualified teachers as a stumbling block to this expansion.

But one area that they saw as particularly encouraging was kindergarten work. It was reported in 1939:

> These little schools should really be called nursery schools, for they are not exactly the same as Kindergartens. Recently, the Kobe school was fortunate enough to be chosen one of the six best for their exhibit of handwork, when an exhibition was held to which many Kindergartens from all over the country sent in specimens of their work. Last March more than ninety children received their diplomas and have gone on to attend Japanese primary school.[67]

That the Kobe school won a prize in competition with other kindergartens indicates that the educational authorities were not averse to giving prizes out to schools for Koreans. The mission continued to stress that "the Nursery Schools are in the hands of capable teachers and meeting a real need. One realizes the greatness of the value of the instruction imparted in the lives of these children, the large majority of whom come from non-Christian homes."[68] The greatest difficulty that the schools faced in 1939 was in securing suitable teachers. Although missionaries could be expected to help in the kindergarten work, they were hard-pressed for time, because they had to devote much time to Japanese-language study in order to meet the government's request that "the national language be used in all church services."[69] The Japanization of the Korean work in Japan was a phenomenon over that the missionaries had little control.

By 1939, the closing of the only Presbyterian seminary in Korea, one of the consequences of the shrine question, meant that the Canadian Presbyterians had to rely solely on Korean graduates of the Japanese Presbyterian seminary in Kobe for their future Korean pastors.[70] More important, however, was the question of union between the Chosen Christian Church and the Nippon

Kirisuto Kyokai (the Japan Presbyterian Church), that had been agreed upon in principle by the Korean Church at its synod in December 1939, with the merger set for the spring of 1940. As both the Japanese Church and the Korean Church in Japan were self-governing, this amalgamation was solely a matter for the two churches to decide. The decision did not involve the Canadian Presbyterians. The Canadians of the six missions that would be associated with the amalgamated church did not envisage any real change as a result of the union. The non-self-supporting Korean congregations and the evangelistic work associated with them would still require the financial and physical help of Canadian missionaries. Yet they did not have long to help, for by February 1941 they had all left Japan. After the Pacific War, Canadian Presbyterians would return to Japan to work among the Korean population there.

CHAPTER SEVEN
Contrast in the Colonies: Educational and Medical Work in Korea, Manchukuo, and Taiwan

Whereas educational work in north Taiwan was curtailed by the shrine question and Government general pressure, United Church missionaries in Korea still struggled to maintain their educational work. The Canadian schools in Korea and over the Manchurian border, like their sister schools in Taiwan, had to conform to educational regulations similar to those imposed on mission schools in metropolitan Japan. Nevertheless, the tasks and challenges that confronted Canadian missionary educators in metropolitan Japan were likely more straightforward than those that their Canadian colleagues had to face on the colonial frontier in Korea. The educational situation in colonial Korea, already exacerbated by the shrine question, did not allow for fence sitting. Yet the Canadian missionaries there showed considerable skill in their dealings with colonial officials, with the result that their schools were still operating at the start of the Pacific War. Because they did not maintain formal secular schools like their fellow Canadians in Korea, the Canadian Presbyterians in Manchukuo avoided difficulties with the Manchukuoan educational authorities. But they encountered problems because of their limited capacity to train sufficient Chinese evangelists to meet the expanding needs of their mission.

As well as its educational work, the United Church mission in Korea undertook medical work until the departure of the last missionary doctor in June 1942. Indeed, the end of the 1930s saw the demand for services provided by the missionary doctors and staff at the Canadian hospitals in Lungchingtsun and Hamheung as strong as it had ever been. Although these hospitals lacked modern equipment, they provided an important alternative to Japanese government hospitals and to traditional Korean medical practices. At a local level, missionary doctors such as Dr. Florence Murray in Hamheung made a significant contribution toward improving the general health of Koreans.

The same can also be applied to Canadian Presbyterian medical work in Taiwan. Even though the mission's educational work in Taiwan was reduced to its specialized theological college and women's school, its medical work continued without undue government interference. This work included not only the Mackay Memorial Hospital in Taipeh but also leper work on the island. The Happy Mount Leprosy Colony was an example of specialized missionary medical work carried on in a colonial setting that helped to draw attention to an important health problem in Taiwan.

For those in Korea, the mid-1930s brought growing financial difficulties that threatened the very existence of the United Church mission in the peninsula. The inevitable retrenchment undertaken to save the Canadian mission brought changes to its educational work.

BUDGETARY CHALLENGES AND EDUCATIONAL WORK IN KOREA

In 1936, at the height of the shrine question, there was a proposal for both male and female boards of the United Church of Canada to withdraw from Korea entirely. Although this proposal was later changed, there was still an unprecedented reduction in the budget, and the Korean mission was instructed by the Policy Committee in Toronto to revise its working program in order to bring it into harmony with the reduced budget.[1] In 1937, to combat cuts to educational grants from Canada as well as to underline the need for the mission's continued existence, the Korean mission compiled comparative statistics revealing that the number of students in Canadian mission schools had steadily increased during the 1930s. In 1937, there were 1,641 students in mission high schools and 4,152 students in mission primary schools. Furthermore, in 1937 the dollar amount that the Korean Church gave to education had more than doubled since 1933 to $50,843.[2] The growth of the educational work in terms of students and financial support was in keeping with the steady, if unspectacular, growth in church membership through the 1930s.[3] Despite all the challenges, Canadian mission schools were growing, as was the church.

In July 1937, Donald Black reported from Lungchingtsun across the border in Manchuria, that, along with the medical and evangelistic work, educational work was enjoying steady expansion. He indicated that both the boys' and the girls' schools had record enrolments and had the active support of their respective parent-teacher associations.[4] Clearly, the figures supported the view of A. E. Armstrong and William Scott that the mission should keep its Korean schools open, in contrast to the policies of their Southern and Northern Presbyterian colleagues.

Yet retrenchment meant that the Canadians did have to reduce their educational work. Although the Korean mission was insistent that its five mission stations remain open, the shortage of male missionaries was a major consideration in closing secondary school education in the three smaller stations.[5] By 1937, the Korean mission had closed its boy's academy and its girls' high school in Wonsan, but it continued to run a primary school for girls. In Sungjin, the boy's school was entirely under the control of the Korean Church. In Hoiryung, the Korean mission resisted, because of its cost and the lack of missionary personnel, the expansion of the girls' school into a full-fledged high school. However, the mission remained firm in its commitment to its boys' and girls' schools in the two major mission centres of Hamheung and Lungchingtsun.

BOYS' AND GIRLS' SCHOOLS IN KOREA AND MANCHUKUO

Canadian schools in Korea were confronted with increasing demands placed upon them by the Japanese colonial authorities. In 1937, Scott, who was in charge of religious education and instructed in the Bible and in English at the mission academy for boys in Hamheung, wrote that "there is evidence of a tightening up of the government's attitude towards religious work in the schools, but I hope that we shall continue to hold as much freedom as we now enjoy."[6] Clearly, the Hamheung school in 1937 was enjoying considerable success, for there had been in the spring almost 700 entrance applicants for 120 places. And, an indication of better times, the general appearance and physical fitness of the boys were improved. It was reported that "the entire student body seemed better fed than formerly."[7] This statement is illustrative of the sharp difference in the standard of living between northern Korea and Japan. Even during the height of the Depression, no student in a Canadian mission school in Japan ever lacked food, but evidently this was not the case in Korea. By 1937, however, economic conditions in northern Korea had improved to such an extent that Korean Christians were able to contribute toward the school's endowment, which stood that year at well over ¥20,000. That so much had been raised was testament to the desire of Koreans in Hamheung to maintain a mission school.

Some Korean pupils were helpful in Christian work. George Bruce, in Lungchingtsun, reported in 1937 that student efforts had brought about the opening of a church building in a village where a night school, Sunday school, and church work were being conducted, and he noted that "it is most gratifying to have some share in the work of a school where boys are doing so much for others. No less than five little groups are being conducted in neighboring villages by the boys of the school."[8]

Whereas students were cooperative in Lungchingtsun, some of the school staff in Hamheung began to cause trouble. These difficulties were doubly disturbing for the Canadians because they involved Kim Kwan Sik, the long-serving principal of the boys' academy and a stalwart Christian. Earl Knechtel wrote from Hamheung at the beginning of 1938 that

> For a long time the head teacher has been making things very difficult for Kim Kwan Sik. He has not been co-operating but rather has been in more or less open opposition and rebellion against the principal. This fall he and two other teachers, Ahn and No, have stirred up no end of trouble. They have accused Kim of being unpatriotic and anti-Japanese. They tried to bring in charges of misuse of funds. They accuse him of inefficiency etc etc.[9]

The school's board decided to support the principal and to dismiss the three teachers. However, the colonial educational authorities in Hamheung were also involved, especially because the charges against Principal Kim included his being anti-Japanese. Knechtel expected, correctly, that the issue would continue for perhaps months. Knechtel also pointed out that Ethel MacEachern, the WMS missionary in charge of the girls' school, was having difficulties with her former head teacher.

The differences between missionaries and staff were not restricted to the two schools, for Murray, the WMS medical doctor in charge of the mission hospital in Hamheung, was having her own troubles with the hospital staff. As well as the shrine question, Knechtel wrote, "War psychology, anti-British sentiment, friction between church and state, the closing of schools on the other side of the country, fear and suspicion all enter the portals of '38 and jostle us right and left. What a venture of faith!"[10] Knechtel was not sure that this venture had the spiritual backing of the whole of the United Church of Canada. Support from home was needed, because more demands were being placed on educational work by the Japanese authorities.

In June 1938, Scott wrote from Hamheung that "the government policy is to amalgamate Korea and Japan. To that end they have dropped the Korean language from the school curriculum, and raised all schools to the same standing as schools in Japan, with similar privileges for their graduates."[11] One ramification of this change was that any Korean organization with international affiliations, such as the YMCA, YWCA, and Sunday School Association, had to disband their overseas connections and allow the Japanese national organization to represent Korean interests abroad. This meant that the ability of Korean groups to project their views to overseas bodies was considerably lessened. However, for missionary educators a more immediate concern was the need to cope with the new regulations. The mission schools in Hamheung and Lungchingtsun were now required, like those in Japan, to form a *zaidan hojin* (a juridical foundation). Money, of course, was needed for the school endowment, and for that purpose the Korean mission asked Toronto for an increase in its grant for 1939. However, money was not uppermost in the mind of Bruce, at the Eunjin school in Lungchingtsun, when he wrote to Armstrong in October 1938. Like Knechtel earlier that year, Bruce was worried about the support of the United Church of Canada for educational work in Korea. His concern was increased because of the slowness of the authorities in Toronto to grant permission to the mission to make an application to form a *zaidan hojin*.[12] Bruce was concerned that the morale of the staff and students at the school would suffer if there was any further delay by Toronto. The American Presbyterians had closed mission schools in western Korea because of the shrine question, and there was a need to reassure those in northern Korea that the Canadian mission schools would remain open. Eventually, Toronto agreed that the Lungchingtsun school should apply to form a *zaidan hojin*.

In June 1939, Black, the Canadian missionary doctor in Lungchingtsun, took the opportunity of seeing his wife and children off to Canada from Kobe to write to Armstrong in Toronto a long and important letter about the situation in Lungchingtsun. Because the letter would be posted in Victoria, Black could put his views on paper without fear that they would be read by Japanese censors. Educational work, that he firmly believed should continue, was uppermost in his mind. The mission had either to form *zaidan hojin* for its two schools in Lungchingtsun or to close them, thus losing everything with little or no compensation. Black thought that "continuance under the Zaidans gave the possibility of maintaining a Christian atmosphere in the schools and considerable hope of extra-curricular classes in Bible etc. I think we feel that the decision to continue was the only possible one."[13] As in the case of the schools in Japan, the constitution of the *zaidan hojin* provided safeguards for the Christian nature of the school board (by a combination of missionary and Korean Christian members) and stipulated that the head teacher be a Christian. Those provisions were opposed by the provincial educational authorities, but the central government, much to the chagrin of its provincial counterpart, accepted the Canadian application without demanding any changes. Again, the local authorities sometimes interpreted regulations differently than did the central government. Yet the response of the central government also suggests that form rather than substance was important. It was sufficient that the Canadians had formed *zaidan hojin* for their schools along the organizational precedents established by mission schools in Japan. When missionaries refused to comply with government regulations and clearly stated policies, as with George S. McCune and Miss V. L. Snook in P'yongyang over the shrine question, a different response was necessary. The authority of the colonial overlords could not be challenged.

Black pointed out that government control over schools was extensive: "no teacher can be engaged until his qualifications, character, past history and 'thoughts' have been approved by the Provincial Educational office. Similarly no teacher can be dismissed without similar permission."[14] This was no different than in Japan. However, in Lungchingtsun, the Canadians were not as lucky with their teachers as was Charles Bates at the Kwansei Gakuin. Black noted that Frances Bonwick, the headmistress of the girls' school, was confronted with a tricky situation in the unsatisfactory performance of one of her teachers. Although temperamentally unsuited for the position, this teacher wanted to become head teacher in the school, and for more than six months he had kept the school in turmoil while trying to get his way. Black wrote that he had been

> increasingly rude and unco-operative in his dealings with Miss Bonwick. He happens to have a Japanese wife and claims influence with the gendarmes. On this basis he has intimidated the whole of the rest of the staff for there are few Koreans who can face a police inquisition without fear. There is no way of getting rid of the man.[15]

When Bonwick decided, as a way of solving the problem, to appoint the principal of the Hoiryung school, who had a strong personality capable of keeping his colleagues in line, as head teacher at her school in Lungchingtsun, there was difficulty obtaining a permit for his employment on the grounds of his advanced age. Age was only an excuse; although the educational authorities in Lungchingtsun eventually did issue him a work permit, they simply did not want a Christian, who had worked for many years with missionaries, in the school. Black, a medical doctor, thought that the strain on Bonwick had been great and that she had come close to having a nervous breakdown.

As to Bonwick's position as headmistress of the girls' school or Bruce's as principal of the boys' academy, Black thought that their jobs were not in jeopardy. In Japan, by contrast missionary principals were stepping down in favour of Japanese replacements. Yet Black made it clear that any other foreigner was unlikely to succeed Bonwick or Bruce because "regulations call for all teachers to pass examinations conducted in the Japanese language. Again English has been taken out of the curriculum of the Girls' School and greatly reduced in the Boys' School so that there would be little they could teach if they were not acting as Principals."[16] All teaching now had to be conducted in Japanese, and no Korean was allowed. It was not uncommon for missionaries in Korea to have some knowledge of Japanese because of the need to deal with colonial officials, but few were fluent enough to teach in Japanese. Their Canadian and English Presbyterian colleagues in Taiwan faced the same problem.

Even though Black was more pessimistic about the future of educational work than some of his missionary colleagues, he did believe that "they are doing excellent work both educationally and evangelistically so there can be little question as to the wisdom of going forward in faith. If they lose their Christian character we can withdraw—though not without difficulty."[17] The main difficulty for the Korean mission, if it did withdraw from educational work, was that its school property would have to be turned over to another body without chance of compensation. At the root of some of the problems that the Canadians faced in their educational work were financial concerns. Black noted that the economic outlook in mid-1939 was grave and that all signs pointed to "a period of uncontrolled inflation and all prices have already risen very greatly. Salaries of Korean employees were never high and are now really inadequate but where are we to secure funds to give living wages?"[18] He believed that the financial problem was greater for the WMS than for Bruce at the boys' school, for he thought that many of the difficulties at the girls' school stemmed from the fact that the salaries that Bonwick could afford to pay were too low to attract good teachers.

Nevertheless, the difficulties with the staff at the girls' school seem to have been overcome relatively quickly. In 1940, it was reported that "we have a full staff of competent Christian teachers who do not begrudge spending many extra hours in order to work out some special project with the girls."[19] A major reason for this sharp change in attitude was the new head teacher. There was every indication–from a full dormitory for out-of-town pupils to students working voluntarily with church groups in and around Lungchingtsun–that the school was doing well. It was noted that "we have a larger enrollment than ever before and the joy of knowing that these girls, future college graduates, church workers, future wives and daughters-in-law, teachers and nurses are receiving their foundational training under Christian influence."[20] Even at the primary school, enthusiasm for work and play characterized the behaviour of its pupils. Behind the positive turn of events at the girls' schools in Lungchingtsun were "unexpected tributes of friendship in moments of discouragement," and the missionaries offered "thanks to God for His guidance through varied experiences."[21] There was a similar thankfulness in the 1939–40 report on boys' educational work in Lungchingtsun, but there was also a feeling reminiscent of the missionary sentiment in Korea and Japan at the beginning of World War 1:

> amid the stress and strain in other parts of the world let it not be forgotten that we are one in Christ and that we have been exhorted to "pray without ceasing," "doing good unto all men especially unto them who are of the household of faith," whatsoever race or creed.[22]

Canada was at war with Germany, and Lungchingtsun was remote from a Canada now turning ploughshares into corvettes. The isolation of missionaries from the national emergency at home, with its unifying spirit of shared national experience, can be detected in the plea that the needs of education in far Manchuria not be forgotten.

Missionaries were also aware that letters and reports sent through the mail were scrutinized by Japanese censors. Care, therefore, had to be taken in how things were phrased. Concerning the boys' academy, it was reported that "the slogan for educational work here today is 'Foster the National Spirit.' The constant effort to build up a strong loyal youth, is ever before us and much time formerly given to a more academic training is now being devoted to this phase of national life."[23] Yet missionaries in Lungchingtsun did not view this development as negative:

> it is our sincere hope that the youth who are gaining their education in our School will go out into life with a deep desire to work for the mutual good of society and self. The spirit of the Master taken into life with the best academic training that one can obtain is the best assurance of valuable service to the State.[24]

It was realized that national spirit in school was best fostered by nationals themselves. The development of national spirit was also perceived to have implications for the Korean Church. Even though the willing handing over of leadership from missionaries to Korean Christians had produced some alarming tendencies, it was noted that "the situation is tending to make the Korean Church more indigenous and is almost certain to aid in the development of a stronger Christian witness."[25] Although national spirit was being drummed into the pupils during school hours, religious education was not hampered by this because it was carried on as an extracurricular activity. The school still aimed to have the boys taught by Christian teachers and to have all boys receive Christian instruction. This aim, however, was seriously challenged by financial problems that made it hard to recruit enough staff.

Unfortunately, better days for the school were not in the offing. In November 1940, Scott wrote that there had been trouble during the summer between the head teacher and the Korean principal at the boys' school in Lungchingtsun. Apparently, the head teacher, in concert with the police and gendarmes, had "fostered a suspicion of the school as a center of foreign influence. Even Mr. Bruce came in for suspicion as a 'spy.' The outcome of all this was a 'strike,' engineered by the head teacher, in that students refused to take religious training, and opposed the principal and the foreign control."[26] This strike brought in the provincial educational authorities. With the intention of taking the school out of Christian hands, the authorities ordered changes to the composition of the *zaidan hojin*. By reducing the missionary representation from four to two, the new board would have four Christian members (two missionary and two from the Korean presbytery) and four non-Christian members, including the principal, the mayor of Lungchingtsun and one representative each from the alumni association and the parents' association. The presence of the mayor was taken to mean that authority over the school would soon be placed completely in non-Christian hands.

The Korean mission wished to avoid this transfer of power at all costs. Negotiations with the provincial educational authorities began, with Scott coming up from Hamheung to lead the missionary side. He was helped by the fact that the vice-governor of the province was a Korean whom he had known in Hamheung and was most helpful in cajoling the educational authorities. Indeed, the vice-governor expressed his "appreciation of the long and helpful service that the mission has rendered the Korean people in Kando."[27] This expression was obviously heartening to Scott, especially when it came with the vice-governor's assurance that the Christian purpose for that the school had been founded and the religious privileges that it had enjoyed would be allowed to continue.

Under the circumstances, the outcome was satisfactory for the Canadians. Scott reported that "the missionaries agreed to withdraw from the board, provided that the government would allow it to continue under the supervision of a Christian board and with the privilege of carrying on Christian work—bible study and worship."[28] The missionaries persuaded Yi Tai Jun, a former schoolteacher and minister who had become a successful businessman, to take over the school from the missionaries. He was appointed founder by the school board and was therefore in control of the school's *zaidan hojin*. Because the Korean mission would no longer be subsidizing the school, Yi would have to find ¥10,000 a year from his own pocket to maintain the school. However, as it was estimated that Yi was worth between ¥300,000 and ¥400,000, this was not seen as too much of a burden for him. Even though he had drifted away from an active role in the Korean Church in recent years, he had first come to Chientao as Rufus Foote's assistant when Foote had established the mission station at Lungchingtsun twenty-seven years before. After working many years for the Canadians, Yi had left to enter business only because the low wages that the Canadians paid meant that he and his family had often gone hungry.[29] Scott had complete confidence that Yi would continue the school as a Christian institution. Indeed, Scott shared the opinion expressed by one of the Korean ministers that the day had been saved for the Christian Church in Chientao and that "our magnanimous offer had borne a witness to the disinterestedness and genuine Christian spirit of the mission that would help greatly to dispel any misconceptions of the mission that still might linger in the minds of officials or general public."[30] Nonetheless, in all dealings with government and educational authorities, so much depended on the attitude of the officials to the missionaries.

DEALING WITH THE COLONIAL AUTHORITIES

Unlike their colleagues in Taiwan, who ran afoul of the colonial educational authorities during the shrine question, the Canadian missionaries in Korea were much more adept at dealing with colonial officials. In part, the problems between Japanese officials and Canadian missionaries in Taiwan revolved around personalities as well as policy. There was unwarranted Japanese suspicion of the Chinese-speaking G. W. Mackay, with his strong familial links to the Chinese community on the island. No Canadian missionary in Korea was regarded with the same suspicion by the Japanese authorities there.

The attitude of the Japanese authorities toward missionaries varied. Scott wrote about Korea:

> The official attitude towards the missionaries differs in different sections of the country. Seoul, Pyengyang, and the South of Korea has been subjected to more suspicion and supervision. In our section of Korea we have enjoyed remarkable goodwill. In several cases where church and missionaries have been molested in other sections of Korea, on orders from above, we have been spared because of our good relationships with the local authorities. No pastors have been imprisoned in our section, and no missionary home has been subject to examination or search. Recently, it would appear that orders have come from higher sources to 'soft-pedel' [sic] the antagonistic attitude towards missionaries. The authorities seem eager to have us stay and carry on as formerly. But this may be dictated by political motives.[31]

In general, the good relations continued to the departure of Canadian missionaries from the peninsula in June 1942. School work continued uninterrupted, and Scott himself taught without any obstacle being placed in his way at the Hamheung boys' school until 8 December 1941. Even though Bruce and Bonwick, respectively, left the boys' academy and the girls' school in Lungchingtsun in early 1941, the Eunjin and Myungsin schools were still operating without interference in March 1942.[32]

It was individual officials who could cause problems, as was the case in November 1941, when a new director of education was appointed in South Hamkyung province, an area that included the southernmost Canadian mission centre at Wonsan. This new director "ordered all mission schools to change their founders from missionaries to nationals, and at the same time required that the new founders should promise that if and when the government wished to make these schools public schools the property would be donated to the municipality without compensation."[33] The Canadians had no objection to the first demand, for they were prepared to be flexible given the different circumstances at their various schools. These changes to the *zaidan hojin* meant that the schools were now independent Korean Christian schools, but the property of the schools remained in the possession of the mission's *zaidan hojin*. Although the Methodist Episcopal Lucy schools in Wonsan[34] had been donated by the Methodist mission's *zaidan hojin* to the government, Scott was unwilling to donate the Canadian property. He stood up to the director of education of South Hamkyung province over this issue, and the man backed down. It was later learned from the Korean secretary of the education department that the government had no intention of taking over mission schools and that "the director of education and his department had been reprimanded by the government general for their action in bringing pressure on the Lucy schools."[35] He had obviously overstepped his authority, but he had also found in Scott a person who would not submit to any browbeating.

The question of property was crucial for the mission. As far as the mission's *zaidan hojin* was concerned, the WMS and the Foreign Mission Board had initially thought it wise to change its constitution to allow the appointment of at least half Korean membership. However, in 1941, when William Scott and E. J. O. Fraser approached the government general for permission to make this change, they were dismayed when it became evident that the government general wanted to make the *zaidan hojin* predominantly or wholly Korean. Therefore, the missionaries delayed taking further action. Scott and his colleagues needed only to look at the example of the Methodist *zaidan hojin*, composed entirely of Koreans, which had buckled under government pressure to donate the Lucy schools in Wonsan. In any case, it was a moot point whether missionary or Korean could have done anything to prevent the colonial authorities from expropriating property.

For some time, the question of mission property in Manchuria had been especially worrisome for the mission. In November 1940, Scott pointed out that this concern arose because the Canadian government did not recognize Manchukuo, and in turn the Manchukuoan government did not recognize the Canadians' property deeds.[36] The Canadian missionaries were aware of the dangers that inaction posed, but they did not act precipitously in regard to their Manchurian property. In September 1941, they were approached by the Lungchingtsun authorities to allow military officers to occupy three residences (leaving a fourth house, the WMS residence where furniture was stored, empty). On the advice of the British consul general in Seoul, the Canadians acquiesced in this proposal, and Scott and Fraser signed a contract with the Japanese mayor of Lungchingtsun to rent the property.[37] Before the departure of the two missionaries from Korea in June 1942, no rent had been collected, but of most importance was that the Japanese recognized that the residences belonged to the Canadians. Following the decision to rent the empty residences in Lungchingtsun, arrangements were made to rent property in Hamheung and Sungjin to the hospital and local church respectively. Renting was only one option adopted by the mission in the fall of 1941.

The uncertainties caused by the war conditions led anxious Korean Christians to put pressure on missionaries to safeguard property for the continued use of the Christian forces by transferring it into Korean hands. Missionaries were hesitant because of their fear that Koreans would not be able to resist Japanese pressure, but they did negotiate some transfers. It was decided to transfer the property of the two high schools in Hamheung to the *zaidan hojin* operating the schools. Likewise, because the Wonsan Bible Training School did not have the endowment to operate independently, the property was transferred to the presbytery *zaidan hojin*. It was also agreed to transfer Bible institute properties to the various presbyteries in that they were located. At the instigation of the Hamheung hospital board, the hospital was handed over to the South Hamkyung Presbytery.[38]

Some property also had to be sold simply because the Korean mission needed money. In the spring of 1941, mission executives decided to make advance payments for two years to all institutions and personnel such as Bible women, provided that this money could be raised from funds already in Korea or through the sale of properties not considered necessary for future Christian work. By July 1941, fifteen months of advance payments—that is, up to 30 June 1942—had been made without the sale of land. However, the Interim Committee wanted to complete the full payment, but it could only raise the remaining nine months of advance payments through selling property. The situation was further compounded in the fall of 1941 by the Wonsan school crisis, that caused the Interim Committee to guarantee grants to its schools until the end of the following school year in March 1943. Mission grants had to be extended to 1943 because schools had to report their budgets to the government a year in advance. In November 1941, the Interim Committee cabled Toronto asking for financial help. But it was not possible for the Foreign Mission Board to send funds through Swiss banks, so the Interim Committee had no alternative but to sell.

It was decided to sell some land and buildings in Sungjin that were going to be affected by new streets that the city was planning. Because a special tax on property was going to be levied to pay for the proposed new streets, it was considered wise to sell before this tax took effect. The Bible institute and its dormitories, the girls' school and dormitory, as well as the missionary residence and its surrounding land, all of that were deemed necessary for the continuance of Christian work, would be kept. However, because it was thought that the sale would not raise enough money, it was also decided to sell all land and buildings within the main compound of Hoiryung. This was by no means all the property that the Korean mission owned in Hoiryung, but the sale of the main compound meant that the city in the future would not be a mission centre with a missionary residence. Even so, this was not considered much of a loss, because Hoiryung was a garrison town, "the conditions created by military occupation there . . . making it the least desirable of the stations for [missionary] residence."[39] It was hoped that the sale of these properties would allow the Interim Committee to meet its financial obligations and to make two grants: ¥10,000 to the North Hamkyung Presbytery in compensation for the sale of the house in Hoiryung, that it used as a Bible institute, and ¥15,000 to the Hamheung hospital for building purposes in accordance with a decision made in the summer of 1940.

The Korean mission still retained a significant financial stake in property. In July 1945, Fraser, the long-serving mission secretary in Korea, put the value of the chief mission properties at $100,000 at Hamheung, $75,000 at Lungchingtsun, $35,000 at Sungjin, $25,000 at Hoiryung, and $25,000 at Wonsan.[40] Because the three missionary residences at Hoiryung were included in this property, Fraser clearly had not known by June 1942, when he had left Hamheung, whether the main compound at Hoiryung had been sold. Similarly, because the Pacific War was still going on, he did not know if the mission property had survived. It was only in a letter of October 1945 that he learned Lungchingtsun had been ravaged by the red army.[41] In his list of Canadian mission property in Korea, Fraser also included $5,000 as the Canadian share of property at the Ehwa College for Women in Seoul. Interestingly, he did not forget to mention that there were approximately sixty buildings in a pine grove at a summer resort at Whachinpo (Wonsan Beach), seventy miles down the east coast from Wonsan. These were cottages privately owned by Western missionaries and businesspeople, that Fraser valued in total at $50,000. Fraser himself probably owned one of those cottages.

Understandably, the Canadians wanted their valuable property restored when hostilities ceased, and the provisions that Fraser and his colleagues made prior to the Pacific War in regard to Canadian property—whether for rent, transfer, or sale—appear to have been made with considerable thought and little rush. Unlike other parts of Korea, where there were real problems between missionaries and government officials, northeast Korea and Chientao enjoyed generally good relations between missionaries and officials. These good relations undoubtedly helped to prevent Canadian missionaries from making sudden and perhaps rash decisions.

When the Canadians left in 1942, the high schools in Lungchingtsun and Hamheung, as well as the primary schools in Wonsan and Hoiryung, were still functioning as Christian institutions. To the best of their abilities, they had made arrangements to safeguard these institutions in a future that they had no way of predicting. Their success owed much to the skill of Scott in dealing with the Japanese colonial authorities. He was called upon to intercede with the provincial educational authorities to save the Lungchingtsun boys' academy as a Christian school and to stand up to the South Hamkyung educational authorities to prevent the loss of the Wonsan school. Moreover, the mission schools in Korea remained open against a background of closure of Christian schools in other parts of the peninsula.

TRAINING EVANGELISTS IN MANCHUKUO

The death of Johnathan Goforth, although on furlough in North America in 1936, was a blow to a Canadian Presbyterian mission that up till then had basked in the limelight of publicity as a result of his international fame. However, evangelistic fire still burned deep among the missionaries and Christians in Manchuria whom he left behind. The mission was driven forward by its desire to preach the Gospel to as many as possible. This desire included starting new work among Mongolians. It was reported in 1937 that "Mongol carts will soon be hauling stone for our first Mongol Church. The land is donated, building materials are planned, the work of building will begin as soon as the severe winter weather is over."[42] One of the evangelists was even prepared to suffer martyrdom in order to bring the Gospel to the Mongolians:

> Abel Chang chose the name "Abel" as a pledge of his willingness to shed his blood on Mongolian soil, as a martyr. He has travelled through all sorts of dangerous places preaching the Gospel, and has come through unscathed. He is as cheerful-looking a prospective martyr as one could wish to see."[43]

New work among Mongolians might have inspired potential martyrs, but opportunities also appeared in other work, especially among women. In 1937, it was proclaimed that "the field is white unto harvest as never before . . . . It has never been easier to reach the Women of Manchuria than it is at present."[44] Such language is reminiscent of the late nineteenth century rather than the latter half of the third decade of the twentieth. Yet the challenge was to train and pay enough Bible women and evangelists to meet the new opportunities for Christian work:

> Reapers are in training—they are in demand everywhere; shall we be able to meet the opportunity—financially? Young women who get the vision, feel the call, and have also the initiative and ability to get their training apart from our exhortations and financial backing, are surely the most promising type. Securing their services for our Mission at the low rate of salary they need, would be an investment of the highest order.[45]

Not only was it hard to secure trained workers, but there were already a large number of workers on the mission payroll. In 1937, the Canadian Presbyterian mission was supporting most of the seventy-six Chinese pastors, evangelists, and Bible women with money from the Goforth Evangelistic Fund. In contrast to its Canadian counterparts in Japan and Korea, which placed such importance on self-support, the Manchurian mission emphasized expansion and paid little attention to self-support. However, the Manchukuo missionaries did realize that the low educational level of many of their Chinese Christian workers was a serious limitation to their effectiveness. Moreover, it was argued that "if we are to build a well-developed, strong, self-supporting church in this part of Manchuria we will have to pursue the policy of raising the general standard of our workers."[46] Yet the Canadian Presbyterians had no educational work of their own and, even more surprisingly, "no organic relations with the educational work of other Missions in Manchuria."[47]

The Canadian Presbyterians attempted to educate evangelists by holding annual short-term training classes for both male evangelists and Bible women. A training class for men was held annually over six weeks in September and October at the major mission centre of Szepingkai. Diplomas were given to those who had successfully completed a four-year course. In 1938, over forty men attended the training class. The best ordained pastors obtainable (mostly from the Scottish or Irish Presbyterian missions) were also used to train the Canadian Presbyterian apprentices at their stations. Furthermore, the Canadians were prepared to send apprentices, after probation, to existing Bible schools and theological seminaries. When money was short, the Canadians tried to encourage workers to pay their own way through these training schools on the understanding that, if possible, they would be hired on graduation by the Presbyterian mission. It was recognized that "both the Mission and the rising indigenous churches have high ideals for their pastors. Self-support, self-administration, native presbyteries, and a well trained ministry are all vitally inter-related. Prospects are as bright as the promises of God."[48] Nevertheless, these high ideals would be hard to meet unless the missionaries made further provisions for the education of their Chinese workers.

There was another problem in increasing the number of evangelists: paying for them. In 1939, it was reported that eight men had completed the four-year training class for evangelists that included not only lectures on the Bible but also the study of Japanese. It was necessary by then for Chinese evangelists in Manchukuo to have some knowledge of Japanese, but most of their wages still had to be borne by the Goforth Evangelistic Fund. In spite of the growing stress placed on the development of self-support, in 1939 only the Szepingkai and Taonan churches completely supported their pastors with help from the weekly offerings of missionaries resident there, and few churches were able to pay a half month or more of their respective worker's salary. It is, in fact, difficult to see how self-support could be quickly achieved given the poverty of many of the Chinese Christians.

One area of Christian work that was popular but did not cost much was kindergartens. In 1939, Mrs. E. H. Johnson noted: "I think sometimes one is just a bit dubious as to the actual Christian good that is accomplished through a kindergarten. Certainly almost everything depends upon the teacher in charge."[49] Here Johnson was voicing a view about kindergartens similar to that held by some of the Canadian Anglican missionaries in Japan. However, she added that the kindergarten in Szepingkai was managed by a very capable young teacher. Johnson described the routine at this kindergarten:

> Every day the children have religious exercises and are told a Bible story. Each week the children learn about five golden texts. On Saturdays, as a special treat, they are given an orange or small biscuit for that they all return thanks. Miss Chang tells them about the One who provides food for them. The children now, in their homes, insist upon saying grace before eating, even in strong Buddhist homes.[50]

Clearly, the level of teaching in this kindergarten was not high. Nevertheless, the children did pick up some ideas along with their oranges. The Canadian Presbyterian kindergartens did not have long to run, because by August 1941, the situation in Japan and the international tension in East Asia had prompted the Canadian missionaries to withdraw. Such was the lack of self-support within the mission churches and the lack of educational and medical institutions that the future must have looked bleak without the Canadians. Indeed, the comment of one of the Chinese pastors to Reverend E. H. Johnson in Szepingkai, shortly before he left Manchukuo, that "you don't need to worry. This is the Church of Jesus Christ and in His strength it will continue. There will necessarily be changes and adjustments but the work will go on"[51] sounds curiously hollow.

MEDICAL WORK IN KOREA

Throughout the 1930s, medical work remained an important aspect of the United Church of Canada mission in northern Korea. Robert Grierson retired from his post in Sungjin during the mid-1930s and was not replaced by a missionary doctor, but Donald Black and Florence Murray remained working in the Lungchingtsun and Hamheung hospitals respectively. Indeed, Murray and Beulah Bourns, a WMS nurse, continued to work at the Hamheung hospital until June 1942, when they were repatriated. Among the most prominent Canadian missionaries was Dr. Stanley Martin, like Dr. Gushue-Taylor in north Taiwan, a Newfoundlander. Murray said of Martin that "his capable hands could do almost anything. Besides being a good mechanic, he was a qualified wireless operator, amateur astronomer, excellent physician, and competent surgeon. He had a heart full of sympathy for the poor and the suffering."[52] Murray was describing the archetypal missionary doctor who had to be a jack-of-all-trades able to overcome a multiplicity of challenges. Martin had planned, built, plumbed, and wired the mission hospital at Lungchingtsun, which Murray deemed "better planned, better built, and better equipped than the older mission hospitals I had seen."[53] On top of all his other skills, Martin was a linguist who spoke fluently not only Korean but also Chinese. However, during the 1930s, perhaps unfortunately for the United Church mission's medical work in north Korea and Manchukuo, he represented the mission on the staff of the Severance Union Hospital and Medical College in Seoul. His chief interest there was the fight against tuberculosis.

As was the case in Japan, tuberculosis in all parts of the body was widespread in colonial Korea. Indeed, Murray believed that it was the greatest public health problem in Korea. In the early 1920s, when she first arrived in Korea, it was considered tantamount to a death sentence for a person to be diagnosed with tuberculosis, and Korean doctors made no attempt to treat tuberculous patients because no one recovered. In the absence of a drug of any value for the treatment of tuberculosis, rest, fresh air, and nourishing food became the mainstays of Murray's treatment of tuberculous patients. However, this approach ran counter to the proclivities of Korean patients "accustomed to being treated with medicine by the bowlful—the worse the taste the more efficacious it was believed to be. But better still a large syringeful of fluid shot directly into the bloodstream."[54] It was sometimes difficult for Murray to convince patients that her method of treatment was more effective in combatting their tuberculosis than massive doses of medicine. Clearly, Western-style hospitals had to adapt to some extent to Korean customs in terms of the treatment and care of patients. The need to take into account Korean sensibilities helped to offset some of the obvious shortcomings that the Canadian mission hospitals had in terms of modern equipment.

The Severance Union Hospital in Seoul was a well-equipped modern hospital where many of the Korean Christian doctors and nurses received their medical training, but the Canadian mission hospitals in Lungchingtsun, Sungjin, and Hamheung were sparse, if not altogether primitive, cottage hospitals with little expensive modern equipment and few facilities. Ruth Compton Brouwer has pointed out that Murray, when she arrived in Hamheung in 1921, was dismayed not only at the conditions at the hospital but also at "the easy tolerance of such conditions evident in the attitude of Dr. Kate McMillan, the resident medical missionary and her Korean colleague, Dr. Pak."[55] Unlike McMillan and Grierson, the Canadian mission's first doctors, who "had made evangelization rather than western standards of medical practice *their* priority," Murray would put her medical work first.[56] The younger generation of missionary doctors, in which Martin should be included, viewed the place of medicine in their missionary work differently than did the older generation.

Yet even Murray had to adjust to the demand of Korean culture that the basic care of the patient was given by family members. This care included, when Murray first started to work in Hamheung, the preparation of meals for patients "by their families: outdoors in summer, in the corridor or ward in winter. Their braziers left many burnt patches on the floor."[57] She tried to restrict the number of family members staying with a patient at the Hamheung hospital to one, but she found it difficult to restrict visitors who came at all hours of the day and night to the hospital. Yet families were important, and during the 1920s the mission hospitals had to rely heavily on help from family members, in part because it was difficult to get competent Korean nurses.

When Murray first arrived in Korea, nursing was not considered a respectable job, for it was unthinkable for a young woman to nurse anyone from another family, especially a man. Thus, few families would permit a daughter to do any sort of work in a hospital—apart from marriage, the only acceptable occupations for young women were teacher or maid. It was extremely difficult to get girls with any education to train as nurses. Such nursing attendants as Murray was able to hire for the Hamheung hospital had to be carefully helped and monitored by her during their first months to ensure that they understood their responsibilities. In order to provide a steady stream of well-trained nurses, it was decided in 1928 to open a school of nursing in Hamheung, with Ada Sandell, a missionary nurse, as principal. By 1941, the school had graduated seventy-five nurses.

Most of the nursing students were graduates of the six-year elementary school course. However, they had to be taught Japanese because the government examination for registration was in Japanese. They also had to learn some English because there were few medical terms in Korean. Apart from these languages, the nursing students studied mathematics and elementary chemistry. Murray and the Korean doctors on the hospital staff taught anatomy and medical subjects, and Sandell trained the students in nursing arts and supervised the nursing in the clinic and the wards. A good deal of emphasis over the three-year course was on practical training on the wards. Interestingly, the government general did not recognize this three-year course, but it did approve two different courses, a one-year course for midwives and a two-year course for nurses.[58] Government regulations apparently did allow women to become registered nurses by studying at home and passing an examination without ever going inside a hospital or obtaining any practical experience. Indeed, according to Murray, many Japanese nurses obtained their licences that way. However, despite their three-year training and their practical experience, the Korean candidates in sharp contrast to the Japanese candidates, usually failed the registration examinations at least once. Murray noted that the Korean students thought that they were being discriminated against by the Japanese colonial regulators, and "they had our [missionary] sympathy, but we could do nothing about it without resorting to bribery."[59] The missionaries made it a habit not to bribe Japanese officials, even though doing so could have smoothed the path for their graduates to obtain their nursing registration. Nevertheless, despite all the difficulties, Murray believed by 1941 that nursing had risen from being a despised occupation to being second only to that of a teacher in public esteem.

The missionary and Korean medical staff also had to deal with family attendants, who customarily took part in nursing patients and observing operations. These attendants had to be closely watched, for they were prone to think "the hospital a fine place to get the household washing done with hospital hot water and soap—luxuries few had at home":

> on late rounds or emergency calls at night, I [Murray] found a home attendant or other visitor in the utility room doing the family wash in the hopper. People accustomed to doing laundry in a river didn't realize that heating water cost money or that hot water wasn't quite as abundant as river water."[60]

Yet, if the family wash cost the hospital money, lack of concern about sanitation shown when the contents of bedpans, for instance, were thrown out the nearest window or shoved under the patient's bed for use again posed a health problem. Teaching patients, family members and new nurses about personal hygiene and taking care when handling dressings was an unending task for Murray, the WMS missionary nurses, and their experienced Korean staff.

A major reason for the unending attempt to teach cleanliness was that infectious diseases were common. Some including typhoid, typhus, diphtheria, leprosy, malaria, sprue, and many parasitic conditions that Murray had not encountered in Canada during her training in Halifax were rife in Korea. Although she never had to treat either cholera or plague, during the early 1920s, when she assisted Martin in Lungchingtsun, she saw her first case of epidemic encephalitis (then often called sleeping sickness). In Lungchingtsun she also saw cases of foot binding among Chinese women, that caused crippling deformity that could not be reversed.

As practitioners of Western medicine, Murray and her colleagues found themselves in competition with practitioners of traditional medicine. Acupuncture, which Murray referred to as "the *chim*," was generally resorted to before people would seek any other form of treatment.[61] Another favoured treatment was what she called "the *doom*," which involved igniting powdered leaves of certain plants on the skin over an affected area. When these traditional treatments proved ineffective, the sick individual often then turned to the missionary doctor for help. However, adhesions from acupuncture or infected doom ulcers often caused serious complications for the surgeon. One of the most frequent operations that Murray performed, often made difficult by prior chim or doom treatment, was the removal of suppurating tuberculous lymph nodes from the neck. It was important to remove such nodes before they ruptured and produced secondary infection. By introducing this secondary infection, acupuncture made surgery more difficult.

Acute infectious diseases had to be reported to the Japanese authorities, as did deaths. Although the Japanese police had a great interest in the movements of missionaries, the authorities, beyond a statistical concern with disease and death, took only a cursory interest in what happened in the hospital itself. Once or twice a year, the police inspected the hospital pharmacy. Murray reported that bottles of medicine not labelled in Japanese were suspect: "the inspector pronounced the drug unfit for use and smashed the container on the floor. We surmised that he knew nothing whatever about the drugs and wished merely to show his authority and make sure we were using the Japanese language on everything."[62] Japanese interest was to ensure that language regulations and licensing standards for doctors and nurses were upheld. In other words, theirs was a bureaucratic concern with adherence to regulations. A major reason for their lack of interest in the mission hospital was that Japanese patients almost invariably went to the Japanese government general hospital in Hamheung. The only Japanese who ever came as patients to the mission hospital were those "suffering from venereal disease who wished to keep their condition a secret in government quarters."[63] Unlike missionary schools, which could become hotbeds of political opposition to Japanese rule, the small mission hospitals were not seen to constitute a political challenge to the colonial overlords. Unable to compete with government general hospitals in terms of equipment and staff or the ability to attract Japanese patients, the mission hospitals were often also not the first choice for Koreans. The Japanese authorities thus saw no real need to interfere with the hospitals.

For their part, missionaries thought that their hospitals were worthwhile. In 1939, Black reported from Lungchingtsun that the past year had been one of the busiest and that

> *St. Andrew's Hospital* has again made records for all its activities, considerably exceeding the high mark set in 1937. Out-patient attendances increased 19 per cent. and in-patient days 12 per cent. over the year before, and when compared with 1936, there were slightly more than twice the number of out-patient and in-patient days [also] showed an increase of 71 per cent.[64]

As well as demonstrating the usual optimism of missionaries for even the smallest increase in their work, his comments show that Koreans were becoming less hesitant to go to a mission hospital. Yet, for the medical missionary, the medical side was only one aspect of the work of the mission hospital. As one doctor wrote in 1941,

> I feel that our hospital carried on not only as an efficient medical institution, but as a place showing forth the Christian spirit to the many thousands who came into contact with it, during the course of the year. . . . It is my sincere hope to make this work [a] still greater blessing, to the large community we serve, in the days to come."[65]

It was the continuing belief that the small Canadian mission hospitals were important in helping to spread the Christian message that sustained Black and

Murray and the WMS missionary nurses in their medical work. Clearly, by the beginning of the Pacific War, their persistence and hard work had begun to change Korean attitudes toward Western-style hospitals and their attendant occupations, such as that of registered nurse for women.

DIFFICULTIES IN TAIWAN

In early 1937, Presbyterian difficulties in Taiwan were reported in the *Fukuin Shimpo*, which implied that the missionaries there looked to the Japanese Presbyterians in the Nippon Kirisutokyokai (the Japanese Presbyterian Church) to help them.[66] The Japanese did help, particularly with finding suitable principals for schools.[67] The Japanese also detected Taiwanese Christian dissatisfaction with the leadership of Western missionaries in the Taiwanese Presbyterian Church. The *Fukuin Shimpo* saw this dissatisfaction and thought that the Japanese colonial authorities were hoping for a Japanese-led church there.[68] Perhaps Japanese Christians saw a parallel between their desire to displace foreign missionaries in metropolitan Japan from their positions of leadership and the perceived discontent with the English and Canadian Presbyterians within the Taiwanese Presbyterian Church. However, if the Japanese had aspirations to replace Canadian and English Presbyterians within the Taiwanese Presbyterian Church, they conveniently overlooked the fact that they were still outsiders to most Taiwanese Christians, who were ethnically Chinese. Nevertheless, as became evident in 1937 at the annual conference of the North Formosa Presbytery, both missionaries and Taiwanese Christians recognized the need to develop close ties with the Nippon Kirisutokyokai. It was decided at this meeting to send four Taiwanese ministers (two of whom spoke Japanese) to visit the Presbyterians in Japan.[69] Furthermore, much attention was given by nearly seventy Taiwanese ministers attending the conference to the question of Taiwanese self-support after they learned that the Presbyterian synod in Japan had announced its decision to become self-supporting in five years. Two years earlier, in October 1935, J. D. Wilkie had stressed that a self-supporting, self-governing, and self-propagating church was the "constant aim in Formosa" of Canadian Presbyterian missionaries. He pointed out that "there is no one who realizes the lethargic effect of too much money from Canada more than the Formosans themselves, and they are determined that the amount of opiate, as they themselves have called it, must gradually be reduced."[70] It was politic to tell the Canadian constituency that the Taiwanese Church was aware of the need to reduce the $10,000 annual grant that it received from Canada. Yet, given the small number of Taiwanese Presbyterians in north Taiwan, some 10,000 out of a total of 15,000 Christians belonging to all denominations in an overall population of 1,500,000, this reduction seemed unlikely. Indeed, at the annual conference in 1937, it was estimated because of the poverty of the Taiwanese congregations that it would take Taiwan another fifteen years to achieve self-support.[71] And, in sharp contrast to the impression given in the *Fukuin Shimpo*, Taiwanese ministers attending conference were in no way dissatisfied with their Canadian missionary colleagues.

Dissatisfaction with Canadian missionaries would probably have meant the existence of factional in-fighting within the Taiwanese Christian membership in north Taiwan. There were two sides of the family of George Leslie Mackay, the pioneer Canadian Presbyterian missionary in Taiwan. One was the Canadian side represented by his son, G. W. Mackay, who was a Canadian Presbyterian missionary and married to a Canadian. The other was the Chinese side represented by G. L. Mackay's two daughters, Mary and Bella, who married into Taiwanese Christian families. The families of Mary Tan and Bella Koa were important within the Taiwanese Christian community in north Taiwan. This importance was recognized by the Japanese authorities, who supported the opening of the Mackay Memorial Library in Tamsui in May 1939. At the opening ceremonies, attended by the governor of Taihoku province and many other Japanese officials as well as the whole student body of the Tamsui Middle School, David Koa, a great-grandson of G. L. Mackay, unveiled a bust of his great-grandfather. Furthermore, everyone present received as a gift a Japanese-language book on the life Mackay.[72] Strange though it might seem at this late date, the Japanese authorities seemed willing to help foster the Mackay legend in colonial Taiwan. Their help might be taken as another sign that the government general's policies toward Christianity were not well thought out.

Although the vitality of the Mackay legend was one sign that Taiwanese Christians in the north were in no hurry to cut their ties with Canadian missionaries, Taiwanese Christians did see the need to create links with other Christian movements, including the Japanese Christian movement. Even though the North Formosa Presbytery saw the need to curry the favour of Japanese Presbyterians, it was also interested in developing close ties with the Korean Presbyterian Church.[73] Hugh MacMillan was one Canadian Presbyterian missionary who thought that the progress made by Korean Presbyterians toward self-support, self-government, and self-propagation could serve as a useful example for the Church in Taiwan.[74] In the months before the outbreak of fighting in north China following the Marco Polo bridge incident, despite the loss of their schools in Tamsui, the evangelistic Canadian Presbyterian missionaries seemed optimistic about the future in Taiwan.

Free from the classroom and school administration, once the Tamsui schools had passed over to government control, missionaries could devote more time to direct evangelistic work. It was reported for 1937 that missionaries had made more evangelistic trips to churches that year than any other in the past decade; these visits not only benefited the churches, but also "the missionaries have found a closer, warmer touch with the people of the church and their problems."[75] Yet there were changes taking place, especially among the young, that caused missionaries to press on with the study of Japanese language. Many Sunday schools were now being conducted in Japanese for the benefit of public school children who knew Japanese. At the same time, however, in many places older Christians were unable to understand sermons in Japanese. Clearly, there were still opportunities to preach in Chinese. Among the most active of missionary evangelists was G. W. Mackay, who, free from his school duties, poured his energy into preaching in churches and homes throughout north Taiwan. Mackay, perhaps aware that his time in Taiwan was coming to an end, was particularly interested in "the carrying out of his long-cherished desire to seek the scattered Pepoan tribe who were once Christians, and to bring them back to the church."[76] The Pepoan aborigines had first been evangelized by his legendary father during the late nineteenth century. It was coming full circle for a Mackay to be taking the Gospel to these people once again.

Even though the evangelistic work was seemingly going well, there were continued difficulties for missionaries because of the climate of suspicion toward British subjects on the island. In October 1936, the Keelung incident, in that three visiting Royal Navy ratings were falsely charged with a petty crime and then beaten (to the point of being tortured) by the police, led to a serious diplomatic problem that threatened to spoil the visit of Prince Chichibu, the brother of the emperor, to Britain in the spring of 1937.[77] Although the Keelung incident was the most serious one involving Britons and the Japanese police in Taiwan, spy fever gripped Taiwan through the fall of 1936 and into 1937, and brought missionaries under suspicion. It is no coincidence that the climax to the Tamsui-schools issue took place against the backdrop of the Keelung incident.

The loss of the schools in Tamsui did not bring about the end of persecution of the work of the Canadian Presbyterian mission by government general officials. In his annual report for 1938, C. H. Archer, the British consul, reported that suspicion of foreigners had become less troublesome than it had been the year before, but he added that, though there had been no proven cases reported of discrimination against British subjects, "some measures taken for other reasons have had a discriminatory effect, and in the case of one of the religious missions a marked unfriendliness has been shown."[78] This, of course, was the Canadian Presbyterian mission. Archer reported that Mackay Memorial Hospital, the Canadian Presbyterian hospital, in Taihoku (Taipeh) had been harshly treated over access to a newly reconstructed road that ran past the hospital's main gate and led to the Taiwan Shinto shrine. To add insult to injury, the Canadians, who had received ¥36,000 in compensation for property expropriated to allow for the widening of the road, were forced to pay back ¥26,000 as a contribution to the expenses of the new road to that they were denied access.[79] Interestingly, the report for Mackay Memorial Hospital for 1938 noted that "the municipal road-widening scheme necessitated demolition and rejuvenation of the entrance to the hospital, with a result that drew favourable comment from no less a personage than the Governor of the Province himself."[80] Although it is likely that the governor did not turn off the road into the hospital, his favourable comment clearly indicated that the matter of the hospital's access to the road had been resolved.

However, it was no coincidence, although the road question was still an issue, that Canadian doctor Eugene Stevens was interviewed by the police on a trumped-up charge. Fortunately, the British consul reported that Stevens had "handled the situation with great tact and good sense, and the case was dropped."[81] Archer believed that such harassment stemmed from the fact that "petty officials with a grudge get away with a good deal, and explains the very unfriendly treatment received by the local mission hospital."[82] Unlike the usually more amenable government general officials that the United Church missionaries encountered in remote northeastern Korea, the minor bureaucrats in Taiwan who had dealings with the Canadian Presbyterians were situated in the capital of the colonial administration. By treating Canadian missionaries harshly, they perhaps thought, they would receive kudos from their superiors. When diplomats or the consul became involved, senior officials normally made amends, as undoubtedly was the case with the Mackay Memorial Hospital main entrance. Before this intervention, the Canadians had to put up with annoyances from petty officials.

Although Mackay Memorial Hospital could not compete with the government general hospitals in Taiwan in terms of facilities and equipment, it still attracted a steady number of Taiwanese patients and continued to do so despite spy fever and the worsening international situation.[83] The hospital kept its fees low and took charity cases where genuine poverty existed.[84] As late as 1941, it was reported that

> in our medical work there has been no lessening of the number of patients because of the times. The hospital has run to its greatest capacity, seeking to meet the spiritual as well as the physical needs of the stream of suffering and afflicted humanity that has daily poured through its doors.[85]

The Canadian Presbyterians took pride in "the reputation which the Mackay Memorial Hospital has built up and maintained over the years as a medical institution in its care for the poor and destitute, its high standard of nursing, its superiority in surgery and general medical standards."[86] It was the presence of Canadian doctors and nurses on staff that made the hospital distinct among the many medical hospitals, both government and private, in north Taiwan. The surgical skill of the Canadian doctors was undoubtedly high, yet the hospital did lack modern equipment.

Above all, what was important to the missionaries was that the hospital work brought evangelistic opportunities. For the missionaries, Mackay

Memorial Hospital was "a centre where the soul may find restoration while the body is engaged in the process of healing."[87] As long as the hospital performed this function to the satisfaction of the missionary medical staff, it was serving a useful role in the life of the Canadian mission in Taiwan. The argument for carrying on medical missions because of "the enormous physical suffering in regions where the Christian Church has responsibility"[88] could not be fully justified in Taiwan, where great strides in public health had been made by the Japanese government general since 1895. In north Taiwan, it was sufficient to say that medical work was traditionally a part of Canadian work and would continue as long as it remained evangelistically valuable. It could be pointed out that the Christian doctor helps to reconcile science and religion: "he believes in Osler's Medicine and in the Bible and uses both. He is acquainted with modern psychology, but he believes that faith in God transcends this. He is instrumental in demonstrating Christianity in action, in its most appealing form."[89] All this was true, but the number of patients seen and operations undertaken at Mackay Memorial Hospital meant that there was precious little time for the missionary doctor to devote to Christian work. The Canadian Presbyterians were able to keep a minimum of one Canadian doctor at the hospital through the 1930s, yet there was a high turnover in doctors, which could be put down not simply to furloughs but to the strain of the job.

THE HAPPY MOUNT LEPROSY COLONY

The Happy Mount Leprosy Colony was one aspect of Canadian Presbyterian medical work that was clearly satisfying to its founder, Dr. George Gushue-Taylor, a Newfoundlander who had worked with lepers in both Japan and Taiwan and who opened Happy Mount in March 1934.[90] Originally, he had wanted to put his colony in southern Taiwan near the English Presbyterian station of Shoka, but when the Japanese authorities objected he chose to build in the north of the island within working distance of Mackay Memorial Hospital.[91] Although the Canadian Presbyterians allowed Gushue-Taylor and his wife to work at the colony, and paid their salaries, the mission in north Taiwan had no responsibility for the colony, an independent Christian institution under Japanese law. It had its own governing body of four Japanese, four Taiwanese Japanese, and four foreigners, of that Gushue-Taylor as chairman of the board and director of the colony was one. Having worked in Japan, he was possibly more adept at working with Japanese officials than were most of his colleagues in north Taiwan. Because it was an independent body, Happy Mount had no official relation to the Christian hospitals in Taihoku and Tainan.[92] This independence was more important to the Japanese authorities than to the Canadian Presbyterian mission. The Canadian Presbyterians got the benefit of having a leper colony for the cost of the missionary doctor's salary and that of a missionary nurse, paid by the WMS. As well as by donations from supporters in Canada and in Newfoundland, the work was supported by funds from the Mission for Lepers, America, Canada, and London.[93]

The legal independence of the colony from the mission also appeared to help with fund-raising from official Japanese sources both inside and outside Taiwan. Even though it had its own leprosy hospital close by, the government general provided a fairly large annual subsidy to Rakusanen, the Japanese name of Happy Mount. In 1930, work among lepers in Taiwan had received an imperial gift from the empress dowager of ¥1,000. A second imperial gift for the same amount was received from the empress dowager in 1937 and presented to Gushue-Taylor by the governor general, Admiral Kobayashi, who visited and inspected the colony so that he could report personally to the empress dowager about the colony on his next visit to Tokyo.[94] Just as a similar gift was an important factor in bringing recognition to the sanatorium at Obuse in Japan, the fact that Happy Mount received imperial gifts showed that the institution was highly regarded by the Japanese authorities. This regard stood in sharp contrast to the Japanese attitude toward the Canadian Presbyterian educational work in Tamsui or even toward Mackay Memorial Hospital. Because Happy Mount was regarded as an independent institution by the Japanese authorities, it would be wrong to assume that the imperial gift was meant to placate the Canadian Presbyterians following the loss of their schools in Tamsui. Moreover, gifts from the imperial household department and from the empress dowager continued to be received. In 1940, the empress dowager donated ¥5,000 to the colony to be paid out in annual instalments of ¥1,000.[95] The continuity of support from the empress dowager lends credence to the idea that it was for altruistic rather than political reasons that the imperial family donated money to Happy Mount.

Like so much of the Canadian Presbyterian mission property, the colony was in a prime location, some fifteen miles from Taihoku (Taipeh) on a forty-six acre site that contained twenty cottages, a hospital, and a church. As well as being close to Taihoku, it could be reached by boat and a short walk from Tamsui.[96] In 1939, the colony estate was described as "situated on the side of a well-wooded hill and a river runs through the valley below, threading its way through lovely green ricefields towards the sea about two miles away. Visitors to the Colony frequently remark on the beauty of the surroundings."[97]

Happy Mount's facilities compared favourably with those of the large government leprosy hospital a few miles away, where the patients lived in crowded barracks. Gretta Gauld, the daughter of one of the early Canadian Presbyterian doctors in north Taiwan and a nurse with the English Presbyterian mission, who looked after Happy Mount while Gushue-Taylor was on furlough, described the living conditions at the colony in her report for 1937–1938: the patients lived in small cottages that were built to hold four occupants. Here they live apart, cooking their own meals, but assemble at certain hours of the day for various meetings in the chapel or central hall, and also unite in different kinds of manual labour for the welfare of their small community.[98]

During the time that she was in charge of the colony, there were sixty-four resident patients, fifty men and fourteen women, all suffering from leprosy but each at a different stage of the disease.

When Gushue-Taylor had first opened the colony, he had hoped to restrict the patients only to early cases, but his Christian compassion had compelled him to admit a large proportion of patients in advanced conditions. Unfortunately, with these advanced cases, Gushue-Taylor could not claim any medical success. He could claim, however, that "we have relieved a volume of human misery, and by kindness and careful treatment have convinced many both inside and outside the colony of the value of Christianity in the community."[99] If appropriate for palliative reasons, Gushue-Taylor would operate to remove dead bone in fingers and toes, but the main course of treatment for leprosy was injections. Unlike the general medical and surgical work that went on at Mackay Memorial Hospital, the medical treatment for patients with leprosy was straightforward and relatively inexpensive. Gushue-Taylor and his wife could therefore devote time and energy to evangelistic work among the patients both at Happy Mount and at the nearby government leprosy hospital. By 1937, the Christian community at Happy Mount, that included nearly all the patients, was large enough to petition the North Formosa Presbytery to be recognized as a congregation and to call for its own pastor.[100] Evangelistic opportunities also existed at the government leprosy hospital, on whose grounds a chapel was erected in 1939. It was reported in 1941 that, among 700 in-patients at the government institution, 100 were Christian.

Although the government leprosy hospital proved to be fertile ground for evangelistic work, its presence also hampered Happy Mount's growth. Despite the imperial gifts, Gushue-Taylor complained in 1941 that from the start of Happy Mount the number of patients had been kept down because of referrals to the government hospital.[101] By the end of 1940, there were only fifty-one resident patients at Happy Mount. If Gushue-Taylor had a regret, then it would be that Happy Mount had failed to grow in patient numbers as he had hoped. Furthermore, he was forced to leave his work in Taiwan at the end of November 1940 before a qualified successor had been appointed.[102] He wrote that, "unfortunately, in the midst of this insane war and rumours of war, it was thought by our people at home that evacuation of British and American nationals was essential."[103] However unwillingly Gushue-Taylor and his wife left, he noted that the leper colony "was founded on the basis of the command of our Lord as recorded in Matthew's Gospel, Chapter ten, verses five to eight" and that "we have the faith to believe that after these seventy-five years of

Christian teaching and witness in the Island, there will be found in that land those followers of our Lord who will continue to bear witness to His Life and Teaching."[104] His work among Taiwanese lepers was grounded in a deep religious faith, and this faith made him confident that Christianity would continue in Taiwan after the sudden withdrawal of the Western missionaries.

Perhaps one of the highlights of Gushue-Taylor's time at Happy Mount was a visit by Mrs. Archer, the wife of the British consul, who came with gifts for each patient. Gushue-Taylor wrote:

> Not only did Mrs. Archer knit and prepare these gift packages, but she personally went and presented them to the patients in the church, going to cottages to present them to patients too ill to come out. I told them that Mrs. Archer was the local representative of our beloved Queen Elizabeth and her action represented what we should like them to feel was the attitude of our country to them in their distress. I have seen few more beautiful acts of Christian charity.[105]

This incident indicates close ties between the Gushue-Taylors and the Archers and shows that the doctor had deep respect for Queen Elizabeth. More importantly, though, the actions of Mrs. Archer revealed that she thought genuine sympathy for the patients.

CHAPTER EIGHT
Missionary Life in Japan and Its Empire

The endeavours of missionaries in mission schools established the rhythm of missionary life, that largely followed the contours of the academic calendar. The long vacation during the hottest and most humid days of summer allowed the exodus of missionaries from the cities to the hill station of Karuizawa, with its temperate climate and sylvan walks, or to the foreign cottage community overlooking Lake Nojiri. As long as the mission schools remained open, the long-established pattern of missionary life continued through the 1930s.

The lifestyle of missionaries acted as a cocoon that protected them from changes taking place outside. Furthermore, the late 1930s saw the publication of several congregational histories marking important anniversaries of individual churches founded by Canadian missionaries. The gratitude expressed by Japanese Christians to Canadian missionaries could only help to bolster the sense of achievement and well-being among missionaries.[1] So calm was day-to-day life that few missionaries recognized before the fall of 1937 that fundamental changes were taking place, against which there would be no protection. Although missionaries themselves saw little of the xenophobic surliness of young non-Christian Japanese, change was noticed by those missionary children who had wider and more indiscriminate contact with Japanese youth.

Little attempt was made by Canadian missionaries in Japan to live like the Japanese. They were foreigners and never attempted to become ersatz Japanese by adopting Japanese dress or mimicking Japanese customs. They were part of the foreign community, indistinguishable in dress from the Western clerks and agents who worked for the foreign shipping lines and trading companies in Tokyo, Yokohama, Osaka, or Kobe.

Yet missionaries were separate. Socially, Canadian missionaries did not rub shoulders with the Western commercial community. This separation was not the result of snobbery by businessmen or the narcissism of missionaries, ever fearful of the scorn of those who questioned the validity of their mission or who did not share their strict moral code. Rather, it was more simply a matter that their paths rarely crossed. Unlike British Anglican missionaries, who saw ministering to the British and Western communities in Japan as a legitimate and important part of their work, United Church or Canadian Anglican missionary work was limited to the Japanese, with the notable exception of the Canadian Academy. Similarly, although the British Anglicans possessed in Walter Weston, Murray Walton, and W. H. Elwin sporting clergymen who joined other foreigners in the pioneer scrambles that opened the vistas of the Japanese Alps and Formosan highlands to the Western world, [2] Canadians could claim few sporting ties with other foreigners.[3]

Social background and educational links through Victoria College led missionaries to have some contact with the small Canadian diplomatic group in Tokyo. Indeed, Sir Herbert Marler, the first minister, was a churchgoer and interested in Canadian missionary work in Japan. However, for the most part, missionaries lived in their own world, for, like their counterparts in private schools in eastern Canada, missionary educators lived on campus, and it was to summer at the cottage at Karuizawa or Lake Nojiri rather than Lake Rousseau or Georgian Bay that they went.

This summer migration from urban campus to hill station, which, at least from the time of World War I, wealthy Japanese were beginning to join, was made possible, in the case of Karuizawa, by the large-scale development of railways during the late Meiji and Taisho periods. The interior of Japan was no longer remote, for regular passenger service connected it to the urban centres on the coast. This also meant that the inconvenience and isolation of missionary work in the cities of mid-Japan were, in the years after World War I, largely things of the past.

Although the experiences of every Canadian missionary in Japan and Korea were distinct, an overall impression of what missionary life was like during the 1930s can be gained by looking at individuals at different stages of life, in different aspects of missionary work, and belonging to different denominations. Furthermore, missionary life in Korea can be contrasted to that in Japan. In both places, missionary life included families. Children were as much a part of the Canadian missionary community in the Japanese Empire as the adults. John Holmes, who grew up in Japan, was among the generation of missionary children who would later serve in the Canadian army in the war against Japan.

GROWING UP IN JAPAN

Although the missionary societies preferred their clerical missionaries to be married, one of the persistent problems for married missionaries was what to do with their children. Missionaries were aware that, unless their children became missionaries themselves,[4] they would have to make their lives in Canada or Britain. Although it was common among Britishers living in Asia to send their children home at a young age to attend boarding school, doing so meant long separations and heavy expenses. The missionary societies realized that allowances had to be made for children. The United Church of Canada went so far as to found the Canadian Academy in Kobe to provide its missionaries with the opportunity to educate their children to school-leaving age in Japan.

The experiences of missionary children growing up in Japan differed according to where they lived and how much contact they had with Japanese. Some parents did not like their children associating with Japanese youngsters for fear of their children acquiring bad habits from them.[5] Others were more tolerant and allowed their children great freedom.

Children were less affected by a sense of cultural isolation than were many missionaries; however, some of those born and brought up in Japan were sensitive enough to be worried about being accepted for what they were. Unlike their parents, who had come to Japan to convert the Japanese to Christianity, missionary children were caught in the dilemma of being born in Japan but not allowed to be of it. Although their parents attempted to fit them into a Western mould, the children also had to contend with Japanese society outside the mission compound. Their parents faced insurmountable cultural barriers erected to protect traditional values against the Christian message, whereas the children faced societal barriers, almost as impenetrable, built simply because they looked different and, therefore, in all aspects must be different.

The case of John Holmes, the son of C. P. Holmes, the veteran United Church missionary in Fukui, illustrates the tensions that a missionary child growing up in a provincial city encountered. Holmes's early friendship with Japanese his own age, his feelings of loneliness, and his desire for acceptance were by no means unique. His experiences and feelings were similar to those of the three children of Dan Norman in Nagano some twenty years before.[6] They were different, however, from those of the American contemporary of the Normans, Edwin Reischauer, who was brought up in Tokyo.[7] Moreover, the rapid modernization of Japan, as well as the introduction of new Western cultural forms (such as Hollywood movies), meant that Japan of the early 1930s was a much different place from that of the early 1910s for a Western boy.

Holmes was born in Fukui in 1918 and spent the first eighteen years of his life in Japan before departing for Canada in 1936, having graduated from the Canadian Academy. He was the only child of parents who were in their midforties when he was born. Perhaps because his parents were older than most, or simply because Fukui was a safe place, young Holmes appears to have been given considerable freedom to roam. His best friend, Anada Shigeru, the son of his parents' cook, was born on the same day.[8] The two of them were inseparable, and Holmes was as much at home in Shigeru's house as in his own. In a community where there were no other Western children, one of his early concerns was that he looked different from his friend and other Japanese boys whom he knew. He wrote:

Until I went to school there was the puzzle of the mirror. Why did I look so different? Everyone had black eyes and black hair—except me. My eyes were blue and hair yellow. My parents looked different because they were different. I was more like my friends so why didn't I look like them? When asked "are your eyes sick?" I replied, "no, they are not sick. They are blue because my soul's eyes are black." There was some talk about souls at home but I was not sure souls had eyes. It stopped the questions for the moment.[9]

Childhood confusion about what his father did can be seen in a description that Holmes wrote about his Fukui home and his father's study in it:

The house was big enough to play real hide and seek. Shigeru liked the game as he could go into rooms he did not usually see. My father's study was out of bounds. My father sat at his desk and wrote for hours, his sermons, I suppose and we were not to disturb him. But that was alright as we did like the study because it had a peculiar smell. Whenever I thought of the odour of sanctity I thought of my father's study. It was his collection of John Wesley's sermons whose covers had absorbed moisture and become mildewed.[10]

As well as the mildew in the study, there were mosquitoes to contend with during the summer. The Holmeses slept under mosquito netting, even though doing so was uncomfortable in hot weather. Their cook held that the mosquitoes preferred *gaijin*.[11] Under the mosquito netting, the Holmeses slept on beds made up with Eaton's best linen sheets, for they came back to Japan after furlough in Canada stocked with six years' supply of sheets, towels, and pillow cases.[12] They lived a Western-style life, and though their house was Japanese built it was outfitted with Western furniture.

Outside the mission compound, however, was the Japanese city. For a boy sent early to bed, the summer night was filled with the sounds of the city. In the early evening, the *ame* (candy) man often stopped close by and attracted children by beating a small drum or even setting up a puppet theatre. Night was ushered in by the bell sounded from the temple. Later, there were the calls of the sweet-bun man selling his wares and those of vendors selling *iwashi* (sardines). The *amma* (masseur) announced his presence by playing a plaintive song on a wooden pipe.[13] As well as tradesmen, groups of people were going home along the street in front of the Holmeses' house from the bathhouse or the nearby sake shop. However, one sound was largely absent: the clatter of geta, the pervading street sound in urban Japan during the 1930s. Fukui had no paved streets, so the clacking of these wooden clogs was muted in summer and absent in winter due to snow. Yet hearing the familiar noises of the summer night before falling asleep undoubtedly helped to give a sense of security and belonging to a boy.

During the day, one of the attractions of the mission residence for the young Holmes was its large grounds, which had a stream running through them.

This stream became an ocean for games with small bamboo-leaf boats that included mock naval battles in that Minamoto and Taira clans fought and refought the famous engagement at Dannoura.[14]

The playful pattern of early childhood changed for Holmes when his family went back to Canada on furlough. His parents "spoke of Canada with longing, a yearning that made memories bigger than life. They said wait until you see Canada. It is so beautiful, a wonderful place."[15] This was little consolation to young John, who was saddened to learn that Shigeru would not be going: "Obasan," Shigeru's mother, tried to comfort Shigeru with a rice ball. But to no avail, because the Holmes family still packed for Canada. Importantly, Holmes, seeing Canada for the first time, saw it through Japanese eyes. He wrote: "I saw Canada with different eyes. It was big. The Rockies were huge. The prairies were flat. The land was empty. Where were all the people? I had yet to learn that bigger had its own grandeur."[16] Banff and Lake Louise reminded him of Japan. He noted that "Canada was where I looked like people around me. I didn't need a mirror to know that. In Toronto, the food was a surprise—pork chops, candies, pies, cakes, fruit and pork chops. Thick pork chops with fat that ran down your chin."[17] There were also relations to meet, for he "had relatives, uncles and cousins and aunts on farms with cows and horses and pigs. My mother's family had a picnic in Woodstock and they called us 'cousin.' We were to eat things I had never seen before," and they asked "'cousin Charlie'—my father—to say grace and he said a beautiful grace—in Japanese. The astonished relatives never said a word. Japanese courtesy must be catching."[18] To ordinary folk in Woodstock and Oxford County, the home of so many of the Canadian missionaries who went to East Asia, it was clearly still exotic to have a missionary in Japan as a cousin, especially a Japanese-speaking one. At the end of their furlough, the Holmeses returned to Fukui. John and Shigeru remained friends, but the close bonds between them had inevitably changed.

The Holmeses followed the normal pattern of missionary life, that took them away from the Japanese in the summer for a two-month stay at the hill station of Karuizawa. In those days, the simplest way of getting to Karuizawa from Fukui was to travel by train. Because the route was indirect, running far to the east along sections of the seacoast before entering the central mountains, the journey was relatively long, taking from midafternoon until early the next morning. For missionaries, the stay in Karuizawa, Holmes noted, was "a time of renewal, reaffirmation of faith, a gathering of the like minded and loneliness for me."[19] Among the Canadian missionaries whom young Holmes especially liked was Dan Norman, whom he respected for "his concern for the Japanese people, especially those of humble calling. He understood to be a missionary was to be kind."[20] Charles Bates, Holmes's father's closest friend, also influenced him as he was growing up. However, Holmes was more critical of Bates, for Bates had once told him that

"I am the least Japanized missionary in this country Japan." I [Holmes] was chagrined. In later years he made little attempt to speak Japanese and when he did his pronunciation made your teeth ache. He was great fun but I faulted him for putting conditions on his ministry—learn English, learn our ways—then you will see the light. It was a time of "preaching God's word to the heathen" in English.[21]

This criticism was a little harsh, for the 1930s were not years when "'preaching God's word to the heathen' in English" was in vogue among missionaries.

Karuizawa was still lonely for young John because there were few foreign children there his own age. He preferred Fukui, where he had his Japanese friends. As Holmes grew older, however, he was able to get a variety of summer jobs in Karuizawa: he guided parties of climbers up Mount Asama, the active volcano close to Karuizawa; collected the premiums for the yearly cooperative fire insurance from the cottagers; and worked at the tennis club. Yet Karuizawa was not all work for the teenage Holmes, for like teenagers in Canada he had his share of high-spirited summer adventures and escapades. One in 1935 resulted in a damaging accident of the speeding car of the vacationing German ambassador after Holmes and a Western friend placed a log on a dead-end road outside Karuizawa that was used by wealthy individuals to test their high-powered cars.[22] Fortunately, most of his boyhood adventures did not end in such a dramatic way.

Like many other young people Western or Japanese, Holmes was fond of films. In 1931, he and his fellow Canadian Academy students were fortunate enough to see one of their favourite film stars when Douglas Fairbanks Sr. visited Kobe. His visit was part of a world tour for the movie *Around the World in Eighty Minutes*.[23] As a teenager who stood six feet tall and could pass for an adult, Holmes adopted the dress and mannerism of his hero when he was away from both the Canadian Academy and his parents' watch. It was not only American movies that he saw, for in 1933 he watched René Clair's *Sous les toits de Paris* at the Kinema Kurabu theatre in Kobe. Even though the film was Western, the theatre was thick with the distinctive Japanese aroma of dried cuttlefish, that the Japanese moviegoer chewed just as his or her counterpart in Canada would savour hot-buttered popcorn as a movie rolled. Holmes described how the Japanese at that time overcame the problem of understanding a film with French dialogue. Because few Japanese could understand French, a *benshi* would be employed to translate the dialogue and explain the action. Holmes wrote that "a benshi could tinge a comedy with tragedy or a drama with farce. The film knew its fate was in the benshi's hands and pleaded for mercy. To no avail, the sound was turned down to give the benshi full sway."[24]

Although Holmes shared with the Japanese a fascination with movies and even with cuttlefish, there remained a gap between him and the Japanese, and he could only wish that the Japanese would accept him as he was. Many long-term foreign residents of Japan or Western students taking postgraduate degrees at Japanese universities have wished that the Japanese would accept them as they were, but it must have been particularly galling for Holmes. After all, he had lived all his young life in Japan except for the brief furlough year in Canada. One of his dreams was to save up money for a hiking expedition up Mount Fuji with Anada Shigeru. However, when Anada won a school competition that had as the prize a trip to Mount Fuji, the Japanese school authorities thought it inappropriate for Holmes as a foreigner to accompany his friend to the sacred mountain.

Like many other foreigners, Holmes preferred rural Japan and its country folk to urban Japan and its city folk. He wrote: "like a knight questing for the Grail I traveled by bicycle about Fukui Prefecture seeking acceptance. In truth the more rural the area the easier my task. Mine was a dialect so rustic it was in part another language and as soon as I spoke there were smiles."[25] Despite the smiles, the unpretentious country folk seemed more willing to accept the teenager as he was.

There came a time, however, and for Holmes it was August 1936, after graduation from the Canadian Academy, when childhood Japan had to be left behind and a new adult life carved out in Canada. When he landed in Vancouver on the Canadian Pacific liner *Empress of Russia*, an unexpected but not uncommon reception for missionary children awaited him. Because he carried a British passport saying that he was a British subject by birth, he was granted permission to enter Canada for one year as a student and nonimmigrant. He noted that "I traveled alone so my parents were unaware that although I looked like people around me I was considered a foreigner. They were right. I felt like a foreigner."[26] The question of granting automatic Canadian citizenship for children born outside Canada to parents one or both of whom were Canadian had not yet been fully resolved.

Despite initially feeling like a foreigner in Canada, Holmes made his life there. With the retirement of his parents from the mission field within months of his arrival in Canada, a connection with Japan, which other missionary children maintained if their parents remained missionaries, was broken. It was only the Pacific War that took him back to East Asia as a Japanese-speaking lieutenant in a special unit of the Canadian Army Intelligence Corps, in that Captain K. C. Woodsworth, a son of H. E. Woodsworth, dean of the Kwansei Gakuin, also served.[27] Holmes was fortunate enough to survive the war, but his boyhood friend, Anada Shigeru, did not live even to see the opening of the Pacific War. Anada was killed in September 1940 when serving as a lieutenant in the Japanese army in north China.

YOUNG AND OLD MISSIONARIES IN JAPAN

Growing up in Japan for a "mish kid" could be filled with adventures interspersed with bouts of loneliness. Living in Japan could also be trying for young and inexperienced missionaries. Howard Norman, the elder son of Dan Norman, the veteran United Church missionary in Nagano, who began missionary in the early 1930s, found missionary life difficult. Writing to his parents-in-law from Tokyo in March 1934, Norman noted: "we were stationed in Nagoya because the teaching in Government schools brought quite an amount of money. However the Middle School that has the most teaching has decided to do without an English teacher."[28] To some extent, where Norman worked depended on getting teaching work to supplement his missionary salary, for the fact that the middle school in Nagoya did not want him raised the question of his posting for the next year. Norman wanted to try rural work, but he hesitated to have his wife and young daughter live in a Japanese house. He could be quite happy, though, living in either Nagoya or Tokyo. One of the attractions of living in Tokyo was the opportunity to enjoy things cultural. Norman reported that "we re-visited the Kabuki-za again a few weeks ago... The bill wasn't as good as when we went last summer, but it was pure joy in spots."[29] Yet living in Tokyo meant not only seeing the famous kabuki actor Ichikawa Sadanji on stage; there was also the chance to see Western films such as Eisenstein's *Thunder over Mexico*, which Norman much enjoyed.

His pleasure in seeing an Eisenstein film was also connected to his desire to become politically involved. He noted: "I would like to work with Iso Abe's (Abe Isoo's) Labour Party if I stayed in Tokyo or went to Nagoya, though I dont know how much the police would welcome that."[30] Abe Isoo's socialism stemmed from Christian socialism and Fabianism, but Norman was also sympathetic to communism. He told his parents-in-law:

> By the way, the last *Contemporary Japan* said the Communist party was dead here. I doubt it very much. Tsarist Russia couldn't stamp it out, and I imagine it carries on the same tenuous, underground existence here, that it did there. Then I heard it said recently that the Japanese Communist Party is regarded as second only to the German C. P. in technique today in the Third Internationale. Two Japanese Christian friends have confirmed this opinion. People who curse the Communists so freely ought to realize that fear of revolution is one of the strongest deterrents of war among the nations of the world today.[31]

Norman was right that the Japanese communist movement continued to exist. However, although many of his contemporaries held a similar idealistic view that fear of communist revolution was one of the strongest deterrents to war, it would prove to be a naïve one. Yet his strong sympathy for communism helped to explain his later desire to join the international brigade during the Spanish Civil War.

Norman's hope of staying either in Tokyo or in Nagoya were dashed. His hope to engage in rural work was also long delayed. The Normans found themselves transferred to the provincial city of Kanazawa. It had been a centre of Canadian missionary work since the 1890s, and during the early 1930s Harper H. Coates, the veteran missionary, had been stationed there.[32] However, Howard Norman, his wife, Gwen, and their young children plainly found living in Kanazawa horrible. Gwen, especially, found it terribly hard. In February 1937, she wrote very candidly to her parents:

> I am becoming more and more of the opinion that missionary life is mentally unhealthy—that is that the mental environment is unhealthy. My opportunities for using Japanese are so limited that as a means of social intercourse it is hopeless—so that outside of my ordinary daily routine and contacts I am practically limited to religious professionals i.e. missionaries. Howie of course isn't quite so hemmed in as I am but the same thing holds true and is more disastrous for him because he hasn't the practical jobs that I have to occupy him.[33]

The letter shows how barren the life of a young missionary couple could become. It was not lack of knowledge about Japan that was the problem, for Gwen Norman was acclimatized to Japan, having already lived there for some four or five years. To some extent, her loneliness was no different than that of a young mother in Canada stuck at home with the children. And she was unsure of herself in bringing them up.[34] There was a universality about her plight.

Undoubtedly, her loneliness was exacerbated in Japan because of the natural reticence of Japanese men and women to speak to the wife of a foreigner to whom they had not been properly introduced. This problem was compounded by the stereotypical attitude that such a foreigner would only speak English in any case. It took time to make Japanese friends, and the Normans had not been long in Kanazawa. However, it does seem somewhat strange that people who knew of the Normans, particularly the members of the local Methodist church and the mothers of the kindergarten children with whom Margaret Norman, the Normans' kindergarten-age child, played, did not have more contact with them.

The high hopes for a satisfying life as a missionary, however sentimentally intertwined they might have been for Howard Norman with memories of growing up in Nagano as the son of a popular missionary, were being shattered through frustration and disappointment. Indeed, Gwen Norman was concerned about what her husband might do in desperation. She wrote that Howard was so frustrated with being unable to do anything constructive in Japan as a missionary that he was considering joining the international brigade as a stretcher bearer.³⁵ Nothing came of this desire to join the international brigade. The idea was irresponsible and impractical for a man with a young wife and family in Japan. Yet the fact that Howard was contemplating going to Spain shows the impact of the Spanish Civil War on his interwar generation and its thinking. Nevertheless, like his more famous younger brother, Herbert, the diplomat and historian who had also considered going to Spain instead of completing his studies at Cambridge, for Howard the idea of joining the international brigade remained merely a dream. "Howie is over tired," Gwen confided to her parents, "and I think a rest will enable him to see more clearly."³⁶

Gwen Norman also mentioned the possibility of not returning to Japan after furlough. She wrote that she often thought that "Howie would be happier in a church at home. For myself I don't know and when Howie asks me the question in general I hate to commit myself for fear that I am unconsciously being influenced by my own desires when the question is really Howie's usefulness."³⁷ It seems that Gwen was sacrificing her own desires and happiness for the sake of her husband's usefulness. Nevertheless, by March 1938, she seems to have come to terms with living in Kanazawa. Some of her time was spent reading: "I'm afraid that the truth the whole truth and nothing but the truth is that I'm too fond of an armchair and a book, and not necessarily a good book: Still I have at last been reading *Seven Pillars of Wisdom*."³⁸ That Gwen was reading this classic work by T. E. Lawrence shows its popularity among the interwar generation.³⁹ She also saw a comparison between what Lawrence wrote about living in the Middle East and her own experiences in Japan. She wrote: "I found what he had to say about living in a foreign land in his first chapter most sympathetic. It is perfectly true that you have to find a sort of balance between the gains and losses involved. Possibly that has something to do with my present unease."⁴⁰ Yet Gwen retained her sense of humour, for she added, poking fun at her husband's enthusiasm for the Oxford Group Movement, "But, tut I am becoming so subjective that I shall be soon fit ground for the seed of the O. M."⁴¹

Despite their trying experience in Kanazawa, the Normans still remained missionaries in Japan. Howard was fortunate to find a niche for himself teaching in the protective environment of the Kwansei Gakuin before and after the Pacific War. The closed academic society of the university in Nishinomiya suited his natural intellectual bent and allowed it to flourish. In postwar Japan, the Kwansei Gakuin also provided a stable setting for Gwen and the young family. Before retiring from the mission field at the mandatory age of seventy in the late 1970s, Howard also achieved one of his earlier ambitions, for his last years in Japan were spent working among rural people.

It was not uncommon for missionary families to encounter difficulties. Horace Watts, one of the most influential clerical Canadian Anglican missionaries in the Japan mission, had the problem of providing for five children. By the late 1930s, he was faced with having to make some provision for the suitable education of his oldest children. His colleague Percy Powles had overcome this problem with his four children by educating them at home in Takata. Mrs. Powles was a trained and talented teacher. The Powleses had made the decision not to be separated from their children as they grew up and ruled out sending them as boarders to the Canadian Academy in Kobe. The only formal schooling prior to university that their children received outside the Maple Leaf Academy in Takata was during the occasional furlough year spent in Canada. Home schooling did not appeal to the Wattses. Horace, an Englishman, possibly carried the view of many middle-class English that their children should be educated in private boarding schools.

During the late 1930s, Watts was stationed at Niigata. Whereas Powles was more than content to work in Takata, far preferring its snowy and bracing climate to that of Tokyo, Watts was less at home in Niigata, possibly because there was little opportunity there to supplement his salary through teaching English. Watts was obviously financially stretched in meeting the needs of his large and growing family. In 1939, a way out of his difficulties appeared: temporary transfer from Japan to the Canadian Anglican mission in Honan. Watts, in his early forties at the end of the 1930s, had worked in Honan prior to joining the Japan mission in the late 1920s. Furthermore, because this area of China was under Japanese military control, the Japanese-speaking Watts could be useful to the Honan mission by being able to act as a liaison between the Canadian Anglican missionaries and their Chinese converts and the Japanese military authorities. He could only contemplate such a transfer, however, if the Canadian Anglicans were willing to increase the allowances for his children.

The Canadian Anglican WA was keen that the Wattses go to China. In fact, the WA was more interested in having Mrs. Watts back in Honan than her clerical husband. In Mrs. Watts, the WA saw a truly outstanding woman in every way. In April 1939, Madeline Wodehouse, the secretary of the WA, wrote to Canon Dixon about Mrs. Watts:

> She is not an ordinary woman. She is a very capable woman and in her quiet way, strikes me as a woman of great strength of character, equal to most emergencies. She has exceptional poise—you have only to see her with her children and to meet them to know that she is a wonderful mother."[42]

Wodehouse thought that she would be an asset to the Canadian Anglican work in China, for Mrs. Watts not only spoke fluent Chinese but also had a keen missionary vision. As was often the case with many missionary wives, she was a much better linguist than her husband. Wodehouse wrote that Horace Watts did not speak Chinese well, "but no doubt his knowledge of Japanese would be of tremendous value in a province under Japanese domination. They both would like to go to Honan but that is out of the question with their present family—five children, the youngest just learning to walk."[43] The cost of the children's education was clearly a very major consideration for the WA and the MSCC. Wodehouse thought that it was unfair to split up the family by having Horace go to China alone while his wife remained in Canada to look after the children. However, the Wattses were finding it difficult to manage in Japan with the family together. They needed financial help and looked to the WA and the MSCC to assist them. Wodehouse indicated that

> Mrs Watts wrote me from Japan asking if the W.A. would help out with the eldest son's education by providing a bursary. At that time Ronnie was under our age limit for acceptance & also because there were so many applications from needy missionaries in the Canadian field—more than we had means to provide for—there was considerable opposition to giving any more bursaries except to the children of clergy in the Canadian North-West.[44]

The WA was also loath to help out because it meant eventually helping with five, if not more, children in one family. Undoubtedly, the WA hoped that the MSCC would step in and help. If not, Mrs. Watts would just have to struggle to make ends meet in Japan with her five children while her husband was in China. Wodehouse wrote that it was a great responsibility to send a woman with five young children to live alone in Japan, but both Mrs. Watts and her children were "exceptional," and she added that, "if it is for the good of the work as it does seem to be, I think it would work out providing the war situation does not become more acute."[45]

As it turned out, neither Canon Dixon nor the missionaries in Japan approved of the idea of Watts being transferred to Honan, however temporarily, for they thought that it would probably mean that he would never return to Japan. By June 1940, Mrs. Watts, who had not been well, was preparing to return to Canada with her children on the advice of the doctor. In informing Toronto of her imminent return, Spencer wrote that it was not only her health "but a number of other things that combine to make her return necessary, e.g. the impossibility of getting a servant, food difficulties and financial difficulties due to the high cost of living and educational fees."[46] It was often the gradual accumulation of small problems that made life difficult for wives and families in Japan.

In mid-October 1940, even though Mrs. Watts had gone home, her husband still angled for more work. He wondered about becoming the chaplain to the Seaman's Mission in Yokohama while retaining his work in Niigata.[47] This scheme also came to nothing because of the decision made before the end of October to withdraw missionaries. By December 1940, however, Watts was teaching English at the Government Commercial College in Nagoya. Spencer, stationed in Nagoya, wanted Watts to be close at hand while the Canadian

Anglican mission shut down. Furthermore, because Watts was still of military age, he had to obtain recognition from the Japanese government to remain in Japan, and his teaching position provided that. Watts noted that

> the College is aware of my intention to leave at the earliest possible date but so many Westerners have left Japan the Principal was as glad to get me, even temporarily, as I was to feel that the closing of the Mission business was less likely to be hampered if I had official recognition.[48]

Despite the international situation, there was still a demand for native-speaking teachers of English.

Even though Watts did not leave Japan until the spring of 1941, it had already been decided that he become the field secretary, working under Canon Dixon, the general secretary, at the MSCC headquarters in Toronto. Watts held this position until 1952 and discharged it with distinction. His return to Canada also alleviated some of the worries about the education of his children. A way was found to send his oldest son, Ronald, to the expensive and elitist Trinity College School in Port Hope, that had close ties to the Anglican Church.[49]

Yet, if things worked out well for Watts, such was not always the case, especially for older missionaries. After expending their working lives in the mission field, it was not unusual for some missionaries to want to remain in Japan for the rest of their lives. A retired missionary was another worker in the field for the missionary society, but there was always concern about his or her health.

John G. Waller, the veteran Canadian Anglican missionary in Nagano,[50] was one missionary who caused some concern for his Canadian Anglican colleagues in Japan. It was hard for Waller, who had been in Japan since 1890, to accept change. In October 1935, he complained about the new rules introduced into the annual mission conference:

> a number of 'rules' for the Conference were passed, the chief object of that seemed to be the control of the Bishop, who becomes nothing but observer. For twenty-three years, since the diocese was set apart in 1912, we have got along without any special rules, and I don't see the need for any now.[51]

These new rules, he thought, could lead to Japanese Christian distrust of missionaries and the loss of influence by the latter. One of his complaints was that, while he and Japanese Christians were desperately trying to raise money for the diocesan endowment, the missionary conference was using diocesan funds to support things outside the diocese. Canadian money was being given to support such things as Christian Fellowship and St. Luke's Hospital in Tokyo without special permission from Toronto to do so.

That Waller complained directly to Canon Gould in Toronto did not lie well with his younger missionary colleagues. They found Waller's propensity to act on his own initiative rather than in consultation with the rest of the Canadian Anglican mission annoying. In August 1936, Spencer wrote to Gould complaining about Waller:

> We have tried to be patient with him because he has been a consecrated worker for Christ so long and because we expected he would retire soon and so not be a cause of trouble to the rest of us any longer. But now we realize his continued presence in Japan after retirement may be an anxiety and trouble to us if he is still a full member of Conference.[52]

Waller was irritating the clerical triumvirate of Spencer, Powles, and Watts who ran the Japan mission and who had introduced the new rules for the mission conference that had upset Waller in September 1935. Waller was particularly friendly with Bishop Sasaki, and it was thought that he could use his influence with the bishop to get his ideas put into effect without referring to the mission executive committee. Spencer wanted to curb some of this influence by preventing Waller as a retired missionary from retaining full membership in the mission conference.

Spencer was also annoyed with Waller earlier when he decided, without consulting the mission, to go on furlough and leave his wife behind in Japan. Spencer noted: "I think we all felt that Mrs. Waller needed a furlough too and ought to take it according to rule, and also that Dr. Waller needed her presence on furlough."[53] Indeed, it did seem unfair for Waller to leave his wife behind in Japan while he journeyed to England to visit his married daughter. Yet even more galling for his colleagues was what Waller did in England. While he was on furlough, Waller, who had served as the chaplain at the New Life Sanatorium at Obuse (only seven miles from Nagano), was temporarily replaced by a British Anglican missionary belonging to the Church Missionary Society (CMS). Once in England, Waller, acting on his own initiative, talked with the authorities at the CMS about their missionary continuing on as the chaplain at Obuse. Spencer thought that Waller was overstepping his position, for he had not consulted with his Canadian colleagues in Japan about this plan. When Waller retired, Spencer wanted his place to be taken by a Canadian missionary couple, not by an English one.

As it turned out, Waller and his wife remained in Japan upon retirement. Then tragedy, no stranger to the Waller family,[54] struck. In 1938, Mrs. Waller died. Even though his clerical son, Wilfrid Waller, whose health had given his parents much concern during the early 1930s, remained in Japan until October 1940, Waller, after his wife's death, was left living alone in Nagano. At one point, he thought about dividing his house in two and letting one-half out to a Japanese family. Spencer thought that this was a bad idea because Waller might not be able to attract suitable tenants. But there was some cause for worry about Waller living alone. Spencer noted in a letter to Watts in early November 1940 that "roughs have been demanding money from him [Waller]"[55] This is one of the few examples of a Canadian missionary being physically threatened during the 1930s. In January 1941, Powles wrote to Spencer: "I will try to look after Dr. Waller, but it is like having a pet flea, sometimes you have him, and then you can't lay a finger on him, just the moment that suits you."[56] Waller was obviously not one to cooperate with those trying to look out for him. He was interned along with other foreign male missionaries and businessmen in the compound of the Canadian Academy in Kobe at the beginning of the Pacific War. Like Waller for the Canadian Anglicans, Mrs. Harper Coates (Agnes Wintemute), a former Canadian Methodist WMS missionary, who had also decided to remain in Japan rather than return to Canada, was a source of concern for United Church missionaries and her Japanese Christian friends.[57]

In 1942, Waller, along with other missionaries, was repatriated to Canada. He had relatives living in the Hamilton area, but his son Wilfrid, as well as his married daughter, were living in England, and another son was a prisoner of the Japanese in Singapore. Waller suffered a stroke in 1943 and was bedridden for the last months of his life before his death in late March 1945.[58]

LIVING AND WORKING IN RURAL JAPAN

Improvements in communications meant that missionaries working in rural Japan during the 1930s were no longer isolated from their colleagues in the coastal cities. Nevertheless, the Canadian missionary in a provincial city worked within the familiar confines of church and Christian community. In the late 1930s, Percy Powles, the Canadian Anglican missionary in Takata in lower Niigata Prefecture, was a mature missionary with a quarter century of experience behind him. Over the years, a strong sense of identification between missionary and the Japanese townspeople had developed. In early 1938, during a wave of anti-British feeling stemming from the war in China, Powles noted that

> despite the fact that I am well known as an Englishman the good people give me the benefit of the doubt around here, and are often amazed when they see me questioned by police and other officers. It just shows how really at home one can make himself, living close to the countryside and it is a great argument for long residence in a place where a tradition can be built up.[59]

After living more than twenty years in Takata, Powles was a familiar figure. It was those who did not know him well who looked upon him with suspicion. In late 1939, he was deeply touched by an incident that probably was a common occurrence at that time:

We must have been talked over in many homes, for one day when I was walking down town and was passing the Normal Training School some little tots of the third year or so passed me by, and as they did so one pointed the finger at me and remarked to her companions 'Look, he is a spy.' Then they all looked towards me as I passed. But one little girl said, 'No such thing! He is our teacher, Mr. Powles.' I think she was one of the little girls who used to attend our Maple Leaf Kindergarten.[60]

Later Powles used the incident for a didactic purpose when speaking to the parents' group at his church; he used the girl's action as "an example of how one little genuine sincere heart could give the lie to what was whispered by thousands, if they had the will to do it."[61] It was also apparent that the camaraderie in Takata was much to his taste. He not only viewed his assistant at the New Life Sanatorium at Obuse as "a good man," but he also had an affection for him because he was "one of my old boys from Takata Church."[62] Powles enjoyed the chattiness of familiar company and the gossip of ordinary things that went with working in a parish in provincial Japan. His fascination with the details of daily life is caught in a letter of November 1940, which also describes the impact of the war in China on business life in Takata. He wrote, after travelling from the Obuse sanatorium home to Takata, that

> I also came up on the train with Ogawa San (one of the biggest confectioners in T. [Takata]) He says he is losing money on his business all the time as he cannot get materials nor sales. Matsuya (our biggest dry goods store, who helped us to get materials for Obuse when there were none to be had elsewhere) has closed down altogether for want of materials and all the stores are in great distress. Our egg man has gone out of business as he cannot get food for his chickens. Eggs are very hard to get. When I took my pen to be fixed they said they could not put a gold nib on it but he managed to fix it up some way and it writes very well.[63]

Despite the shortages caused by the war, the tradesmen, with whom he had obviously been dealing for years, did their best to help him. The war in China exacerbated the poverty of his part of the Diocese of Mid-Japan.

Powles, who liked to see himself as "a country evangelist,"[64] repeatedly referred to the rural poverty of lower Niigata Prefecture surrounding Takata. With his family roots in Shawville in rural Quebec, he possibly retained an affinity with the feelings of farming folk despite the citified education that he had received in Montreal. Just as climate affected agriculture along the banks of the Ottawa River, so it contributed to rural poverty around Takata. In late 1939, in discussing the building of a rural evangelistic centre, Powles wrote that the region

> is able to take only one crop a year from the ground on account of the heavy

snowfall. The parish of Iiyama in Nagano also shares this difficulty. The result is that money is scarce and of much greater value than around Nagoya, or any other place on the other side of the Main Island. When you couple with this money stringency the expense of clearing the roofs and walks of snow you will have some idea of church expense. Fire insurance also is high on account of the poor buildings and the lack of protection.[65]

Despite the hardships that the farmers had to endure, which meant that they had little to give to the church, Powles felt much at home among these people. There is a smack of Barsetshire about the Diocese of Mid-Japan that fades differences of place, culture, race, and language. Powles was as much at ease in his mission parish in lower Niigata Prefecture as ever Trollope's Archdeacon Grantly was in rural Barsetshire. It was a measure of his empathy for the ordinary people whom he served that Powles could turn the bleak prospects of evangelizing provincial Japan into a deeply pleasing life work that only the approach of the Pacific War threatened to cut short.

By early 1941, Powles had found that "there is evident malice against us Britishers, of that we are not unaware."[66] Some of the hostility came from the fact that he was trying to get money out of Japan before his departure. War seemed imminent:

judging by the papers and remarks in general the war stage seems to be set for April, and there is an evident spurring up of the feelings that it cannot be avoided. Of course it can if this party here can be brought to its senses. But it seems very unwilling.[67]

As it turned out, war did not break out for another seven months.

CONTRAST IN THE JAPANESE EMPIRE

Missionary life in Korea, Manchukuo, and Taiwan did not greatly differ in outline from that in Japan. Like their colleagues in metropolitan Japan, Canadian missionaries in the Japanese Empire attempted to live in a Western lifestyle. Similarly, because many missionaries in Korea and Taiwan were engaged in educational work, for many the rhythm of life was dictated by the school calendar. Moreover, just as most missionaries in Japan quickly developed strong feelings of sympathy and affection for the Japanese, so too did those living in the colonies. However, geography, climate, and surrounding culture did make a difference to the way in that missionaries lived. The standard of living of Koreans, Manchukuoans, and Taiwanese was not as high as that of the Japanese, so the conditions that the missionaries faced in conducting their work in Korea, Manchukuo, and Taiwan were often more physically difficult than those in Japan. Likewise, because there were diseases such as malaria in Korea and Taiwan, and even plague in Manchuria into the 1920s, precautions had to be taken in order to protect the health of missionaries.

The Canadian mission compound at Tamsui, with its beautiful views, showed that early arrival sometimes enabled missionaries to gain possession of property that later became highly desirable real estate. The need for space for their vegetable gardens and fruit trees (in order to ensure a supply of wholesome vegetables and fruit), as well as for school buildings and missionary residences, often resulted in the early missionary compounds being sizable properties. This was the case with the compound at Lungchingtsun, for Manchuria, in contrast to crowded Japan, had a lot of space. When some of these larger compounds were originally established, they were intended to be as self-sufficient as possible. As health standards improved in Taiwan and Korea, there was less need for such large properties. In 1937, when the Canadian Presbyterians stationed at Szepingkai in Manchukuo moved into new accommodations, Mrs. H. E. Johnson wrote that

> The new houses, unlike most mission houses, do not stand out as large mansions towering above tiny native dwellings. There are many Japanese houses in the neighborhood that also have two storeys, and are not unlike many of our western homes in outside appearance. Being on the edge of town, the air is far cleaner than the air we had last year—living on one of the busiest and dustiest streets of the town. We are away from unpleasant, loud noises, and we are within sight of one of the town parks. We have ample space inside our homes, and the plumbing facilities are quite modern and far superior to the minus drains, minus hot water system of former years. A small garden is a great asset, not only from the point of having a few flowers and perhaps tomato plants, but in providing a safe play-place for children.[68]

Although the Canadian Presbyterian missionaries in Szepingkai worked to convert the Chinese, they lived in the Japanese quarter of the city. Clearly, the housing and the general living conditions were better in those neighbourhoods where the Japanese lived. Because missionaries could fall sick as easily as anyone else from diseases caused by poor sanitary conditions, it was in their interest to have good plumbing facilities. Moreover, because foreign children especially would excite the curiosity of many of the ordinary people on the street, a garden where children could play out of public view was obviously desirable.

Although the Canadian Presbyterians in Szepingkai were fortunate to find reasonable housing, there were often disadvantages to some of the places where missionaries lived. Florence Murray pointed out that the compounds at Hamheung, Hoiryung, and Lungchingtsun were adjacent to cemeteries or crematoriums. This was one reason why the Canadians were able to buy such properties. Writing of her first visit to Hoiryung in 1921 on her way to

Lungchingtsun, Murray provided a depressing picture of the mission compound:

> The Hoiryung mission station was a bare, dreary place surrounded on three sides by Chinese gardens, chiefly characterized by the smell of human waste that was used as fertilizer. On the third side stood the city crematory whose odor did nothing to overcome the other smells. The missionary's wife said she had gotten used to it, but not to the nighttime howls of wild animals that she feared were wolves, hyenas, or tigers in the hills. The high winds that blew almost constantly came right through the flimsily built houses. The walls were only one brick thick, plastered on the inside with mud, over that was a thin coat of plaster. Furnaces, just arrived from Canada and soon to be installed, gave hope of more comfort. The couple's eleven-year-old had been lonely with his brother at school in Japan. His mother was teaching him at home that year. He had shot several pheasants that were delicious eating and had twice the meat of domesticated fowls.[69]

In commenting about the house in Hamheung where the single female missionaries lived in 1921, Murray noted that, "though the mud walls and ceiling of the house were nicely whitewashed, this failed to mute the musty smell of mud and straw that pervaded the place."[70] The mission compound at Hamheung left almost as much to be desired as that at Hoiryung as far as its buildings were concerned. Murray wrote:

> The women's house was surrounded by a mud wall topped with tiles. Over the wall I saw the thatched mud houses of our neighbors. There were similar houses inside the compound too—one for the "outside man," another for the cook and her household. Other houses from which the partitions had been removed served as classrooms for the primary department of the school. The high school was a rectangular two-story building of such flimsy construction that the weight of the tile roof had caused the walls to bulge. They were kept relatively near their original position by metal bars running the length and width of the building, although the heavy tiles had been replaced by lighter corrugated iron.[71]

The mission hospital, where Murray was to spend most of the next twenty years working, was situated "on rising ground across a little gully" and was "a two-story, red brick building with a sagging wood verandah in front."[72] Concerning Hamheung beyond the mission compound's mud walls, she wrote that

> Except for a few two-story buildings along the main streets, most construction consisted of one-story earthen houses. The well-to-do had tile roofs, the rest straw thatch. Street signs were in Chinese characters. There was no paving and no street lighting. Wind raised dust in clouds. In residential areas the streets were lined with mud walls. Wooden gates opened into courtyards which could not be seen from the street. Windows of paper admitted some light, but

excluded curious stares of passersby.[73]

When Murray first went to Korea in the early 1920s, Lungchingtsun and Hoiryung were still difficult to reach from Hamheung (itself a day's rail journey from Seoul). On her first journey to Hoiryung from Hamheung, Murray travelled south to Wonsan and from there took a coaster north to the port of Chungjin, the terminus for a narrow-gauge railway that followed the Tumen River to Hoiryung. To go from Hoiryung to Lungchingtsun meant crossing the Tumen, that was frozen in winter, and then travelling by foot, bicycle, or Korean cart. All manner of transportation—bicycles, carts, horses, palanquins, and Korean porters—was utilized by Duncan MacRae on his many evangelistic trips and excursions into the northern interior during the early twentieth century. By the 1930s, the Japanese had built a railway north into the Chientao region from Hoiryung, and it greatly facilitated travel to Lungchingtsun as well as stimulated trade.

By that time also, there were other forms of travel. Murray, then stationed in Hamheung, had acquired a 1928 Ford, a gift from the young people of the United Church in Prince Edward Island. She noted that "Driver's licenses were difficult to obtain unless one took the Japanese police officer who gave the driving tests out to dinner several times and plied him with liquor or gave him money with that to entertain himself and his friends."[74] Corruption, albeit at a minor level, was an accepted fact within the Japanese police in Korea. Because Murray refused to bribe the policeman, it took her three tries—and the test was only given once in six months—before she received her licence. She reported that driving was always adventurous because the roads were narrow, crooked, and unpaved. Moreover, it was often necessary, when journeying into the countryside, to ford streams and to negotiate the banks of canals, because the villagers would often remove bridges to prevent their loss during the rainy season and sometimes not bother to replace them.[75] Because cars were rare in northern Korea, Murray's car itself became an attraction and had to be guarded to prevent curious children from draining the battery by turning on and off the lights or from letting the air out of the tires. Having a car, however, did facilitate her work. She wrote that, because transportation was no longer a major problem, meetings could be held in village churches to teach not only the Gospel but also health:

> Children would be there in swarms. After teaching them a song, telling Bible stories, and giving a simple health talk, we tried to send them home. It didn't work. No child would leave. By the time the adult meeting was half over, the youngsters were either restless or asleep, but to go home before they saw a moving car was unthinkable.[76]

As well as the car, a slide show to illustrate Bible stories or a health lecture often attracted people from surrounding villages and audiences of several hundred. Clearly, a little modern technology went a long way in bringing out the curious and helping to knit them to the world outside their rural villages.

Indeed, by the 1930s, the isolation of northern Korea was being broken. Although there were fewer Western amenities available in northern Korea in comparison to cosmopolitan Tokyo or Kobe, the building of new railway lines meant that train service connected the northern Canadian mission centres to P'yongyang and to the colonial capital of Seoul. Even though the Pacific War and later the Cold War once again cut off the provincial towns of northern Korea and Manchuria from the West, during the decade prior to Pearl Harbor they were being integrated into a railway network that stretched throughout Korea and Manchuria and allowed passage even beyond via the Trans-Siberian line to Europe. Lungchingtsun, Hoiryung, and Hamheung were distant, but they were not remote as they had been before World War I. The train also made it easier for missionaries to reach the summer hill stations.

Just as summer resorts and holidays were a feature of missionary life in Japan, so too were they elsewhere in East Asia. In 1934, Peter Fleming, the British writer, visiting the summer resort of Kuling on Mount Lushun close to the Yangtse River in 1933, said that place "owes both its name and its popularity as a summer resort to missionary enterprise, which has found an anomalous outlet in the field of real estate."[77] What happened in China also occurred in Korea. Indeed, the protection of the cottages of Canadian missionaries at Wonsan Beach, the favourite summer haunt of missionaries in Korea, was a concern for United Church missionaries who remained in the peninsula past the outbreak of the Pacific War.[78] Missionaries in Taiwan tended to go to Karuizawa in Japan for their summer holidays. Those in Manchukuo went to metropolitan China. Rosalind Goforth, in her biography of her husband, noted that in the summer of 1932, after six months of vigorous evangelistic work, the Goforths had:

> the most delightfully quiet, refreshing holiday of their life, by the sea at Peitaiho, the most beautiful summer resort in the Far East. Each evening towards sundown, chairs were drawn together on the west veranda and here we sat drinking in the marvellous beauty of the scene before us. The wide, deep valley, reaching far westward to the mountain ranges beyond.[79]

The missionary resorts were geared toward the needs of the adults, and it was the loneliness of the missionary children that especially struck Fleming, an upper-class outsider, who looked at the antics of the vacationing missionaries during his 1933 visit to Kuling with an unflattering and satirical eye. He wrote that "the foreign children were all pale and mostly querulous. One could not help feeling sorry for them, condemned by a combination of heroism and piety in their parents to exchange the untasted fields and friendships of their native land in a country which offers few amenities to a child."[80] The case of John Holmes in Japan or the boy in Hoiryung showed that children had to develop an independent streak or a knack at hunting game in order to combat the loneliness of living in provincial Japan or Korea.

Just as at Karuizawa, the gathering of missionaries at Wonsan Beach during the summer allowed for "the annual obligatory mission meeting."[81] In 1930, MacRae, who had returned to Korea after his furlough without his wife and family, went from Lungchingtsun to Wonsan Beach to attend the mission's annual meeting, and "for the months of July and August he was able to enjoy fellowship with missionaries from Australia, the United States, and those of his own mission from other missions."[82] At the end of the 1930s, the Japanese authorities moved the missionaries off Wonsan Beach, but as late as July 1941 Murray and some other missionaries still in Korea were able to go to Whajinpo Beach, where many Westerners also had summer cottages.[83] The Japanese were loath to allow foreigners in places where they might observe naval or military movements, and most likely this was the reason why Wonsan Beach was closed to foreigners. During normal times, however, it was a place for fellowship that might or might not have been relaxing.

Fellowship was also apparent at Christmas. In 1921, her first Christmas in the mission field and at Lungchingtsun, Murray was invited on Christmas Eve to dinner at Dr. Stanley Martin's house, and she wrote that,

> for this family occasion, all who were far from home had been invited; among them, Mr. Grierson, a lonely and somewhat recluse Englishman, Mr. Hansen, a Scandinavian, and Mrs. Nadarov, a Russian woman who lived at Kookjaka, about fifteen miles away. After an excellent dinner of pheasant, we played games, heard music, and sang carols.[84]

Christmas Day celebrations

> began at four in the morning with carols sung under our windows and outside all the Christian homes in the town by the boys and girls of the mission schools. They came in separate groups, a proper distance apart, and sang in the below zero cold till their throats were hardly fit to take part in the regular Sunday morning service which was a special Christmas celebration.[85]

Many of those who packed the church for the Korean Christmas service had never attended a Christmas service before but had come out of curiosity or to hear their children sing. The importance of singing as both a part and an attraction of Christian services should not be underestimated. The joyfulness of this first Christmas in the mission field, as well as the novelty of attending not only Korean services but also a Chinese Christian service followed by a Chinese meal with the Chinese pastor and his congregation,[86] made a lasting impression on Murray. It was the contact with ordinary Koreans (or, in this case, Chinese) that helped to deepen the affection with that Murray came to regard Koreans. The busy life of a missionary doctor, with its constant medical demands, often meant that there was little time for Christian work even within the hospital, let alone beyond it. The lack of opportunity to engage in direct Christian work was often one of the nagging disappointments for missionary doctors. The Koreans with whom Murray had the most contact were the Korean doctors and staff at the Hamheung hospital.

Whereas Murray looked after the maternity, gynecology, and tuberculosis departments within the hospital, a Korean doctor was normally employed to deal with general male surgery. Yet Murray did not restrict herself to treating women only.[87] Indeed, she saw it as her goal to alter the perception, prevalent when she first arrived in Korea as a result of the example of Dr. Kate McMillan, her predecessor at Hamheung, as well as other female missionary doctors in Korea, that "the term 'woman doctor' [was] a byword for inferior standards."[88] Over the course of her long and distinguished missionary career in Korea, which lasted into the 1960s, she was able to achieve her goal.

Sometimes it was difficult to keep Korean doctors, because good surgeons were at a premium, and there was the pull to return to work at the Severance Union Medical Hospital in Seoul, the alma mater of those who came to Hamheung. This was the case with Dr. Koh, Murray's particular friend, who—after serving at the hospital in Hamheung for a number of years—was transferred to the Severance Union Medical Hospital in 1936. Koh was a competent surgeon and a person whose judgment Murray could unhesitatingly trust. It proved difficult to find a suitable replacement for him. In 1941, when it became evident that Murray or any other foreigner could not act as the superintendent of the Hamheung hospital, Dr. Koh, who had adopted the Japanese name of Takahashi (as Koreans were required to do by law), was persuaded to return from Seoul to take charge. Another Korean doctor with whom Murray got on well was Dr. Kim Hyo-Soon, a female staff doctor, who helped with the maternity cases. And a Korean on whom Murray relied for sound advice and help was Elder Lee of the YMCA in Hamheung, whose son was the doctor in charge of the hospital's Ear, Nose, and Throat Department.[89] In difficult times, such as when Scott and Fraser—on a trip to Lungchingtsun in October 1941—failed to return to Hamheung at the arranged time, Murray worried that they had been arrested by the Manchukuoan authorities, she turned to Elder Lee for advice as to what was the best thing to do.

As well as her Korean friends, Murray was close to Ada Sandell and her successor, Beulah Bourns, who worked as nursing superintendents at the hospital and lived in the single missionary woman's residence with Murray in the Hamheung compound. As a single woman, her closest Western friends were other Canadian WMS missionaries. Ruth Compton Brouwer has pointed out that Murray, during her first missionary term in Korea, had been very lonely and had escaped from the overcrowded conditions and the tensions in the WMS residence at Hamheung by living as well as working in the hospital.[90] In normal times, there seems to have been little social contact with the married missionaries and their families. Necessity threw Murray and Bourns together with Scott and Fraser in the Hamheung compound after the start of the Pacific War.

Murray also had some contact with the Japanese. On one occasion in the early 1930s, she was invited with other dignitaries in charge of hospitals or schools to attend a celebratory party given by the provincial governor on the occasion of the emperor's birthday. Unfortunately, the party was ruined for Murray by an irritating and drunk Japanese army officer who made unwelcome advances.[91] What dealings she had with the Japanese, and they were restricted to police and officials, were almost always unpleasant. Murray believed that because she was a woman she did not count for much in Japanese eyes,[92] and this misogyny is likely why Japanese did not pay attention to her. During the late 1930s, like other missionaries, however, she was watched and followed by the police when she made trips into the countryside, and probably the Koreans whom she spoke to were later questioned. Nevertheless, apart from the occasional unexpected police visit to the hospital to ensure that the proper blackout measures had been carried out, there were few problems with the Japanese.

Although the experiences of a medical missionary in colonial northern Korea were different from those of the missionaries in Japan, a deep current of affection for and strong commitment to ordinary Japanese or Koreans runs through all of them. All the missionaries were changed by their experiences living among the Japanese or Koreans. The missionaries lived a privileged life in comparison to that of many of the Japanese or Koreans whom they wished to convert. However, it was a life that often meant long separations from children and family in Canada. Despite the loneliness, most missionaries were prepared to spend the rest of their working lives in the mission field, but the start of the Pacific War shattered their world and forced them to return home. Their lifestyle had helped to shield them from the political changes that were taking place in Japan and East Asia during the 1930s. As a result, it was all the more shocking for missionaries to feel in the late 1930s open hostility to foreigners in Japan. They had allowed themselves to believe that the political difficulties of the moment would pass.

CHAPTER NINE
Canadian Missionary Attitudes to Politics in Japan

The Manchurian incident of 1931 showed that missionaries and Japanese Christians alike held strong views on the actions of the Japanese government and military. Yet, because the opinions of Canadian missionaries about events taking place in Chientao and Manchuria in the aftermath of the Manchurian incident also indicate, missionaries were concerned primarily with the political or military actions that had an immediate impact on their Christian work. Once the international crises over the Manchurian incident, the Shanghai crisis of 1932, and the subsequent formation of Manchukuo had subsided, the political changes in Japan during the early 1930s attracted little attention from missionaries. Japan's withdrawal from the League of Nations did not excite much comment. Perhaps one reason was the death in 1933 of Nitobe Inazo, a key Japanese Christian link with the league and a man who had looked favourably on missionaries.[1]

Because the arrests of Chinese Christians in Mukden in October 1935 or the difficulties that confronted Mackay and other missionaries at the Tamsui Middle School vividly illustrate, the sensitivity of Japanese colonial or military authorities to any perceived anti-Japanese feeling by Chinese Christians or Canadian missionaries could result in serious problems for the Christian and missionary movements. It was not without reason that Canadian Presbyterians in Manchuria and north Taiwan, because well as their United Church colleagues in northern Korea, eschewed political comment. Understandably, it was the missionaries in the centre of the empire, in metropolitan Japan, who retained the freedom, though letters mailed through the Japanese-controlled post could be censored, to comment in private letters to their superiors in Toronto about the changing political situation in Japan during the second half of the 1930s.

There was no theological imperative for missionaries to comment on or to press for political change. Canadian Anglicans steered clear of observations on political events in their correspondence and reports concentrating instead on their Christian work. Yet United Church missionaries in Japan took a different line, partly because their superiors in Toronto were interested in knowing what was going on in Japan. This knowledge was important to them, for the actions of the Japanese government and military had profound implications for the Canadian missionary movement not only in Japan and its colonies but also in metropolitan China. Just as important, however, the United Church missionaries in Japan thought obliged to explain their perceptions of the Japanese side of events in Japan and East Asia to those in Toronto, partly to sustain support for missionary work in Japan at a time when Japanese actions in China were being criticized overseas. Japan missionaries also attempted to supply information to counter, or at least to balance, the views of China missionaries in regard to the crisis in East Asia. This was an uphill battle, one that Japan missionaries had lost by 1940.

Despite the efforts of the Japan missionaries, however, by the summer of 1940 Jesse Arnup, the United Church missionary society secretary, had thrown his influential support behind Chiang Kai-shek. The Chinese Kuomintang (KMT) leadership put considerable stock in gaining the moral support of North American and European Christians in their struggle against Japan, and in this of course, they were immeasurably helped by the fact that Chiang Kai-shek publicly professed to be a Christian, and a Methodist to boot. For their part, the Japanese were also conscious of the need to ensure that their Christians supported Japan. Christian support for China in Canada and the West had consequences for the missionary movement in Japan. Although there was a definite connection between diplomatic tensions between Japan and Britain or Canada and subsequent difficulties for Christians, Japanese authorities did not differentiate between the statements of diplomats, politicians, and religious leaders. Because their export of state Shinto to Korea and Taiwan or their championing of Confucian ceremonies in Manchuria reveals, the Japanese authorities thought that religious organizations and ideas were tools to be controlled and used by the state for national purposes. So, when the archbishop of Canterbury prominently participated in a meeting at Albert Hall in late 1937 that chastised Japanese actions in China, it was understood that he was expressing the official view of the Church of England and, implicitly, the view of the British government. It is not surprising, then, that following the Albert Hall meeting Japanese Anglicans and Western Anglican missionaries in Japan found themselves in difficulties with the Japanese authorities.

United Church missionaries obviously wanted to avoid similar difficulties for Japanese Methodists as a result of United Church leaders supporting China. Perhaps it is to go too far to suggest that Western Christian support for China resulted in the destruction of the Western missionary movement in Japan. Yet it is no coincidence that the intense Japanese Christian drive to forge church union in Japan late in the summer of 1940 took place in the wake of the arrest of British subjects in Japan and Japanese associated with them, among whom were British Salvation Army missionaries and Japanese Salvationists. Although these arrests demonstrated Japanese displeasure with British diplomatic policy toward China, the arrest of the Salvationists might also be taken as an expression of Japanese displeasure with Christian support for China.

The situation in China was the central concern of Canadian missionary comment in the late 1930s. Missionaries in Japan were blinkered by their deep affection for and loyalty to ordinary Japanese and therefore could not see that the Japanese government was motivated by aggressive and deceitful ambitions, both internally and externally. Furthermore, missionaries remained naïvely optimistic, until the fall of 1940, that a peaceful resolution to the Sino-Japanese War could be reached. Unfortunately for them, because they were perceived as being blatantly pro-Japanese at a time when there was widespread criticism of Japan in Canada as a result of the actions of the Japanese army in China, their ability to influence missionary leadership in Toronto to take a broad and balanced view of the crisis in East Asia was limited.

Although missionaries in Japan were pro-Japanese, in the second half of the 1930s they began to notice the changing atmosphere in Japan, of which the shrine question was only one manifestation. For the first time since the Manchurian incident, they began to express concern about political trends. Among the most prominent and disturbing of these new political trends was the rise of Japanese ultranationalism, that was seen, at least initially, in the old-fashioned terms of the challenge that it posed to Christianity and to Christian work in Japan.

DARKENING CLOUDS OF ULTRANATIONALISM

The difficult political circumstances under that missionary work was being conducted was described in no uncertain terms in *The United Church of Canada Year Book, 1936*:

> The work in Japan of the United Church has been carried out against the dark background of national and international unrest that beclouds the Far East. It is impossible for a mission to carry on its work detached from the swift currents of life and thought that are sweeping through the country. The intensifying of extreme nationalism has made more difficult the propagation of a faith that knows no national boundaries. The open preparation for possible war does not harmonize with the gospel of peace.[2]

It was also noted that the Church in Japan was feeling "the pressure of ultranationalism." Christian publications were carefully scrutinized by the authorities, and Christian speakers had to be guarded in what they said. It was only natural that Japanese Christians should be influenced by the ultranationalistic feelings within Japanese society, but the meaning of ultranationalism appears to have evaded missionaries. It was accepted naïvely that the impact of ultranationalistic feelings on Japanese Christians expressed itself in a positive response to the Japanization of the Christian movement. Ultranationalism led, according to the Canadian missionary report, to a legitimate desire in Japanese Christians to "want to feel that they are Christians and Japanese. They want their church to be a Japanese church, their schools to be Japanese schools, the Christian movement to be a Japanese movement," and "the missionary must recognize this as natural and inevitable, and have understanding and sympathy enough to make his leadership inconspicuous, and to sink his personal ambitions completely."[3] The invidious nature of ultranationalism was not understood, especially in terms of its potentially destructive consequences for both the Japanese Christian movement and the foreign missionary movement.

However, some missionaries recognized that the prevailing atmosphere left many Japanese Christians confused. In January 1936, Dan Norman wrote to Arnup in Toronto a letter in that he enclosed a newspaper clipping about a memorial service for the souls of rats; Norman thought that the article might interest Arnup because, coupled with "the intense military-nationalistic air that prevails," it would give him "some idea of the conditions of things out here just now ... and for some time past." Norman added that "the majority of Christian pastors and workers are bewildered or benumbed and have no positive message of life and salvation."[4] Clearly, he was concerned more with the need for Japanese Christian workers to find a positive message of life and salvation in the military-nationalistic atmosphere than with the political roots of the changing conditions in Japan.

Some attempt was made to try to understand changing Japanese thought. In January 1936, Muto Takeshi, the American-university-educated Japanese pastor in charge of the Central Tabernacle Church, gave a paper, clearly directed toward a foreign missionary audience, on the Christian message and its relation to Japanese thought. In explaining why "among us Japanese people it has become almost a vogue to study afresh the Japanese mind and character," Muto argued that "a cause of this situation is the problem of economic distribution or of social justice."[5] Just as was the case in other countries, he noted, "in connexion with the distribution of wealth, we were presented with two opposing standards:—the one is *capitalism*, the other, *communism*."[6] Although the vogue in studying the Japanese spirit was seemingly a reaction against these Western standards, Muto still believed that the rampant nationalism of Japan was closely linked to important Western ideas. He believed that "the most prominent nationalistic thinkers in Japan learned their nationalism from the western countries. ... In explaining their principle, they, without exception, use the philosophy of the west— Hegelianism mostly."[7] The use of Western ideas to support nationalism also meant that there was still a chance for Christianity.

THE 26 FEBRUARY 1936 INCIDENT
AND ITS AFTERMATH

On 26 February 1936 in Tokyo, young officers assassinated members of the cabinet in an attempt to stage a coup d'etat.[8] E. C. Hennigar, a United Church missionary in Tokyo, was caught up in the excitement of the incident; like thousands of other Tokyoites, he could not resist the temptation to go downtown to Tokyo Station and witness the drama first-hand. Hennigar noted about sightseers around Tokyo Station on February 27 that "every student in town had turned out to 'have a look see.'"[9] Yet, interestingly, writing on February 29 to Arnup, he believed that those in Toronto probably knew more about what was really happening in Tokyo than he did because the news in Japan was heavily censored. The assassination of the finance minister and a former prime minister had been kept a secret for twenty-four hours because of the effect that it might have on the stock market. Hennigar did not know how many others had been killed or why the incident had taken place. He conjectured that "the result of last week's elections was not pleasing to the conservative party in the army. It seems that some young officers in the Azabu regiment who were on duty during the night of the 25th–26th ordered the men out at 4 a.m. ostensibly for maneuvers."[10] Apart from what he garnered downtown, his information came from listening to sporadic radio broadcasts (the radio was off the air for two days at the beginning of the crisis) and from reading the papers. Despite censorship, Hennigar reached a reasonable assessment of what had happened. Clearly, there was a serious division in the army:

> One group, all *young* officers, wish to eliminate "those who stand between the Emperor and the people." That is what they say; whether they would go to the extreme of doing away with parliamentary government or not is not certain. I imagine what they want is army rule in the name of the Emperor. How widespread this is in the army we do not yet know. Rumour has it that certain regiments ordered to the city yesterday to put down the disturbance refused to come. Now whether that is true no one, least of all we foreigners, has any way of knowing.[11]

Even though the incident had thrown political and military Tokyo into turmoil, life for most people went on almost as normal. Hennigar noted that "orders are taken over the phone and goods delivered to our door as if nothing were happening. Some of the delivery boys from down town have had to come by roundabout routes but a slight delay is all the inconvenience we have thought."[12] That Tokyoites went about their normal business likely tended to mask the seriousness of the crisis.

At the end of March 1936, Dan Norman linked the motives behind the February 26 incident to the malaise that he saw affecting Christian work. About the participants in the incident, he wrote that "some wanted to foment war with Russia & some opposed it & paid for their efforts to keep the peace with their lives," and he added that "nationalism and militarism explains the dumbness, badness & ineffectiveness of the Church here."[13] In Norman's view, nowhere was this ineffectiveness more evident than at the Kwansei Gakuin.

Hennigar was more positive about the overall impact of the February 26 incident, for he wrote in May 1936 that

> the Diet, now in session, has really ushered in a new day for liberalism in Japan. I feel more hopeful now than at any time in the past five or six years. We are seeing the resurrection of liberalism and free speech. The recent election let into the Diet a stream of new life. No doubt of that. And the way the newspapers, the Nichi Nichi (the Army organ, if there is one) have endorsed these speeches is really most encouraging.[14]

He was particularly heartened by the death sentence given to Colonel Aizawa, whose arrest after murdering General Nagata Tetsuzan had been one of the causes of the February uprising, as a step in the right direction.[15] A year later, however, Howard Outerbridge was more cautious about the political future but pinned some hope on the new prime minister, Konoe Fujimaro. In June 1937, Outerbridge wrote that there was a new cabinet, but he thought that any sudden change would be unlikely:

> our new Premier, Prince Konoe, is broad-minded and well-read. He has a son in Princeton, and made a special study of Marxianism during his student days. He is conservative, but appreciates the liberal point of view, and respects the opinion of the people. So we're hoping. How he will make out, wedged between the military party on the one hand and the popular will on the other, remains to be seen.[16]

Unfortunately, the hopes that Outerbridge held for Konoe were quickly dashed.

THE MARCO POLO BRIDGE INCIDENT AND WAR IN NORTH CHINA

It was the sudden outbreak of war in China following the Marco Polo bridge incident of July 1937 that sparked renewed missionary interest in political and military affairs. Prior to this incident, there was some missionary sympathy for Chiang Kai-shek, the Chinese Nationalist leader, particularly at the time of the

Sian incident of late 1936, when the generalissimo was kidnapped by Chinese communists.[17] They staged the Sian incident in order to try to convince Chiang to form a united front with them to combat Japanese aggression in north China.[18] After agreeing to the united front, and by doing so gaining his freedom, Chiang publicly declared that his Christian faith had helped to sustain him during the time that he was kidnapped.[19] His claim might have gained support for the Nationalists among missionaries, but events in north China were bringing about a major confrontation between China and Japan. In the wake of the first news of the Marco Polo bridge incident, Outerbridge wrote to Arnup that he hoped common sense would prevail:

> Certainly China has everything to lose by starting anything just at this stage. They would be further ahead if they used their ancient more patient methods for a while longer, no matter what Japan has done. Their only hope is to get help from Russia, and she will be no more helpful an overlord than Japan has been,— quite possibly a worse.[20]

There was some logic to this idea in light of the long-standing Russo-Japanese rivalry for control over north China.

Outerbridge received information about the fighting in north China from the *Japan Advertiser*, from English-language magazines, and from reprints of vernacular press editorials, for he sent clippings from these sources to Arnup in Toronto. In August 1937, Outerbridge wrote to Arnup that Japan seemed preparing for a long and hard war. In his opinion, the only reason for the extensive preparations being made as well as the large number of troops being sent overseas was that Japan thought that it would have to face both China and Russia before the conflict ended. He lamented that, "if she would only realize that no one wins a war today, and be satisfied to strengthen herself economically for a decade or two more and give her people a chance, she would be much wiser. But she will have to go her own way, I suppose."[21] Arnup appreciated Outerbridge's "guarded comments on the war situation," for he was hearing a different point of view from China missionaries on furlough.[22] Information about what was going on was clearly in short supply in Japan, for Outerbridge thought, in early September 1937, that Arnup probably knew as much about the war situation as he did.[23] Yet what Outerbridge could provide Arnup with was a sense of Japanese attitudes toward the war:

> To the casual observer there is an entire unanimity of purpose, and a gradual awakening to the conviction that it is a big drive that is on, which may take a long time. Most of the people see only the censored reports and have no basis for objection even if they felt inclined to make any, which they do not. Among some of the Christian people, especially the young and idealistic, there is a good deal of real agony of spirit over the whole affair. They know however that any expressed opposition would be summarily dealt with, and so are for the most

part silent.[24]

Outerbridge recognized that Japanese people ran the risk of getting into serious trouble with the authorities if they openly criticized Japanese actions and that missionaries also had to be careful about what they wrote, for the mail was censored. There was no knowing what might happen to Japanese Christians if a missionary wrote something about the war to which the censors took exception. However, in late September 1937, Outerbridge took the opportunity to send a letter to Arnup through E. J. O. Fraser, the United Church Korea missionary, passing through Kobe on his way home to Canada; Outerbridge expressed his deeply held opinions about the war in China in considerable detail. The letter illustrates the dilemma for Canadian missionaries concerning the war, for though they might condemn the actions of the Japanese army in China, they were unable to condemn the Japanese people.

It was clear to Outerbridge that the Japanese army had been planning their advance into north China for some years and perhaps that this action would have taken place in 1935 or 1936 except for the restraint put on the army by the more liberal statesmen.[25] He reported that he had been told that an article in the daily newspaper, the *Asahi Shinbun*, had warned the girls attending the YWCA summer conference that "they must not believe the reports of the papers that Japan had been forced into this thing, or had any altruistic purpose in it all. This was merely the next stage of the great push for empire." Outerbridge added:

> In this conviction I believe all intelligent people are united, unfortunately however there are not so many of them, or at least, they don't like to admit it when they are constantly being bombarded through radio, press and addresses with the claim that it is a righteous war of self-defence to keep the peace of the far east. People naturally hate to admit that their government is deliberately deceiving them, and hope for the best, and refuse to admit the worst, in spite of their convictions that it is true.[26]

Yet the war in north China made surprisingly little difference to the normal pattern of life for those in Japan. Outerbridge pointed out that, apart from troop trains being much in evidence, together with flag-waving crowds of people who had been detailed to see them off, there was little apparent change from peacetime. This situation made it all the more difficult to elicit what Japanese people really thought about the war.

In private, Japanese people would talk frankly to Outerbridge about the current ideas on the China situation, but few were prepared to do more than that. However, although people might not be willing to speak openly about the war, they did hold views about the future. There was some suspicion about the call-up of men to the colours, because it had drawn from a broad pool that included the old and the young, and so, for example, relatively few students at the Kwansei Gakuin had been drafted up to that time. The explanation was that Japan anticipated a more difficult enemy in the future, namely the Soviet Union. Outerbridge thought that a Russo-Japanese war was "one of those inevitable things that we must expect sooner or later, much as we may dread it."[27] Although there was a conviction in the army that "Russia is now extremely weak because of the internal troubles, and the recent 'purge,' and that there will never be a better time," Outerbridge thought otherwise: "I am not so sure of Russia's feebleness . . . and fear that the task may be more difficult than many now believe." He added that some were greatly alarmed at the possible outcome of such a war, "predicting Japanese cities destroyed, widespread havoc and ultimate revolution among the people of this country. I cannot find any reasonable basis for such fears however. Certainly Russian airplanes will come over, but I don't think we need to anticipate any widespread destruction or an uprising of the people."[28] Outerbridge was correct in his view that the Japanese were greatly underestimating the strength of the Soviet Union, as the Japanese defeat at the battle of Nomonhan in 1939 vividly illustrated. Yet it is clear that he—and most people at that time—underestimated the damage that air raids could cause to Japanese cities.

Outerbridge believed that the Japanese would gain much more Western sympathy for their war in China if they stopped engaging in weak propaganda about the menace to Japan's lifeline in Manchuria or about preventing China and Russia from uniting to spread communism throughout East Asia and truthfully put the war down to economic need caused by the immigration and trading practices of Western nations. He argued that "Japanese make poor liars, which proves perhaps that they are fundamentally honest, but I think that in this case if they told the truth there would be much more foreign sympathy than they can expect on the basis of their present apologetic."[29] At the same time, in regard to Western attitudes toward Japan, he argued that "the one place where *we* fall down is in expecting Japan, a non-Christian nation, to show to the world an example of unselfishness and Christian pacifism that no Christian nation has yet reached."[30] Adopting a common tack to counter Western criticism of Japanese actions in China, Outerbridge pointed to examples of questionable behaviour by the United States and Britain—including American actions in the Philippines, Panama, and Nicaragua and British ones during the Boer War and at Amritsar—to show that the Western powers had skeletons in their own closets and should not be so critical of Japan.

Outerbridge remained fervently loyal to the Japanese people. As much as he hated what was going on in China, he wrote that

> I can't shut my eyes to the fact that we have here a people of wonderful energy and intelligence and determination, loyally determined to make their land and their nation second to none, and ready to toil and die like the microscopic coral insects, in order that sometime there may rise above the waves something that

is beautiful and good and enduring.

He went on to reiterate that

> for what Japan is doing in China I have no apology. It may be economic necessity, but if so it is devilish in its method. But for the Japanese people as a whole, for what they are and are willing to endure, for their loyalty and their native kindliness and charm, I have only kind thoughts and feelings. If this nation could only become truly Christian,—what a wonderful nation it would be.[31]

Despite the actions of the Japanese military in China, Outerbridge and his fellow Canadian missionaries in Japan continued to hold the Japanese people in the highest regard.

Yet, whereas missionaries remained loyal to the Japanese, the latter seemingly were prone to anti-Western feelings. In October 1937, Outerbridge mentioned that

> there was a strong anti-British tide of feeling flowing in from somewhere. I am not sure just where. If it comes from the War-office it may presage something unpleasant in the future for all of us. Some even go so far as to say that Britain is the real enemy of Japan, more so than China or Russia.[32]

The timing suggests that this wave of Anglophobia in Japan was related to the archbishop of Canterbury's actions concerning the war in China. Despite the current anti-British feeling among the Japanese, Outerbridge was encouraged by the attempt of Matsuoka Yosuke, a leading Japanese political figure, to justify Japan's actions along economic lines. This move struck him as

> a far better approach to the problem for American consumption than most of the propaganda the Foreign Office is pulling out. The fundamental need for raw materials and markets, coupled with the defence that is the method always used up to date, is probably the best that can be said. I don't think they will ever convince the world that the Chinese drove them into it.[33]

In early January 1938, Outerbridge took heart from the fact that Japanese attitudes toward Britain were becoming milder and that, with Japan's hands full with the war in north China, the danger of a clash with the Soviet Union was diminishing. He was hopeful that "1938 may not be so disastrous a year as a month or two ago seemed inevitable. But there—my wife tells me that I am 'disgustingly optimistic,' and although I do not admit that charge, I will admit that my prophecies are usually wrong."[34] At the end of January 1938, although Anglo-Japanese relations continued to improve, Outerbridge perceptively noted that the main trouble still remains. Britain is still at Shanghai, still holds Hongkong and the Singapore base. Until she gets out Japan feels she has a grievance,—at least the extremists do. One hears frank statements from time to time that the Orient must be left for the orientals, which means that France Holland and Great Britain must get out. I think that many of the people really feel that the very existence of these countries out here in the Far East constitutes a sort of insult and a grave threat to Japan's existence. It is not clearly argued, and certainly would not be admitted by most statesmen, but it is there in the minds of a great many people of the rightest group.[35]

He went on to stress that there was a general feeling of pessimism among his Western friends about the future, and his Japanese ones thought that "the 'net is tightening' and they feel the pressure increasing all the time."[36] For Japanese Christians, the pressure was to show themselves patriotic in the face of outside secular criticism. Outerbridge certainly thought that any movement that had patriotism attached to it would likely find supporters.

Yet the patriotic feeling in Japan was conducive to the success of the national spiritual mobilization campaign that the government began in the fall of 1937. Outerbridge wrote that the government was "very anxious that the 'spiritual mobilization' of the country,—the complete unification of everybody to meet the present emergency,—shall not be in any way interfered with. In this they have been remarkably successful. Externally at least there is complete uniformity."[37] He explained that "the majority accept without question what they are told, as they see no inconsistency in the situation whatever."[38] In a conversation with Dean Kanzaki at the Kwansei Gakuin, Outerbridge had been told simply that "these are abnormal times, when normal principles and methods of conduct do not hold. The country is at war, and we must fit ourselves into that abnormal situation."[39] One Japanese Christian teacher expressed to Outerbridge a concern that had a universal ring to it: his greatest fear was not for the soldiers at the front but the impact of the war on children, learning to play with guns and to hate the Chinese as their enemies.[40] This fear struck a responsive cord in Outerbridge because he remembered similar things happening to Canadian children during World War I.

Canadian missionaries were swift to draw parallels between what was going on in Japan and what had happened in Canada during the Great War. The spectre of that war and its impact upon Canadian society, as well as their sense of having been betrayed by British and Canadian political leaders because they had failed to make good on the promises of a better postwar world, clouded missionary judgment about what was going on in Japan. In drawing parallels between the Great War and the situation in Japan in early 1938, Outerbridge conveniently overlooked the fact that Canadian youth had gone to war for very different reasons than the Japanese who were fighting an aggressive war in north China.

Although Japanese children were learning to shoot Chinese in their playground games, Outerbridge mentioned that the Chinese in Kobe were still being well treated, though they were required to pledge their allegiance to the new provisional government in north China or face deportation.

Missionaries found it hard to accept that a war was going on in that Japan was seen as the aggressor by the rest of the world. In October 1937, Melvin Whiting, writing from the campus of the Canadian Academy in Kobe, pointed out to friends in Canada that

> We who love Japan and her people, we who have given years of our lives in service in this country regret very much that at this time she has lost the sympathy and support of so many of the nations. The Japanese are a wonderful people and do not want war.... The situation takes us back twenty years when an unscrupulous war propaganda, without any regard for facts, was sweeping our own western lands. At that time the people in our own fair Canada saw things that were black as if they were pure white. A narrow, prejudiced, arrogant, violent nationalism swept us off our feet. Our British spirit of love was submerged beneath a mass of propaganda. We went into a war to end war, but how we were deceived! People are still being deceived. It is the same old game over again. "How long, O Lord...."[41]

Having been deluged by the propaganda of the Great War, many Canadian missionaries in Japan saw the anti-Japanese reports in the Western press through jaundiced eyes. Whiting was not alone among Canadian missionaries in expressing pacifist feelings. As late as June 1938, Alfred Stone wrote from Nagano to friends in Canada that he had taken a pacifist stand for the last fifteen years but still believed that "Japan (who has only 75 years of Protestant Christian History) is now doing what all the 'Christian' nations of the 19th Century did without apology. That does not make Japan right; for war is wrong; but it does mean that we Westerners have to be humble as we criticise."[42] Sybil Courtice, also in June 1938, wrote to Mrs. Taylor of the United Church WMS in Toronto in much the same vein as Stone. Courtice noted that war could not be justified but that,

> with facts of history before us, we cannot but see Japan's case and there is no escaping the fact that there is some responsibility even on the part of our own loved land for the circumstances which led inevitably to the present situation between these two neighbouring countries of China and Japan. And that fact cuts like a knife into the heart. Just a day or two ago we read in the [*Japan*] *Advertiser* the statement that America, and the same comes often from Britain too, will protect her nationals and her *trade* wherever they may be. It sounds like the same old story.[43]

She admitted having her own style of pacifism, but she said that the more I think of it, the more I see that Dr. Kagawa struck the nail on the head when he said, "Tell your people to keep on loving." The way of the loving heart is the only way for the true peacemaker, who shall be called the child of God.[44]

Most importantly, Courtice wrote that "we do not love war—but we do love the Japanese people and we can see that there is a long history leading up almost inevitably to the present situation."[45] The problem was that missionaries seemingly could not distinguish between the Japanese people, whom they genuinely loved, and the actions of the Japanese government and military.

THE NANKING ATROCITIES AND THE CONTINUING WAR

By June 1938, missionaries had been aware for some months of the behaviour of the Japanese army in China. The atrocities committed by the Japanese army in Nanking were well known to Canadian missionaries. In February 1938, Hennigar wrote to Arnup in Toronto that

> it seems that our Japanese army absolutely ran amok in Nanking. We had heard similar stories from Tientsin last fall, but I almost refused to credit the stories of rape and looting we heard then, I could not bring myself to believe that these nice Japanese boys that we know so well could do the things told of them.[46]

Because Hennigar's source of information about the Nanking atrocities came from a parcel of uncensored mail from China containing letters from missionaries in the Chinese interior as well as Nanking itself, there was no denying the veracity of the reports. What happened in Nanking lent credence to a report that Hennigar heard through his friends in the Purity Society, that brothel keepers in Japan were recruiting, with the connivance of the Japanese army, 3,000 Japanese women to take to Shanghai to comfort the soldiers. Some Japanese people opposed such recruiting through the Home Office, but the officials there had no power to stop it. Apparently, according to Hennigar's sources, half the men in hospital in Japan had venereal disease, and the conditions among the troops in China had become extremely bad.[47] The Nanking atrocities, in other words, served to bring to the fore in missionary minds other questionable practices of the Japanese army that might have passed unnoticed. This recruitment must have been all the more shocking to Hennigar, who had devoted many years of his life to fighting prostitution in Japan. (The issue of the recruitment of Korean women to comfort Japanese soldiers during the later Pacific War—a practice that until recently the Japanese government denied ever took place—became a serious postwar political and diplomatic issue between Japan and the Republic of Korea.)

Outerbridge at the Kwansei Gakuin received the same information as Hennigar from missionary friends in China and was also appalled by what he read. He wrote to Arnup that "they tell a fearful tale of war at its very worst, and as the report is that of eyewitnesses, men of irreproachable honesty, one of whom I know personally, I am afraid there is little room for doubt." He went on to say that

> the most convincing perhaps consists of the correspondence between the Chairman of the Emergency Committee of Nanking University and the Japanese Consul at Nanking,—letters that show that the soldiers who took Nanking were absolutely out of control. The consular authorities seem to have made efforts, but they were utterly helpless.[48]

Outerbridge's friend among the eyewitnesses was, it can reasonably be assumed, Searles Bates, the American missionary who would in June address a meeting of missionaries in Karuizawa that Courtice, among others, attended. The story that the troops, on capturing Nanking, were given "three days 'holiday' without military discipline!!!!" was also mentioned by Hennigar, who believed that the China incident would quickly be over because he had been told that the treasury department could only guarantee the yen until midsummer, and as a result the army would try to end the war before the Japanese currency collapsed.[49] As it turned out, the war in China dragged on.

In early January 1939, Whiting at the Kwansei Gakuin was still hoping that the fighting would be over before the next Christmas. Interestingly, he also attempted to explain why Japanese Christians did not openly oppose the war by pointing out the reply of one of the Japanese Kwansei Gakuin professors to that question:

> if a German, or a Frenchman, or a Czechoslovakian wishes to oppose the policy of his government, he may do so, and then get out of the country, if necessary, and go to America or England, but if I should lose my position I have no place to go. We Japanese have NOWHERE TO GO.[50]

The Japanese professor was taking the easy way out, but Whiting still had great sympathy for him. People such as Yanaihara Tadao, who was prepared to put his Christian principles before his professorial post, were rare.

What made it all the more difficult to oppose the war in China was that there were few obvious signs that a war was going on. It had started a year and a half before, and Japan had sent overseas a million and a half soldiers; nevertheless, Whiting wrote that "If you were to ride on the trains or cars, or go shopping in Kobe or Osaka today, you would never know the country was at war."[51] Although prices were a little higher than before, there were no real shortages of goods. A few months later, in June 1939, Albright indicated that he and other foreigners were being asked to declare all their gold holdings except for dental fillings in preparation for a possible attempt by the government to extract gold from resident foreigners. Although the Japanese government had recently ordered the pegging of commodity prices, salaries, land and house rents, and freights, Albright noted that there was a shortage of sugar and that his grocer had told him that his butter would be partly margarine. Fruit was expensive, but Albright put this down to drought that had also caused electricity and water shortages, rather than the war.[52] Missionaries were also beginning to face considerable and irritating supervision of their movements from the police and authorities.

The red tape and inconveniences that Donald Black, the United Church medical missionary in Lungchingtsun in Manchukuo, mentioned to Armstrong in June 1939 could apply to missionaries in Japan as well as those working in the peninsula. These inconveniences included obtaining permission from the police in order to travel as well as putting up with visits of police detectives to their homes. Black wrote that "every time we wish to leave the town we must go *in person* to the police station in advance and have an entry made in our Residence Certificate as to our date of leaving, date of return, object, etc. We answer various questions and finally get the police seal affixed."[53] Once missionaries embarked on a trip, they could expect to be stopped and questioned and to have their luggage searched. Black also noted, correctly, that "many of the officials would be only too glad to have all foreigners out of the country," but he added that "the common people want us."[54] Nevertheless, Black and most foreign missionaries in either Korea or Japan were prepared for the sake of their Christian work to tolerate such petty annoyances and inconveniences.

CHANGKUFENG, NOMONHAN, AND FEAR OF THE SOVIET UNION

For missionaries, news of the outside world was difficult to obtain. This was especially true of the situation in China. In June 1939, Albright admitted that was very difficult to get direct information about China from the local newspapers. Yet he believed that the situation in China was not good and that what was happening there

> may be another undeclared war in Mongolia and the beginning of a long drawn-out struggle between this country and England-France and perhaps America, resulting in an anti-Japanese combination similar to the anti-German-Italy combination in Europe over the concessions as to the remnant of the open door in China.[55]

Albright also pointed out that there was growing concern about relations with the United States and that the appointment of Admiral Nomura as ambassador there was intended to address that problem. But China and the Soviet Union remained primary concerns. Albright reported that "Wang Ching Wei is being given every possible support in his efforts to form a union government in the occupied territory. The truce with Soviet Russia is welcomed, but her attitude and practice in Poland does not make for confidence. Stalin has out-hitlered Hitler."[56]

In early July 1939, Albright mentioned that

> the European situation has had its repercussions in extraordinary activity in Outer Mongolia. The reports of this which reach us and the reports printed in Shanghai are diametrically opposite. Probably both are coloured, but it is the relative situations of the two forces after the affair is over that counts. And after the so-called victory of Changkufeng Hill affair last year, the Russians still occupied the Hill and Japan had to give up her demand that she count for two in the negotiations to delimit the boundary. This time there may be the same immediate military outcome but a different sequel.[57]

As well as the fighting between the Soviet Union and Japan in Mongolia, Albright reported that negotiations between Britain, France, and Japan were about to start in Tokyo. These talks were apparently intended to solve the crisis in China with a fresh partition of China between the interested parties. Albright thought that Britain would be expected to withdraw from north China but would still be left as the chief exploiter of the Yangtse, whereas France would remain in South China. He believed that the British and French would accept such terms and that Chiang Kai-shek could be persuaded by the British and French to agree to them also. He realized that

> there will be a struggle in Tokyo and it will not be entirely between Britain and Japan, but also between various factions and policies here. But in spite of the uncompromising attitudes announced in advance, I would not be at all surprised to see an outcome such as the above. Indeed it is the only way I can envisage an end to the Incident, now or in the near future.[58]

The settlement of the crisis in north China and the termination of military operations there would leave Japan free to turn its attention to Russia with no third powers present

> to impede her progress or thwart her ambitions. And although North China constitutes a blunt wedge between Communist [sic] China and Soviet Russia, Japan will never feel safe until outer Mongolia is rendered innocuous and the problems of the Northern Fisheries and Saghalien settled, not to mention the

Maritime Provinces themselves.[59]

The mention of the northern fisheries has a contemporary ring to it, because it remains an issue between Japan and Russia. It is interesting that Albright saw north China in terms of a wedge between the Chinese-communist- controlled region of northwestern China centred on Yenan and Soviet Russia. He was undoubtedly expressing a Japanese view of the crisis in north China, and one might conclude that Japan's fight was not with Chiang Kai-shek but with his relatively new allies in Yenan led by Mao Tse-t'ung. This view suggests that the Japanese would have been willing to come to terms with Chiang and the Nationalist government but would have been anxious to gain control of outer Mongolia. This control would inevitably have led to conflict with the Soviet Union, because the Mongolian communist regime was closely allied to Moscow, but outer Mongolia was important because it bordered not only Manchuria but also Chinese-communist-controlled China.

Albright saw that the struggle in China was bringing about profound economic, racial, political, and social changes in Japan. Apparently, the newspapers were talking of a shortage of over 1 million labourers in Japan and claiming that the solution was to bring workers over from Korea. Albright reported that "the gradual application of the Mobilization Bill is changing the whole political and economic organization of life into a more and more regimented state, the effects of which are now beginning to reach the classes most free hitherto—teachers and students."[60] The changes taking place only confirmed in Albright a belief that the Japanese people during the 1930s had jumped from the frying pan into the fire as far as individual freedom was concerned. He recalled that, ten years before,

> one of the first words I had to learn was "ikitsumatta" or "stifled." Everything, Church and state, industry and society, was in a bottle-neck and there was no way to get out. Now Japan has broken out, but in the very doing so, has imposed on herself new bonds of regimentation.[61]

These new bonds meant that all life would be guided and disciplined for state ends. This development, of course, did not augur well for the Christian movement in Japan. A solution to the crisis in China would certainly have helped.

Thus, Albright hoped for a settlement to the crisis through the upcoming negotiations in Tokyo between Britain, France, and Japan. If his premise—that outer Mongolia and the Soviet Union were Japan's primary concerns and not any further expansion south in China—was accepted, then the chances of success in these negotiations would have been reasonable. However, Hennigar reported a different opinion from the streets of Tokyo. Writing three days after Albright, he reported that Tokyo was plastered with anti-British posters calling for Britain to be pushed out of Asia and that there was no room for compromise.[62] Given the anti-British atmosphere, and the Japanese unwillingness to make concessions, the negotiations in Tokyo seemed doomed before they began, despite Albright's optimism for them.

Yet, although political Tokyo was displaying its anti-British fervour, the visit of the Vancouver basket ball team was clearly welcomed. Hennigar noted enthusiastically about the team that

> we have met them at the Legation and sat near, or, once, on their bench at the games. We saw the two games when they won. I guess we had better try to go tonight, for we seem to bring them luck. Three of them tell me they are U. C. C. boys. They are awfully nice boys.[63]

Although it might appear strange that international basketball games could go on quite happily despite the politically inspired anti-British sentiment, personal relations between missionaries and Japanese seemingly remained cordial. In December 1939, Outerbridge noted that his personal relations had never been better, and "in fact there is a general desire on the part of most people to improve relations as much as possible with other countries,—a sentiment that we may expect to grow, if the victory of the allies in Europe seems to become more certain."[64] He was correct to see that improved relations with Britain and Canada had much to do with the estimation of the Japanese government as to the outcome of the war in Europe. Yet he was not so naïve to think that public opinion was naturally in favour of Britain. In writing about the attitude of the Japanese newspapers toward the war in Europe, Outerbridge commented that, even though they claimed strict neutrality, they favoured Germany rather than England. The reason was that

> they had been so emphatic for so long on the superiority of German methods, institutions and armament, and the effete character of poor old worn-out England, that it is hard for them to readjust themselves to the idea of an Anglo-French victory. They were quite clear on the injustice of the Russian invasion of Finland, but not quite so clear about the German aggression in Poland, and other similar events in recent years. There is a very real fear of Russia especially since the Nomonhan incident. That is pretty generally admitted to have been a very unfortunate and unexpected sort of incident, though the word defeat is not used. It has been followed by a greatly accelerated desire to come to terms with Russia on all the outstanding issues.[65]

The extent of the Japanese reverse at the hands of the Soviet army at Nomonhan had been made public in October. In that month, Albright had written that "the losses at Nomonhan are now admitted to be 18,000 casualties and the assurance of superiority of equipment and invincibility of fighting forces has been checked. With over 6,000 miles of border to defend that becomes very significant."⁶⁶ Yet, if Russian success at Nomonhan, in Outerbridge's view, had made Japan seek a settlement with the Soviet Union, then it was also implicitly clear that the British and French would have to demonstrate on the battlefield that they could defeat the Germans before the Japanese would come to terms with them.

The Japanese also faced difficulties in their dealings the United States. Although the Japanese were trying to restore good relations by paying indemnities to the American universities in China whose property had been damaged during the fighting there, the termination of the trade agreement between the two countries in January 1940 was a cause of friction. Many Japanese were upset with the Americans for ending this agreement, and Outerbridge stated that "there seems to be strong tension between two desires, not to kowtow to anyone, on the one hand, and not to lose the trade which is so vital to their well being on the other. And there seems to be likelihood that these can both be very preserved."⁶⁷ Unlike the Russians, whom the Japanese now feared after Nomonhan, the Americans inspired in the Japanese only resentment.

CHIANG KAI-SHEK AND THE CHINA CRISIS

Despite the tensions between Japan and the Western powers, Japan's war in China continued. Outerbridge thought that there was a growing restlessness among the people because of the continued delay in reaching a settlement with Chiang Kai-shek. This restiveness was accentuated, according to Outerbridge, because there were increasing shortages of many goods, particularly those that could be profitably exported or were imported, including coffee, raisins, coconuts, foreign drugs, and groceries. These shortages affected foreigners, with their Western diets, more than Japanese, but Outerbridge also knew that rice was scarce and had heard rumours of the possibility of rice riots, but perhaps even more important was the shortage of coal for heating during the winter. Despite the current difficulties, he reported,

> the merchants . . . predict that next autumn will be the time of most serious shortage and crisis. Just how they know however is hard to tell. Government officials keep warning the people to expect even worse times in the next few years, so evidently they feel that they are in a tight jam.⁶⁸

However, the shortages did not translate into open opposition to the fighting in China. Outerbridge explained that, though the fear that the campaign was not going well in China was becoming more widespread, the Japanese "seem incapable of even considering any solution of the situation but a Japanese victory. They can't stop till they have done something to Chiang, and he seems very hard to do anything to."⁶⁹ In a private conversation with a Japanese friend whom Outerbridge considered an ultranationalist, the Japanese admitted to Outerbridge that

> we know that we can never conquer China. It's too big. You will find that when the final terms are reached, N. China down to the Yellow River will be under one government, friendly to Japan, tho not so closely interwoven with Japanese control as Manchuria. Central and South China will be as independent as they have ever been, except that the rulers must agree to friendly trade relations with Japan.⁷⁰

The sticking point of this partition of China, similar to the terms mentioned by Albright in July before the Anglo-French-Japanese negotiations in Tokyo, was Chiang Kai-shek. According to Outerbridge's friend, "Chiang Kai Shek will probably disappear for a few years, in order to save the face of the Japanese and of the temporary administration. Later he may appear again and become the real ruler of China. There is no one else who can do it as well."⁷¹ Put in those terms, Chiang had only temporarily to step down to save Japanese face and the China problem would seemingly disappear.

In emphasizing the key position that Chiang Kai-shek held in the China crisis in Japanese eyes, Outerbridge quoted Kagawa as saying in a private conversation that "Chiang Kai Shek has already defeated us. We cannot hope to win against him, for we Japanese have not the moral character to win."⁷² Kagawa was too wise to say the same thing publicly in front of a Japanese audience. One of the difficulties for Outerbridge and other missionaries in trying to fathom what was going on was that prominent Christian figures such as Kagawa, whom they had long admired, would tell missionaries one thing in private and Japanese another thing in public.

Although Japanese Christian leaders attempted privately to reassure Canadian missionaries about Japan's intentions in China, Chiang Kai-shek actively curried the support of Christians and foreign missionaries in China for his continued resistance. In an interview with two missionary spokesmen reported in the *Chinese Recorder* of May 1939, Chiang was quoted as saying:

> Christians have left no stone unturned to show their growing interest in the material as well as the spiritual welfare of our suffering people. Missionaries, in particular, have never hesitated to take even the greatest personal sacrifices to heal the wounded and succour the distressed. I welcome this opportunity, therefore, to reiterate the previously expressed appreciation of myself and my countrymen for the unqualified endorsement of our resistance that has come to us so spontaneously and in such unstinting measure from the Christian world.⁷³

The contrast between this expression of gratitude and the actions of the

Japanese authorities toward missionaries in the Japanese Empire could not have been sharper. Madam Chiang Kai-shek made a personal effort to garner the support of the United Church of Canada as well as other missionary groups. She was in correspondence with Arnup and believed, correctly, that he and the Foreign Mission Board of the United Church of Canada stood firmly on China's side in the struggle against Japan. In November 1939, Madam Chiang went so far as to ask Arnup to convey to the Foreign Mission Board "the appreciation of the Generalissimo and myself for the sympathy and help which you have accorded China and her cause since Japan began her aggression on our country."[74] Although Arnup did have sympathy for the Chinese, it would have made his relations with the missionaries in Japan exceedingly difficult if the support that he gave to China was as great as her appreciation implied. In her letter to Arnup, Madam Chiang pointed out that the Chinese had defeated Japanese military drives to take Sian and Changsha and had inflicted upon the Japanese large casualties. Heartened by these successes, she stressed that "the human suffering that has been inflicted upon us and the tremendous losses surely justify the Democracies in at last rendering assistance to us to crush this originator of treaty violation and ruthless aggression in spite of all international laws to safeguard humanity."[75] Madam Chiang was obviously looking to Arnup and his colleagues on the Foreign Mission Board to put pressure on the Canadian government to stop trading with Japan. What is clear from her letter is that she was a consummate propagandist for the Chinese cause.

For their part, Albright and his colleagues in Japan were aware that their attempts to impress upon those at home the need for patience and tolerance in regard to Japan and the war in China could be misunderstood by Arnup and others who were inclined to support China. Indeed, Arnup, in throwing his support behind the Chinese, was likely aware that the possibility of a compromise between China and Japan was remote. Nonetheless, Albright continued to press Japan's case. Indeed, in early February 1940, he even admonished Arnup by saying, "how easy it is to misinterpret when one has a prejudice or is not in sympathy with another."[76]

TYPHOON WEATHER

Albright was increasingly pessimistic by early 1940 about the prospects for peace in East Asia, but there were still signs, albeit weak ones, that the political and military situation in which Japan found itself ensnared would change for the better. Albright and his fellow Canadian missionaries undoubtedly agreed with the view of Bishop Abe Yoshimune of the Japan Methodist Church that Japan was going through typhoon weather, that would eventually play itself out. In any case, missionaries were infused with long-term hope for their Christian work and were used to putting a positive spin even the tiniest indication that their hope was justified. The Saito affair was one incident taken as an indication that there remained a chance for political change.

Albright took heart in the interpellation of Saito Takao, an MP whose speech in the Diet "revealed that there are or were differences of opinion as to the expressed aims of the war even in government circles."[77] Albright was not the only one who saw the Saito case and its consequences as important. A few days after his letter of mid-March, Gwen Norman, writing from Kanazawa, reported that Saito "had the temerity to inquire in the Diet about the China incident. The most pertinent of his questions being how long and whither. Of course he simply voices the opinions of many whispered behind closed doors."[78] His actions led to immediate calls for his expulsion from both the Diet and the Social Mass Party, to which he belonged. Yet the Saito case showed that there were still some people willing to stand up, however unsuccessfully, against the army. Norman took heart in the fact that "there are a few Pyms and Hampdens here."[79] Yet it would turn out to be a forlorn hope that the few Japanese Pyms and Hampdens could achieve anything.

As might be expected, Albright still hoped for a settlement in China. He argued in February 1940 that the statement of the Konoe cabinet in regard to the situation in China "represents an amazingly liberal attitude of any government at war" and that "with such indications of deeper reflection and self-criticism we may expect a growth in sober and reasonable attitudes all along the line."[80] Yet, as always, the problem with Japanese attitudes failed to take into account Chiang Kai-shek; Albright believed that,

> should he [Chiang] continue his resistance, it is difficult to see how there can be much cessation or decrease of the present campaigns. But we are all apt to be like Micawber at times, hoping that something will turn up. Perhaps the psychology which often decides elections is at work, anything for a change.[81]

Yet there was little hope for real change. As Albright wrote in late March, "Chungking seems as resolute as ever and appears to be growing stronger month by month and year by year."[82] According to Albright, the attitude of the United States in lending $20 million to the Chinese, and the policy of France in supporting Chiang by allowing supplies to flow from Indo-China into Yunnan, were important factors in the situation in East Asia. He thought that the end of the Finnish-Soviet War could also result in greater Soviet help for China, and he added that "in other words it is a race between some kind of extrication from the China impasse and vicious inflation resulting in social unrest leading to unpredictable political changes. Certainly such changes would not be in the direction of greater liberalism."[83] He believed that the political parties had been further discredited because of their time-serving attitude over the Saito expulsion case and that there were ambitious men who wanted to see the Diet system eclipsed by a grand council. In regard to Japanese views of Western countries, Albright mentioned that "the attitude toward Germany is still one of pathetic desire to make the best of an uncertain friendship. On the other hand there is still the attempt to blame Britain for Japan's difficulties. Toward America there is rising resentment."[84] One might surmise from this that Albright thought that the United States and Britain were increasingly unable to bring about an end to the situation in China.

The Japanese attempt to create a new regime in China under Wang Ching-wei was apparently not going well, and Albright was worried about the future in China: "there is a strain of fanaticism here that would rather suicide than surrender, and I just wonder. We can only hope and pray that wise counsels will prevail, that the terms of the Konoe policy will be put into effect."[85] Albright hoped that there would be an increasing realization in Japan, China, and the foreign powers concerning the need for conciliation leading to the creation of programs of mutual benefit in north China that would exceed those in Taiwan, Korea, and Manchukuo. Otherwise, he could not envisage a new order in East Asia that would bring either peace or prosperity. Clearly, he had come to the conclusion that Konoe's policy for the creation of a new order in East Asia held the best hope for peace.

While peace was proving elusive in China, serious fighting broke out in Europe. Reminiscent of the difficulty for missionaries to comprehend what was happening in Flanders during World War I, Albright wrote in April 1940 that, "with our garden blossoming and cherry, magnolia, and peach trees burgeoning, it is hard to realize that the Allies, augmented by Norway, are locked in mortal conflict with Germany along the coasts of Denmark and Norway, and no doubt in Sweden long before this reaches you. Japan remains calm."[86] Yet, as far as China was concerned, though he approved of the fact that Japan had omitted a full president and a separate flag and virtually excluded north China from the new regime that it had established in China, he remained worried about possible Soviet incursions. He wondered: "will she [Soviet Russia] strike here or there or press at half a dozen points at once up to the very limit of safe aggression?"[87]

The problems of Korea also gave Albright food for thought during the spring of 1940. In May, the arrival of Black from Lungchingtsun and three female missionaries from other Canadian stations in north Korea on their way home to Canada allowed Albright the opportunity not only to find out what was happening in north Korea but also to send uncensored letters home with them. Both Black and Mary Thomas from Hoiryung emphasized that there was a growing problem with bandits on the border (an area that had been generally free of such activity since the 1930s), for one of the consequences of the Sino-Japanese War was the withdrawal of Japanese troops from the Manchukuo-Korean border. Other issues were also causing problems in Korea, such as the pressure from the government general to induce Koreans to take Japanese names. The changing of names was not a simple matter, and it caused a great deal of work because, according to Albright, "under the exogamic system all members of the same clan are cousins and while specially liable to help one another, may not marry. Hence it is important that in changing names, the members of the same clan should choose the same two-syllable name."[88] Yet it was the shrine question and its relation to the spiritual mobilization campaign that brought the most significant comment from Albright. Quite rightly, he saw the shrine question as only one element in the larger problem of national assimilation in Korea and spiritual mobilization in metropolitan Japan "in the interests of a near-absolute state and a very ambitious continental program."[89] Albright hoped that there would be a lessening of emphasis on the shrine question in Korea and on spiritual mobilization in Japan once the 1940 celebrations for the 2,600th anniversary of the imperial line were over and the war in China had ended. He went so far as to suggest that

> there may even be a reaction before the China Affair is liquidated. For any failure to realize the program on the continent would react upon its authors and the highest authorities ultimately involved. The Army Pamphlet issued in China seems to recognize this possibility and warns against careless words and acts on the part of returning soldiers.[90]

This was wishful thinking.

In August 1940, Albright argued that state Shinto, and Japanese exploitation of Confucianism in Manchukuo, were essential elements in the maintenance of the Japanese Empire. He wrote that they provided the cement that held the empire together.[91] To Albright, as far as Christianity was concerned, "the real question is how far can an independent ethics, religious education or evangelism function in an increasingly totalitarian (Japanese model) state or bloc?"[92] In answer to his own question, he suggested that there was still a possibility for Christianity as long as the government allowed independent ethics or religion to exist within the state framework. For the moment at least, this was the state of affairs in Japan.

However, part of Albright's concern over the ability of Christianity to survive within the Japanese Empire also came from continued anti-British feeling. Fortunately, according to Albright, anti-British demonstrations seemed to be "concomitant of the hot weather. But at least that is the best time for them for us, when we are away from our stations and the necessity of meeting our Japanese colleagues."[93] By the time missionaries returned from their summer vacations in Karuizawa in the autumn, the situation had usually calmed down. August 1940 saw the arrest of a few Japanese citizens in London and other parts of the British Empire in response to the arrest of British citizens in Japanese territory. Among those caught up in the anti-British feeling in Japan was the Salvation Army, that saw five of its senior Japanese officers taken into custody during the summer. The connection between religion and national security was not lost on the Japanese military. Albright quoted from a release by the War Office stating that

> Religion, it goes without saying, is essential to national life. The Army, which has grave concern about defense of the country in the field of thought, is impelled to take action against those who, under the cloak of religion, compromise the intelligence services, by taking positions in the forefront of foreign drives against Japanese thought, or by allowing themselves to become a hotbed of foreign intrigue against Japanese thought, apart from the question of the religion in which they happen to believe.[94]

Albright's comment about this statement was that "responsible Japanese make no distinctions between espionage and propaganda, or between political propaganda and the propagation of religion."[95] To emphasize further the seriousness of the situation, Albright also quoted from a Japanese newspaper, the *Domei*, that the Ministry of Education had

> long been investigating the inner organization of all foreign religious bodies in the country. As almost all of the Christian sects in this country have doctrines and theories that are not in harmony with the national policy [polity?] of Japan, as well as with the traditional thought of the people, who have been brought up in a Buddhist atmosphere, they will have to be reformed to harmonize perfectly with Japanese ideas in the future.[96]

Without the war in China and the resultant deterioration of Anglo-Japanese relations because of Japan's resentment over Britain's perceived support of China, it seems doubtful that the Ministry of Education and the army would have been so intent on harmonizing Christianity with Japanese ideas.

In early September, Albright reported that a more realistic attitude was developing in Japan toward Europe and the United States, in part because of the good understanding between the United States and Britain coupled with the growing American defence budget. Nevertheless, the Japanese government was going ahead with the creation of a new political structure, that saw the disbandment of political parties in the Lower House of the Diet. Moreover, there was growing pressure on foreigners to leave Japan. Albright pointed out that

> it looks as though the Military Police, who are increasing their units far beyond barracks towns and their functions altogether outside of army discipline, would like to get all the [Anglo-American] foreigners out of the country, no doubt under German influence and even pressure. Their technique seems to be to create the impression that all foreigners must leave, in the hope that many will do so voluntarily as a result of veiled threats.[97]

Japanese authorities were bringing pressure on missionaries to give up Christian education and return home. Again, the pressure on the Japanese Christian movement to form a united Protestant Church was another manifestation of the government's desire to rid Japan of foreigners and foreign influence. Albright reported that Hennigar had told him that Bishop Abe of the Japan Methodist Church regarded "the present as typhoon weather, which will blow over."[98] Although Albright partially agreed with that view, he believed that it was too optimistic.

Yet Albright did not give up hope. He downplayed the importance of the tripartite agreement between Japan, Germany, and Italy. At the end of September, he wrote:

> I cannot get excited over the Tri-partite Agreement, since a former Cabinet deliberated on the same general problem in over seventy sessions, before the German-Soviet alliance was announced. And in spite of the latter we have known that there has been a growing trend toward the Axis, because there was nowhere else to go.[99]

Although he believed that Japan would not benefit from the agreement between Germany and Vichy France over Indo-China, he did not see that the new arrangements would make any real difference to American aid to Britain. He believed that it would take six months or so to see whether the new political structure in Japan and the new foreign alliance worked as well as the Japanese anticipated.

In late November, Albright took heart from the fact that Admiral Nomura had agreed to become ambassador in Washington, for that gave diplomacy a chance.[100] He thought that the appointment of Nomura, who knew President Roosevelt personally, gave Japan a respite of six months in which to tackle the numerous complex issues between it and the United States. However, he did think it probable that Nomura would fail to bring about any substantial change in Japanese-American relations, "and if Nomura does fail, after that the deluge."[101] As it turned out, Nomura took his time in taking up his position in Washington, for, much to Albright's frustration, he was still in Japan in January 1941.

Albright saw the policies of Japan and the United States as diametrically opposed. He believed that concessions might be made but that neither country was prepared to give up its policy as such. He wrote that, "on this side, what we have seen recently is changes of internal organization and modifications of external policy, as in the N.E.I., but no change of heart,—in basic reliance upon force—control, regimentation, unification at home, and conquest, subordination and absorption abroad."[102] Fundamental change in Japan, Albright believed, could only come if there was a national awakening due to an overwhelming political crisis or a religious revival, but there was little chance of either happening. He thought that state Shinto was stronger than ever as the inspiration of Japanese nationalism, and "Christianity in Formosa and Korea and Japan has been weakened by the withdrawal of missionaries and almost the debacle of some missions, although the rising national churches are thus far much more amenable to government direction than the Buddhist and Shinto sects."[103] Clearly, there was little chance of a religious revival. However, he was confident enough about the future of missionary work in Japan to contemplate a forthcoming furlough in Canada.

At the end of 1940, Albright noted that,

> in spite of cabinet strengthening, mortgage-bank and trust company mergers and continued emphasis on the new subsidiary political-economic structure, the old stresses and strains remain between the services, the civil government and the forces, the officials and business men, city and country, and there are new lines of cleavages between the Diet and the Throne Assistance Organization.[104]

The prospects were equally as strained and bleak in terms of relations with Russia. Albright wrote that "southern skies are fairer but the situation in N. W. China and vis a vis Russia looks rather threatening, and it is not entirely the usual year-end controversy over the renewal of fishing rights but a growing sense of rivalry and incompatibility."[105] The political difficulties gave no sign of averting the collision course that Japan was on with the United States. However, Albright could hardly have imagined that within a few weeks he would be advocating the withdrawal of Canadian United Church missionaries from Japan.

Throughout the late 1930s and 1940, Outerbridge and Albright had attempted to see some signs of hope in the political changes in Japan. They believed that change was possible as long as the war in China could be ended. They seemed to be well informed as to what was happening in China, despite complaints of censorship by the Japanese authorities. Because both Outerbridge and Albright lived in Nishinomiya, they had plenty of opportunities to meet missionaries from China and Korea who landed at Kobe on their way to or from their mission fields. Indeed, it was only possible for Albright to make the comments that he did on political developments without fear of reprisal because missionary friends returning home could carry uncensored letters from him. Yet much of his information about politics in Japan came from the *Japan Times*, an English-language newspaper known to follow the government line. Nonetheless, it was possible for him to find out about Japanese military reverses—like that at Nomonhan—that, reasonably, the military would want to keep secret. Hence, censorship was not complete. To some extent, this made the task of judging what was happening all the more difficult for missionaries living in the comfortable cocoon of the Kwansei Gakuin campus.

The war in China was at the heart of all the changes in Japan and the Japanese Empire after 1937. The political, social, and religious changes as well as the anti-British feeling that punctuate Albright's comments were all related to the situation in China. Until August 1940, Albright held out hope that a resolution to the conflict in China could be found. From his Japan-centred point of view, Chiang Kai-shek was the major stumbling block to peace in metropolitan China. Ironically, though, Albright did not see Chiang as Japan's primary enemy (and in this he was merely expressing a Japanese view). That figure was the man whom Albright described as "the Spider of the Kremlin," who was ever "weaving his web in such a way that he can run out on either of his main threads of intrigue to entangle either China or Japan or possibly both in his toils."[106] It might be expected that Albright as a Christian missionary would look upon Stalin with some disdain. From the fall of 1940, there is a change in the tone of Albright's comments about politics in Japan. For one thing, his letters contain little reference to China, a sign that he had given up hope for any quick end to the situation there. He therefore viewed the new political structures and developments with increasing pessimism.

It was no coincidence that Albright's pessimism during the fall of 1940 about political events coincided with the climax of negotiations concerning church union, that had profound ramifications for the future of the missionary movement in Japan. Pressure for Christianity in Japan to harmonize its views with those of the rest of Japan was put on the Japanese Christian leadership. Church union was their answer.

CHAPTER TEN
Growing Pressure for Church Union in Japan

As the international crisis in China and East Asia deepened during the late 1930s, the Japanese government intensified its efforts to bring Japanese religions, including Christianity, under its control. After the Marco Polo bridge incident in the summer of 1937, this control became part of the government's endeavour to mobilize the Japanese people in support of the war effort. This chapter will analyse the growing pressure for church union up to the mass meeting on 17 October 1940 of Japanese Christians at Aoyama Gakuin to celebrate the 2,600th anniversary of the founding of the Japanese Empire.

During this time, Japanese Christians strove to demonstrate their loyalty to the state by participating in the government's campaign for national spiritual mobilization. Furthermore, they showed their enthusiastic support for the government's call for a new order in East Asia by attempting to expand missionary work in Korea, Manchuria, and north China in the wake of the Japanese military advance. Japanese expansion did provide tantalizing new opportunities for the Japanese Christian movement both at home and abroad. Overseas opportunities were seen to provide Japanese Christianity with a world role. As well as direct appeals to Japanese nationalism and patriotism by the authorities, the emergence of *Nipponteki Kirisutokyo* (Japanese Christianity) as a potent force within the intellectual milieu of the Christian movement helped to provide a theological rationale for those wishing to harmonize the goals of the Christian movement in Japan with those of the state. *Nipponteki Kirisutokyo* was particularly useful in helping to justify increased Japanese Christian missionary work overseas.

The new responsibilities of the Japanese Christian movement in East Asia were one factor in bringing about increasing pressure for church union. The amalgamation of Protestant churches would obviously help to facilitate government control over the organizational structure of Christianity in Japan. In that respect, church union was the capstone to a government effort already manifested in the shrine question and in the Japanization of the curricula and leadership of Christian and mission schools in order to rid Christianity of foreign influences and leadership. The international crisis, in which the Western powers, especially the United Kingdom, were seen to be adopting an anti-Japanese position, was another factor in making Japanese Christians wish to rid the Christian movement in Japan of all foreign influence. For example, as will be seen below, the Salvation Army crisis of August 1940 taught Japanese Christian leaders that the authorities were prepared to arrest Japanese Christians believed to have strong ties to Britain or other foreign countries. The threat of imprisonment was an added impetus to the movement for church union.

Following the Salvation Army Crisis, for some two months from mid-August until mid-October 1940, the NCC held a frantic succession of meetings between denominational representatives concerning amalgamation. Missionaries were informed of the dramatically swift decisions taken by Japanese Christian leaders but were powerless to influence the course of events. However, the place of foreign missionaries within any new Protestant union remained unresolved. Although the major Japanese denominations supported union, during this two-month period differences in attitude toward union movement between Japanese bishops within the NSKK came to a head. The position taken by Bishop Sasaki of the Diocese of Mid-Japan had profound consequences for Canadian Anglican missionaries.

As the issue of church union was debated through the 1930s, Canadian missionaries continued their evangelistic and social work. Although the educational work of missionaries was clearly changing as the process of handing over leadership to the Japanese proceeded, the specialized nature of slum or abolition work was largely protected from the winds of change. However, there were casualties, notably the disappearance of Canadian missionaries in charge of pastorates in the interior provincial cities as the older generation of male missionaries—such as Dan Norman, Harper Coates, and John Holmes, whose service in Japan stretched back three or four decades—retired. Whereas the WMS maintained its stations and work in the interior, male missionaries were replaced by Japanese pastors. In any case, the sense of identification between Norman and Nagano or Holmes and Fukui, built up over long years of continuous residency, could not be easily replaced even if funds and personnel were available.

The tranquillity of normal missionary life in Japan helped to obscure the developments that led to the sudden crisis surrounding church union, that came to a head in the summer of 1940. Canadian missionaries, despite the long debate over church union and their awareness of the political situation in Japan, were seemingly caught off-guard by the rapidity of events.

THE TWISTS AND TURNS ON THE ROAD TO CHURCH UNION

Church union reflected a long-term ideal of many Japanese Christians, including, as we have seen, such luminaries as Nitobe Inazo and Ebina Danjo. One of its major advocates, Bishop Abe Yoshimune of the Japan Methodist Church, claimed in January 1941 that the movement had "arisen, not because of pressure from above, but 'at the urge of self-respect, as Japanese.'"[1] On the other hand, a more cynical point of view suggests that it *was* pressure from above that brought about church union, because, particularly after the Marco Polo bridge incident in 1937, the union movement became increasingly identified with Japan's national cause. Clearly, however, both the ecumenicalists among the Japanese Christian leadership and the government authorities achieved their goals with the creation of a united Protestant Church in Japan.

In investigating the various reasons and motives behind the formation of the *kyodan*, the atmosphere within the Japanese Christian world during the late 1930s and early 1940s should be considered. In a recent study arguing that the Japan of the 1930s was a logical outcome of Meiji policy, Kisaka Junichiro writes that "the 1930s can be described as a period of war and fascistization."[2] Professor Kisaka asserts that during the late 1930s and early 1940s Japan's government was consolidated under the leadership of the military and bureaucracy by national-movement organizations that replaced dissolved parliamentary political parties and disbanded labour and farmers' unions. During these years, the history of the Japanese Christian movement is, in large part, one of the struggle for the integration of Christianity into the national movement. Reflecting this effort, in 1965 Motoi Takamichi gave "Christianity in the Stream of Fascistization" as the English title to an article on the background to the 1939 Religious Bodies Law.[3] This title suggests that Japanese Christian leaders were powerless and were being pulled by the irresistible political current into the disastrous maelstrom of war. However, the Pacific War was not seen as inevitable to most people living on either side of the Pacific before its outbreak on 8 December 1941.

Gonoi Takashi, in his recent history of Japanese Christianity, captures much of the atmosphere in the Christian world in Japan during the 1930. He argues that a dark age, reminiscent of the witch hunts of European medieval society, began after the Manchurian incident. In keeping with this medieval motif, Professor Gonoi compares the government's persecution of new religions to the persecution of Christians during the Tokugawa period.[4] The selective nature of the government persecution, as well as the latitude of individual officials in their application of government policies, have to be taken into account; if the intention of persecution was to instil fear into Japanese Christians and to make them compliant with government directives, then it succeeded. Among Japanese Christians, there was much more fear of consequences than actual persecution.

By 1934, *lese-majesty* and the Peace Preservation Law were being misused against religious groups.[5] A tougher stance toward religion by the thought-control police occurred in December 1935 with the arrest of some thirty leaders of Kodo Omotokyo, a new religion stemming from Shinto. In 1936, the *tokko keisatsu*, the thought-control police, began an investigation of the tendencies of religious groups.[6] In the mid-1930s, Roman Catholic missionaries were forced to discontinue some of their work in southern Kyushu on the ground of national security. Furthermore, the shrine question had led both to tension between Roman Catholics and the government at Jochi (Sophia) University and to problems at the Anglican Rikkyo University, but these tensions and problems had been resolved through discussion. A hint of military pressure might be detected in the fact that the Roman Catholics, as a sign of their patriotism, raised nationally in 1935 some ¥52,000 for the army and the navy.[7]

As far as the Christian movement was concerned, the Marco Polo bridge incident of July 1937 marked the beginning of a more active period of government persecution. The open fighting in north China led to a strengthening of wartime controls in Japan, especially in terms of thought control. This control led to the virtual extinction of the communist movement and the suppression of the ideas of class conflict and internationalism. Likewise, anti-*kokutai* (national polity) thought was rejected and antiwar or antimilitary thought stamped out as national treachery.[8] The ideas of certain Christian groups, particularly those associated with politically or socially active intellectuals, came under government scrutiny after July 1937. Among those singled out were people associated with the Christian socialist movement, with Kagawa and his social reform movement, or with the antiwar thought of Yanaihara Tadao and other members of the Mukyokai (Non-Church Movement) influenced by the pacifist ideas of Uchimura Kanzo.[9] The government was also suspicious of Christians opposed to attendance at state Shinto ceremonies. Two larger and well-established organizations also came under the scrutiny of the thought-control police. They were the Salvation Army and the NSKK, which fell under suspicion because they were linked to international bodies headquartered in Britain.

It was in this atmosphere of growing suspicion that the drive for Protestant amalgamation continued. Following the failure of the negotiations between the Kumiai Church and the Presbyterians in 1933, the union movement lost some of its momentum. But NCC kept interest alive. Whereas Presbyterian enthusiasm for union cooled after 1933, Japan Methodist interest increased, as seen in the election of Abe Yoshimune to chair the executive board of the NCC in 1937.[10] William Axling and Charles W. Iglehart, two American missionaries, were among the most active foreign missionary supporters of the NCC, but United Church of Canada missionaries in Japan were not opposed to the idea of church union. This was to be expected, as the formation of the United Church of Canada in 1925 was held up as a model for Protestant denominations in Japan to follow. The NCC clearly looked to the United Church for support. In January 1936, Ebisawa Akira of the NCC wrote to Jesse Arnup in Toronto that a recent all-Japan conference of the NCC had discussed the two problems of church union and a union evangelistic campaign to follow up the Kingdom of God movement. Ebisawa noted that conference delegates had unanimously agreed to the principle that church union was inevitable and had established a special commission to study and promote union as well as to investigate further the policies, creed, and order of a united church.[11] Another committee had also been organized to lay out a new three-year union evangelistic campaign to follow up the Kingdom of God movement. Because Kagawa was to visit Canada later in 1936, Ebisawa and the NCC were obviously looking to Arnup and the United Church of Canada for strong support.

At the beginning of 1936, while Ebisawa was looking overseas for support, there was reason for some concern about the Japanese Christian movement at home. In his annual report for 1936, Leland Albright dwelt on the political and economic situation, in Japan and then turned to the religious situation, which looked increasingly gloomy. He indicated that the Buddhist revival of the early 1930s had lost its momentum and that several new sects of Shinto had come under government suspicion. "Christianity," he noted, "senses the coming tension, and the laymen are urging Church Union within ten years."[12] But supporters of church union were persistent. In September 1938, a *Fukuin Shimpo* editorial, which warned against the rash behaviour of unionists, noted that the most important issue, certain to occur at the annual denominational fall conferences, was church union.[13] Albright, of course, could not peer into the future.

Despite the difficulties that the Japanese Christian movement had faced in 1936, there was some hope for the movement in Japan during the early months of 1937. Those months were a time of contrasts for Japanese Christians. On the one hand, February had seen the beginnings of Yuasa Hachiro's difficulties at Doshisha over alleged disrespect to the Imperial Rescript on Education. Yet, on a much more positive note, the end of April saw the Anglicans come together in a conference to celebrate the fiftieth anniversary of the founding of the NSKK.[14] In May, the 150th anniversary of the Presbyterian North mission work was commemorated.[15] Moreover, church union pressed forward, but not without some missionary eyebrows being raised about its financial cost. In April 1937, Outerbridge pleaded ignorance on both his and Bates's part concerning a rumour that Arnup in Toronto had heard that the NCC was spending a quarter of a million yen a year to further the cause of church union.[16] Yet the spark that did away with any consideration of money by Japanese Christian leaders who advocated union was the Marco Polo bridge incident, that marked the beginning of open and sustained fighting between Japanese and Chinese in north China.

THE MARCO POLO BRIDGE INCIDENT AND ITS AFTERMATH

The initial response of the Japan Methodist Church was to issue a statement calling for peace and stressing the support of Japan Methodists for Japan's national spirit.[17] In late September 1937, however, in analysing the response of Japanese Christians to the beginning of open war in north China, Outerbridge noted that

> the Government has said in effect "we know that you Christians preach love and peace and good-will. We have no objection in peace time. But Japan is now at war, and if you say a word to obstruct or weaken us at this time, we will crush your Christians and your churches out of existence."[18]

This was one view of the government attitude toward Christianity that was widely held by both missionaries and Japanese Christians, and it goes far to explain their actions in response to government policies toward religions during the next few years. But it was a rather extreme view that exaggerated the danger of Christian extinction. It was fear of what might happen to Christianity, much more than actual government policies and actions, that sapped the spirit of both Japanese Christians and foreign missionaries.

Outerbridge clearly hoped that Japanese Christians would take a pacifist position in regard to the war in China. The experience of the Great War was for him evidence enough that war was not beneficial. However, he realized that it would be difficult to convince Japanese Christians of this because Japan had not suffered as greatly as Canada had during the Great War and had not learned the Canadian lesson that "even victors are losers and that war doesn't pay."[19] In looking for support for his pacifist viewpoint, Outerbridge turned to Kagawa, who had lamented at a Kagawa Fellowship meeting that he was "a man half-dead. My body is alive, but my soul died when Japanese guns began to shoot my Chinese friends."[20] In looking at Kagawa's attachment to pacifism throughout the wartime period, Ota Yuzo has concluded that "the most balanced view of Kagawa with respect to pacifism is to see him as inclined towards it but neither consistent nor resolute in it."[21] It is undoubtedly true, however, that what Kagawa said in September 1937 expressed his genuine feeling at the time.

Outerbridge knew of other Japanese Christians who came out strongly for pacifism. He noted that, at a conference in September 1937 in Odawara, the gateway to the beautiful Hakone region near Tokyo, a church leader had told him that many young Japanese Christians "cannot reconcile this cruel war with the love and brotherhood and spirit of forgiveness that Jesus taught. If we [pastors] try to teach them that the purposes of the Government are right,—well we will lose our young people. They do not believe it."[22] Many young Japanese Christians were privately opposed to the war in China, but most Japanese pastors preferred to sit on the fence rather than take a strong position with regard to the war. Most preachers, Outerbridge maintained, were "doing just what all our men in Canada did during the world war, justifying it when they can. When they can't praying for peace. I have never yet heard a preacher pray for victory however. (Many may have done so.) They carefully pray for peace to come."[23] Yet, when it came to making a public statement that the authorities might take note of, the same pastors came out with a politic response.

At yet another conference, this time in Gotemba, Outerbridge noted that

> the phrase "prays for the peace in the Far East for that our soldiers are fighting" was finally adopted, though the last phrase was strongly objected to by some. Most of them firmly believe that the only way to get that peace is by some such way as they are now following.[24]

While Outerbridge was putting forward a pacifist position, it was evident from the conferences at Odawara and Gotemba that the response of Japanese Christians and pastors to the war in north China was muted. As he admitted, Japanese pastors needed only to look to their Canadian or American counterparts during the Great War for models to copy should they wish to support Japan's war effort in China. Although he did mention the possibility of government reprisals against Christians and their churches, no widespread persecution of Christians belonging to larger orthodox denominations had as yet taken place.

Outerbridge did not mention, however, an important factor that obviously concerned many Japanese Christians. On 15 July 1937, the weekly Christian journal *Fukuin Shimpo* carried an editorial that called for peace in East Asia. The editorial also revealed that Japanese Christians were very conscious of criticism coming from the United States and other Western countries (where there were many anti-Japanese Chinese students) as well as the strong anti-Japanese feeling within metropolitan China itself.[25] In August 1937, an editorial in *Kirisutokyo Sekai*, another influential Christian weekly, dealing with the meaning of the north China incident, saw the historical actions of the Western imperialist countries and the more recent activities of Westerners, particularly the Russians, as contributing causes of the crisis.[26] Just as with the earlier Manchurian incident, there was the danger that too much adverse criticism from foreigners might drive moderate Japanese Christians to support openly their government's military policies.[27]

Whereas some Japanese Christians were prepared to take a pacifist line, the NCC was more ambivalent in its attitude. Within days of the beginning of open fighting in China, the Ministry of Education approached Japanese Christian leaders to take part in the national spiritual mobilization campaign.[28] The importance of obtaining the support of Japanese religious groups, including the Christians, was underlined by the head of the ministry's religions bureau in mid-September 1937. Japanese Christians were susceptible to appeals to their patriotism.[29] The NCC, for its part, was willing to participate in the campaign. Early October 1937 was the season for important general meetings, including the fifty-third general conference of the Kumiai Church and the fifty-first general conference of the Nippon Kirisutokyokai (Presbyterians). Both conferences emphasized the need for renewed evangelistic effort, and the Kumiai Church threw its support behind the national spiritual mobilization campaign.[30]

Yet many Japanese Christians remained largely unenthusiastic about Japan's actions in China. However, the mood of Christians began to change dramatically in October. The critical moment was October 3, when Cosmo Lang, the archbishop of Canterbury, chaired a meeting at Albert Hall in London that condemned Japanese actions in China.[31] Archbishop Lang's stand made the position of the NSKK much more difficult, and an Anglican crisis in Japan was averted only after the Japanese clergy of the NSKK insisted on a stand of enthusiastic support for the government's position on the China issue. The Albert Hall incident also had ramifications that went beyond simply increasing the desire of some Japanese Anglicans for complete independence for the NSKK, for it brought the church to the attention of the *tokko keisatsu* (the thought-control police) and ultimately led to the arrest of Bishop Samuel Heaslett, a British bishop of the NSKK, and others on charges of spying.[32] Moreover, the incident had an impact on Japanese Christians outside the NSKK, for it was considered to be unwarranted interference by a foreign religious leader into the affairs of Japan. Lang's support for China was taken as representative of a broader British anti-Japanese feeling, for the archbishop's condemnation of Japan was not separated from Japanese perceptions of the official British position, that after long years of Anglo-Japanese friendship had now seemingly become anti-Japanese. Just as had happened midway through the Manchurian crisis of 1931–32, adverse criticism, perceived as anti-Japanese in a racist sense, coming this time from a prominent British religious figure, turned moderate Japanese Christians into supporters of their government's actions in China.

After October 1937, the NSKK underwent a rapid internal process of disassociating itself from the Church of England (with that it had always maintained close ties) and replacing British and American missionary bishops with Japanese ones. The Canadian diocese, of course, already had a Japanese bishop, but it was still dependent on Canadian funds. Like the Anglicans, the Salvation Army came under great pressure to sever all connections with Britain.[33] The Salvation Army also suffered because of its name and the military-style ranks of its officials, that could unwittingly lead to misinterpretations of its function. Its evangelistic concern with the underprivileged in Japanese society also made it suspect.

It was no coincidence that at the end of November 1937 the NCC published a Christian view of the China incident that came out strongly in support of Japanese government and military actions.[34] In December, the NCC launched a nationwide evangelistic movement, which differed from the earlier Kingdom of God campaign in that it hoped to correct the "present perilous thought currents" and provide a basis for "fostering a devout and unalloyed sentiment" among the people.[35] This new evangelistic movement was a concrete commitment by the NCC to participate in the spiritual mobilization campaign promoted by the government. The NCC was no longer challenging Japanese military and government policies but had come out in support of them.

The change in NCC attitude toward the war in China was vividly illustrated in December 1937 in an English-language open letter signed by forty-five prominent Japanese Christians and sent to foreign Christians.[36] In this letter, the Japanese Christian leaders deplored the loss of life in the fighting in China but defended Japan's actions because the "anti-Japanese policy of the Nanking government on the one hand, a policy utilized as a means of consolidating that nation, and China's policy of cooperating with Communism with its anti-religious materialism on the other hand, directly threatened her [Japan's] national foundation and endanger her very existence."[37] The Japanese Christian leaders wanted peace, but it was peace on Japanese terms. It was profoundly regretted that "the present complicated international situation has arisen largely because of the failure of the Christian forces to apply the teachings of Christ to the thought and culture of contemporary minds and to secure their realization in practice."[38] The implication was that Chinese Christians (including Chiang Kai-shek) as well as Western Christians had contributed to this failure. In a paper given to foreign missionaries, Tagawa Daikichiro, the former president of Meiji Gakuin, warned missionaries against accepting the Chinese interpretation of events and speaking out against Japan, for "the whole of Japan is now resorting to a procedure unanimously supported by our people, and not a single soul is suffered to protest."[39] The pacifist voice, in which Outerbridge barely three months earlier had put so much hope, was now silent. In their dealings with church leaders in North America and Europe, though condemning the loss of life caused by fighting in north China, Japanese church leaders now steadfastly defended the righteousness of Japan's cause.

Yet, despite the views of Japanese Christian leaders, missionaries still had to depend upon them. In March 1938, Albright wrote that, in light of the declining influence of missionaries, "we must place the burden of student leadership soon on the shoulders of the Christian professors and teachers of our Mission and of Government Schools."[40] It was all the more important that missionaries help prepare Japanese Christian instructors to conduct Christian work among students, for "there is not much left but religion, and we must make the most of it. For life has lost its meaning for many people and students have no reason to anticipate a bright future under existing trends."[41] However, the ability of Japanese Christian professors to influence their students was much in doubt owing to the threat of government persecution. Albright was very concerned about the muzzling of free speech and its possible impact upon Christian work and education.

Nevertheless, in spite of the continuing crisis in China and worries over free speech, some Japanese Christian leaders remained appreciative of missionary efforts. In February 1939, Bishop Kugimiya Tokio of the Japan Methodist Church reassured Canadian missionaries that they "need not worry about the internal situation. That was a local national matter. There was no longer necessity for special reticence. Missionaries could be bold in the presentation of the Gospel."[42] Kugimiya saw that there were still evangelistic opportunities for Canadian missionaries, especially in rural work, and he thought that missionaries might usefully be stationed in rural Yamanashi Prefecture and in the countryside east of Toyama. Nevertheless, even though personal relations with missionaries were warm, Kugimiya and others toed a strongly national line when it came to China.

NIPPONTEKI KIRISUTOKYO AND OVERSEAS EVANGELISM

Although Japanese Christian leaders might want to appear in the eyes of an English-speaking audience to be placating Western Christian opinion in regard to Japan's reasons for fighting in north China, there was considerable hostility toward Britain and the United States in the Japanese Christian press. Equally important was the contradiction, even at this early stage, between the conciliatory attitude of the Japanese Christian leadership in its English-language correspondence with church leaders in North America and Europe and the hostility toward Western Christianity in the Japanese-language Christian press. There were few Japanese defenders of Western Christianity in the Japanese-language Christian publications.

In December 1937, the influential *Fukuin Shimpo* criticized Britain and the United States and their role in East Asian Christianity. The connection between Western Christianity, Western politicians, and Western cultural values was disparaged. Moreover, it was pointed out that what happened in East Asia would not be decided in the West.[43] The unease with that Japanese Christians looked upon Western Christianity was further underlined in another article in the same issue of *Fukuin Shimpo,* one that dealt with the thoughts of Japanese Christianity (*Nipponteki Kirisutokyo*).[44] Clear in these articles was the desire of Japanese Christians to distance themselves from Western Christianity and its cultural values and to stress a Japanese Christianity that took into account the particular aspirations of the Japanese people. As it emerged in the late 1930s, *Nipponteki Kirisutokyo* was an attempt to join Christianity with Japan's traditional spirit, thought, and religion.[45] The views expressed in the 16 December 1937 issue of *Fukuin Shimpo* were important, not the least because of their timing. They were representative of the opinions of many Japanese Christians, and they had significant implications for the Western missionary movement in Japan.

Yet *Nipponteki Kirisutokyo* implied different things to different people at different times. In analysing the phenomenon of *Nipponteki Kirisutokyo* and the NSKK, Tsukada Osamu has argued that the *Nipponteki* of *Nipponteki Kirisutokyo* at first meant an indigenous and independent church on the model of a grafted tree (that is, a Western organizational structure). Tsukada maintained that this meaning later led the way to acceptance of *tennosei* by Japanese Anglicans (and, by analogy, by other Christians).[46] It is not surprising, therefore, especially after the Marco Polo bridge incident, that there would be renewed interest in *Nipponteki Kirisutokyo* as a stream of Christian thought compatible with Japanese national ambitions in East Asia. However, even as late as the early 1930s, *Nipponteki Kirisutokyo* seemed innocuous. In 1934, Yanaihara Tadao published a short article entitled "Nipponteki Kirisutokyo" in that he defended the patriotism of Japanese Christians against the views, such as that held by Kato Hiroyuki at the time of the Russo-Japanese War, of those who believed that Christianity was opposed to Japan's *kokutai*.[47] According to Fujita Wakao, to Yanaihara "Japanese Christianity meant in essence that Japan would become a genuine peace-loving Christian country while maintaining the basic political structure of the imperial system and its unique cultural tradition."[48] As a Mukyokai Christian, Yanaihara was influenced deeply by Uchimura Kanzo's idea of the "2 Js"[49] as well as by his views that the organization of the church should be independent of Western missionaries. As well as arguing that Japanese Christians were true patriots, Yanaihara believed that a new Christian age was dawning in that the light would come from the East.[50] Implicit in this belief was the idea that Japanese Christians would play a significant role in the Christian future in East Asia. This was by no means a new or unusual idea. For instance, during the Meiji period, Imai Judo, the influential Japanese Anglican priest, had held that Japan had a special calling to bring enlightenment and Christianity to East Asia.[51] What was largely absent in Imai's thinking or in that of Yanaihara's *Nipponteki Kirisutokyo* was any overt hostility toward the West.

By the late 1930s, however, the rise of militarism and authoritarianism at home combined with the international situation in East Asia to transform the meaning of *Nipponteki Kirisutokyo*. The new interpretation supported Japanese national policies both religious and secular. Japanese conquests in north China, in effect, gave the Japanese Christian movement the opportunity to fulfil its special calling to bring enlightenment and Christianity to East Asia. By 1940, there were some in Japan's religious world who went so far as to advocate an imperial Christianity (*kodo Kirisutokyo*). At the least, it was hoped that in the future Christianity in Japan would no longer be a colony of British and American Christianity.[52]

Missionaries in Japan made an attempt to understand the Japanese attitude toward Christianity in the missionary press. In January 1940, the *Japan Christian Quarterly* published a translated excerpt from Hiyane Antei's *Kirisutokyo no Nihon-teki Tenkai* entitled "National Spirit and the Christian Faith."[53] This article was important not only because Hiyane was a well-known and respected Christian scholar but also, as a faculty member of Aoyama Gakuin, because his views might be taken to represent a Japan Methodist position. Hiyane, to some extent, was merely reiterating long-held Japanese Christian views, for he thought that with belief in God "we should be awakened to a new consciousness of our national being, based upon the holy desires of God."[54] This idea was reminiscent of early Meiji Japanese Christians, who saw that Christianity's moral code could practically benefit Japan and its society. However, Hiyane saw the development of a Christianity in Japan that was in complete harmony with the Japanese national spirit. The same fate awaited Christianity in Japan, he argued, that had befallen Buddhism and Confucianism, both of which, he believed, had reached their highest state of perfection in Japan. He stated that "the ability of the Japanese to consummate the essence of Buddhism and Confucianism has been abundantly proved. Our ability to assimilate Christianity will doubtless be demonstrated in the future."[55] Hiyane also strongly believed that Christian Japan had evangelistic obligations overseas. He suggested that "it is not a dream to hope that we Japanese may be able to propagate and preach the Gospel to the world more vigorously than others, in the same way that we did Buddhism and Confucianism."[56] He held that "Japan is the pivot of the world. It is the task of Japanese Christians to adjust the pivot properly. Nichiren, the Buddhist prophet of the Kamakura period said, 'I must be the pillar of Japan, and its eye.' We Christians should exert ourselves in the same spirit that moved Nichiren."[57] Implicit in this for Hiyane was that Christianity should be not only at peace with Japanese national feeling at home but also ready to take on overseas responsibilities. His views were clearly shared by many other Japanese Christians. Indeed, Aasulv Lande has pointed out that Hiyane's views were similar to many of those of Tagawa Daikichiro.[58]

Whereas Hiyane escaped missionary criticism for his views, Tagawa did not. In July 1940, an editorial in the *Japan Christian Quarterly* took exception to Tagawa's "conviction that religion strengthened national morality."[59] The editorial called attention to the danger in his position of

> allowing Christianity to become the hand-maiden of a particular political order that defines the type of morality desired for the preservation of such a social system and then calls upon religion to undergird and support that specific moral code. If and when Christianity bows to such enslavement, it has betrayed its true genius and function.[60]

Whether or not Christianity in Japan had already betrayed its true genius and function was a moot point. However, the *Japan Christian Quarterly* was deeply concerned that there was "growing evidence that the cleavage in ideologies along cultural and national lines is very deep and tends to make difficult in certain lands all forms of Christian endeavor by workers of different traditions and standards."[61] Obviously, there was some missionary self-interest involved in not wanting to see such cleavages, for they would spell the end of foreign missionary opportunity.

Yet it appears that this was what Japanese Christians had been doing since 1937, for the *Japan Christian Quarterly* stated that many missionaries had come to believe that, with the outbreak of war in China,

> Japanese Christians and churches of many denominations turned away from the primary concerns of the New Testament gospel to considerations that, even if worthy, are of secondary importance in the strategy of the Christian faith. To some this may even seem to violate the very spirit of the Gospel and to be cutting the spiritual and ethical nerve of the church.[62]

The *Japan Christian Quarterly* also made a stinging attack on the attempt of Japanese Christians to harmonize Christianity with Japanese national spirit, that was at the heart of *Nipponteki Kirisutokyo*:

> to our Japanese brethren such accommodation to circumstances seems not only the counsel of expediency but the true and only way to bring about a genuine indigenization of the Christian movement in this and other Oriental lands. Accordingly we are informed that the populace is yearning for the assurances of religion's essential harmony with the native Japanese spirit and that when they see how Christianity really undergirds and supports the national morality, they will flock to our churches.[63]

The *Japan Christian Quarterly* held that there were other more pressing priorities for Christians in Japan. It argued that "what Japan needs today from Christian pastors, missionaries, and churches is not more harmonization of religion and national culture, but more of the ethically bold and prophetic gospel of Jesus Christ."[64]

Much as missionaries desired more preaching of the Gospel, Japanese Christian leaders were more concerned with harmonization. By the end of the 1930s, some missionaries thought that the NCC was in the vanguard of harmonizing Christian ideas with those of Japanese national objectives both internally and in China. The annual report of the British Anglican Church Missionary Society for 1939–1940 perceptively stated that Japanese Christians, along with the vast majority of Japanese, were imbued with a sense of

> "Japan's great mission to bring peace and order in East Asia." The National Christian Council places in the forefront of its programme this aim: "To stress the harmony between Christianity and the national objectives." The campaign in China and their country's mission have been presented to the Japanese in such a light that very few Christians are aware of any conflict between full loyalty to God and to the State.[65]

The difficulty for Japanese Christians, one unnamed British Anglican missionary pointed out, was that "'For the sake of Japan' is for some a more compelling motive than 'for Christ's sake.'"[66] Such had always been a challenge for Japanese Christians during a time of war. For the ordinary Japanese Christian, the challenge was all the more difficult because of the strong appeals to the sense of duty of Christian individuals in regard to Japanese nationalism made by Japanese Christian leaders, such as Bishop Kugiyama, who fully endorsed government policies for spiritual mobilization in support of the war effort in China.[67] However, the crisis in China had other important ramifications for Japanese Christians. It was further noted in the Church Missionary Society's annual report that most Christian leaders accepted the official interpretation of the government's actions in China and supported the construction of a new order in East Asia. It stated that

> The conventional Christian view is, that this is in line with God's will for the Far East, and that no human power can therefore hinder its fulfilment. There is also a real earnestness of intention that the Christian Church should bear a brave part in reconciling China to the new order, and a call for sacrifices to that end, considerable keenness is shown in extending work among Japanese residents on the continent, and a vague conviction that witness should be extended to the Chinese themselves, when that becomes opportune.[68]

Increasingly, as time went on, some Japanese Christian leaders came to see that divine purpose was behind Japanese actions in East Asia. By 7 July 1939, Bishop Kugimiya was saying that "we believe that the august will of God is using our race for a great purpose here in East Asia" and was urging "his people to pray that 'our soldiers may be given power to conquer themselves and also the enemy.'"[69] By the second anniversary of the Marco Polo bridge incident, Ebizawa, the secretary of the NCC, was reported to have said "that

God is using Japan for the establishment of His Kingdom in Asia, but that only the 'pure in heart' can appreciate this fact."[70] As the crisis in China deepened, Japanese Christians became increasingly convinced that Japan indeed had a special role to play in the establishment of God's kingdom in Asia, and this role meant undertaking evangelistic work not only in Japanese colonies and in Manchukuo, that had already been conducted for a long time, but also in the newly conquered areas of China. Underpinning this overseas evangelistic effort was the desire of the Japanese Christian leadership, especially after the Marco Polo bridge incident, to show Christian support for Japan's national objectives, including those in metropolitan China. This desire was also buttressed by the ideas of *Nipponteki Kirisutokyo*.

Among the Protestant denominations, the Presbyterians believed that they had a responsibility to undertake evangelistic work on the Asian continent.[71] They were aware that the disorder in north China had led to Western missionaries giving up their work, and there was a danger that all would be lost unless somebody stepped in. The Japanese Methodists were also active in calling for missionary work in China. The *Nippon Mesojisuto Jiho*,[72] the weekly newspaper of the Japanese Methodist Church, was particularly in favour of missionary work in China. In January 1938, it solicited ¥1,000 for missionary work, of which ¥200 would go to north China, where Japanese Methodists had been undertaking evangelistic work since the fall of 1937 in addition to their existing endeavours in Manchuria, Hokkaido, and elsewhere. Work was being undertaken "for the sake of Christ, Church and the Fatherland."[73] Yet, because many Methodist churches in Japan had still to achieve self-support, this new missionary work obviously placed another heavy demand on the already stretched funds of Japanese Christians. In early February 1938, an editorial made it clear that the Japanese Methodists saw their role in north China as one of reconciling Chinese and Japanese and promoting peace. By undertaking this role, the Methodists thought that they were actively participating in Japan's national spiritual mobilization. Furthermore, this Japanese Christian endeavour was a demonstration of Japan's leadership within a new international order.[74] These were, indeed, to be abiding themes in the appeals of those advocating the extension of missionary work.

As well as among Chinese and Japanese civilians, Bishop Kugimiya believed that the Methodist Church had a responsibility as part of its national spiritual mobilization to undertake Christian work among members of the imperial forces and their families by way of consoling the bereaved and providing comfort for the wounded.[75] In April 1938, it was argued that the responsibility to spread the Christian message was an essential duty of the national church.[76] This work might take different forms—for instance, helping the Manchurian Christian movement with its Japanese Sunday school educational program as part of the Methodist Church's effort to highlight Sunday school education in conjunction with the celebration of Children's

Day.[77] In such a way, the local needs of the overseas mission field were kept before Japanese Methodists. Yet Methodists were also continuously being rallied to make new evangelistic efforts through the well-worn appeal to the uniqueness of Japan's place in world Christianity, especially in the East.[78] In September 1938, the *Nippon Mesojisuto Jiho* saw Japan as the big brother in East Asia, with Korea as "Japan's Ireland" and Manchukuo particularly important because of the opportunity to build up a spirit of cooperation between its constituent five ethnic groups.[79] Undoubtedly, Christian success in ethnically diverse Manchukuo could be taken as a portent of future success in metropolitan China.

China itself continued to hold the attention of the Methodist leadership. In June 1939, Kugimiya took the opportunity of Asia Development Public Service Day to describe Methodist missionary activities in Peking, Tientsin, and elsewhere in north China, which he had recently visited.[80] Far from being pessimistic, he emphasized that the prospects for the future were good. Christian work in north China was under the control of the Japanese authorities, and their policies appear to have followed closely the pattern of control already adopted in Manchukuo, Korea, and Taiwan. The key to this control was seen to be education. In describing church work in occupied areas of China in its January 1939 issue, the *Chinese Recorder* reported that churches in the cities continued to carry out their work almost as before but that educational work was under the control of the Japanese authorities, who had ordered middle school principals to attend "a special period of training with certain Japanese documents and thoughts. The text books used in schools are published in Peking under the approval of the Japanese authorities."[81] For the moment, Christian congregations were left alone. However, there were problems in rural areas where churches had difficulties in carrying out their programs because "constantly there is guerilla-fighting with the Japanese. Sometimes the church leaders of the rural districts are suspected by the Japanese of being communists."[82] This situation was reminiscent of that in rural Manchuria during the 1930s. Yet the spirit of Chinese Christians in the occupied areas of north China appears to have been unbroken. The *Chinese Recorder* reported that "the spirit of our people is still one, in one fellowship, in one great hope for the final victory of China, in the struggle for perfect freedom and peace for their life in the future."[83] In March 1939, another report on conditions in occupied areas of China noted that "the people in the occupied areas are living a double life."[84] Given this situation, it was unlikely that Japanese missionaries in north China, despite the optimism of Bishop Kugimiya in June 1939, would be able to achieve any abiding success either in reconciling Chinese and Japanese or in promoting peace.

Nevertheless, the Methodist leadership was undeterred. In November 1939, the support of *Nipponteki Kirisutokyo* and the new order in East Asia was underlined.[85] In February 1940, while discussing the mission of the Methodist

Church and the 2,600th year of the imperial era, Bishop Abe pointed out that, just as Luther's religious revolution had helped to provide the spiritual foundation for the establishment of Germany and Wesley's religious revival had been the basis of the building of Great Britain during the eighteenth century, so, too, in the twentieth century the establishment of Christian Japan must become the spiritual foundation of the great work of building the new order in East Asia.[86] In asserting such an opinion, Abe clearly identified himself with the ideas of *Nipponteki Kirisutokyo*.

The desire to expand overseas missionary work was not restricted to the Japan Methodists, Presbyterians, and Congregationalists, for the NSKK was also deeply interested in such an expansion. The same reasoning that motivated the Japanese Methodists and the others to follow in the wake of the Japanese army in north China was evident in Japanese Anglican thinking. Following the Marco Polo bridge incident, the Japanese Anglican bishops did not object, for instance, to the NSKK establishing the "Spiritual Prayer for the China Incident," and in November 1938 Bishop Matsui Yonetaro, accompanied by Yashiro Hinsuke, made an extended tour of Manchuria and north China to investigate the problem of evangelistic work in those two regions.[87] In his report, Yashiro realized that there were three major difficulties in regard to work conducted by the NSKK in those areas: first, there was the question of jurisdiction, for north China and Manchuria were in the Diocese of North China's Bishop Norris, the SPG (British Anglican Society for the Propagation of the Gospel in Foreign Parts) missionary bishop resident in Peking; second, there was the problem of getting permission from the Japanese army to undertake work; and third, there was the danger of Japanese missionaries being killed by anti-Japanese Chinese.[88] Yet, in early January 1939, the *Kirisutokyo Shuho*, in an editorial dealing with the "Light from the East," pointed out that the Konoe government was urging Japan to take part in the building of a new Asia.[89] Matsui's trip to investigate the possibilities of evangelistic work in Manchuria and north China should be seen, like the interest of other denominations in the same areas, as a response to the appeal of the government to help build a new order in Asia. In February 1939, Bishop Heaslett, the missionary bishop of South Tokyo and primate of the NSKK, published two articles in the *Kirisutokyo Shuho* dealing with the Korean Anglican Church and with potential evangelistic work in Korea, Manchuria, and north China.[90] Heaslett obviously decided to comment on the idea of extending Japanese Anglican evangelistic work into Korea, Manchuria, and north China, an idea advocated by the NSKK's Young People's Alliance (*Seinenkai*) and pursued by Matsui because he thought that certain facts were being overlooked. Heaslett pointed out that the Korean Anglican Church was independent and that Manchuria and north China fell under the jurisdiction of Bishop Norris. Heaslett hoped that the new political situation in north China would lead to friendly relations between the Chinese Anglican Church and the NSKK, but a new relationship and greater cooperation between the two churches would have to be worked out.[91] Even though he was pouring cold water on expansion by stressing the clear jurisdictional boundaries that were already in place, he realized that the church's youth organization was particularly keen to extend Japanese Anglican work in Korea.[92]

In March 1939, a member of the Young People's Alliance made it clear, however, that the *Seinenkai* was not concerned with the niceties of jurisdictional distinctions but simply wanted to press ahead in Korea, as well as Manchuria and north China, with evangelistic work in accordance with the view expressed at the NSKK's nineteenth general conference.[93] The response of the young Japanese Anglican was illustrative of a growing Japanese restiveness with foreign missionary leadership. Although the issue of jurisdiction continued to receive attention over the next few months,[94] it could not prevent the continued advocacy of the extension of missionary work in Manchuria and north China. Indeed, it was reported in April 1939 that the NSKK already had missionaries working in Dairen and Mukden and were starting work in Shinkyo, the capital of Manchukuo. Furthermore, a missionary from Dairen and Mukden had been sent to make contacts in the Tientsin and Peking areas in the hope of extending work there in the future.[95] As well as this work on the northeastern Asian continent, the NSKK continued its long-established missionary work in Taiwan, that had been conducted under the jurisdiction of the Diocese of Osaka since the 1890s.[96] The desire to expand overseas missionary endeavour was taking place at a time when the NSKK was not close to achieving self-support in metropolitan Japan, and the added financial needs of overseas mission fields made self-support even more difficult to achieve.

Even though political considerations played a key part in why Japanese Anglicans were so eager to follow in the wake of Japanese military expansion in China, they were quick to criticize the use of a church platform for perceived political purposes by others. In early June 1939, the *Kirisutokyo Shuho* pointed out that Neville Chamberlain, the British prime minister, had addressed the general assembly of the Presbyterian Church meeting in Edinburgh and had taken the opportunity to call for the cooperation of the whole church in that time of international dangers.[97] The *Kirisutokyo Shuho* argued that religionists were not politicians and that Chamberlain was overstepping his place in trying to use a church meeting for political purposes.[98] Ever since Archbishop Lang had involved himself in the Albert Hall meeting in 1937, Japanese Anglicans were obviously chary of British religionists or politicians making statements to church or public audiences that might be construed as criticism of Japanese actions in China. Moreover, the comment in *Kirisutokyo Shuho* was in keeping with the wave of anti-British feeling in Japan that summer. Clearly, this criticism of Chamberlain reflected a desire among Japanese Anglicans to distance themselves from their British and other foreign connections.[99] What was ironic, of course, was that the NSKK itself was being manipulated by

Japanese politicians and bureaucrats to further their political goals in China.

The expansion of missionary work in China remained of great interest to the NSKK. In October 1939, Maejima Kiyoshi, who visited Peking in the autumn of 1939 as a representative of the NSKK, stressed that the Chinese Anglican Church needed the help of the NSKK and wanted or needed to cooperate with the Japanese church in matters of theology, funding, life, and missionaries.[100] Cooperation between the NSKK and the Anglican churches on the northeast Asian continent was stressed. In late October 1939, it was reported that a special festival had taken place at the Yasukuni Ginja in that Korean residents in the Japanese Empire had participated with perfect equality with the Japanese. The meaning for Japanese and Korean Anglicans was that there was nothing to be worried about when the merger of the NSKK and Korean Seikokai took place—all the more so because it was stressed that Japanese and Koreans alike were building a new order in East Asia.[101]

The importance of overseas missionary work as a rallying point for Japanese Christians in helping to create a new order in East Asia cannot be overestimated. Participation in missionary work in the effort to establish a new order was one way in which Japanese Christians could demonstrate their loyalty to the state. Likewise, the significance of the ideas of *Nipponteki Kirisutokyo* as a theological underpinning of Japanese Christian endeavour in East Asia should not be overlooked. It was a *Japanese* Christianity that was to be propagated in the wake of Japan's continental expansion. The demands of overseas missionary work added impetus to the church movement in Japan, all the more so because the leading proponents of overseas missionary endeavour and of church union at home were often the same people. This was the case with Kozaki Michio of the Kumiai Church and Bishop Abe of the Japan Methodist Church.

GROWING PRESSURE FOR UNION

The change in leadership within the Japan Methodist Church was to prove significant for the future of both the Japan Methodist Church and the Western missionary movement in Japan. In October 1939, however, the Canadian impression of Bishop Abe was highly favourable. Indeed, the trust that United Church missionaries placed in his judgment and integrity was rivalled only by their loyalty to Kagawa. Whether or not their trust was ultimately justified is debatable. Abe's attachment to *Nipponteki Kirisutokyo* suggests that it was not. Nevertheless, his appointment as the new bishop was warmly welcomed. Charles Bates was pleased that Bishop Kugiyama Tokio's place was being taken by Abe, the president of Aoyama Gakuin and the son-in-law of Honda Yoichi, the first bishop of the Japan Methodist Church. Bates believed that "the

Church is fortunate to have so good a man available for the position at this time" and that Abe "will bear the torch with daring and success."[102] Certainly, Abe bore the torch with daring, but, as a fervent unionist, it would ultimately be at the expense of the Japan Methodist Church. One of his important attributes, however, which put him in good stead when dealing with Western missionaries, was his familiarity with the United States.

Although Japanese Christians, by the end of 1937, had come to support Japanese war aims in north China, the government still put informal pressure on the Christian movement to ensure that its thinking remained correct. One manifestation of this pressure was the questionnaire sent out to Christian organizations in the Kansai region, including the NSKK, in March 1938 by the *tokko kacho* of the Osaka gendarmerie that Professor Hori of the Kwansei Gakuin was asked to answer. Increasingly, it became clear that it was a government goal to eliminate foreign influences and control of Christian denominations. This agenda had an impact upon all denominations helped by foreign missionaries and outside funds. Even missionaries of the Roman Catholic Church, that was under the special protection of the Italian government, were ultimately affected.[103]

While it was gaining the support of the Japanese Christian movement for its policy of military expansion in China, the government was also bringing forward legislation to tighten its control over religious organizations. Even though attempts in 1929 and before had failed, the government still remained concerned with getting a religious bodies bill passed through the Diet. In late 1935, the Okada cabinet created a committee to draft a new religious bill. The bill was intended to consolidate and rationalize the existing rules and regulations concerning religious organizations and to place the supervision of religious bodies under the Ministry of Education. It was also directed toward enforcing a more rigid control over religious organizations and eliminating pseudoreligious orders and "fly-by-night" religious promoters. In the context of the mid-1930s, this bill implied the government's wish to have greater power to control new religions such as Omotokyo or Tenrikyo rather than to crimp the natural development of mainstream Buddhism, Shinto, and Christianity. In early 1937, however, the first Konoe cabinet, that had inherited the draft bill, decided to withdraw it.

The outbreak of war in China revived the government's interest in passing a religious bodies law as part of its overall policy of national mobilization for war.[104] The importance that the military placed on control of education and religion was clearly indicated in May 1938, when General Araki Sadao became minister of education in the first Konoe cabinet and remained as such until the fall of the Hiranuma cabinet at the end of August 1939. Above all, General Araki stood for the government's desire to control and utilize religious bodies to bolster government policies.

Under Article 28 of the Meiji Constitution, the government had the ability to restrict religious freedom in order to preserve law and order. As a result, the government could demand that religious organizations receive permission to exist from both the education minister and the regional authorities. Once that permission was granted, religious organizations could be given tax exemption. Article 28 allowed the government to apply pressure on religious associations. At the same time, the issue of the qualifications of priests, that could have become contentious on the ground of religious freedom, was avoided if the religious organization made provisions for adherence to national policies.[105]

In May 1938, the *Fukuin Shimpo* worried that religious freedom, guaranteed in the Meiji Constitution, was not being upheld, and it raised the question of the administration of religions and religious freedom. There was concern that the officials responsible for making religious policy did not understand religious people,[106] and this concern was repeatedly raised. When the draft of the Religious Bodies Law was made public in July 1938, it was sharply criticized in the *Fukuin Shimpo*, that published a series of articles commenting on the draft. They challenged the contention that Christianity so disturbed public order that it needed supervision from above and argued that an investigation into the real situation would show that the freedom of worship was being trampled on. The *Fukuin Shimpo* contended that the people who had devised the draft misunderstood religion and Christianity and that the bill was dangerous and should be eliminated.[107] Although the Konoe cabinet had temporarily retracted its previous bill, it was realized that in a period of increasing control and with Araki Sadao as minister of education such an abandonment would be more difficult. Yet the stakes were high.[108]

Although the draft bill was criticized in the pages of the *Fukuin Shimpo*, such criticism was rare. When the bill was introduced into the seventy-fourth Imperial Parliament in January 1939 by the new Hiranuma cabinet, only one question was raised in the Diet. Sugiyama Genjiro, a close associate of Kagawa and a member of the House of Representatives,[109] inquired why state Shinto was not included in the bill. Araki replied that state Shinto was special and that the bill was designed to protect and to supervise religion.[110] The long-held government position was that state Shinto was suprareligious. In regard to bodies that it considered religious, the ministry's view was that the law was needed to ensure the public peace. The bill was passed without difficulty, and on 23 March 1939 it became law. The law came into effect on 1 April 1940.

It is somewhat surprising that the 1939 legislation should pass with so little protest considering the long history of opposition inside and outside the Diet, dating back to the Meiji period, from Christianity and other religions to any such law. Even the *Fukuin Shimpo* was moderate in its views on the Religious Bodies Law, and, in an editorial at the end of March 1939, it saw the new legislation as being advantageous to Christianity because the writ explicitly recognized the Christian movement.[111] There were some, however, who did express concern. It was reported that Tomita Mitsuro, the moderator of the Church of Christ in Japan (Presbyterian), saw two different attitudes toward the law: one that feared that it would secularize the church, and one that thought that during the national emergency the church must cooperate with the national polity. Tomita worried that the church would lose even more power than it already had if it became a tool of the government.[112] A different tack was taken in a leading article in the Christian publication *Kirisutokyo Sekai*, which noted three main points about the law: first, that it was a religious bodies law and not a religions law; second, that it was to control or supervise all religious organizations; and third, that "it is to encourage religious organizations and so expect them to approve government policies and cultivate the spirit of the people."[113] That the government was now involved in legislating religious organizations was not considered improper. The trauma of the international situation, that provoked the government to call for national solidarity, had clearly reduced the will of the Japanese Christian movement to resist. Another reason for Christian acquiescence was that the NCC, for instance, was under the illusion that, because the law included Buddhism and shrine Shinto, Christianity was being given national recognition.[114] The lack of Christian opposition to the Religious Bodies Law, in such contrast to the stance of Christians ten years before, dramatically reveals the changes in society in the intervening years.

The issue of recognition was particularly significant. As Bishop Abe explained to an American audience in May 1941, "this law, for the first time in the history of the Christian Movement in Japan, gave Christianity a legal status and put it on the statute books as an indigenous religion of the Empire."[115] It was important for Japanese Christians, especially at a time when Japan was fighting a war in China, to gain legal recognition for their religion, because it removed any doubt about their patriotism and loyalty. For Abe, an added benefit of legal recognition was that it could prove "an impetus to the Christian Church to send its roots deeper into its native soil and to orientate itself more fully as an integral part of the nation's life."[116]

What was not foreseen by the Japanese Christian leadership was that religious organizations might have difficulty obtaining permission from the government to exist. In April 1940, when the Religious Bodies Law came into effect, all religious bodies were granted one year's grace during that they could operate under their old charters, but they could not exist beyond that point without first obtaining permission from the government. In June 1940, it was unofficially passed on to a member of the NCC that the Ministry of Education had decided to recognize only Christian denominations that had at least fifty churches and no fewer than 5,000 members.[117] This meant that, of the forty or more Protestant denominations, charters would only be granted to about ten. By August 1940, "it was understood that seven churches,—Presbyterian-Reformed, Methodist, Congregational, Episcopal-Anglican, Holiness (the moderate wing), Baptist and Lutheran,—would be accorded status as recognized denominations.

Each of these was well on the way toward completion of a revised constitution acceptable to the Ministry of Education."[118] Most of these larger denominations looked forward to having their new constitutions adopted during the annual conference season in the fall.

Realizing that they might not receive recognition, the smaller denominations had begun the process of amalgamation. In January 1940, the East and West Conferences of the Japan Baptist Church amalgamated, and in April the sixty-three Korean churches in Japan of the Korean Presbyterian Church, as well as its evangelistic work in Japan, were amalgamated into the Nippon Kirisutokyokai, the Japanese Presbyterian Church. This activity was followed by a flurry of unions as smaller churches, under the threat of nonrecognition, scrambled to amalgamate with larger ones. In 1937, most of the Japan Universalist Christian Church had amalgamated with the Kumiai Church, but a recalcitrant rump in Tokyo remained. In September 1940, it joined the Japan Methodist Church. In the same month, the East and West Conferences of the Nazarene Church amalgamated.[119]

By late 1940, it was clear that the Ministry of Education's original intention of giving official recognition to the largest denominations had given way to a greater plan of combining all the Christian churches. However, further pressure had to be applied before the larger denominations would find the atmosphere conducive to amalgamation.

THE SALVATION ARMY CRISIS

At the end of July 1940, the thought-control police arrested four members of the headquarters of the Salvation Army in Japan, including Victor Leach, an Englishman who worked in its financial department, on charges of spying.[120] Even though they were released quickly, the incident showed that the Tokyo *Kempetai* (military police) was deeply suspicious of the Salvation Army because its international headquarters were in London. Pressure was put on the Salvation Army to reform itself and to denounce its British connections.[121] The arrests had the desired effect, for the Salvation Army swiftly changed its name from Kyuseigun to Kyuseidan (Salvation Group), broke off all its connections with Britain, and did away with its distinctive military-style uniforms and terminology. The arrests had a wide impact, for all denominations with foreign connections began to think about severing them. For churches with foreign links, such as the NSKK and the Japan Methodist Church, the lesson drawn from what had happened to the Salvationists was the need to give up not only financial support from abroad but also foreign missionaries.

It was in an atmosphere of tension caused by the Salvationists' arrest that the NCC held a crucial conference on 17 August 1940 attended by fifty representatives from various denominations. The conference was called to discuss the Salvation Army crisis, the internal and external strains facing the Japanese Christian movement, and inevitably church union.[122] From this conference came a commitment by representatives from the Japan Methodist and Kumiai Churches to begin unofficial discussions about union. Once started, the discussions between these two major denominations developed a momentum of their own, and the drive for church union accelerated to an almost breathless pace.

Between August 22 and 24, the All Japan Cooperative Evangelistic Conference held a consultative meeting in which the establishment of a new structure for Japanese Christianity was discussed.[123] As if to inject another vial of fear into the already frightened veins of Japanese Christians, the Shibuya *kempetai* arrested Kagawa and Ogawa Kiyozumi, one of Kagawa's close colleagues, on August 25.[124] As to the reason for Kagawa's arrest, Albright "understood that the immediate cause was the Kagawa Calendar that consists largely of extracts from his new book, though there may be other older scores as well."[125] Kagawa and Ogawa were quickly released, but the arrests had come on the eve of yet another consultative meeting held by those sponsoring amalgamation. Importantly, the delegates discussed the problem of getting rid of foreign support and gaining independence from Western missionaries.[126] This discussion was part and parcel of the main concern of the meeting—the establishment of a new structure for Japanese Christianity. In light of the recent experience of the Salvationists, the question of gaining independence from foreign missions continued to loom large.

At the same meeting, the Methodists and Kumiai representatives were joined by the Presbyterians in union discussions. Although the year before, in 1939, the Presbyterians had called for a new Christian alliance, they continued to have serious reservations about union because of the difficulty of reconciling articles of faith.[127] Substantial discussions about breaking down theological differences between the major denominations were now taking place.

UNITED CHURCH MISSIONARIES AND THE IMPENDING UNION

On September 2, the NCC sponsored an interdenominational conference at the Tokyo YMCA, and it was attended by some 120 representatives from various churches. It was agreed at this meeting to gain independence from foreign missions and to announce the determination of various churches to amalgamate on October 17 at the All Japan Christian Conference, to be held at Aoyama Gakuin in Tokyo to celebrate the 2,600th anniversary of the founding of the imperial throne.[128] It was also decided to establish a union-preparations committee with members from some thirty-five denominations as well as observers from the NSKK, the Fukyu Fukuin Kyokai, and other groups.[129] As well as pro-union Christians, the Ministry of Education looked favourably upon the progress of preparations for amalgamation and the creation of a new Christian structure. This endorsement was important because it reinforced the view of Abe and his unionist colleagues that they were doing the correct thing.

Writing from his summer cottage at Lake Nojiri about what was happening in Tokyo, Albright reported to Arnup that the NCC-sponsored conference had resulted in a general agreement to effect church union and to eliminate foreign subsidies, but it had not resulted in a decision to ask foreign missionaries to withdraw. Albright indicated that the final decision concerning church union would take place at a mass meeting of Christians in Tokyo on October 17, but it was a foregone conclusion that all objections would be swept aside. Most important for Albright and other United Church missionaries was what the unionized future might hold for them. They looked to Abe for reassurance, because evidently there was mounting pressure from the military police to get Westerners out of Japan. Abe reassured missionaries that they would be well treated, and Albright hoped that "we shall not be intimidated into playing into the hands of those who would like to get rid of us, by means of the mild terrorism that is being adopted under Axis tutelage at the present time."[130] Abe appeared to be optimistic about the future and thought that missionaries would be given time to make the necessary adjustments caused by the need for the church in Japan to become self-supporting.[131] Given the pace at which meetings about church union were taking place, it is difficult to see how the missionary movement would be given the time necessary to make adjustments.

On September 6, Bishop Abe called a meeting of six missionary representatives from the three male boards and the three WMS boards that supported the Japan Methodist Church. Abe began by outlining recent developments, including the Salvation Army trouble, the Anglican Church problem, and the spy scare. He noted that "there had been many extreme rumours that had no basis, but there was underneath it all a strong movement that would have permanent results."[132] The first such result was that the Japan Methodist Church would enter the church union. In the interim, the Nihon Mesujisuto Kyokai (Japan Methodist Church) would change its name to a Japanese one.[133] The Japanese name Kanri Kyokai used in Korea was not popular, so it was suggested that the new name be Toa Kirisuto Kyokai (East Asia Christian Church), which, indeed, would underline the imperial aspirations of the Japan Methodists.

As far as money from abroad was concerned, Abe thought subsidies from the mission boards must be discontinued, although the exact date for their termination had not been determined. The stoppage of funds included some ¥112,000 from the Board of Ministerial Support, of that ¥50,000 was for Bible women. However, importantly, at this stage the termination of foreign subsidies did not include money for special things such as the Central Tabernacle, rural work, social work, and kindergartens.[134] Clearly, this was not a complete discontinuation of foreign financial support. The Japan Methodist Church was obviously trying to avoid suspicion that its pastors and evangelists were in the pay of foreigners, but it still wanted to receive the money from overseas that was directed toward institutions or programs supporting evangelistic and social work. In the future, even this support would have to be discontinued, possibly at the time of church union, because it was thought that the government also wanted kindergartens, hospitals, rural enterprises, and social work institutions to give up foreign subsidies. Nevertheless, the Japan Methodist Church "wanted Missionary Cooperation to continue, by all means."[135]

As to the place and work of missionaries, it was pointed out that "the church cannot accept any financial help for any of its work, but the missionary can carry on as a side line such work as correspondence evangelism, social service work, and even preaching places, if he finances them himself."[136] The continuation of missionary evangelistic work at the local level was also dependent on whether the various district superintendents wanted missionaries working in their districts. As far as educational and social work missionaries were concerned, Abe thought that there was no need for immediate concern.

At the same time as Bishop Abe was attempting to reassure missionaries about educational work, another meeting was taking place involving Christian school principals. This meeting reiterated that all presidents, deans, and departmental heads of Christian schools in Japan had to be Japanese and that these institutions had to free be from foreign financial help. It emphasized that Christian schools should contribute as much as they could to spiritual culture as part of the effort to establish the new order in East Asia. Importantly for missionaries, the Ministry of Education had not decided either whether foreigners should be prohibited from teaching in middle schools or if foreigners of all nationalities should be allowed to teach "thought subjects." Furthermore, the ministry had made no decision about Bible teaching or chapel services.[137] Nevertheless, the meeting of Christian school principals the same day as Bishop Abe's unofficial conference could have done little to lift the hearts of United Church missionaries in Japan or to alleviate their concerns for their future.

On September 17, Bishop Abe, in his role as chairman of the NCC, called a special meeting of all the missionary delegates to that council. He told the assembled missionaries the general consensus of opinion among the Japanese about recent decisions concerning church union. Until this point, missionaries had not been officially informed by the NCC of the results of the many meetings that had taken place. Iglehart, the American missionary, reported that "he [Abe] also expressed the view that in order best to integrate with the life of the new united church some closer-knit inter-mission organization might be needed, though each mission, also, would make its decisions and maintain its traditional relations with its own Japanese church group."[138] The precise relationship between missionaries, missionary societies, and the proposed union church still had to be determined. As ever, Abe was vague about details.

In analysing the problems that faced the Japan Methodist Church and its supporting missions in October 1940, Outerbridge thought that three things should be distinguished even though they were all working toward the same end. The first was the efforts of the churches to attain self-support; the second was the Religious Bodies Law, which necessitated a large number of changes in organization and method including the relationship of the missionary and the mission to the church; and the third was the *shintaisei,* or new structure policy, of the government. Outerbridge argued that the changes that the church in Japan and Christian schools were making were due to pressure from the Ministry of Education, not from specific laws or regulations. He maintained that the ministry was attempting to get the churches and schools to modify organization and method to avoid attack from extremists: "the Educ'l Dept. say 'we are a fire wall trying to protect you from those on the other side who would destroy you. You must support us and make it possible to do so.'"[139] It is difficult to see the ministry as the protector of the Japanese Christian movement.

Outerbridge stressed that Japan Methodist officials wanted "to save the Church from attack if possible."[140] This was a common explanation for the actions of Japanese Christian leaders, yet it had profound consequences for Canadian missionaries. Outerbridge observed that every missionary was considered a spy by Japanese extremists and that all churches, schools, or individuals associated with missionaries were suspect. Furthermore, some Japanese pastors saw missionaries as possible causes of embarrassment because, in some cases, church members had been questioned by the gendarmes about their connections with missionaries. In particular, missionaries who lived in strategic zones such as Shizuoka and Niigata Prefectures and certain parts of Kyushu were having difficulties. As a result of the embarrassment caused by missionary presence, some Japanese Christians wanted the curtailment of missionary evangelistic activities. Outerbridge reported that only one of the thirteen district superintendents in the Japan Methodist Church wanted missionaries to conduct evangelistic work. This was Ono Zentaro of Kofu, one of the great characters among Japanese pastors on the Canadian side of the Japan Methodist Church. It was perfectly in keeping with his personality that he should go against the current and ask for evangelistic missionaries for Kofu.[141] However, the Shizuoka District wanted no missionaries, and the Nagano and Kanazawa Districts wanted Canadian missionaries to restrict their activities to those cities and not to go into the countryside. Considering the earlier success of rural work, in particular in Nagano Prefecture, this restriction was obviously disappointing for the United Church mission. Clearly, unless the political situation changed drastically, there was little future for United Church missionaries in evangelistic work outside Tokyo.

Despite all this, it was stated in a Japanese Methodist newspaper that the church's cooperative policy with missionaries had not changed. After achieving self-support and independence, it was believed, "with thankful hearts for all the beautiful history of the past seventy years of cooperation, this relationship can be preserved without change. Bearing our common burdens in love, it is our fixed purpose to carry on as heretofore with our missionary friends residing in Japan."[142] The Japanese Methodist leadership was either deluding itself or wanted to delude its membership, because it is difficult to see how the relationship could be preserved "without change." If it was simply a matter of continuing Canadian goodwill toward the Japanese Methodist Church, then that was possible. In spite of everything, United Church missionary confidence in Abe remained as strong as ever.

Whereas Outerbridge believed that the future was bleak for American and Canadian missionaries working with the Japan Methodist Church in the provinces, Iglehart regarded developments in the Japanese Christian movement as a whole in a much more positive light. Reporting about the crisis in the movement in October 1940, the American wrote that amid the press of Japanese Christian meetings that had been taking place

> one hears on all sides the expression "hammered into one ball" (*utte ichi-gan*) as the object and the method of conference. In these almost continuous meetings of the past six weeks the corners of difference have been rubbed off while pressures without and within have formed a solid amalgam of unity.[143]

Iglehart obviously thought that these meetings were achieving something positive. His interpretation of the motives behind this intense activity was very different from that of Outerbridge, for the American sympathetically noted that

> It is also impossible to weigh the precise degree of spontaneity and of coercion in it all. To loyal citizens of a country in its fourth year of a life and death conflict no sharp line between these two can seem real. Irresistible currents are sweeping the members of the Christian movement, who cannot live in a vacuum just because they are Christians. Those who are aware of the meaning of the present events do not care to wait till freedom of action becomes impossible.[144]

During early October 1940, there was a series of crucial annual conferences that had the question of union as the chief item on their agendas. These conferences ranged from those of the Methodist, Kumiai, and Presbyterian Churches, the three major denominations, to those of numerically smaller ones such as the Nippon Seikyokai, an offshoot from the Holiness Church, the Baptists, and the Japan Brethren.[145] The support of the three major denominations was, of course, most important, and it was given. The Kumiai Church fully approved Christian unification, that it believed was in keeping with the spirit of the new national structure. The Methodist general conference passed a resolution to refuse all foreign aid. At their annual conference, the Presbyterians also voted to do away with assistance from foreign missions. Even though articles of faith remained a problem, definite ideas for church organization were pressed at the Presbyterian conference.[146] In its unanimous approval of union with other denominations, the Methodist conference suggested that the Apostles' Creed be the basis of faith, that the union be organic rather than federal, and that the name Nippon Kirisuto Kyodan (Japan Church of Christ) be adopted for the new church.[147] The one fly in the ointment was the NSKK, whose bishops wrestled with the question of joining the union as late as the night of October 16 before a decision on the matter was reached.

THE PREDICAMENT OF THE NSKK

The divisive issue of whether or not to join the proposed church union came about with little warning. The quiet tenor of Canadian Anglican missionary work continued relatively undisturbed until the fall of 1940. The Diocese of Mid-Japan was a quiet backwater marked by patient evangelistic and medical work and free from controversy. As late as August 1937, there was every indication that relations between Canadian Anglican missionaries and Japanese Anglicans were untroubled. In that month, in a letter to Canon Gould in Toronto, Daito Chusaburo, the chairman of the Central Committee of the fiftieth anniversary celebration of the NSKK, stated that the missionaries from Canada were "visible signs of the spirit of Christ that more than words teaches us the meaning of the Kingdom of God in that all men, no matter what different races and colors, they may be, are one family."[148] The Canadian Anglican contribution to the development of the NSKK was recognized as having been of some help.

An inkling of problems ahead came in early November 1937, when there was a meeting of all the missionaries in Mid-Japan (some twenty, in fact, attended) at the Tokyo residence of Bishop Samuel Heaslett, the presiding bishop of the NSKK, to discuss the difficulties that had arisen in the NSKK because of the Albert Hall incident.[149] The action of Archbishop Lang marked the beginning of major problems for foreign missionaries associated with the NSKK.

However, Lang's comments did not have an immediate effect on the work of Canadian Anglicans in Mid-Japan, largely because Canadian Anglican work was distant from the centre of change in Tokyo. In October 1937, it was not the political crisis but the calling of hundreds of thousands of reservists to active service, including Japanese Anglican priests, that was causing immediate difficulties for Christian work in the countryside. Furthermore, it was emphasized that the continued poverty of rural Japan was greatly aggravated by the loss of trade caused by the situation in China.[150] A different note was struck by Percy Powles, writing from Takata in February 1938. Powles pointed out that 1937 had not been easy and that Japanese Christians had suffered a mild form of persecution because they were suspected of disloyalty given of their Christian affiliations.[151] This was particularly distressing to Japanese Christians, because this type of persecution had not occurred for many years.

Despite the "wartime conditions of the countryside," Powles thought that there were many opportunities for evangelistic work.[152] He had received numerous invitations to speak, and one of his successes was the development of movie work, for there had been a number of chances to run "Kagawa's *A Grain of Wheat* in the country schools and cooperatives. The subject of the film being the improvement of the villages it lends itself especially well to rural evangelism."[153] The popularity of Kagawa's film could not stop, however, a small reduction in the number of church members in 1937. The cause was the migration of people to the major urban centres and elsewhere. Powles wrote that "our trouble, as always, is the constant removal to Tokyo and other big cities of the Empire. Some of our young people have gone as far as Formosa and some to Manchuria."[154] This problem was not unique to Takata, yet it shows that in spite of the war there was migration both within Japan and to the colonies.

There remained, nevertheless, the missionary hope that the Christian message would succeed. In 1939, Nora Bowman wrote from Nagoya that

> there is a great undercurrent of unrest among the rising generation now, and we believe it is only the Gospel of Christ and the hope of His Second Coming that can stabilize this people. Help us all both Japanese and Canadians to hold forth the banner of our Lord because of the Truth.[155]

Miss F. Hamilton, who arrived from furlough in Canada to take up a new post in Matsumoto in September 1939, was less optimistic, reporting that " though the people here are not on the whole opposed to Christianity they are mostly indifferent to any religion."[156] However, far from retrenchment, the Canadian Anglicans were advocating expansion.

In December 1939, Powles, home in Canada on furlough since June, came out strongly for the continued need for Canadian missionaries in Japan.[157] His view demonstrated a dramatic difference between Canadian Anglicans and their United Church colleagues, for the latter saw no prospect for new missionary work. As far as his work in Takata was concerned, Powles thought that "the Church in her activities had not suffered from war conditions as much as many feared."[158] Although Takata was a garrison town, and a number of factories were off-limits because they had been converted to munitions production, Powles noted:

> I felt myself or my work was not blocked or set back by official or public

antipathy, and I had the satisfaction of knowing that my colleagues could go to many centres and carry on for me where it was wiser for me to stay at home or go in another direction.[159]

Yet there were some difficulties emerging in evangelistic work. One was that the number of enquiring young people was limited because so many were going into the military. Another, rather extraordinary, difficulty was that people were often too tired to listen to public preaching. Powles explained that because of the frequent public meetings

> for regimenting the national feeling ... our Church public preaching gets little response from a tired out people. Even in regard to national gatherings the response to them seems largely based upon the principle of delegation, and one will be sent to represent a family or a village or just a firm or organization.[160]

The government's campaign to mobilize the national spirit was thus both rather ham-fisted and losing momentum. Although public Christian preaching was also failing to reach the now overregimented Japanese, Powles indicated that the number of those who came to his house for interviews was not slackening. Even though a war was going on in China, Christian work continued in Takata without undue difficulty.

Powles was away on furlough in Canada for over a year. During this time, he faced anti-Japanese prejudice from church members in Canada. As he wrote in July 1940,

> It has never been my lot to run up against this prejudice in Church House 'since the Incident began' but I have hit it hard in other quarters, as was to be expected when Japan is an aggressor. One good lady in the W.A. (just an ordinary member) said quite frankly to my wife and me after a meeting that she supposed we were part of the Japanese propaganda machine.[161]

Powles added that "it was pretty clear to me how confused is the thinking of many of our clergy on the actual question of Nationalism and Missions."[162] He tried to avoid making any cultural link between the two, which undoubtedly was hard not to do. Most people did make such a link.

When Powles arrived back in Japan in late October 1940, he found himself in the middle of a major crisis that threatened to end the missionary connection with the NSKK. The immediate cause of the crisis was the Salvation Army incident at the beginning of August. This affair frightened the two senior Japanese bishops, Matsui Yonetaro of Tokyo and Naide Yasutaro of Osaka, into precipitous action.[163] Since the promulgation of the Religious Bodies Act in 1939, there had been a strong movement within the NSKK to reform the church along the lines of the new structure set out in the law. A major barrier to successful restructuring was the episcopal system. The Salvation Army incident

GROWING PRESSURE FOR CHURCH UNION 269

provided Matsui and Naide with the opportunity to force the resignation of the foreign bishops within the NSKK and to initiate reform. In the middle of August, Naide told a meeting of the NCC that the NSKK had rejected foreign financial assistance, and he asked for the withdrawal of missionaries. Although he later attempted to retract his statement about financial assistance and was criticized for his premature call for missionary withdrawal, the Central Committee of the NSKK, of that Naide was a member, announced immediate self-autonomy and self-support. These were difficult times of change in that sudden decisions were often made. As Bishop Abe of the Japan Methodist Church stressed at a meeting with missionaries on September 6, "Japan is at present in the midst of changes equal to those at the Meiji Restoration. The common-sense of yesterday is not that of today or tomorrow, and likewise with the subjects of conversations."[164]

The NSKK and the Holiness Church hung back from union, but there was pressure on them to join. There was a danger that the NSKK might be left out completely if Japanese Anglicans did not agree to join the union committee by October 17. This question was to bedevil the Japanese bishops of the NSKK until the last moment. The Central Committee had entrusted the House of Bishops to make the decision of whether or not to join the union. At the October 16 meeting of the five Japanese bishops who made up the NSKK House of Bishops, it was argued by Naide, together with Bishops Matsui and Yanagihara Sadajiro, that joining the union would save the NSKK. Bishops Sasaki and Yashiro strongly opposed it on the ground that the historic episcopate had to be preserved.[165] Despite the fact that Vice-Minister of the Navy Matsuyama Tsunejiro went to the House of Bishops and threatened to report them to the military police unless all the bishops agreed at once to join the union,[166] Sasaki and Yashiro continued their opposition. The result was that the NSKK did not join the other major denominations in announcing its intention to join the church union at the mass meeting at Aoyama Gakuin on October 17.

Some six weeks before this disagreement in the House of Bishops, Sasaki tried to clarify the situation within the NSKK for Canadian Anglican missionaries. He claimed that Naide's reasons for demanding the resignations of the foreign bishops "simply boiled down to fear of government pressure due to the suspicion of spying by the missionaries and their 'employees.'"[167] The NSKK also wanted to adopt a policy of self-support. This policy Sasaki supported, for he believed that in regard to "the problem of church union—the NSK cannot make an independent stand for truth as long as it is dependent on foreign money—its stand would be regarded as foreign-inspired rather than being of the nature of its own position."[168] The Japanese Anglicans saw Western missionaries and their financial support as impediments to the NSKK's receiving recognition and permission from the government to operate as a distinct and separate church outside the Protestant union. An argument was made by Sasaki and other bishops that the NSKK was neither a Roman Catholic nor a Protestant church and, therefore, should be regarded as a distinct religious organization.[169] Clearly, the NSKK was nearly granted distinct status. The Ministry of Education's religious department changed its attitude regarding granting the NSKK recognition as a separate body only because "a few people within the NSKK who urged unification and later developed its movement very enthusiastically, had by their activities influenced the authorities."[170]

Although Sasaki and Yashiro wanted the NSKK to remain outside the church union, they and the other Japanese bishops remained staunch Japanese nationalists. There was never any doubt about their loyalty to Japan. They took umbrage from the fact that Britain and America were apparently taking China's side in the Sino-Japanese War. Their Japanese nationalism did have a strong bearing on their view of the nature of the NSKK. At the September meeting with Sasaki, the Canadians had a long discussion with him about the implication of the word *Catholic* as it was used in the Anglican Communion. The position that Sasaki took was that the NSKK "must be 'catholic minded' but need not have any connection with non-Japan bodies in order to retain its catholicity. The church can be absolutely separate from any Christian body outside of Japan, and have no fraternal relationships with them, and yet remain catholic."[171] There was a strong hint in this of a unique Japanese Anglicanism separate from outside movements. This achievement would be in keeping with the creation of a *Nipponteki Kirisutokyo*, that had influenced Japanese Anglican thinking since the days of Imai Judo.

Yet the immediate cause of the crisis that greeted Powles on his return to Japan stemmed from the mass meeting of Christians at Aoyama Gakuin in Tokyo at that Bishop Abe had announced that a union church would be formed. On October 17, Horace Watts and Victor Spencer represented Canadian Anglicans at a meeting of some sixty missionary representatives called in Tokyo by Darley Downs and Iglehart, the only two foreign members of the National Christian Council. The purpose was to find out what had happened and what might happen to the missionary movement. Even though the experiences of the various denominations varied, one thing became clear during this meeting: concerning union, "not one society was enthusiastic. Those who had gone in had done so with 'mental reservation' and a feeling of no alternative—as well now as later."[172] Perhaps the most devastating part of the meeting for the future of Canadian Anglican missionaries was the heated discussion stemming from the reading of a report from the American ambassador, Joseph Grew, that recommended the withdrawal of missionaries from Japan.[173] A few days later, Watts would advocate evacuation for Canadian Anglicans. Even if missionaries did remain, changes would have to be made. For instance, Watts noted that "it was mentioned that the word 'Jehovah' was to be eliminated from the Hymn Book."[174] In that connection, Bishop Sasaki later pointed out that "the officials aren't allowing anything that isn't purely Japanese, even though it is 'tadashii' (right, correct, proper, lawful, just)," and he added that "there has actually been no official word at all—just subtle, broad hints, e.g. International law affects the Japanese in U.S.A. and Americans have a right to remain in Japan so the Government can't take an official stand without international complications. So an official gives an unofficial order."[175] So much of what was happening to the Japanese Christian movement and the missionary movement in Japan was the result of "unofficial" orders or vague suggestions emanating from unnamed Ministry of Education officials. It seems that the meeting of missionary representatives in Tokyo on October 17 did little other than unsettle missionaries about their future in Japan.

The missionaries were unprepared for the rapid series of changes that the Japanese Christian leadership decided upon during the two months prior to the mass meeting of Japanese Christians at Aoyama Gakuin to celebrate the 2,600th anniversary of the founding of the Japanese Empire. The missionaries had placed too much trust in Japanese Christian leaders, particularly in the case of the United Church missionaries in Bishop Abe. Yet, his advocacy of *Nipponteki Kirisutokyo* seemingly offered little reason to believe that he would act in the best interests of foreign missionaries. Furthermore, the publication of Hiyane's *Kirisutokyo no Nihon-teki Tenkai* clearly indicated that one of the leading Japanese Christian specialists on religion saw the development of a Christianity in Japan in complete harmony with the Japanese national spirit. Indeed, the reaction of the Japanese Christian leadership to hostilities in north China following the Marco Polo bridge incident, and their enthusiastic support for the creation of a new order in East Asia and for the extension of Japanese Christian missionary work behind the advance of the Japanese army, should have served to warn missionaries to expect the worst.

Although the *Japan Christian Quarterly* carried some translations from the Japanese Christian press, missionaries were apparently not familiar with the debates over missionary work or church union in their own Japanese-language denominational newspapers. It was only in the NSKK's *Kirisutokyo Shuho* that a missionary, the British Anglican Bishop Heaslett of South Tokyo, intervened to counter Japanese views concerning jurisdiction in Chinese or Korean dioceses. No attempt was made by United Church missionaries to challenge the positions taken by Japanese correspondents in the *Nippon Mesojisuto Jiho*. In restricting their attention to the English-language explanations offered by Abe and other Japanese Christian leaders, Canadian and other foreign missionaries unwittingly isolated themselves from ordinary Japanese Christians whose opinions might have differed from those of their leaders.

CHAPTER ELEVEN
Union and Withdrawal

Despite Anglican rejection of church union, the Christian celebration of the 2,600th anniversary of the founding of the Japanese Empire went ahead on the campus of Aoyama Gakuin in Tokyo. The clear public signal given at this mass meeting—that church union was going to take place—set in motion the final negotiations that would lead to the formation of the Nippon Kirisutokyodan (Kyodan) by the summer of 1941. For foreign missionaries, it became clear that there was little possibility for them to continue evangelistic work under the new church. However, it was less clear whether or not specialized missionary work like that carried on in east Tokyo or at Obuse would also have to be stopped. Furthermore, whereas the Japanese Christian leadership was publicly keen to do away with foreign financial support, both the United Church and Canadian Anglican missions were prepared to make generous provisions through the transfer and sale of mission property to lessen the immediate impact of the termination of foreign support.

    As the bargaining between Japanese denominations concerning the nature of the *kyodan* was going on, the growing crisis in East Asia and the increasing likelihood of an Anglo-Japanese war erupting at any moment led the Canadian government to recommend in late 1940 the voluntary withdrawal of missionaries from Japan and its colonies. The missionary societies took heed of this diplomatic advice, and missionaries rapidly began leaving Japan. Some missionaries thought that it was premature to leave Japan and its colonies, but by the summer of 1941 the vast majority of Canadians had left. The speed with that missionaries left inevitably meant that many issues were left unresolved. This was especially true in the case of the relationship of the Nippon Seikokai to the new church, which had not been decided by the time that Canadian Anglicans left Japan. Likewise, the majority of United Church missionaries in Japan had also gone home before the final structure of the *kyodan* had been confirmed. The same was true of the Canadian Presbyterians, who had withdrawn their missionaries from Taiwan, Manchukuo, and Japan by the early summer of 1941. The Canadian Presbyterian decision to withdraw from the three mission fields was made in Toronto. Although Canadian Presbyterian missionaries in Taiwan and Manchukuo remained optimistic about Christian prospects, especially in Manchukuo, they still faced great difficulties in those mission fields. Whereas the Canadian Presbyterians had been prepared to see their mission to the Koreans in Japan amalgamate with the Japanese Presbyterian Church in 1940, they opposed the formation of the *kyodan*. Furthermore, regulations that made the Japanese language mandatory in church services contributed to making the work among Koreans in Japan more difficult.

In October 1940, however, few Canadian missionaries would have believed that within six or seven months their work in Japan would end, at least until the end of the Pacific War. Even in the wake of the mass meeting at Aoyama Gakuin, missionaries were still hopeful that adjustments could be made to allow mission work to continue.

MAKING MISSIONARY ADJUSTMENTS

Even though it had rained the night before and the day itself was chilly and cloudy, an estimated 20,000 Christians were present at the anniversary celebration at Aoyama Gakuin. Arthur Berry, who taught in the theological department of Aoyama Gakuin, noted that "most of them had to sit on the wet ground on thin rough matting. Surely none but a Japanese Christian crowd could have sat on that cold wet ground through the hours of forenoon and afternoon sessions in such enthusiastic patience."[1] Bishop Abe preached, and many other Christian leaders took part, as well as a chorus of 1,500 young people who led the singing, for it was "a day of Christian worship as well as national celebration."[2] Abe capped the proceedings with the announcement that all Protestant churches in Japan would be united into an organic whole. Although this decision was ostensibly the result of voluntary action, according to a contemporary American diplomatic report it was in fact an arbitrary decision handed down by the government authorities through Bishop Abe.[3] Given the intense activity by the NCC and pro-unionists over the past two and a half months, this view was somewhat unfair to Abe. However, it is easy to see why there was some suspicion of the role played by Abe, because prayers for the imperial family were offered. Furthermore, the prime minister and the education minister both sent congratulatory messages to the meeting. There was a hint of blackmailing government interference in this, for the Ministry of Education had made it clear beforehand that the meeting would not receive a congratulatory message from the prime minister unless the intention of church union was announced.

The Japanese Christian leaders did more than just that. The question of the responsibility of the Japanese Church to undertake missionary work on the Asian continent and to provide money to support that endeavour was also raised.[4] This issue underlined the fact that overseas missionary work was a prime reason for church union. For Abe, evangelistic work on the East Asian continent within the Greater East Asia Co-Prosperity Sphere was the crucial factor that joined the two threads leading from his vision of Japanese Christianity (Nipponteki Kirisutokyo).[5] Moreover, public expression of the Japanese Christian movement's commitment to missionary work overseas would clearly show to the government that Japanese Christians were fully committed to helping the Japanese effort in China. Through their efforts in the overseas empire and conquered territories, Japanese Christians were demonstrating their support of the government's spiritual mobilization campaign. Equally clear was that there was little room for Western missionaries in this Japanese missionary endeavour.

On October 18, the first meeting of a new Union Preparations Committee was held at the Tokyo YMCA. This committee was made up of eighty members representing the various denominations. Abe was named chairman, and Tomita Mitsuro, Kozaki Michio, and Ebisawa Akira were among its other officials. These Christian leaders, who had led the drive for union, remained in charge as the final period of preparation for union was entered. By March 1941, the committee made public the union regulations of the new church.[6] It took a surprisingly short time to create regulations acceptable to denominations with sometimes widely differing doctrinal and liturgical views. Yet there were a good many loose ends. Not the least was the question of the relationship of missionaries to the new church structure.

As early as September 1940, Sybil Courtice, the secretary-treasurer of the WMS in Japan, thought that church union was a foregone conclusion, but she understood that "as simple a plan as possible is being worked out for the legal structure and this, if acceptable to the authorities, it is hoped will not too greatly affect the different units in their responsibilities."[7] This was perhaps wishful thinking; even though Abe had asked the Canadian missionaries to remain, Outerbridge believed that, "as we see it however, our presence could scarcely fail to be a serious embarrassment to those who were our friends, or who thought obligated to help us. We feel that the kindest thing we could do is to relieve them of that responsibility."[8] This widely held view would also be used as a common justification for missionary withdrawal. In a sense, though, it obfuscated the situation, which put bluntly was that missionaries were simply not wanted.

The situation for missionaries working in schools was little better than that of their evangelistic counterparts. Although many missionary teachers had gone back to their schools in the fall and had been courteously received by their Japanese colleagues, there were indications that in the new academic year beginning in April 1941, the Ministry of Education would restrict foreign teachers to teaching English language and only at the college and university levels. The one area where missionaries were seemingly least affected by church union or government directives and principles was in social work, because it was thought that the renovation of the national structure had not yet encompassed such activities. As far as evangelistic missionaries were concerned, it was rumoured that only those missionaries who derived their support from the Japanese Church would be allowed to continue work.[9] If that was the case, then few missionaries would be able to remain working in Japan.

The obviously difficult situation facing the missionary movement in Japan was not helped by alarmist rumours coming from outside Japan. On October 17, Jesse Arnup thought it necessary to issue a letter of information and reassurance to friends and relatives of missionaries in Japan, Korea, and north and south China. Arnup pointed out that the Department of External Affairs in Ottawa was prepared to guide to Canadian missionaries in case of evacuation and had established a small emergency committee with the power to act if the need arose.[10] Indeed, the missionary authorities in Toronto authorized the early evacuation of women and children from the mission fields. The replies of the various missions showed that Toronto was overreacting, for "Korea—advises partial evacuation at once; Honan—sent word 'temporarily undisturbed;' Japan—all single women report that all will stay on field as long as the church wants them and the government permits."[11] In early November, some missionary wives and children did return to Canada. For those missionary men and women who remained in Japan, there was little physical danger. It was a matter of waiting to find out more about the new church structure and their place in it.

As part of the process of the United Church headquarters coming to grips with the situation in Japan, an unsigned statement obviously culled from various missionary letters was written in early December 1940. It began by pointing out that, because of "its recent emergence from feudalism, the strength of its prevailing religions, the acceptance of the divine origin of the Emperor and the practice of loyal obedience as the primary virtue, Japan has always been one of our most difficult fields."[12] Nonetheless it was still asserted that "the Japanese are not outside the loving purpose of our Heavenly Father. We look upon it as one of those kingdoms that must become the Kingdom of our God and of His Christ."[13] Missionary optimism remained intact. As to the causes of the current difficulties that missionaries confronted in Japan, the stock answers of nationalism, the new Religious Bodies Law, and the new structure policy of the government were given. However, a further cause was "international strain vis-a-vis Great Britain and the United States. This aggravates the nationalistic attitude, accentuates the totalitarian emphasis and has created some genuine anti-foreign feeling."[14] It was also pointed out that progress toward the formation of a single Protestant denomination had been made but that there seemed to be little place for missionaries in it, so missionaries must be prepared for the worst. Still, there was always the possibility that circumstances would change.

At the end of December 1940, Leland Albright wrote that, even though the diplomatic, political, and economic situation in Japan was worsening, the religious and mission school situation was somewhat better than before. He still thought that "Union will be a federation rather than organic union, in reality, and that may be a good thing, for organic unions take time to mature."[15] There was some hope for missionaries in this form of organization, and the Presbyterian mission had decided to make a place for its missionaries. Albright thought that United Church missionaries might also find a place within the Methodist bloc. In the meantime, provisions had to be made for ongoing missionary work, even though the mission was down to half its normal size and most families were separated. He believed that the best policy was for the mission to concentrate temporarily in two main centres so that

> provision can be made for fellowship and the work shared and reshuffled as people leave *or* others return, from time to time. At the same time, we must do our best to keep or to provide as soon as possible an F. M. B. missionary in or near each W. M. S. station during this ensuing period of still further uncertainty.[16]

Albright was looking forward to a Japan mission council meeting at the beginning of January at that the placement of missionaries would be discussed. However, much depended upon the opinion of Bishop Abe.

The stationing of WMS missionaries proved to pose little difficulty. Indeed, Albright noted about Abe in January 1941 that "his attitude is fine and he understands our situation," and later in the same letter to Arnup he added that "it was almost uncanny and shows how well he knows our field and personnel."[17] It proved more difficult to appoint male missionaries within the Methodist bloc. Abe, perhaps conscious of the Ministry of Education watching over his shoulder, was in no rush to do this. Albright remained optimistic, although he realized how much depended upon Abe personally. He wrote that, so long as Abe remained in office, the missionaries had little to fear, but he added: "In fact our only standing in the united or federated church *may* be just his appointment to this work or that. Even in the continuing Methodist bloc, our status is not *assured*, except in so far as we are appointed to this station or that."[18] This was not altogether a reassuring reality at the beginning of the new year.

Nevertheless, Albright and his fellow Canadian missionaries in Japan retained their great faith in Abe. In January 1941, William Scott, visiting Japan from Korea, noted that "our Canadian missionaries know that Bishop Abe is sincere in this desire [to continue to cooperate with missionaries], and the confidence with that they face the future of their work in Japan rests, to a great degree, upon their faith in this wise, able and gracious Christian leader." He added that Abe was "thought of as a gift of God, a man raised for such a time as this, whose wise judgement, gracious personality and able leadership will steer his [Methodist] church through the present crisis."[19] It is striking, however, in light of Abe's speech at Aoyama Gakuin and his subsequent authoritarian actions in regard to union, that the Canadians should still hold that opinion.

Yet part of the reason why Scott and other Canadian missionaries retained their faith in Abe was a feeling in January 1941 that political change was in the air in Japan. Scott wrote that "no one minimized the menace to Christian faith and fellowship of the present state domination, anti-foreign drive and exaggerated nationalism. But one and all asserted that these were passing phases, superimposed from above and encouraged from without, that did not reveal or alter the real Japan."[20] To the missionary, "the real Japan" was one in that missionary work was welcomed by Japanese Christians. Indeed, influential church leaders such as Abe kept missionary hopes alive by stressing that there was still a place for missionaries.[21] Of the mood of the conference that he had attended in Japan, Scott noted that the "prevailing note was one of confidence: confidence in the work of the years; confidence in the Japanese church and her leadership; confidence in the continuity of the Christian fellowship through missionary service."[22] Such confidence would turn out to be misplaced, but the time it only confirmed in Scott the belief that Canadian missionaries should remain in the mission field.

Abe could do little to spare Canadian missionaries from the distressing visit of Bishop Baker and Dr. Diffendorfer, representing the American Methodist Episcopal missionary societies. They came to Japan with the mandate to evacuate their missionaries from Korea and Japan. Albright wrote damningly that Baker and Diffendorfer had not seemed "to get the situation in Japan; then rather suddenly the situation seemed to get them, and they appeared to us to be more panicky than missionaries in general, not to say government school teachers or business people," and he added that "the missionary groups seemed to be much calmer than our visiting executives."[23] Possibly he thought that calmer heads might have prevailed had Arnup and Mrs. R. D. Taylor, the WMS secretary in Toronto, both of whom had been invited by Abe to visit Japan with the Americans, been able to come.[24] The visit of Baker and Diffendorfer coincided with the pull-out of American Methodist missionaries in Korea, with which Scott and the small group of remaining Canadians did not agree. To Albright, the situation in Japan was not grave enough for the full evacuation of missionaries. He thought that "missionaries in near-totalitarian states will just have to be a bit thick-skinned in some matters, and very sensitive on essentials. And I believe that far more serious than any embarrassment caused by our presence, would be the disappointment at our withdrawal, before absolutely necessary."[25] Given the problems over the stationing of male missionaries, Albright was giving the benefit of the doubt to the Japanese when he thought that they wanted missionaries to stay as long as possible. Despite all the difficulties that he was facing, he still had time to read. At the end of a letter to Arnup written toward the end of January 1941 in which he gave his thoughts on the ongoing political and international situation in Japan and East Asia, Albright noted that he was going to "read another chapter of Herbert Norman's book, 'Japan's Emergence As A Modern State.' It is quite good for an understanding of present day Japan in its political, economic, social and agrarian phases."[26] Norman, serving at the Canadian Legation in Tokyo, was well known to all United Church missionaries in Japan because of his family connections.

For most Canadian missionaries, the question of withdrawal could not be answered by reading history. Outerbridge was more sympathetic than Albright to Baker and Diffendorfer and their argument for withdrawal. Yet he was also opposed to complete withdrawal. One reason why he did not believe that the remaining Canadian missionaries should leave was that "in our own UCC group we are, or will be in a couple of months, reduced to an irreducible minimum. Those who remain are trying to hold up all the props that support the structure, but if they go, it must fall."[27] Yet, for Outerbridge, the most important argument against withdrawal was sentimental:

> Our Japanese Christian people are feeling very lonely and apprehensive concerning the future. They look to us for that intangible sort of encouragement which comes from a sense of camaraderie, of conscious unity in support of a common cause. It is all so entirely unexpressed, and they do not feel that they can express it, under the circumstances, but it is extremely clear, I think, to all of us who have remained. To leave at this time before there is a clear mandate to leave would be to make them feel forsaken by those in whom they trusted.[28]

Despite the public pronouncements of Japanese Christian leaders, some Japanese Christians remained strongly attached to individual missionaries, such as Outerbridge, whom they might have known for many years. This sentimental attachment should not be dismissed. Yet feelings could be played the other way, especially the reticence of the Japanese to be frank in their opinions due to their innate politeness. Outerbridge believed that Baker and Diffendorfer were returning to the United States

> with a distinct impression that some leaders in the church feel that it would be less embarrassment if we were all to leave at this time. They are inclined to wonder if that is not true everywhere, and if Japanese politeness has not prevented some other leaders from expressing their true feelings.[29]

Even Outerbridge, however, admitted that there was a possibility of war, which would necessitate missionaries to leave: "if our prophets, both in America and Japan are right, that gives us from two to three months still to stay here. But of course they may all be wrong, and the final show-down indefinitely postponed or averted."[30] If the war prophets turned out to be wrong, then missionaries would be thankful that they had stayed. Whether war broke out sooner or later, the authorities in Toronto were informed that nearly fifty percent of WMS missionaries had indicated to Courtice that they preferred to remain in Japan even under war conditions. Outerbridge noted that "some of the WMS ladies are much more closely absorbed in the details of their work than we are, and much less conscious of the political and international movements taking place and the implications of those movements than we are."[31] Even he admitted that there might be some danger if some WMS missionaries did decide to stay after the outbreak of war. In the event of war, he thought that the WMS should be unequivocal in demanding every missionary to withdraw. Indeed, as early as October 1940, the Department of External Affairs in Ottawa had been trying to impress upon the WMS that its missionaries in Japan were "running chances that may well result in complications and trouble for the Government as well as hardship and, perhaps, danger for themselves" by continuing their work as long as possible.[32] In February 1941, Norman Robertson, the acting deputy minister of state for external affairs, wrote to Taylor in Toronto stating that the department was disturbed that WMS missionaries in Japan without exception had decided to remain at their posts. Robertson stressed that the situation in East Asia, increasingly more threatening, should not be underestimated. He pointed out that war would probably come suddenly and that it would be impossible for the Canadian government to bring out any Canadian missionaries or nonofficials caught in Japan or occupied areas at that time. Robertson also thought that Canadians would be badly treated if they were caught in Japan at the outbreak of hostilities:

> It is sometimes suggested that because the Germans who were caught in Japan during the last war were not badly treated, it would probably not be very serious if Canadians should have to remain in Japan during a war between that country and the British Commonwealth. This argument is completely fallacious. In the last war the Japanese were only meagre participants and they were not seriously aroused by the points at issue. If a war should come now Japan would be fighting for her life and fighting, so far as the ruling groups are concerned, with a bitterness unparalleled in the history of that country. It might be a very seriousthing to be a Canadian in Japan during such a war.[33]

Although Robertson believed that the Japanese government would observe the niceties of international law in reference to the personal rights of members of the diplomatic corps, he also thought that "the present Japanese Government and those upon whose support it chiefly rests could be expected to treat non-diplomatic Canadian nationals with great severity—or what would appear to be great severity to those who experience it."[34] In hindsight, Robertson was mostly correct in his views. Canadian diplomats were treated well, but he was proved wrong concerning the treatment of Canadian missionaries by the Japanese authorities after the war began. They were not mistreated. The wrath of the Japanese government and its military did, however, fall on Canadian prisoners of war, who were cruelly and criminally mistreated. Robertson did his best to warn the WMS of the consequences probably in store for those missionaries who did not return to Canada. Indeed, it must have been annoying for the Department of External Affairs, in the midst of dealing with all the problems stemming from the war in Europe and the Atlantic, that it should have to remind female missionaries in far-off Japan of the dangers of staying on, which should have been as patently evident to them as it was to the mandarins in wintry Ottawa.

The male missionaries were all prepared to return to Canada at such a time, and already the tying up of loose ends, in regard to schools and the transfer of mission property to the Japan Methodist Church, was well in hand. Yet Outerbridge remained firm in his belief that the Japan Methodist Church and the Kwansei Gakuin wanted Canadian missionaries to stay in Japan as long as possible.

At the Foreign Mission Board executive meeting held at the Kwansei Gakuin on 3 February 1941, it was again pointed out that Abe wanted Canadian missionaries to go on with their normal work as long as conditions allowed. If the situation became critical, Abe thought, then it would be best for missionaries to concentrate in Tokyo and be prepared to evacuate without embarrassment when war appeared imminent. Although the Japan Methodist Church would do its best for any who were unable to get away, it was pointed out that, "if any remain during the war on principle, this will constitute a real embarrassment for the Church, but the Church will share the difficulty involved."[35] Noticeably, the point of embarrassment to the Japanese Church was brought up again. In any case, in the middle of February, a telegram was sent from Toronto calling for the complete evacuation of women from Japan and Korea and strongly urging the early evacuation of men.[36] This message did not sit well with the WMS missionaries, but the headquarters in Toronto had decided that they must be evacuated.

The February meeting also considered the transfer of title on lesser pieces of missionary property that had not yet been passed over to the Japan Methodist Church's *iji zaidan* (support foundation). Furthermore, there were requests and demands for continued missionary financial support or gifts. It was calculated that the financial obligations of the mission up to March 1942 were ¥55,760. This amount included a grant of ¥24,000 to the Japan Methodist Church, as well as grants of ¥10,000 to both the Central Tabernacle and the East Tokyo Social Service Centers.[37] In all, ¥56,000—of that the ¥24,000 was the first instalment—was to be paid to the Japan Methodist Church, the equivalent of two years of support, "to make possible the adjustment of the pastors' salaries without too much suffering and injustice."[38] After this final payment, the United Church mission was only obligated to pay pensions to the widows of three former Canadian Methodist pastors, which only amounted to some ¥960 per year. The Central Tabernacle received three years of funding as well as the final grant of ¥10,000. The financial cushion that the United Church mission was providing to the Japan Methodist Church and its institutions was considerable and would allow the Japanese Church to operate for a couple of years without too much strain.

By the beginning of March, Abe had come to the conclusion that it was inevitable that missionaries should leave Japan. He wrote to Arnup in Toronto on March 4: "I am sorry that a number of missionaries are leaving the country but I take it this is inevitable for them. Still, the sentiment of our church is unchanged; they will be welcomed back to Japan again and to their stations when they can return." He went on to state: "I also hope the day will soon come when all our missionaries may continue their work undisturbed by wars and rumours of war."[39] As a sign of his goodwill toward missionaries, Abe made the effort to ensure that missionaries retained their active status and their respective stations in Japan while they were temporarily back home.[40] This status would allow missionaries to return to work in Japan without having to be reappointed.

In early March 1941, a report on the United Church mission's financial situation pointed out that "for about a year no drafts have been sold, and the missionary salaries, the grants to various institutions, and the regular working budget have all been met out of the proceeds of the sale of property,—both mission and personal."[41] In other words, the United Church mission was able to finance itself in the past year without having to draw on money from Canada. The mission continued to hold property, with a total value of ¥700,000 or $182,000, consisting mainly of the Canadian Academy property, the Koishikawa Mission House property in Tokyo, and various missionary residences in Nagano, Kanazawa, Fukui, and Shizuoka. All this property had been registered in the mission *shadan*, or juridical person, made up of missionaries for the purpose of holding property. In the absence of missionaries from Japan, the Canadian Legation had been appointed to be the mission's representative. The reason was to ensure, should the property be confiscated, the mission's right to it. At the end of hostilities, the mission could therefore claim compensation for any loss of or damage to its property.

WITHDRAWAL FROM MID-JAPAN

On 22 October 1940, there was an emergency two-day meeting in Nagoya of the Canadian Anglican mission, with virtually all missionaries, both male and female, as well as Bishop Sasaki, in attendance.[42] This meeting was held in the wake of the round of church union meetings in Tokyo that had culminated in the mass meeting at Aoyama Gakuin. The Canadian Anglicans wanted Sasaki to explain what had happened at the recent discussions in Tokyo and the response of the NSKK to the question of church union. Moreover, the

Canadians were looking to the bishop for reassurance about their own role in the Diocese of Mid-Japan. This emergency meeting turned out to be one of the most significant meetings in the history of the Canadian Anglican mission in Japan. According to Percy Powles, it got off to a bad start. Despite an agenda that put the simplest business first in order to create a momentum before tackling more difficult questions, the missionaries were seemingly unable to reach any final decisions because of the need to refer matters to the diocese and the bishop. Powles wrote:

> when we adjourned for a short breathing space I suggested to Horace Watts that the apparent flagging was due to the indecision of the Bishop, and with most questions I thought there was a graver question which must be settled first—the future of our work as priests of the Diocese.[43]

Consequently, Powles drafted a letter of resignation that he and Watts showed first to Victor Spencer and then to the WA missionaries before finally presenting it to Sasaki. This action provoked criticism from the WA missionaries, who did not think that the immediate situation warranted such precipitous action. There was little in their daily contact with Japanese in their kindergarten or evangelistic work to suggest that wholesale resignation served any useful purpose at that time. Perhaps WA missionaries were not as aware of the seriousness of the international situation as their male clerical colleagues, but like their WMS counterparts in the United Church mission they preferred to stay on rather than being rushed into leaving what they still considered valuable work. Furthermore, they were only consulted after the male clerical missionaries had decided to offer their resignations. Powles wrote that "the ladies did not take any part in this definite action, as we did, in putting their resignations at the disposal of the Bishop, and I believe that some of them are rather grieved that the Bishop grouped us all together in asking us to go home."[44] Despite objections from the WA missionaries, the letter was given to Sasaki, who told the men that the matter would be discussed that evening at a meeting of the diocesan Standing Committee.

The next morning, when the missionary meeting reconvened, the bishop was asked if he had anything to report. His response was that "he wanted to talk to us in a very frank manner and forthwith proceeded to give us an outline of the situation at the present moment and our relation to it."[45] Sasaki began by reviewing the events of August 1940 concerning the movement for self-support for the church and the elimination of foreigners from official positions. He mentioned that "there was a private order issued by the Military Police about August 22-23rd but because of the previous decision of the church no one was arrested by them."[46] Sasaki did not clarify this private order of the *kempetai* or how, as nobody was arrested, it had become public knowledge. However, this order obviously acted as a spur for reforming the NSKK. At the meeting of the

House of Bishops on October 3, the resignations of the foreign bishops (all except Bishop Basil Simpson of Kobe, who was gravely ill and hospitalized at the Mayo Clinic in the United States) were accepted and were to take effect that month.[47] Until the general synod, to be called in March 1941, Matsui of Tokyo was put in charge of the Dioceses of Hokkaido and South Tokyo; Sasaki of Mid-Japan had Tohoku and North Tokyo added to his responsibilities; Naide of Osaka was given Kyoto; Yanagihara of Osaka became responsible for the missionary districts of Taiwan, Korea, and Manchukuo; and Yashiro of Kobe was to supervise Kobe and Kyushu.[48] There was also the question of financial self-support. This goal was not easy, at least, for the Diocese of Mid-Japan. Even with supplementary support from the richer Dioceses of Tokyo and Osaka, there would barely be enough money to support twenty clergy in Mid-Japan at a minimum of ¥50 per month. Yet it was the question of union that was the major concern for the Japanese bishops.

Sasaki told the Canadian Anglican missionaries that "the political aspect of the situation is that they [the authorities] want a purely Japanese church in accord with the new regime."[49] At first, Bishops Matsui and Naide were in favour of joining the union if the *torisha* (titular head) would be ordained in accordance with NSKK conventions. As a result, the rumour got around that the NSKK was joining the union. However, within the Anglican Church, the question of union became bogged down in controversy over how the *torisha* should be elected. More important, however, was a general feeling at the meeting of the Executive Committee of the general synod held on October 3 that the best option for the NSKK was to get recognition as a distinct organization. In order to resolve the issue of union, the Executive Committee gave full authority to the House of Bishops, and the foreign bishops in their turn gave full authority to the five Japanese bishops to decide the question, so that it could not be said that the foreign bishops dictated any decision against union. The Japanese bishops believed that the Lambeth Quadrilateral was the only basis on that the NSKK could enter the church union, but they did not know whether this basis would be acceptable to the NCC. On October 4 and 5, the bishops went to the NCC and to the Ministry of Education to tell them that they had decided not to join the union church. Both groups urged the Japanese Anglicans to reconsider and to join. In particular, the NCC was afraid that the Presbyterians would also reject union if they heard that the Anglicans were not joining, so the bishops were asked to delay their final decision until the last moment.

Importantly, there was also the threat of arrest if the bishops did not agree to join the union. Sasaki returned home on October 14 and deliberately changed into his winter clothing because "he had received word that he would be arrested if he continued to oppose union—two Presbyterian and Congregational men in authority opposed the Bishop's stand and said they'd have him arrested."[50] Just who these men were or how they would have Sasaki arrested was not made clear, but even the suggestion raises the spectre of quislings within the Japanese Christian movement.

Despite this threat, the position of the majority of the bishops did not change. Sasaki reported that there was the danger of a split within the church, because two bishops took the position that "we believe we are saved by Jesus Christ and the outward church form has no connection with that essential fact; they said that those opposing did so just because they didn't want to lose their positions as bishops."[51] However, eventually they were won over, and all agreed to vote against union. Sasaki made it clear that it was for doctrinal reasons that he and his fellow bishops opposed union. Nevertheless, there remained the issue of the NSKK as a separate entity receiving recognition and permission to operate from the government. The question was raised that, "if the Bishops have no real reason for not going into the union, then they may not receive official recognition," but it was added that "this is not directed solely at the Christian Church because Buddhists and Shintoists are also being required to unite and are finding the same difficulties and opposition from sects."[52] Sasaki mentioned that the Roman Catholics, who had eighteen dioceses in Japan, had been asked by the authorities to reduce that number and to appoint Japanese bishops. Furthermore, the Apostolic delegates had been demoted to advisers. The NSKK had, in fact, done much the same as the Roman Catholics. Indeed, now that church union was rejected, it was the implied hope of Japanese Anglicans that they would be treated by the Ministry of Education in the same way as the Roman Catholics. However, a response from the ministry was not expected until March 1941, when the general synod of the NSKK would also meet.

Powles wrote about Sasaki's report that apparently there was not "much room for us [missionaries] out here politically nor any desire on the part of the Church that we should stay and invite and share such persecution as came along."[53] Not only that, but Sasaki also believed that the foreign missionaries in Japan "aggravated the situation and made matters difficult in a number of ways. He particularly stressed the English connection and the economic power of help coming from abroad to support the Church."[54] Sasaki was determined that the church would become independent in the matter of clerical salaries from January 1941 on, and Powles added about missionaries that "as our manner of living was too extravagant compared with that of the Japanese clergy we would only irritate the situation and make it very difficult for those who were trying in various ways to support themselves."[55] It was clear to him that "the Japanese authorities in the Diocese did not want us and . . . that there would be little we could do. Many questions were asked of the Bishop along this line until it became increasingly evident as to what was wanted of us."[56] As missionaries talked with the bishop, Powles noted that emotions began to rise: "I felt my throat closing up and one could sense that everybody was very much moved. Horace Watts rose to move a motion of withdrawal and feelings began to run rather high so I suggested from the chair that we pause and sing a hymn."[57] Such was the emotional strain, Powles noted, that "we all began to break down, realizing that another chapter in our lives was about to be finished, and finished before we had the chance to put on any finishing touches."[58] He felt special sympathy for Watts and the position on withdrawal that he had taken:

> I have never seen Horace Watts so deeply moved. He was quite broken up because some had bitterly attacked him for moving a motion of withdrawal "willingly." They thought we should have waited to be put out. But it seems to me that Horace was perfectly right, and no gentleman who for years has been working more or less in the spirit of a guest and helper is going to wait until he is put out. His feelings as both guest and gentleman tell him the time to come and go. When we were acting as a Mission, seeking to build the bottom foundations of the Church, I would say that it were a flaw too in our sense of duty had we laid our tools down and fled. We would not have been missionaries in the real sense of the word. But that day is over, and when all control, even to a complete Japanese Standing Committee [Spencer was compelled to resign] and Bishop, is in the hands of the Japanese surely we work as a helper and servant and not as an architect and finisher.[59]

Another factor weighed on the missionary decision to withdraw, and that was the political situation. Powles wrote that the consul general had twice warned them about the gravity of the international situation, but "it was better, to my mind, to keep the two issues quite separate for one would hate to think that we were returning just out of 'fear' of war."[60] This was wishful thinking, for without the political changes taking place internally and externally, Canadian Anglicans would have been welcome to carry on their work.

That was certainly the tenor of the response of the Standing Committee to the letter of resignation from the missionaries, even though it favoured missionary withdrawal. The standing committee pointed out in its address to the missionaries that "a completely new state of affairs, a new condition and atmosphere, have arisen in Japan, and there is much doubt, whether, until this is fully comprehended in other countries, foreigners can fit into the new movement."[61] It was further stressed that "nationalism is just now so strong in Japan that if our Nippon Seikokwai has close connection with foreigners, even missionaries, she will be suspected and shunned by the people," but it was added: "if, however, conditions in the world, and in Japan especially, should revert to what has been, we trust that we shall again be closely united in heart and work with our Mother Church as we have been hitherto."[62] In the interim, the diocese wanted, in church matters, to achieve self-support and independence.

As Powles well knew, not all missionaries were in favour of resigning or withdrawing. On October 29, Miss Gertrude Hamilton wrote privately to Canon Dixon in Toronto that "as you already know we have resigned, though a number of us women had different ideas about that. The men seemed to think quite differently about some things."[63] By this time, however, it was too late to complain. The men had cabled to Toronto that "all Canadian missionaries should return to Canada by April and the mission properties be handed over to the Diocese."[64] Moreover, an emergency meeting of the subexecutive of the MSCEC had been called in Toronto by Dixon, which the retired Bishop Hamilton attended as adviser at the primate's request. After careful consideration, the subexecutive had acquiesced to the gradual return of missionaries.[65] A statement to the Canadian press released on October 26 said that the twenty-six missionaries (six of whom were on furlough in Canada) would all be back in Canada by April.[66] Another statement announcing the mission's withdrawal was published in the *Japan Advertiser* on October 27, stating that,

> in view of the changed circumstances in Japan, circumstances over that we have no control, and that show no indication of change for a number of years we realize that our presence in this country will not be of sufficient help to the Nippon Seikokwai to justify our remaining in Japan.[67]

The Canadians also informed the senior foreign Anglican missionary in Japan, Bishop Heaslett, the presiding bishop of the NSKK, of their decision. Heaslett responded to the news by writing to Spencer in Nagoya that

> your p.c. is very very sad reading. The end of a great & noble effort to found a Church in Japan. But only a material end, the spiritual effort lives & will grow—& in some ways, yet unseen to us, in the future, we may be allowed again to help them from our inherited spiritual riches.[68]

A few days later, Heaslett wrote again to Spencer that he had heard in detail from Reg Savary, one of the younger Canadian Anglican missionaries, about the missionary conference: "it must have been an intense 3 days for all of you. I found Savary much moved & could guess what the seniors must have thought."[69] It was obviously a blow to the American and British missionaries in the NSKK that the Canadians had decided to withdraw, because it made their own staying on more difficult.

As it turned out, however, the Canadians were not alone in their decision, for the American Church mission had also begun making preparations to leave. There was exasperation at what was going on in Japan at the headquarters of the Protestant Episcopal Church in New York. At the end of October 1940, John Wood, the executive secretary of the Protestant Episcopal Church Department of Foreign Missions, wrote to Dixon in Toronto that, "at a long meeting yesterday, I failed to get any useful information with regard to the situation."[70] Obviously, the authorities in New York found it difficult to keep abreast of the rapidly changing circumstances in Japan. This uncertainty was also true of the United Church of Canada headquarters, that precipitously issued telegrams ordering withdrawal when its missionaries in Japan saw no need for it. In the case of the Anglicans, the situation was the opposite, for the decision to withdraw was made by missionaries in the field rather than at head office. Indeed, given the diocesan structure and the recognized rights of bishops and clergy within it, it would have been surprising if Church House on Jarvis Street had either demanded the withdrawal of its missionaries or objected to their decision to return home. Yet what Jarvis Street did possess beyond moral persuasion was the power of the purse to influence events. In that respect, it was useful for Dixon to learn that the three American missionary bishops were leaving behind for their dioceses in Japan "a 'parting gift,' with the understanding that there will be no further appropriations for Japanese Evangelistic workers."[71] He knew, therefore, how much the Canadian Anglicans would have to pay on leaving. This amount was important, because the Canadian Church itself was hard pressed, for grants from Britain had gone to help support some of the dioceses in Canada itself.

The issue of money and the transfer of property were not simple matters. Hamilton, the WA missionary, for instance, was worried by Sasaki's apparent intention, after hearing that the Canadian Anglican property was being transferred to the diocese, to sell the kindergarten training school property in Nagoya, to lay off a number of workers and Bible women, and to use the profits and savings to build a cathedral.[72] In transferring property to the diocese, the Canadian Anglicans also wanted some payment from the Japanese for the return passage of missionaries to Canada. The Japanese, for their part, expected ¥40,000 in cash from Canada as a parting gift "either for the Bishop's Endowment or to swing the transfer of the regimes."[73] On learning of the financial difficulties of the Canadian Church, the Japanese did not press for the bishop's endowment. As a quid pro quo, the missionaries thought that they could only ask for ¥36,000 from the diocese to assist in paying for their passages home. The missionary residences were the only things that Powles did not want Sasaki to liquidate, because he hoped that they could be held as a future tie between the churches in Canada and Japan.[74] However, he realized that it was difficult to tie the hands of a future regime by fixing conditions to the transfer of property.

The tuberculosis sanatorium at Obuse was also of some concern. The wholesale withdrawal of Canadian Anglican missionaries meant that Dr. Richard Start and the missionary staff at the sanatorium would also pack up and go home. Powles noted:

> I doubt if the Bishop or Diocese wanted the staff to withdraw from Obuse or the grant to cease in 1941. He seemed to think it might carry on with both foreign staff & grant, being of social service & no promise having complicated things. However now the international situation makes it inevitable.[75]

There is a hint in this that a mistake, albeit in the form of a misunderstanding, had been made. Powles and Watts thought of withdrawal in terms of total withdrawal, but the Japanese had a compartmentalized view, that the WA missionaries possibly understood better than their male clerical colleagues (thus their objection to being lumped with the men in having to resign). Although the Japanese saw self-support and independence in terms of congregations and clerical freedom from foreign direction, specialized social work and medical work existed in separate compartments. The latter were judged by different criteria. As Wood, the Protestant Episcopal executive secretary in New York, pointed out, "the Japanese seem to be making a clear cut distinction between mission activities that are described as 'thought' activities and those that are of a more purely humanitarian character. Wherever the activity involves the influencing of 'thought' the tendency is to replace the foreigner at an early date."[76] The tuberculosis sanatorium at Obuse was clearly a humanitarian activity.

Yet there was always the political situation to fall back on. At the beginning of November, Powles said that "twice I have received notifications about evacuation and I may have to flee suddenly to Australia if we are called out."[77] Hindsight suggests that the diplomats were premature in advocating the evacuation of Britons and Canadians, but the Canadian Anglicans obviously followed their advice. Spencer, Watts, and Powles planned to stay in Japan until April 1941 in order to wind down mission affairs, but the rest were going as quickly as they could find passage home. The personal cost of leaving a life's work was high. Powles wrote to his sons:

> I know you will be bitterly disappointed that Mother and I will not be able to continue what we thought was a life-task in Japan but it may be that you will have the joy of doing something for Japan that we have never had. Evidently God wants us to lay down our tools and look for another job, and when the Japanese have finished making the foundation secure that you will be able to help with more of the superstructure or even future foundations.[78]

In early December, Powles, acting as chaplain at the Obuse sanatorium, wrote: "at present I am suffering from a bad attack of helplessness and every day is a great struggle to keep God at the centre of things. Our Obuse hospital is feeling the tremors just like all other places and the whole staff is wondering what is going to happen."[79] Although his presence at Obuse could help to keep the institution on an even keel, he was deeply concerned about both the future of the NSKK and the actions of Sasaki in particular. About the church, he wrote:

> From what I can see and read we are in the midst of a great earthquake in Church and State, and what will be the eventual shape of the mountain when all the land has slipped and found its centre of gravity I do not know. One feels tremors and shivers in all quarters and wherever you happen to be there is a

feeling of nervousness among our clergy which is preventing them from taking a sense of permanency in their work.[80]

Powles believed that he knew where the earthquake had started, and it was a place where missionaries no longer had much influence: "I do not like to say so, but the earthquake seems to have started with our Bishops. Perhaps they knew what they were doing. I cannot tell, but undue haste on their part seems to have shaken things up badly."[81]

Yet his sharpest criticism was reserved for Sasaki:

> Even our own Bishop whom I trusted as a solid and very composed man is just through with nationalism and allows it to influence him in ways which I would never have suspected. And it is all the more incomprehensible in view of his rather extreme views on the Church. How he harmonized them is a continual puzzle to me.[82]

Sasaki had been bishop of Mid-Japan since 1935, and until October 1940 his tenure had been marked by no major crisis within the diocese. Furthermore, he had always been able to look to Spencer, a member of the diocesan Standing Committee and the senior Canadian Anglican missionary in Nagoya, for advice. After October 1940, Sasaki was much on his own and was obviously revealing a side of himself that had not surfaced before. Powles noted that

> the isolation of the authorities in the State from the people seems to carry over into the Church and we have there a similar situation, the one acting almost independently of the other and in no way reflecting the popular opinion. When I say the authorities I must include the Standing Committees of the various Dioceses."[83]

Worry about Sasaki's actions continued for Powles. In late January 1941, he noted that Sasaki

> seems to be standing very much aloof from us missionaries at this time when a little more friendly counsel would be good for us both. All men complain that he is too autocratic and makes all decisions himself and gives them without any opportunity of talking things over. One man said to me, 'He is our Hitler Bishop.'"[84]

Given his national proclivities and their impending withdrawal, it is not surprising that the bishop stood aloof from the missionaries. However, he was also not getting on with his own clergy. Part of the problem, Powles thought, was the fact that "many of the men would like to bring their grievances to some of us, or to the Mission, for help in their time of stress," but he added that "it simply cannot be done if things are to be readjusted, and so we are better out of the way."[85] It is interesting that some of the Japanese clergy had looked to the Canadians in the past to counter the power of the bishop and the Standing Committee. Nevertheless, Powles reaffirmed his view that the decision to withdraw was the correct one. He believed that the question of withdrawal was vexing, but he held that "it is almost necessary for a proper reorientation of the Church work. What I mean is that all the different attitudes or loyalties have to be readjusted and it is not easy while we are present."[86]

With the missionaries gone, the Japanese Anglicans could not take their grievances to the mission instead of their bishop. It seems, however, that Powles had more faith in the ordinary church member to do the right thing in terms of Christianity than in their "Hitler Bishop." A case in point was the reaction of church members to rumours about the creed of the union church. Powles wrote:

> Bishop Abe of the Methodists said that pressure has been brought to bear on them about the elimination of the Virgin Birth, the Resurrection and the Last Judgement. Certainly I know our church members will not broke any interference with the Apostles Creed. Any to whom I have spoken have said, We might as well become heathen again as surrender those 3 vital points. We would not be Christians at all, for they are just the things which make Christianity. It bucked me up greatly to hear them speak that way, and they meant it too, I could see.[87]

There was certainly a keen desire by the ordinary Japanese Anglican in Mid-Japan to help the Canadian missionaries in any way that he or she could. There would have been more help, but Sasaki had not bothered to keep the ordinary clergy and lay people in the diocese informed about what was going on, so they were ignorant of all the problems leading to the withdrawal of the Canadian missionaries. In mid-February 1941, Powles noted that "this attitude of keeping everything to himself makes it very hard on the Bishop himself and hard on everybody else."[88] It does seem odd that the reasons for the Canadian mission pulling up stakes in Mid-Japan were not publicized. Many people were surprised when they learned that Powles himself was leaving Japan at the end of February. Much of the blame for this and much else was put at the feet of Sasaki. Powles had the chance to see Bishop Basil (Simpson) of Kobe just before he left Japan in February 1941 for what was to be his final visit to the Mayo Clinic. Powles discussed Sasaki with Bishop Basil, and they came to a damning conclusion. Powles wrote: "He [Basil] says that he has found, as I have, that Bishop Sasaki is the man on whom we pinned our faith only to be disappointed & utterly chagrined."[89] Since the fateful meeting with Canadian missionaries in October 1940, Sasaki's actions did appear erratic. Moreover, his performance was pleasing neither missionaries nor his own Japanese clergy. In this crisis, Sasaki was out of his depth.

There was no turning back from the decision to leave. At the end of February 1941, Powles noted that the many presents that well-wishers gave to him on leaving the Obuse sanatorium show "what a feeling there is hidden behind all this useless upheaval."[90] Briefly visiting Takata to deal with some final property matters and then leaving for the last time, Powles wrote: "What a feeling to leave the place you have lived in for 24 years. I just thought sick. Only a small group knew that I was leaving on that train, but they were at the station to see me off. It was hard but it had to be gone through."[91] It was a sad experience to leave and in doing so to bring to an end fifty-three years of continuous Canadian Anglican missionary activity in Japan.

By April 1941, the departure of Protestant missionaries of all denominations was in full flood. The *Christian Century* reported that by the end of April only some 200 missionaries would be left in Japan, whereas the previous year there had been as many as 800 missionaries working in Japan and Taiwan.[92] The Anglicans, Methodist Episcopalians, and United Church of Canada missionaries were seen, by the editor of the *Japan Christian Quarterly*, to be at the forefront of the exodus, goaded on, in the case of the latter two missions, by instructions from their headquarters in New York and in Toronto.[93]

CANADIAN PRESBYTERIAN EVACUATION FROM TAIWAN, MANCHUKUO, AND JAPAN

By February 1941, the Canadian Presbyterian mission in north Taiwan had come to an end. In light of the increasingly hostile international situation, it was reported that every missionary had to make the decision either to stay on despite the antiforeign feeling manifested by the military and police and the increasing restrictions on missionary work or to withdraw quietly and by doing so relieve "the Church of the constant suspicion directed toward it because of its being associated with foreigners."[94] The missionaries in Taiwan reached the decision that it was better for them to leave the island. To a far greater degree than their colleagues in metropolitan Japan, they had found themselves the butt of growing Japanese anti-foreign feeling. Reportedly, "it was intimated everywhere that all foreigners were spies, or potential spies, and was announced in a government-sponsored radio program in the Formosan language that missionaries were the worst of all spies, and warned the people to have nothing to do with them."[95] In those circumstances, it was obviously trying for missionaries to conduct evangelistic work, all the more so because Taiwan was a colony under military control. Moreover, like the Canadian Anglicans, who also paid attention to diplomatic opinion, the Canadian Presbyterians were aided in their decision to withdraw by the advice of C. H. Archer, the British consul, who urged them to leave the island as soon as possible, and this advice was reinforced by the fact that the American State Department was urging all US citizens to leave Japanese-controlled areas. Duncan McLeod, one of the senior Canadian missionaries, attempted to remain in Asia by asking to be transferred from Taiwan to the continuing English Presbyterian work in Singapore, but the majority of missionaries returned home to Canada. In reality, ever since their difficulties with the colonial authorities over the shrine question and the subsequent closure of their educational work, the Canadian Presbyterians had been slowly winding down their mission. It was admitted that "pressure of circumstances has caused the missionaries to hand over complete responsibility for the work to the native church sooner than they would have voluntarily done so, although that had already become a policy of the Mission, and a start had been made in that direction."[96] The start was a ten-year plan begun three years earlier that aimed at making the Taiwanese Presbyterian Church completely self-supporting. It was hoped, perhaps a little optimistically, that the withdrawal of Canadian missionaries would not upset this plan, because the sale of mission property was intended to provide sufficient funds for the completion of this ten-year plan.[97] Likewise, property had been set aside to be sold in order to provide an endowment for the theological college and the women's Bible school. As they returned home to Canada, a year short of the seventieth anniversary of the founding of the Canadian Presbyterian mission in Taiwan, the missionaries obviously tried to put the best face possible on what they had left behind. What they could not have foreseen was that the future of the Taiwanese Presbyterian Church lay with church union in Japan.

On the heels of the news of Canadian Presbyterian withdrawal from Taiwan came the announcement of a second Presbyterian evacuation, this one from Manchukuo. In April 1941, the Presbyterian mission board advised its missionaries in Manchukuo to return home. The decision to withdraw came quickly, for as late as February 1941 Allan Reoch, the missionary in Szepinkai, wrote that "we will carry on here as long as it is possible to do so and have no intention of evacuating or leaving the work. Please continue to pray for us."[98] At that time, Reoch's evangelistic work was still going well. This was in keeping with the annual report for 1940, in which progress was stressed: "there have been a large number of converts and baptisms, but the most notable advance in 1940 was in the line of church organization."[99] This advance alluded to a conference of local church representatives that met for the first time in 1940 a few days before the annual meeting of the presbytery. This conference provided delegates with an opportunity to discuss their local work and to make suggestions in a Christian forum that was wider than their own congregations.[100] Although this conference did represent progress and was a laudable achievement, it was also indicative of the organizational weakness of the Manchukuo mission. The mission simply did not have the trained Manchukuoan pastors (it had only nine of them) and elders that its colleagues in north Taiwan, Korea, and Japan possessed. Granted, Canadian Presbyterian work in

Manchukuo was of recent origin, and it took time to develop a strong church organization. However, the Canadian Presbyterian missions in north Taiwan and Korea, at a similar time in their development, were better able to develop a strong church organization than the solely evangelistic Manchukuo mission because they had stressed from the start educational work and the training of pastors. Nevertheless, Reoch and his fellow missionaries in Manchukuo seemed confident that the prospects for Christian work remained good.

In early 1941, despite a dramatic rise in the cost of living that necessitated increasing the wages of the Manchukuoan evangelists and Bible women, the Presbyterians were able to meet their costs because of the Goforth Evangelistic Fund, which brought in money from American and Canadian sources. In contrast to the Canadian Presbyterians in Taiwan, who had set aside property to help sustain the Taiwanese Presbyterian Church, the Canadians in Manchukuo had sufficient funds only to meet the needs of 1941. Even so, there were some missions in Manchukuo that were in worse financial condition than that of the Canadian Presbyterians. In February 1941, Reoch mentioned that friends in the United States had lent $200 to help the Danish Lutherans and that the Norwegian missionaries were even worse off financially.[101] Within a few weeks, however, the Canadian Presbyterians would not be in any position to help other missions. Ironically, as both Denmark and Norway were occupied by Germany during the early part of World War II, Danish and Norwegian missionaries were allowed to continue work after the start of the Pacific War.

It was the Presbyterian mission board in Toronto that requested the return of missionaries, for the same reasons as the missionaries in Taiwan had been asked to come home. Once the missionaries were out of Manchukuo, it was reported that "for many months it has been apparent that mission evacuation would probably become necessary, and much thought and planning of mission Chinese leaders has been given to prepare for it."[102] Furthermore, details of the severe persecution of Christians in Manchukuo since 1935 were made public. Although the Canadian Presbyterian mission operated in the interior of Manchukuo, where circumstances might have been different, the conditions in Mukden and other regions were likely much more difficult for Christians than the positive reports of missionaries prior to their withdrawal would indicate. There was, however, some display of goodwill between Japanese Christians and missionaries. In spite of the actions of government authorities, many Japanese Christian ministers in Manchukuo did as much as they could to help not only Chinese Christians but also Irish and Scottish Presbyterian missionaries caught in the mission field at the beginning of the war. In 1943, after his repatriation, one of those British missionaries acknowledged the kindness of Japanese ministers toward him and his fellow missionaries and noted that "an astonishing amount of co-operation proved possible even in wartime, and the willingness of the Japanese Church and Japanese Christians in Manchuria to do all in their power to help the Manchurian Church and the missionaries should never be forgotten."[103] As well as helping the Manchukuoan Church, the Japanese Christian leadership in Manchukuo was determined to see that the union church, formed out of all the Protestant denominations in Manchukuo like its model in Japan, was "a real church."[104] Nevertheless, it was equally clear that, unlike many Christians in Japan who favoured the formation of the *kyodan*, Chinese Christians in Manchukuo did not strongly believe in their union church. Indeed, the *International Review of Missions* accurately argued that "the Manchurian union is much more definitely a union brought about by force majeure" and that it was only held together by government pressure.[105] In other words, it was believed that the union church in Manchukuo would not continue to exist after Japan's defeat. It is reasonable to assume that Canadian Presbyterian missionaries held a similar view. After its return to Manchuria at the end of the war, the Canadian Presbyterian mission, like other foreign missions, saw that its future lay in joining the North-Eastern Synod of the Church of Christ in China rather than in a union Manchurian church.[106]

The Canadian Presbyterians also withdrew their missionaries to the Koreans in Japan. For Canadian Presbyterians, the reasons why they and so many other missionaries had left Japan by the end of 1940 were straightforward. These reasons included "the decision of the Japanese Church to be independent of the foreign missionary and foreign funds . . . and the hostile attitude of the government toward the Christian movement and missionaries, making it exceedingly difficult for the native worker to have the missionary assist him in his church work;" moreover, "repeated reminders from the British and American consuls to their respective nationals to evacuate, when at all possible, are the direct causes of the evacuation of most of the missionaries."[107] In July 1941, Gordon K. Chapman, an American Presbyterian North missionary serving as the acting superintendent of the Canadian Presbyterian mission, pointed out in the *Japan Christian Quarterly* that "the major problems of this Mission have had to do with the various adjustments involved in the union of the Korean Church in Japan with the Nippon Kirisuto Kyokai."[108] Initially, at least, this amalgamation, brought on by the requirements of the Religious Organizations Law of 1939, that caused all small denominations to merge with larger ones prior to applying by April 1940 to be registered as a religious organization, worked well.

According to the terms of amalgamation between the Korean Church and the Japanese Presbyterian Church, the self-supporting Korean churches were given the same status in the new church as similarly self-supporting Japanese congregations. The nonself-supporting Korean congregations were put under a cooperating committee made up of Japanese Presbyterians and missionary representatives. In keeping with the overall Presbyterian desire to do away with foreign support, by December 1940 the Japanese Presbyterian Church had taken over responsibility from the Canadian Presbyterian mission for the support of all twenty-three Korean pastors working with the mission. However, because the

Korean pastors of the Canadian Presbyterian mission were mainly graduates of the Presbyterian seminary in Kobe, that was supported by the missions of both the American North and South Presbyterian Churches, it was thought that in the future there might be difficulty obtaining new ministers.

However, there were also more immediate difficulties for the Canadian Presbyterian mission and its Korean Presbyterian members. Not the least of these difficulties were new regulations concerning the use of Japanese in church services. These regulations, to come into effect in April 1941, were in fact enforced in Osaka, one of the main centres of Canadian Presbyterian work, from August 1940 on. The regulations made it difficult for many of the Korean Bible women who had to lead church services for congregations lacking a regular minister. Most importantly, it was very trying for ordinary Korean church members. It was reported that

> the use of the Japanese language was a great trial indeed for the older women members of the congregations, who, if willing to attend at all, must listen to services conducted in an unknown tongue, and their church life that had been the one bright spot in their lives was now strange and unreal, and the joy that the coming of the Lord's Day had always brought, was dimmed.[109]

Canadian Presbyterian missionaries and Korean Presbyterians were also strongly opposed to the formation of the union church. The key issue for them concerning the *kyodan* was the question of the lack of a creed, and negotiations for the union nearly stopped. Furthermore, the Canadian Presbyterians, reflecting the interests of their Korean constituents, could see little advantage for their church members in another amalgamation when already they were prohibited from participating in church services in their own Korean language. By the time that the annual report for 1940 was published in 1941, all Canadian Presbyterian missionaries were safely home in Canada, and no words were minced about the possibility of "a church composed of all the Protestant denominations of Japan, with rank rationalism and servile attitude to state control rampant as it is in some of them;" it "would be another monstrosity such as the state church of Germany is at the present time."[110] This was a very different view from that of United Church missionaries, who were by and large supportive of the *kyodan* and who never compared it with the state church in Germany. Whereas most missionaries in Japan left the country with feelings of sympathy for the plight of Japanese Christians, the Canadian Presbyterians obviously had much more ambivalent feelings about the Japanese as they went home.

CHAPTER TWELVE
Into the Fires of War

As the withdrawal of missionaries from the Japanese Empire was taking place in early 1941, a deputation of leading Japanese Christians travelled to the United States to explain the proposed church union and to try to make American Christians understand the difficulties that Japanese Christians faced. Although the deputation put a brave face on Christian developments in Japan, the charismatic Kagawa Toyohiko and his Japanese colleagues came away concerned about the growing nationalism in the United States and the danger of it to peace in East Asia. Despite the prospect of war breaking out, some missionaries had decided by the spring of 1941 that they should remain in the mission field rather than return home. This was especially true of female educational missionaries, who believed that there was still a place for them in the new system. Indeed, Abe Yoshimune and other leading Japanese Christians certainly gave the impression that they wanted educational missionaries to continue to their work. The last months before the attack on Pearl Harbor and Hong Kong were marked by amicable relations between Japanese Christians and missionaries. The start of the war came as a surprise to both.

During the summer of 1941, the Nippon Kirisutokyodan finally came into being, even though it was December 1941 before the Japanese government formally recognized it. Although the new union church had a centralized leadership, its sectional structure allowed the joining denominations to retain a degree of autonomy. The NSKK had chosen not to join the *kyodan*, and in September 1942 the Anglicans learned that they would not be granted permission to form their own religious body. This denial precipitated serious debate between those Anglicans who wanted the NSKK to amalgamate with the *kyodan* and those who were equally opposed to union. The belief that it was their patriotic duty to conform to the desires of the government to create a single Japanese Protestant church was a major motive behind the actions of Anglicans who advocated union. Equally as patriotic as their unionist opponents, Anglicans who nonetheless resisted union held that the main reason for their stand stemmed from their opposition to too much state intervention in religion. Although their position cannot be attributed to the teaching of Canadian Anglican missionaries, Bishop Sasaki Shinji, who served as presiding bishop of the NSKK throughout much of the war, and the congregations of the Diocese of Mid-Japan were among those Japanese Anglicans most adamantly opposed to union. The irreconcilable differences between these two camps of Anglicans ultimately led to schism and to persecution for some of those who refused to join the *kyodan*.

For missionaries, the beginning of hostilities meant internment and, for most, eventually repatriation on one of the exchange ships. In sharp contrast to the brutal treatment of Allied prisoners of war, Canadian missionaries were generally reasonably treated during their internment.

THE JAPANESE CHRISTIAN DEPUTATION

At the end of March 1941, an eight-member Japanese Christian Fellowship Deputation was sent to the United States by the NCC to explain the proposed church union and to impress upon North American Christians the enormous problems that Japanese Christians were facing. Small though it was, the deputation was made up of the best-known Japanese Christian leaders, including Abe, Kagawa, and Kozaki, and was accompanied by William Axling, the American Baptist missionary. As well as its Christian purpose, the deputation obviously hoped to win understanding and to promote goodwill for Japan among North Americans. Although the point should not be belaboured, in view of the deteriorating relations between Japan and the United States, such a prominent group of Japanese Christians could only have gone to the United States with the blessing of the Japanese government.

The deputation went armed with the knowledge that on March 26 forty-two Protestant denominations and bodies had unanimously decided to form one church in Japan. The prospect of a meeting between Japanese and American Christians was welcomed, but the *Christian Century*, the American weekly Christian magazine, asked hard questions about what was to be discussed. It queried whether or not the Japanese delegates were interested in

> peace for the sake of peace, with injustices such as the rape of China and the Japanese exclusion act unremedied? Do they think of the extension of the Kingdom of God as merely the exploitation of spheres of influence in a system of competing religious imperialisms that offer a thin coat of respectability to armed conquest? Is their highest loyalty to the religions of nationalism, whose symbol is either a god-emperor or a god-flag? If so, then the meeting is sure to end in disunion and had better never be held.[1]

The Japanese group met with American church leaders at conferences in

Riverside, California, in Atlantic City, New Jersey, and in Chicago during April and May. There were also opportunities for the Japanese Christian leaders to give speeches to interested bodies and to meet missionary society representatives. Kagawa, certainly, took advantage of being in the United States to speak to different groups and to give interviews. He chose not to discuss politics with Americans, but he did let it be known that he had profound misgivings about the future of Japanese-American relations. In an interview published in the *Christian Century*, it was reported that Kagawa sensed the changed mood of the United States and the possibility of war: "Kagawa dreads what he sees will happen to Christianity in Japan and throughout Asia if present trends lead this country to war. No more than one in a thousand Japanese wants war with the United States, he says."[2] Interestingly, Kagawa saw the Americans becoming involved in a war in the Pacific as a result of being dragged into the ongoing conflict in Europe and failed to mention that the Japanese might also bear some responsibility for bringing about war. However, he was obviously playing to American Christians with pacifist or isolationist tendencies. As to the formation of the union church, Kagawa used the argument that it was

> an effort on the part of Japanese Christians to prepare Christianity in that country to survive, no matter what happens. This it could not hope to do under foreign control, especially if relations between Japan and America further deteriorate. Accordingly longtime trends in the direction of Christian unity were brought to a culmination last fall when Christian leaders, noting the movement of international affairs, anticipated measures of compulsion which the new forces at work in their own government might have been disposed to use and on their own initiative set up the Japan Christian Church.[3]

Kagawa's explanation did not fully convince his interviewer, who thought that the similar drive for union among Japanese Buddhist sects left some doubt as to whether "the primary impulse and control came from the Japanese government."[4] The doubt about the impulses behind church union can be taken as one sign that the Japanese Christians ultimately failed to convince North American Christians that the Japanese desired peace.

It was Abe's intention to visit Toronto, but visa regulations would not have permitted him to reenter the United States had he crossed into Canada. A visit to Canada by Abe might have reassured those who had missionary relatives in Japan about their safety. However, it is unlikely that Canadians would have been any more sympathetic than Americans to his Japanese Christian message. The Japanese Christian leaders tried to put the best face possible on their visit to the United States. Saito Soichi, writing in the *Japan Christian Quarterly* after the deputation's return to Japan, noted that it was timely for a visit to the United States in order to "'give expression to the gratitude of Christians of Japan for all that American Mission Boards and American Christians have done for the furthering of the Christian movement in Japan during the past eighty years.' Ingratitude is alien to the Japanese character."[5] However, the Japanese Christian leaders had to go beyond expressing their gratitude—they had to explain the motives behind church union. The American side suggested that it was government pressure that was bringing about church union. Kozaki and Abe, though admitting that the situation in Japan stimulated the union movement, argued that the primary motive behind church union was the desire to preserve Christian belief. The Japanese were also questioned on the problem of nationalism and religion, especially in regard to the shrine issue and *tennosei*.[6] The Japanese were by no means given an easy time of it.

For their part, there was a trace of exasperation at the inability of American churchleaders to appreciate the depth of the difficulties that the Christian movement faced in Japan. In a speech in New York, Abe stated:

> I want you to understand it is not an easy job in Japan. I quite often envied you, especially as I sat in the meeting of the bishops one night in Nashville. I envied them their freedom, freedom from care. I don't know that they are free of care; but in an enviable sense they are free from care. As soon as I go back to Japan I have to face an entirely different atmosphere, a different sentiment.[7]

Yet, if Abe found the Methodist Episcopalian South bishops in Nashville free from care, he also found young Americans to be disturbingly nationalistic. He remarked that since he had come to the United States he had met "young people who are becoming nationalistic. I am surprised that these young Americans speak to me and ask me very nationalistic questions—I would not say selfish, but self-centred. Even in this country your young people are feeling the tension more and more. Why not in Japan?"[8] American nationalism ran counter to the need for an "international mindedness" that he thought future American missionaries in Japan could help to stir up among Japanese youth. In this respect, Abe was arguing in a similar vein to Kagawa by putting the blame for difficulties between Japan and the United States on rising American nationalism. Once he returned to Japan, Abe expressed his continuing concern with American nationalism. Although he had come to realize more than ever before that the United States was a land of freedom and rich resources, he could not help but be concerned about America's future. He noted that, "unless, both as individuals and as a nation, America succeeds in getting rid of her present extreme, self-centred, nationalistic trend, her future is fraught with danger. Herein lies the great need of emphasizing the Christian philosophy of life and its international message."[9] What Abe said about nationalism in the United States could equally have applied to Japan. Going to the United States, he stressed the international message of Christianity to his English-speaking audiences. He called upon American Christians to be internationally minded and decried American nationalism. In Japan, of course, Abe preached a particular

Japanese Christianity in that any sense of internationalism outside the Greater East Asia Co-Prosperity Sphere was noticeably absent. It is difficult to see where his *Nipponteki Kirisutokyo* contained any inkling of internationalism as it was generally understood in the West. Although Kozaki was "reassured" that "there is no difference of East and West in Christ,"[10] the Japanese Christian leaders were unable to bring American audiences around to their international point of view. They could not offer any hope of an early return to the mission field to the many missionaries who had by now left their work in Japan, Korea, and north China. Their message was out of step with the news from China and Southeast Asia that Americans heard or read about on a daily basis.

WORKING ON IN JAPAN AND KOREA

United Church WMS missionaries in Japan were saddened and dismayed over the message from Toronto calling for their withdrawal.[11] They had resolutely resisted the idea of withdrawal, but some were leaving Japan temporarily. In March 1941, Arthur McKenzie, who, together with Ernest Bott of the east Tokyo mission work, had long thought that the conservative group in Japan would be able to avoid war with England or the United States, found it expedient to leave Japan temporarily. Yet McKenzie still clung to the idea that there remained opportunities in Japan for Christianity and for missionaries. He wrote from the safety of Vancouver in April 1941 that he believed that the responsibilities of and opportunities for missionary work in Japan, especially in educational work, were greater than ever. However, he noted that "we must meet the totalitarian challenge on the ideological front. There we can win, and there we must win if the one truly great and homogeneous bloc of liberalism in the East is to be vitalized and imbued with the saving spirit of Christ."[12] Despite everything that had happened in recent months, he clung to the belief that "Christianizing the culture of the East lies chiefly with the numerically strong but at present politically weak mass of educated liberal Japanese. A complete defeat of Japan would be disastrous for our Mission in Asia"[13] because of the impact that such a defeat would have on China. McKenzie astutely pointed out that "China, relieved of Japanese pressure would at once revert to its old cultural patterns—civil war and anti-foreignism would be in full swing within six months, while the northern areas would quickly be overrun and dominated by the Soviets."[14] By the Soviets, he was clearly referring to the Chinese communists in Yenan and north China rather than the Soviet Union. He added that "if the Japanese should be thoroughly defeated there is an even greater danger to Asia and to the Christian forces, than any opposition contained in the present set-up, and that is the inevitable push of the Soviets to the Pacific and the China Seas."[15] McKenzie was accurately predicting the course of the final phase of the Chinese Revolution, which would begin after the thorough defeat of the Japanese in 1945. Yet his faith in the future resurgence of liberalism in Japan, and with it great opportunities for Christianity, remained firm. In April 1941, he also noted that "there will be many frightful wounds that Christ alone can heal. In that day the new organization of the Christian Church in Japan will be discovered to be a great advantage."[16]

At the end of May 1941, although the Japanese Christian leaders were still in the United States, McKenzie was becoming less optimistic about the future as he prepared to return to Japan and to teaching at the Kwansei Gakuin. In a letter to Jesse Arnup, he described what he thought were the difficulties awaiting him in Japan. His opinions would have confirmed the worst fears of Norman Robertson at the Department of External Affairs. Moreover, he revealed the height of the barriers of hate and spite that would meet any attempt at "international mindedness" on the part of North American Christians:

> In all our work these days in Japan we are gambling on vestiges of liberal sentiment and uncertainty about the future of Japan vis-a-vis the gold bloc democracies in the Pacific. . . . If Japanese officialdom ever becomes totally Nazi in its heart or completely certain of its security within the Tripartite Treaty we shall get short shrift indeed. I often envy the lot of our brethren in China, though I deeply commiserate their sufferings due to the war. In these difficult days they at least have the full and sincere moral support of the Chinese authorities. To the Japanese official we are the barely tolerated enemies of the state, and we live in a continual nightmare of suspicion and distrust, and in the case of the younger officials and the younger officers of the army and navy of hardly disguised Nazi-inspired hatred.[17]

McKenzie painted a grim picture of the atmosphere in Japan, one that would inevitably lead to war. However, in sharp contrast to his broad picture, Sybil Courtice, still working at the Toyo Eiwa Jo Gakko, described, also at the end of May, a different atmosphere within the Christian community in Tokyo. Writing to Mrs. Taylor in Toronto, she stated that "there is no lack of expression of cordiality and kindness on the part of our church and school friends and co-workers and indeed one constantly meets with unexpected and marked kindness from utter strangers."[18] The conviviality between Japanese Christians and Canadian missionaries was demonstrated by a large party of missionaries and Japanese members of the three girls' school boards to celebrate the seventy-seventh birthday of Principal Shimizu of the Azabu Middle School, who also served as the chairman of the boards of the three girls' schools. Courtice and her WMS colleagues might not have paid as much attention to political trends as their male counterparts, but clearly there was a sharp difference of opinion as to the climate for missionaries in Japan between those in Tokyo and those looking at Japan from Canada. In June 1941, Ishiwara Ken, the president of Tokyo Joshi Daigaku, was pressing for the return of

Constance Chappell to her duties in the college's English department at the end of her furlough. It was explained that, "in this college that stands for Christianity and where we have a strong English Department, she is greatly needed both as an efficient and experienced teacher of English and also as a leader in various religious and musical functions of the college."[19] Ishiwara possible thought that Chappell—born in Japan and a WMS missionary since 1912—was so unobtrusively a part of the good-mannered and well-educated Japan of Tokyo Joshi Daigaku that it was unimaginable that either any government regulation should prevent her from teaching or any harm would come to her. In June 1941, the Japanese assessment of current social and political circumstances, in contrast to that of External Affairs in Ottawa or missionary authorities in Toronto, probably saw nothing that would inhibit a Canadian teacher from continuing to do useful work. Indeed, as late as mid-October 1941, the Toyo Eiwa Jo Gakko was requesting that a second missionary teacher of English be appointed[20]—a reflection, perhaps, of how unexpected the Pacific War was to many Japanese despite months of rumours about its inevitability.

In a synopsis of the United Church of Canada mission work in the July 1941 issue of the *Japan Christian Quarterly*, Courtice mentioned with obvious relief that the complete evacuation of the mission had been averted and that one missionary family and six single female missionaries remained at work.[21] The dramatic reduction in the number of United Church missionaries at work was put down entirely to the international crisis. Although the status of missionaries within the framework of church union was still definitely to be decided, it appeared to Courtice that there would be no further restrictions on missionaries other than those already agreed upon by the various denominational bodies. In the main, these restrictions were financial independence and the transfer of all leadership positions in Christian organizations to Japanese from missionary hands. To Courtice, at least, this transfer was by no means disastrous to missionary work. She pointed out that the transfer of institutional leadership provided some missionaries with more time for evangelism and that, "where difficulties have arisen, the place of work has been responsible for lack of opportunity for some, while matters of personnel have made cooperation somewhat difficult for others."[22] The last point hints at some friction between Japanese faculty and missionary teachers at the three girls' schools, but Courtice did not elaborate. The one area in that the transfer of administrative posts to Japanese had a considerable impact upon the mission was in kindergarten administration. There had been forty-eight kindergartens, including nursery schools and day nurseries, associated with WMS work, and all of them had passed into Japanese Christian hands. Yet even here Courtice thought that the missionary connection could have been maintained by retaining a missionary as a member of the board of each kindergarten; had that been done, there "would probably have been great opportunity here for a time at least if the mission workers had been allowed to remain."[23] In her opinion, it was the premature withdrawal of WMS missionaries rather than any policy by the Ministry of Education or the Japan Methodist Church that had spelled the end of kindergarten work. Even though kindergartens had to be self-supporting, or close to it, by 1943, Courtice was gratified by the response of parents to necessary fee increases caused by the end of WMS financial support. Although some might close, she thought that a large number of them would manage to become self-supporting before the deadline.

By July 1941, Courtice and the WMS had adjusted to the new circumstances caused by church union and the drive for the Japanization of Christian organizations. Work for those who remained in Japan continued as normal, largely unaffected by the stresses and strains of the changing international situation. In mid-September 1941, Courtice reported of a gathering of some fifty kindergarten principals and teachers in Kanazawa that she and Ella Lediard had attended that "It was a very good, inspiring and helpful meeting to all concerned."[24] It hardly seems that the world beyond Kanazawa was in crisis.

Some of the United Church missionaries in Korea were also determined to stay on in the peninsula even though other American missions thought that missionaries should withdraw.[25] What was frustrating for the Canadian missionaries in Korea was that the missionary authorities in Toronto were not as clear about withdrawal. In March 1941, William Scott complained to A. E. Armstrong that there was a lack of coordination in Toronto in regard to the withdrawal of Canadian missionaries from Korea. Scott had received a cable from Toronto calling for Canadian withdrawal, whereas the Presbyterian North mission had not only reconsidered its decision to withdraw but also had indicated that it was going to send five men back to Korea in the fall. As Scott noted, "even the [British] consul referred with surprise to the casual manner in that missionaries had left their posts—their work and their property. All of that got under our skins and made us feel the pricks."[26] Withdrawal ran against the grain for Scott, who had consistently opposed large-scale withdrawal because it would "seriously compromise our Christian witness."[27] He was going to endure to the end. To stay on in Korea could only be done at some personal cost. His wife was already in Canada, and he obviously disliked being separated from his family. In January 1941, he learned that his son was getting married, and he did not even know the name of his prospective daughter-in-law.[28] That separation from family, especially children, was an accepted part of missionary service in East Asia did not make it any easier. Yet Scott remained in Korea.

THE NIPPON KIRISUTOKYODAN AND THE NSKK

On 24 and 25 June 1941, a general meeting was held and ended with a gathering of 3,000 Christians to celebrate the formation of the Nippon Kirisutokyodan (Kyodan). At this meeting, Tomita Mitsuru of the Presbyterian Church was elected the *torisha* (head) of the new organization, Kozaki Michio became the assistant to the *torisha*, and Abe Yoshimune was named chairman of the general conference. The *torisha*, who had powers of control and discipline over churches and ministers comparable to those of the *kancho* of a Buddhist sect,[29] was elected for a renewable term of two years. As it turned out, Tomita was the first and last *torisha*. He represented the church in its relations with the government and the general public and was responsible as head of the union church to the general conference. His election revealed the important position that the Presbyterian group had within the *kyodan*.[30] Abe retained his influence over the former Japan Methodist Church as superintendent of Section 2, but the ascendancy of Tomita marked the beginning of Abe's withdrawal from centre stage in the affairs of the Japanese Christian movement. Later in 1941, Abe went to Shanghai to become the chairman of the Central China Religious Alliance and to work for the Chinese Church.[31] This move underlined the great importance attached by the Japanese Christian movement to its role of leading Christian movements in Japanese-occupied areas. It also freed Abe from the constant pressure of dealing with Japanese government officials over the future of the union church.

The two-day meeting also formalized the organization of the new united church, which was initially divided into eleven sections that largely followed denominational lines. Section 1 consisted of the Japan Presbyterian and Reformed Churches, Section 2 consisted of the Japan Methodist and Methodist Protestant Churches, and so on down to Section 11, the Salvation Army.[32] These sections were regarded as temporary bodies and were to be amalgamated into a single unit within three years. Even in the interim, the *kyodan* was a single church with one name, one general conference, one creed, and one head. The Japanese Empire was split into twelve regional conferences (which included Korea, Taiwan, and Manchuria—the last one being a missionary conference—as well as metropolitan Japan). The *kyodan* was an imperial church with the twelve regional conferences responsible for electing 300 delegates to the general conference. The union church functioned through eight administrative departments: general affairs, finance, foreign missions, home missions, social welfare, education, women's work, and publications. These departments operated from the headquarters in Tokyo.

The union church maintained the traditional emphasis and basis of universal Christendom by making the Old and New Testaments its standard of faith and practice and by placing the historic Apostles' Creed at the centre of its confession of faith. Obviously, details of the faith of the union church took second place to the formulation of an organizational structure in discussions concerning the creation of the church. Initially, only a general statement of faith was submitted to the Ministry of Education on the understanding that a more detailed creed would be drawn up after the organization of the new church had been effected.[33] Indeed, the problem of its creed was one of the major weaknesses of the *kyodan*, and it was still being resolved when the Pacific War ended. As a result, the creedal commitments of the individual congregations tended more to reflect those of their previous denominational affiliations than a distinct new creed to that the whole union church could subscribe. One thing that all were required to subscribe to was the first article of the bylaws for believers (*seito no seikatsu kitei*), that decreed that church members supported and gave reverence to the emperor. The inclusion of such an article has been taken to indicate that the new church was prepared to bend its Christian beliefs in the face of government pressure for the control of religion.[34]

One of the most pressing issues for the new union church was to obtain Ministry of Education approval of its regulations. Initially, this approval was anticipated by mid-July, but it was withheld. In October 1941, the *Asahi Shinbun*, the influential daily newspaper, reported that the ministry deemed the organization of the union church unsatisfactory.[35] The major reason was that the ministry wanted the quasi-denominational sections to be dissolved quickly.[36] At the end of November 1941, the *Fukuin Shimpo* saw that the most important issue to be discussed at the first conference of Section 1, which was to convene at the beginning of December, was the abolition of the sections within the church.[37] It was seen that this question was clearly linked to official approval of the union church. Furthermore, it was suggested 100 years from then pride would still be taken at the efforts made to preserve the church.[38] The seriousness of the situation facing the *kyodan* was underlined during the conference when Tomita, the *torisha*, described this period as the most difficult time for Christianity since the Meiji era.[39] In December 1941, five months after it was established, the *kyodan* was finally and officially recognized by the Ministry of Education.

The opening of the Pacific War on 8 December 1941 brought new challenges for the union church. Its leadership was quick to stress that its members wanted Japanese success.[40] In January 1942, Tomita went on a pilgrimage to the imperial shrine at Ise to pray for Japan's victory. Although this act showed that the leadership was completely at one with Japan's war aims, there was a need to ensure that the ordinary ministers understood the war's meaning and its relation to the Japanese spirit. In June 1942, the first training conference for priests was held for six days in Tokyo, at which historians, army officers, and Ministry of Education bureaucrats lectured those who attended on the government'' view.[41] Following the Tokyo conference, other priest-training conferences were held in different parts of Japan. Clearly, the Ministry of Education wanted to ensure that the *kyodan* and the Japanese Christian movement supported the Japanese spirit and the national endeavour during the war.

The consequences of not supporting the war effort were seen in June 1942, when ninety-six members of Section 6 (the former Nippon Seikyokai) and Section 9 (the former Kiyome Kyokai) were arrested. These two sections were formed from churches that were offshoots from the Holiness Church. Those arrested were charged under the Peace Preservation Law on the grounds of profanity at shrines and their belief that the Pacific War was a prelude to the last judgment.[42] These arrests had serious implications for the union church. They made something of a mockery of the efforts of Tomita to show that the union church was completely in support of the war effort. More importantly, they led Ministry of Education officials to urge swift progress on the dissolution of the sections. It was under this cloud that the first general conference of the *kyodan*, since its official approval, was held in late November 1942. It was no surprise that the decision was made to dissolve the sectional structure by 1 April 1943. At this meeting, the YMCA, the YWCA, and the Japan Christian Women's Moral Conference became associated with the *kyodan*. On the last day of the General Conference, Tomita, in company with some forty representatives from Shinto and Buddhist sects, was received by the emperor. Reputedly, inclusion in this audience greatly enhanced Tomita's authority, because "he and other Christians made much of the affair as betokening an official recognition of Christianity by the state such as it had never had before and interpreted it as entitling the church to take a firm stand against harassments by local and military police."[43] Despite numerous instances of official recognition since the granting of religious freedom under the Meiji Constitution, Tomita and others were still concerned with this question.

Official recognition as a religious organization was what the NSKK wanted to receive. However, in September 1942, it was informed by the Ministry of Education that its application for recognition as a separate religious body, presented as early as March 1941, had not been accepted.[44] The failure of the NSKK to receive official recognition placed Japanese Anglicans in great difficulties. It isolated them from Japanese Christians who had signalled their belief in a single, pure Christianity in Japan by joining the union church. Importantly, for people so concerned with nationalism, the isolation of Japanese Anglicans reflected badly on their loyalty to Japan and their solidarity with Japan's national goals. Furthermore, the arrest of the former Nippon Seikyokai and Kiyome Kyokai members of the *kyodan* could well have been interpreted by Japanese Anglicans as a warning of what might happen to Christians whose ideas and actions displeased the authorities. In more practical terms, failure to be recognized as a religious organization meant that individual churches within the NSKK did not receive tax relief or other privileges, including exemption from military service for priests, that *kyodan* pastors received.

As a result, there was renewed interest among Anglicans, particularly in the Diocese of Osaka,[45] in joining the union church. A schism began to appear in NSKK ranks between those who were pro-union and those who were anti-union.[46] In early September 1942, Bishop Naide of Osaka expressed his support for affiliation with the *kyodan*, and in this he had the support of virtually all the clergy in his diocese.[47] There was also support for union in the Diocese of Tokyo. Indeed, on September 16, at the Central Committee conference of the NSKK, held to deal with the problem of official recognition, a proposal was put forward that the conference should proceed to join the whole of the NSKK with the *kyodan*. Although this proposal was rejected, the conference did decide to abandon the use of the NSKK's system of church government, which meant that the NSKK would cease officially to exist as dioceses and as a province.[48] This can be seen as a victory for the pro-unionists, because the power of the bishops, the majority of whom opposed union, would seemingly disappear. In any case, because the NSKK's application for legal recognition had been rejected, the House of Bishops had no legal jurisdiction over the churches and was not allowed to maintain lateral contact between dioceses or churches. To get around this obstacle, the NSKK claimed authority for the bishops based only on Christian faith.[49] This point was emphasized when the House of Bishops decided in December 1942 to change the title of bishop from the usual term *kantoku* to *shukyo*, a title that underlined the spiritual aspect of their position.

The issue of union, however, could not be avoided. In early October, the Diocese of Osaka officially announced that it had decided to affiliate with the *kyodan*.[50] In a letter to both clerical and lay members of the NSKK, the diocese argued that, by dissolving Christian denominations that had developed in the West, and "by tracing Christianity back to its origins, and by training the minds of the people with the Japanese nationalistic spirit we intend to build up Imperial Christianity by realizing the religion of the true person of Jesus Christ."[51] Such a statement dramatically reveals the desire in the diocese for the creation of a *Nipponteki Kirisutokyo* that would harmonize Christianity with the Japanese national spirit.

As Diocese of Osaka was moving toward its decision, the pro-union forces in the Diocese of Tokyo were also active. In early October, a consultative meeting was held in Tokyo at that an association to further church union (Nippon Kirisutokyodan Kanyu Kisei Domei) was formed.[52] This new association quickly issued a proposal for unification with the *kyodan* and called for the establishment of a pure Christianity free of British and American influence.[53] In contrast to the Osaka diocese, however, where the impetus for union came mainly from the clergy, in the Tokyo diocese it was lay people who took the lead in the drive for union.[54] This initiative allowed the pro-unionists to criticize the anti-union bishops for failing to take into account the wishes of ordinary lay church members and clergy. In the case of Bishop Sasaki of Mid-Japan, for instance, one of the Canadian missionary criticisms of him was that he sometimes acted in an authoritarian fashion that upset some of his clergy.

In spite of the pressures for union, Sasaki, also now serving as the presiding bishop of the NSKK, firmly rejected union. At the end of October, a meeting of bishops was convened in Nagoya to discuss the matter of the Diocese of Osaka's decision concerning the *kyodan*. As a result of discussions there, in early November Sasaki issued a statement, signed by the majority of Japanese bishops, that was openly critical of the Osaka movement. This statement upheld the authority of the episcopacy and apostolic succession and pointed out the impossibility of uniting with the *kyodan* because of its failure to adopt the Apostles' Creed as one of its main theological tenets.[55] The *kyodan* did eventually adopt the Apostles' Creed as the centre of its confession of faith, but at this time the Anglican bishops were obviously unclear about the kyodan's position on the creed. Naturally, Naide, and the associate bishop of Osaka, Yanagihara Sadajiro, did not sign the bishops' statement, but Matsui of Tokyo did. However, Matsui had second thoughts, for within days of signing he abruptly withdrew his signature and declared his support for union.[56] In doing so, he advised the clergy in the Tokyo diocese to follow his lead. From that moment on, there was little possibility of compromise between the pro-union and anti-union groups.

Indeed, in early December, Professor Saeki Yoshiro, a prominent layman in the NSKK in Tokyo, accused the six anti-union bishops of breaking the law and requested their public prosecution in the Tokyo criminal court.[57] Although this accusation was not prosecuted, it did serve to open the way for the later prosecution and imprisonment of clergy and bishops. Saeki attacked Sasaki and his five episcopal colleagues as being antinationalistic, and he emphasized their past relationship with Western bishops as well as castigated them for ignoring the lay movement for amalgamation.[58] In bringing up the links between the anti-union Japanese bishops and Britain and America, Saeki was confirming the worst suspicions of the military police. Their reports concerning the anti-union group in the NSKK repeat the connection between the NSKK and Britain and, to a lesser extent, the United States.[59] Despite such attacks, Sasaki remained adamantly opposed to union.

Frustrated by such opposition, in late January 1943 Naide, relying on his prestige as a former presiding bishop, went so far as to announce publicly that the NSKK had ceased to exist as early as 31 March 1942.[60] Again, he intimated that union with the *kyodan* meant the creation not only of a union church but also a Christianity for the imperial state that was based not on foreign denominations but on the Japanese spirit.[61] Furthermore, he advocated union in compliance with the wishes of the government. In contrast, the anti-union bishops, such as Yashiro of Kobe, argued for the freedom of the church from undue interference from the state and pointed out that the creation of a national

Japanese church through union did not serve the interests of either the Christian faith or the Japanese state.[62] If Naide had hoped to undermine the authority of the anti-union bishops by declaring that the NSKK no longer existed, he failed. However, the pro-union forces were gaining support. Thus, in order to blunt the pro-union efforts to bring the NSKK into the *kyodan*, it was finally decided at a Central Committee conference held at the beginning of February 1943 to dissolve the organization of the NSKK. One reason for this dramatic decision was to preempt the church's possible dissolution by government authorities, that some within the pro-union group had been strongly advocating. It was feared that, if the government ordered the dissolution, then church funds would be distributed to the pro-union churches. Already in September 1942 the decision to terminate the system of church government had been made, and measures had been taken over that winter to change individual dioceses "into either a 'Society of Friendly Mutual Aid' or a 'Society of Fraternal Order'—instead of using the term, 'diocese'—and the bishops became their leaders."[63] Thus, the February 1943 dissolution of the NSKK's organization altered little. However, this situation did not last for long because pressure from the pro-union group continued. As a result, over the next few months, the individual dioceses or fraternal societies felt obliged to dissolve formally their organizations and to distribute their funds among the congregations. This dissolution that individual churches were free to decide about joining the *kyodan*.

By the spring of 1943, however, amalgamation with the *kyodan* was becoming less attractive, especially for a centre group of moderate Anglicans who hoped that the NSKK could be resurrected within the sectional organization of the *kyodan*. This centre group had gone so far as to get Tomita, the *torisha*, to agree in early February 1943 to give Anglican bishops the authority to perform ordinations. Although this was still not enough to sway the anti-union bishops, who also wanted the acceptance of the pastoral rights of the episcopacy, it was a positive step in the direction of resolving the issues that were stopping the bishops from giving their consent to amalgamation. However, the hopes of the centre group were dashed in April 1943 when the Ministry of Education decided to abolish the denominational sections within the *kyodan*. This meant that the possibility of maintaining the NSKK intact within the *kyodan* was gone.

By the end of August 1943, Naide and the other two pro-union bishops had grown tired of waiting for the NSKK churches to join the *kyodan*. To hasten union, the three bishops decided to take the extraordinary step of secretly consecrating seven new bishops at St. Saviour's Church, Osaka.[64] This consecration was irregular, because it did not follow the established NSKK procedures for the selection and consecration of bishops and was done without the knowledge or consent of the six non-union bishops. It has been argued that Naide and Matsui, who were both old men, wanted to increase the number of bishops before joining the *kyodan*.⁶⁵ Moreover, the seven new bishops would ensure that the pro-union bishops would have a majority in the House of Bishops. However, the immediate Anglican reaction to the consecrations once they had been made public was hostile, and a number of churches decided in protest to cancel their applications to join the *kyodan*. Despite this reaction, the pro-union forces remained adamant in their desire to enter the united church. In late November 1943, the second conference of the *kyodan* formally recognized the amalgamation of the NSKK's pro-union churches within it. In all, some eighty-three churches, including four in Taiwan, representing one-third of all NSKK churches, joined the *kyodan* at this time.⁶⁶ The whole of the Osaka diocese joined (including its missionary churches in Taiwan), half the churches in the Tokyo diocese joined, and a varying number in all other dioceses except Mid-Japan joined. Just as all the Osaka churches followed Naide's lead, it was a testament to the influence of Sasaki that none of the churches in the Diocese of Mid-Japan chose to join.⁶⁷ Likewise, only five churches out of nineteen in the Kobe diocese entered the *kyodan*,⁶⁸ a reflection of the influence of Yashiro, who, together with Sasaki, was one of the strongest opponents of union among the Anglican bishops.

Clearly, the influence of individual bishops was significant in whether or not a church joined the *kyodan*. It is much more difficult to determine whether or not the long-term influence of missionaries also helped in shaping the path that bishops and clergy chose to follow. Certainly, the theological thinking of Herbert Kelly, the British Anglican missionary monk, greatly influenced the thinking of Yashiro and Nosse Hidetoshi,⁶⁹ an anti-union clergyman in the Diocese of South Tokyo who, like Yashiro, had studied under Kelly at Kelham. It is much more difficult to say that Sasaki resisted union because of the influence that Victor Spencer, Percy Powles, or other Canadian Anglican missionaries had upon him. Clearly, the Canadians did not have the charisma of Kelly. Nevertheless, Powles, Spencer, and Bishop Heber Hamilton had been able to develop strong ties with individual Japanese clergy in Mid-Japan, and these ties might have been a reason why some of the clergy and churches in Mid-Japan rejected union. It is also true that leading anti-union Anglicans such as Sasaki, Yashiro, and Nosse possessed strong personalities and were truly tough-minded, some would say obstinate, when it came to the question of joining the *kyodan*. And, as well as being sincere Christians, they were patriotic Japanese. Indeed, Yashiro, as has been shown, believed that union was counter to the interests not only of Christianity in Japan but also of Japan itself. During the early Meiji period, concern for the well-being of Japan was one reason why some young Japanese converted to Protestantism. For Yashiro, and equally for Sasaki and Nosse, this well-being provided a reason why they should stand firm against not only the policies of the state, directed toward the creation of a union church, but also the majority of Protestants who accepted, if not welcomed, the creation of the *kyodan*. Yet Yashiro was no pacifist; he might have preferred to remain working as a priest and bishop in Kobe, but he did not avoid military service. When he was eventually called to the colours in late 1944, he went. Likewise, during the height of the Allied bombing of Tokyo in 1945, Sasaki thought that his place was to remain in Tokyo to share the sufferings of Anglicans there. Nevertheless, regardless of the personal consequences, Sasaki, Yashiro, and Nosse held to the principle that religion should not be unduly interfered with by the state.

Those NSKK churches that remained outside the *kyodan* were faced with a grim future. Although Canadian Anglicans had made provisions that would help for two years to soften the financial blow to the Diocese of Mid-Japan caused by the loss of foreign subsidies, by the fall of 1943 all churches would be in severe financial straits. When the formal structure of the NSKK had disappeared, the churches of the diocese were held together by voluntary associations and the personality of the bishop. In January 1944, in addition to his responsibilities in Mid-Japan, Sasaki was installed as bishop of Tokyo to replace Matsui, who had joined the *kyodan*. In March 1944, the Ministry of Education ordered the closure of the NSKK's theological college in Tokyo. This decision was based on the military police's long-held belief that the NSKK had close ties with Britain and the United States as well as on the ministry's view that the small number of students did not warrant the existence of a separate Anglican theological college. Clearly, the ministry wanted all Protestant theological students to attend *kyodan* theological institutions.[70]

During late 1944, Sasaki and Bishop Sugai Todomu of South Tokyo were examined on numerous occasions by government prosecutors about their religious views. In February 1945, Sasaki was detained by the Tokyo *kempeitai* and put under house arrest for a month before being released. He was free only a few weeks before being arrested once again and imprisoned until mid-June 1945. During much of the same period, Sugai was also jailed at the Sugamo prison. Both men were in poor health when they were released.[71] NSKK priests were also suspected of being spies or defeatist in attitude, and some—including Nosse, Matsumoto Fumishi, Shimizu Fumio, and Shikutani Shigeru—spent some time in prison during the last months of the war.[72] Whereas Japanese Anglicans did suffer persecution, other Christian groups—especially the Holiness Church, the Seventh Day Adventists, the Salvation Army, and the Lighthouse Society (Jehovah's Witnesses)—suffered even more.[73] However, it was a measure of the growing desperation of the authorities in trying to maintain Japanese morale, as Tokyo and other major cities were being destroyed by Allied bombing during the last months of the war, that they began imprisoning NSKK priests.

The Japanese Christians in the NSKK and the *kyodan* had to face the trials and sufferings of the Pacific War alone. With the opening of the Pacific War, those missionaries remaining in Japan were interned by the authorities.

INTERNMENT

On 8 December 1941, the United Church of Canada had only eight missionaries still working in Japan, of whom six were WMS missionaries. There were also two retired WMS missionaries, Mrs. Harper Coates (the former Agnes Wintemute) and Margaret Armstrong, still living in Japan. By September 1942, Coates was the only Canadian of the twenty female and two male American, British, or Canadian missionaries still in Japan out of a total of thirty-nine Protestant missionaries.[74] Even though Armstrong was still living in Toyama, she was not included in this list of missionaries because she had taken the extraordinary step of becoming a Japanese citizen after retiring from the WMS in 1940.[75] As such, she was free to remain in Japan.

For Ernest Bott and his wife, Edith, who were teaching English in Tokyo as well as watching over the east Tokyo mission, it was four or five days after the beginning of the war before the police came to see them. By that time, the Botts had learned from the radio that "all enemy aliens who were to be interned were now in custody and that all foreigners of whatever nationality still at large were under no suspicion whatever and were free to go about their business."[76] Indeed, even though their residence was searched by the police, who only came to visit them three times, the Botts were never put under any form of arrest prior to their repatriation in the middle of 1942. Their telephone was bugged, but they still received mail. For his own safety, Bott was told by the authorities at Waseda University, where he taught, not to come in for classes. For her part, Edith continued to teach at the Women's Higher Normal School until the end of December 1941, when the Ministry of Education decreed that no foreigner was allowed to teach in government schools. Indeed, the only constraints on the Botts' freedom of action were self-imposed. Ernest was free to travel about Tokyo, and he went to church headquarters on a number of occasions. However, they decided that it was wise not to attend church or for Ernest to visit the east Tokyo mission or any of the social work institutions that he had been associated with in order not to embarrass the Japanese workers. The only time that he was engaged in mission business was when he, as residuary director of the Canadian Academy *shadan*, refused to sign over the ownership of the Canadian Academy to an interim board of directors of that school.[77] Why the Botts were treated well probably stemmed from the wide discretion that the local police possessed in dealing with enemy aliens. Although he had served in the Canadian army during World War I and was still young enough to join it again, Ernest had worked for twenty years in the slums of east Tokyo and was well known to many of the welfare officials who worked in the metropolitan Tokyo government. It was their goodwill toward him personally that allowed the Botts to remain free.

This was not the case across Tokyo at the Toyo Eiwa Jo Gakko, where Sybil Courtice and her two WMS colleagues were put under house arrest and then eventually placed in the Sumire internment camp.[78] This camp was on the grounds of a Roman Catholic institution and held some 124 women, including some twenty French Canadian nuns. Because her Japanese was excellent, Courtice was appointed the interpreter for the camp by the commandant, whose daughter was a student at the Toyo Eiwa Jo Gakko, and whose wife was a graduate of the Shizuoka Eiwa Jo Gakko. Conditions in the camp were not harsh, and the internees were well treated by their guards. The camp food usually consisted of a small piece of fish and all the bread that internees could eat, but the three Canadians were able to supplement this diet to some extent because they received a monthly allowance of three pots of marmalade from the Swiss Embassy. At other times, they also received parcels from the British Red Cross. Beyond that, they were able to obtain occasionally food from outside the camp. Nevertheless, the internees did suffer from shortages not only of food but also of fuel, but it was obvious that the Japanese in Tokyo were also enduring similar scarcities. Fortunately, for Courtice and her companions, their internment came to an end with their repatriation on board the Swedish exchange ship the *Gripsholm* in September 1942. Prior to boarding the ship in Yokohama, the WMS missionaries were allowed to return to the Toyo Eiwa Jo Gakko to pick up some of their personal belongings and to say goodbye to their friends there.

When the Pacific War broke out in December 1941, Florence Murray and nurse Beulah Bourns were at the Hamheung hospital and continued to work there until the end of May 1942. William Scott was teaching at the Hamheung boys' school and his colleague, E. J. O. Fraser, was still acting as mission secretary. Even after the declaration of war, Japanese gendarmes treated Murray and Bourns with great civility. Although they were not allowed out of the mission compound, they were allowed to work in the Hamheung hospital until they left Hamheung in June 1942. Their confinement was lax enough to allow Korean friends to stay surreptitiously with them at night so that the missionaries would not feel too lonely for lack of company. Christmas dinner 1941 was eaten at Scott's house in the compound in the presence of three armed Japanese guards, and it was then that they learned of the surrender of Hong Kong to the Japanese.[79] After Christmas, the female missionaries were permitted to visit Scott and Fraser, and in that way they kept each other's spirits up and exchanged news. The Japanese had confiscated their radios, but Scott had found one, which the Japanese had overlooked, so they were able to get some news of the outside world beyond that provided by the English-language Japanese papers that they were able to obtain.[80] While the four Canadian missionaries were under house arrest, they were well treated and came to no harm. When the time came for them to leave Hamheung, some of their Korean friends, hearing of their departure, risked punishment by going to the train station to bid them farewell. The missionaries were first taken to Seoul, then travelled to Japan, and from there via the *Gripsholm* returned to North America.

Like the Canadians in Hamheung, Courtice and the other WMS missionaries were able to leave Japan before the darkest days of the war. However, Armstrong remained in Japan throughout the war. It was a reflection of how attached she had become to Japan that she chose to remain there. Moreover, after many years of working in Japan, some missionaries had lost their close family ties to Canada and preferred to retire in Japan rather than face loneliness at home. Armstrong had a close friend and companion in Ichikawa Yayoi, and the two women faced the hardships of war together. Instead of staying in the relative safety of Karuizawa, as Courtice had wanted her to do, Armstrong spent the war in Toyama. However, her Japanese citizenship and long residency in Toyama did not stop the police from viewing her with suspicion. Some time after the end of the war, she wrote that on 8 December 1941 the police had examined her house and kindergarten to see if there were any radio connections to outside countries. She also remembered that the same day "one Christian friend, who spent eight years in America, said 'I tell everyone to read American history, and to remember the kindness, too, of America at the time of our great earthquake. If they do, they couldn't credit the propaganda against America carried on by the war-mongers.'"[81] Some of her friends were obviously sympathetic, at least when with her, toward the United States. She claimed that one young Japanese, whom she described as an artist, told her: "I'm waiting to be summoned to serve in the army; but I'll never, never fight against America, or against Chinese either. I will shoot myself before I shoot my fellowmen."[82] Armstrong also recorded that an elderly Christian woman had told her that "I'm for America, not for Japan. I pray that America may conquer. Then the Japanese would turn to God."[83] Although such statements might be naïve, they do show that the police had reason to worry that some of the Japanese Christians associated with Armstrong were not wholeheartedly behind Japan's war effort. Possibly for that reason, the police restricted her ability to undertake evangelistic work. She was not allowed to teach Christianity except at the house of refuge and the reformatory, and even there she was not permitted to mention the name of Jesus but could teach Old Testament stories as ethics. This restriction must have been tremendously trying for such a sincere and committed Christian who had spent her life attempting to convert people and was now prohibited from doing so.

Armstrong herself noted: "I was quite ready to go to prison or to any fate,—with my loving Father; but I was careful and tongue-tied to a great extent for the sake of the kindergarten."[84] She believed deeply that her kindergarten work had to go on. As the war continued, air raids posed new dangers for the kindergarten. She mentioned that "the radio was on all the time. Whenever the B29 aeroplanes were within a few hours of Toyama, the children were hurried off to their homes, or into an air-raid shelter half full of water."[85] The threat of fire was great because so many buildings were built of wood. Indeed, it was the fire bombing of Toyama on 1 August 1945 that forced Armstrong and her companion, Ichikawa, together with the kindergarten janitor and her young son, to take refuge at the home of a former kindergarten teacher in the countryside some ten miles from Toyama. The four of them were lucky to have left, because both the kindergarten and the residence were destroyed by fire.

It was in the countryside that Armstrong learned of the end of the war. She wrote:

> the night of August 15th 1945, after listening to much bitter talk, I lay down on my poor pallet under the net. The very heavens seemed to open and shower blessings upon us but to save my friends, I remained silent. That night, I spent in prayer, especially entreating for the Americans that they would be merciful to the Japanese.[86]

The war was over, but it was two weeks before it was deemed safe for them to return to Toyama. In the interim, Ichikawa was very concerned that Armstrong might be murdered by somebody who was distraught by the end of the war and saw her only as an American. She thought correctly that Armstrong would be safer near Toyama, where she was known, rather than in the country, which was filled with refugees, many of whom were starving. Nobody harmed Armstrong, but the two weeks after the end of the war were the only time when she might have been in danger from the Japanese. Once the American military arrived in Japan, things changed. Not surprisingly, Armstrong noted that "English, that had been taboo during the war, suddenly sprang into popularity."[87] Even less surprising, when a group of American military officers arrived in the fall of 1945 to set up the occupation government for the prefecture, the mayor of Toyama asked Armstrong to be among others at the station to meet them.[88] She found that her services as an English teacher for the Japanese, and as a Japanese translator for the American occupation forces, were much in demand. Indeed, for three years, Armstrong served as the official interpreter for the occupation government in Toyama Prefecture. In time, the kindergarten and residence were rebuilt by the city of Toyama, and Armstrong returned to her Christian work until her death in 1960.

The help and kindness of long-suffering Japanese friends proved insufficient to prevent the death of the other Canadian woman who remained in Japan during the war, Mrs. Coates. Coates died in the temporary hospital on the premises of St. Nicholas Church, the famous Russian Orthodox cathedral in Tokyo, only two months before the end of the war.[89] At that time, conditions for everyone in Tokyo were appalling, and food was desperately scarce, and Coates was in her early eighties.

HOPING FOR THE BEST

Although it was only at the end of the war that the fate of Armstrong and Coates was learned, during the war the missionaries in Toronto tried as best they could to find out what was happening to their churches in Japan. The first concrete information came with the exchange of missionaries in the late summer of 1942. Ernest Bott was able to reassure missionaries that the missionaries held in Japan had been well looked after. In October 1942, he wrote to Charles Iglehart in New York that schools such as Aoyama Gakuin and social work endeavours in Tokyo were still going strong. Furthermore, he noted that the Ministry of Finance held the attitude that all property belonging to enemy aliens should be protected against the day of settlement after the war. To ensure that this was done, the ministry had appointed the *kyodan* as custodian of all property belonging to mission *shadans*.[90] There were certain areas of concern, though. Bott pointed out that a large number of rural preaching places had been discontinued because of lack of funds and a shortage of ministers and female evangelists. He thought that "it is one of the most unfortunate aspects of the situation that the church will become very largely urban."[91] He also reported that he had seen Abe a number of times since the outbreak of the war and that, on those occasions, he "was always very cordial and helpful."[92] Indeed, he had a farewell dinner with Abe and a number of other former Methodist leaders the day before he left Japan. He learned that Abe had become involved with work in China, but he was not quite sure just what his title or duties were in regard to this work. Bott noted that Abe was a member of a committee representing the cooperation of the three religions in East Asia and that he was acting as a mediator between Chinese Christians in occupied China and the Japanese authorities. Bott pointed out that "some of the China Missionaries are inclined to question his judgement if not his motives."[93] Unfortunately for Abe, it was not only missionaries in China who questioned his judgment. Bott also indicated that some of his Japanese colleagues criticized Abe for doing two jobs (he was still in charge of the Methodist section of the *kyodan*), one of that involved long absences from Japan. But Bott clearly still held Abe in high regard.

John Waller, the retired Canadian Anglican priest, who had been under house arrest in Nagano and then interned with other male missionaries at the Canadian Academy in Kobe, was able in September 1942 to provide some information about the state of the NSKK and the Diocese of Mid-Japan. He was optimistic about the NSKK, perhaps partially because "the result of 'Christian Union' in Japan forced on a lot of reluctant bodies by an anti-Christian Government looks not very hopeful. It will be only by God's special mercy that it will become a success."[94] Clearly, Waller was an opponent of union.

Nevertheless, even though the NSKK had yet to be recognized as a *kyodan* in its own right, he gave the impression that the Anglican churches of Mid-Japan were faring well. Great strides toward self-support had been made, and he noted that two years before there had only been one self-supporting church in Mid-Japan, but when he left Japan there were thirteen. Although the pay of parish priests was low, ranging between ¥100 and ¥65, parsonages allowed most of the priests to live rent free. As far as he knew, Sasaki also had sufficient money to pay for his expenses, including travel costs. Waller mentioned that "Bishop Sasaki works as hard as ever (he had a severe breakdown, Jan. 1939) and travels constantly over much of the main island. He is the most prominent and effective of the Nippon Sei Ko Kwai Bishops."[95] Waller had always been one of the staunchest missionary supporters of Sasaki, and his only complaint against the bishop was his emphasis on money. He commented that, when this emphasis was not accompanied by an equal amount of evangelistic work, "it becomes a dangerous evil. And as yet the Gospel is not preached with equal vigour. Repeatedly I warned our Bishop and clergy about this. Unless you control a man's heart, you will not long control his purse."[96]

At the time that Waller left Japan, the NSKK had not made any approach, to his knowledge, toward the *kyodan*. Interestingly, but not altogether unreasonably, Waller was asked if the NSKK had made any approach toward the Roman Catholic Church, that it had not. The only worrisome thing, Waller reported, was that church attendance, as might be expected, was generally poor. More detailed information on the condition of the NSKK and former American Church institutions in Japan was provided by Paul Rusch, an American Church missionary who had been repatriated, like Waller, on the *Gripsholm*.[97] Again, the news from Rusch was reassuring and indicated that schools and hospitals associated with the NSKK were still functioning. Indeed, Rusch had learned that the Ministry of Education had granted a licence for the formation of a medical college into that Rikkyo and St. Luke's International Medical Center were to merge. New buildings were to be built on the Sumida River grounds of the hospital to house the new medical college.

United Church missionaries, for their part, felt confident in the leadership of the *kyodan*. In April 1942, at a conference on "Mission Policy as Affected by the War," Charles Bates gave a paper on "The Church in Japan" in that he expressed great confidence in the leaders of the *kyodan*:

> Today there are such men as Tomita the official head of the new United Church and the representative of the Presbyterian branch of that Church, Bishop Abe who represents Methodism therein, Kozaki of Congregational heritage, Chiba, a Baptist leader a man of finest Christian humility and devotion, and many others with Kagawa as the outstanding evangelist and social worker. We believe that the interests of the Cause of Christ is as safe in their hands as it could be in any under the governance and guidance of God.[98]

Bates retained great faith in the Japanese Christian leadership despite the war, clearly he was looking to a time when missionaries could return to their work in Japan once hostilities ceased.

Other missionaries were not as optimistic about the future. Emma Palethorpe, a veteran WMS missionary in Korea who had been evacuated from the peninsula in 1941, speaking at the same conference as Bates, was much less sanguine about the future prospects of missionary work in Korea. Correctly, she saw that this work was shrouded with uncertainty. Nevertheless, like Bates in terms of the Japanese, Palethorpe gave credit to the Korean Christian leadership, telling her audience: "let us not forget that the leaders are carrying unaccustomed responsibilities—and *that* at a time of extreme difficulty and danger. They are subject to insidious and subtle temptation such as we in free Canada have not yet had to face."[99] Yet, most of all, Palethorpe was impressed by the spirit and courage of the ordinary Korean Christian:

> No one who has had fellowship with the humble, faithful Korean Christians, scattered through the mountain valleys of Korea and Manchuria can doubt that the Korean Church will survive the present wave of suppression and oppression. These Christians have come into vital, personal contact with the Living Christ and would die rather than deny Him. They carry in their hearts a treasure of which even a totalitarian government cannot deprive them. Surely this makes the work of the past worth while and insures at least a remnant, for the future.[100]

Palethorpe was giving a stereotypical characterization of Korean Christians as people prepared to suffer and, if need be, to die to remain true to their faith. Even before the opening of the Pacific War, Korean Christians demonstrated their fierce loyalty to Christianity in the face of persecution by the Japanese army and colonial authorities over the shrine issue. Although some Japanese Christians did endure great suffering for their religious beliefs during the war, few missionaries in Japan, if any, had ever described Japanese Christians in the same way as Palethorpe saw "the humble, faithful Korean Christians scattered through the mountain valleys of Korea and Manchuria." Plainly, the Japanese Christians were different. The sophisticated academic and urban world inhabited by Bates and the Japanese Christian leaders whom he admired so deeply and sincerely was far removed from the harsh life of the Korean farming communities clustered around Lungchingtsun, where Palethorpe had toiled for many years. Bates was smugly confident that the interests of Christianity in Japan were safe in the hands of a small group of outstanding Christian leaders. In contrast, the only certainty that Palethorpe saw in Korea was that a remnant of Christianity would survive in spite of suppression and oppression.

By 1942, other missionaries were also thinking about the future in the mission field after the defeat of Japan. In late December 1942, O. R. Avison, a Canadian who had worked for many years for the American Presbyterian mission at the Severance Union Medical College in Seoul, wrote to A. E. Armstrong pressing the case of the Christian Friends of Korea, a political lobby group for the creation of an independent Korea. In particular, this lobby group championed the political cause of Syngman Rhee (Rhee Syngman), the elderly Korean nationalist leader and a Christian, whom Avison had known for over forty years. Avison told Armstrong that he believed that, "if Korea is not rendered Independent, Japan may be just as cocky in regard to Korea as she is now and has been."[101]

In the past, Armstrong had been very supportive of lobby groups such as the American Committee for Non-Participation in Japanese Aggression, a pro-Chinese organization.[102] Clearly, he was also personally sympathetic to both the Christian Friends of Korea and Korean independence. He believed that after the war Korea should be either granted independence or put under the supervision of the United Nations Association until the country had the capacity to administer its own affairs and to form a competent government.[103] Although Armstrong was prescient in seeing a role for the United Nations in postwar Korea, he still thought that there might be a different future for Korea. He believed that there was "at least a strong possibility that in the political bargaining that may follow this war Korea might be left under the Japanese" and that under this circumstance "formal membership in a society whose objective is the political freedom of Korea might constitute a very real barrier to entrance into the country."[104]

For this reason Armstrong refused to become a member of Avison's organization. To become a member would be tantamount to giving the United Church of Canada's blessing to the organization's postwar political objectives. Obviously, Armstrong thought that the Allies would not demand Japan's unconditional surrender but that there would be negotiations following Japan's defeat. Either he underestimated the will of the Allies to achieve a complete victory or his view merely underlined the foolishness of Japan in fighting a war that became more hopeless every day. Indeed, even in early 1943, it is rather surprising that Armstrong thought that Japan would be allowed to retain such power in Korea that the Japanese would be able to prevent pro-independence missionaries from entering the peninsula. Yet this concern was echoed by Florence Murray and other missionaries in the closing months of the war.[105] Interestingly, Armstrong objected to membership in the Christian Friends of Korea not because it was so closely identified with Rhee, whose politics not everybody in Korea would have approved of, but for the sake of those missionaries who might want to return to Korea. Whereas Scott was prepared to join Avison's organization, Armstrong held that United Church missionaries who hoped to return to Korea after the war preferred not to join. Undeterred, Avison continued to appeal to Armstrong for support.[106]

Although Avison and others were lobbying for the future, a limited amount of information about what was happening to the Christian movement in Japan became available at missionary headquarters in Toronto. This information came through the New York-based Committee on East Asia of the Foreign Missions Conference of North America, that had access to transcripts of Japanese government broadcasts to Latin and North America and, on occasion, to those of metropolitan Japanese radio. Although much of the news about the Christian movement was propaganda, efforts were made to interpret this "news" in order to establish what was actually happening. This was the case in September 1944, when a news release issued by the Office of Wartime Information reported that Christian churches in Japan had been dissolved. However, the Committee on East Asia, after examining the complete text of the Japanese Domei broadcast on that the release had been based as well as those of other Japanese-language broadcasts on the same subject, concluded that the Japanese had formed a single "Wartime Patriotic Society" and had dissolved all other religious patriotic societies, but there had been no dissolution of Christian churches.[107]

Transcripts of broadcasts also brought news that needed no interpretation. In August 1944, Kagawa, incensed by the skull incident involving *Life* magazine, was quoted as saying in a sermon that "it is reported that bones and even skulls of Japanese soldiers killed in battle have been sent to America as souvenirs. This is incredible to the Oriental mind, a kind of savagery comparable to the lowest cannibalism."[108] Recalling his visit to the United States with the Christian deputation in 1941, Kagawa went on to claim:

> I travelled in many cities in America which proclaimed its plea for a real civilization that can never come to doubt the concept of love and cooperation. Today I see America as a white grave. I cannot believe that the Almighty of all the earth will permit the success of their inordinate ambitions for world domination which forged the spirit of racial superiority, but at the same time talks of freedom and liberty, using these words while waging this unjust war on the Oriental race. Ah, woe to America for so degrading the name of Christ by this butchery.[109]

Kagawa was not the only Japanese Christian leader who made broadcasts attacking the United States and the behaviour of the Allies. Tomita, the leading figure in the *kyodan*, made a number of broadcasts at the request of the Army General Staff Headquarters. In January 1945, following the bombing of the outer shrine of Ise, Tomita made a broadcast titled "The Americans Who Lost God," in that he was supposed to have said that

> the enemy bombing of the outer shrine of Ise really indicated that Americans have lost their religion, and there is no other violent blasphemy against God than this. The Christians in Japan have completely lost faith in the religion of the Americans, and I believe that this holds true for the rest of the people of the world.[110]

Tomita, who had visited Ise earlier in the war, held that the bombing of Ise enraged the Japanese people more than the bombing of the Vatican had angered Catholics. He added that:

> Christians in Japan have come to realize that the religion of Americans is nothing but an external form. The enemy in the past has sent a number of missionary workers to China and other southern areas in order to spread Christianity, but the religion was utilized to execute the U. S. policy: therefore, as soon as war was declared, without any hesitation she took off her mask, and complacently defiled God and exposed her shamelessness. Such defilement against God by the Americans is to indicate to the world that the United States has lost her right for leadership. Our public enemy United States, a race which desecrates God surely will be annihilated in the fearful flame of sins.[111]

Clearly, Tomita had become a mouthpiece for Japanese wartime propaganda, and to a lesser extent so had Kagawa. In contrast to Tomita and Kagawa, whose hostility to the Allies seemed to increase as the war continued, the growing persecution of Japanese Christians in the last months of the war indicated the existence among some ordinary Christians of a defeatist view—that it might be best for Japan to end its war with the United States.[112] Whether or not the mission headquarters in Toronto were aware of the anti-American statements of Christian leaders on whom they had pinned so much faith to keep the cause of Christ safe, once the war ended all was swept aside.

This was transparent in the first postwar letter that Armstrong wrote to Kagawa. In October 1945, Armstrong expressed his happiness at being able to write to Kagawa once again:

> I rejoice that even the terrible conflict has not broken the bond of love which we Christians in North America have toward the Christians of Japan and they, I am sure, toward us. The fellowship of the Christian faith is a very precious thing: "Nothing can separate us from the love of God." Nor can anything separate those who are members of the world family of Christians from one another. It is gratifying that throughout the war years this bond was held between Christians who are in Europe or in Asia or in North America. The ecumenical church is a reality.[113]

It did not matter that Kagawa's behaviour during the Pacific War revealed that the bond of his love for Christians in North America had been stretched perilously thin, for Armstrong believed that it had remained strong.

Indeed, as early as January 1945, the fear of offending the Japanese was evident among former missionaries during a meeting in Toronto concerning their possible return to Japan at the war's end. One of the missionaries' worries was that their work would be identified with that of Allied government agencies. If this connection was made, then their Christian efforts would suffer the same fate as Japanese Christian work in China. Attention was drawn to the fact that "Japanese Christian workers who went to China with the best of intentions met a feeling of distrust and suspicion that would likely be ours if we returned to Japan in connection with government agencies."[114] Such a comparison was of dubious validity, but the phrase "the best of intentions" in regard to Japanese Christian actions in China is striking. It gives them the benefit of any doubt about the motives behind their work in China. Apparently, that the missionaries were prepared to overlook the war. One of the first postwar reports about the Christian churches in Japan during the war was written by an American diplomat, who noted that "the national leadership of the Church of Christ in Japan is in the hands of sincere pastors but men who have been so tied up with government regulations, control and bureaucracy that they seem to have lost sight of the larger vision to a certain extent."[115] No blame was seemingly attached to these sincere pastors for what had taken place during the war years. When it came to the return of missionaries to Japan, weight was even given to the opinion of Tomita, who was still head of the *kyodan* and understandably extremely cautious about their return.[116]

In sharp contrast to the reaction of the Japanese Christian leadership, all church leaders in Korea were anxious that former missionaries return to the peninsula as soon as possible.[117] Canadian missionaries were eager to get back to work; however, as they indicated in a wartime questionnaire about the future of missionary work in Korea, it all depended upon the status of Korea at the end of the war.[118] Indeed, should Korea be granted independence from Japan, some missionaries, Murray among them, thought that there would be a need for more Canadian missionaries than before. Nevertheless, Murray thought that Armstrong and the missionary society authorities were leaning toward sending back to Korea fewer but more highly qualified missionaries.[119] The possibility of the occupation of northern Korea by the Soviet army, and what consequences this occupation might have on the future of missionary work, were understandably never considered before the end of the war. Missionaries simply had little information about conditions in Korea during the war and none about the plans for postwar Allied military policies there. In the first news after the war that Toronto received about the situation of the Korean Christian movement, it was pointed out that

> in the northern areas, occupied by Russian forces, the Koreans are under the severe handicap of rough treatment that is being given. Many pastors have come to ask if something could be done about that, but we have no control over the area. At the same time, much of the support previously given to the Communist teaching has been discredited by the actions of the Russian soldiers.[120]

The belief that returning missionaries could protect Korean Christians was echoed by Reverend Chairin Moon, who wrote to Armstrong from

Lungchingtsun in late October 1945, stating that "the Christians in Kanto and Korea, especially in North Korea are waiting [for] your missionaries because they have some trouble from the R. Movement."[121] In the past, Canadian missionaries had done their best to protect Korean Christians from the Japanese military or communist partisans. Moon in Lungchingtsun and his fellow Christians in north Korea saw the role of Canadian missionaries as protectors of Korean Christians continuing. When they did eventually return to Korea and Manchuria, Scott, Murray, and other Canadian missionaries did their best before the Korean War intervened.

Although missionaries in Canada hoped for the best for Christians in the Japanese Empire, many of the Japan missionaries in Canada were deeply concerned about the plight of Japanese Canadians.[122] Among the most active was the Percy Powles family, late of Takata, who did much to help ease the difficulties of nisei relocated to Montreal.[123] Constance Chappell, who had taught at Tokyo Woman's Christian College before the war, was another outspoken critic of the treatment of Japanese Canadians. Other former missionaries, such as Howard Norman, who spent much of the war as a civilian instructor at the Canadian Army Japanese Language School in Vancouver, commanded by his missionary colleague, McKenzie, a World War I army captain and a holder of the Military Cross, who had been recalled to the colours and rose to the rank of lieutenant-colonel in the Intelligence Corps, helped Japanese Canadians as much as they could.[124] Indeed, the realization that Japanese Canadians had been mistreated by their fellow Canadians might well have coloured missionary attitudes toward Christians in metropolitan Japan and reinforced the prevalent missionary view that the Japanese Christian leadership was blameless of any wrongdoing during the war.

The future held that the *kyodan* should continue to exist, with Kozaki replacing Tomita as its head at the first postwar general conference in June 1946. Kozaki and the *kyodan* leadership lent the support of the Christian movement to the building of a new Japan and expressed their hope for peace.[125] The NSKK moved to heal its wounds by allowing those who had defected to the *kyodan* during the war the opportunity to return to the Anglican Church. However, such were the appalling conditions in Tokyo and in Japan as a whole that the primary concern was the relief effort. In April 1946, Bott, the first United Church missionary to return, landed in Japan. Immediately, he threw his prodigious energies into relief work in conjunction with LARA (Licensed Agencies for Relief in Asia), the major organization through that private relief supplies for the civilian population were funnelled. The hardships of the 1930s and the horrors of the Pacific War were things of the past as Canadian missionaries returned to help build for the future.

The future would prove unkind to Canadian missionaries who returned to Manchuria and northern Korea, for the new age that began with the end of the Pacific War brought revolution and war. The Korean Christian world of

Lungchingtsun, of Chientao province, and of Tiger Mountain long familiar to generations of Canadian Christians through church group meetings and missionary publications was soon shuttered tight behind a bamboo curtain that cut the Korean peninsula at the thirty-eighth parallel. The evangelistic hopes of the Canadian Presbyterian missionaries who returned to Szepinkai in a Manchuria once again part of China to carry on the work that Goforth had begun were quickly dashed. The link between Canadians and ordinary folk in rural northeast Asia was extinguished and lost. Those who went back to north Taiwan also soon found themselves caught in a revolution that brought the defeated Chinese Nationalists en masse to the island in 1949. It was only in postwar Japan that there was peace and opportunity.

Conclusion

Canadian missionaries entered the 1930s with a considerable record of achievement behind them. As well as direct evangelistic work, missionary activity encompassed mission schools, hospitals, kindergarten-teacher training institutes, and social welfare organizations. Canadian missionaries took a prominent role in an impressive variety of different causes, from the purity movement, to the founding of farmers' institutes, to the fight against tuberculosis and leprosy. Nevertheless, evangelism was always the central task, with education looked upon as an adjunct. When, as occurred in Japan, evangelism did not go as well as expected and competition with government education made missionary educational work more difficult, the social gospel came to the rescue by providing a Christian motive for social work. In Korea, evangelistic and educational work was more successful, and in Taiwan, which remained a shoestring operation, social work was not developed to the same extent as in metropolitan Japan. Yet, by their actions, Canadian missionaries showed ordinary people in the Japanese Empire that they were not only sympathetic to their problems but also prepared to strive to improve their material well-being and their physical health. Moreover, Canadian missionary work was expanding in new directions, for during the late 1920s Johnathan Goforth had moved from metropolitan China to begin new evangelistic work in Manchuria, and other Canadian Presbyterians had commenced work among the Koreans living in Japan. At the same time, the mission schools and other educational institutions maintained by Canadians in the Japanese Empire continued to flourish. At the beginning of the 1930s, the opportunities for a Christian revival in Japan and its empire, if they could only be grasped, seemed as tantalizingly close as they had ever been since the arrival of the first Canadian missionaries.

Ordinary Japanese Christians responded positively and gratefully to the actions of Canadian missionaries. This response can be clearly seen in the anniversary histories of local churches and in Kuranaga Takashi's history of the Canadian Methodist mission that were published during the late 1930s. The selfless work of Canadian female missionaries working in kindergartens in the cities and towns of central Honshu left an indelible mark on the minds of their small charges that many have tenaciously held on to throughout their lives. The contributions of the United Church educational missionaries to the development of their respective institutions are still remembered. This is true not only of the procession of missionary principals at the *eiwa* schools or Charles Bates of the Kwansei Gakuin but also of other missionary teachers such as Constance Chappell, who influenced successive generations of students at the Tokyo Woman's Christian College. The work of Annie Allen and the staff at the Aiseikan in Kameido ward helped to highlight the need to improve the living and working conditions of female factory workers and others in the east Tokyo slums. The contributions of the independent Canadian missionary Caroline Macdonald to the development of the YWCA in Japan and to prison reform are also remembered. The Japanese clergy in the Diocese of Mid-Japan looked to Percy Powles (the high Japanese regard for whom was later dramatically illustrated when he was made a bishop in postwar Japan) and other Canadian Anglican missionaries for help in dealing with some of the more high-handed actions of Bishop Sasaki Shinji. The work of Richard Start, the medical doctor at the Obuse sanatorium, was widely admired both inside and outside the Christian community. Even after the Pacific War had begun, the treatment of Ernest Bott and his wife during their internment by the authorities in Tokyo revealed their continuing respect for what the Botts had done to help the poor in east Tokyo. Furthermore, the courageous help of Japanese friends shielded Margaret Armstrong from harm after she decided to become a Japanese citizen and to remain in Japan during the war.

Despite their good personal relations with individual Japanese Christians and their own continued optimism for the future, however, missionaries were faced from the early 1930s on with serious internal and external challenges. One of the most important came from within the missionary movement itself in the form of reduced budgets owing to the Depression. Initially, the Depression in Japan resulted in an increased openness to the Christian message, that did much to bolster missionary optimism. However, this openness was not so much the result of the spiritual attraction of Christianity as of a search by Japanese to find relief from the difficulties that many encountered during the early years of the Depression. As well as its effect on the lives of ordinary Japanese, the Depression had an adverse and more permanent impact on the missionary movement. Understandably, the Depression in Canada led to fewer donations in support of foreign missions. The impact of this shortage caused retrenchment and the downsizing of the Canadian missions in the Japanese Empire. This process was most evident in the United Church of Canada mission work in both Japan and Korea. Indeed, so acute was the financial situation that the closure of the entire mission in Korea was threatened with closure. Because Korea had long been considered the most successful field of missionary endeavour in East Asia, it would have been more reasonable to close the mission in Japan. However, financial expediency, not logic, drove the missionary authorities in faraway Toronto to threaten to terminate the mission in Korea. As it turned out, of course, closure was averted, and Canadian missionary work in the peninsula continued.

In the case of United Church work in Japan, the missionary staff involved in education or social welfare was virtually untouched by retrenchment. Seasoned evangelistic missionaries in provincial Japan were cut and not replaced. In doing so, the United Church mission largely did away with the one pillar of the trinity of evangelism, education, and social work that had characterized its work from the beginning. One result of moving away from evangelistic activity was the isolation of United Church missionaries from ordinary Japanese Christians at the parish level. Missionaries thus became more dependent on the approval and goodwill of the small and sometimes fickle Japanese Christian leadership. Furthermore, giving up evangelistic work represented a retreat from rural Japan despite the positive signs that farmers' institutes and other aspects of rural evangelistic endeavour were attracting a number of enquirers. However, the United Church mission chose to withdraw to the urban centres of Tokyo and Osaka-Kobe and to continue to support their specialized activities. Consequently, the ability of the mission to take advantage of a revival to increase the number of Japanese Christians was limited.

Whereas Canadian missionary effort in rural evangelism among the Japanese virtually stopped, the Canadian Academy, that provided private school education for foreign children in Kobe, was maintained. The main emphasis of United Church mission work had therefore begun to shift from trying to convert the Japanese to providing specialized services on the periphery of the Christian endeavour in Japan. This shift could be interpreted as showing the willingness of the United Church mission to pass the baton of responsibility for Christian expansion from the missionary movement to the Japanese Christian movement. However, Canadian missionaries revealed no pressing desire to give up their deanships, principalships, and other positions to their Japanese colleagues. Indeed, they had no intention of ending United Church mission work in Japan in the near future. Missionaries were open to new and fashionable ideas, as the attraction of some to the Oxford Group Movement attested (perhaps to the detriment of clear-sightedness about their role as missionaries), but there remained no doubt that they were in Japan to stay.

The Canadian Anglican mission offered a different approach to mission work. Largely unencumbered by the physical plant of mission schools and welfare institutions, the Canadian Anglicans maintained their parish-based work in Mid-Japan and in doing so retained their links with Japanese Christians and clergy at the grassroots. A relatively small mission, the Canadian Anglicans were also able to avoid, through the careful juggling of exchange rates, the full impact of reduced budgets caused by the Depression in Canada. Likewise, the retirement of Bishop Heber Hamilton opportunely allowed the Canadians to fill his position with a Japanese, which represented not only a saving in salary to the mission but also that they were in favour of more Japanese bishops in the NSKK. At the same time, Sasaki's elevation to bishop did not alter the fact that the Canadian Anglicans still controlled the purse strings of the Mid-Japan diocese. The early 1930s also saw the fulfilment of Hamilton's long-held dream with the opening of the tuberculosis sanatorium at Obuse. In the absence of a Canadian Anglican bishop to give a distinct Canadian identity to missionary work in Mid-Japan, Obuse came to serve as a focal point for a continued Canadian Anglican presence in and commitment to the diocese.

While the Canadian Anglicans in Mid-Japan continued their evangelistic work as before, United Church missionaries enthusiastically turned to the Kingdom of God movement, led by the charismatic Kagawa Toyohiko, to fill the evangelistic vacuum in their mission work. Their reliance on Kagawa's movement conveniently allowed the United Church mission to trim its budget at the expense of its own evangelistic work. However, it is no coincidence that the most enthusiastic supporters of Kagawa among United Church missionaries in Japan were not evangelistic missionaries but rather Bates, the president of the Kwansei Gakuin, and Percy Price, who was involved in specialized temperance and purity work. The invitations extended to Kagawa to conduct evangelistic campaigns in Canada also revealed that Kagawa was seen as a Christian of international significance. Indeed, some of United Church missionaries believed that he was so prominent an Asian figure that he should be compared with Mahatma Gandhi. The Kingdom of God movement did achieve some success in attracting enquirers to meetings in both urban centres and rural towns, but it was the Holiness Church, not the orthodox denominations that supported the Kingdom of God movement, that made the most converts of all Protestant groups during the early 1930s.

Despite the evangelistic dynamism of Kagawa and the Kingdom of God movement, the United Church decision to sacrifice evangelistic work and to maintain mission schools was arguably incorrect. The early history of the Canadian work in Japan suggests that it was more productive for missionaries to concentrate on evangelistic instead of educational work. During the late nineteenth and early twentieth centuries, Canadian missionaries had been more effective than Japanese evangelists in attracting Japanese enquirers. Through the strength of their personalities, the power of their learning, and the fact that they were foreigners, George Cochran, Davidson Macdonald, and Charles Eby, the pioneer Canadian Methodist missionaries, had been able to draw Japanese to their preaching places. It was at the second stage, once the enquirer had expressed an interest in Christianity, that the Japanese pastor took on a crucial role in explaining the subtleties of Christianity to the potential convert. Conversion was usually not only a long process but also a bilingual one. Indeed, the success of a Canadian missionary at making conversions was most times only as good as his or her Japanese helper. However, even during the 1930s, as the example of Goforth and his Canadian Presbyterian colleagues clearly revealed in Manchuria, foreign missionaries had little difficulty in attracting audiences in rural areas. Similarly, the example of Manchuria indicated that the evangelistic zeal of missionaries was important in inspiring their Chinese evangelists and Bible women.

Whereas missionaries were able to accomplish much in evangelistic work, Japanese were more effective than missionaries in educational work. Naturally, money or the lack of it often played a vital part in determining the reputation of any mission or Christian school. Yet, in general, institutions with a Japanese principal usually enjoyed a higher reputation than their counterparts with a foreign missionary principal. In the late 1890s, the success of the Azabu Middle School under the headmastership of Ebara Soroku illustrated the drawing power of a well-known and respected name. Tsuda College and Tokyo Woman's Christian College, the two most prestigious Christian institutions for women's higher education, owe much to the reputations of Tsuda Umeko and Nitobe Inazo respectively. Likewise, Doshisha University in Kyoto, the most famous Christian university in Japan, is associated with Neeshima Jo, its Japanese founder. Tokyo Woman's Christian College was a union institution supported by five different missions, including the United Church, but A. K. Reischauer, the senior American Presbyterian missionary, associated with the development of the college during the 1920s and 1930s, devoted his attention to fund-raising and teaching and left public relations to successive Japanese presidents. To some Japanese, a missionary principal was a sign of foreign control of and influence in education in Japan, but a Christian school with a Japanese principal indicated Japanese mastery of Western-style education and independence from foreign control.

Canadian missionaries did not fully appreciate how chary the Japanese were about foreign influence in education. The Japanese authorities saw education as a means to inculcate loyalty in Japanese citizens. Thus, it was vital for them to have control over curricula, and to prevent the teaching of foreign ideas seen to challenge the state orthodoxy or to provide an alternative to it. By the end of the 1930s, government regulations concerning curricula and qualifications of teachers, particularly linguistic ones, did much to squeeze foreigners out of mission schools.

The need to comply with government standards in education also meant that missionary principals had to deal with the Japanese authorities. At once, many of them were at a disadvantage because of language. Bates of the Kwansei Gakuin, for instance, was a poor Japanese linguist. However, the linguistic situation was further complicated in Korea and Taiwan, where—beyond having to master Korean or Chinese—it was also useful for missionaries to know Japanese, the language of the colonial government. William Scott and E. J. O. Fraser in Korea, neither of whom had any deep knowledge of Japanese, had the good fortune of negotiating with reasonable, if not sympathetic, bureaucrats. This was certainly not the case in Taiwan, where G. W. Mackay, who had no Japanese, was faced with hostile colonial civil servants. Undoubtedly, some of his difficulties with the colonial authorities stemmed from linguistic misunderstandings and misinterpreted cultural nuances. Moreover, there might have been some racial antipathy toward Mackay by some of the Japanese officials because his mother was Chinese. What is clear, however, is that local officials and gendarmes in both Taiwan and Korea, as well as metropolitan Japan itself, had broad discretion in interpreting and implementing government regulations. Some of the petty colonial officials were open to bribery on small matters, such as issuing drivers' licences, as Florence Murray in Hamheung found out, but most were simply concerned with fulfilling their bureaucratic obligations and expected a modicum of compliance to regulations from missionaries. Only in Taiwan was there outright and unprovoked hostility toward missionaries and their mission schools by lesser colonial officials.

There were times when officials felt obliged to take forceful measures to ensure that government policy was followed. The shrine question was an issue over that the authorities could not give ground. Their interpretation of the meaning of the shrine ceremonies had to be accepted by missionaries and Christians, especially in Korea and Taiwan, where the policies of the colonial government general required the transformation of Koreans and Taiwanese into compliant subjects of the Japanese Empire.

The stand over the shrine question taken by the Canadian missionaries in Korea was very different from that taken by George S. McCune and Miss V. L. Snook in P'yongyang, who had the support of the majority of American missionaries and many Korean Christians. In sharp contrast to the Americans, the Canadians were not prepared to close their schools in protest; they were willing, like their United Church colleagues in Japan, to accept the government's position that the shrine ceremonies were not religious. As a result, the Canadian mission in Korea remained on good terms with the government general and local Japanese officials, and the shrine question caused little disruption to Canadian mission schools. For Scott and his fellow Canadians, and Howard Outerbridge in Japan, who held a similar opinion, the consequences for Korean schoolchildren of closing Canadian mission schools were far greater than the impact on them of attending shrine ceremonies. However, the protest over these ceremonies did lead to the closure of much of the mission school network throughout the peninsula and to the persecution of Korean Christians. It left the missionary movement in disarray and much weakened to face the severe challenges from the Japanese authorities at the end of the 1930s.

Unfortunately, the reputations of missionaries rose or fell in the eyes of many Korean Christians on the public expression of their support for Korean national goals. This was certainly the case in the 1 March 1919 Independence Movement, when missionaries who did not publicly condemn Japanese actions and declare their sympathy for Korean independence ran the risk of being pilloried as pro-Japanese. This happened to the Canadian independent missionary James Scarth Gale and to the British Anglican mission in Korea as a whole. Likewise, the lack of resistance by Canadian missionaries to the shrine question could have been interpreted by Korean Christians as a sign that Canadian missionaries were pro-Japanese. Such a charge would have been unjustified, of course, because Canadian missionaries in Korea were anything but pro-Japanese. Many Korean Christians failed to appreciate that Canadian missionary attitudes toward the actions of the Japanese colonial or military authorities depended upon whether missionaries considered these actions harmful or beneficial to Korean Christians and not upon their consequences for Korean national aspirations. Thus, it was perfectly understandable and logical for Canadian missionaries in Korea to condemn the brutalities of the Japanese in the wake of the 1 March 1919 demonstrations and to respond favourably to the Japanese intervention in Manchuria in 1931. Many of the Canadian missionaries believed that the Japanese military represented the best chance to bring about peace and security for Korean Christians in an area along the Manchurian-Korean border that was disturbed by the activities of Korean nationalist partisans. By this time, Canadian missionaries had come to see Korean communists, who were leading the armed struggle for national liberation from the Japanese, as a danger to Korean Christians and to the Christian movement in Korea.

The Canadian response to the shrine question in Korea was also coloured by an important difference between the younger generation of Canadian missionaries and their American counterparts in Korea. Whereas many American missionaries tended to be theologically conservative (and P'yongyang was a centre of this conservatism), United Church missionaries were liberals in theology. The attacks by Duncan MacRae, the pioneer Canadian missionary in Hamheung, on his younger colleagues over the shrine question, which he carried on long after his retirement to Cape Breton, can also be seen as a conflict of conservative and liberal ideas within the United Church mission itself. Scott and other Canadians played a significant role in introducing liberal theology into Korea, but whether their position on the shrine question hampered the acceptance of liberal theological ideas in Korea cannot be answered. However, the mainstream of the Korean Christian movement was and remains theologically conservative. The sulphuric combination of theological conservatism and Korean nationalism goes far to explain the bitter and sometimes tragic Korean Christian opposition to attending ceremonies at state Shinto shrines, opposition that continued long after McCune and Snook had left Korea.

Although the Canadian mission schools in Korea remained open, the Tamsui Middle School in Taiwan did not survive the shrine question, which was interwoven with other issues, not the least of that was the severe anti-British feeling running through some elements in the island. The Keelung incident, which involved the detention and beating of visiting British bluejackets, revealed the seriousness of this anti-British sentiment. Because the Tamsui Middle School and its counterpart for girls occupied a prime site overlooking the Keelung River, the colonial authorities, for military security reasons, wanted to and eventually did terminate the missionary presence there. The shrine question served to embarrass Mackay and his missionary teachers, but there was no doubt that the Japanese wanted the missionaries away from that area. Once Mackay had vacated the property at Tamsui, the authorities did not object to him undertaking extensive evangelistic trips into the interior of northern Taiwan. As C. H. Archer, the British consul in Taiwan, well understood, the actions of the Japanese against Mackay and his fellow Canadian missionary educators were politically motivated. Indeed, as the colonial attitude toward George Gushue-Taylor and the Happy Mount Leper Colony indicated, where there was no political bone of contention good relations could be maintained. Whether they liked it or not, Canadian missionaries were affected by the vagaries of Anglo-Japanese relations. During the halcyon days of the Anglo-Japanese alliance, this relationship had worked to their benefit. During the late 1930s, however, the fluctuating fortunes of Anglo-Japanese relations at times worked against missionary interests.

Even though the impact of anti-British feeling on mission schools was felt more sharply on the colonial frontier in Taiwan than in metropolitan Japan, mission schools in Japan still had to comply with stringent government regulations. The long line of Canadian WMS principals of the three *eiwa* schools as well as Bates at the union Kwansei Gakuin generally proved to be competent administrators. They did their best to protect Canadian interests and to ensure that Canadian money was wisely spent. The Kwansei Gakuin under Bates developed steadily in its academic offering and its student numbers. Importantly, in the early 1930s, the Kwansei Gakuin, that had been held back because of the United Church's inability to provide its half share of the necessary endowment, was able to achieve university status. Furthermore, during the late 1930s, the Kwansei Gakuin was able to avoid the faculty and student strife that Doshisha University experienced, that led to the public resignation of Yuasa Hachiro, its president. That Bates was able to escape a similar humiliation was due in part to his sympathetic and avuncular personality. More important, however, was the positive attitude of the officers on the retired list, who served as the military instructors on the Kwansei Gakuin staff, toward him and his United Church and American Methodist Episcopal South missionary colleagues. It was their military instructor counterparts at Doshisha University who had precipitated the crisis that brought down Yuasa.

The apparent lack of political tension on campus leaves the impression that the Kwansei Gakuin was an oasis of academic tranquillity even though the rest of the Japanese Christian community and much of society at large were in turmoil. The calm at the Kwansei Gakuin likely enabled the sustained growth in student numbers in the late 1930s. Despite this growth in size, however, the number of students converted to Christianity remained disappointingly low. Even though its effectiveness as an evangelistic tool might have been questioned, Canadian missionaries believed that the Kwansei Gakuin provided a highly useful service to society by offering an alternative to the state educational system, in that places became increasingly limited as students moved upwards from primary school. Similarly, the Kwansei Gakuin helped to broaden the opportunities for higher education by providing an alternative to private secular secondary and postsecondary institutions. Indeed, the growing student population indicated that the Kwansei Gakuin was filling a need for education.

The three *eiwa* schools for girls also enjoyed steady growth throughout the 1930s and into the war years. During the early 1930s, the Toyo Eiwa Jo Gakko in Tokyo, that had long suffered from overcrowding, built fine new school buildings (that have only recently been demolished after sixty years of use to make way for more modern facilities). Almost immediately after the new school buildings were opened, they were filled to capacity. Similar success in attracting students was experienced in the schools in Shizuoka and Kofu. Despite this numerical success, the opportunities for missionary teachers at the *eiwa* schools shrank dramatically as a result of government regulations. It became difficult at the middle school level for missionaries to teach music, which—along with English—had been one of the staple occupations for the missionary teacher. The result was that there was increasingly little contact between missionaries and Japanese pupils in the classroom at the lower levels. Indeed, by squeezing missionary teachers out of the classrooms of middle and high schools, the government was achieving much of its aim to remove foreign influence in education, even in mission schools. Contact between missionaries and Japanese pupils now had to take place largely outside school hours. Japanization at the highest administrative levels also rapidly gained momentum. The most obvious casualties of government pressure were the WMS principals at the *eiwa* schools, who were replaced by male Japanese successors. Nevertheless, all was not bleak for missionary educators, for teaching opportunities still existed beyond the middle and high school levels at union colleges such as Tokyo Woman's Christian College. Indeed, one of the prime impulses to develop schools of higher learning was to circumvent the strict government regulations on curricula and teaching staff, regulations that were not as rigidly applied to tertiary schools as they were to secondary schools. Similarly, specialized education, such as the training of kindergarten teachers, was less regulated by the government authorities. Because the WMS missionaries maintained their kindergarten-teacher training program as a higher department of the Toyo Eiwa Jo Gakko, Canadian missionaries were able to maintain a presence at the school until the beginning of the Pacific War. Likewise, there was little government pressure for the Canadian Anglicans to close their kindergarten-teacher training institute in Nagoya, that trained Japanese teachers for the network of Anglican kindergartens in the Mid-Japan diocese.

Likewise, the specialized social work of Canadian missionaries at the Aiseikan and at the East Tokyo Mission in Nippori continued without undue government interference until the Pacific War began. Local officials saw the work of Canadians in the slums of east Tokyo not only as a helpful complement to their own social work but also as being of practical benefit to the destitute. The Obuse sanatorium was also clearly regarded by the health authorities in Nagano Prefecture as a useful institution that helped sick Japanese and reduced the strain on similar government facilities. Furthermore, these activities did not impinge in any obvious way on national security or morale and so did not automatically attract the attention of the *kempeitai* or the military authorities in the way that schools did. The work of Canadian missionaries in the temperance and purity movements went against the cultural proclivities of the Japanese. In the mid-1930s, however, there was fairly wide support within secular Japanese society for temperance. Indeed, after 1937 some elements in the Japanese army saw that support of the temperance and purity movements could be of help to their military efforts in China. Conscious of the problems of prostitution and disease that travelled with the Japanese army overseas, the temperance and purity movements were more than willing to mobilize their resources to help the national war effort.

In contrast to Japan, there was little emphasis on specialized social welfare work in Korea or Taiwan. In both colonies, United Church and Canadian Presbyterian missionaries concentrated on educational and medical work. In their educational work, the chief difficulty was to adapt it to meet regulations similar to those enforced in metropolitan Japan. This adaption required hiring Japanese-speaking staff and changing the curricula of schools accordingly. This process led to difficulties at the Tamsui Middle School, where a Japanese staff member levelled criticism at the school at the time of the so-called airplane incident (involving the charge of disrespect to the visiting Manchukuo emperor). Moreover, in both Taiwan and Korea, many parents and students expected mission schools to teach Japanese language. Indeed, in order to attract students, as well as to comply with government general regulations, mission schools were forced to develop Japanese-language programs. In Korea, these demands were put on mission schools at a time when the United Church mission was hard-pressed for funds. One difference, however, between Korea and Taiwan was that the colonial educational authorities in Korea were generally less doctrinaire and difficult for Canadians to deal with. As in Japan, the Canadian mission schools in northern Korea and Lungchingtsun provided a Christian alternative both to Japanese government general and to Korean secular private schools.

Medical work in Korea also provided an alternative to Japanese colonial and private Korean hospitals. Although the Canadian hospitals attracted a steady flow of patients, they were not the first choices for many sick Koreans, who would go to a mission hospital only after traditional Korean medical treatments had failed. Likewise, only those Japanese who suffered from venereal disease or other diseases that they wanted to keep private would deign to venture into a mission hospital. Nevertheless, Murray and the other missionary doctors performed a useful role not only in surgery but also in broadening the knowledge of Koreans in the countryside about public health. Murray saw herself as a doctor first and an evangelist second. Similarly, she saw her work as a doctor catering to all Koreans, irrespective of gender. In part, this was a reaction against the practices of the first generation of female missionary doctors in Korea, who had received a mixed reputation in regard to their medical competence. However, increasingly stringent government regulations meant that all missionary doctors and nurses had to meet rising professional standards and the challenges of modernization in order to remain in general medical work or medical teaching.

In northern Korea and Manchuria, medical work was often an effective evangelistic tool. Mackay Memorial Hospital in Taiwan, although it could not rival the Japanese government hospitals in terms of equipment, attracted many Taiwanese. Although Sherwood Hall, an independent Canadian missionary, made a lasting name for himself in helping to treat tuberculosis in Korea, the United Church mission itself did not conduct any specialized medical work beyond its hospitals. The Canadian Presbyterians in north Taiwan did and supported the Happy Mount Leper Colony. Although it competed directly with extensive work undertaken by the government general in Taiwan to combat leprosy, the work of Gushue-Taylor for lepers proved to be a worthwhile Christian endeavour appreciated by the colonial authorities. Because it was less demanding medically, working among lepers allowed Gushue-Taylor more time for the evangelistic side of missionary medical work.

While the medical work of missionaries went on largely unimpeded throughout the 1930s, the political situation in East Asia worsened. For most missionaries in Japan, their lives were measured by the academic calendar, that allowed them to exchange the cloister of the mission school campus for the summer cocoon of missionary Karuizawa. Hence, the events taking place in China did not affect their way of life until long after the Marco Polo bridge incident. Yet one of the most obvious responses of United Church missionaries to the growing crisis after 1937 was to put their trust in the wisdom and goodwill of Japanese Christian leaders. This trust reflected the changing relationship between the missionary movement and the Japanese Christian movement during the 1930s.

From the late nineteenth century on, the Japanese Christian movement was led by impressive first-generation leaders who articulated a broad range of theological views. Yet these early leaders also revealed a high degree of unanimity on key questions concerning Japanese Christians, such as the need for Japanese Christians to demonstrate patriotism and loyalty to Japan, especially in time of war. Furthermore, there was a broad consensus among

Japanese Christian leaders on the necessity for church independence from foreign control as well as the desirability of church union. Nevertheless, there was no apparent hurry to achieve these goals at the expense of the missionary movement, partly because of close personal ties between many of the early Japanese Christian leaders and missionaries. During the early 1930s, this situation changed.

A major cause of this change was the emergence of a second generation of Japanese Christian leaders. Many of them were highly educated and often familiar with North America through travel or study, but compared with their predecessors they had fewer personal ties of loyalty to missionaries. As a result, they were more willing than the first generation of leaders to sacrifice the missionary movement and its financial support in order to achieve the goal of ridding the Japanese Christian movement of foreign control and influence. Already evident among the first generation of Protestant leaders as they grew older, the desire for respectability was pronounced among the second generation. This desire was seen in their continual concern (despite the guarantee of religious freedom in the Meiji Constitution) to see Christianity accepted as one of the three major religions in Japan, along with Buddhism and Shintoism. Added to this concern was their constant preoccupation with being regarded as loyal and patriotic Japanese. Although many of the early Protestant leaders viewed the Meiji oligarchy with antipathy because they had belonged to the losing Tokugawa side at the time of the Meiji Restoration, the second generation of Protestant leaders had no such antipathy toward the Showa government. The new leaders were the beneficiaries of the unparalllelled success of the Meiji government that had made Japan a world power. The government could provide them with the respectability and recognition that they so wanted.

Missionaries, moreover, could and did give these new leaders their trust. United Church missionaries had absolute trust in the Japanese Christian leadership, a trust that would transcend the trials of war and continue during the Allied occupation. Indeed, it was fortunate for the reputations of the wartime Japanese Christian leaders that the most influential English-language postwar history of the Protestant movement in Japan was written by Charles Iglehart, who, together with William Axling, another prolific writer on Japanese Christianity, was one of the most intimately involved of American missionaries with the NCC. Kagawa was the most obvious beneficiary of missionary trust. Nevertheless, missionaries (not only United Church ones but also Americans such as Axling and Helen Topping) seemingly fashioned Kagawa into such a Christian giant that he could not possibly live up to his overseas reputation. Indeed, his actions during the Pacific War clearly showed this inability. As it was, his international reputation was much higher than his national reputation, especially outside Christian circles. Indeed, the gap between the missionary perception and that of the Japanese about Kagawa might lead one to query missionary judgment about Japanese personality. Importantly, the missionary trust of the Japanese Christian leadership was not so wholeheartedly shared by many Japanese Christians, as some of the debate over church union in the Japanese Christian press during the late 1930s indicates. United Church missionaries also had a slavish admiration for Bishop Abe Yoshimune of the Japan Methodist Church. In this respect, it is interesting that Bishop Sasaki of Mid-Japan had his detractors among Canadian Anglican missionaries, who might have had a more honest appreciation of the qualities of this courageous Japanese Anglican.

As well as the emergence of this second generation of Japanese Christian leaders, a new interpretation of *Nipponteki Kirisutokyo* appeared; it attempted to harmonize Christianity with the Japanese national spirit, thought, and religion and to make it compatible with *tennosei*. The acceptance of this new interpretation made Japanese Christians more amenable to the religious proposals that the Japanese government put forward. The *Nipponteki Kirisutokyo* of the late 1930s had its roots in the desire of Meiji Protestants both to free Christianity in Japan from foreign control and to see it fulfil a special calling to bring enlightenment and Christianity to East Asia. Yet it took these ideas to a new extreme by proposing what was tantamount to stripping away all foreign influence from Japanese Christianity. Likewise, it lent its support to Japanese national policies both religious and secular. In particular, Japanese conquests in north China provided the Japanese Christian movement with the opportunity to fulfil its special calling to bring enlightenment and a Japanese Christianity to East Asia. Whether or not Manchurian or Chinese Christians would accept Japanese Christian leadership imposed on them by conquest was of little concern. Indeed, as time went on, some Japanese Christian leaders came to see that divine purpose was behind Japanese actions in East Asia. Others went so far as to advocate an imperial Christianity (*kodo Kirisutokyo*). In any case, the desire to assume Christian leadership in those areas of continental East Asia and later Southeast Asia under Japanese control must be regarded as one of the prime motives behind the formation of the Nippon Kirisutokyodan. Japan was the centre of an empire, and what happened in Japan politically, militarily, economically, or religiously had consequences for the colonies or regions under Japanese control. Japanese Christian leaders were fully aware of their position at the centre of empire and of their concomitant responsibilities.

Although missionaries criticized the concept of *Nipponteki Kirisutokyo*, they failed to see that it might also provide the philosophical underpinning to and find practical expression in the Japanese-language pronouncements of trusted leaders such as Abe. It was undoubtedly difficult for missionaries to pick up subtle distinctions across cultural boundaries, especially when the individuals involved were thought to share views similar to their own. The gulf between the proponents of *Nipponteki Kirisutokyo* in the leadership of the Japan Methodist Church and United Church missionaries can be seen in Outerbridge, who—having lived through the World War I, during which so many of his generation of Canadians had been killed—thought that the Christian response to the Sino-Japanese War should be a pacifist one. For Japanese Christians, World War I had provided no similar trauma that would incline them toward pacifism. Quite the opposite, war supplied an opportunity for Japanese Christians to demonstrate their loyalty. Moreover, expanding their missionary work in regions of China occupied by the Japanese army allowed the Japanese Christian movement to show the government that Christians were patriotically supporting its policies.

Whether influenced or not by *Nipponteki Kirisutokyo*, virtually all Japanese Christians were patriotic and nationalistic (which suggests that the government's effort to bring the Christian movement completely under its control through the formation of the *kyodan* was largely unnecessary, except in terms of bureaucratic convenience). Indeed, even the patriotism of Sasaki, who suffered imprisonment during the war, cannot be questioned. His opposition to the entry of the NSKK into the *kyodan*, that rested on the issue of state interference in religion as well as concerns over the authority of the episcopacy and apostolic succession, was partially justified by the patriotic argument that the continuation of the NSKK as a separate *kyodan* was in Japan's best interest. Sasaki's stand was broadly in keeping with that long-standing stream of Japanese Anglican thought associated with Imai Judo (who had died as early as 1919), that advocated an indigenized and independent NSKK with a Western organizational structure. The call by Professor Saeki Yoshiro in December 1942 for the public prosecution of Sasaki and his five anti-union episcopal colleagues on the grounds that they were being anti-nationalistic and had past relations with Western bishops was unjustified.

The degree to that government pressure forced the creation of the *kyodan* remains controversial. It is easy with the benefit of hindsight to underestimate the difficulties and the stress under which Japanese Christian leaders worked as they struggled to reach decisions that would have far-reaching consequences for the future of Christianity in the Japanese Empire. The persecution of Salvationists as well as members of other religions brought home the possibility of imprisonment for Christians who did not comply with the wishes of the government. There was no time for quiet reflection amid the flurry of meetings leading to the Aoyama Gakuin mass meeting in September 1940. In language that evokes the fevered atmosphere under that difficult decisions were made, Axling, the American Baptist missionary who had close ties with the NCC, argued after the Pacific War that

> The Fascist Revolution that came to a head in 1937 resulted in the centralization and regimentation of every phase in the nation's life. The Japanese Christian leaders forewarned by fellow Christians in government service of hostile undercover activities on the part of anti-Christian groups and reading the signs of the times decided that the hour had struck to close in their ranks and build a

united front. Failure to act involved the danger of being engulfed in the Fascist tide, being robbed of freedom to build a church structure true to the fundamentals of the Christian tradition and being deprived of the right to formulate a distinctively Christian confession of faith.[1]

In the mid-1950s, when Axling wrote the above, the continued existence of the *kyodan* had long been assured. Moreover, in the wake of the Korean War, he was deeply worried by the menace of communism in Japan, against that the *kyodan* was a bulwark. It is not surprising, therefore, for him to argue that the "Fascist Revolution" had only meant that the timing of union was not an act of the Protestant community. Axling maintained that "the impression in western church circles that this union of thirty-four denominations into an integrated unified body came wholly as the result of governmental pressure leaves out of account most of the causative factors involved in this venture."[2] The ecumenical movement and the desire for church union had deep roots in Japanese Protestantism, and the government was able to exploit this history in pressuring the Japanese Christian movement to unite. Indeed, it is remarkable how conveniently the goals of the government and the aspirations of the Japanese Christian leadership dovetailed in regard to church union. Axling is correct to assert, of course, that there were other causes than government pressure in bringing about the *kyodan*. Nonetheless, "the impression in western church circles" was closer to reality than Axling would have liked to admit. The aims and goals of the Japanese Christian leadership came to be closely identified with those of the Japanese government. To the Japanese Christian leadership, conscious of the leading role that the Japanese Christian movement had to play in East Asia, the union church was needed in order to marshal Christian resources in support of this continental effort in the wake of Japanese military advance. The price, however, was to dispense with the foreign missionary movement and its financial support.

Many United Church missionaries were not opposed to church union and accepted the interpretation of it as given by the Japanese Christian leadership. Nevertheless, Canadian missionaries had no influence in the debates, meetings, and decisions that led to the formation of the *kyodan*. Indeed, union was presented to missionaries as a fait accompli, and it was clear to them that they had no place in the amalgamated church. This was a striking indication of the isolation of the missionary movement from the Japanese Christian movement. The news that church union was going to take place was quickly followed by the withdrawal of most of the Canadian missionaries from the Japanese Empire. Although disappointment with the future prospects of the missionary movement within the context of the union church and a genuine concern that continued missionary presence might jeopardize the safety of Japanese Christians were factors in causing Canadian missionaries to leave, the main reason for their withdrawal in late 1940 was that they heeded diplomatic advice. Before they left, however, Canadian missionaries made generous provisions that cushioned the financial shock of missionary withdrawal for two years.

As well as giving financial support to the Japanese Christian movement, during the 1930s Canadian missionaries in Japan attempted to counter the anti-Japanese stance of Canadian missionaries in China. The Canadian missionaries in Japan stood for fair play and balance, and that meant putting forward the Japanese view of events. In doing so, the missionaries endangered their reputation as respected experts on Japan, because they were perceived by many Canadians as being overly pro-Japanese. However, the political situation in Japan was fluid and difficult to judge even for seasoned diplomats. Likewise, the quixotic hope that peace could be achieved in China remained strong in many missionaries in Japan despite mounting evidence after Nanking that peace was unlikely. There were signs that Canadian missionaries misjudged the characters of some of Japan's political leaders, just as they did those of some of its Christian leaders. They had, for instance, a misplaced trust in Konoe Fumimaro, the sometimes prime minister, and his ability to bring an end to the crisis in China. Leland Albright was more sanguine than many of his missionary colleagues in China and Canada concerning Chiang Kai-shek. It was extremely difficult for missionaries in Japan to distinguish between their genuine feelings of sympathy and affection for Japanese people and the motives of Japanese political and military leaders in their handling of the East Asian crisis and the war in China. Missionaries wanted to show their fellow Christians in Canada that Japan did have legitimate grievances and reasons behind its actions in Manchuria, Mongolia, and north China. Even though Canadian missionaries in Japan had been appalled by the news of the atrocities committed by the Japanese army in Nanking during early 1938, they attempted to convey the Japanese standpoint. It was difficult for Outerbridge or Albright living at the Kwansei Gakuin to comprehend the extent of the devastation wrought on China by the Japanese army. Thus, Albright stressed the dangers posed by Stalin and the Soviet Union to peace in East Asia and downplayed the threat posed by the Japanese. The Canadian missionaries in Japan stood for peace, but at times they grasped at straws. This was clearly the case in the late winter of 1940, when there was hope that the appointment of Admiral Nomura Naokuni, a personal friend of President Roosevelt, to Washington might lead to peace and understanding between Japan and the United States. By early 1941, however, Albright had come to the conclusion that a trans-Pacific war was inevitable.

In the struggle to win favourable public opinion in North America to the stand against Japanese aggression, the Chinese government deliberately curried the favour of the foreign missionary movement in China. The Japanese government took an opposite position; it deliberately threw away any advantage that the support of the missionary movement in Japan might have given in the contest to win the hearts and minds of North Americans. In pursuing a calculated policy to rid the Christian movement in Japan of foreign influence and to organize a single Japanese Protestant denomination at the expense of the foreign missionary movement, Japanese policy makers failed to comprehend the importance of this movement in the East Asian crisis. Even though the Japanese authorities had managed by late 1940 to force the withdrawal of the missionary movement from the Japanese Empire, they had also lost the battle for public opinion in North America. In terms of the East Asian crisis, the importance of foreign missionaries was not their impact in Japan but their influence on public opinion at home. Chiang Kai-shek and the Chinese Nationalists realized this importance and they won the support of North American public opinion.

The failure of the Japanese to gain public sympathy in North America was strikingly evident during the visit of the Japanese Christian deputation to the United States in the spring of 1941. This visit left Abe berating Americans for their narrow-minded nationalistic feeling and their intolerance toward Japan, attitudes that he thought posed real dangers to peace. In holding these views, Abe stood at the opposite pole from that of the majority of Canadian and American missionaries by seeing the United States, not innocent Japan, as the main obstacle to reconciliation between the two countries. The failure to receive an expected outpouring of sympathy from American Christians for the hardships of the Japanese Christian movement as the process of Japanization reached its climax with the formation of the *kyodan* must have been galling for Abe and the other members of the deputation. They had never before been rebuffed by North American audiences. For the first time, of course, the Japanese Christian leaders were faced with the ire of missionaries in China; likewise, they could expect little sympathy from missionaries only recently withdrawn from their life's work in Japan.

The end of the Pacific War saw Canadian missionaries return to Japan. The devastation of the cities of Japan and the suffering of ordinary Japanese resulted in an outpouring of sympathy. Missionaries strove to help the Japanese rebuild their society and to fashion a new country free and prosperous. With the peace, a new era began in modern Japanese history as the country grew strong under the umbrella of the *pax Americana*. Although the Canadian missionary movement continued to operate in Japan after 1945, it would never regain the status and numerical strength that it had enjoyed at the beginning of the 1930s. As Japanese-Canadian relations became increasingly complex, the role that Canadian missionaries had traditionally played as ambassadors of goodwill between neighbours across the Pacific as well as messengers of the cross diminished. The changing concerns of churches in Canada meant that much of the effort and resources channelled before World War II into the foreign missionary endeavour was now redirected toward meeting new challenges at home. The expansive and optimistic spirit of Victorian Canada, that had brought it into the vanguard of the attempt to conquer the world for Christianity, had begun to falter and to fade. The long missionary age in Japanese-Canadian relations was over.

Notes

INTRODUCTION

1   The most recent academic study of the earlier history of the Canadian Protestant missionary movement in Japan is A. Hamish Ion, *The Cross and the Rising Sun: Volume 1: The Canadian Protestant Missionary Movement in the Japanese Empire, 1872–1931* (Waterloo: Wilfrid Laurier University Press, 1990). A detailed church-sponsored study of the 100 years of the United Church of Canada mission in Japan is G. R. P. Norman and W. H. H. Norman, *One Hundred Years in Japan, 1873–1973* (Toronto: Division of World Out-Reach, United Church of Canada, 1981). An earlier Canadian Methodist missionary account written at the time of the Methodist jubilee in Japan that is of some interest is John W. Saunby, *The New Chivalry in Japan* (Toronto: Methodist Publishing House, 1923). For A. C. Shaw's career in Japan, see C. H. Powles, *Victorian Missionaries in Meiji Japan* (Toronto: University of Toronto-York University Joint Centre for Modern East Asia, 1987). For Canadian missionaries in Korea, see William Scott, *Canadians in Korea: Brief Historical Sketch of Canadian Mission Work in Korea: Part One to the Time of Church Union* (Toronto: United Church of Canada Board of World Mission, 1970). For a recent study on the impact of the first Canadian independent missionaries in Korea, see Young-sik Yoo, "The Impact of Canadian Missionaries in Korea: A Historical Survey of Early Canadian Mission Work 1888–1898," unpublished PhD diss., Centre for the Study of Religion, University of Toronto, 1996. For a recent biography of one of the Canadian Presbyterian pioneer missionaries in Korea, see Helen Fraser MacRae, *A Tiger on Dragon Mountain: The Life of Rev. Duncan M. MacRae, D.D.*, ed. Ross Penner and Janice Penner (Charlottetown: A. James Haslam, QC, 1993). The standard Japanese-language survey of the Canadian Methodist work in Japan remains Kuranaga Takashi, *Kanada Mesojisuto Nihon Dendo Gaishi* (Tokyo: Kanada Godo Kyokai Senkyoshika, 1937). A useful summary is Bamba Nobuya, "Nika kanke no gendai teki igi," *Kanada Kenkyu Nenpyo—Nika Gakujitsu Kaigi Tokushu* (Tokyo: Nihon Kanada Gakkai, 1981). Japanese writings reflect an interest in the activities of Canadian missionaries and their converts at the local level, especially during the Meiji period, as seen, for instance, in Ota Aito, *Meiji Kirisutokyo no Ryuiki: Shizuoka Bando to Bakushintachi* (Tokyo: Tsukiji Shokan, 1979) or in the recent article by Takashima Yuichiro, "Kanada Mesijisuto Kyokai no Nihon senkyo hoshin no keisei—C. S. Ebi no katsudo o te ga kari to shite," *Kirisutokyo Shakai Mondai Kenkyu*, [hereafter cited as *KSMK*] 40.3 (1992), pp. 100–35. In terms of the background of the Canadian Methodist women's missionary movement, a useful introduction is Rosemary B. Gagan, *A Sensitive Independence: Canadian Methodist Women Missionaries in Canada and the Orient, 1881–1925* (Montreal: McGill-Queen's University Press, 1992). Caroline Macdonald, the independent Canadian missionary, has been the subject of a recent and outstanding biography, Margaret Prang, *A Heart at Leisure from Itself: Caroline Macdonald of Japan* (Vancouver: University of British Columbia Press, 1995). Ruth Compton Brouwer has

also written articles on Florence Murray, the United Church missionary doctor in Korea; see "'Home Lessons, Foreign Tests': The Background and First Missionary Term of Florence Murray, Maritime Doctor in Korea," *Journal of the CHA*, new series, 6 (1995), pp. 103–28, and "Beyond 'Women's Work for Women': Dr. Florence Murray and the Practice and Teaching of Western Medicine in Korea, 1921–1950," unpublished thirty-eight page typescript in the possession of the author. For an interesting paper on Canadian Anglican work among Japanese Canadians in Vancouver, see Norman Knowles, "A Selective Dependence: Vancouver's Japanese Community and Anglican Missions, 1903–42," unpublished paper given at the Canadian Historical Association Conference, Calgary, June 1994.

2   John Hilliker, *Canada's Department of External Affairs: Volume 1: The Early Years, 1909–1946* (Montreal: McGill-Queen's University Press, 1990), p. 163. For a memoir of the early days of the Canadian Legation in Japan, see Hugh L. Keenleyside, *Memoirs: Volume 1: Hammer the Golden Day* (Toronto: McClelland and Stewart, 1981), pp. 246–85. Keenleyside was the first secretary at the Legation when it opened.

3   Robert Wright, *A World Mission: Canadian Protestantism and the Quest for a New International Order, 1918–1939* (Montreal: McGill-Queen's University Press, 1991), p. 256.

4   Arthur Menzies, the Canadian diplomat and East Asian authority, has noted that "the young academics—Hugh Keenleyside, Lester Pearson, Hume Wrong and Norman Robertson—that Dr. O. D. Skelton had been bringing into the Department of External Affairs were influenced by and had a continuing interaction with academics who contributed to the CIIA and IPR conferences and publications." A. R. Menzies, "Canadian Views of United States Policy toward Japan, 1945–1952," in A. Hamish Ion and Barry D. Hunt, eds., *War and Diplomacy across the Pacific, 1919–1952* (Waterloo: Wilfrid Laurier University Press, 1988), pp. 155–172, p. 157. Canadian writings on Canada and East Asia during the 1930s include Henry F. Angus, "Responsibility for Peace and War in the Pacific," *Canadian Papers, Yosemite Conference 1936* (Toronto: CIIA, 1936); Henry F. Angus, *The Problem of Peaceful Change in the Pacific Area* (London: 1937); and Henry F. Angus, *Canada and the Far East 1940-1953* (Toronto: 1953); J. Bartlet Brebner, "Canada, the Anglo-Japanese Alliance and the Washington Conference," *Political Science Quarterly*, 50 (1935); E. Brown, *Canada and Japan* (Toronto: 1932); A. R. M. Lower, *Canada and the Far East–1940* (New York: 1941); N. A. M. MacKenzie, "Canada and the Changing Balance of Power in the Pacific," *Canada Papers, Yosemite Conference 1936* (Toronto: CIIA, 1936); J. W. Pickersgill, "International Machinery for the Maintenance of Peace in the Pacific Area," *Canada Papers, Yosemite Conference 1936* (Toronto: CIIA, 1936); H. Soward, "Canada and the Far Eastern Crisis," paper presented to the Institute of Pacific Relations Conference, at Banff, 1935; William Strange, *Canada, the Pacific and War* (Toronto: 1937); K. W. Taylor, "The Far East," in Violet Anderson, ed. *World Currents and Canada's Course* (Toronto: T. Nelson, 1937), pp. 20–48; C. J. Woodsworth, *Canada and the Orient* (Toronto: 1941). More recent surveys of Canada and Japan include Michael G. Fry, "The Development of Canada's Relations with Japan, 1919–1947," in Keith A. J. Hay, ed., *Canadian Perspectives on Economic Relations with Japan* (Montreal: 1980), pp. 7–67; Michael G. Fry, "Canada and the Occupation of Japan: The MacArthur-Norman Years," in Thomas W. Burkman, ed., *The Occupation of Japan: The International Context: Proceedings of the Fifth Symposium Sponsored by the MacArthur Memorial* (Norfolk, VA: 1984), pp. 129–49; Hamish Ion, "Canada and the Occupation of Japan," in Ian Nish, ed., *The British Commonwealth and the Occupation of Japan* (London: ICERD, 1983); Gregory A. Johnson, "Canada and the Far East during the 1930s," in John Schultz and Kimitada Miwa, eds., *Canada and Japan in the Twentieth Century* (Toronto: Oxford

University Press, 1991), pp. 111–25; Alan Mason, "Canadian-Japanese Relations, 1930–1941," University of Toronto Research Paper, 1973; Alan Mason, "Canada and the Manchurian Crisis," in Robert Bothwell and Norman Hillmer, eds., *The In-Between Time: Canadian External Policy in the 1930's* (Toronto: Copp Clark, 1975), pp. 113–19.

5 See Johnson, "Canada and the Far East during the 1930s," p. 125. Much recent writing on Canadian-Japanese relations has laid stress on economic relations. See Frank Langdon, *The Politics of Canadian-Japanese Economic Relations 1952–1982* (Vancouver: University of British Columbia Press, 1984); and Klaus H. Pringsheim, *Neighbours across the Pacific: The Development of Economic and Political Relations between Canada and Japan* (Westport, CT: Greenwood Press, 1983). Of interest regarding the treatment of Japanese Canadians in Canada and Canadian military and civilian prisoners in Japan during the Pacific War is Patricia E. Roy, J. L. Granatstein, Masako Iino, and Hiroko Takamura, *Mutual Hostages: Canadians and Japanese during the Second World War* (Toronto: University of Toronto Press, 1990).

6 Among significant Canadian missionary writings on Japanese culture, religion, and literature are Egerton Ryerson, *The Netsuke of Japan* (London: G. Bell, 1958); H. H. Coates and Ryugaku Ishizuka, *Honen, the Buddhist Saint* (Kyoto: Chionin, 1924); Robert Cornell Armstrong, *Just before the Dawn: The Life and Work of Nimomiya Sontoku* (New York: Macmillan, 1912); and Robert Cornell Armstrong, *Light from the East: Studies in Japanese Confucianism* (Toronto: University of Toronto Press, 1914); and *Hell Screen*, W. H. H. Norman, trans. (Tokyo: Hokuseido, 1948). James Scarth Gale, a Canadian who served for many years as a missionary with the American Presbyterian North mission in Korea, was one of the greatest Western pioneers of Korean studies. His many writings on things Korean includes *The History of the Korean People* (Seoul: Christian Literature Society, 1927).

7 Gagan, *A Sensitive Independence*, p. 205.

8 Brouwer, "Beyond 'Women's Work for Women,'" p. 1.

9 For Frank Schofield, see Doretha E. Mortimore, "Dr. Frank W. Schofield and the Korean National Consciousness," in C. I. Eugene Kim and Doretha E. Mortimore, eds., *Korea's Response to Japan: The Colonial Period 1910–1945* (Kalamazoo: Center for Korean Studies, Western Michigan University, 1977), pp. 145–67; see also Frank Baldwin, "Missionaries and the March First Movement: Can Moral Man Be Neutral?" in Andrew C. Nahm, ed., *Korea under Japanese Colonial Rule: Studies of the Policy and Techniques of Japanese Colonialism* (Kalamazoo: Center for Korean Studies, Western Michigan University, 1973). For E. H. Norman, the most recent article is Miwa Kimitada, "E. H. Norman Revisited," in Schultz and Miwa, eds., *Canada and Japan in the Twentieth Century*, pp. 48–58. See also Roger W. Bowen, ed., *E. H. Norman: His Life and Scholarship* (Toronto: University of Toronto Press, 1984); Roger W. Bowen, *Innocence Is Not Enough: The Life and Death of E. H. Norman* (Vancouver: Douglas and McIntyre, 1986); James Barros, *No Sense of Evil: The Espionage Case of E. Herbert Norman* (New York: Ivy Books, 1987). For Norman Bethune, see Ted Allan and Sydney Gordon, *The Scalpel, the Sword: The Story of Doctor Norman Bethune*, rev. ed. (New York: Monthly Review Press, 1973).

10 In her definition of *tennosei*, Janet E. Hunter states that "the official ideology stressed loyalty and piety within the family, and this was transferred upwards to the nation, which was regarded as one large family (*kazoku kokka*—family state) presided over by the emperor to whom loyalty at all levels was promoted." Janet E. Hunter, comp., *Concise Dictionary of Modern Japanese History* (Berkeley: University of California Press, 1984), p. 39. A brief but useful discussion of the prewar role of *tennosei* ideology can be found in the epilogue of Carol Gluck, *Japan's Modern Myth: Ideology in the Late Meiji Period* (Princeton: Princeton University Press, 1985), pp. 279–86. Tsukada Osamu has stressed

that the denominational and liturgical legacy of the missionary movement might also have contributed to the ready acceptance by Japanese Christians to emphasize loyalty to the state and its political leaders. This was a factor in the response to the crisis of the late 1930s of the NSKK, the Japanese Anglican Church, founded in part by British missionaries belonging to the state Church of England. See Tsukada Osamu, *Shocho Tennosei to Kirisutokyo* (Tokyo: Shinkyo Shuppansha, 1990), pp. 121–25.

11 Sandra C. Taylor, in her study of Sidney L. Gulick, the American missionary statesman, points out that his ability to influence American opinion about Japan was lessened as friends of Japan became increasingly suspect in the United States during the interwar years. See Sandra C. Taylor, *Advocate of Understanding: Sidney Gulick and the Search for Peace with Japan* (Tokyo: Kent State University Press, 1984), p. xii.

CHAPTER ONE

1   Dohi Akio, "1930 nendai no Purotesutanto Kirisutokyokai (1)," *KSMK* 25.12 (1976), pp. 187-217, especially p. 189.
2   Among the important leaders who died during this period were Uemura Masahisa (Presbyterian, 1858–1925), Motoda Sakunoshin (Anglican, 1870–1928), Uchimura Kanzo (Mukyokai [Non-Church Movement], 1861–1930), Hiraiwa Yoshiyasu (Methodist, 1858–1933), Nitobe Inazo (Quaker, 1862–1933), Ebina Danjo (Congregationalist, 1857–1937), Kozaki Hiromichi (Congregationalist, 1858–1938), and Yamamuro Gunpei (Salvation Army, 1872–1940). These figures belonged to the first generation of Japanese Protestants and most had become Christians during the halcyon days of the 1870s. Of particular importance for his connection with Canada was Hiraiwa Yoshiyasu, converted to Christianity in 1875 by George Cochran, the Canadian Methodist pioneer missionary. See Ebisawa Arimichi and Oouchi Saburo, *Nihon Kirisutokyo Shi* (Tokyo: Nihon Kirisutokyodan Shuppan Kyoku, 1971), p. 542.
3   For a general account of the Christian century in Japan, see Christopher R. Boxer, *Christian Century in Japan, 1540–1650* (Berkeley: University of California Press, 1957). For a recent study of a leading Jesuit missionary official, see Joseph F. Moran, *The Japanese and the Jesuits: Alexandro Valignano in Sixteenth-Century Japan* (London: Routledge, 1993). For the political motives behind the initial proscription of Christianity, see Mary Elizabeth Berry, *Hideyoshi* (Cambridge: Harvard University Press, 1982), especially pp. 91–93, pp. 225–28.
4   Ebisawa and Oouchi, *Nihon Kirisutokyo Shi*, p. 167.
5   Sumiya Mikio, *Nihon no Shakai Shiso: Kindaika to Kirisutokyo* (Tokyo: Tokyo Daigaku Shuppansha, 1968), pp. 8–9.
6   Kenneth Ballhatchet and Helen Ballhatchet, "Asia," in John McManners, ed., *The Oxford Illustrated History of Christianity* (Oxford: Oxford University Press, 1992), pp. 488–518, p. 513.
7   Kudo Eiichi, *Nihon Kirisutokyo Shakai Keizei Shi Kenkyu* (Tokyo: Shinkyo Shuppansha, 1980), p. 23. See also Yamaji Aizan, "Gendai Nihon Kyokai Shiron," *Gendai Nihon Bungaku Taikei 6: Kitamura Tohoku, Yamaji Aizan Shu* (Tokyo: Tsukiji Shobo, 1970), pp. 223–71, especially pp. 230–31. For a recent translation of Yamaji's "Gendai Nihon Kyokai Shiron," see Graham Squires, "Yamaji Aizan's 'Essays on the History of the Modern Japanese Church'—An Introduction and Translation," unpublished PhD diss., University of Newcastle, Australia, 1995.
8   Ebisawa and Oouchi, *Nihon Kirisutokyo Shi*, p. 169. See also Kudo, *Nihon Kirisutokyo*

Shakai Keizei Shi Kenkyu, p. 29; Yamaji, "Gendai Nihon Kyokai Shiron," p. 231; and Matsuzawa Hiroaki, "Kirisutokyo to Chishikijin," in Iwanami Koza Nihon Rekishi, 16, kindai 3 (Tokyo: Iwanami Shoten, 1976), pp. 182–320, p. 291.

9   For the *Shichi Ichi Zappo*, see Doshisha Daigaku Jinbun Kagaku Kenkyujo hen, *Shichi Ichi Zappo no Kenkyu* (Kyoto: Domeiya Shuppan, 1986). See also Nihon Kirisutokyo Rekishi Dai Jiten Henshu Iinkai, *Nihon Kirisutokyo Rekishi Dai Jiten* (Tokyo: Kyobunkan, 1988) [hereafter cited as *NKRDJ*], p. 615.

10 Sumiya, *Nihon Shakai to Kirisutokyo*, 1956 ed., pp. 13–14.

11 Matsuzawa, "Kirisutokyo to Chishikijin," p. 285.

12 See Ota Yuzo, *E. S. Mozu: "Furuki Nihon" o tsutaeta shin-nichi kagakusha* (Tokyo: Liburo Poto, 1988), pp. 40–44. See also Helen Ballhatchet, "The Religion of the West versus the Science of the West: The Evolution Controversy in Late Nineteenth Century Japan," in John Breen and Mark Williams, eds., *Japan and Christianity: Impacts and Responses* (Basingstoke: Macmillan Press, 1996), pp. 107–21.

13 *KSMK*, 30.2 (1982), contains a number of interesting articles dealing with the *Rikugo Zasshi*. See also *NKRDJ*, pp. 1494–95.

14 Yamaji, "Gendai Nihon Kyokai Shiron," p. 243.

15 For a summation of Yasui Sokken's ideas in *Benmo*, see Dohi Akio, *Nihon Purotesutanto Kirisutokyo Shi* (Tokyo: Shinkyo Shuppansha, 1982), p. 39. See also Yamaji, "Gendai Nihon Kyokai Shiron," pp. 232–38; Yamamoto Yukinori, "Yasui Sokken no [Bemmo] to Meiji Shonen no Kirisutokyokai," *KSMK*, 32.3 (1984), pp. 68–128, 84–91; and Otis Cary, *A History of Christianity in Japan: Roman Catholic, Greek Orthodox, and Protestant Missions, Vol. 2: Protestant Missions* (Rutland, VT: Charles E. Tuttle, 1982), pp. 103–04.

16 For this incident, see Suzuki Norihisa, *Uchimura Kanzo* (Tokyo: Iwanami Shinsho, 1992), pp. 51–56. See also Matsuzawa Hiroaki, ed., *Nihon no Meicho 38: Uchimura Kanzo* (Tokyo: Chuo Koron Sha, 1971), pp. 26–28. The Mukyokai (Non-Church Movement) which Uchimura founded, was a Christian movement that had no church organization but merely consisted of people who came together to study the Bible. This movement completely dispensed with links to the Western missionary movement.

17 Janet Hunter, *The Emergence of Modern Japan: An Introductory History since 1853* (London: Longman, 1989), p. 191. For an excellent brief account of the Japanese state's attitude toward religions in Japan including Christianity, see Sheldon Garon, *Molding Japanese Minds: The State in Everyday Life* (Princeton: Princeton University Press, 1997), pp. 60–87.

18 Yamaji, "Gendai Nihon Kyokai Shiron," p. 264. See also Ebisawa and Oouchi, *Nihon Kirisutokyo Shi*, p. 283; and Cary, *A History of Christianity in Japan*, pp. 242–43.

19 Dohi Akio, *Nihon Purotesutanto Kyokai no Seiritsu to Tenkai* (Tokyo: Nihon Kirisutokyodan Shuppan Kyoku, 1975), p. 145.

20 Ibid.

21 William R. Hutchinson, "Modernism and Missions: The Liberal Search for an Exportable Christianity, 1875–1935," in John K. Fairbank, ed., *The Missionary Enterprise in China and America* (Cambridge: Harvard University Press, 1974), pp. 110–31, p. 118.

22 Richard Henry Drummond, *A History of Christianity in Japan* (Grand Rapids: William B. Eerdmans, 1971), p. 218.

23 Tasuku Harada, *The Faith of Japan* (New York: Macmillan, 1914), pp. 182–83.

24 Yamamoto Taijiro and Muto Yoichi, comps., *Uchimura Kanzo Eibun Shosaku Zenshu* (Tokyo: Kyobunkan, 1971–72), 7 vols., vol. 1, *How I Became a Christian: Out of My Diary*, p. 190.

25 F. G. Notehelfer, "Review of *Nitobe Inazo: Japan's Bridge*," *Journal of Japanese Studies*, 22.2 (1996), pp. 450–53, p. 453.

26 See Nitobe Inazo, *Bushido: The Soul of Japan* (New York: G. Putnam, 1905). For an analysis of Nitobe's writings and ideas and their impact on the West, see Ota Yuzo, *Taiheyo no Hashi to shite Nitobe Inazo* (Tokyo: Misuzu Shobo, 1986). See also Nitobe Inazo, *Japan: Some Phases of Her Problems and Development* (London: Ernest Benn, 1931), especially pp. 366–72, pp. 371–72.
27 Quoted in A. Hamish Ion, *The Cross and the Rising Sun: Volume 2: The British Protestant Missionary Movement in Japan, Korea, and Taiwan, 1865–1945* (Waterloo: Wilfrid Laurier University Press, 1993), p. 121.
28 See Sumiya, *Nihon no Shakai Shiso*, pp. 48–57, pp. 139–61.
29 Among leading figures in the Japanese socialist movement was Katayama Sen (1859–1933), who studied theology in the United States and later was one of the founders of the Japanese Communist Party; see *NKRDJ*, p. 297. Katayama Tetsu (1887–1978), the first postwar socialist prime minister of Japan, was also a Christian; see *NKRDJ*, p. 297. See also Cyril H. Powles, "Abe Isoo and the Role of Christians in the Founding of the Japanese Socialist Movement, 1895–1905," in *Papers on Japan*, vol. 1 (Cambridge: 1961), pp. 89–109. Among the most famous of those Christians active in the early labour movement was Suzuki Bunji.
30 Sumiya, *Nihon no Shakai Shiso*, p. 16. The importance of Suzuki Bunji and of Uchimura Kanzo is clearly seen in their inclusion in Professor Matsuo Takayoshi's recent study of individuals who helped to shape the nature of the Taisho period. See Matsuo Takayoshi, *Taisho Jidai no Senkotachi* (Tokyo: Iwanami Shoten, 1993), pp. 1–78.
31 Quoted in Charles H. Germany, *Protestant Theologies in modern Japan: A History of Dominant Theological Currents from 1920–1960* (Tokyo: International Institute for the Study of Religions Press, 1965), p. 34. The importance of both Kagawa Toyohiko and Sugiyama Motojiro in rural evangelism is underlined by Iinuma Jiro's study of rural evangelism in Japan. See Iinuma Jiro, *Nihon Noson Dendo Shi Kenkyu* (Tokyo: Nihon Kirisutokyodan Shuppan Kyoku, 1988), 113–33. Kagawa played an important role as a labour organizer, making his name in the drawn-out 1919 Kawasaki Shipyard strike. However, Sumiya has pointed out that Kagawa cannot be considered as one of the leading Japanese figures in the labour movement during the 1910s and 1920s. See Sumiya, *Nihon no Shakai Shiso*, pp. 133–36, especially pp. 133, 135.
32 Powles, "Abe Isoo," p. 117.
33 Dohi Akio, "Christianity and Politics in the Taisho Period of Democracy," *Japanese Religions*, 7.3 (1972), pp. 42–68, especially p. 42.
34 Ibid., pp. 52–53. See also Yoshino Sakuzo, "Demokurashi to Kirisutokyo," in Takeda Kyoko, ed., *Gendai Nihon Shiso Taikei, 6: Kirisutokyo* (Tokyo: Chikuma Shobo, 1975), pp. 236-41, p. 240. See also Peter Duus, "Yoshino Sakuzo: The Christian as Political Critic," *Journal of Japanese Studies*, 4.2 (1978), pp. 301–26, p. 323.
35 Matsuo Takayoshi, "Nihon Kumiai Kirisutokyokai no Chosen dendo," *Shiso* (July 1968), pp. 949–65, p. 951. For an interesting account of the beginnings of the missionary society of the Kumiai Church and its efforts to become self-supporting and independent, see Shigeru Yoshiki, "Nippon Kirisuto Dendokaisha no dokuritsu to Ebina Danjo," *KSMK*, 24.3 (1976), pp. 83–132.
36 Nitobe's ideas concerning Korea can be found in Tanaka Shiitchi, "Nitobe Inazo to Chosen," *San Sen Ri*, 34 (Natsu 1983), pp. 88–97, especially p. 95. See also Mark R. Peattie, "Japanese Attitudes toward Colonialism, 1895–1945," in Ramon H. Myers and Mark R. Peattie, eds., *The Japanese Colonial Empire, 1895–1945* (Princeton: Princeton University Press, 1984), pp. 80–127, especially pp. 99–100. For a more detailed and recent study of Nitobe's views on colonialism, see Kitaoka Shinichi, "Nitobe Inazo ni okeru Teikokushugi to Kokuseishugi," in *Iwanami Koza Kindai Nihon to Shokumichi, 4: Togo to Shihai no Ronri* (Tokyo: Iwanami Shoten, 1993), pp. 179–203.

NOTES TO CHAPTER ONE

37. For Yoshino Sakuzo's views, see Matsuo Takayoshi, "Yoshino Sakuzo to Chosen: San Ichi Undo no chushin ni," in Yui Masatomi, ed., *Taisho Demokurashi* (Tokyo: 1957), pp. 243–64, p. 245.
38. Ibid.
39. Matsuo, "Nihon Kumiai Kirisutokyokai no Chosen dendo," p. 952.
40. Ibid., pp. 957–60.
41. Kozaki Hiromichi, *Reminiscences of Seventy Years: The Autobiography of a Japanese Pastor* (Tokyo: Kyobunkwan, 1934), p. 282.
42. Dohi, *Nihon Purotesutanto Kyokai no Seiritsu to Tenkai*, pp. 173–74.
43. Matsuo, "Yoshino Sakuzo to Chosen," pp. 254–55.
44. Fujita Wakao, *Yanaihara Tadao: Sono Shogai to Shinko* (Tokyo: Kyobunkan, 1967), pp. 30–34.
45. Fujita Wakao, "Yanaihara Tadao: Disciple of Uchimura Kanzo and Nitobe Inazo," in Nobuya Bamba and John F. Howes, eds., *Pacifism in Japan: The Christian and Socialist Tradition* (Vancouver: University of British Columbia Press, 1978) pp. 199–219, p. 206.
46. Wakao Fujita, "Yanaihara Tadao: Disciple of Uchimura Kanzo and Nitobe Inazo," p. 207. In an article on Japanese political parties in the 1930s, George Totten has argued that there was a ground rule within the political process that "was none other than reverence for the emperor (abroad often called 'emperor worship'), summed up in the theory of *kokutai*, which held that Japan was unique in being ruled by an unbroken line of good emperors from time immemorial." See George O. Totten III, "Japan's Political Parties in Democracy, Fascism and War," in Harry Wray and Hilary Conroy, eds., *Japan Examined: Perspectives on Modern Japanese History* (Honolulu: University of Hawaii Press, 1983), pp. 258–68, p. 260.
47. Fujita, "Yanaihara Tadao: Disciple of Uchimura Kanzo and Nitobe Inazo," p. 207.
48. Arthur Judson Brown, *The Mastery of the Far East* (New York: Scribner's Sons, 1919), p. 660.
49. J. R. Mott, *Addresses and Papers*, vol. 2 (New York: 1941), 2 vols., p. 437.
50. Brown, *The Mastery of the Far East*, p. 632.
51. Miyakoda Tsunetaro, ed., *Nihon Kirisutokyo Godo Shiko* (Tokyo: Kyobunkan, 1967), pp. 73–78.
52. Dohi, "1930 nendai no Purotesutanto Kirisutokyokai (1)," p. 198.
53. Shigeru Yoshiki, "1930 Nendai no Kirisutokyo Janarizumu *Kirisutokyo Sekai* no baii," *KSMK*, 25.12 (1976), pp. 47–82, p. 58.
54. Dohi, "1930 nendai no Purotesutanto Kirisutokyokai (1)," p. 198.
55. Ibid., pp. 209–11.
56. Howard Outerbridge outlined Bates's views in a letter to Jesse Arnup in Toronto. United Church of Canada Board of Foreign Missions [hereafter cited as UCC BFM] Japan, Box 4 File 81, Outerbridge to Arnup, 30 April 1937, p. 7. C. J. L. Bates (1877–1963) was born in rural Ontario and went to Japan in 1902. In 1920, he became the fourth principal of the Kwansei Gakuin, a position that he held until 1940. See *NKRDJ*, p. 1261.
57. Dohi, "1930 nendai no Purotesutanto Kirisutokyokai (1)," p. 211.
58. Ibid., p. 206.
59. *Renmei Jipo* [hereafter cited as *RJ*], 15.ii. (1932), p. 9; 15.iv. (1932), p. 5.
60. Shigeru, "1930 Nendai no Kirisutokyo Janarizumu *Kirisutokyo Sekai* no baii," p. 52. For Kashiwagi Gien (1860–1938), see *NKRDJ*, p. 293. Although it does not deal with his views on the Manchurian incident, the study of Kashiwagi Gien by Sugai Kichiro is useful for its insights into Kashiwagi's ideas about war. See Sugai Kichiro, *Kashiwagi Gien* (Tokyo: Shunju Sha, 1972).
61. Shigeru, "1930 Nendai no Kirisutokyo Janarizumu *Kirisutokyo Sekai* no baii," p. 54.
62. Ibid.

63 Ibid., p. 58.
64 Yamamoto Hideteru, *Nippon Kirisuto Kyokai Shi* (Tokyo: Nippon Kirisuto Kyokai Jimusho, 1929), especially pp. 509-32. For Yamamoto Hideteru (1857–1943), see *NKRDJ*, p. 1448. For Ebisawa Akira (1883–1959), see *NKRDJ*, p. 194.
65 Yamamoto, *Nippon Kirisuto Kyokai Shi*, pp. 67–68; see also pp. 111–21.
66 Nitobe Inazo, "The Penetration of the Life and Thought of Japan by Christianity," *Japan Christian Quarterly* (from now on cited as *JCQ*) (spring 1981), pp. 68–75, p. 74. This article was originally published in October 1929.
67 Ibid., p. 75.
68 Miyakoda, *Nihon Kirisutokyo Godo Shiko*, p. 114.
69 Nihon Kirisutokyodan Shi Hensan Iinkai Hen, *Nihon Kirisutokyodan Shi* (Tokyo: Nihon Kirisutokyodan Shuppanbu, 1967), p. 68 [hereafter cited as *Nihon Kirisutokyodan Shi*].
70 Danjo Ebina, "The Distinctive Message of Christianity for the Present Situation," *JCQ* (spring 1981), pp. 76–80, p. 80. This article was first published in July 1931.
71 For Kozaki Michio (1888–1973), see *NKRDJ*, p. 520. For a sympathetic look at Kozaki's ecumenical activities after the Pacific War, see Dohi Akio, *Kozaki Michio no Kodo to sono Rikai* (Tokyo: Nihon Kirisutokyodan Reinanzaka Kyokai, 1972). See also Takenaka Masao, "Natanaeru no Shinko: Ekyumenikuru undo ni okuru Kozaki Hiromichi," *KSMK*, 32.3 (1984) pp. 1–36.
72 Shigeru, "1930 Nendai no Kirisutokyo Janarizumu *Kirisutokyo Sekai* no baii," p. 59.
73 For the beginnings of Canadian missionary work in Japan, see A. Hamish Ion, *The Cross and the Rising Sun: Volume 1: The Canadian Protestant Missionary Movement in the Japanese Empire, 1872–1931* (Waterloo: Wilfrid Laurier University Press, 1990).
74 For the history of the NSKK, see Nippon Seikokai reklishi hensan iinkai, *Nippon Seikokai Hyakunen Shi* (Tokyo: Nippon Seikokai Kyomuin Bunshokyoku, 1959) [hereafter cited as *Nippon Seikokai Hyakunen Shi*]; also of interest is Tsukada Osamu, *Nippon Seikokai no Kisei to Kadai* (Tokyo: Seikokai Shuppan, 1979).
75 See Mayama Mitsuya, *Owari Nagoya no Kirisutokyo—Nagoya Kyokai no Sosoki* (Tokyo: Shinkyo Shuppansha, 1986), p. 67.
76 Rosemary R. Gagan, "Two Sexes Warring in the Bosom of a Single Mission Station: Feminism in the Canadian Methodist Japan Mission, 1881–1895," unpublished thirty-one page typescript in the author's possession. See also Rosemary R. Gagan, *A Sensitive Independence: Canadian Methodist Women Missionaries in Canada and the Orient, 1881–1924* (Montreal: McGill-Queen's University Press, 1992), especially pp. 65–114.
77 See Ushiyama Setsuai, *Kirisutokyo Shinko Dendo Shi: Wara Choro, Dendo no Kiseki* (Nagano: Ginga Shobo, 1980), pp. 35–39.
78 See Sumiya's comment in Kuyama Yasushi, ed., *Kirisutokyo Kyoiku Shi: Shicho Hen* (Tokyo: Sobunsha, 1993), p. 102.
79 For a history of the Toyo Eiwa Jo Gakko, see Toyo Eiwa Jo Gakuin hyakunen shi hensan jikko iinkai, *Toyo Eiwa Jo Gakuin Hyakunen Shi* (Tokyo: Toyo Eiwa Jo Gakuin hyakunen shi hensan jikko iinkai, 1984)[hereafter cited as *Toyo Eiwa Jo Gakuin Hyakunen Shi*].
80 For a history of Shizuoka Eiwa Jo Gakko, see Shizuoka Eiwa Jo Gakuin hachijunen shi hensan iinkai, *Shizuoka Eiwa Jo Gakuin Hachijunen Shi* (Shizuoka: Shizuoka Eiwa Jo Gakuin, 1971) [hereafter cited as *Shizuoka Eiwa Jo Gakuin Hachijunen Shi*]. A briefer account of the school is found in Shizuoka Eiwa Jo Gakuin hyakunen shi hensan iinkai, *Shizuoka Eiwa no Hyakunen* (Shizuoka: Shizuoka Eiwa Jo Gakuin hyakunen hensan iinkai, 1988).
81 For a history of the Yamanashi Eiwa Jo Gakko, see Yamanashi Eiwa Gakuin shi hensan iinkai, *Yamanashi Eiwa Gakuin Hachijunen Shi* (Kofu: Yamanashi Eiwa Gakuin, 1969) [hereafter cited as *Yamanashi Eiwa Gakuin Hachijunen Shi*].
82 For Caroline Macdonald (1874-1931), see John MacNab, *The White Angel of Tokyo: Miss*

Caroline Macdonald (Toronto: Centenary Committee of the Canadian Churches, n.d.). See also *NKRDJ*, p. 1312. For a recent study of Caroline Macdonald, see Margaret Prang, *A Heart at Leisure from Itself: Caroline Macdonald of Japan* (Vancouver: University of British Columbia Press, 1995).

83   Gagan, *A Sensitive Independence*, p. 49.
84   The Commission of Appraisal [William Ernest Hocking, chairman], *Re-Thinking Missions: A Laymen's Inquiry after One Hundred Years* (New York: Harper and Brothers, 1932), p. 85.
85   Ibid., p. 66.
86   UCC BFM Japan, Box 2 File 34, Bates to Arnup, 12 July 1932.
87   For a recent history of Korean Christianity up to 1945, see Sawa Masahiko, *Mika no Chosen Kirisutokyo Shi* (Tokyo: Nihon Kirisutokyodan Shuppan Kyoku, 1991). Another useful history, which continues its investigation beyond 1945, is Min Kyon Be, *Kankoku Kirisutokyo Shi: Kankoku Minzoku Kyokai Kisei no Katai*, Kim Chyun Iru, trans. (Tokyo: Shinkyo Shuppansha, 1981). Allen D. Clark, *A History of the Church in Korea* (Seoul: Christian Literature Society, 1971), remains a good standard English language general history.
88   Information concerning the beginnings of Canadian missionary work in Korea can be found in Ion, *The Cross and the Rising Sun*, vol. 1.
89   The decision of Duncan M. MacRae (1868–1949) to become a missionary in Korea as well as later life in Korea are vividly described in Helen Fraser MacRae, *A Tiger on Dragon Mountain: The Life of Rev. Duncan M. MacRae, D.D.*, ed. Ross Penner and Janice Penner (Charlottetown: A. James Haslam, Q. C., 1993).
90   For a recent history of Korean religions, see James Huntley Grayson, *Korea: A Religious History* (Oxford: Oxford University Press, 1989). His short chapter on Christianity is a useful summary of many of the main trends in Korean Christian history from the seventeenth century onward.
91   The Korean nationalist movement in Chientao is described in Paul Hobom Shin, "The Korean Colony in Chientao: A Study of Japanese Imperialism and Militant Korean Nationalism, 1905–1932," unpublished PhD diss., University of Washington, 1980.
92   See Hara Kishi, "Kyokuto Roshia ni okeru Chosen dokuritsu undo to Nihon," *San Sen Ri*, 17 (Tokushu San Ichi Undo Rokyu Shunen) (1979), pp. 47–53.
93   See George Leslie Mackay, *From Far Formosa: The Islands, Its People*, ed. J. A. Macdonald (Chicago: Fleming H. Revell, 1896).
94   For the English Presbyterian mission in Taiwan, see Edward Band, *Working Out His Purpose: The History of the English Presbyterian Mission 1847–1947* (Taipeh: Ch'eng Wen Publishing Company, 1972). See also Ion, *The Cross and the Rising Sun*, vol. 2.
95   Dr. James Rohrer made this suggestion during a presentation entitled "The Triumph and Tragedy of G. L. Mackay and the North Formosa Mission," given at a symposium entitled George Leslie Mackay and His Legacy in Taiwan and Canada, Victoria College, University of Toronto, April 1997.
96   Alvyn J. Austin, *Saving China: Canadian Missionaries in the Middle Kingdom 1888–1959* (Toronto: University of Toronto Press, 1986), p. 32.
97   Ibid., pp. 32–33.

CHAPTER TWO

1. Dohi Akio, "1930 nendai no Purotesutanto Kirisutokyokai (1),"*KSMK*, 25.12 (1976), pp. 187–217, p. 193.
2. Horinesu Bando Showa Kirisutokyo Danatsu Shi Kankokai, *Horinesu Bando no Kiseki: Ribaibaru to Kirisutokyo Danatsu* (Tokyo: Horinesu Bando Danatsu Shi Kankokai Hen, 1983), p. 84.
3. William Axling, *Kagawa* (London: Student Christian Movement, 1932), p. 133.
4. C. J. L. Bates, "The One Million Souls Campaign," *JCQ* (January 1929), pp. 59–68, p. 68.
5. Ibid., pp. 60, 63.
6. UCC BFM Japan, Box 4, Bates to Young People of the Ottawa Presbytery, 24 November 1936.
7. Bates, "The One Million Souls Campaign," p. 63.
8. Ibid.
9. Ibid.
10. Ibid., pp. 63–64.
11. Rev. P. G. Price, "A Report of Mr. Kagawa's Evangelistic Campaign," *JCQ* (April 1929), pp. 130–37. Price was influential in establishing the Airindan, the Canadian Methodist centre for slum work in Nippori, in 1920. See Airindan entry, *NKRDJ*, p. 16.
12. Ibid., p. 137.
13. The United Church of Canada Year Book, 1931, p. 115 [hereafter cited as *UCCYB* with appropriate date].
14. *UCCYB* 1933, p. 121.
15. *UCCYB* 1934, p. 107.
16. *UCCYB* 1935, p. 123. The Oxford Group (also known as Buchmanism and Moral Rearmament) was a modern revival movement founded by Frank N. D. Buchman (1878–1961) in the United States. The movement called on God's guidance, moral absolutes, and change in the lives of individuals through personal work. In the early 1930s, the Oxford Group through the means of conferences, so-called house parties, were able to attract some interest in Japan. See *NKRDJ*, pp. 262–63.
17. UCC BFM Japan, Box 2 File 30, Gressit to Arnup, 25 March 1932.
18. UCC BFM Japan, Box 2 File 30, "Kagawa of Japan: A Modern Apostle."
19. Ibid. During his early life, Kagawa was deeply influenced in his Christian faith by two missionaries, Charles Logan and Harry Myers. See Robert M. Fukada, "C. A. Rogan to H. W. Maiyasu: Kagawa Toyohiko o meguru senkyoshitachi," *KSMK*, 32.3 (1984), pp. 129–45.
20. UCC BFM Japan, Box 2 File 36, Kagawa to Arnup, 2 May 1932.
21. Ibid.
22. Robert Wright, *A World Mission: Canadian Protestantism and the Quest for a New International Order, 1918–1939* (Montreal: McGill-Queen's University Press, 1991), p. 193.
23. UCC BFM Japan, Box 2 File 36, Kagawa to Arnup, 2 May 1932. Kagawa was aware that the Kingdom of God movement in Canada was stimulated by and modelled on the movement in Japan. See Toyohiko Kagawa, "The Kingdom of God Movement: Its Future Programme and Philosophy," *JCQ* (spring 1982), pp. 81–88, p. 85. This article was originally published in July 1931.
24. See Axling, *Kagawa*, p. 137.

25 See, for instance, UCC BFM Japan 1926, Box 1 File 1, Armstrong to Endicott, 15 January 1926.
26 Ibid. For Kobayashi Yataro (1888–1969), see *NKRDJ*, p. 536. As well as the Central Tabernacle and the Nippori slum work, Kobayashi was deeply involved with the YMCA and the development of its boys' work camps, in which he was helped by George Sutton Patterson (1887–1953), a former Canadian Methodist missionary in Japan. For Patterson, see *NKRDJ*, p. 1116. Concerning Patterson's and Kobayashi's YMCA boys' work activities, see Naratada Gotaro, *Nihon YMCA Shi* (Tokyo: Nihon YMCA Domei Shuppanbu, 1959), pp. 261–65.
27 For the Aiseikan, see under Kyoaikan, *NKRDJ*, p. 376.
28 Annie Whitburn Allen (1878–1973) was a graduate of the University of Toronto and went to Japan in 1905 to teach first at the Toyo Eiwa Jo Gakko and then at the Yamanashi Eiwa Jo Gakko. During World War I, however, Allen began to concentrate full time on evangelistic work among factory girls, who were then pouring into Tokyo. See *NKRDJ*, p. 72. See also John W. Saunby, *The New Chivalry in Japan* (Toronto: Methodist Publishing House, 1923), p. 142.
29 Saunby, *The New Chivalry in Japan*, pp. 164–65.
30 Kuranaga Takashi, *Kanada Mesojisuto Nihon Dendo Gaishi* (Tokyo: Kanada Godo Kyokai Senkyoshika, 1937), pp. 211–12.
31 Ibid., p. 213. See also *Toyo Eiwa Jo Gakuin Hyakunen Shi*, pp. 169–73.
32 UCC BFM Japan 1926, Box 1 File 3, "The Mission Field of the United Church in Japan."
33 UCC BFM Japan 1927, Box 1 File 8, Holmes to Arnup, 1 September 1927.
34 Ibid.
35 UCC BFM, Japan 1928, East Tokyo, P. G. Price, "Report of East Tokyo Mission for 1928: Leaven at Work in a Great City."
36 Ibid.
37 Ibid.
38 E. C. Hennigar, "Abolition of Licensed Prostitution," *JCQ* (April 1929), pp. 174–76, p. 176.
39 Akisada Yoshikazu, "1934 zengo no haisho undo," *KSMK*, 39.3 (1991), pp. 50–71, p. 71.
40 G. R. P. Norman and W. H. H. Norman, *One Hundred Years in Japan, 1873–1973* (Toronto: Division of World Out-Reach, United Church of Canada, 1981), p. 388.
41 E. C. Hennigar, "Some Suggestions for Temperance Work," *JCQ* (April 1934), pp. 168–73, p. 172.
42 *UCCYB* 1930, p. 148.
43 D. Norman, "An Institute School of Rural Evangelism," *JCQ* (April 1929), pp. 147–51, p. 148.
44 For the Farmers Gospel School Movement and Sugiyama Motojiro's relationship to it, see Inuma Jiro, *Nihon Noson Dendo Shi Kenkyu* (Tokyo: Nihon Kirisutokyodan Shuppan Kyoku, 1988), pp. 31–62, especially p. 43. The Nagano school was the fourth such rural evangelistic school established, although many other schools were founded in the early 1930s.
45 D. Norman, "An Institute School of Rural Evangelism," p. 150–51.
46 A. R. Stone, "Difficulties in Christian Rural Permeation (The Disillusions of a Tamed Ruralist)," *JCQ* (April 1934), pp. 14–21, p. 16. For Alfred Russell Stone (1902–54), see *NKRDJ*, pp. 727–28.
47 Ibid., p. 16.
48 Ibid., p. 17.
49 Ibid.
50 *UCCYB* 1934, p. 112.

51 *UCCYB* 1935, p. 108.
52 *UCCYB* 1928, p. 179. By way of comparison, the mission in Korea received $79,131.73 and the work in Taiwan $2,718.75.
53 *UCCYB* 1935, p. 67. The Korean mission also received a slight increase, getting $56,636.83. The obligations to Taiwan, however, only amounted to $421.62.
54 UCC William Howard Heal Norman Personal Papers [hereafter Norman Papers], Box 1 File 8, Howie [Howard Norman] to Dr. and Mrs. Roberts, 2 March 1934.
55 Ibid.
56 *UCCYB* 1934, p. 111.
57 Missionary Society of the Church of England in Canada [hereafter cited as MSCEC] Japan files, Bishop H. J. Hamilton, GS 75-103 Series 3-2 Box 64, Hamilton to Gould, 15 March 1927.
58 Ibid.
59 MSCEC Japan files, Bishop H. J. Hamilton, GS 75-103 Series 3-2 Box 64, Notes on Mid- Japan for Anglican National Commission, signed 6 December 1930.
60 Ibid.
61 MSCEC Japan files, Bishop H. J. Hamilton, GS 75-103 Series 3-2 Box 64, Hamilton to Gould, 8 May 1931.
62 Ibid.
63 MSCEC Japan files, Bishop H. J. Hamilton, GS 75-103 Series 3-2 Box 64, Hamilton to Gould, 26 September 1932.
64 MSCEC Japan files, Bishop H. J. Hamilton, GS 75-103 Series 3-2 Box 64, Hamilton to Gould, 15 February 1934.
65 MSCEC Japan files, Miscellaneous, GS 75-103 Series 3-2 Box 65. Sasaki Shinji (1885–1946) was born in Azabu, Tokyo, and had studied theology in England. See *NKRDJ*, p. 572.
66 MSCEC Japan files, J. G. Waller, GS 75-103 Series 3-3 Box 88, "Japanese Bishops," dated 1943.
67 MSCEC Japan files, Sydney Gould, GS 75-103 Series 3-2 Box 65, Gould to Sasaki, 30 May 1935.
68 MSCEC Japan files, Bishop H. J. Hamilton, GS 75-103 Series 3-2 Box 64, Hamilton to Gould, 14 January 1930.
69 Ibid.
70 MSCEC Japan files, Bishop H. J. Hamilton, GS 75-103 Series 3-2 Box 64, Hamilton to Gould, 11 May 1933.
71 MSCEC Japan files, Bishop H. J. Hamilton, GS 75-103 Series 3-2 Box 64, Hamilton to Gould, 15 February 1934.
72 MSCEC Japan files, Bishop H. J. Hamilton, GS 75-103 Series 3-2 Box 64, Hamilton to Gould, 14 January 1930.
73 MSCEC Japan files, Bishop H. J. Hamilton, GS 75-103 Series 3-2 Box 64, Hamilton to Gould, 26 October 1931.
74 MSCEC Japan files, Bishop H. J. Hamilton, GS 75-103 Series 3-2 Box 64, Hamilton to Gould, 5 January 1932.
75 MSCEC Japan files, Bishop H. J. Hamilton, GS 75-103 Series 3-2 Box 64, Bishop Hamilton letter of 20 September 1927, quoted in Report of Executive Committee re Cost of Living in Japan as compared with that in Canada.
76 MSCEC Japan files, Bishop H. J. Hamilton, GS 75-103, Series 3-2 Box 64, Diocese of Mid-Japan 1935 Suggested Budget.
77 *Acts and Proceedings of the Fifty-Seventh General Assembly of the Presbyterian Church in Canada*, 1931 [hereafter cited as *APPCC* with appropriate year]. For Caroline Macdonald and the Japanese YWCA, see Nihon YWCA hachi nen shi henshu iinkai,

NOTES TO CHAPTER TWO 355

Mizu o Kaze o Hikari o: Nihon YWCA 80 Nen 1905–1985 (Tokyo: Nihon Kirisutokyo Joshi Seinen Kai, 1987), especially pp. 79–81. Macdonald was the first general secretary of the Japanese YWCA. She resigned in 1916 in order to devote more energy toward helping factory girls. See also Prang, *A Heart at Leisure from Itself.*
78 *APPCC* 1929, p. 82. See also Prang, *A Heart at Leisure from Itself*, pp. 222–23.
79 *APPCC* 1930, p. 102.
80 For a brief description of Macdonald's prison work, see Margaret Prang, "Caroline Macdonald and Prison Work in Japan," Working Paper Series 51, University of Toronto-York University Joint Centre for Asia Pacific Studies, 1988.
81 *APPCC* 1935, p. 63.
82 Ibid.
83 J. A. Foote, "Evangelistic Work among Koreans in Japan," *JCQ* (spring 1981), pp. 113–18, p. 115. This article was first published in January 1930.
84 Ibid., p. 117.
85 *APPCC* 1933, p. 42.
86 *APPCC* 1930, p. 102.
87 Ibid.
88 *APPCC* 1934, p. 35.
89 Ibid., p. 36.
90 *APPCC* 1935, p. 64.
91 Ibid.

CHAPTER THREE

1 *UCCYB* 1928, p. 282.
2 In October 1919, the Presbyterian Church reported that 3,804 of its members had been arrested, including 134 pastors or elders, and that 202 leaders of other denominations had been arrested. See Ji Myon Kuwan [Chi Mekan], *Kankoku Gendai Shi to Kyokai Shi* (Tokyo: Shinkyo Shuppansha, 1975), p. 121.
3 Ibid., p. 128. As Professor Kenneth M. Wells has noted, "'culturalism' meant commitment to constructing a new culture as the necessary foundation for independent statehood and democracy." Kenneth M. Wells, *New God, New Nation: Protestants and Self-Reconstruction Nationalism in Korea 1896–1937* (North Sydney, Australia: Allen and Unwin, 1990), p. 106.
4 See Cho Juhun, *Kankoku Minzoku Undo Shi*, Kato Haruko, trans. (Tokyo: Korai Shorin, 1975), p. 197.
5 See, for instance, Chosen Sotokufu, *Chosen no Tochi to Kirisutokyo* (Keijo: Chosen Sotokufu, 1920).
6 Ji, *Kankoku Gendai Shi to Kyokai Shi*, p. 130.
7 See Zai Kanto Nippon Soryojikan, *Kanto Jijo Kogai* (n.p.: n.p., 1932), p. 3. [Hokkaido University Library call number 915 Ka].
8 Shinkyo Tetsuro Kyoku, *Kanto Chiho Gaiyo* (n.p.: n.p., May 1934), pp. 107, 113–14. There were some 33,560 Korean believers belonging to various religions: 22,430 Christians, 6,518 Confucianists, 2,256 Buddhists, and 1,346 Tendokyoists. There were 138 Christian churches in the Chientao region out of a total of 183 religious houses. Of Christian groups, the Canadian mission had 55 churches, the Roman Catholics 35, the Southern Methodists 20, and the Toa Kirisutokyo Ha (Holiness Church) 20. The German Roman Catholic missionaries, with some 9,700 adherents, were the only other Western

missionaries in the immediate Lungchingtsun district.
9. Zaigai Senjin Chosa Hokoku, *Mammo no Beisaku to Iju Senno Mondai* (n.p.: n.p., 1927), p. 139. [Hokkaido University Library call number 633 cho]. It can be assumed that the book was published by the government general of Korea.
10. See Ann Trotter, ed., *British Documents on Foreign Affairs: Reports and Papers from the Foreign Office Confidential Print* [hereafter cited as *BDFA*], vol. 10 Japan [F1387/1387/23], Snow to Henderson, 22 January 1931. Enclosure, Annual Report on Affairs in Korea during 1930, p. 100.
11. Robert A. Scalapino and Chong-sik Lee, *Communism in Korea, Part 1: The Movement* (Berkeley: University of California Press, 1972), pp. 156–57. For a brief description of the 30 May 1930 revolt in Lungchingtsun and the Chientao region, see Kan Juon, *Chosen Kindai Shi* (Tokyo: Heibonsha, 1986), pp. 284–88.
12. UCC BFM Korea, Box 2 File 47, Bruce to Armstrong, 18 January 1931.
13. Grierson felt bitter regret that this incident took place. However, he believed that the individual had badly let down the boys' school by leaving the teaching staff without warning after the Canadian mission had paid for special training for him. See Robert Grierson, "Episodes on a Long, Long Trial," ninety-one page typescript in the possession of A. H. Ion, pp. 87–90.
14. UCC BFM Korea, Box 2 File 45, MacDonald to Armstrong, 27 April 1931.
15. UCC BFM Korea, Box 2 File 45, Rogers to Armstrong, 11 May 1931.
16. UCC BFM Korea, Box 2 File 2, MacDonald to Armstrong, 1 September 1931.
17. Ian Nish, *Japan's Struggle with Internationalism: Japan, China, and the League of Nations, 1931–3* (London: Kegan Paul International, 1993), pp. 23–24. Other useful studies of the Manchurian crisis include Christopher Thorne, *The Limits of Foreign Policy* (London: Hamish Hamilton, 1972); Sadako N. Ogata, *Defiance in Manchuria* (Berkeley: University of California Press, 1964); and James B. Crowley, *Japan's Quest for Autonomy* (Princeton: Princeton University Press, 1966).
18. UCC BFM Korea, Box 2 File 2, MacDonald to Armstrong, 13 October 1931.
19. UCC BFM Korea, Box 2 File 45, Armstrong to MacDonald, 19 October 1931.
20. UCC BFM Korea, Box 2 File 53, MacDonald to Armstrong, 13 January 1932.
21. UCC BFM Korea, Box 2 File 54, Fraser to Burns, 16 January 1932.
22. UCC BFM Korea, Box 2 File 55, Ross to Armstrong, 13 February 1932. For Canadian missionaries, it was primarily the methods that the Korean communists employed that appalled them. Concerning the Shanghai incident, Armstrong wrote in reply to Ross's letter that "Japan had some rights in Manchuria and she had the sympathy of most of the world in that connection but she greatly injured her case when her navy, perhaps in jealousy of the army, wantonly and cruelly bombarded civilians in Shanghai." At least at the missionary society headquarters in Toronto, sympathy for Japan over Manchuria was slipping away because of the actions in Shanghai. UCC BFM Korea, Box File 55, Armstrong to Ross, 22 March 1932.
23. UCC BFM Korea, Box 2 File 55, Ross to Armstrong, 13 February 1932. In his reply to Ross, Armstrong was very sympathetic to any effort that Ross had made to help the refugees around Lungchingtsun. UCC BFM Korea, Box 2 File 55, Armstrong to Ross, 22 March 1932.
24. UCC BFM Korea, Box 2 File 55, Ross to Armstrong, 13 February 1932. See also UCC BFM Korea, Box 2 File 54, Fraser to Armstrong, 6 December 1932.
25. UCC BFM Korea, Box 2 File 54, Fraser to Burns, 18 April 1932.
26. UCC BFM Korea, Box 2 File 55, Bruce to Friends, 28 June 1932. The British consul in Dairen believed that Rapp had been killed by Japanese soldiers, although his murder could not be proved. See *BDFA*, vol. 12 Japan [F1683/1683/23], Lindley to Simon, 8 February 1933. Enclosure, Austin to Lindley, 31 December 1933 [sic], Report on the

Kwantung Leased Territory and Japanese Activities in Manchuria during the Year 1932, p. 203. See also UCC BFM Korea, Box 2 File 63, Bruce to Armstrong, 17 January 1933, in which Bruce emphasized the stress that Canadian knowledge of the Japanese killing of Rapp had on missionaries in Lungchingtsun. In early 1933, Armstrong in Toronto expressed concern about the safety of Canadian missionaries. See UCC BFM Korea, Box 2 File 66, Armstrong to Robb, 3 January 1933.

27 UCC BFM Korea, Box 2 File 55, Bruce to Friends, 28 June 1932. Consul Austin at Dairen mentioned that 1932 had seen "incessant guerilla warfare against the established State," a constant and difficult problem for Japanese troops. See Report on the Kwantung Leased Territory and Japanese Activities in Manchuria during the Year 1932, p. 28. The dangers to missionaries were further underlined in the fall of 1932 when an American Presbyterian North missionary, Lloyd P. Henderson, who worked at Sinpin in West Manchuria, was killed by bandits during an itinerant journey.
28 UCC BFM Korea, Box 2 File 56, Kim to Armstrong, 31 October 1932.
29 Ibid.
30 UCC BFM Korea, Box 2 File 55, Robb to Armstrong, 30 November 1932.
31 Ibid.
32 UCC BFM Korea, Box 2 File 54, Fraser to Armstrong, 6 December 1932.
33 Scalapino and Lee, *Communism in Korea*, pp. 161–63.
34 UCC BFM Korea, Box 2 File 65, Armstrong to MacRae, 27 January 1933.
35 UCC BFM Korea, Box 2 File 66, Robb to Armstrong, 2 February 1933.
36 UCC BFM Korea, Box 2 File 60, Armstrong to Black, 29 March 1933.
37 UCC BFM Korea, Box 2 File 62, Bruce to Armstrong, 1 October 1933.
38 Ibid.
39 UCC BFM Korea, Box 2 File 61, Black to Armstrong, 15 October 1933.
40 Ibid.
41 Robert Wright, *A World Mission: Canadian Protestantism and the Quest for a New International Order, 1918–1939* (Montreal: McGill-Queen's University Press, 1991), p. 205.
42 UCC BFM Japan, Box 2 File 35, Whiting to Arnup, 16 August 1932.
43 UCC BFM Japan, Box 2 File 35, Woodsworth to Arnup, 8 October 1932.
44 Wright, *A World Mission*, p. 206.
45 See *RJ*, 15 February 1932, p. 9; 15 April 1932, p. 5.
46 UCC BFM Japan, Box 2 File 34, Bates to Arnup, 12 July 1932.
47 "Minzoku to Kaikyu to Senso," in Yoshino Sakuzo, *Chugoku: Chosenron*, ed. Matsuo Takayoshi (Tokyo: Heibonsha, 1970), pp. 333–47, p. 38. This article was first published in the magazine *Chuokoron* in January 1932. Fujita Wakao, *Yanaihara Tadao: Sono Shogai to Shinko* (Tokyo: Kyobunkan, 1967), p. 23. Yanaihara's study of the Manchurian situation was published in 1934.
48 Dohi Akio, *Nihon Purotesutanto Kyokai no Seiritsu to Tenkai* (Tokyo: Nihon Kirisutokyodan Shuppan Kyoku, 1975), pp. 174–75. The Japanese Presbyterian mission in Manchuria to which Hayashi was attached received some financial support from the South Manchurian Railway, and this support might have influenced his opinion and those of his colleagues involved in Manchurian work.
49 Sandra Wilson, "The Manchurian Crisis and Moderate Japanese Intellectuals: The Japan Council of the Institute of Pacific Relations," *Modern Asian Studies* 26.3 (1992), pp. 507–44, p. 519. For a recent article that analyses Nitobe's attitude toward the Manchurian problem, see George Oshiro, "The End: 1929–1933," in John F. Howes, ed., *Nitobe Inazo: Japan's Bridge across the Pacific* (Boulder: Westview Press, 1995), pp. 253–78, especially pp. 255–58.
50 Goforth was one of the great missionary heroes of the Canadian Presbyterian Church.

Drawn into mission work after hearing an appeal by the legendary George Leslie Mackay of Formosa in the late 1880s, he was one of the founders of the North Honan mission. See *Presbyterian Record* [hereafter cited as *PR*], 55.8 (August 1930), p. 230.
51 Alvyn J. Austin, *Saving China: Canadian Missionaries in the Middle Kingdom 1888–1959* (Toronto: University of Toronto Press, 1986), pp. 220–21.
52 Austin Fulton, *Through Earthquake, Wind, and Fire: Church and Mission in Manchuria 1867–1950: The Work of the United Presbyterian Church, the United Free Church of Scotland, the Church of Scotland, and the Presbyterian Church in Ireland with the Chinese Church in Manchuria* (Edinburgh: Saint Andrew Press, 1967), pp. 48–49.
53 *PR*, 52.9 (September 1927), pp. 282–83.
54 *PR*, 52.12 (December 1927), p. 375.
55 Ibid.
56 *APPCC* 1930, p. 103.
57 *APPCC* 1933; for instance, see pp. 36–37.
58 Ibid., p. 41.
59 Ibid., p. 36.
60 Ibid.
61 *APPCC* 1932, pp. 43–44.
62 Fulton, *Through Earthquake, Wind, and Fire*, pp. 87–89.
63 Letter from A. A. Fulton to A. H. Ion, 21 August 1978; in the possession of A. H. Ion.
64 Fulton, *Through Earthquake, Wind, and Fire*, pp. 92–111. E. H. Johnson, "The Manchurian Church in Crisis," *PR*, 66.4 (August 1941), pp. 227–30, p. 96. Johnson, writing almost six years after the events, gave the number of Christians arrested as eighty.
65 Fulton, *Through Earthquake, Wind, and Fire*, pp. 92–111.
66 Ibid.
67 *Chinese Recorder* (hereafter cited as *CR*), 67.1 (January 1936), p. 57. See also *CR*, 66.12 (December 1935), p. 765.
68 *PR*, 66.4 (August 1941), p. 229.
69 Letter from A. A. Fulton to A. H. Ion, 21 August 1978; in the possession of A. H. Ion.
70 Ibid.
71 Ibid. Fulton provided an example of the generous interpretation of regulations by the Japanese civilian authorities in the case of income tax on missionary salaries.
72 Ibid.
73 UCC BFM Korea, Box 3 File 69. Information about Armstrong's itinerary and activities during his visit to Korea in the late summer of 1934 is found in MacDonald to Endicott, 6 October 1934.
74 UCC BFM Korea, Box 3 File 69, Armstrong to Scott, 22 January 1934.
75 UCC BFM Korea, Box 3 File 75, Minute, April 1935.
76 UCC BFM Korea, Box 3 File 75, "Appropriations for 1935."
77 UCC BFM Korea, Box 3 File 77, Pastor Pak of Hoiryung quoted in Burbridge to Armstrong, 27 July 1935.
78 Ibid. Pastor Kim Kwan-sik quoted.
79 UCC BFM Korea, Box 3 File 77, "Open Letter to Friends in Canada."
80 Ibid.
81 UCC BFM Korea, Box 3 File 77, Bates quoted in Armstrong to Burbridge, 13 September 1935.
82 *UCCYB* 1936, pp. 94–95. As well as the return to Canada of Grierson and MacRae, who were retiring in any case, the number of missionaries was further reduced by the deaths of Robb, who had spent thirty-four years as a missionary in Korea, and a WMS nurse, Mabel Young.
83 *APPCC* 1925–26, p. 14.

NOTES TO CHAPTER THREE 359

84 *APPCC* 1927, p. 39.
85 *PR*, 55.2 (February 1930), letter from Dr. M. G. Graham, p. 51.
86 See A. Hamish Ion, *The Cross and the Rising Sun*, vol. 2, p. 142.
87 *APPCC* 1929, p. 48.
88 *RP*, 55.11 (November 1930), p. 278.
89 *BDFA*, vol. 10 Japan [F1394/1394/23], Snow to Henderson, 27 January 27 1931. Enclosure, Consul A. R. Ovens to Snow, Annual Report on the Island of Formosa for the Year 1930, p. 118.
90 Ibid., p. 119.
91 Ibid., p. 118. See also *BDFA*, vol. 10 Japan [F579/289/23], Snow to Henderson, December 1931. Enclosure, Lieutenant C. R. Boxer's report on "The Formosan Aborigines and the Outbreak of October 1930," p. 87.
92 *BDFA*, vol. 10 Japan[F579/289/23], Simon to Snow, 17 December 1930, p. 85.
93 Hollington K. Tong, *Christianity in Taiwan: A History* (Taipeh: China Post, 1972), pp. 139–41. In his annual report on Taiwan for 1932, the British consul in Tamsui reported about the Musha tribe that the only survivors were women and children. See *BDFA*, vol. 12 Japan [F987/420/23], Lindley to Simon, 16 January 1933. Enclosure, Annual Report on the Island of Formosa for the Year 1932, p. 149.
94 *PR*, 55.10 (October 1930), p. 309.
95 *PR*, 56. 3 (March 1931), "Evangelism in Formosa," by J. Douglas Wilkie, p. 85. Wilkie gave figures of 150,000 aborigines, 4,000,000 ethnic Chinese, and 200,000 Japanese as the population of the island in 1931.
96 *PR*, 56.12 (December 1931), p. 372.
97 Tong, *Christianity in Taiwan*, p. 141.
98 Ibid., p. 143.
99 *APPCC* 1932, p. 37.
100 *APPCC* 1933, pp. 32–33.
101 Ibid., p. 33.
102 *APPCC* 1934, p. 29.
103 *APPCC* 1935, p. 54.
104 Ibid.
105 Ibid., p. 55.
106 Ibid., p. 61.

CHAPTER FOUR

1 Tomura Masahiro, ed., *Jinja Mondai to Kirisutokyo: Nihon Kindai Kirisutokyo Shi Shiryo 1* (Tokyo: Shinkyo Shuppansha, 1976), p. 3.
2 Ibid.
3 Helen Hardacre, *Shinto and the State 1868–1988* (Princeton: Princeton University Press, 1990), p. 27.
4 Ibid., p. 29. For a detailed analysis of Japanese government Shinto policy from the Meiji Restoration onward, see Tomura, *Jinja Mondai to Kirisutokyo*, pp. 3–33.
5 Hardacre, *Shinto and the State 1868–1988*, p. 32.
6 Ibid., pp. 32–33.
7 Ebisawa Arimichi and Oouchi Saburo, *Nihon Kirisutokyo Shi* (Tokyo: Nihon Kirisutokyodan Shuppan Kyoku, 1971), pp. 370–71.
8 Hardacre, *Shinto and the State 1868–1988*, pp. 124–25.

9   Ibid., p. 125.
10 B. H. Chamberlain, *The Invention of a New Religion* (London: Rationalist Press, 1912).
11 Dohi Akio, *Nihon Purotesutanto Kirisutokyo Shi* (Tokyo: Shinkyo Shuppansha, 1982), p. 134.
12 Ebisawa and Oouchi, *Nihon Kirisutokyo Shi*, p. 475.
13 A. Hamish Ion, *The Cross and the Rising Sun: Volume 2: The British Missionary Movement in Japan, Korea, and Taiwan, 1865–1945* (Waterloo: Wilfrid Laurier University Press, 1993), p. 121.
14 Tsukada Osamu, *Shocho Tennosei to Kirisutokyo* (Tokyo: Shinkyo Shuppansha, 1990), p. 121.
15 Ibid., p. 123.
16 Tsukada Osamu, *Shoki Nippon Seikokai no Keisei to Imai Judo* (Tokyo: Seikokai Shuppan, 1992), p. 223.
17 Ibid., pp. 100-07.
18 Tsukada, *Shocho Tennosei to Kirisutokyo*, p. 123.
19 Tsukada Osamu, *Tennoseika no Kirisutokyo: Nippon Seikokai no Tataki to Kunan* (Tokyo: Shinkyo Shuppansha, 1981), p. 82.
20 Hardacre, *Shinto and the State 1868–1988*, pp. 93–94.
21 Kasahara Yoshimitsu, "Nippon Kirisutokyodan Seiritsu no Mondai: Shukyo Tosei ni tai sure Junno to Teiko" in Doshisha Daigaku Jinbun Kagaku Kenkyu Hen, *Senjika Teiko no Kenkyu: Kirisutokyosha, Jiyushugisha no Baii*, 2 vols (Tokyo: Misuzu Shobo, 1978), vol. 1, pp. 155–57.
22 Kudo Hiroshi, "Senjika no *Kirisutokyo Sekai* o yomu—1936 nen kara 1941 made no, Tennosei oyobi senso kanren kiji," *KSMK*, 42.7 (1993), pp. 25–55, pp. 53–54.
23 D. C. Holtom, "Modern Shinto as a State Religion," *The Japan Mission Year Book* 1930, (Tokyo: Kyobunkwan, 1930), pp. 38–61, p. 60.
24 *BDFA*, vol. 12: Japan [F8922/8922/23], Lindley to Simon, 24 November, 1932, p. 59.
25 Ibid.
26 National Archives of Canada (hereafter cited as NAC) RG 25 G1, vol. 1668, file 547, Skelton to Marler, 7 January 1936.
27 Ibid.
28 NAC, RG 25 G1, vol. 1668, file 547, Marler to Secretary of State, 21 May 1936. Sir Herbert Marler (1876–1940) was a former political colleague of Prime Minister Mackenzie King and Canada's first minister to Japan between 1929 and 1936. For a brief description of Marler's tenure as minister in Japan, see Eber H. Rice, "Sir Herbert Marler and the Canadian Legation in Tokyo," in John Schultz and Kimitada Miwa, eds., *Canada and Japan in the Twentieth Century* (Toronto: Oxford University Press, 1991), pp. 75–84.
29 NAC, RG 25 G1, vol. 1668, file 547, Marler to Secretary of State, 21 May 1936.
30 Ibid.
31 Ibid.
32 NAC, RG 25 G1, vol. 1668, file 547, Marler to Secretary of State, 22 May 1936.
33 Ibid. The Dr. Batchelor referred to was John Batchelor (1854–1944), the British Anglican missionary famous for his work among the Ainu of Hokkaido.
34 UCC BFM Japan, Box 4 File 74, Arnup to Hennigar, 19 March 1936.
35 Even though Bruce and his wife were personally well liked in Tokyo, his tenure as minister between 1936 and 1938 was neither a diplomatic success nor a happy period for him. His replacement was a career diplomat, D'Arcy McGreer, who held the rank of charge d'affaires. See John Hilliker, *Canada's Department of External Affairs, vol. 1: The Early Years, 1909–1946* (Montreal: McGill-Queen's University Press, 1990), pp. 182–83, pp. 186–87, pp. 190–91.
36 Doshisha Daigaku Amerika Kenkyukai hen, *Aru Ribarisuto no Kaiso: Yuasa Hachiro no*

Nihon to Amerika (Tokyo: Nihon YMCA Domei Shuppanbu, 1977), pp. 47–48.
37 Ibid., pp. 47–48, pp. 52–54. See also Dohi, *Nihon Purotesutanto Kirisutokyo Shi*, pp. 366–68; Wada Yoichi, "Sen Kyu Hyaku Sanju Nananen Natsu no Doshisha Chaperu Rojo Jiken," *KSMK*, 8.4 (1964), pp. 99–113. For a brief biographical description of Yuasa Hachiro (1890–1981), see *NKRDJ*, pp. 1451–52.
38 Doshisha Daigaku Amerika Kenkyukai hen, *Aru Ribarisuto no Kaiso*, pp. 54–56.
39 Dohi, *Nihon Purotesutanto Kirisutokyo Shi*, p. 368. For Kimura Shigeharu (1874–1967), see *NKRDJ*, pp. 368–69.
40 Dohi, *Nihon Purotesutanto Kirisutokyo Shi*, pp. 368–69.
41 Yuasa clearly thought that the military officers attached to the Doshisha faculty stirred up trouble against him. He also condemned the Ministry of Education for failing to stand up to either individual military officers or the Ministry of War behind them. Doshisha Daigaku Amerika Kenkyukai hen, *Aru Ribarisuto no Kaiso*, pp. 46–47.
42 UCC BFM Japan, Box 4 File 81, Outerbridge to Arnup, 6 and 9 April 1937.
43 Ibid.
44 Ibid.
45 UCC BFM Korea, Box 3 File 72, Bruce to Armstrong, 15 January 1934.
46 Ibid.
47 Spencer J. Palmer, "Korean Christians and the Shinto Shrine Issue," in C. I. Eugene Kim and Doretha E. Mortimore, eds., *Korea's Response to Japan: The Colonial Period 1910–1945* (Kalamazoo: Center for Korean Studies, Western Michigan University, 1977), pp. 139–61, p. 140.
48 Sawa Masahiko, *Mika no Chosen Purotesutanto Shi* (Tokyo: Nihon Kirisutokyodan Shuppan Kyoku, 1991), pp. 231–32.
49 Kai Kanto Nippon So Ryojikan, *Kanto Jijo Kogai*, pp. 74–75.
50 Wi Jo Kang, "Religion and Politics under Japanese Rule," in C. I. Eugene Kim and Doretha E. Mortimore, eds., *Korea's Response to Japan: The Colonial Period 1910–1945* (Kalamazoo: Center for Korean Studies, Western Michigan University, 1977), pp. 103–38, p. 114.
51 Sawa, *Chosen Purotesutanto Shi*, pp. 232–33.
52 Ji Myon Kuwan [Chi Mekan], *Kankoku Gendai Shi to Kirisutokyo Shi* (Tokyo: Shinkyo Shuppansha, 1975), p. 143.
53 Allen D. Clark, *A History of the Church in Korea* (Seoul: Christian Literature Society, 1971), p. 223.
54 Archives of the Presbyterian Church in Canada [hereafter cited as APCC], Formosa File re Shrine Question 1935–37, "'A Warning to Dr. G. S. McCune, Principal of the Sujitsu School.' Copy of a statement handed to Dr. G. S. McCune, to Mr. T. S. Soltau and to J. G. Holdcroft by H. E. T. Watanabe, Director of the Educational Bureau of The Government General of Chosen, December 30th 1935."
55 Ibid.
56 Helen Fraser MacRae, *A Tiger on Dragon Mountain: The Life of Rev. Duncan M. MacRae, D. D.*, ed. Ross Penner and Janice Penner (Charlottetown: A. James Haslam, QC, 1993), p. 200.
57 APCC Formosa File re Shrine Question 1935–37, George S. McCune to H. E. H. Yasutake, 18 January 1936.
58 Ibid.
59 APCC Formosa File re Shrine Question 1935–37, "Religious Liberty under Japanese Rule: Summary of the Present Situation in Korea, Manchukuo, and Japan," dated February 1936.
60 Clark, *A History of the Church in Korea*, p. 224.
61 Palmer, "Korean Christians and the Shinto Shrine Issue," p. 145.

62   Ibid., p. 146.
63   Kan Wijo, *Nihon Tojika Chosen no Shukyo to Seiji* (Tokyo: Seibunsha, 1976), pp. 70–72.
64   Sawa, *Mika no Chosen Kirisutokyo Shi*, p. 266.
65   Kurata Masahiko, *Tennosei to Kankoku Kirisutokyo* (Tokyo: Shinkyo Shuppansha, 1991), p. 143.
66   Ibid.
67   APCC Formosa File re Shrine Question 1935–37, Armstrong to McAfee, 29 February 1936.
68   Ibid.
69   Ibid.
70   APCC Formosa File re Shrine Question 1935–37, McAfee to MacNamara, 2 March 1936.
71   APCC Formosa File re Shrine Question 1935–37. Gould to MacNamara, 11 March 1936.
72   UCC BFM Korea, Box 3 File 81, Burbridge to Armstrong, 1 March 1936.
73   UCC BFM Korea, Box 3 File 83, Black to Armstrong, 24 October 1936. In February 1936, the acting British consul general in Mukden reported that "the elevation of Confucianism, upon which the nebulous doctrine of Wangtao is claimed to be based, to the status of a national religion is proceeding according to the Kwantung Army's programme, and the spring and autumn festivals are being observed with a solemnity unknown in China proper, sheep and oxen being publicly sacrificed and partaken of by the congregations. The position of Christian missionary schools is consequently becoming more difficult." *BDFA*, vol. 15 Japan [F1051/1051/10], Knatchbull-Hugessen to Eden, 6 January 1937. Enclosure, Morland to Knatchbull-Hugessen, 22 December 1936, Annual Report on Manchukuo for 1936, p. 316.
74   APCC Formosa File re Shrine Question 1935–37, "Religious Liberty under Japanese Rule." Acting consul general Morland reported that the Scottish and Irish missions considered that "it would be impossible for them to remain and tolerate the presence of their students at sacrificial observances, even if an official declaration were made that these observances had no more than a patriotic and commemorative meaning." *BDFA*, vol. 15 Japan [F1051/1051/10], Knatchbull-Hugessen to Eden, 6 January 1937. Enclosure, Annual Report on Manchukuo for 1936, p. 316. As early as January 1936, the *Chinese Recorder* had reported that "the Japanese are also pressing for the establishment of Confucian worship. In Kirin they demanded that a Christian school send its students to a Confucian temple. The principal (a missionary) said that non-Christian children could go but that the Christians did not have to. As a result the government grant and the Japanese teacher were withdrawn and the school has been threatened with closure." *CR*, 57.1, (January 1936), p. 57.
75   APCC Formosa File re Shrine Question 1935–37, "Religious Liberty under Japanese Rule." Acting consul general Morland thought that "as the predominant official feeling, especially in the Kwantung Army, is anti-Christian the departure of the missions would be not unwelcome to the authorities." *BDFA*, vol. 15 Japan [F1051/1051/10], Knatchbull-Hugessen to Eden, 6 January 1937. Enclosure, Annual Report on Manchukuo for 1936, p. 316. See also Austin Fulton, *Through Earthquake, Wind, and Fire: Church Work and Mission in Manchuria 1867–1950: The Work of the United Presbyterian Church, the United Free Church of Scotland, the Church of Scotland, and the Presbyterian Church in Ireland with the Chinese Church in Manchuria* (Edinburgh: Saint Andrew Press, 1967), p. 93.
76   APCC Formosa File re Shrine Question 1935–37, "Religious Liberty under Japanese Rule."
77   *BDFA*, vol. 15 Japan [F1051/1051/10], Knatchbull-Hugessen to Eden, 6 January 1937. Enclosure, Annual Report on Manchukuo for 1936, p. 316.
78   UCC BFM Korea, Box 3 File 86, Scott to Armstrong, 13 December 1936.

NOTES TO CHAPTER FOUR 363

79 Ibid.
80 Ibid.
81 Quoted in MacRae, *A Tiger on Dragon Mountain*, p. 200.
82 Ibid., p. 201.
83 Ibid.
84 UCC BFM Korea, Box 3 File 25, Armstrong to MacRae, 26 February 1936.
85 UCC BFM Korea, Box 4, Armstrong to Fraser, 9 April 1938.
86 UCC BFM Korea, Box 3 File 86, Scott to Armstrong, 13 December 1936.
87 UCC BFM Korea, Box 3, Armstrong to Hooper, 12 September 1938. J. L. Hooper was the acting secretary for the Chosen mission of the Presbyterian Church in the United States.
88 Ibid.
89 UCC BFM Korea, Box 4 File 106, Underwood to Armstrong, 28 March 1939.
90 UCC BFM Korea, Box 3 File 86, Scott to Armstrong, 13 December 1936.
91 Ibid.
92 Ibid.
93 *BDFA*, vol. 12 Japan [F7866/2094/23], Lindley to Simon, 11 October 1932. Enclosure, Memorandum respecting Education in Formosa, p. 49.
94 Ibid., see Enclosure, Graves to Lindley, 29 September 1932.
95 Ibid., see Enclosure, Memorandum respecting Education in Formosa, pp. 49–50.
96 *BDFA*, vol. 15 Japan [F5146/1233/23], Clive to Eden, 29 July 1936, pp. 143–44.
97 *APPCC* 1933, p. 34.
98 *PR*, 59.1 (January 1934), p. 26.
99 *APPCC* 1935, p. 57.
100 *APPCC* 1936, p. 46.
101 Ibid., p. 47.
102 Ibid.
103 APCC Formosa File re Shrine Question 1935–37, "Mr. Mackay's Historical Statement."
104 APCC Formosa File re Shrine Question 1935–37, "Historical Statement of Events in Connection with the 'Shrine Question' as It Concerns the Tamsui Girls' School."
105 FO 371/19364, Clive to Foreign Secretary, 15 July 1935. Enclosure, Archer to Clive, 25 June 1935, memorandum on position and prospect of the British religious missions in Formosa.
106 Ibid.
107 Ibid.
108 Ibid. See also Ion, *The Cross and the Rising Sun*, vol. 2, p. 244.
109 APCC Formosa File re Shrine Question 1935–37, "Mr. Mackay's Historical Statement."
110 Ibid.
111 APCC Formosa File re Shrine Question 1935–37, "Historical Statement of Events in Connection with the 'Shrine Question' as It Concerns the Tamsui Girls' School."
112 APCC Formosa File re Shrine Question 1935–37, "Mr. Mackay's Historical Statement."
113 Ibid.
114 APCC Formosa File re Shrine Question 1935–37, "Statement by Jean Ross Mackay on the 'Shrine Question,' Written June 27, 1935."
115 Ibid.
116 Ibid.
117 Ibid.
118 APCC Formosa File re Shrine Question 1935–37, "Personal Statement by Hildur K. Hermanson, Signed June 27, 1935."
119 APCC Formosa File re Shrine Question 1935–37, "Personal Statement by Alma M. Burdick, Signed June 27, 1935."

120 APCC Formosa File re Shrine Question 1935–37, "Personal Statement by Phyllis Argall, Signed June 27, 1935."
121 Ibid.
122 APCC Formosa File re Shrine Question 1935–37, "Historical Statement of Events in Connection with the 'Shrine Question' as It Concerns the Tamsui Girls' School."
123 Ibid.
124 APCC Formosa File re Shrine Question 1935–37, "Mr. Mackay's Historical Statement."
125 APCC Formosa File re Shrine Question 1935–37, "Historical Statement of Events in Connection with the 'Shrine Question' as It Concerns the Tamsui Girls' School."
126 APCC Formosa File re Shrine Question 1935–37, "Mr. Mackay's Historical Statement."
127 *APPCC* 1937, p. 44. See also *BDFA*, vol. 15 Japan [F5696/1233/23], Clive to Eden, 25 August 1936. Enclosure, Archer to Clive, 7 July 1936, Political Report on Formosa for June Quarter, 1936, p. 157.
128 *APPCC* 1937, p. 44.
129 *BDFA*, vol. 15 Japan [F5696/1233/23], Clive to Eden, 25 August 1936. Enclosure, Political Report on Formosa for June Quarter, 1936, p. 157.
130 Ibid.
131 F0 371/2029, I. J. Thyne Henderson minute on Clive to Eden, 26 August 1936.
132 *APPCC* 1937, p. 44.
133 *BDFA*, vol. 15 Japan [F7396/1233/13], Clive to Eden, 28 October 1936. Enclosure, Archer to Clive, 3 October 1936, Political Report on Formosa, July 1–October 1, 1936, p. 222.
134 Ibid., p. 46.
135 FO 371/21043, Clive to Eden, 16 February 1937. Enclosure, His Majesty's Consul, Tamsui, Annual Report for the Year 1936.
136 FO 371/20291, Clive to Eden, 26 August 1936.
137 *APPCC* 1937, p. 44.
138 Ibid.
139 Ion, *The Cross and the Rising Sun*, vol. 2, p. 245.

CHAPTER FIVE

1 *Toyo Eiwa Jo Gakuin Hyakunen Shi*, p. 282.
2 Toyo Eiwa Jo Gakuin Nanajunen Shi Henshu Iinkai, *Toyo Eiwa Jo Gakuin Nanajunen Shi* (Tokyo: Toyo Eiwa Jo Gakuin, 1955), p. 27 [Hereafter cited as *Toyo Eiwa Jo Gakuin Nanajunen Shi*]. For Frances Gertrude Hamilton (1888–1975), see *NKRDJ*, p. 1131.
3 *Toyo Eiwa Jo Gakuin Hyakunen Shi*, p. 229.
4 Ibid.
5 *Toyo Eiwa Jo Gakuin Nanajunen Shi*, p. 27.
6 See Frances Gertrude Hamilton's report on the Toyo Eiwa Jo Gakko in "New Buildings for Three Women's Colleges," *JCQ*, 9 (1934), pp. 211–23, pp. 215–18, p. 216. See also *Toyo Eiwa Jo Gakuin Hyakunen Shi*, pp. 246–50. The Torii Zaka is close to the present Roppongi Subway Station in what is now a fashionable entertainment district of Tokyo. This school building remained in use for sixty years, until 1993, when it was demolished to make way for new buildings.
7 Hamilton, "New Buildings for Three Women's Colleges," p. 217.
8 *Toyo Eiwa Jo Gakuin Hyakunen Shi*, pp. 248–49. Howard Norman noted that the cost of the new property was $75,000, to which the alumnae contributed a third, and that the

home board paid $300,000 for the new buildings. See G. R. P. Norman and W. H. H. Norman, *One Hundred Years in Japan, 1873–1973* (Toronto: Division of World Out-Reach, United Church of Canada, 1981), p. 344.

9   Ibid. Other Christian schools had formed much earlier *zaidan hojin*, including Doshisha in Kyoto in 1900, Aoyama Gakuin in Tokyo in 1916, Kobe Jo Gakuin in Kobe in 1920, and Tohoku Gakuin in 1929. However, the mid- and late 1930s saw a rush of mission girls' schools forming *zaidan hojin*, including Heian Jo Gakuin and Fukuoka Jo Gakuin as well as the three Canadian schools. See *Yamanashi Eiwa Gakuin Hachijunen Shi*, pp. 258–59.

10   The required reserve fund was ¥30,000, but the Depression in Canada made it difficult for the WMS to meet quickly its commitment of ¥10,000. The directors of the *zaidan hojin* numbered fourteen. Seven were United Church missionaries, of whom five were WMS missionaries and the other two represented the general board. The other seven members were Japanese, of whom one represented the Japan Methodist Church, two were from the Alumnae Association of the Toyo Eiwa Jo Gakko, and the remaining four were brought in for their financial or other special knowledge. See *Toyo Eiwa Hyakunen Shi*, pp. 250–51.

11   Ibid., pp. 242–43.

12   Ibid., pp. 238–51.

13   *Toyo Eiwa Jo Gakuin Nanajunen Shi*, p. 38.

14   *Toyo Eiwa Hyakunen Shi*, p. 327. A *tsubo* is a unit of approximately thirty-six square feet.

15   Ibid.

16   Ibid., pp. 240–41.

17   Ibid., pp. 223–24.

18   UCC BFM Japan, 1926–66, Series II Reports and Minutes, Box 3 File 38, Sybil R. Courtice, "Our Educational Work in Japan," n. d. For Sybil R. Courtice (1884–1980), see *NKRDJ*, p. 526.

19   For Katherine Drake (1878–1957), see *NKRDJ*, p. 967. See also UCC WMS, Dominion Board, Missionary Biographies, Copy 1 A-C, Copy D-K, Miss Katherine Drake.

20   For Marie Melissa Staples (1889–1966), see *Toyo Eiwa Jo Gakuin Hyakunen Shi*, p. 224. See also UCC WMS, Dominion Board, Missionary Biographies, Copy L-Q, R-Z, Miss Marie Staples.

21   For Lois A. Lehman (1897–?), see *NKRDJ*, p. 1518.

22   *Toyo Eiwa Jo Gakuin Hyakunen Shi*, pp. 221–22.

23   Ibid., pp. 314–16. For Gertrud E. Kuechlick (1897–1976), see *NKRDJ*, p. 375.

24   *Toyo Eiwa Jo Gakuin Hyakunen Shi*, p. 231. For Mary Ada Robertson (1869–1950), see *NKRDJ*, pp. 1528–29.

25   *Toyo Eiwa Jo Gakuin Hyakunen Shi*, p. 316.

26   See Kuyama Yasushi, ed., *Kirisutokyo Kyoiku Shi: Shicho Hen* (Tokyo: Sobunsha, 1993), pp. 452–54.

27   *Toyo Eiwa Jo Gakuin Hyakunen Shi*, p. 317. See also pp. 312–14.

28   Ibid., pp. 317–18.

29   UCC BFM Japan, 1926–66, Series II Reports and Minutes, Box 3 File 38, Sybil R. Courtice, "Our Educational Work in Japan." The policy of replacing missionary principals with Japanese ones was by no means restricted to the Canadian WMS. Of sixty-three missionary-affiliated schools in 1932, twenty-seven had missionary principals. By 1939, only ten out of sixty-six schools had missionary principals. By 1941, there were no foreign principals. See *Yamanashi Eiwa Gakuin Hachijunen Shi*, p. 276.

30   Ibid., p. 348. Despite the Pacific War, the school went on growing until 1943, when there were 685 students in the high school and 256 in the primary school.

31   *Shizuoka Eiwa Jo Gakuin Hachijunen Shi*, p. 207.

32 Ibid., p. 267.
33 Ibid., p. 204. In 1932, the total expenditures for the school stood at ¥20,000, of which the WMS paid about ¥1,000. In 1929, the Shizuoka Prefecture educational authorities also began to give grants to private middle and high schools, and in 1932 this was a little over ¥300. See pp. 208–09.
34 Ibid., p. 289. In 1938, the WMS's contribution was ¥5,312, 27.6 percent of the total receipts.
35 UCC WMS, Dominion Board, Overseas Missions, Japan, Correspondence of Executive Secretary with Japan 1937, Box 1 [Box 73] File 9, Courtice to Taylor, 24 February 1937.
36 *Shizuoka Eiwa Jo Gakuin Hachijunen Shi*, pp. 254–56. As in the case of the Toyo Eiwa Jo Gakko, the Shizuoka Eiwa Jo Gakko's *zaidan hojin* was made up of six missionaries (four WMS, two general board) and six Japanese (two from the Alumnae Association, three from the board of directors, and one from the Japan Methodist Church). See p. 258.
37 Ibid., p. 263.
38 For Murota Tamotsu (1881–1965), see *NKRDJ*, p. 1390. See also Kirisutokyo Gakko Kyoiku Domei hen, *Nihon Kirisutokyo Kyoiku Shi: Jinbutsu Hen* (Tokyo: Sobunsha, 1977), pp. 469–70.
39 *Shizuoka Eiwa Jo Gakuin Hachijunen Shi*, p. 266.
40 Isabel Govenlock, quoted in UCC WMS, Dominion Board, Overseas Missions, Japan, Correspondence of Executive Secretary with Japan 1937, Box 1 [Box 73] File 10, Courtice to Friends at Home, 17 June 1938.
41 Ibid.
42 For Isabel Govenlock (1883–1974), see *NKRDJ*, p. 281. *Shizuoka Eiwa Jo Gakuin Hachijunen Shi*, pp. 239–41.
43 For Mary Jane Cunningham, see *NKRDJ*, p. 315. Rosemary R. Gagan has stressed Cunningham's feminist views as a reason for her recall to Canada. See Rosemary R. Gagan, *A Sensitive Independence: Canadian Methodist Women Missionaries in Canada and the Orient, 1881–1925* (Montreal: McGill-Queen's University Press, 1992), p. 78.
44 For Olivia Lindsay, see UCC WMS, Dominion Board, Missionary Biographies, Copy L-Q, R-Z, Rev. Olivia Lindsay. See also Gagan, *A Sensitive Independence*, p. 38.
45 *Shizuoka Eiwa Jo Gakuin Hachijunen Shi*, pp. 234–6.
46 Ibid., pp. 210–11. The average size of the graduating class in the sample was twenty. The other middle schools that Shizuoka Eiwa Jo Gakko was compared with included the Miyagi Girls' School thirty percent, Hokuriku Girls' School twenty-three percent, and Kobe Girls' School twenty-one percent.
47 Ibid., p. 212.
48 This was a church that despite the war between Japan and Canada, held on 19 April 1942 a commemorative service for the beginning of Davidson McDonald's work in Shizuoka. See Fukumchi Masakatsu, *Nihon Kirisutokyodan Shizuoka Kyokai Hachiju Gonen Shi* (Shizuoka: Nihon Kirisutokyodan Shizuoka Kyokai, 1959), p. 123.
49 *Shizuoka Eiwa Jo Gakuin Hachijunen Shi*, pp. 241–44.
50 *Yamanashi Eiwa Gakuin Hachijunen Shi*, p. 521.
51 Ibid., p. 259.
52 For Katherine Martha Greenbank (1891–1983), see UCC WMS, Dominion Board, Missionary Biographies, Copy 1 A-C, Copy 1 D-K, Katherine M. Greenbank. See also *NKRDJ*, p. 467; and *Yamanashi Eiwa Gakuin Hachijunen Shi*, pp. 186–91.
53 *Yamanashi Eiwa Gakuin Hachijunen Shi*, pp. 190–93.
54 Ibid., p. 240.
55 Ibid., p. 203.
56 Ibid., pp. 206-13.
57 For Amemiya Keisaku (1879–1964), see *NKRDJ*, pp. 56–57. See also *Yamanashi Eiwa*

Gakuin Hachijunen Shi, p. 202, pp. 269–75.
58 For Shinkai Eitaro (1864–1935), see *NKRDJ*, p. 691.
59 Courtice reported to Mrs. Taylor in Toronto in 1937 that the government was pressing to have the endowment for the *zaidan hojin* in 1938 owing to circumstances arising from the death of Shinkai Etaro. Courtice requested that ¥10,000, which the WMS had promised, be paid in 1938 instead of 1939. UCC WMS, Dominion Board, Overseas Missions, Japan, Correspondence of Executive Secretary with Japan 1937, Box 1 [Box 73] File 9, Courtice to Taylor, 24 February 1937; *Yamanashi Eiwa Gakuin Hachijunen Shi*, pp. 260–61, pp. 267–68. The composition of the *zaidan hojin* was similar to the ones at the Tokyo and Shizuoka schools, with eight missionary members (six from the WMS, two from the general board), one member from the Alumni Society, two representatives from the Japan Methodist Church, and four members from the board of directors.
60 For Ogata Kiyo (1907–55), see *NKRDJ*, p. 240. See also Kirisutokyo Gakko Kyoiku Domei hen, *Nihon Kirisutokyo Kyoiku Shi*, pp. 474–5.
61 The characters *eiwa* stood for English-Japanese (Anglo-Japanese). The character for *ei* was changed from *ei* (English) to *ei* (prosperity, glorious). In 1941, the Toyo Eiwa Jo Gakko in Tokyo changed its *ei* (English) to *ei* (eternity). The character *wa* remained the same, as it could be taken to refer either to the Japanese or to peace or harmony. In changing its name, the Shizuoka Eiwa Jo Gakko went the furthest, choosing in late 1940 the name Seiryo Koto Jo Gakko. The characters for *seiryo* were made up of the *shizu* (the first character of Shizuoka) and *ryo* (the character for imperial tomb). See *Shizuoka Eiwa Jo Gakuin Hachijunen Shi*, pp. 277–78.
62 See *Yamanashi Eiwa Gakuin Hachijunen Shi*, pp. 244–52.
63 Ibid., p. 284.
64 Ibid., pp. 291–94.
65 Tokyo Joshi Daigaku Gojunen Shi Hensan Iinkai, *Tokyo Joshi Daigaku Gojunen Shi* (Tokyo: Tokyo Joshi Daigaku, 1968), pp. 20–21.
66 UCC WMS, Dominion Board, Overseas Mission, Japan, Correspondence of Executive Secretary with Japan Mission 1927, 1928, Box 1 File 1, Chappell to Langford, 14 June 1927. For Constance Chappell (1892–1989), see under Benjamin Chappell, *NKRDJ*, p. 868.
67 UCC WMS, Dominion Board, Overseas Mission, Japan, Correspondence of Executive Secretary with Japan Mission 1927, 1928, Box 1 File 1, Chappell to Langford, 14 June 1927.
68 For August Karl Reischauer (1879–1971), see *NKRDJ*, p. 1481.
69 Yasui Tetsu (1870–1945) was one of the most distinguished female Japanese educators by the time that she became principal of Tokyo Union Woman's College in 1923 in succession to Nitobe Inazo. She remained principal until 1940. See *NKRDJ*, p. 1420. See also Otsuka Noyuri, "Yasui Tetsu: Joshi Koto Kyoiku no Kaitakusha," in Kirisutokyo Bunka Gakkai Hen, *Purotesutanto Jinbutsu Shi: Kindai Nihon no Bunka Keisei* (Tokyo: Yorudansha, 1990), pp. 399–420. In May 1941, when Dr. Yasui was helping at the Tokyo school during the illness of Principal Ono, Courtice wrote that "it is a wonderful help to the school to have her and she is most generous in giving her time, refusing any remuneration." UCC WMS, Dominion Board, Overseas Mission, Japan, Correspondence of Executive Secretary to Japan, Box 1 [Box 73] File 13, Courtice to Taylor, 26 May 1941.
70 For a recent study of John Leighton Stuart, see Yu-ming Shaw, *An American Missionary in China: John Leighton Stuart and Chinese-American Relations* (Cambridge: Harvard University Press, 1992).
71 Quoted in Norman and Norman, *One Hundred Years in Japan*, pp. 344–45.
72 *UCCYB* 1930, p. 150.

73 Norman and Norman, *One Hundred Years in Japan*, p. 345. For Howard Wilkinson Outerbridge (1886–1976), see *NKRDJ*, p. 17.
74 Norman and Norman, *One Hundred Years in Japan*, p. 346.
75 Ibid.
76 Soritsu Hyaku Shunen Kinen Gigyo Iinkai/Kinen Shuppan Senmon Iinkai, *Kwansei Gakuin no Hyakunen* (Osaka: Kwansei Gakuin, 1989), p. 184 [hereafter cited as *Kwansei Gakuin no Hyakunen*].
77 *UCCYB* 1928, p. 282.
78 *UCCYB* 1930, pp. 149–50.
79 *Kwansei Gakuin no Hyakunen*, p. 66.
80 *UCCYB* 1930, p. 150. The Departments of Literature and Commerce and Economics were referred to as colleges in missionary reports to denote the fact that they, together with the Department of Theology, had been recognized by the Ministry of Education as having higher specialty status as *senmon gakko*.
81 *UCCYB* 1932, p. 121.
82 *UCCYB* 1933, p. 121. The Ministry of Education had relaxed its regulations regarding institutions of higher learning gaining university status in 1918. As a result, a number of leading private schools gained university status in 1920. Among them was the most famous Christian college in Japan, Doshisha College in Kyoto, which became a university in April 1920. See Yamazumi Masami, *Nihon Kyoiku Shoshi: Kin: Gendai* (Tokyo: Iwanani Shoten, 1987), p. 96.
83 *Kwansei Gakuin no Hyakunen*, p. 80.
84 For Kikuchi Shichiro (1877–1958), see *NKRDJ*, p. 355. Kikuchi was known as being very considerate to the students and for possessing a strong Christian spirit. See *Kwansei Gakuin no Hyakunen*, p. 72.
85 *UCCYB* 1933, p. 123.
86 Kirisutokyo Kyoiku Domei Hen, *Nihon Kirisutokyo Kyoiku Shi*, p. 432.
87 *UCCYB* 1933, p. 121.
88 *Kwansei Gakuin no Hyakunen*, p. 78. For Harold Friedrich Woodsworth (1883–1939), the brother of the famous pacifist politician, see *NKRDJ*, p. 178. For Kanzaki Kiichi (1884–1959), see *NKRDJ*, p. 345.
89 There was an overlap of staff between the university and the *senmon gakko* courses. For Imada Megumi (1894–1970), see *NKRDJ*, p. 134.
90 *UCCYB* 1935, p. 123.
91 *UCCYB* 1934, p. 112.
92 Norman and Norman, *One Hundred Years in Japan*, p. 363. For Arthur Pearson McKenzie (d. 1960), the son of Daniel R. McKenzie (1861–1935), see *NKRDJ*, p. 1324.
93 *UCCYB* 1940, p. 113.
94 *UCCYB* 1934, p. 113. For Melvin Mansel Whiting (1885–1955), see *NKRDJ*, p. 1296.
95 *Kwansei Gakuin no Hyakunen*, p. 60.
96 For Hata Kanzo (1880–1957), see *NKRDJ*, p. 1115.
97 *Kwansei Gakuin no Hyakunen*, p. 82. See also Norman and Norman, *One Hundred Years in Japan*, p. 369.
98 *Kwansei Gakuin no Hyakunen*, p. 82.
99 *UCCYB* 1936, p. 93.
100 Ibid. In four years, the general board mission had been reduced from supporting twenty-two missionary families to only fifteen.
101 Ibid., p. 94.
102 *UCCYB* 1937, p. 77.
103 *UCCYB* 1939, p. 66.
104 Ibid.

105　Ibid.
106　Ibid., p. 66.
107　Ibid., p. 67.
108　*UCCYB* 1940, p. 112.
109　Ibid.
110　Ibid., p. 113.
111　*UCCYB* 1941, p. 107.
112　Ibid.
113　Ibid.
114　Ibid., pp. 107–08.
115　Ibid., p. 108.
116　Ibid.
117　Ibid.
118　Quoted in Norman and Norman, *One Hundred Years in Japan*, p. 365.
119　*Kwansei Gakuin no Hyakunen*, p. 58.
120　UCC BFM Japan 1926–66, Box 2 File 16, Minutes of FMB Council, January 1941, Report of Kobe District Conference, 8 January 1941.
121　*UCCYB* 1934, p. 111.
122　*RJ*, 15 November 1932, p. 8.
123　Kirisutokyo Gakko Kyoiku Domei hen, *Nihon Kirisutokyo Kyoiku Shi*, p. 419.
124　Norman and Norman, *One Hundred Years in Japan*, p. 362.
125　UCC BFM Japan 1926–66, Box 5, Whiting circular letter, 24 October 1937.
126　*UCCYB* 1939, p. 66.
127　*Kwansei Gakuin no Hyakunen*, p. 184.
128　See A. Hamish Ion, *The Cross and the Rising Sun: Volume 2: The British Protestant Missionary Movement in Japan, Korea, and Taiwan 1865-1945* (Waterloo: Wilfrid Laurier University Press, 1993), p. 215.
129　UCC BFM Japan 1926–66, Box 5 File 90, Outerbridge to Arnup, 18 May 1938. Enclosure, answers of Mr. Hori.
130　Ibid.
131　Ibid.
132　Ibid.
133　Ibid.
134　Ibid.
135　Ibid. See also *UCCYB* 1939, p. 66.
136　See Ion, *The Cross and the Rising Sun*, vol. 2, p. 215.
137　UCC BFM Japan 1926–66, Box 2 File 16, Report of Kobe District Conference, 8 January 1941.
138　Ibid.
139　Ibid.
140　Ibid.
141　*Kwansei Gakuin no Hyakunen*, p. 92.
142　Ibid., p. 184.
143　UCC BFM Japan 1926–66, Box 3 File 38, Kwansei Gakuin Board of Directors, President's Report for 1939–40, 7 May 1940.

CHAPTER SIX

1. *UCCYB* 1933, p. 120.
2. *UCCYB* 1936, p. 34.
3. *UCCYB* 1935, pp. 122-23.
4. Ibid., p. 123.
5. *UCCYB* 1934, p. 113.
6. *UCCYB* 1941, p. 108.
7. UCC BFM Japan 1926–66, Box 2 File 16, Report of Kobe District Conference, 8 January 1941.
8. Ibid.
9. UCC BFM Japan 1926–66, Box 2 File 24, Report of the Acting Principal to the Canadian Academy Council, 20 February 1941.
10. Ibid.
11. UCC BFM Japan 1926–66, Box 2 File 24, Mr. S. Otani's Report to the Canadian Academy Committee Meeting of 4 September 1941.
12. Ibid.
13. Ibid.
14. See A. Hamish Ion, *The Cross and the Rising Sun: Volume 1: The Canadian Protestant Missionary Movement in the Japanese Empire 1872–1931*, (Waterloo: Wilfrid Laurier University Press, 1990), p. 135. See also *NKRDJ*, p. 366, p. 481. For A. F. Chappell (?–1945) and Mori Kenji (1855–1914), see *NKRDJ*, p. 868, p. 1408.
15. *Nippon Seikokai Hyakunen Shi*, p. 295.
16. MSCEC Japan Files, Japan Mission Conference Minutes, GS75-103 Series 3-2 Box 63A, Meeting of All Foreign Missionaries in Mid-Japan, 3 November 1937. See also *Nippon Seikokai Hyakunen Shi*, p. 294.
17. MSCEC Japan Files, Japan Mission Conference Minutes, GS75-103 Series 3-2 Box 63A. In the 20 November 1940 minutes of the Personal Relations Committee, it was carried that it should be recommended to the WA that a yearly donation of $200 be made to the Gifu Kumoin as a suitable expression of the mission's continued fellowship with the Diocese of Mid-Japan.
18. MSCEC Japan Files, Miss N. F. Bowman, GS75-103 Series 3-3 Box 85, Bowman Annual Report 1938–39. Bowman mentioned that the three kindergartens in Nagoya of which she had been principal had a combined enrolment of 278 in 1939.
19. Ibid.
20. Ibid.
21. MSCEC Japan Files, V. C. Spencer, GS75-103 Series 3-3 Box 87 File 6, V. C. Spencer Annual Report 1939.
22. MSCEC Japan Files, Miss N. F. Bowman, GS75-103 Series 3-3 Box 85, Bowman Annual Report 1938–39.
23. MSCEC Japan Files, V. C. Spencer, GS75-103 Series 3-3 Box 87 File 6, V. C. Spencer Annual Report 1939.
24. MSCEC Japan Files, P. S. C. Powles, GS75-103 Series 3-3 Box 86, Powles to Dixon, 2 March 1939.
25. MSCEC Japan Files, Adelaide Moss, GS75-103 Series 3-3 Box 85, Takata, Japan, WA Report for 1939.
26. Ibid.
27. MSCEC Japan Files, Marie Foerstel, GS75-103 Series 3-3 Box 85 File 7, Marie Foerstel

Annual Report 1939.
28 Ibid.
29 Ibid.
30 MSCEC Japan Files, V. C. Spencer, GS75-103 Series 3-3 Box 87 File 6, Spencer Annual Report 1939.
31 Ibid.
32 Ibid.
33 MSCEC Japan Files, M. Clench, GS75-103 Series 3-3 Box 85, Clench to Spencer, 27 March 1939.
34 MSCEC Japan Files, M. Clench, GS75-103 Series 3-3 Box 85, Clench to Spencer, 1 May 1939.
35 MSCEC Japan Files, Helen Bailey, GS75-103 Series 3-3 Box 85, Bailey Annual Report 1939.
36 MSCEC Japan Files, Helen Bailey, GS75-103 Series 3-3 Box 85, Spencer to Bailey, 21 February 1940.
37 MSCEC Japan Files, Helen Bailey, GS75-103 Series 3-3 Box 85, Bailey Annual Report 1939.
38 MSCEC Japan Files, Helen Bailey, GS75-103 Series 3-3 Box 85, Bailey to Spencer, 23 February 1940.
39 Ibid.
40 MSCEC Japan Files, Helen Bailey, GS75-103 Series 3-3 Box 85, Bailey to Spencer, [received] 1 April 1940.
41 MSCEC Japan Files, Miss N. F. Bowman, GS75-103 Series 3-3 Box 85, Bowman Annual Report 1938–39.
42 MSCEC Japan Files, Helen Bailey, GS75-103 Series 3-3 Box 85, Spencer to Bailey, 21 February 1940.
43 See A. Hamish Ion, *The Cross and the Rising Sun: Volume 2: The British Protestant Missionary Movement in Japan, Korea, and Taiwan 1865-1945* (Waterloo: Wilfrid Laurier University Press, 1993), pp. 177–79.
44 *Nippon Seikokai Hyakunen Shi*, p. 300.
45 MSCEC Japan Files, J. G. Waller, GS75-103 Series 3-2 Box 65, Waller to Gould, 10 October 1935.
46 MSCEC Japan Files, Richard Start, GS75-103 Series 3-3 Box 88 File 2, Start to Gould, 15 March 1937.
47 Ibid. Because they were paid directly through the mission, Start naturally did not include his own salary or those of the missionary chaplain and the WA missionary in his budget estimates. However, the salaries of the Japanese doctors, nurses, chaplain, and other staff were included.
48 Ibid.
49 MSCEC Japan Files, P. S. C. Powles, GS75-103 Series 3-3 Box 86, Powles to Gould, 25 February 1938.
50 MSCEC Japan Files, P. S. C. Powles, GS75-103 Series 3-3 Box 86, Powles to Dixon, 30 December 1939.
51 Ibid.
52 Ibid.
53 Ibid.
54 MSCEC Japan Files, Richard Start, GS75-103 Series 3-3 Box 88 File 2, Start to Dixon, 14 December 1939.
55 Ibid.
56 Ibid.
57 Ibid.

58 MSCEC Japan Files, Richard Start, GS75-103 Series 3-3 File 2, Start to Dixon, 28 December 1939.
59 Ibid.
60 MSCEC Japan Files, Richard Start, GS75-103 Series 3-3 File 2, Start to Dixon, 16 November 1940.
61 Ibid.
62 MSCEC Japan Files, P. S. C. Powles, GS75-103 Series 3-3 Box 86, Powles to Dixon, 1 November 1940.
63 MSCEC Japan Files, P. S. C. Powles, GS75-103 Series 3-3 Box 86, Powles to Dixon, 28 January 1941. Even so, as late as 1939 the Canadian Presbyterians estimated that there were 200,000 Koreans in Osaka alone. See *APPCC* 1940, p. 85.
64 *APPCC* 1938, pp. 55–56.
65 *APPCC* 1938, p. 53.
66 Ibid.
67 *APPCC* 1939, p. 45. The Canadian Presbyterians maintained six nursery schools in 1938 with a total of 215 students. See p. 48.
68 *APPCC* 1940, p. 55.
69 Ibid., p. 84.
70 Ibid., p. 53.

CHAPTER SEVEN

1 UCC BFM Korea, Box 4 File 87, Covering Letter Explaining the Following Resolution Adopted at Council Meeting July 1937: "That we adopt as our definite policy for the future the continuance of the present five stations," signed W. A. Burbridge.
2 UCC BFM Korea, Box 4 File 92, Comparative Statistics 1899 to 1937. In 1928, there were 443 students in mission high schools, rising to 1,050 in 1933. The number of pupils in mission primary schools rose from 3,263 in 1928 to 3,709 in 1933. Based on the exchange rate of one dollar to two yen, the contribution in dollars of the Korean Church to education rose from $17,790 in 1928 to $18,519 in 1933.
3 Ibid. The size of the total Christian community and the number of total baptized Christians rose from 17,426 and 7,794 in 1928 to 22,813 and 8,548 in 1933 and to 27,909 and 9,434 in 1937. The numbers associated with the Canadians made up less than ten percent of the total Christian community associated with the Presbyterian Church of Korea in 1937, which numbered 356,281.
4 UCC BFM Korea, Box 4 File 89, Black to friends, 13 July 1937.
5 UCC BFM Korea, Box 4 File 87, Covering Letter. In Wonsan, the one male missionary, Fraser, was going on furlough for a year in 1937. There had not been a male missionary in Sungjin since the departure of Dr. Grierson in 1935. The number of missionaries—men and women—had fallen from forty-eight in the decade from 1923 to 1933 to forty-four in 1937. See UCC BFM Korea, Box 4 File 92, Comparative Statistics 1899 to 1937. The number of missionaries associated with the Foreign Mission Board stood at twenty-six in 1937. See UCC BFM Korea, Box 12 File 242, Diagram Illustrating Increase in Foreign Mission Staff from 1927 to 1939.
6 UCC BFM Korea, Box 4 File 90, Scott to Armstrong, 13 May 1937.
7 *UCCYB* 1937, pp. 79–80.
8 Ibid., p. 80.
9 UCC BFM Korea, Box 4, Knechtel to Armstrong, 3 January 1938.

NOTES TO CHAPTER SEVEN 373

10 Ibid.
11 UCC BFM Korea, Box 4 File 90, Scott to Armstrong, 23 June 1938.
12 UCC BFM Korea, Box 4 File 96, Bruce to Armstrong, 9 October 1938.
13 UCC BFM Korea, Box 4, Black to Armstrong, 14 June 1939.
14 Ibid.
15 Ibid.
16 Ibid.
17 Ibid.
18 Ibid.
19 UCC BFM Korea, Box 4, Station Report 1939–40, Lungchingtsun, Manchukuo.
20 Ibid.
21 Ibid.
22 Ibid.
23 Ibid.
24 Ibid.
25 Ibid.
26 UCC BFM Korea, Box 4 File 112, Scott to Armstrong, 29 November 1940.
27 Ibid.
28 Ibid.
29 Ibid.
30 Ibid.
31 UCC BFM Korea, Box 4 File 1942 Aug. [misfiled in Box 4, no file number except pencil word *food*], Report of the Interim Committee of the Korean Mission of the United Church of Canada, August 1942.
32 Ibid.
33 Ibid. The Canadians preferred to have the Presbytery *zaidan hojin* named as a founder.
34 See Charles August Sauer, *Methodists in Korea 1930-1960* (Seoul: Christian Literature Society, 1973), pp. 60–61.
35 UCC BFM Korea, Box 4 File 1942 Aug. Report of the Interim Committee.
36 UCC BFM Korea, Box 4 File 112, Scott to Armstrong, 29 November 1940.
37 UCC BFM Korea, Box 4 File 1942 Aug. Report of the Interim Committee.
38 Ibid.
39 Ibid.
40 UCC BFM Korea, Box 5 Korea 1945, Fraser to Young, 6 July 1945. See also UCC BFM Korea, Box 5 Korea 1945, Youn and Han to Board of Foreign Missions, Presbyterian Church, 1 October 1945.
41 UCC BFM Korea, Box 5 Korea 1945, Fraser to Young, 6 July 1945.
42 *APPCC* 1937, p. 39.
43 Ibid.
44 Ibid.
45 Ibid. In 1936, the Goforth Evangelistic Fund turned $14,150.63 (in Manchurian currency) into the mission treasury. In 1937, the fund put in $12,000 (in Manchurian currency) to the mission. The Goforth Evangelistic Fund Association received donations from supporters in the United States, Canada, England, Japan, China, Manchuria, and Hong Kong. In 1936, the largest amount came from supporters in the United States. See *APPCC* 1937, p. 40. The salaries of missionaries were paid by the Canadian Presbyterian Church.
46 *APPCC* 1938, p. 38. In regard to the educational qualifications of the Chinese workers, it was recorded in 1937 that, out of a total of 76, 10 were theological graduates, 9 Bible school graduates, 2 high school graduates, 7 lower high school graduates, 14 primary school graduates (high school entrance), and 28 not up to high school entrance standard. See *APPCC* 1938, p. 37. In regard to how long these workers had been Christians 8 had

been baptised as children, 10 baptised 20 or more years earlier, 9 baptised from 10 to 19 years earlier, 24 baptised from 5 to 9 years before, and 25 baptised from 3 to 4 years before. See *APPCC* 1938, p. 38.
47   Ibid., p. 38.
48   *APPCC* 1939, p. 30.
49   Ibid., p. 32.
50   *PR*, 66.8 (August 1941), p. 228.
51   Ibid., p. 230.
52   Florence J. Murray, *At the Foot of Dragon Hill* (New York: E. P. Dutton, 1975), p. 27.
53   Ibid. See also Ruth Compton Brouwer, "Home Lessons, Foreign Tests: The Background and First Missionary Term of Florence Murray, Maritime Doctor in Korea," *Journal of the CHA*, new series, 6 (1995), pp. 103–38, p. 117.
54   Murray, *At the Foot of Dragon Hill*, p. 42.
55   Brouwer, "Home Lessons, Foreign Tests," p. 117.
56   Ibid.
57   Murray, *At the Foot of Dragon Hill*, p. 130.
58   Ibid., p. 12.
59   Ibid., pp. 162–64.
60   Ibid., p. 42.
61   Ibid., p. 207.
62   Ibid., p. 208.
63   *UCCYB* 1939, p. 70.
64   *UCCYB* 1941, p. 110.
65   *FS*, 21 January 1937, p. 1 (33), p. 6 (38).
66   Hollington K. Tong, *Christianity in Taiwan: A History* (Taipeh: China Post, 1972), pp. 73–74. This was seen in the appointment of Uemura Tamaki, the daughter of the famous minister Uemura Masahisa, as principal of the English Presbyterian girls' school in Tainan during 1937.
67   *FS*, 21 January 1937, p. 6 (38).
68   *PR*, 62.7 (July 1937), p. 212.
69   *PR*, 60.10 (October 1935), p. 311.
70   *PR*, 62.3 (March 1937), p. 83. At this stage, only nineteen or twenty churches out of seventy-eight churches or preaching stations were self-supporting. By July 1937, the figure of fifteen years to become self-supporting had been extended to twenty. The plan was to reduce the grant from the Canadian Presbyterians to the Taiwanese Church from its current level of some $10,000 by $2,500 every five years until it completely disappeared. *PR*, 62.7 (July 1937), p. 212.
71   *PR*, 64.12 (December 1939), pp. 370–71.
72   *PR*, 62.12 (December 1937), pp. 369–70.
73   Ibid., p. 370.
74   *APPCC* 1938, p. 41.
75   Ibid., p. 42.
76   *BDFA*, Japan vol. 15 [F 6996/6182/23], Clive to Eden, 17 October 1936. Enclosure, Archer to Kobayashi, 13 October 1936, pp. 202–03. See also *BDFA*, Japan vol. 15 [F 2090/147/23], Clive to Eden, 12 April 1937, pp. 420–21. The Japanese foreign ministry officially regretted that the unpleasant incident at Keelung had ever occurred, and the governor general of Taiwan reprimanded the offending police officer for improper conduct.
77   *BDFA*, Japan vol. 18[F 2030/2030/23], Craigie to Halifax, 31 December 1938. Enclosure, Archer to Craigie, 22 December 1938, p. 75.
78   Ibid., p. 76.

79 *APPCC* 1939, p. 37.
80 *BDFA*, Japan vol. 18 [F 2030/2030/23], Craigie to Halifax, 31 December 1938. Enclosure, Archer to Craigie, 22 December 1938, p. 76.
81 Ibid., p. 75.
82 Statistics show the number of in-patients and major operations as 1936: 1,116 and 177;1937: 1,410 and 465; 1938: 1,506 and 592; 1939: 1,256 and no figure. See *APPCC* 1937, p. 50; *APPCC* 1938, p. 49; *APPCC* 1939, p. 38; and *APPCC* 1940, p. 44.
83 *APPCC* 1937, p. 49.
84 *APPCC* 1941, p. 49.
85 Ibid., pp. 49–50.
86 *PR*, 64.9 (December 1939), p. 276.
87 *PR*, 65.9 (September 1940), p. 278.
88 Ibid., pp. 278–79.
89 *PR*, 59.5 (May 1934), p. 149.
90 *PR*, 55.10 (October 1930), p. 307.
91 *PR*, 62.5 (May 1937), p. 150.
92 *APPCC* 1937, pp. 52-3,
93 *PR*, 62.5 (May 1937), p. 150.
94 *PR*, 66.5 (May 1941), pp. 147–48.
95 *PR*, 59.5 (May 1934), pp. 149–50.
96 *PR*, 64.6 (June 1939), p. 170.
97 *APPCC* 1939, p. 30.
98 *APPCC* 1937, p. 51.
99 *PR*, 62.7 (July 1937), p. 211.
100 *PR*, 66.5 (May 1941), p. 101.
101 *APPCC* 1941, p. 52.
102 Ibid.
103 Ibid. Importantly, for medical and leper work; Mathew 10.8, King James version, states: "heal the sick, cleanse the lepers, raise the dead, cast out devils; freely ye have received, freely give."
104 *PR*, 66.5 (May 1941), p. 148.
105 Ibid.

CHAPTER EIGHT

1 Among these was the standard Japanese account of the early Canadian connection with the Japan Methodist Church: Kuranaga Takashi, *Kanada Mesojisuto Nihon Dendo Gaishi* (Tokyo: Kanada Godo Kyokai Senkyoshika, 1937). Kuranaga also wrote a biography of Hiraiwa Yoshiyasu, the convert of George Cochran who later became bishop of the Japan Methodist Church: Kuranaga Takashi, *Hiraiwa Yoshiyasu den* (Tokyo: Kyobunkan, 1938). In his own right, Kuranaga was an example of a long-serving pastor who remained loyal to Canadian Methodist missionaries who had been his teachers. For Kuranaga Takashi (1867–1949), see *NKRDJ*, p. 461. There were also local histories written in the late 1930s that paid tribute to the work of early Canadian missionaries. Nihon Mesojisuto Shitaya Kyokai rokujinen shi hensan iinkai shusai, *Nihon Mesojisuto Shitaya Kyokai rokujunen shi* (Tokyo: Rekishi hensan iinkai, 1939), emphasizes the role played by George Meacham in the founding of the church. Shizuoka Mesojisuto Kyokai rokujunen shi hensan iinkai, *Shizuoka Mesojisuto Kyokai rokujunen*

shi (Shizuoka: Shizuoka Mesojisuto Kyokai, 1937), remains one of the most detailed accounts of Davidson McDonald and the formation of the Shizuoka Christian Band.

2. For a study of the contribution of one British Anglican missionary, Walter Weston, to the development of mountaineering as a popular sport in Japan, see A. H. Ion, "Mountain High and Valley Low: Walter Weston (1861–1940) and Japan," in Sir Hugh Cortazzi and Gordon Daniels, eds., *Britain and Japan 1859–1991: Themes and Personalities* (London: Routledge, 1991), pp. 94–106.

3. A tenuous claim can be made for Canadian participation in the introduction of baseball into Korea. James Scarth Gale, one of the early Canadian missionaries in Korea, includes in his interesting novel of missionary life in 1890s Korea a description of one of the first baseball games in the peninsula in which one of the fictional players is a thinly disguised William J. McKenzie, the first missionary from Canada in Korea. See James Scarth Gale, *The Vanguard* (New York: Fleming H. Revell, 1904).

4. A number of missionary children did follow their parents into the mission field; among them were R. D. M. Shaw (son of Archdeacon A. C. Shaw, a Canadian who was the pioneer SPG missionary in Japan); A. P. McKenzie (son of D. R. McKenzie, the long-time secretary-treasurer of the United Church mission in Japan); Wilfrid Waller (son of John Waller, the Canadian Anglican missionary in Nagano); and Howard Norman (son of Dan Norman, the United Church missionary in Nagano). After World War II, Cyril H. Powles (son of P. S. C. Powles, the Canadian Anglican missionary in Takata) followed in his father's footsteps to become a Canadian Anglican missionary in Japan.

5. See A. Hamish Ion, *The Cross and the Rising Sun: Volume 1: The Canadian Protestant Missionary Movement in the Japanese Empire, 1872–1931* (Waterloo: Wilfrid Laurier University Press, 1990), p. 106.

6. For a description of the life of the Dan Norman family in Nagano, see ibid., pp. 104–06. See also W. Howard Norman, *Nagano no Noruman*, H. Hirabayashi, trans. (Tokyo: Fukuinkan, 1965).

7. Edwin O. Reischauer, *My Life between Japan and America* (Tokyo: John Weatherhill, 1986), especially, pp. 20–27.

8. This information is found in John Holmes, "Shigeru," seventeen-page typescript in the possession of the author.

9. Ibid., p. 5.

10. Ibid., p. 4.

11. See John Holmes, "Eine Kleine Nachtmusik," p. 3, six-page typescript in the possession of the author.

12. See John Holmes, "Fire," p. 2, three-page typescript in the possession of the author.

13. Ibid., pp. 2–4. The *amma* profession was reserved for the blind, who usually plied their trade after dark and made house calls.

14. See Holmes, "Shigeru," pp. 4–5.

15. Ibid., p. 6.

16. Ibid.

17. Ibid.

18. Ibid., pp. 6–7.

19. Ibid., p. 7.

20. J. W. Holmes [on Dan Norman] to author, n. d. In the possession of the author.

21. Ibid.

22. See John Holmes, "And Some Have Greatness Thrust upon Them," three-page typescript in the possession of the author.

23. See John Holmes, "Hero Worship," three-page typescript in the possession of the author.

24. See John Holmes, "Sous Les Toits de Paris," p. 1, five-page typescript in the possession

25 Ibid., p. 2.
26 See Holmes, "Shigeru," pp. 16–17.
27 Stuart Robert Elliot, *Scarlet to Green: A History of Intelligence in the Canadian Army 1903–1963* (Toronto: Canadian Intelligence and Security Association, 1981), p. 666.
28 UCC G. R. P. Norman and W. H. H. Norman Personal Papers [hereafter cited as Norman Papers], Box 1 File 8, Howie to Dr. and Mrs. Roberts, 2 March 1934.
29 Ibid.
30 Ibid.
31 Ibid.
32 For Harper H. Coates (1865–1934), see *NKRDJ*, pp. 524-25.
33 Norman Papers, Box 1 File 7, Gwen to Mamsie and Dadsie, 8 February 1937.
34 Norman Papers, Box 1 File 8, Gwen to Pegs, 18 March 1938. She wrote: "the more books that I read about the upbringing of children the more pathetic do I appear to myself. What I want to know is how do other people do it. I plan to do this and that with the children but there never seems to be any time."
35 Norman Papers, Box 1 File 7, Gwen to Mamsie and Dadsie, 8 February 1937.
36 Ibid.
37 Ibid.
38 Norman Personal Papers, Box 1 File 8, Gwen to Pegs, 18 March 1938.
39 *The Seven Pillars of Wisdom*, T. E. Lawrence's account of Arab revolt and his part in it, was first published in a limited edition for private circulation in 1927. It was only in 1935, the year of Lawrence's death, that it was made available for the general public.
40 Norman Papers, Box 1 File 8, Gwen to Pegs, 18 March 1938.
41 Ibid.
42 MSCEC Japan Files, H. G. Watts, GS75-103 Series 3-3 Box 88 File 4, Wodehouse to Dixon, 3 April 1939.
43 Ibid.
44 Ibid.
45 Ibid.
46 MSCEC Japan Files, Victor Spencer, GS75-103 Series 3-3 Box 88 File 1, Spencer to Dixon, 29 June 1940.
47 MSCEC Japan Files, H. G. Watts, GS75-103 Series 3-3 Box 88 File 4, Watts to Spencer, 14 October 1940.
48 MSCEC Japan Files, H. G. Watts GS75-103 Series 3-3 Box 88 File 4, Watts to Dixon, 7 December 1940.
49 Ronald Watts went on to become a distinguished political scientist and university administrator. While Watts was principal of Queen's University at Kingston during the 1980s, two other Japan mish kids, sons of Dan Norman and Percy Powles respectively, were also members of that university's faculty.
50 For John Gage Waller (1863–1945), see *NKRDJ*, pp. 167–68.
51 MSCEC Japan Files, J. G. Waller, GS75-103 Series 3-2 Box 65, Waller to Gould, 10 October 1935.
52 MSCEC Japan Files, Victor Spencer, GS75-103 Series 3-2 Box 65, Spencer to Gould, 19 August 1936.
53 Ibid.
54 A son had been killed in World War I, and another had died in Japan.
55 MSCEC Japan Files, H. G. Watts, GS75-103 Series 3-3 Box 88 File 4, Spencer to Watts, 7 November 1940.
56 MSCEC Japan Files, P. S. C. Powles, GS75-103 Series 3-3 Box 86, Powles to Spencer,

16 January 1941.
57 Mrs. Coates was the widow of Harper Coates, the veteran Canadian Methodist missionary who had served for many years in Hamamatsu. Mrs. Coates remained in Japan until her death in the last months of the Pacific War.
58 MSCEC Japan Files, J. G. Waller, GS75-103 Series 3-3 Box 88 File 3, Lucy A. Waller to Dixon, 23 March 1945.
59 MSCEC Japan Files, P. S. C. Powles, GS75-103 Series 3-3 Box 86, Powles to Dixon, 25 February 1938.
60 MSCEC Japan Files, P. S. C. Powles, GS75-103 Series 3-3 Box 86, Powles to Dixon, 30 December 1939.
61 Ibid.
62 MSCEC Japan Files, P. S. C. Powles, GS75-103 Series 3-3 Box 86, Powles to Dixon, 25 Februrary 1938.
63 MSCEC Japan Files, P. S. C. Powles, GS75-103 Series 3-3 Box 86, Powles to Dixon, 2 November 1940.
64 MSCEC Japan Files, P. S. C. Powles, GS75-103 Series 3-3 Box 86, Powles to Dixon, 30 December 1939.
65 Ibid.
66 MSCEC Japan Files, P. S. C. Powles, GS75-103 Series 3-3 Box 86, Powles to Dixon, 12 February 1941.
67 Ibid.
68 *APPCC* 1938, p. 33.
69 Florence Murray, *At the Foot of Dragon Hill* (New York: E. P. Dutton, 1975), p. 20. In her account of her father's life in Korea, Helen Fraser MacRae includes a photograph dated 1912 that shows a young Douglas Young petting a frozen Siberian tiger with two young MacRaes looking on. See Helen Fraser MacRae, *A Tiger on Dragon Mountain: The Life of Rev. Duncan M. MacRae, D. D.*, ed. Ross Penner and Janice Penner (Charlottetown: A. James Haslam, QC, 1993), photograph between pp. 150–51. Obviously, wild animals posed some danger.
70 Murray, *At the Foot of Dragon Hill*, p. 7.
71 Ibid., p. 8.
72 Ibid.
73 Ibid., p. 9.
74 Ibid., p. 150.
75 Ibid., p. 155.
76 Ibid., p. 157.
77 Peter Fleming, *One's Company: A Journey to China Made by the Author in 1933* (Harmondsworth: Penguin Books, 1956), p. 180.
78 At Wonsan Beach, there were cottages in a cool pine forest, a sandy beach, and the sea. See Ion, *The Cross and the Rising Sun*, vol. 1, p. 109.
79 Rosalind Goforth, *Goforth of China* (Minneapolis: Dimension Books, n. d.), p. 311.
80 Fleming, *One's Company*, p. 184.
81 Murray, *At the Foot of Dragon Hill*, p. 54. For those like Murray and other medical missionaries, who did not stop for the summer, going to Wonsan Beach for the annual mission meeting might well have been an unwanted imposition on their time and energy.
82 MacRae, *A Tiger on Dragon Mountain*, p. 182.
83 Murray, *At the Foot of Dragon Hill*, p. 228. Murray also wrote that, when she and her friends were at Whajingo Beach in July 1941, they saw Japanese ships going north day and night loaded, she supposed, with troops and war supplies. She later learned that the movement of troops was due to a clash with Russia along the border, in which Japan took

many casualties.
84 Ibid., p. 30. Mrs. Nadarov was the wife of the former imperial Russian consul at Kookjaga; she was friendly with Canadian missionaries at Lungchingtsun.
85 Ibid.
86 The Chinese congregation was not a part of the Canadian mission, which was solely directed toward Koreans, but associated with the Irish Presbyterian mission in Manchuria. However, because Martin could speak Chinese, he was undoubtedly well known to this congregation.
87 Ruth Compton Brouwer, " Beyond 'Women's Work for Women:' Dr. Florence Murray and the Practice and Teaching of Western Medicine in Korea, 1921–1950," unpublished thirty-eight-page typescript in the possession of the author, p. 36.
88 Ruth Compton Brouwer, "Home Lessons, Foreign Tests: The Background and First Missionary Term of Florence Murray, Maritime Doctor in Korea," *Journal of the CHA*, new series, 6 (1995), p. 120.
89 Murray does not provide full names for either Dr. Koh or Elder Lee. Without a doubt, Elder Lee was Yi Man-ok, who had been associated with the Canadian mission in Hamheung from 1900 and had a son, Alexander Lee (Yi Choon-chul), who was a doctor. It is reasonable to suggest that Dr. Koh was Dr. Mo Hak-pok. See MacRae, *A Tiger on Dragon Mountain*, p. 80, p. 99, p. 148, pp. 220–21.
90 Brouwer, "Home Lessons, Foreign Tests," p. 121.
91 Murray, *At the Foot of Dragon Hill*, p. 230.
92 Ibid., pp. 209–10.

CHAPTER NINE

1 See Nitobe Inazo, *Japan: Some Phases of Her Problems and Development* (London: Ernest Benn, 1931), p. 367.
2 *UCCYB* 1936, p. 91.
3 Ibid.
4 UCC BFM Japan 1926–66, Box 4 File 75, Norman to Arnup, 19 January 1936.
5 Muto Takeshi, "The Christian Message in Relation to Japanese Thought—Backgrounds," enclosure in UCC BFM Japan 1926–66, Hennigar to Arnup, 31 January 1936. For Muto Takeshi (1893–1974), see *NKRDJ*, pp. 1383-84.
6 Ibid.
7 Ibid.
8 For a detailed account of the 26 February 1936 Incident, see B. A. Shillony, *Revolt in Japan: The Young Officers and the February 26, 1936 Incident* (Princeton: Princeton University Press, 1973).
9 UCC BFM Japan 1926–66, Box 4, Hennigar to Friends, 29 February 1936.
10 Ibid.
11 Ibid.
12 Ibid.
13 UCC BFM Japan 1926–66, Box 4 File 75, Norman to Arnup, 28 March 1936.
14 UCC BFM Japan 1926–66, Box 4, Hennigar to Arnup, 12 May 1936.
15 Ibid. For a brief description of the impact of the assassination of General Nagata of the Military Affairs Bureau on political and military affairs in Japan, see Janet Hunter, *The Emergence of Modern Japan: An Introductory History since 1853* (London: Longman, 1989), pp. 277–78.

16. UCC BFM Japan, Box 4 File 81, Outerbridge to Arnup, 2 June 1937.
17. UCC BFM Japan, Box 4 File 81, Outerbridge to Arnup, 30 April 1937. Enclosure, statement of Chiang Kai-shek.
18. For a brief synopsis of the Sian incident, see Immanuel C. Y. Hsu, *The Rise of Modern China*, 2nd ed. (New York: Oxford University Press, 1975), pp. 677–79.
19. UCC BFM Japan, Box 4 File 81, Outerbridge to Arnup, 30 April 1937. Enclosure, statement of Chiang Kai-shek.
20. UCC BFM Japan, Box 4 File 81, Outerbridge to Arnup, 14 July 1937.
21. UCC BFM Japan, Box 4 File 81, Outerbridge to Arnup, 11 August 1937.
22. UCC BFM Japan, Box 4 File 81, Arnup to Outerbridge, 30 August 1937.
23. UCC BFM Japan, Box 4 File 81, Outerbridge to Arnup, 6 September 1937.
24. Ibid.
25. UCC BFM Japan, Box 4 File 81, Outerbridge to Arnup, 22 September 1937.
26. Ibid.
27. Ibid.
28. Ibid.
29. Ibid.
30. Ibid.
31. Ibid.
32. UCC BFM Japan, Box 4 File 81, Outerbridge to Arnup, 14 October 1937.
33. Ibid. Matsuoka Yosuke (1880–1946) was at this time the president of the South Manchurian Railway Company and a cabinet adviser. In 1940, he would become foreign minister in the second Konoe cabinet.
34. UCC BFM Japan, Box 5 File 90, Outerbridge to Arnup, 14 January 1938.
35. UCC BFM Japan, Box 5 File 90, Outerbridge to Arnup, 25 January 1938.
36. Ibid.
37. Ibid.
38. Ibid.
39. Ibid.
40. Ibid.
41. UCC BFM Japan 1926–66, Whiting, Circular Letter Extracts, 24 October 1937.
42. UCC BFM Japan, Box 5 File 91, Stone to Friends in Canada, 4 June 1938.
43. UCC WMS Dominion Board, Overseas Mission, Japan, Correspondence of Executive Secretary to Japan Mission 1938, Courtice to Taylor, 17 June 1938.
44. Ibid.
45. Ibid.
46. UCC BFM Japan, Box 5 File 91, Hennigar to Arnup, 11 February 1938.
47. Ibid.
48. UCC BFM Japan 1926–66, Box 5, Outerbridge to Arnup, 11 February 1938.
49. UCC BFM Japan 1926–66, Box 5 File 91, Hennigar to Arnup, 11 February 1938. The above comment was added in a postscript dated 18 February 1938. Hennigar sent his letter to Arnup via Miss Hamilton, the WMS missionary, who was sailing on February 19 for Los Angeles. Because the letter would not be censored by the Japanese, as normal post often was, Hennigar could be candid in his opinions.
50. UCC BFM Japan, Box 5 File 98, Whiting to the Young People of the Elgin Presbytery, 2 January 1939.
51. Ibid.
52. UCC BFM Japan, Box 5 File 97, Albright to Arnup, 28 June 1939.
53. UCC BFM Korea, Box 4 File 102, Black to Armstrong, 14 June 1939.
54. Ibid.

NOTES TO CHAPTER NINE 381

55 UCC BFM Japan, Box 5 File 97, Albright to Arnup, 28 June 1939. Albright's reference to an undeclared war in Mongolia is clearly to the major battle between Soviet and Japanese forces at Nomonohan.
56 Ibid.
57 UCC BFM Japan, Box 5 File 97, Albright to Arnup, 10 July 1939. Changkufeng Hill was the site of a battle in 1938 between Japanese and Soviet forces on the Manchurian-Siberian border close to the Korean frontier. The Japanese claimed victory.
58 UCC BFM Japan, Box 5 File 97, Albright to Arnup, 10 July 1939.
59 Ibid.
60 Ibid.
61 Ibid.
62 UCC BFM Japan, Box 5 File 99, Hennigar to Arnup, 13 July 1939.
63 Ibid. At the time that Hennigar was writing, the Vancouver team had played four games and, surprisingly perhaps, had lost two of them. However, amateur sports leagues were highly developed in Japan. It is clear from the *Japan Advertiser*, the leading independent English-language daily newspaper in Tokyo, that basketball and other Western sports including soccer, rugby, American football, and baseball were popular not only among expatriates but also within the Japanese university and school community. Tokyo was to have been the venue for the 1940 Olympic Games.
64 UCC BFM Japan, Box 5 File 99, Hennigar to Arnup, 13 July 1939.
65 UCC BFM Japan, Box 5 File 97, Outerbridge to Arnup, 19 December 1939.
66 UCC BFM Japan, Box 5 File 97, Albright to Arnup, 16 October 1939. Interestingly, Albright held that "the drift in Europe shows that Japan backed the wrong horse and perhaps made peace with Soviet Russia prematurely. We shall know better at the end of the year when the fishery treaty and the Saghalien issue come up again." Two months later, Outerbridge was taking a different point of view by stressing Japan's eagerness to come to terms quickly with the Soviet Union.
67 UCC BFM Japan, Box 5 File 97, Outerbridge to Arnup, 19 December 1939. In February 1940, Albright told Arnup that there was a proposal in the Diet to grant ¥10,000,000 to American missionaries working in China as compensation for war damage. UCC BFM Japan, Box 5 File 69, Albright to Arnup, 19 February 1940. In July 1939, the United States announced that it would abrogate its 1911 Treaty of Commerce and Navigation with Japan in January 1940. Although Japanese trade with the United States had declined during the Depression, Japan depended upon the United States for strategically important materials, including petroleum and scrap iron. See Shiniichi Kitaoka, "Diplomacy and the Military in Showa Japan," in Carol Gluck and Stephen R. Graubard, eds., *Showa: The Japan of Hirohito* (New York: W. W. Norton, 1992), pp. 155–76, pp. 166–7.
68 UCC BFM Japan, Box 5 File 97, Outerbridge to Arnup, 19 December 1939.
69 Ibid.
70 Ibid.
71 Ibid.
72 Ibid.
73 *CR*, 70.5 (May 1939), p. 268. The interview was conducted by E. H. Cressy and J. W. Decker.
74 UCC BFM Japan, Box 12 File 237, Mayling Soong Chiang to Arnup, 1 November 1939.
75 Ibid. The importance of capturing the hearts of foreign missionaries was even recognized apparently by President Roosevelt of the United States. Albright noted in February 1940 that the *Japan Times* carried "a report of a Peace plan on the part of President Roosevelt, which includes the project of rallying 10,000 Protestant missionaries throughout the world 'in a spiritual drive for peace through a Christian Foreign Service Convocation' sponsored

by the Foreign Missions Conference of North America." UCC BFM,Box 5 File 100, Albright to Arnup, 19 February 1940. Albright was sceptical about this peace plan.
76 UCC BFM Box 5 File 100, Albright to Arnup, 8 February 1940.
77 Ibid. Saito Takao (1870–1949) led the criticism of the National Mobilization Law in the Diet in 1938. For Saito Takao, see Ueda Seiji et al. *Konsaisu Jinmei Jiten: Nihon Hen* (Tokyo: Sanseido, 1976), p. 489.
78 UCC Gwen R. P. Norman Papers, Box 1 File 8, Gwen to Pegs, 18 March [1938 handwritten in; however, the correct year would be 1940, because the expulsion of Saito Takao from the Diet took place on 7 March 1940].
79 Ibid.
80 UCC BFM, Box 5 File 100, Albright to Arnup, 19 February 1940.
81 Ibid.
82 UCC BFM, Box 5 File 100, Albright to Arnup, 17 March 1940.
83 Ibid.
84 Ibid.
85 Ibid.
86 UCC BFM, Box 5 File 100, Albright to Arnup, 12 April 1940.
87 Ibid.
88 UCC BFM, Box 5 File 100, Albright to Arnup, 7 May 1940.
89 Ibid. The annoyance of Koreans at having to take Japanese names is also mentioned by Florence J. Murray. See Florence J. Murray, *At the Foot of Dragon Hill* (New York: E. P. Dutton, 1975), p. 226, p. 228.
90 UCC BFM, Box 5 File 100, Albright to Arnup, 7 May 1940.
91 UCC BFM, Box 5 File 101, Albright to Arnup, 7 August 1940. Albright's comments on the shrine question in both May and August were stimulated by reading two articles in the *International Review of Missions* on this question.
92 Ibid.
93 Ibid.
94 Ibid.
95 Ibid.
96 Ibid.
97 UCC BFM, Box 5 File 101, Albright to Arnup, 5 September 1940.
98 Ibid.
99 UCC BFM, Box 5 File 101, Albright to Arnup, 30 September 1940.
100 UCC BFM, Box 5 File 101, Albright to Arnup, November 29 1940.
101 Ibid.
102 Ibid.
103 Ibid.
104 UCC BFM, Box 5 File 101, Albright to Arnup, 28 December 1940.
105 Ibid.
106 UCC BFM, Box 6 File 108, Albright to Arnup, 20 January 1941.

CHAPTER TEN

1 UCC BFM Korea, Box 4 File William Scott, Scott to Armstrong, 20 January 1941.
2 Kisaka Junichiro, "The 1930s: A Logical Outcome of Meiji Policy," in Harry Wray and Hilary Conroy, eds., *Japan Examined: Perspectives on Modern Japanese History* (Honolulu: University of Hawaii Press, 1983), pp. 241–51, pp. 250–51.

3   Takamichi Motoi, "Fashizumu taisei Ka no Shukyo," *KSMK*, 9.4 (1965), pp. 45–56. Japanese-language accounts of Christianity in the 1930s, especially those written in the 1960s and 1970s, make constant use of the term "fascism" and its derivatives to describe the political atmosphere and repetitively employ the words *dan-atsu* (pressure, oppression, suppression) or the slightly less powerful *appaku* (pressure, coercion, oppression) in reference to government actions and policies toward the Christian movement. Although there was certain persecution of religionists, including Christians, in Japan, such language tends to exaggerate the physical dangers faced by the ordinary Japanese Christian or priest.
4   Gonoi Takashi, *Nihon Kirisutokyo Shi* (Tokyo: Yoshikawa Ko Bunkan, 1990), p. 293.
5   Ibid., p. 297.
6   Dohi Akio, *Nihon Purotesutanto Kyokai no Seiritsu to Tenkai* (Tokyo: Nihon Kirisutokyodan Shuppan Kyoku), p. 215.
7   Gonoi, *Nihon Kirisutokyo Shi*, p. 296.
8   Sasaki Toshiji, "Nikka Jihen Ka no Purotesutanto Kyokai," *KSMK*, 9.4 (1965), pp. 16–44, p. 17.
9   Ibid., p. 18.
10 Miyakoda Tsunetaro, *Nihon Kirisutokyo Godo Shiko* (Tokyo: Kyobunkan, 1967), p. 124.
11 UCC BFM Japan, Box 4 File 78, Ebisawa to Arnup, 24 January 1936.
12 UCC BFM Japan, Box 4 File 80, L. S. Albright, Annual Report 1936.
13 *FS*, 15 September 1938, p. 1 (401).
14 *Nippon Seikokai Hyakunen Shi*, pp. 176–79.
15 The Presbyterian Church of the United States began work in Japan with the arrival of James Curtis Hepburn in Yokohama on 18 October 1859.
16 UCC BFM Japan, Box 4 File 81, Outerbridge to Arnup, 30 April 1937.
17 See the Japan Methodist's statement reprinted in *NMJ*, 18 March 1938, p. 2.
18 UCC BFM Japan, Box 4 File 81, Outerbridge to Arnup, 22 September 1937.
19 Ibid.
20 Ibid.
21 Ota Yuzo, "Kagawa Toyohiko: A Pacifist?," in Nobuya Bamba and John F. Howes, *Pacifism in Japan: The Christian and Socialist Tradition* (Vancouver: University of British Columbia Press, 1978), pp. 169–97, p. 197.
22 UCC BFM Japan, Box 4 File 81, Outerbridge to Arnup, 22 September 1937.
23 Ibid.
24 Ibid.
25 *FS*, 15 July 1937, p. 1 (403). On July 22, the Japan Methodist Church also called for peace and stressed its support of the national spirit. See report in *NMJ*, 18 March 1938, p. 2.
26 *Kirisutokyo Sekai*, 12 August 1937, p. 1, [hereafter cited as *KS*].
27 See, for instance, *KS*, 20 July 1937, p. 1. See also *NMJ*, 23 July 1937, p. 1. The American Christian weekly journal, the *Christian Century*, which regularly contained news from Japan, for instance, came out strongly against the Japanese in the wake of the Marco Polo bridge incident. See the *Christian Century*, editorial, 28 July 1937, pp. 942–44; E. Stanley Jones, "An Open Letter to the People of Japan," *Christian Century*, 15 September 1937, pp. 1131–33; and Reinhold Niebuhr, "America and the War in China," *Christian Century*, 29 September 1937, pp. 1195–96.
28 *FS*, 23 September 1937, p. 1 (553).
29 See, for instance, the article by Bishop Kugimiya Tokio entitled "Seishin Hhokoku to Kirisutokyo no Shimei," *NMJ*, 26 November 1937. For Kugimiya Tokio (1872–1947), see *NKRDJ*, p. 446. As well as individuals, Christian organizations, such as the WCTU

(Women's Christian Temperance Union), were also susceptible to the government's appeals. For the WCTU, see Nihon Kirisutokyo Fujin Tafu Kai Hyakunen Shi Henshu, *Nihon Kirisutokyo Fujin Tafu Kai Hyakunen Shi* (Tokyo: Nihon Kirisutokyo Fujin Tafu Kai, 1986), especially pp. 616–88.

30 *FS*, 7 October 1937, p. 1 (573). See also Ebisawa Arimichi and Oouchi Saburo, *Nihon Kirisutokyo Shi* (Tokyo: Nihon Kirisutokyodan Shuppan Kyoku, 1971), p. 549.

31 See *KS*, 7 October 1937, p. 2; *FS*, 21 October 1937, p. 1 (597). See also Tsukada Osamu, *Tennoseika no Kirisutokyo: Nippon Seikokai no Tatakai to Kunan* (Tokyo: Shinkyo Shuppansha, 1981), p. 184.

32 Tsukada, *Tennoseika no Kirisutokyo*, p.185.

33 Doshisha Daigaku Jinbun Kagaku Kenkyujo/Kirisutokyo Shakai Mondai Kenkyukai, *Senjika no Kirisutokyo Undo: Tokko Shiryo ni joru: 1: Showa Juichi Nen—Showa Jugo Nen* (Tokyo: Shinkyo Shuppansha, 1972), pp. 286–91. See A. Hamish Ion, *The Cross and the Rising Sun: Volume 2: The British Protestant Missionary Movement in Japan, Korea, and Taiwan 1865-1945* (Waterloo: Wilfrid Laurier University Press, 1993), p. 239.

34 *Nippon Kirisutokyo Renmei: Shina Jiken to Kirisutokyo Undo Gaikyo* (Tokyo: n. p., 1937).

35 See *Kirisutokyo Nenkan 1937*.

36 The Japanese version of this letter was published in the December 1937 issue of *Renmei Jipo*. An English-language version can be found in UCC BFM Japan, Box 5 File 96.

37 UCC BFM Japan, Box 5 File 96.

38 Ibid.

39 UCC BFM Japan, Box 5 File 96, "Paper Presented to a Group of Foreign Missionaries by D. Tagawa." For Tagawa Daikichiro (1869–1947), see *NKRDJ*, p. 831.

40 UCC BFM Japan, Box 5 File 92, Albright to Arnup, 2 March 1938.

41 Ibid.

42 UCC BFM Japan, Series II Reports and Minutes, Japan 1926–66, Box 2 File 21, Minutes of BFM Executive, 25 February 1939.

43 *FS*, 16 December 1937, p. 1 (685).

44 See Murakishi Kiyohiko, "Nipponteki Kirisutokyo ni oite no kanso," *FS*, 16 December 1937, p. 2 (686).

45 Kasahara Yoshimitsu, " 'Nipponteki Kirisutokyo' Hihan," *KSMK*, 22.3 (1974), pp. 114–39, p. 115. This is a useful article in terms of the evolution of *Nipponteki Kirisutokyo* during the 1930s. For a brief summary of *Nipponteki Kirisutokyo*, see also *NKRDJ*, p. 1063.

46 Tsukada, *Tennoseika no Kirisutokyo*, p. 33. See also Aasulu Lande, *Meiji Protestantism in History and Historiography: A Comparative Study of Japanese and Western Interpretation of Early Protestantism in Japan* (Frankfurt am Main: Verlag Peter Lang, 1989), p. 133.

47 Yanaihara Tadao, "Nipponteki Kirisutokyo," in Yanaihara Tadao, *Kokka no Riso: Senji Hyoron Shu* (Tokyo: Iwanami Shoten, 1982), pp. 116–20, p. 118.

48 Fujita Wakao, "Yanaihara Tadao: Disciple of Uchimura Kanzo and Nitobe Inazo," in Nobuya Bamba and John F. Howes, eds., *Pacifism in Japan: The Christian and Socialist Tradition* (Vancouver: University of British Columbia Press, 1978), p. 209.

49 Yanaihara, "Nipponteki Kirisutokyo," p. 116. Yanaihara gives Uchimura's dictum as *koku no tame, Kirisuto no tame*.

50 Ibid., p. 120.

51 See Tsukada Osamu, *Shoki Nippon Seikokai no Keisei to Imai Judo* (Tokyo: Seikokai Shuppan, 1992), pp. 142–46.

52 State Decimal File 394.006318, National Archives, Washington DC, Grew to Hull, 10

October 1940, No. 5050, on "The 'New Structure' and Christian Missionaries in Japan."
53 Hiyane Antei, *Kirisutokyo no Nihonteki Tenkai* (Tokyo: Kirisutokyo Shiso Sosho Kanko Kokai Hakko, 1938). This book paid considerable attention to Confucianism and Shintoism and their relationship to Christianity in Japan. It stressed the influence of bushido on Christianity. It also pointed out the patriotic characteristics of Japanese Christians and emphasized the example of Honda Yoichi, the first Japan Methodist bishop. Clearly, the book was an attempt to downplay foreign influence on Christianity in Japan and to emphasize its uniquely Japanese characteristics. The importance of Japanese Christianity to the future of world Christianity was underlined. See, for instance, pp.172–74. Antei Hiyane, "National Spirit and the Christian Faith," *JCQ*, 15 (January 1940), pp. 42–49, p. 44. For Hiyane Antei (1892–1970), see *NKRDJ*, pp. 1166–67.
54 Hiyane, "National Spirit and the Christian Faith," p. 49.
55 Ibid.
56 Ibid., p. 48.
57 Ibid.
58 Lande, *Meiji Protestantism in History and Historiography*, p. 125. Although Lande admits that Hiyane "had some rather unguarded nationalist statements, there are reasons to believe that they should not be overemphasized when the basic and underlying viewpoints of Hiyane are described," and, in fact, Hiyane "did not approve of 'Japanese Christianity.'" Ibid., p. 126. Lande is too lenient on Hiyane.
59 *JCQ*, 15.3, (July 1940), p. 211.
60 Ibid.
61 Ibid., p. 205.
62 Ibid.
63 Ibid.
64 Ibid., p. 206–07.
65 *Annual Report of the Church Missionary Society for Africa and the East* 1939–40, p. 48.
66 Ibid.
67 See, for instance, *NMJ*, 29 March 1938, p. 2.
68 *Annual Report of the Church Missionary Society for Africa and the East* 1939–40, pp. 44–45.
69 UCC BFM Japan, Box 5 File 99, Hennigar to Arnup, 13 July 1939.
70 Ibid.
71 See *FS*, 18 November 1937, p. 1 (641).
72 The *Nippon Mesojisuto Jiho* was generally twelve to fourteen pages long. It had a first-page editorial. As well as articles on aspects of Christian faith, it contained resumes concerning local church work. The newspaper paid close attention to the utterances of the head office of the church. Indeed, particularly after Bishop Abe assumed power in 1939, it seemed to be the vehicle of the leadership. The *Nippon Mesojisuto Jiho*, in general, lacked the weekly political comment found in the *Fukuin Shimpo*.
73 *NMJ*, 21 January 1938, p. 1.
74 *NMJ*, 4 February 1938, p. 1. See also *NMJ*, 25 February 1938, p. 1.
75 *NMJ*, 18 March 1938, p. 1.
76 *NMJ*, 29 April 1938, p. 4.
77 *NMJ*, 3 June 1938, p. 8.
78 *NMJ*, 1 July 1938, p. 1.
79 *NMJ*, 16 September 1938, p. 1. The five ethnic groups were Japanese, Manchurian, Chinese, Korean, and Mongolian. The importance of missionary work in Manchukuo and the strides that the Japanese had made there were emphasized again in an editorial written by a Japanese Methodist missionary in June 1939. See *NMJ*, 23 June 1939.

80 *NMJ*, 30 June 1939.
81 *CR*, 70.1 (January 1939), p. 51. The *Chinese Recorder* was published in Shanghai, the western part of which was already occupied by the Japanese military. In that sense, too much Christian missionary criticism of Japanese policies toward Chinese Christians in the occupied areas might have had repercussions on congregations there. No mention was ever made of Japanese Christian missionary work in the occupied areas.
82 Ibid., p. 52.
83 Ibid.
84 *CR*, 70.3 (March 1939), p. 191.
85 *NMJ*, 24 November 1939.
86 *NMJ*, 9 February 1940, p. 1.
87 *Kirisutokyo Shuho*, 25 November 1938, p. 3, [hereafter cited as *KS*(NSKK)]. The *Kirisutokyo Shuho* was the weekly newspaper of the NSKK. It had begun publishing in 1900 and continued to be published until March 1943, after which it was succeeded by the *Kirisuto Koho*, which was still being published in 1944. See *NKRDJ*, pp. 427–28. The newspaper was normally eight pages long, with an editorial on the first page.
88 *KS*(NSKK), 6 January 1939, p. 1.
89 Ibid.
90 *KS*(NSKK), 17 February 1939, see p. 1 and p. 5.
91 Ibid., p. 5.
92 Ibid.
93 *KS*(NSKK), 10 March 1939, p. 5.
94 See, for instance, *KS*(NSKK), 17 March and 24 March 1939.
95 *KS*(NSKK), 14 April 1939, p. 7.
96 *KS*(NSKK), 5 May 1939, p. 7.
97 *KS*(NSKK), 2 June 1939, p. 1.
98 Ibid. During the summer of 1939, the *Kirisutokyo Shuho* was paying attention to British government policy, for in July it commented on changing British policy toward the war in China. See *KS*(NSKK), 10 July 1939, p. 1.
99 If foreign missionaries did not involve themselves in political debate, their views were still welcomed, as was seen in the fact that C. K. Sansbury, the British Anglican missionary and chaplain to the British Embassy, wrote a series of six weekly articles in October and November 1939 dealing with considerations about Gospel writings.
100 *KS*(NSKK), 13 October 1939, p. 2. Maejima Kiyoshi (1888–1944) was a leading Japanese Anglican priest from Nagano Prefecture. During the 1930s, he served as chaplain at Rikkyo University and sometime editor of the *Kirisutokyo Shuho*. See *NKRDJ*, p. 1306.
101 *KS*(NSKK), 20 October 1939, p. 1.
102 UCC BFM Japan, Box 5 File 99, Bates to Arnup, 26 October 1939.
103 Kasahara Yoshimitsu, "Nihon Kirisutokyodan Seiritsu no Mondai: Shukyo Tosei ni tai suru Junno to Teiko," in Doshisha Daigaku Jinbun Kagaku Kenkyu Hen, *Senjika Teiko no Kenkyu: Kirisutokyosha, Jiyushugisha no Baii* (Tokyo: Misuzu Shobo, 1978), 2 vols., vol. 1, pp. 140–87, p. 157.
104 Ibid., p. 158.
105 Ibid.
106 *FS*, 19 May 1938, p. 8 (219).
107 See also Kasahara, "Nihon Kirisutokyodan Seiritsu no Mondai" p. 159.
108 *FS*, 4 August 1938, p. 8 (340).
109 For Sugiyama Genjiro (1885–1964), see *NKRDJ*, p. 717.
110 Kasahara, "Nihon Kirisutokyodan Seiritsu no Mondai," p. 160. See also Takamichi, "Fashizumu taisei Ka no Shukyo," pp. 47–48.

111 *FS*, 30 March 1939, p. 1 (137). See also Kasahara's comment about and quotation from this *Fukuin Shimpo* editorial, Kasahara, "Nihon Kirisutokyodan Seiritsu no Mondai," p. 161.
112 For Tomita Mitsuro (1883–1961), see *NKRDJ*, p. 956. Tomita's opinion appears in William Woodard, comp., "The Religious Press," *JCQ*, 15.1 (January 1940), pp. 67–76, p. 68. See also *FS,* 10 December 1939.
113 Woodard, "The Religious Press," p. 73.
114 Kasahara, "Nihon Kirisutokyodan Seiritsu no Mondai," p. 160.
115 UCC, Dominion Board, Overseas Mission, Japan Correspondence of Executive Secretary with Japan Mission, Box 1 File 14a (Box 73), Address Given by Bishop Y. Abe, of the Japan Methodist Church, at a Luncheon Meeting, 21 May 1941, at the Aldine Club, New York, NY.
116 Ibid.
117 Sasaki, "Nikka Jihen Ka no Purotesutanto Kyokai," p. 35.
118 Charles Iglehart, "Crisis in the Japan Christian Movement," *JCQ*, 15 (October 1940), pp. 315–26, p. 317. For Charles Wheeler Iglehart (1883–1969), see *NKRDJ*, p. 10.
119 Kasahara, "Nihon Kirisutokyodan seiritsu no mondai," pp. 163–64.
120 Doshisha Daigaku Jinbun Kagaku Kenkyujo/Kirisutokyo Shakai Mondai Kenkyukai, *Senjika no Kirisutokyo Undo: Tokko Shiryo ni yoru* (Tokyo: Shinkyo Shuppansha, 1972), 3 vols., vol. 1, p. 181, pp. 286–91.
121 Kasahara, "Nihon Kirisutokyodan Seiritsu no Mondai," p. 164.
122 Ibid., p. 165.
123 Dohi Akio, *Nihon Purotesutanto Kyokai no Seiritsu to Tenkai* (Tokyo: Nihon Kirisutokyodan Shuppan Kyoku, 1975), p. 215.
124 Nihon Kirisutokyodan Shi Henshu Iinkai hen, *Nihon Kirisutokyodan Shi* (Tokyo: Nihon Kirisutokyodan Shuppanbu, 1967), p. 92. For Ogawa Kiyozumi (1886–1954), see *NKRDJ*, pp. 246–47.
125 UCC BFM Japan, Box 5 File 101, Albright to Arnup, 5 September 1940. Albright describes Ogawa as Kagawa's "right-hand man."
126 Kasahara, "Nihon Kirisutokyodan Seiritsu no Mondai," p. 165.
127 Ibid.
128 Nihon Kirisutokyodan Shi Henshu Iinkai hen, *Nihon Kirisutokyodan Shi*, p. 95.
129 Kasahara, "Nihon Kirisutokyodan Seiritsu no Mondai," p. 166. For a brief description of the German-founded Fukyu Fukuin Kyokai, see *NKRDJ*, p. 1198.
130 UCC BFM Japan, Box 5 File 101, Albright to Arnup, 5 September 1940.
131 Ibid.
132 UCC BFM Japan, Series II Reports and Minutes 1926–66, Box 3 File 38, "Outline Report of Unofficial Conference with Bishop Abe, September 10th, 1940."
133 It was somewhat ironic that when the name Japan Methodist Church was chosen in 1876, it was supposed to make clear that the church was a Japanese church and not part of the Canadian Methodist church, which it was de jure. See A. Hamish Ion, *The Cross and the Rising Sun: Volume 1: The Canadian Protestant Missionary Movement in the Japanese Empire, 1872–1931* (Waterloo: Wilfrid Laurier University Press, 1990), p. 63.
134 UCC BFM Japan, Series II Reports and Minutes 1926–66, Box 3 File 38, "Outline Report of Unofficial Conference with Bishop Abe, September 10th, 1940."
135 Ibid.
136 Ibid.
137 Ibid.
138 Iglehart, "Crisis in the Japan Christian Movement," p. 321.
139 UCC BFM Japan, Box 5 File 102, Outerbridge to Arnup, 8 October 1940.

140 Ibid.
141 For Ono Zentaro (1875–1965), see *NKRDJ*, p. 265.
142 UCC BFM Japan, Series II Reports and Minutes 1926–66, Box 2 File 22. Enclosure with BFM Executive Minutes, Koshikawa, 6 November 1940, "Translation of an Excerpt from 'The Bishop's Room' in the *NMJ*, Oct. 11 '40."
143 Iglehart, "Crisis in the Japan Christian Movement," p. 321.
144 Ibid.
145 Nihon Kirisutokyodan Shi Henshu Iinkai hen, *Nihon Kirisutokyodan Shi*, pp. 97–98.
146 Ibid., p. 166.
147 UCC WMS, Dominion Board, Overseas Mission, Japan, Correspondence of Executive Secretary with Japan Mission 1940, Box 1 [Box 73] File 12, "Special Session of the Japan Methodist Church Held at Aoyama Gakuin Tokyo Oct. 14–16, 1940."
148 MSCEC Japan Files, Miscellaneous, GS75-103 Series 3-2 Box 65, Daito to Gould, 7 August 1937. Daito Chusaburo (1874–1961) was one of the senior Japanese clergymen on the American Church side of the NSKK.
149 MSCEC Japan Files, Japan Mission Conference Minutes, GS75-103 Series 3-2 Box 63A, Meeting of All Foreign Missionaries in Mid-Japan, 3 November 1937.
150 MSCEC Japan Files, J. A. Waller, GS75-103 Series 3-2 Box 65, Waller to Williams, 20 October 1937.
151 MSCEC Japan Files, P. S. C. Powles, GS75-103 Series 3-3 Box 65, Powles to Gould, 25 February 1938.
152 Ibid.
153 Ibid.
154 Ibid.
155 MSCEC Japan Files, Miss N. F. Bowman, GS75-103 Series 3-3 Box 85, Bowman Annual Report 1938–39.
156 MSCEC Japan Files, Miss F. Hamilton, GS75-103 Series 3-3 Box 85, Hamilton Annual Report 1939.
157 MSCEC Japan Files, P. S. C. Powles, GS75-103 Series 3-3 Box 86, Powles to Dixon, 30 December 1939.
158 Ibid.
159 Ibid.
160 Ibid.
161 MSCEC Japan Files, P. S. C. Powles, GS75-103 Series 3-3 Box 86, Powles to Dixon, 19 July 1940.
162 Ibid.
163 For Bishop Matsui Yonetaro (1869–1946), see *NKRDJ*, p. 1319: for Bishop Naide Yasutaro (1866–1945), see *NKRDJ*, pp. 970–71, p. 255. For a description of the background to this incident from the perspective of British Anglican missionaries attached to the NSKK, see A. Hamish Ion, *The Cross and the Rising Sun: Volume 2: The British Protestant Missionary Movement in Japan, Korea, and Taiwan 1865-1945* (Waterloo: Wilfrid Laurier University Press, 1993), pp. 239–41; and John Mitsuru Oe, "The Conflict of Church Views in Japan during Wartime 1940–1945: The Unification Problem of the Anglican Church in Japan (The Nippon Sei Ko Kwai)," *Anglican and Episcopal History*, 58.4 (December 1989), pp. 448–497, especially p. 455.
164 MSCEC Japan Files, Japan Mission Conference Minutes, GS75-103 Series 3-2 Box 63A, Meeting with Bishop on 5 September 1940.
165 Oe, "The Conflict of Church Views in Japan during Wartime 1940–1945," p. 457. The position of the NSKK regarding church unity was based on the Chicago-Lambeth Quadrilateral, among whose four elements was the historic episcopate. Professor Oe has

pointed out that "it was obvious that the NSKK would find it difficult to affiliate with the United Church of Japan unless a church order was presented which included reference to the historic episcopate." Ibid., p. 458.
166 Ibid.
167 MSCEC Japan Files, Japan Mission Conference Minutes, GS75-103 Series 3-2 Box 63A, Meeting with Bishop on 5 September 1940.
168 Ibid.
169 See Oe, "The Conflict of Church Views in Japan during Wartime 1940–1945," pp. 454–455, p. 458. This view was widely held, and as late as 17 July 1942 the *Kirisutokyo Shuho*, the weekly NSKK newspaper, in an editorial on the central characteristics of the Seikokai, argued this point. See *KS*(NSKK), 17 July 1942, p. 1.
170 MSCEC Japan Files, Japan Mission Conference Minutes, GS75-103 Series 3-2 Box 63A, Notes on Mr. Watt's Report of the Meeting of Mission Representatives, Tokyo, 17 October 1940.
171 Ibid.
172 Ibid.
173 Ibid.
174 Ibid.
175 Ibid.

CHAPTER ELEVEN

1   UCC BFM Japan, Box 6 File 127, Berry to Friends across the Seas, 5 December 1940.
2   Ibid.
3   State Decimal File, 394.0063/9, National Archives, Washington DC, Grew to Hull, 28 October 1940, No. 5092, on "Church Union in Japan."
4   Kasahara Yoshimitsu, "Nihon Kirisutokyodan Seiritsu no Mondai: Shukyo Tosei ni tai suru Junno to Teiko," in Doshisha Daigaku Jinbun Kagaku Kenkyu Hen, *Senjika Teiko no Kenkyu: Kirisutokyosha, Jiyushugisha no Baii* (Tokyo: Misuzu Shobo, 1978), 2 vols., vol. 1, pp. 140–87, p. 167.
5   Tsukada Osamu, *Tennoseika no Kirisutokyo: Nippon Seikokai no Tatakai to Kunan* (Tokyo: Shinkyo Shuppansha, 1981), pp. 169–71. One thread of Abe's Japanese Christianity had its basis in loyalty to Christ and ultimately led to the development of a church of Japanese people (and church union). The other thread stressed loyalty to the emperor and the unique characteristics of the Japanese people and ultimately moved toward the union of peoples. Both threads served to emphasize that Japanese Christians had a responsibility for the evangelization of people in the Greater East Asia Co-Prosperity Sphere.
6   Kasahara, "Nihon Kirisutokyodan Seiritsu no Mondai," pp. 167–68.
7   UCC WMS, Dominion Board, Overseas Mission, Japan, Correspondence of Executive Secretary with Japan Mission 1941, 1942, 1946, Box 1 [Box 73] File 12, Courtice to Taylor, 9 September 1940.
8   UCC WMS, Dominion Board, Overseas Mission, Japan, Correspondence of Executive Secretary with Japan Mission 1941, 1942, 1946, Box 1 [Box 73] File 12, Outerbridge to Arnup, 15 November 1940.
9   Charles Iglehart, "Crisis in the Japan Christian Movement," *JCQ*, 15 (October 1940), pp. 315–26, pp. 324–25.
10 UCC BFM Japan, Box 5 File 101, To Friends and Relatives of Missionaries in Japan,

Korea, North and South China, Circular from Arnup, 17 October 1940.
11　Ibid.
12　UCC BFM Japan, Box 5 File 101, Statement on the Situation in Japan, December 1940.
13　Ibid.
14　Ibid.
15　UCC BFM Japan, Box 5 File 101, Albright to Arnup, 28 December 1940.
16　Ibid.
17　UCC BFM Japan, Box 6 File 108, Albright to Arnup, 4 January 1941.
18　Ibid.
19　UCC BFM Korea, Box 4 File William Scott, Scott to Armstrong, 20 January 1941.
20　Ibid.
21　UCC BFM Korea, Box 4 Korea 1941 File William Scott, Scott to Armstrong, 2 March 1941. See also William Axling, "Japan's Christians Unite," *Christian Century*, 25 June 1941, pp. 826–27; and Paul S. Mayer, "Church Union and Its Possible Implications for the Missionary," *JCQ*, 16.3 (July 1941), pp. 215–23.
22　UCC BFM Korea, Box 4 Korea 1941 File William Scott, Scott to Armstrong, 2 March 1941.
23　UCC BFM Japan, Box 6 File 108, Albright to Arnup, 13 January 1941.
24　UCC WMS, Dominion Board, Overseas Mission, Japan, Correspondence of Executive Secretary with Japan Mission 1941, 1942, 1946, Box 1 [Box 73], Abe to Arnup, 12 October 1940; Courtice to Taylor, October 18 1940.
25　UCC BFM Japan, Box 6 File 108, Albright to Arnup, 13 January 1941.
26　UCC BFM Japan, Box 6 File 108, Albright to Arnup, 20 January 1941.
27　UCC WMS, Dominion Board, Overseas Mission, Japan, Correspondence of Executive Secretary with Japan Mission 1941, 1942, 1946, Box 1 [Box 73] File 14a, Outerbridge to Arnup, 19 January 1941.
28　Ibid.
29　Ibid.
30　Ibid.
31　Ibid.
32　UCC WMS, Dominion Board, Overseas Mission, Japan, Correspondence of Executive Secretary with Department of External Affairs, 1940–41. Box 1 [Box 73] File 13, Skelton to Taylor, 24 October 1940.
33　UCC WMS, Dominion Board, Overseas Mission, Japan, Correspondence of Executive Secretary with Department of External Affairs, 1940–41. Box 1 [Box 73] File 13, Robertson to Taylor, 10 February 1941.
34　Ibid.
35　UCC BFM Japan, Series II Reports and Minutes 1926–66, Box 2 File 23, Minutes of BFM Executive Meeting, 3 February 1941. The BFM executive meeting on 1 March 1941 passed a motion giving permission for missionaries to return to Canada when they considered it advisable and declaring that it was not in the best interest of either the church or the mission for missionaries to remain in Japan in case of war. UCC BFM Japan, Series II Reports and Minutes 1926–66, Box 2 File 23, Minutes of BFM Executive Meeting, 1 March 1941.
36　UCC WMS, Dominion Board, Overseas Mission, Japan, Correspondence of Executive Secretary with Japan mission 1941, 1942, 1946, Box 1 [Box 73] File 14a, Marconigram from Taylor, Arnup to Japan and Korea.
37　UCC BFM Japan, Series II Reports and Minutes 1926–66, Box 2 File 23, Minutes of BFM Executive Meeting, 3 February 1941.
38　UCC BFM Japan, Series II Reports and Minutes 1926–66, Box 2 File 23, Report of

Financial Situation, Japan Mission, 10 March 1941.
39 UCC WMS, Dominion Board, Overseas Mission, Japan, Correspondence of Executive Secretary with Department of External Affairs, 1940–41. Box 1 [Box 73] File 13, Abe to Arnup, 4 March 1941.
40 Ibid. See enclosure, Japan Methodist Church, Shibuya, Tokyo, Office of the Bishop, 22 February 1941.
41 UCC BFM Japan, Series II Reports and Minutes 1926–66, Box 2 File 23, Report of Financial Situation, Japan Mission, 10 March 1941.
42 MSCEC Japan Files, Japan Mission Conference Minutes, GS75-103 Series 3-2 Box 63A, Emergency Conference of Japan Mission, MSCC, Nagoya, 22 October 1940.
43 MSCEC Japan Files, P. S. C. Powles, GS75-103 Series 3-3 Box 86, Powles to Dixon, 1 November 1940.
44 Ibid.
45 Ibid.
46 MSCEC Japan Files, Japan Mission Conference Minutes, GS75-103 Series 3-2 Box 63A, Gist of Bishop Sasaki's Report, Nagoya, 22 October 1940.
47 Bishop Basil, who died of cancer in 1942, never did resign, nor is it likely—had he been in good health—that he ever would have resigned in such circumstances or under such pressure. He stood on principle.
48 Bishop Yanagihara Teijiro (1886–1973) became the assistant bishop of Osaka (his father-in-law was Bishop Naide) in June 1940. See *NKRDJ*, pp. 1425–26. Before leaving Japan, Bishop Basil arranged for the election of Yashiro Hinsuke (1900–1970) as his assistant bishop, and he was consecrated as such on 29 September 1940. See *NKRDJ*, pp. 1419–20.
49 MSCEC Japan Files, Japan Mission Conference Minutes, GS75-103 Series 3-2 Box 63A, Gist of Bishop Sasaki's Report, Nagoya, 22 October 1940.
50 Ibid.
51 Ibid.
52 Ibid.
53 MSCEC Japan Files, P. S. C. Powles, GS75-103 Series 3-3 Box 86, Powles to Dixon, November 1 1940.
54 Ibid.
55 Ibid.
56 Ibid.
57 Ibid.
58 Ibid.
59 Ibid.
60 Ibid.
61 MSCEC Japan Files, Japan Mission Conference Minutes, GS75-103 Series 3-2 Box 63A, A Translation of the Address by the Standing Committee of the Missionary District of Mid-Japan to the MSCC Mid-Japan Conference, 23 October 1940.
62 Ibid.
63 MSCEC Japan Files, Reports WA, GS75-103 Series 3-3 Box 85, F. Hamilton.
64 MSCEC Japan Files, Conference Minutes, GS75-103 Series 3-2 Box 63A, To the Relatives and Friends of MSCC Missionaries in Japan, 26 October 1940.
65 Ibid.
66 MSCEC Japan Files, Japan Mission Conference Minutes, GS75-103 Series 3-2 Box 63A, Statement Given to the Press, Saturday, 26 October 1940.
67 MSCEC Japan Files, Japan Mission Conference Minutes, GS75-103 Series 3-2 Box 63A, Statement in the *Japan Advertiser*, Sunday, 27 October 1940.
68 MSCEC Japan Files, S. Heaslett, GS75-103 Series 3-3 Box 85, Heaslett to Spencer, 24

69 MSCEC Japan Files, S. Heaslett, GS75-103 Series 3-3 Box 85, Heaslett to Spencer, 29 October 1940.
70 MSCEC Japan Files, Japan Mission Conference Minutes, GS75-103 Series 3-2 Box 63A, Wood to Dixon, 31 October 1940.
71 Ibid.
72 MSCEC Japan Files, Reports WA, GS75-103 Series 3-3 Box 85, F. Hamilton.
73 MSCEC Japan Files, P. S. C. Powles, GS75-103 Series 3-3 Box 86, Powles to Dixon, 1 November 1940.
74 Ibid.
75 Ibid.
76 MSCEC Japan Files, Japan Mission Conference Minutes, GS75-103 Series 3-2 Box 63A, Wood to Dixon, 31 October 1940.
77 MSCEC Japan Files, P. S. C. Powles, GS75-103 Series 3-3 Box 86, typewritten two-page note, headed Takata, 2 November 1940.
78 Ibid., extract of a letter to Cyril and Bill.
79 MSCEC Japan Files, P. S. C. Powles, GS75-103 Series 3-3 Box 86, Powles to Dixon, 4 December 1940.
80 Ibid.
81 Ibid.
82 Ibid. John Mitsuru Oe has argued that Sasaki and the other bishops opposed to union with the *kyodan* believed in the coexistence of church and state but were not prepared to tolerate undue interference by the state in regard to the freedom of the Church. Professor Oe has pointed out that Sasaki and his fellow anti-union bishops were not completely opposed to the New Organized Movement (*Shintaisei*), for their views, in common with those of other churches, were premised by the Religious Organizations Law in terms of the foundation of the church-state relationship. Importantly, Professor Oe has emphasized that, with the exception of the Watch Tower Society, "there was little difference among the opinions of the churches about the political situation in Japan. That is, they believed that the war for 'Greater East Asia' was a holy war to release Asian countries from the chains forged by European countries and the United States, though it was in fact a Japanese war of aggression against Asian countries." John Mitsuru Oe, "Church and State in Japan, 1940–1945," *Anglican and Episcopal History*, 59.2 (June 1990), pp. 202–23, pp. 210–11.
83 MSCEC Japan Files, P. S. C. Powles, GS75-103 Series 3-3 Box 86, Powles to Dixon, 4 December 1940.
84 MSCEC Japan Files, P. S. C. Powles, GS75-103 Series 3-3 Box 86, Powles to Dixon, 28 January 1941.
85 Ibid.
86 Ibid.
87 MSCEC Japan Files, P. S. C. Powles, GS75-103 Series 3-3 Box 86, Powles to Dixon, 12 February 1941.
88 Ibid.
89 Ibid.
90 MSCEC Japan Files, P. S. C. Powles, GS75-103 Series 3-3 Box 86, Powles to Dixon, 25 February 1941.
91 Ibid.
92 *Christian Century*, 19 March 1941, p. 383.
93 "The Tragedy of Missionary Evacuation," editorial *JCQ*, 16.2 (April 1941), pp. 101–06, pp. 102–03.

94   *PR*, 66.2 (February 1941), p. 36.
95   Ibid., p. 35.
96   Ibid., p. 36.
97   Details of the disposal of mission property are given in *PR*, 66.4 (April 1941), pp. 115–16.
98   *PR*, 66.5 (May 1941), p. 151.
99   *APPCC* 1941, p. 36.
100 *PR*, 66.5 (May 1941), p. 151.
101 *APPCC* 1941, p. 37.
102 E. H. Johnson, "The Manchurian Church in Crisis," *PR*, 66.8 (August 1941), pp. 227–30, p. 230.
103 Missionary quoted in "Developments in Japan and Manchuria," *International Review of Missions*, 32 (April 1943), pp. 122–34, p. 124.
104 Ibid., pp. 124–25.
105 Ibid., p. 134.
106 Austin Fulton, *Through Earthquake, Wind, and Fire: Church and Mission in Manchuria 1867–1950: The Work of the United Presbyterian Church, the United Free Church of Scotland, the Church of Scotland, and the Presbyterian Church in Ireland with the Chinese Church in Manchuria* (Edinburgh: Saint Andrew Press, 1967), p. 204.
107 *APPCC* 1941, p. 58.
108 See report by Gordon K. Chapman in "The Crisis and Our Missions as Reported by Mission Secretaries," *JCQ*, 16.3 (July 1941), pp. 235–60, p. 260.
109 *APPCC* 1941, p. 60.
110 Ibid., p. 58.

CHAPTER TWELVE

1   Harold E. Fey, "Kagawa Revisits America," *Christian Century*, 21 May 1941, pp. 684–86, p. 685.
2   Ibid.
3   Ibid.
4   Ibid.
5   Saito Soichi, "The Significance of the Japanese Christian Deputation,"*JCQ*, 16.3 (July 1941), pp. 225–29, p. 226. For Saito Soichi (1886–1960), see *NKRDJ*, p. 556.
6   Dohi Akio, *Kozaki Michio no Kodo to sono Rikai* (Tokyo: Nihon Kirisutokyodan Reinanzaka Kyokai, 1972), p. 33.
7   UCC, Dominion Board, Overseas Mission, Japan Correspondence of Executive Secretary with Japan Mission. Box 1[Box 73] File 14a, Address Given by Bishop Y. Abe, of the Japan Methodist Church, at a Luncheon Meeting, 21 May 1941, at the Aldine Club, New York, NY.
8   Ibid.
9   Ibid.
10   Saito, "The Significance of the Japanese Christian Deputation," p. 229.
11   UCC WMS, Dominion Board, Overseas Mission, Japan, Correspondence of Executive Secretary with Japan Mission 1941, 1942, 1946, Box 1 [Box 73] File 14a, Courtice to Taylor, 1 March 1941.
12   UCC BFM Japan, Box 6 File 116, McKenzie to Arnup, 22 April 1941.
13   Ibid.

14 Ibid.
15 Ibid.
16 Ibid.
17 UCC BFM Japan, Box 6 File 116, McKenzie to Arnup, 27 May 1941.
18 UCC WMS, Dominion Board, Overseas Mission, Japan, Correspondence of Executive Secretary with Japan Mission 1941, 1942, 1946, Box 1 [Box 73] File 14a, Courtice to Taylor, 26 May 1941.
19 UCC WMS, Dominion Board, Overseas Mission, Japan, Correspondence of Executive Secretary with Japan Mission 1941, 1942, 1946, Box 1 [Box 73] File 14a, Ishiwara to Courtice, 20 June 1941.
20 UCC WMS, Dominion Board, Overseas Mission Japan, Correspondence of Executive Secretary with Japan Mission 1941, 1942, 1946, Box 1 [Box 73] File 14a, "News Items from Recent Letters from Japan," entry for 16 October.
21 Sybil R. Courtice, "The United Church of Canada Mission," *JCQ*, 16.3 (July 1941), pp. 252–54, p. 252. In 1940, there had been eleven families and twenty-seven single women in the field, with two families and eight single women on regular furlough.
22 Ibid., pp. 252–53.
23 Ibid., p. 253.
24 UCC WMS, Dominion Board, Overseas Mission, Japan, Correspondence of Executive Secretary with Japan Mission 1941, 1942, 1946, Box 1 [Box 73] File 14a, Courtice to Taylor, 15 September 1941.
25 UCC BFM Korea, Box 4 Korea 1941 File William Scott, Scott to Armstrong, 2 March 1941.
26 Ibid. In January 1941, Scott reported that of 416 foreign missionaries on the rolls, only 125 remained in Korea; of these, 20 were Canadians. UCC BFM Korea, Box 4 Korea 1941File William Scott, Scott to Armstrong, 20 January 1941.
27 Ibid.
28 Ibid.
29 Richard Henry Drummond, *A History of Christianity in Japan* (Grand Rapids: William B. Eerdmans, 1971), pp. 260–61. The torisha"s powers were similar to those, but on a grander scale, that Abe had acquired as head of the Japan Methodist Church.
30 A very sympathetic picture of the senior officers of the *kyodan* as well as biographical details can be found in Royal H. Fisher, "Introducing the Officers of the Church of Christ in Japan," *JCQ*, 16.4 (October 1941), pp. 314–20.
31 See *NKRDJ*, p. 52.
32 Kasahara Yoshimitsu, "Nihon Kirisutokyodan Seiritsu no Mondai: Shukyo Tosei ni tai suru Junno to Teiko,"in Doshisha Daigaku Jinbun Kagaku Kenkyu Hen, *Senjika Teiko no Kenkyu: Kirisutokyosha, Jiyushugisha no Baii* (Tokyo: Misuzu Shobo, 1978), 2 vols., vol. 1, pp. 140–87, pp. 170–71. See also Miyakoda, *Nihon Kirisutokyo Godo Shiko* (Tokyo: Kyobunkan, 1967), pp. 221–35.
33 *RJ*, 207 (July 1941), p. 10.
34 Kasahara, "Nihon Kirisutokyodan Seiritsu no Mondai," p. 171.
35 *Asahi Shinbun*, evening ed. 30 October 1941.
36 *RJ*, 207 (July 1941), p. 9.
37 *FS*, 27 November 1941, p. 1 (485).
38 Ibid.
39 *FS*, 11 December 1941, p. 1 (505). For a summary of the conference, see *FS*, 11 December 1941, p. 7 (511). See also Kasahara, "Nihon Kirisutokyodan Seiritsu no Mondai," p. 174.
40 Ibid., p. 175. In its 18 December 1941 issue, the *Fukuin Shimpo* made its first mention of

NOTES TO CHAPTER TWELVE 395

the start of the Pacific War and supported Japan's cause. See *FS*, 18 December 1941, p. 1 (517).
41 Kasahara, "Nihon Kirisutokyodan Seiritsu no Mondai," p. 175.
42 Ibid., p. 176.
43 Drummond, *A History of Christianity in Japan*, p. 268.
44 John Mitsuru Oe, "The Conflict of Church Views in Japan during Wartime 1940–1945: The Unification Problem of the Anglican Church in Japan (The Nippon Sei Ko Kwai)," *Anglican and Episcopal History*, 58.4 (December 1989), pp. 448–497, p. 461.
45 Tsukada Osamu, *Tennoseika no Kirisutokyo: Nippon Seikokai no Tatakai to Kunan* (Tokyo: Shinkyo Shuppansha, 1981), pp. 191–93. See also Oe, "The Conflict of Church Views in Japan during Wartime 1940–1945," p. 469.
46 Kasahara, "Nihon Kirisutokyodan Seiritsu no Mondai," p. 177. For a chart that shows the key differences between pro-union and anti-union supporters, see Tsukada, *Tennoseika no Kirisutokyo*, p. 198. For a military police report on the attitudes of the various Anglican dioceses to union in 1942, see Doshisha Daigaku Jinbun Kagaku Kenkyujo / Kirisutokyo Shakai Mondai Kenkyukai, *Senjika no Kirisutokyo Undo: Tokko Shiryo ni joru: 1: Showa Juichi Nen—Showa Jugo Nen* (Tokyo: Shinkyo Shuppansha, 1972), vol. 2, pp. 186–208.
47 Oe, "The Conflict of Church Views in Japan during Wartime 1940–1945," p. 469. See also *Nippon Seikokai Hyakunen Shi*, p. 193.
48 Oe, "The Conflict of Church Views in Japan during Wartime 1940–1945," p. 462.
49 Ibid., p. 468.
50 Tsukada, *Tennoseika no Kirisutokyo*, p. 192.
52 Excerpt of a letter from the Diocese of Osaka to all clergy and laity of the NSKK, dated 11 October 1942, translated and quoted in John Mitsuru Oe, "Church and State in Japan, 1940–1945," *Anglican and Episcopal History*, 59.2 (June 1990), pp. 202–23, p. 206.
52 Tsukada, *Tennoseika no Kirisutokyo*, p. 193.
53 Oe, "Church and State in Japan," p. 206.
54 Oe, "The Conflict of Church Views in Japan during Wartime 1940–1945," p. 463.
55 Ibid., pp. 463–65. See also Tsukada, *Tennoseika no Kirisutokyo*, pp. 193–94.
56 Ibid., p. 194.
57 For Saeki Yoshiro (1871–1965), see *NKRDJ*, p. 560. Doshisha Daigaku Jinbun Kagaku Kenkyujo, *Senjika no Kirisutokyo Undo*, vol. 2, pp. 197–98.
58 Oe, "The Conflict of Church Views in Japan during Wartime 1940–1945," p. 467.
59 See, for instance, Doshisha Daigaku Jinbun Kagaku Kenkyujo, *Senjika no Kirisutokyo Undo*, vol. 2, p. 86, p. 88, pp. 199–208.
60 Tsukada, *Tennoseika no Kirisutokyo*, p. 196.
61 Oe, "Church and State in Japan," p. 208.
62 Ibid., p. 211.
63 Oe, "The Conflict of Church Views in Japan during Wartime 1940–1945," p. 470.
64 Ibid., p. 472.
65 Ibid., p. 473.
66 Ibid. See also Tsukada, *Tennoseika no Kirisutokyo*, p. 211.
67 The influence of Sasaki on Mid-Japan's anti-union stand in 1942 in the eyes of the *kempeitai* is shown in Doshisha Daigaku Jinbun Kagaku Kenkyujo, *Senjika no Kirisutokyo Undo*, vol. 2, p. 192.
68 Tsukada, *Tennoseika no Kirisutokyo*, p. 212; see also the table on p. 213.
69 For Nosse Hidetoshi (1892–1974), see *NKRDJ*, p. 1088.
70 *Nippon Seikokai Hyakunen Shi*, p. 199.
71 Oe, "The Conflict of Church Views in Japan during Wartime 1940–1945," p. 450. See

also *Nippon Seikokai Hyakunen Shi*, pp. 200–01.
72 *Nippon Seikokai Hyakunen Shi*, p. 200. See also Doshisha Daigaku Jinbun Kagaku Kenkyujo, *Senjika no Kirisutokyo Undo*, vol. 2. p. 306.
73 Kasahara, "Nihon Kirisutokyodan Seiritsu no Mondai," p. 182. See also National Archives, Washington, DC, Record Group 243, Records of the US Strategic Bombing Survey "Religious Movements," 14h(57). See also A. Hamish Ion, *The Cross and the Rising Sun: Volume 2: The British Protestant Missionary Movement in Japan, Korea, and Taiwan 1865-1945* (Waterloo: Wilfrid Laurier University Press, 1993), pp. 253–54.
74 National Archives, Washington, DC, Record Group 226, OSS 61445, "Report of the Christian Movement in Japan since June, 1942."
75 Norman suggested that the only reason that she was able to get Japanese citizenship "was that she was a woman and had lived so long in Toyama that she was almost a civic institution." G. R. P. Norman and W. H. H. Norman, *One Hundred Years in Japan, 1873–1973* (Toronto: Division of World Out-Reach, United Church of Canada, 1981), p. 411. Courtice, the WMS secretary-treasurer in Tokyo, was not totally sympathetic toward Armstrong's naturalization. See UCC WMS, Dominion Board, Overseas Mission, Japan, Correspondence of Executive Secretary with Japan Mission 1941, 1942, 1946, Box 1 [Box 73] File 14a, Courtice to Taylor, 11 February 1941. For Margaret Elizabeth Armstrong (1877–1960), see *NKRDJ*, p. 56.
76 Quoted in Norman and Norman, *One Hundred Years in Japan*, pp. 405–06. For the treatment of the Botts in Tokyo, see also pp. 405–07.
77 Ibid., p. 407.
78 Ibid. For description of Courtice's experiences at the Sumire camp, see pp. 409–11.
79 Florence J. Murray, *At the Foot of Dragon Hill* (New York: E. P. Dutton, 1975), pp. 234–35.
80 Ibid., p. 237.
81 "'I Was There,' by Margaret Armstrong," UCC WMS, Dominion Board, Overseas Missions, Japan Missionaries, Miss Margaret Armstrong, Box 3 [Box 75], File 39b.
82 Ibid.
83 Ibid.
84 Ibid.
85 Ibid.
86 Ibid.
87 Ibid.
88 Norman and Norman, *One Hundred Years in Japan*, p. 414.
89 See *NKRDJ*, p. 169.
90 UCC BFM Japan, Box 6 File 132, Bott to Iglehart, 20 October 1942.
91 Ibid.
92 Ibid.
93 Ibid.
94 MSCEC CEA File, Information re Japan 1942–45, GS75-103 Series 3-3 Box 89, Answer by Dr. Waller, 4 September 1942.
95 Ibid.
96 Ibid.
97 MSCEC CEA File. Information re Japan 1942–45, GS75-103 Series 3-3 Box 89; see Watt to Dixon, 29 October 1942.
98 UCC BFM General 1942, Box 16 File 322, Conference on "Mission Policy as Affected by the War," 2 April 1942. "The Church in Japan," conference paper by C. J. L. Bates.
99 UCC BFM General 1942, Box 16 File 322, Conference on "Mission Policy as Affected by the War," 2 April 1942. "The Future of the Korean Church," conference paper by

Emma Palethorpe.
100 Ibid.
101 UCC BFM General 1942, Box 16 File 333, Avison to Armstrong, 29 December 1942.
102 See UCC BFM General 1939, Box 12 File 253, Price to Friends and Supporters, 15 September 1939; Armstrong to Price, 6 December 1939.
103 UCC BFM General 1942, Box 16 File 333, Armstrong to Avison, 7 January 1943.
104 Ibid.
105 UCC WMS, Dominion Board, Overseas Missions, Korea 1945, Box 4 File 70, Correspondence re Postwar Work in Korea.
106 See, for instance, UCC BFM General 1942, Box 16 File 333, Avison to Armstrong, 22 March 1943.
107 MSCEC CEA File, Information re Japan 1942–45, GS75-103 Series 3-3 Box 89, Committee on East Asia Bulletin, 13 October 1944.
108 Ibid. In saying this, Kagawa conveniently forgot that the Japanese had engaged in similar practices in the past. During their invasions of Korea in the 1590s, for instance, the Japanese cut off the heads of slain Koreans, pickled them, and sent them back to the headquarters of Toyotomi Hideyoshi in Japan. See Herman Ooms, *Tokugawa Ideology: Early Constructs, 1570–1680* (Princeton: Princeton University Press, 1985), p. 44.
109 Ibid.
110 National Archives, Washington, DC, Record Group 245, Records of the US Strategic Bombing Survey (RR9–RR13), "Overseas Broadcasts by Directors of the Japan Christian Federation."
111 Ibid.
112 National Archives, Washington, DC, Record Group 245, Records of the US Strategic Bombing Survey, "Recent Trends of Christians That Require Vigilance." For a more detailed survey of the persecution of Christians and other religionists during the last years of the war based on the records of the thought-control police, see Okashi Hirotaka and Matsura Sozo, eds., *Showa Tokko Danatsu Shi, 4: Shukyojin ni Taisuru Danatsu* (Tokyo: Daihei Shuppansha, 1975).
113 UCC BFM General 1945, Armstrong to Kagawa, 11 October 1945.
114 MSCEC CEA File, Information re Japan 1942–45, GS75-103 Series 3-3 Box 89, Committee on East Asia Bulletin, 24 January 1945. The meeting took place at the Royal York Hotel in Toronto on 8 January 1945.
115 UCC BFM 1945, Box 6 File 143, "Christian Churches in Japan and the War," by Russell L. Durgin, five-page typescript. Durgin was a US Foreign Service officer who was a member of the staff of the US political adviser in Tokyo.
116 Ibid.
117 UCC WMS, Dominion Board, Overseas Missions, Korea 1945, Box 4 File 70, Lamps to Board of Foreign Missions, Presbyterian Church in the United States, 22 September 1945. Henry W. Lamps was in the chaplain section of the U S Army 24th Corps and had been in Seoul for a week at the time that he wrote this short letter explaining the immediate situation facing the Christian church in Korea.
118 UCC WMS, Dominion Board, Overseas Missions, Korea 1945, Box 4 File 70, Correspondence re Postwar Work in Korea.
119 Ibid.
120 UCC WMS, Dominion Board, Overseas Missions, Korea 1945, Box 4 File 70, Lamps to Board of Foreign Missions, Presbyterian Church in the United States, 22 September 1945.
121 UCC BFM Korea 1945, Box 6, Moon to Armstrong, October 26 1945. See also A. Hamish Ion, *The Cross and the Rising Sun: Volume 1: The Canadian Protestant Missionary Movement in the Japanese Empire, 1872–1931* (Waterloo: Wilfrid Laurier

University Press, 1990), p. 218.
122 The question of the wartime treatment of Japanese Canadians is beyond the scope of this study.
123 See mention of the work of Mrs. P. S. C. Powles in Patricia E. Roy, J. L. Granatstein, Masako Iino, and Hiroko Takamura, *Mutual Hostages: Canadians and Japanese during the Second World War* (Toronto: University of Toronto Press, 1990), p. 149.
124 For more information on McKenzie's wartime activities and the Canadian Army Japanese Language School, see Stuart Robert Elliot, *Scarlet to Green: A History of Intelligence in the Canadian Army 1903–1963* (Toronto: Canadian Intelligence and Security Association, 1981).
125 Dohi, *Kozaki Michio*, p. 42.

CONCLUSION

1 William Axling, *Japan at the Midcentury: Leaves from Life* (New York: American Baptist Foreign Mission Society, 1955), p. 198.
2 Ibid.

Select Bibliography

PRIVATE PAPERS

1. *In the possession of John Holmes*

John Holmes, "And Some Have Greatness Thrust upon Them," three-page typescript.
——————, "Eine Kleine Nachtmusik," six-page typescript.
——————, "Fire," six-page typescript.
——————, "Hero Worship," three-page typescript.
——————, "Shigeru," seventeen-page typescript.
——————, "Sous Les Toits de Paris," five-page typescript.

ARCHIVES

1. General Synod Archives, The Anglican Church of Canada, Church House, 600 Jarvis Street, Toronto, Ontario, Canada

Annual Reports of the Missionary Society of the Church of England in Canada.
Bishop H. J. Hamilton Notebook.
Missionary Society of the Church of England in Canada, GS75-103.
Series 1: Board of Management and Executive Committee 1884–1969 [Boxes 1–8].
Series 2: Committees 1903–68 [Boxes 9–32].
Series 3: General Secretary's Material 1897–1976 [Boxes 33–98], 3.1 Lewis Norman Tucker 1903–12, 3.2 Sydney Gould 1910–38, 3.3 Leonard Alexander Dixon 1939–59.
Series 4: Field Secretary's Files, 1941–59, 4.1 Horace Godfrey Watts 1941–52.
Series 5: Financial 1877–1963.
Series 6: Overseas Personnel, 1907–40.
Series 7: Publications Department 1943–57.
Series 8: Publications—Official Records 1901–58, 8.5 Printed Reports of the General Secretary 1907–45.
Official Minutes of the Missionary Society of the Church of England in Canada.

2. *National Archives of Canada, Ottawa, Ontario, Canada*

RG 7 G21. Governor General's Office.
RG 25 G1. External Affairs Central Registry Files.

3. *National Archives, Washington, DC, United States of America*

State Department Decimal Files, 394.0063; 894.404
Record Group 226 OSS.
Record Group 243 Records of the US Strategic Bombing Survey.

4. *Nippon Seikokai Kanko Jimusho, Yuraicho, Tokyo, Japan*

Kirisutokyo Shuho, 1931–44 (weekly newspaper of approximately eight pages).
Nichiyo Soshi, 1892–(monthly magazine of approximately thirty-five pages that has some interesting short articles).
Missions in Japan: The Guild of St. Paul Magazine (quarterly magazine). Originally, the magazine was directed to the support of missions connected with the Diocese of South Tokyo, but in the 1930s its scope was extended to the whole of Japan.

5. *Archives of the Presbyterian Church of Canada, Knox College, University of Toronto, Toronto, Ontario, Canada*

Formosa File re Shrine Question 1935–37.
"Historical statement of Events in Connection with the 'Shrine Question' as It Concerns the Tamsui Girls' School."
"Mr. Mackay's Historical Statement."
"Personal Statement by Phyllis Argall, signed June 27 1935."
"Personal Statement by Alma M. Burdick, signed June 27 1935."
"Personal Statement by Hildur K. Hermanson, signed June 27 1935."
"Religious Liberty under Japanese Rule: Summary of the Present Situation in Korea, Manchukuo, and Japan," dated February 1936.
"Statement by Jean Ross Mackay on the "Shrine Question," written June 27, 1935."
"A Warning to Dr. G. S. McCune, Principal of the Sujitsu School. Copy of a statement handed to Dr. G. S. McCune, to Mr. T. S. Soltau and to J. G. Holdcroft by H. E. T. Watanabe, Director of the Educational Bureau of The Government General of Chosen, December 30th 1935."

6. *United Church of Canada Archives, Victoria College, University of Toronto, Toronto, Ontario, Canada*

i) Correspondence and Reports

a) United Church of Canada Board of Foreign Missions, Japan.
Series 1: Correspondence 1926–66 [Boxes 1–23], Correspondence 1926–48.
Series 2: Minutes and Reports 1926–66 [Boxes 24–39].

SELECT BIBLIOGRAPHY

b) United Church of Canada Board of Foreign Missions, Korea.
Board of Foreign Missions: Correspondence 1925–44.
Board of Overseas Missions: Correspondence 1944–45.

c) United Church of Canada Women's Missionary Society Dominion Board, Overseas Mission, Japan.
Correspondence of Overseas Mission Executive Secretary with Japan 1930–42.
Minutes of Japan Mission, annual meetings and executive committee.
Missionaries Files.

d) United Church of Canada Women's Missionary Society Dominion Board, Overseas Mission, Korea.
Correspondence of Overseas Mission Executive Secretary with Korea.
Minutes of Japan Mission, annual meetings and executive committee.

ii) Microfilmed Materials

UCC BFM Japan 1926–53 [Boxes 1–9] (files 1–218).
UCC BFM Korea 1926–53 [Boxes 1–7] (files 1–173).

iii) Personal Papers

J. Endicott and J. Arnup Papers.
D. M. MacRae Papers.
G. R. P. Norman and W. H. H. Norman Papers.
F. C. Stephenson Papers.

MICROFILM AND BOUND DIPLOMATIC CONFIDENTIAL PRINT

British Foreign Office, Japan: FO 46, 1894–1904.
British Foreign Office, Japan: Correspondence FO 371, 1930–41.
British Documents on Foreign Affairs: Reports and Papers from the Foreign Office Confidential Print, Part 1: From the Mid-Century to the First World War, Series E: Asia, 1858–1914, ed. Ian H. Nish.
British Documents on Foreign Affairs: Reports and Papers from the Foreign Office Confidential Print, Part II: From the First to the Second World War, Series E: Asia, 1914–1939, ed. Anne Trotter.
Confidential US Diplomatic Post Records, Japan, 1914–41.
OSS/State Department Intelligence and Research Reports: Japan and Its Occupied Territories during World War II.

SPECIAL LIBRARY COLLECTIONS

1. *Hokkaido University Library, Kita-ku, Sapporo, Japan*

Shinkyo Tetsuro Kyoku, *Kanto Chiho Gaiyo* (n.p.: n.p., 1934). Call number 915 Mi.
Zai Kanto Nippon Soryojikan, *Kanto Jijo Kogai* (n.p.: n.p.,1932). Call number 915 Ka.
Zaigai Senjin Chosa Hokoku, *Mammo no Beisaku to Iju Senno Mondai* (n.p.: n.p., 1927). Call number 633 Cho.

2. *Institute for Comparative Studies of Culture Library, Tokyo Women's Christian University, Suginami-ku, Tokyo, Japan*

Sumiya Bunko
Uemura Kinen Sawa Bunko

3. *International Christian University, Mitaka-shi, Tokyo, Japan*

Papers of the Japan Mission of the American Board of Commissions for Foreign Missions (microfilm).

DICTIONARIES AND ENCYCLOPEDIA

Fujio, Ikado, and McGovern, James R. *A Bibliography of Christianity in Japan: Protestantism in English Sources*. Tokyo: Committee on Asian Cultural Studies, International Christian University, 1966.
Hunter, Janet E., comp. *Concise Dictionary of Modern Japanese History*. Berkeley: University of California Press, 1984.
Institute of Asian Cultural Studies, International Christian University. *Comparative Chronology of Protestantism in Asia 1792–1945*. Tokyo: Institute of Asian Cultural Studies, International Christian University, 1984.
Krummel, John W. *Rainichi Mesojisuto Senkyoshi Jiten 1873–1993 nen: A Bibliographical Dictionary of Methodist Missionaries to Japan 1873–1993*. Tokyo: Kyobunkan, 1996.
Nihon Kirisutokyo Rekishi Dai Jiten Henshu Iinkai. *Nihon Kirisutokyo Rekishi Dai Jiten*. Tokyo: Kyobunkan, 1988.
Nihon Kirisutokyo Rekishi Dai Jiten Henshu Iinkai. *Nihon Kirisutokyo Shi Nenpyo*. Tokyo: Kyobunkan, 1988.
Ueda, Seiji, et al. *Konsaisu Jinmei Jiten: Nihon Hen*. Tokyo: Sanseido, 1976.

NEWSPAPERS AND JOURNALS

Acts and Proceedings of the General Assembly of the Presbyterian Church in Canada.
Anglican and Episcopal History.
Canadian Church and Mission News.
Canadian Historical Review.
China Recorder and Educational Review.
Christian Movement in Japan, Korea, and Formosa.
Christian Century.
Fukuin Shimpo.
Japan Advertiser.
Japan Mission Year Book.
Kirisutokyo Shakai Mondai Kenkyu.
Mission World.
New Outlook.
Presbyterian Record.
Rikugo Zasshi.
Shichi Ichi Zappo.
Shin Gaku.
United Church of Canada Year Book.
Far Eastern Quarterly.
Fukuin to Sekai.
Japan Christian Quarterly.
Journal of Japanese Studies.
Kirisutokyo Shuho.
Modern Asian Studies.
Nippon Mesojisuto Jiho.
Renmei Jipo.
San Sen Ri.
Shiso.

BOOKS

Allan, Ted, and Sydney Gordon. *The Scalpel, the Sword: The Story of Doctor Norman Bethune.* Rev. ed. New York: Monthly Review Press, 1973.

Anderson, Robert K. *My Dear Redeemer's Praise: The Life of Luther Lisgar Young.* Halifax: Lancelot Press, 1979.

Anderson, Violet. *World Currents and Canada's Course.* Toronto: T. Nelson, 1937.

Angus, Henry F. *The Problem of Peaceful Change in the Pacific Area.* London: Oxfo—rd University Press, 1937.

——————, *Canada and the Far East 1940–1953.* Toronto: University of Toronto Press, 1953.

Armstrong, Robert Cornell. *Just before the Dawn: The Life and Work of Nimomiya Sentoku.* New York: Macmillan, 1912.

——————. *Light from the East: Studies in Japanese Confucianism.* Toronto: University of Toronto Press, 1914.

Austin, Alvyn J. *Saving China: Canadian Missionaries in the Middle Kingdom 1888–1959.* Toronto: University of Toronto Press, 1986.

Axling, William. *Kagawa.* London: Student Christian Movement, 1932.

Bamba, Nobuya, and John F. Howes, eds. *Pacifism in Japan: The Christian and Socialist Tradition.* Vancouver: University of British Columbia Press, 1978.

Band, Edward. *Working Out His Purpose: The History of the English Presbyterian*

Mission 1847–1947. Taipeh: Ch'eng Wen, 1972.
Barros, James. *No Sense of Evil: The Espionage Case of E. Herbert Norman*. New York: Ivy Books, 1987.
Berry, Mary Elizabeth. *Hideyoshi*. Cambridge: Harvard University Press, 1982.
Best, Ernest E. *Christian Faith and Cultural Crisis: The Japanese Case*. Leiden: E. J. Brill, 1966.
Bickle, George B., Jr. *The New Jerusalem: Aspects of Utopianism in the Thought of Kagawa Toyohiko*. Tucson: Arizona University Press, 1976.
Bothwell, Robert, and Norman Hillmer, eds. *The In-Between Time: Canadian External Policy in the 1930s*. Toronto: Copp Clark, 1975.
Bowen, Roger W., ed. *E. H. Norman: His Life and Scholarship*. Toronto: University of Toronto Press, 1984.
——————. *Innocence Is Not Enough: The Life and Death of E. H. Norman*. Vancouver: Douglas and McIntyre, 1986.
Boxer, Christopher R. *Christian Century in Japan, 1540–1650*. Berkeley: University of California Press, 1957.
Breen, John, and Mark Williams, eds. *Japan and Christianity: Impacts and Responses*. Basingstoke: Macmillan Press, 1996.
Brown, Arthur Judson. *The Mastery of the Far East*. New York: Scribner's Sons, 1919.
Burkman, Thomas W. *The Occupation of Japan: The International Context: Proceedings of the Fifth Symposium Sponsored by the MacArthur Memorial*. Norfolk, VA: Old Dominion University, 1984.
Canadian Papers, Yosemite Conference 1936. Toronto: CIIA, 1936.
Cary, Otis. *A History of Christianity in Japan: Roman Catholic, Greek Orthodox, and Protestant Missions, Vol. 2: Protestant Missions*. Rutland, VT, and Tokyo, Japan: Charles E. Tuttle, 1982.
Chamberlain, Basil Hall. *The Invention of a New Religion*. London: Rationalist Press, 1912.
Cho, Juhun. *Kankoku Minzoku Undo Shi*. Kato Haruko, trans. Tokyo: Korai Shorin, 1975.
Chosen Sotokufu. *Chosen no Tochi to Kirisutokyo*. Keijo: Chosen Sotokufu, 1920.
Clark, Allen D. *A History of the Church in Korea*. Seoul: Christian Literature Society, 1971.
Coates, H. H., and Ryugaku Ishizuka. *Honen, the Buddhist Saint*. Kyoto: Chionin, 1924.
Cortazzi, Sir Hugh, and Gordon Daniels, eds. *Britain and Japan 1859–1991: Themes and Personalities*. London: Routledge, 1991.
Crowley, James B. *Japan's Quest for Autonomy*. Princeton: Princeton University Press, 1966.
Dixon, William Gray. *The Land of the Morning: An Account of Japan and Its People Based on a Four Years' Residence in That Country, Including Travels into the Remotest Parts of the Interior*. Edinburgh: James Gemmell, 1882.
Dohi, Akio. *Kozaki Michio no Kodo to sono Rikai*. Tokyo: Nihon Kirisutokyodan Reinanzaka Kyokai, 1972.
——————. *Nihon Purotesutanto Kirisutokyo Shi*. Tokyo: Shinkyo Shuppansha, 1982.
——————. *Nihon Purotesutanto Kyokai no Seiritsu to Tenkai*. Tokyo: Nihon

Kirisutokyodan Shuppan Kyoku, 1975.
Doshisha Daigaku Amerika Kenkyukai hen. *Aru Ribarisuto no Kaiso: Yuasa Hachiro no Nihon to Amerika*. Tokyo: Nihon YMCA Domei Shuppanbu, 1977.
Doshisha Daigaku Jinbun Kagaku Kenkyujo/Kirisutokyo Shakai Mondai Kenkyukai. *Senjika no Kirisutokyo Undo: Tokko Shiryo ni yoru*. 3 vols. Tokyo: Shinkyo Shuppansha, 1972.
Doshisha Daigaku Jinbun Kagaku Kenkyujo hen. *Senjika Teiko no Kenkyu: Kirisutosha. Jiyushugisha no baai*. 2 vols. Tokyo: Misuzu Shobo, 1978.
——————. *Shichi Ichi Zappo no Kenkyu*. Kyoto: Domeiya Shuppan, 1986.
Drummond, Richard Henry. *A History of Christianity in Japan*. Grand Rapids: William B. Eerdmans, 1971.
Ebisawa, Arimichi, and Oouchi Saburo. *Nihon Kirisutokyo Shi*. Tokyo: Nihon Kirisutokyodan Shuppan Kyoku, 1971.
Elliot, Stuart Robert. *Scarlet to Green: A History of Intelligence in the Canadian Army 1903–1963*. Toronto: Canadian Intelligence and Security Association, 1981.
Evans, Paul M., and Michael B. Frolic, eds. *Reluctant Adversaries: Canada and the People's Republic of China 1949–1970*. Toronto: University of Toronto Press, 1991.
Fairbank, John K., ed. *The Missionary Enterprise in China and America*. Cambridge: Harvard University Press, 1974.
Fairbank, John K., Edwin O. Reischauer, and, Albert Craig, eds. *East Asia: The Modern Transformation*. Boston: Houghton Mifflin, 1965.
Faulds, Henry. *Nine Years in Nipon: Sketches of Japanese Life and Manners*. Wilmington, DE: Scholarly Resources Reprint, 1973.
Fenwick, Malcolm C. *The Church of Christ in Corea: A Pioneer Missionary's Own Story*. New York: George H. Doran, 1911.
Fleming, Peter. *One's Company: A Journey to China made by the author in 1933*. Harmondsworth: Penguin Books, 1956.
Fujita, Wakao. *Yanaihara Tadao: Sono Shogai to Shinko*. Tokyo: Kyobunkan, 1967.
Fukumchi, Masakatsu. *Nihon Kirisutokyodan Shizuoka Kyokai Hachiju Gonen Shi*. Shizuoka: Nihon Kirisutokyodan Shizuoka Kyokai, 1959.
Fulton, Austin. *Through Earthquake, Wind and Fire: Church Work and Mission in Manchuria 1867–1950: The Work of the United Presbyterian Church, the United Free Church of Scotland, the Church of Scotland and the Presbyterian Church in Ireland with the Chinese Church in Manchuria*. Edinburgh: Saint Andrew Press, 1967.
Gagan, Rosemary B. *A Sensitive Independence: Canadian Methodist Women Missionaries in Canada and the Orient, 1881–1925*. Montreal: McGill-Queen's University Press, 1992.
Gale, James Scarth. *The History of the Korean People*. Seoul: Christian Literature Society, 1927.
Garon, Sheldon. *Molding Japanese Minds: The State in Everyday Life*. Princeton: Princeton University Press, 1997.
Gendai Nihon Bungaku Taikei 6: Kitamura Tohoku, Yamaji Aizan Shu. Tokyo: Tsukiji Shobo, 1970.

Germany, Charles H. *Protestant Theologies in Modern Japan: A History of Dominant Theological Currents from 1920–1960.* Tokyo: International Institute for the Study of Religions Press, 1965.

Gluck, Carol. *Japan's Modern Myth: Ideology in the Late Meiji Period.* Princeton: Princeton University Press, 1985.

Gluck, Carol and Stephen R. Graubard, eds. *Showa: The Japan of Hirohito.* New York: W. W. Norton, 1992.

Goforth, Rosalind. *Goforth of China.* Minneapolis: Dimension Books, n.d.

Gonoi Takashi. *Nihon Kirisutokyo Shi.* Tokyo: Yoshikawa Ko Bunkan, 1990.

Grayson, James Huntley. *Korea: A Religious History.* Oxford: Oxford University Press, 1989.

Hall, Rosetta (Sherwood), ed. *The Life of Rev. William James Hall, M. D., Medical Missionary to the Slums of New York; Pioneer Missionary to Pyong Yang, Korea.* New York: Eaton and Mains, 1897.

Harada, Tasuku. *The Faith of Japan.* New York: Macmillan, 1914.

Hardacre, Helen. *Shinto and the State 1868–1988.* Princeton: Princeton University Press, 1990.

Hay, Keith A. J., ed. *Canadian Perspectives on Economic Relations with Japan.* Montreal: Institute for Research on Public Policy, 1980.

Hell Screen. W. H. H. Norman, trans. Tokyo: Hokuseido, 1948.

Hewat, Elizabeth G. K. *Vision and Achievement 1796–1956: A History of the Foreign Missions of the Churches United with the Church of Scotland.* Edinburgh: Nelson and Sons, 1960.

Hine, Leland D. *Axling: A Christian Presence in Japan.* Valley Forge: Judson Press, 1969.

Hiyane, Antei. *Kirisutokyo no Nihonteki Tenkai.* Tokyo: Kirisutokyo Shiso Sosho Kanko Kokai Hakko, 1938.

——————. *Nihon Kinsei Kirisutokyo Jinbutsu Shi.* Tokyo: Kirisutokyo Hakkosha, 1935.

Holtom, D. C. *The National Faith of Japan: A Study of Modern Shinto.* New York: E. P. Dutton, 1938.

Horinesu Bando Showa Kirisutokyo Danatsu Shi Kankokai. *Horinesu Bando no Kiseki: Ribairu to Kirisutokyo Danatsu.* Tokyo: Horinesu Bando Danatsu Shi Kankokai Hen, 1983.

Howes, John F., ed. *Nitobe Inazo: Japan's Bridge across the Pacific.* Boulder: Westview Press, 1995.

Hunter, Janet E. *The Emergence of Modern Japan: An Introductory History since 1853.* London: Longman, 1989.

Iglehart, Charles W. *A Century of Protestant Christianity in Japan.* Tokyo: Charles E. Tuttle, 1959.

——————. *Cross and Crisis in Japan.* New York: Friendship Press, 1957.

Iinuma, Jiro. *Nihon Noson Dendo Shi Kenkyu.* Tokyo: Nihon Kirisutokyodan Shuppan Kyoku, 1988.

Ion, A. Hamish. *The Cross and the Rising Sun: Volume 1: The Canadian Protestant Missionary Movement in the Japanese Empire, 1872–1931.* Waterloo: Wilfrid Laurier University Press, 1990.

——————. *The Cross and the Rising Sun: Volume 2: The British Protestant*

Missionary Movement in Japan, Korea, and Taiwan, 1865–1945. Waterloo: Wilfrid Laurier University Press, 1993.

Ion, A. Hamish, and Barry D. Hunt, eds. *War and Diplomacy Across the Pacific, 1919–1952*. Waterloo: Wilfrid Laurier University Press, 1988.

Iwanami Koza Kindai Nihon to Shokumichi, 4: Togo to Shihai no Ronri. Tokyo: Iwanami Shoten, 1993.

Ji, Myon Kuwan [Chi Mekan]. *Kantoku Gendai Shi to Kyokai Shi*. Tokyo: Shinkyo Shuppansha, 1975.

Kagawa, Toyohiko. *Before the Dawn*. I. Fukumoto and T. Satchell, trans. New York: George H. Doran, 1924.

Kan, Juon. *Chosen Kindai Shi*. Tokyo: Heibonsha, 1986.

Kan, Wijo. *Nihon Toji Shita Chosen no Shukyo to Seiji*. Tokyo: Seibunsha, 1976.

Kaneta, Ryuichi. *Senjika Kirisutokyo no Teiko to Zasetsu*. Tokyo: Shinkyo Shuppansha, 1985.

——————. *Showa Nihon Kirisutokyo Shi: Tennosei to Ju Gonen Senso no moto de*. Tokyo: Shinkyo Shuppansha, 1996.

Kankoku Kirisutokyo Rekishi Kenkyujo. *Kankoku Kirisutokyo Shi 1919–45*. Han Shyuki and Kuroda Masahiko, trans. Tokyo: Shinkyo Shuppansha, 1995.

Kim, C. I. Eugene, and Doretha E. Mortimore, eds. *Korea's Response to Japan: The Colonial Period 1910–1945*. Kalamazoo: Center for Korean Studies, Western Michigan University, 1977.

Kirisutokyo Bunka Gakkai hen. *Purotesutanto Jinbutsu Shi: Kindai Nihon no Bunka Keisei*. Tokyo: Yorudansha, 1990.

Kirisutokyo Gakko Kyoiku Domei hen. *Nihon Kirisutokyo Kyoiku Shi: Jinbutsu Hen*. Tokyo: Sobunsha, 1977.

Kozaki, Hiromichi. *Reminiscences of Seventy Years: The Autobiography of a Japanese Pastor*. Tokyo: Kyobunkan, 1934.

Kudo, Eiichi. *Nihon Kirisutokyo Shakai Keixei Kenkyu*. Tokyo: Shinkyo Shuppansha, 1980.

Kuranaga, Takashi. *Hiraiwa Yoshiyasu Den*. Tokyo: Kyobunkan, 1938.

——————. *Kanada Mesojisuto Dendo Shi*. Tokyo: Kanada Godo Kyokai Senkyoshika, 1937.

Kurata, Masahiko. *Tennosei to Kankoku Kirisutokyo*. Tokyo: Shinkyo Shuppansha, 1991.

Kuyama, Yasushi, ed. *Kirisutokyo Kyoiku Shi: Shicho Hen*. Tokyo: Sobunsha, 1993.

Lande, Aasulv. *Meiji Protestantism in History and Historiography: A Comparative Study of Japanese and Western Interpretation of Early Protestantism in Japan*. Frankfurt am Main: Verlag Peter Lang, 1989.

Langdon, Frank. *The Politics of Canadian-Japanese Economic Relations 1952–1982*. Vancouver: University of British Columbia Press, 1984.

Lower, Arthur R. M. *Canada and the Far East—1940*. New York: Institute of Pacific Relations, 1941.

MacNab, John. *The White Angel of Tokyo: Miss Caroline Macdonald*. Toronto: Centenary Committee of the Canadian Churches, n.d.

Mackay, George Leslie. *From Far Formosa: The Islands, Its People*. Ed. J. A. Macdonald. Chicago: Fleming H. Revell, 1896.

MacRae, Helen Fraser. *A Tiger on Dragon Mountain: The Life of Rev. Duncan M.*

MacRae, D. D. Ross Penner and Janice Penner, eds. Charlottetown: A. James Haslam, QC, 1993.

Matsuo, Takayoshi. *Taisho Jidai no Senkotachi.* Tokyo: Iwanami Shoten, 1993.

Matsuzawa, Hiroaki, ed. *Nihon no Meicho 38: Uchimura Kanzo.* Tokyo: Chuo Koron Sha, 1971.

Mayama, Mitsuya. *Owari Nagoya no Kirisutokyo—Nagoya Kyokai no Sosoki.* Tokyo: Shinkyo Shuppansha, 1986.

McCully, Elizabeth A. *A Corn of Wheat; Or, The Life of Rev. W. J. McKenzie of Korea.* Toronto: Westminster Press, 1904.

McManners, John, ed. *The Oxford Illustrated History of Christianity.* Oxford: Oxford University Press, 1992.

Min, Kyon Be. *Kankoku Kirisutokyo Shi: Kankoku Minzoku Kyokai Kisei no Katai.* Iru Chyun Kim, trans. Tokyo: Shinkyo Shuppansha, 1981.

Miyakoda, Tsunetaro, ed. *Nihon Kirisutokyo Godo Shiko.* Tokyo: Kyobunkan, 1967.

Moran, Joseph F. *The Japanese and the Jesuits: Alexandro Valignano in Sixteenth Century Japan.* London: Routledge, 1993.

Mott, J. R. *Addresses and Papers.* 2 vols. New York: 1941.

Murray, Florence J. *At the Foot of Dragon Hill.* New York: E. P. Dutton, 1975.

Myers, Ramon H., and Mark R. Peattie, eds. *The Japanese Colonial Empire, 1895–1945.* Princeton: Princeton University Press, 1984.

Nahm, Andrew C., ed. *Korea under Japanese Colonial Rule: Studies of the Policy and Techniques of Japanese Colonialism.* Kalamazoo: Center for Korean Studies, Western Michigan University, 1973.

Naratada, Gotaro. *Nihon YMCA Shi.* Tokyo: Nihon YMCA Domei Shuppanbu, 1959.

Nihon Kanada Gakkai Henshu Iinkai. *Kanada Kenkyu Nenpyo—Nika Gakujitsu Kaigi Tokushu.* Tokyo: Nihon Kanada Gakkai, 1981.

Nihon Kirisutokyo Fujin Tafu Kai Hyakunen Shi Henshu. *Nihon Kirisutokyo Fujin Tafu Kai Hyakunen Shi.* Tokyo: Nihon Kirisutokyo Fujin Tafu Kai, 1986.

Nihon Kirisutokyodan Shi Hensan Iinkai Hen. *Nihon Kirisutokyodan Shi.* Tokyo: Nihon Kirisutokyodan Shuppanbu, 1967.

Nihon Mesojisuto Shitaya Kyokai Rokujinen Shi Hensan Iinkai Shusai. *Nihon Mesojisuto Shitaya Kyokai Rokujunen Shi.* Tokyo: Rekishi hensan iinkai, 1939.

Nihon YWCA Hachinen Shi Henshu Iinkai. *Mizu o Kaze o Hikari o: Nihon YWCA 80 Nen 1905–1985.* Tokyo: Nihon Kirisutokyo Joshi Seinen Kai, 1987.

Nippon Kirisutokyo Renmei: Shina Jiken to Kirisutokyo Undo Gaikyo. Tokyo: Nippon Kirisutokyo Renmei, 1937.

Nippon Seikokai Rekishi Hensan Iinkai. *Nippon Seikokai Hyakunen Shi.* Tokyo: Nippon Seikokai Kyomuin Bunshokyoku, 1959.

Nish, Ian, ed. *Britain and Japan: Biographical Portraits.* London: Japan Library, 1994.

———. *Japan's Struggle with Internationalism: Japan, China, and the League of Nations, 1931–33.* London: Kegan Paul International, 1993.

Nitobe, Inazo. *Bushido: The Soul of Japan.* New York: G. Putnam, 1905.

———. *Japan: Some Phases of Her Problems and Development.* London: Ernest Benn, 1931.

Norman, G. R. P., and W. H. H. Norman. *One Hundred Years in Japan, 1873–1973.* 2 vols. Toronto: Division of World Out-Reach, United Church of Canada, 1981.

Norman, W. Howard H. *Nagano no Noruman.* H. Hirabayashi, trans. Tokyo: Fukuinkan, 1965.
Notehelfer, Fred G. *American Samurai: Captain L. Janes and Japan.* Princeton: Princeton University Press, 1985.
Ogata, Sadako N. *Defiance in Manchuria.* Berkeley: University of California Press, 1964.
Oka, Yoshitake. *Konoe Fumimaro: A Political Biography.* Okamoto Shumpei and Patricia Murray, trans. Tokyo: University of Tokyo Press, 1983.
Ooms, Herman. *Tokugawa Ideology: Early Constructs, 1570–1680.* Princeton: Princeton University Press, 1985.
Ota, Aito. *Meiji Kirisutokyo no Ryuiki: Shizuoka Bando to Bakushintachi.* Tokyo: Tsukiji Shokan, 1979.
Ota, Yuzo. *E. S. Mozu: "Furuki Nihon" o Tsutaeta Shin-Nichi Kagakusha.* Tokyo: Liburo Poto, 1988.
―――――. *Taiheyo no Hashi to shite Nitobe Inazo.* Tokyo: Misuzu Shobo, 1986.
Parker, F. Calvin. *Johnathan Goble of Japan: Marine, Missionary, Maverick.* Lanham, MD: University Press of America, 1990.
Powles, Cyril H. *Victorian Missionaries in Meiji Japan.* Toronto: University of Toronto-York University Joint Centre for Modern East Asia, 1987.
Prang, Margaret. *A Heart at Leisure from Itself: Caroline Macdonald of Japan.* Vancouver: University of British Columbia Press, 1995.
Pringsheim, Klaus H. *Neighbours across the Pacific: The Development of Economic and Political Relations between Canada and Japan.* Westport, CT: Greenwood Press, 1983.
Rawlyk, George A., ed. *The Canadian Protestant Experience 1760 to 1990.* Montreal: McGill-Queen's University Press, 1990.
Reader, Ian. *Religion in Contemporary Japan.* Basingstoke: Macmillan, 1991.
Reischauer, Edwin O. *My Life between Japan and America.* Tokyo: John Weatherhill, 1986.
Roy, Patricia E., J. L. Granatstein, Iino Masako, and Takamura Hiroko. *Mutual Hostages: Canadians and Japanese during the Second World War.* Toronto: University of Toronto Press, 1990.
Ryerson, Egerton. *The Netsuke of Japan.* London: G. Bell, 1958.
Sapporo Shi Kyoiku Iinkai Shu. *Oyatoi Gaikokujin.* Sapporo: Hokkaido Shimbunsha, 1982.
Sauer, Charles August. *Methodists in Korea 1930–1960.* Seoul: Christian Literature Society, 1973.
Saunby, John W. *The New Chivalry in Japan: Methodist Golden Jubilee.* Toronto: Methodist Publishing House, 1923.
Sawa, Masahiko. *Mika no Chosen Kirisutokyo Shi.* Tokyo: Nihon Kirisutokyodan Shuppan Kyoku, 1991.
Scalapino, Robert A., and Lee Chong-sik. *Communism in Korea, Part 1: The Movement.* Berkeley: University of California Press, 1972.
Schultz, John, and Miwa, Kimitada, eds. *Canada and Japan in the Twentieth Century.* Toronto: Oxford University Press, 1991.
Scott, William. *Canadians in Korea: Brief Historical Sketch of Canadian Mission Work in Korea: Part One to the Time of Church Union.* Toronto: United Church

of Canada Board of World Mission, 1970.
Shaw, Yu-ming. *An American Missionary in China: John Leighton Stuart and Chinese-American Relations.* Cambridge: Harvard University Press, 1992.
Shillony, Ben-Ali. *Revolt in Japan: The Young Officers and the February 26th, 1936, Incident.* Princeton: Princeton University Press, 1973.
Shiono, Kazuo. *Nihon Kumiai Kirisutokyokai Shi Kenkyu Josetsu.* Tokyo: Shinkyo Shuppansha, 1995.
Shizuoka Eiwa Jo Gakuin Hachijunen Shi Hensan Iinkai. *Shizuoka Eiwa Jo Gakuin Hachijunen Shi.* Shizuoka: Shizuoka Eiwa Jo Gakuin, 1971.
Shizuoka Eiwa Jo Gakuin Hyakunen Shi Hensan Iinkai. *Shizuoka Eiwa no Hyakunen.* Shizuoka: Shizuoka Eiwa Jo Gakuin Hyakunen Hensan Iinkai, 1988.
Shizuoka Mesojisuto Kyokai Rokujunen Shi Hensan Iinkai. *Shizuoka Mesojisuto Kyokai Rokujunen Shi.* Shizuoka: Shizuoka Mesojisuto Kyokai, 1937.
Soritsu Hyaku Shunen Kinen Gigyo Iinkai/Kinen Shuppan Senmon Iinkai. *Kwansei Gakuin no Hyakunen.* Osaka: Kwansei Gakuin, 1989.
Strange, William. *Canada, the Pacific, and War.* Toronto: T. Nelson, 1937.
Sugai, Kichiro. *Kashiwagi Gien.* Tokyo: Shunju Sha, 1972.
Sumiya, Mikio. *Kagawa.* Tokyo: Nihon Kirisutokyodan Shuppanbu, 1966.
—————. *Nihon no Shakai Shiso: Kindaika to Kirisutokyo.* Tokyo: Tokyo Daigaku Shuppansha, 1968.
—————. *Nihon Shakai to Kirisutokyo.* Tokyo: Tokyo Daigaku Shuppankai, 1956.
Suzuki, Norihisa. *Uchimura Kanzo.* Tokyo: Iwanami Shinsho, 1992.
Takeda, Kyoko, ed. *Gendai Nihon Shiso Taikei, 6: Kirisutokyo.* Tokyo: Chikuma Shobo, 1975.
Taylor, Sandra C. *Advocate of Understanding: Sidney Gulick and the Search for Peace with Japan.* Tokyo: Kent State University Press, 1984.
The Commission of Appraisal [William Ernest Hocking, chairman]. *Re-Thinking Missions: A Laymen's Inquiry after One Hundred Years.* New York: Harper and Brothers, 1932.
Tiedemann, Arthur E., ed. *An Introduction to Japanese Civilization.* New York: Columbia University Press, 1974.
Thorne, Christopher. *The Limits of Foreign Policy.* London: Hamish Hamilton, 1972.
Tokyo Joshi Daigaku Gojunen Shi Hensan Iinkai. *Tokyo Joshi Daigaku Gojunen Shi.* Tokyo: Tokyo Joshi Daigaku, 1968.
Tomura, Masahiro, ed. *Jinja Mondai to Kirisutokyo: Nihon Kindai Kirisutokyo Shi Shiryo 1.* Tokyo: Shinkyo Shuppansha, 1976.
Tong, Hollington K. *Christianity in Taiwan: A History.* Taipeh: China Post, 1972.
Toyo Eiwa Jo Gakuin Hyakunen Shi Hensan Jikko Iinkai. *Toyo Eiwa Jo Gakuin Hyakunen Shi.* Tokyo: Toyo Eiwa Jo Gakuin Hyakunen Shi Hensan Jikko Iinkai, 1984.
Toyo Eiwa Jo Gakuin Nanajunen Shi Henshu Iinkai. *Toyo Eiwa Jo Gakuin Nanajunen Shi.* Tokyo: Toyo Eiwa Jo Gakuin, 1955.
Tsukada, Osamu. *Nippon Seikokai no Kisei to Kadai.* Tokyo: Seikokai Shuppan, 1979.
—————. *Shocho Tennosei to Kirisutokyo.* Tokyo: Shinkyo Shuppansha, 1990.
—————. *Shoki Nippon Seikokai no Keisei to Imai Judo.* Tokyo: Seikokai Shuppan, 1992.

———. *Tennoseika no Kirisutokyo: Nippon Seikokai no Tatakai to Kunan.* Tokyo: Shinkyo Shuppansha, 1981.
Tsurumi, Shunsuke. *An Intellectual History of Wartime Japan 1931–1945.* London: KPI, 1986.
Ushiyama, Setsuai. *Kirisutokyo Shinko Dendo Shi: Wara Choro, Dendo no Kiseki.* Nagano: Ginga Shobo, 1980.
Wells, Kenneth M. *New God, New Nation: Protestants and Self-Reconstruction Nationalism in Korea 1896–1937.* North Sydney, Australia: Allen and Unwin, 1990.
Whyte, Bob. *Unfinished Encounter in China and Christianity.* London: Fount Paperbacks, 1988.
Woodsworth, C. J. *Canada and the Orient.* Toronto: Macmillan, 1941.
Wray, Harry, and Hilary Conroy, eds. *Japan Examined: Perspectives on Modern Japanese History.* Honolulu: University of Hawaii Press, 1983.
Wright, Robert. *A World Mission: Canadian Protestantism and the Quest for a New International Order, 1918–1939.* Montreal: McGill-Queen's University Press, 1992.
Yamamoto, Hideteru. *Nippon Kirisuto Kyokai Shi.* Tokyo: Nippon Kirisuto Kyokai Jimusho, 1929.
Yamamoto, Taijiro, and Muto Yoichi, comps. *Uchimura Kanzo Eibun Shosaku Zenshu.* Tokyo: Kyobunkan, 1971–72. 7 vols. *Vol. 1: How I Became a Christian: Out of My Diary. Vol. 3: Alone with God and Me. Vol. 4: The Japan Christian Intelligencer.*
Yamanashi Eiwa Gakuin Shi Hensan Iinkai. *Yamanashi Eiwa Gakuin Hachijunen Shi.* Kofu: Yamanashi Eiwa Gakuin, 1969.
Yamazumi, Masami. *Nihon Kyoiku Shoshi: Kin: Gendai.* Tokyo: Iwanani Shoten, 1987.
Yoshino, Sakuzo. *Chugoku: Chosenron.* Matsuo Takayoshi, ed. Tokyo: Heibonsha, 1970.
Yui, Masatomi, ed. *Taisho Demokurashi.* Tokyo, 1957.

ARTICLES, DISSERTATIONS, AND MAGAZINES

Akisada, Yoshikazu. "1934 Zengo no Haisho Undo." *KSMK,* 39.3 (1991), 50–71.
Angus, Henry F. "Responsibility for Peace and War in the Pacific." *Canada Papers, Yosemite Conference 1936.* Toronto: CIIA, 1936.
Axling, William. "Japan's Christians Unite." *Christian Century,* 25 June 1941, 826–27.
Baldwin, Frank. "Missionaries and the March First Movement: Can Moral Man Be Neutral?" In Andrew C. Nahm, ed. *Korea under Japanese Colonial Rule: Studies of the Policy and Techniques of Japanese Colonialism.* Kalamazoo: Center for Korean Studies, Western Michigan University, 1973. 185–219.
Ballhatchet, Kenneth, and Helen Ballhatchet. "Asia." In John McManners, ed. *The Oxford Illustrated History of Christianity.* Oxford: Oxford University Press,

1992. 488–518.
Ballhatchet, Helen. "The Religion of the West versus the Science of the West: The Evolution Controversy in Late Nineteenth Century Japan." In John Breen and Mark Williams, eds. *Japan and Christianity: Impacts and Responses.* Basingstoke: Macmillan Press, 1996. 107–21.
Bamba, Nobuya. "Nika Kanke no Gendai Teki Igi." In *Kanada Kenkyu Nenpyo—Nika Gakujitsu Kaigi Tokushu.* Tokyo: Nihon Kanada Gakkai, 1981.
Bates, C. J. L. "The One Million Souls Campaign." *JCQ* (January 1929), 59–68.
Best, Antony. "Sir Robert Craigie as Ambassador to Japan, 1937-1941." In Ian Nish, ed. *Britain and Japan: Biographical Portraits.* London: Japan Library, 1994. 238–51.
―――. "'Straws in the Wind': Britain and the February 1941 War-Scare in East Asia." *Diplomacy and Statecraft,* 5. 3 (November 1994), 642–65.
Brebner, J. Bartlet. "Canada, the Anglo-Japanese Alliance and the Washington Conference." *Political Science Quarterly,* 50.1 (1935).
Brouwer, Ruth Compton. "Beyond 'Women's Work for Women': Dr. Florence Murray and the Practice and Teaching of Western Medicine in Korea, 1921–1950." Unpublished article in the possession of the author.
―――."Home Lessons, Foreign Tests: The Background and First Missionary Term of Florence Murray, Maritime Doctor in Korea." *Journal of the CHA,* new series, 6 (1995), 103–28.
Dohi, Akio. "Christianity and Politics in the Taisho Period of Democracy." *Japanese Religions,* 7.3 (July 1972), 42–68.
―――. "1930 Nendai no Purotesutanto Kirisutokyokai (Part 1)." *KSMK,* 25.12 (1976), 187–217.
Duus, Peter. "Yoshino Sakuzo: The Christian as Political Critic." *Journal of Japanese Studies,* 4.2 (summer 1978), 301–26.
Eayrs, James. "The Atlantic Conference and Its Charter: A Canadian's Reflections." In Douglas Buckley and David R. Facey-Crowther, eds. *The Atlantic Charter.* New York: St. Martin's Press, 1994. 151–71.
Ebina, Danjo. "The Distinctive Message of Christianity for the Present Situation." *JCQ* (spring 1981), 76–80.
Foote, J. A. "Evangelistic Work Among Koreans in Japan." *JCQ* (spring 1981), 113–18.
Fry, Michael G. "The Development of Canada's Relations with Japan, 1919–1947." In Keith A. J. Hay, ed. *Canadian Perspectives on Economic Relations with Japan.* Montreal: The Institute for Research on Public Policy, 1980.
―――. "Canada and the Occupation of Japan: The MacArthur-Norman Years." In Thomas W. Burkman, ed. *The Occupation of Japan: The International Context: Proceedings of the Fifth Symposium Sponsored by the MacArthur Memorial.* Norfolk, VA: Old Dominion University, 1984.
Fisher, Royal H. "Introducing the Officers of the Church of Christ in Japan." *JCQ,* 16.4 (October 1941), 314–21.
Fujita, Wakao. "Yanaihara Tadao: Disciple of Uchimura Kanzo and Nitobe Inazo." In Bamba Nobuya and John F. Howes, eds. *Pacifism in Japan: The Christian and Socialist Tradition.* Vancouver: University British Columbia Press, 1978. 198–219.

Fukada, Robert M. "C. A. Rogan to H. W. Maiyasu: Kagawa Toyohiko o Meguru Senkyoshitachi." *KSMK,* 32.3(1984), 129–45.
Gagan, Rosemary B. "Two Sexes Warring in the Bosom of a Single Mission Station: Feminism in the Canadian Methodist Japan Mission, 1881–1895." Unpublished thirty-one-page typescript in the author's possession.
Grierson, Robert. "Episodes on a Long, Long Trial." Ninety-one page typescript in the author's possession.
Hara, Kishi. "Kyokuto Roshia ni Okeru Chosen Dokuritsu Undo to Nihon." *San Sen Ri* 17 (Tokushu San Ichi Undo Rokyu Shunen) (1979), 47–53.
Hennigar, E. C. "Abolition of Licensed Prostitution." *JCQ* (April 1929), 174–76.
———. "Some Suggestions for Temperance Work." *JCQ* (April 1934), 168–73.
Hiyane, Antei. "National Spirit and the Christian Faith." *JCQ,* 15.1 (January 1940), 42–49.
Holtom, D. C. "Modern Shinto as a State Religion." In *The Japan Mission Year Book 1930.* Tokyo: Kyobunkan, 1930. 38–61.
Howes, John F. "Uchimura Kanzo: The Bible and War." In Bamba Nobuya and John F. Howes, eds. *Pacifism in Japan: The Christian and Socialist Tradition.* Vancouver: University of British Columbia Press, 1978. 191–222.
Hutchinson, William R. "Modernism and Missions: The Liberal Search for an Exportable Christianity, 1875–1935." In John K. Fairbank, ed. *The Missionary Enterprise in China and America.* Cambridge: Harvard University Press, 1974. 110–31.
Ion, A. Hamish. "Canada and the Occupation of Japan." In Ian Nish, ed. *The British Commonwealth and the Occupation of Japan.* London: ICERD, 1983. 44–68.
———. "Mountain High and Valley Low: Walter Weston (1861-1940) and Japan." In Sir Hugh Cortazzi and Gordon Daniels, eds. *Britain and Japan 1859–1991: Themes and Personalities.* London: Routledge, 1991. 94–106.
Johnson, E. H. "The Manchurian Church in Crisis." *PR,* 66.4 (August 1941), 227–30.
Johnson, Gregory A. "Canada and the Far East during the 1930s." In John Schultz and Miwa Kimitada, eds. *Canada and Japan in the Twentieth Century.* Toronto: Oxford University Press, 1991. 110–26.
Kagawa, Toyohiko. "The Kingdom of God Movement: Its Future Programme and Philosophy." *JCQ* (spring 1982), 81–88.
Kasahara, Yoshimitsu. "Nihon Kirisutokyodan Seiritsu no Mondai: Shukyo Tosei ni tai suru Junno to Teiko." In Doshisha Daigaku Jinbun Kagaku Kenkyu Hen. *Senjika Teiko no Kenkyu: Kirisutokyosha, Jiyushugisha no Baii.* 2 vols. Tokyo: Misuzu Shobo, 1978. Vol. 1, 140–87.
———. "'Nipponteki Kirisutokyo' Hihan." *KSMK,* 22.3(1974), 114–39.
Kisaka, Junichiro. "The 1930s: A Logical Outcome of Meiji Policy." In Harry Wray and Hilary Conroy, eds. *Japan Examined: Perspectives on Modern Japanese History.* Honolulu: University of Hawaii Press, 1983, 241–51.
Kitaoka, Shinichi. "Diplomacy and the Military in Showa Japan." In Carol Gluck and Stephen R. Graubard, eds. *Showa: The Japan of Hirohito.* New York: W. W. Norton, 1992. 155–76.
———. "Nitobe Inazo ni Okeru Teikokushugi to Kokuseishugi." In *Iwanami Koza Kindai Nihon to Shokumichi, 4: Togo to Shihai no Ronri.* Tokyo:

Iwanami Shoten, 1993. 179–203.

Knowles, Norman. "A Selective Dependence: Vancouver's Japanese Community and Anglican Missions, 1903–42." Unpublished paper given at the Canadian Historical Association Conference, Calgary, June 1994.

Kudo, Hiroshi. "Senjika no *Kirisutokyo Sekai* o Yomu—1936 Nen kara 1941 made no, Tennosei Oyobi Senso Kanren Kiji." *KSMK,* 42.7 (1993), 25–55.

Macdonald, Caroline. "The Twentieth Century Christ," *JCQ* (April 1929), 103–07.

MacKenzie, N. A. M. "Canada and the Changing Balance of Power in the Pacific." *Canada Papers, Yosemite Conference 1936.* Toronto, CIIA, 1936.

Mason, Allan. "Canada and the Manchurian Crisis." In Robert Bothwell and Norman Hillmer, eds. *The In-Between Time: Canadian External Policy in the 1930's.* Toronto: Copp Clark, 1975.

———."Canadian-Japanese Relations, 1930–1941." University of Toronto Research Paper, 1973.

Matsuo, Takayoshi. "Nihon Kumiai Kirisutokyokai no Chosen Dendo." *Shiso* (July 1968), 949–65.

————————————. "Yoshino Sakuzo to Chosen: San Ichi Undo no Chushin ni." In Yui Masatomi, ed. *Taisho Demokurashi.* Tokyo: 1957, 243–64.

Matsuzawa, Hiroaki. "Kirisutokyo to Chishikijin." In *Iwanami Koza Nihon Rekishi, 16, kindai 3.* Tokyo: Iwanami Shoten, 1976. 182–320.

Mayer, Paul S. "Church Union and its Possible Implications for the Missionary." *JCQ,* 16.3 (July 1941), 215–23.

Menzies, A. R. "Canadian Views of United States Policy toward Japan, 1945–1952." In A. Hamish Ion and Barry D. Hunt, eds. *War and Diplomacy across the Pacific, 1919–1952.* Waterloo: Wilfrid Laurier University Press, 1988. 155–72.

"Minzoku to Kaikyu to Senso." In Yoshino Sakuzo. *Chugoku: Chosenron.* Matsuo Takayoshi, ed. Tokyo: Heibonsha, 1970. 333–47.

Mitchell, Peter M. "The Missionary Connection." In Paul M. Evans and B. Michael Frolic, eds. *Canada and the People's Republic of China 1949–1970.* Toronto: University of Toronto Press, 1991. 17–40.

Miwa, Kimitada. "E. H. Norman Revisited." In John Schultz and Miwa Kimitada, eds. *Canada and Japan in the Twentieth Century.* Toronto: Oxford University Press, 1991. 48–58.

Mortimore, Doretha E. "Dr. Frank W. Schofield and the Korean National Consciousness." In C. I. Eugene Kim and Doretha E. Mortimore, eds. *Korea's Response to Japan: The Colonial Period 1910–1945.* Kalamazoo: Center for Korean Studies, Western Michigan University, 1977.

Motoi, Takamichi. "Nikka Jihen Shita no Purotesutanto Kyokai." *KSMK* 9.4 (1965), 16–44.

Murakami, Katsuhiko. "Yanaihara Tadao ni Okeru Shokuminron to Shokumin Seisaku." *Iwanami Koza, Kindai Nihon to Shokuminchi, Vol. 4: Togo to Shihai no Ronri.* Tokyo: Iwanami Shoten, 1993. 205–37.

"New Buildings for Three Women's Colleges." *JCQ,* 9 (1934), 211–23.

Nitobe, I. "The Penetration of the Life and Thought of Japan by Christianity." *JCQ* (spring 1981), 68–75.

Norman, D. "An Institute School of Rural Evangelism." *JCQ* (April 1929), 147–51.

Notehelfer, F. "Ebina Danjo: A Christian Samurai of the Meiji Period." *Papers on*

Japan. Vol. 2, Cambridge, 1963.
Oe, John Mitsuo. "Church and State in Japan, 1940–1945." *Anglican and Episcopal History,* 59.2 (June 1990), 202–23.

———. "The Conflict of Church Views in Japan during Wartime 1940–1945: The Church Unification Problem of the Anglican Church in Japan (The Nippon Sei Ko Kwai)." *Anglican and Episcopal History,* 58.4 (December 1989), 448–97.

Oshiro, George. "The End: 1929-1933." In John F. Howes, ed. *Nitobe Inazo: Japan's Bridge across the Pacific.* Boulder: Westview Press, 1995, 253–78.

Ota, Yuzo. "Kagawa Toyohiko: A Pacifist." In Bamba Nobuya, and John F. Howes, eds. *Pacifism in Japan: The Christian and Socialist Tradition.* Vancouver: University of British Columbia Press, 1978. 169–97.

Otsuka, Noyuri. "Yasui Tetsu: Joshi Koto Kyoiku no Kaitakusha." in Kirisutokyo Bunka Gakkai Hen. *Purotesutanto Jinbutsu Shi: Kindai Nihon no Bunka Keisei.* Tokyo: Yorudansha, 1990.

Peattie, Mark R. "Japanese Attitudes Toward Colonialism, 1895–1945." In Ramon H. Myers and Mark R. Peattie, eds. *The Japanese Colonial Empire, 1895–1945.* Princeton: Princeton University Press, 1984. 80–127.

Palmer, Spencer J. "Korean Christians and the Shinto Shrine Issue." In C. I. Eugene Kim and Doretha E. Mortimore, eds. Korea's Response to Japan: The Colonial Period 1910–1945. Kalamazoo: Center for Korean Studies, Western Michigan University, 1977. 139–161.

Pickersgill, J. W. "International Machinery for the Maintenance of Peace in the Pacific Area." *Canada Papers, Yosemite Conference 1936.* Toronto: CIIA, 1936.

Powles, Cyril H. "Abe Isoo and the Role of Christians in the Founding of the Japanese Socialist Movement, 1895–1905." *Papers on Japan,* Vol. 1. Cambridge: 1961. 89–109.

———. "Abe Isoo: The Utility Man." In Bamba Nobuya and John F. Howes, eds. *Pacifism in Japan: The Christian and Socialist Tradition.* Vancouver: University of British Columbia Press, 1978. 142–67.

———. "The Development of Japanese-Canadian Relations in the Age of Missionary Activity, 1873–1930." *Kanada Kenkyu Nenpo,* 2 (1980), 146–65.

Prang, Margaret. "Caroline Macdonald and Prison Work in Japan." Working Paper Series 51, University of Toronto-York University Joint Centre for Asia Pacific Studies, 1988.

Price, P. G. "A Report of Mr. Kagawa's Evangelistic Campaign." *JCQ* (April 1929), 130–37.

Rice, Eber H. "Sir Herbert Marler and the Canadian Legation in Tokyo." In John Schultz and Miwa Kimitada, eds. *Canada and Japan in the Twentieth Century.* Toronto: Oxford University Press, 1991. 75–84.

Rideout, Katherine. "A Woman of Mission: The Religious and Cultural Odyssey of Agnes Wintemute Coates." *Canadian Historical Review,* 71.2 (June 1990), 204–44.

Sasaki Toshiji, "Nikka Jihenka no Purotesutanto Kyokai." *KSMK,* 9.4 (1965), 16–44.

Sawa, Masahiko. "Kankoku Kyokai to Minzoku Shugi." *Shin Gaku,* 34–35 (1973), 1–59.

Schwantes, Robert S. "Christianity versus Science: A Conflict of Ideas in Meiji

Japan."*Far Eastern Quarterly,* 12 (1952–53), 123–32.
Shigeru, Yoshiki. "Nippon Kirisuto Dendokaisha no dokuritsu to Ebina Danjo." KSMK, 24.3 (1976), 83–132.
———. "1930 Nendai no Kirisutokyo Janarizumu *Kirisutokyo Sekai* no Baii." KSMK, 25.12 (1976), 47–82.
Shimada, Keiichiro. "1930 Nendai e no Michi: Kagawa Toyohiko no Baii." *KSMK,* 25.12 (1976), 20–46.
Shin, Paul Hobom. "The Korean Colony in Chientao: A Study of Japanese Imperialism and Militant Korean Nationalism, 1905–1932." Unpublished PhD diss. University of Washington, 1980.
Soward, H. "Canada and the Far Eastern Crisis." Paper presented to the Institute of Pacific Relations Conference, Banff, 1935.
Squires, Graham. "Yamaji Aizan's 'Essays on the History of the Modern Japanese Church'—An Introduction andTranslation." Unpublished PhD diss. University of Newcastle, New South Wales, Australia, 1995.
Stone, A. R. "Difficulties in Christian Rural Permeation (The Disillusions of a Tamed Ruralist)." *JCQ* (April 1934), 14–21.
Storry, Richard. "The Road to War: 1931–1945." In Arthur E. Tiedemann, ed. *An Introduction to Japanese Civilization.* New York: Columbia University Press, 1974. 248–76.
Takashima, Yuichiro. "Kanada Mesijisuto Kyokai no Nihon Senkyo Hoshin no Keisei—C. S. Ebi no Katsudo o te ga kari to shite." *KSMK,* 40.3 (1992), 100–35.
Takenaka, Masao. "Natanaeru no Shinko: Ekyumenikuru Undo ni Okuru Kozaki Hiromichi." *KSMK,* 32.3 (1984). 1–36.
Tanaka, Shiitchi. "Nitobe Inazo to Chosen." *San Sen Ri,* 34 (1983). 88–97.
Taylor, K. W. "The Far East." In Violet Anderson. *World Currents and Canada's Course.* Toronto: T. Nelson, 1937. 20–48.
Totten, George O., III. "Japan's Political Parties in Democracy, Fascism, and War." In Harry Wray and Hilary Conroy, eds. *Japan Examined: Perspectives on Modern Japanese History.* Honolulu: University of Hawaii Press, 1983. 258–68.
Waller, J. G. "Our Canadian Mission in Japan." Toronto: Joint Committee on Summer Schools and Institutes of the Church of England in Canada, 1930.
Wada, Yoichi. "Nippon. Katoriku Sanjunendai Zenhan no Kuno." *KSMK,* 25.12 (1976), 1–19.
———. "Sen Kyu Hyaku Sanju Nananen Natsu no Doshisha Chaperu Rojo Jiken." *KSMK,* 8.4 (1964), 99–113.
Wi, Jo Kang. "Religion and Politics under Japanese Rule." In C. I. Eugene Kim and Doretha E. Mortimore, eds. *Korea's Response to Japan: The Colonial Period 1910–1945.* Kalamazoo: Center for Korean Studies, Western Michigan University, 1977. 103–38.
Wilson, Sandra. "The Manchurian Crisis and Moderate Japanese Intellectuals: The Japan Council of the Institute of Pacific Relations." *Modern Asian Studies,* 26.3 (1992), 507–44.
Wright, Robert A. "The Canadian Protestant Tradition 1914–1945." In George A. Rawlyk, ed. *The Canadian Protestant Experience 1760–1990.* Montreal: McGill-Queen's University Press, 1990. 139–97.
Yamaji, Aizan. "Gendai Nihon Kyokai Shiron." *Gendai Nihon Bungaku Taikei 6:*

Kitamura Tohoku, Yamaji Aizan Shu. Tokyo: Tsukiji Shobo, 1970. 223–71.
Yamamoto, Yukinori. "Yasui Sokken no [Bemmo] to Meiji Shonen no Kirisutokyokai." *KSMK,* 32.3 (1984), 68–128.
Yoo, Young-sik. "The Impact of Canadian Missionaries in Korea: A Historical Survey of Early Canadian Mission Work, 1888–1898." Unpublished PhD diss. Centre for the Study of Religion, University of Toronto, 1996.
Yoshino, Sakuzo. "Demokurashi to Kirisutokyo." In Takeda Kyoko, ed. *Gendai Nihon Shiso Taikei, 6: Kirisutokyo.* Tokyo: Chikuma Shobo, 1975. 236–41.

Index

Abe, Isoo, 191
Abe, Yoshimune, Bishop, 230, 234, 238, 241, 253, 256, 258, 261–264, 268–271, 271–273, 276–277, 281, 290, 297–300, 304, 316–317, 337, 341
Ainsworth, Bishop, 128
Aiseikan, 39–41, 326
Akazawa, Bishop Motozo, 114
Akigawa, Shunko, 115
Albert Hall incident (1937), 245, 255, 266
Albright, Leland, 224–226, 228–236, 241, 246, 260–261, 275–278, 340
All Japan Christian Cooperative Conference, 18, 260
Allen, Annie, 26, 39–41, 326
Amaterasu Omikami, 82
Amemiya, Keisaku, 124–125
American Church mission, 51, 142, 151
American "Laymen's Mission," 21, 27
American Presbyterians, in Korea, 28, 94–96, 99, 112, 126, 159, 294, 319
Anada, Shigeru, 188, 190, 192
Anglican Church of Canada, missionaries, 1; *see* Canadian Anglicans
Anglo-Japanese, Alliance, 58; tensions, 139, 331–332
Anne of Green Gables, 3
Aoyama Gakuin, 25, 86, 127, 237, 269–270, 272–273, 277, 316, 338
Apostles' Creed, 264, 305, 308
Araki, Sadao, General, 121, 256
Archer, C. H., 102–104, 180–181, 291, 332
Archer, Mrs C. H., 185
Argall, Phyllis, 104, 106–107
Armstrong, A. E., 33, 64–65, 72–74, 96, 99, 159, 161, 303, 319, 322
Armstrong, Margaret, 314–315, 326

Arnup, Jesse, 38, 213, 215–216, 221, 229, 241–242, 275, 277, 281, 301
Around the World in Eighty Minutes, 191
Asahi Shimbun, 215
Ashio Copper Mine, pollution at, 13
Atlantic City, 298
Australia, 206, 288
Avison, O. R., 318–319
Axis-powers, 139
Axling, William, 241, 297, 336, 338–339
Azabu Middle School, 126, 301, 329

Baddeck, Cape Breton Island, 99
Bailey, Helen, 149–150
Baker, Bishop, 277–278
Ballhatchet, Kenneth and Helen, 10
Bamboo Curtain, 2
Band, Edward, 103, 110
Barsetshire, 201
Barth, Karl, 133
Bates, Charles, 19, 27, 36–37, 67, 74, 127, 129, 131–136, 140, 163, 190, 242, 256, 317–318, 326, 328–329
Bates, Searles, 222
Bemmo, 11
Berry, Arthur, 273
Bethune, Dr Norman, 5
Black, Donald, 65–66, 96–97, 160, 162–164, 174, 177, 223, 232
Blackmore, Isabella, 118, 126
Boer War, 218
Bonwick, Frances Evelyn, 163–164, 168
Bott, Edith, 312
Bott, G. E., 41–42, 312, 316, 323
Book of Common Prayer, 84
Bourns, Beulah, 173, 208–209, 313
Bowman, Nora, 147–150, 266
Britain, 2, 59–60, 63, 100, 102–104, 109, 139, 169, 231–237, 241, 245, 247, 250, 253, 260, 271, 275, 287–288, 303, 308, 311, 331–332

INDEX

British Anglican missionaries in Japan, 84–85, 142, 151, 186, 199, 226, 310. *See also* Church Missionary Society, Heaslett
Brouwer, Dr Ruth Compton, 174, 208
Bruce, G. F., 60, 65, 161–162, 164, 166, 168
Bruce, Robert Randolph, 90
Brunner, 133
Buddhism, 3, 11–12, 42, 82–84, 86, 138, 249, 258–259, 284, 298, 336; Korean, 28; Nicheren sect, 249
Burbridge, Wilfred Arnold, 96
Burdick, Alma M, 106–107
Burma Road, 139
Burns, Chalmers, 32
bushido, 12–13, 138

Canada, 1–7, 13, 78, 127, 133, 143, 160, 165, 179, 189–190, 192, 195, 200, 211, 226, 232, 235, 240, 243, 267, 272, 279–280, 298, 314, 318 340–341; Army, 192, 323; Department of External Affairs, 2, 275, 279–280, 301; diplomatic relations with Japan, 2, 5, 8–9, 139, 280, 301, 341
Canadian Academy, 25–26, 132, 142–146, 188, 191, 220, 312, 316, 327
Canadian Anglicans, missionaries in Japan, 1, 22, 26, 35, 47–52, 96, 142, 146–154, 195–202, 210, 265–271, 281–291, 296, 326–328, 337; missionary work in Honan, 196, 275; in Taiwan, 33, 75
Canadian Anglican Blind School (Gifu), 26, 147–148
Canadian Anglican Kindergarten Training School (Nagoya), 142, 146–151
Canadian Army Japanese Language School, 323
Canadian Institute of International Affairs, 3
Canadian Methodists, 22; missionaries in Japan, 22–25, 29, 39, 113, 143. *See also* United Church of Canada missionaries
Canadian Presbyterians, 1–2; missionaries, among Koreans in Japan, 4, 35, 53–56, 143, 155–156, 272, 291–294, 326–327; in Korea, 4, 27–31, 57–58; in Manchukuo, 4, 28, 30-31, 57, 68–72, 78, 171–72, 202–203, 210, 272, 292–293, 328, 334–335; in North Honan, 68; in Taiwan, 4, 31–34, 57, 74–80, 100–112, 164, 178–85, 272, 291–294, 334–335
Canterbury, Archbishop of (Cosmo Lang), 217, 244–245, 255
Cartmel, Martha, 113
Central China Religious Alliance, 304
Central Tabernacle Church, 39, 212, 280
Chamberlain, Basil Hall, 84
Chamberlain, Neville, 255
Chang, Abel, 171
Changkufeng Hill, 224
Chappell, A F, 146
Chappell, Constance, 126, 302, 323, 326
Chiang Kai-shek, 215, 225, 227–230, 246, 340–341
Chiang, Madam, 229
Chicago, 298
Chichibu, Prince, 180
Chientao (Kanto), 30–31, 59–62, 64–66, 324. *See also* Lungchingtsun
China, 7, 28, 30, 59–62, 64, 68–72, 85, 133–134, 143, 166, 192, 195–196, 200–201, 207, 210–211, 215–221, 231–237, 242–247, 252, 272–273, 275, 294, 300–301, 306, 316, 319, 321–323, 325, 327, 337, 340–341
Chinese Anglican Church, 254–256
Chinese Recorder, 252–253
Chi-oang, 77
Chondokyo, 28
Chosen Christian Church, 156
Chosen Christian College (now Yonsei University), 29, 72, 99
Chosen *jinja*, 93
Christian Century, 298
Christianity, 3, 5–6, 9–18, 20–21, 23, 27–28, 31–32, 34–37, 39, 42, 44, 46–48, 51, 58–59, 63, 73–74, 78–79, 83–85, 87–89, 93, 125, 132–133, 136–138, 142, 178, 182, 184–185, 188, 212–213, 233–235, 237, 239, 242–243, 247, 240–250, 252, 256–261, 267, 271, 298–300, 306–311, 321, 336–338, 341; and support of Japanese spirit and national endeavour during war,

305–306
Chungking, 231
Church Missionary Society (CMS), 199, 250–251
Church union, in Canada, 241, in Japan, 237–295
Clair, René, 191
Clench, Miss, 149
Clive, Sir Robert, 109
Coates, Harper H., 193, 238
Coates, Mrs. (Agnes Wintemute), 199, 312, 315
Cold War in East Asia, 2
Commission on Christian Education in Japan, 36–37
Communism, in China, 215; in Japan, 87, 193, 213, 246; Korean, 59–60, 63–65, 92, 331; Russian, 44
Confucianism, 20, 23, 28, 97–98, 232, 249
Cornwell Legh, Mary, 142
Courtice, Sybil, 117, 121, 221–222, 274, 279, 301–303, 313–314
Creighton, W. B., 67
Cunningham, Mary, 121

Dairen, 251
Daito, Chusaburo, 265
Dalhousie University, 29
Dannoura, 189
Department of Education, Japanese, 81, 83.
 See also Ministry of Education; Ontario, 25
Depression, The, 35–36, 39, 45, 47, 130, 160, 326
Diffendorfer, Dr., 277–278
Dixon, Canon, 154, 196–200, 285–286
Dohi, Akio, 19
Domei, 233
Doshisha University, iv; 90–91, 130, 135, 138, 140, 242, 329, 332
Do–wai, 77
Downs, Darley, 269
Drake, Katherine, 117

East Tokyo mission in Nippori ward, 26, 41–42, 47, 314–315
Eaton's, 189
Ebara, Soroku, 126, 329

Ebina, Danjo, 21, 238
Ebisawa, Akira, 20, 241–242, 274
Edinburgh Conference (1910), 10, 17; Continuation Committee of, 17
Ehwa College for Women (Seoul), 170
Eisenstein, 193
Elizabeth, Queen, 185
Elwin, W. H., 186
Empress of Asia, 135
Empress of Russia, 192
emperor system. *See tennosei*
Endicott, James, 33
England, 138, 143
English Presbyterians, missionaries in south Taiwan, 31–32, 79, 103, 110–111, 178, 199, 291
Eunjin school, 161
Evangelical Church of North America mission, 118

Farmer Gospel Schools, 18, 44
Farmers Institute, 43
Federal Council of Churches and Missions in Korea, 53
Finnish-Soviet War, 229
1 March 1919 independence demonstrations, 7, 30, 58, 329
Fleming, Peter, 206
Foerstel, Marie, 148–149
Foote, J.A., 54
France, 138, 226, 231
Fraser, Edward James Oxley, 62–64, 73, 161–169, 208–209, 216, 313, 329
Free Methodists, 36
Fujimori, 150
Fujita, Shizuo, 114
Fujita, Wakao, 16, 246
Fukui, 41, 54, 188–190, 281
Fukuin Shimpo, 179, 242, 244, 247, 257–258, 305
Fulton, Austin, 70–71

Gale, James Scarth, 330
Gandhi, Mahatma, 36, 328
Gauld, William, 32
Gagan, Dr Rosemary, 22, 26
Germany, 65, 138–139, 164, 191, 253, 293
Gloucester, Duke of, 144

INDEX 421

Goforth, Johnathan, 57, 68–72, 206, 325
Goforth, Rosalind, 68–69, 170, 206
Gonoi, Takashi, 239
Gould, Canon, 50, 96, 198
Govenlock, Isobel, 121, 141
Gow, Dr. Ian M, iv
Grantly, Archdeacon, 201
Great Kanto earthquake, 41, 128, 151
Greater East Asia Co-Prosperity Sphere, 274
Greenback, Katherine, 123–124, 141
Grew, Joseph, Ambassador, 270
Grierson, Dr. Robert, 61, 74, 174–175
Gushue-Taylor, Dr. G., 79, 174, 182–185, 335
Gripsholm, 314

Hall, Sherwood, 335
Hamamatsu, 41
Hamheung, 28, 63, 153, 157–162, 166, 169–171, 174–178, 203–205, 207–208, 313–314, 329, 331; Boy's School, 63
Hamilton, F., 266
Hamilton, Gertrude, 114–116, 118–119, 124, 285
Hamilton, Heber J., Bishop, 48–52, 143, 286, 311, 327
Hankyu Company, 128
Happy Mount Leprosy Colony, 79, 157, 182–185, 335
Harbin, 62
Heaslett, Samuel, Bishop, 50, 245, 254, 266, 271, 286
Hennigar, E C, 43–44, 213–214, 221–222, 226, 234
Henty, A. M., 151
Hermanson, Hildur K., 106–107
Higuchi, 150
Hikawa Maru, 154
Hilburn, S. M., 134
Hiranuma, cabinet, 257–258
Hitler, 224
Hiyane, Antei, 248–249, 270
Hoiryung, 28, 163, 169–170, 203–204, 206
Hokkaido, diocese of, 283
Holiness Church, 36, 38, 47, 150, 259, 265, 268, 314, 330
Holmes, C P, 41–42, 187, 189–190, 238
Holmes, John, iv, 187–192

Holtom, D.C., 87
Honaman, Dr William F., iv
Honda, Yoichi, 256
Hong Kong, 297
Hongo Church (Tokyo), 39, Chosen Mondai Kenkyukai at, 28
Hori, Professor, 137–138, 140, 256
Howes, Professor John, iv
Hunter, Dr. Janet, 11

Ichikawa, Yayoi, 314–315
Ichikawa, Sadanji, 193
Ichinomiya, 150
Iglehart, Charles W., 241, 264, 269, 316, 336
Imada, Megumi, 130
Imai, Judo, 24, 85, 248, 269, 338
Imperial Ancestors, 137
Imperial Rescript on Education (1890), 11–12, 108, 119, 138, 242
Institute of Pacific Relations, 4
International Christian University, iv
International Labour Conference (Geneva), 53
International Review of Missions, 294
International Missionary Conference, 18
Irish Presbyterian mission (Manchuria), 68, 70, 82, 97–98, 171, 294
Ise shrine, 323
Ishiwara, Ken, 301
Italy, government, 256
Ito, Dr "Canada," 153, 155

Japan, 1–4, 6, 9–11, 13, 17, 20, 22–28, 35–56, 59, 67, 81–92 112–156, 161, 164–186, 208–292, 296–341; Army, 71, 190, 208, 216, 339; colonial policies in Korea, 15, 58–59, 92–100, 166–170, 303; colonial policies in Taiwan, 77–78, 100–112, 166, 178–185; shrine question in, 81–92
Japan Advertiser, 216
Japan Baptist Church, 259, 265, 320
Japan Brethren, 265
Japanese Christian movement, 1–2, 6, 9, 11–12, 14–17, 19–20, 35–39, 58, 67, 81–92, 113–156, 198, 210–292, 296–341; early development of,

10–22; missionary work in Korea, 14–16, 252–255, 294; missionary work in Manchuria, 16, 252–254, 262; missionary work in South Seas, 15–16; missionary work in Taiwan, 14, 178, 252
Japan Christian Quarterly, 19, 43–44, 248–250, 270, 298, 302
Japanese culture, needed Christianity to perfect it, 24
Japan Federation of Churches, 17
Japan Methodist Church, 9, 22, 37, 40–41, 47, 113–146, 230, 241–242, 246, 248, 251–253, 253, 259–265, 268, 273–276, 280, 303, 336–338
Japan Temperance League, 43
Jerusalem Conference (1928), 17, 18–19
Jochi University (Sophia University), 87, 239
Johnson, E. H., 173
Johnson, Mrs E. H., 173, 203
Johnson, Dr. Gregory A., 3
Jones, Stanley, 36

Kabuki-za, 193
Kagawa Toyohiko, 14–15, 18, 35–38, 46–48, 50–51, 55, 73, 132, 136, 221, 241–243, 258, 260, 266, 296–298, 317, 320–322, 328, 336; in Canada, 38
Kanazaki, Kiichi, 130
Kanazawa, 41, 193, 195, 230, 264, 281
Kangwha, Treaty of (1876), 14
Kanri Kyokai, 262
Karafuto, 36
Karuizawa, 186–187, 190–191, 206, 222, 314, 335
Kashiwagi, Gien, 20
Kato, Hiroyuki, 248
Kato, Chotaro, 110
Keelung incident, 180, 331
Kelham, 310
Kelly, Herbert, 310
Kellogg Pact, 20
Kim Hyo–Soon, 208
Kim Iktoo, 55

Kim Kwan sik, 63, 160
King Edward VIII, 99–100
King George V, 85, 144
Kingdom of God Movement, 10, 18–19, 35, 37–39, 46–48, 241–242, 245, 265, 328; in Canada, 38
Kirisutokyo Kyoiku Domei Kai, 125
Kirisutokyo no Nihon-teki Tenkai, 248, 270
Kirisutokyo Sekai, 21, 244, 258
Kirisutokyo Shuho, 254–256, 271
Kisaka, Junichiro, 239
Kiyome Kyokai, 306
Knechtel, Earl, 160–161
Koa, David, 179
Kobayashi Ichizo, 128
Kobayashi, Yataro, 39, 41
Kobe, 54, 128, 130, 135, 140, 143–145, 155, 186, 191, 205, 317; diocese of, 282, 308, 310–311
kodo Kirisutokyo, 248, 337
Kofu, 4, 113, 123–26, 264, 333
Kofu Methodist Church, 125
kokutai, 16
Kokutai no Hongi, 136
Konoe, Fujimaro, 215; cabinet, 230, 254, 258
Korea, 1–3, 5–8, 10, 14, 17–18, 27–31, 36, 53–74, 81–82, 85, 92–100, 144, 157–178, 203–210, 231–232, 237, 252, 254–256, 262, 271–272, 291–295, 300–303, 314, 318–320, 322–323, 324–326, 329–331, 334; annexation of (1910), 15; Japanese colonial authorities in, 14, 29, 57–74; shrine question in, 7, 81–82, 92–100, 111
Korean Anglican Church, 254–55, 271
Korean Christians, 7–8, 14–15, 27–31, 53–74, 92–100, 111, 157–178, 318, 325, 329–331; in Japan, 53–56, 143, 155–156, 294; Presbyterians, 180
Kozaki, Hiromichi, 21
Kozaki, Michio, 21–22, 253, 274, 297, 299–300, 318, 324
Kuechlich, Gertrud, 118
Kugiyama, Tokio, Bishop, 246–247, 251–253, 256
Kumiai Kyokai (Congregationalist), 9, 20–21, 130, 241, 244, 257, 259–260, 265; missionary work in Korea,

15–16
Kunmoin. *See* Canadian Anglican Blind School (Gifu)
Kuranaga, Takashi, 325
Kwansei Gakuin, 19, 25, 29, 60, 67, 74, 91, 111, 127–141, 144–145, 162, 192, 195, 214, 217, 223, 256, 280, 301, 325, 328–329, 332, 338
Kwantung army, 60–61, 68
Kyoto, 54, 130, 133, 140, 329; diocese of 283
Kyoto Imperial University, 130
Kyushu, diocese of, 283

Lambeth Quadrilateral, 283
Lawrence, T. E., 195
Lea, Arthur, Bishop, 26
League of Nations, 20, 62, 64–65, 68, 210
Lehman, Lois, 118
leper work, 142, 151, 157, 182–185
Licensed Agencies for Relief in Asia (LARA), 323
Life, 321
Liggins, John, 51
Lighthouse Society (Jehovah's Witnesses), 311
Livingstone, David, 32
Lindsey, Olivia, 121–22
Lower, Prof A. R., 3,
Lungchintsun, 28, 30, 34, 59–60, 62, 65–66, 157–160, 163–169, 174, 176, 203–205, 207–208, 223, 319, 324, 334
Luther, Martin, 253
Lutheran Church, 259
Lytton Commission, 64, 71

Macdonald, Caroline, 26, 53, 326
MacDonald, Donald A., 61–62, 65
Mackay, George Leslie, 2, 31–32, 75, 110, 171; daughters Bella and Mary, 179
Mackay, George W., 32–33, 75, 101, 103–105, 107–108, 166, 179–180, 182–183, 211, 329, 331
Mackay, Mrs Jean Ross, 105–106
Mackay Memorial Hospital, 33, 79–80, 157, 181–182, 335
Mackay Memorial Library, 179
MacMillan, Hugh, 180

Madras Conference (1938), 17
Maejima, Kiyoshi, 255
Manchuria (Manchukuo), 1, 7, 16, 27, 30–33, 36, 56–57, 59, 61–72, 78, 81–82, 92, 95–98, 107–108, 155, 157, 160–168, 170–173, 202–203, 223, 230–232, 237, 239, 245, 251–53, 266, 291, 304, 318–319, 323–324, 329, 334–335, 341; Japanese missionary work in, 16, 36, 252–253, 306
Manchurian (Mukden) incident (1931), 1, 6, 16, 20–21, 57, 61–65, 70, 95, 123, 210, 239, 245
Maple Leaf Academy, 195, 200
Marco Polo Bridge incident (1937), 21–22, 136, 140, 237–238, 241–247, 253
Marler, Sir Herbert, 88–90, 187
Martin, Dr Stanley S., 174, 176, 207
Marxism, in Japan, 44, 136, 215; in Korea, 59. *See also* Communism
Matsui, P. Y., Bishop, 86, 253–254, 268, 283, 308, 311
Matsumoto, 41, 43, 48, 266
Matsumoto, Fumishi, 311
Matsuyama, Tsunejiro, 268
Matsuzawa Hiroaki, iv, 11
McCune, George S., 94–95, 111, 162, 330
McKenzie, Arthur P., 130–131, 136, 300–301, 323
McKenzie, William, 72
McLeod, Duncan, 292
McMillan, Dr. Kate, 175, 207
McRae, Duncan M., 64, 98–99, 206, 331
Meiji Constitution (1889), 10; and religious freedom, 5, 11, 257, 305, 336
Meiji Gakuin, 91, 246
Meiji Restoration (1868), 10–11, 21, 81–82, 268, 336
Meiji Shrine, 85, 115
Methodist Church of Canada, 22. *See* Canadian Methodists
Methodist Episcopal North mission, in Japan, 25, 126–127, 278; in Korea, 167
Methodist Episcopal South, 296; mission in Japan, 25, 127–128, 332
Mickle, J. J., 130
Mid-Japan, diocese of, 35, 47–52, 142,

147–151, 200–201, 265–271, 281–291, 296, 311, 317, 326–27, 336. *See also* Canadian Anglicans
Ministry of Education, Japanese, 24, 83, 87, 114–116, 123, 129, 131, 148, 233, 242, 244, 257, 259, 261–263, 270, 273–274, 284, 305–306
Mino-Hide earthquake (1891), 26
Missionaries: *See* Canadian Anglicans, Canadian Presbyterians, Canadian Methodists, United Church of Canada and under individual denominations
Missionary Society of the Church [of England] in Canada, MSCC, 194–195. *See also* Canadian Anglicans
Missouri, USS, 4
Mitsui, 15
Mongol Church, 170
Mongolia, 224–226, 340
Montreal, 199, 323
Moon, Chairin, 322
Mori, Kenji, 146
Moss, Adelaide, 147
Motoi, Takamichi, 239
Motoda, Bishop J. S., 85
Mott, John R., 17–19
Mount Allison University, 126
Mount Fuji, 192
Mukden, 68, 71, 254, 293
Mukyokai (Non-Church Movement), 11, 241, 248
Murota Tomotsu, 120–121
Murray, Dr Florence, 153, 157, 161, 173–178, 203–209, 313, 322–323, 330, 335
Muto, Takeshi, 213
Myungsin school, 167

Nagano, 41, 44, 188, 192–194, 198, 201, 264, 281
Nagoya, 41, 54, 142, 146, 147–150, 155, 197, 201, 267, 286
Naide, Yasutaro, Bishop, 268, 283, 307–309
Nanking, 221–222, 340
Nashville, 128, 299
National Council of Churches (NCC), 6, 17–20, 35, 47, 51, 67, 155, 238, 241–242, 244–245, 250, 258–259, 261, 263, 268–270, 273, 336
National Diet, 43
Nazerene Church, 36
Neeshima, Jo, 329
Negishi, 41
Nevius Method, 28
New Life sanatorium (Obuse), 48, 142, 151–154, 199–201, 287–288, 326, 333
New Outlook, 65, 67
Newspaper evangelism, 43
Nihon Kirisuto Kyokai (Presbyterian), 9, 156, 178, 241, 244, 258–259, 261, 265, 272, 294, 304; missionary work in Manchuria, 16
Nihon Purotesanto Shi Kenkyukai, iv
Niigata, 195–196; prefecture, 200–201, 263
Nine-Power Treaty, 20
Nippon Kirisuchan Kyokai, 21
Nippon Kirisutokyodan (*kyodan*), 6, 22, 265, 272, 296, 304–311, 316–318, 321, 324, 337–339
Nippon Mesojisuto Jiho, 251–252, 271
Nippon Seikokai (NSKK), 9, 17–18, 22, 35, 48–52, 80, 84–86, 238–242, 244–245, 247–248, 253–256, 259–260, 265–273, 281–291, 296, 304–311, 317–318, 324, 327, 337–339; Provincial Office, iv
Nippon Seikyokai, 265, 306
Nippon Seishin, 138
Nipponteki Kirisutokyo, 237, 247–256, 269, 300, 307, 337–338
Nippori, 41
Nitobe Inazo, 12, 15, 20–21, 68, 126, 138, 210, 238, 329
Nojiri, Lake, 186–187, 260
Nomin Fukuin Gakko, 44,
Nomonhan, 218, 224–227
Nomura, Naokuni, Admiral, 234–235, 340
Norman, Dan, 44–46, 188, 192–194, 238
Norman, Egerton Herbert, 5, 194, 278
Norman, Mrs, Gwen R P, 193–195, 230
Norman, W. H. H. (Howard), 46, 192–195
Norris, Bishop, 254
North America, anti-Japanese feeling in, 7, 297–300
North Formosa presbytery, 178
North Hamkyung presbytery, 169
North Tokyo, diocese of, 283

INDEX

Nosse, Hidetoshi, 310–311
Notehelfer, Professor Fred, 12
Nova Scotia, 28, 99

Odawara, 243
Ogata, Kiyo, 125
Ogawa, Kiyozumi, 260
Okada, cabinet, 257
Okaya, 149–150
Okuma Shigenobu, 15
Omotokyo, 5, 239, 257
One Cent Society, 97
Ono, Zentaro, 264
Osaka, 54, 128, 130, 136, 140, 143–144, 155, 186, 268, 295; diocese of, 283, 308–309; gendarmerie, 136, 138, 257
Osaka Imperial University, 153
Ota, Yuzo, 243
Ottawa, 275, 280; river, 201
Outerbridge, H.W., 91–92, 128, 133, 135, 139, 215–217, 220, 222, 226–227, 235–244, 247, 263–264, 278, 280, 330, 337
Oxford Group Movement (Moral Re-Armament), 37, 46, 73, 132, 328

Pacific War, 1, 4–5, 7–8, 19, 28, 31 78, 125–126, 140, 156–157, 169, 178, 192, 195, 206, 239, 273, 305, 311, 324, 326, 333, 335, 340–341
pacifists, 12, 243–244, 338
Pak, Dr., 175
Palethorpe, Emma, 318
Palmer, Spencer J., 93
Pan-Anglican Conference at Lambeth (1907), 17
Parker, Kenneth, 143
Peace Police Law (1900), 83
Peace Preservation Law (1925), 239
Pearl Harbor, 4, 205
Peking, 254–256
Pepoan aborigines, 180
Perry, Commodore Matthew, 1, 3
Popular Rights Movement, 13
Powell, Miss, 151
Powles, Dr Cyril H., 13
Powles, P. S. C. (Percy), 49, 148, 151–152, 154, 195, 199–201, 266–268, 282, 284–285, 287–291, 310, 323, 325
Powles, Mrs., 195
Presbyterian Church in Canada, missionaries, 1–2. *See* Canadian Presbyterians
Presbyterians, Japanese, 42
Price, P. G., 37–38, 41–42, 46, 328
Prince Edward Island, 6, 205
prostitution, 43
Purity Society, 43
Pu Yi, Henry, 97, 107
P'yongyang, 28–29, 61, 63, 72, 94–96, 99, 162, 330; American school in, 145

Red Cross, British, 313
Reischauer, A. K., 126, 329
Reischauer, E. O., 126, 188
Religious Organizations Bill (1900), 83; (1929), 86
Religious Bodies Law (1939), 239, 256–258, 263, 268, 275
Reoch, Allan, 69, 293
Rhee, Syngman, 319
Riddell, Helen, 142
Residency Generalcy (Korea), 28
Rikkyo University, 91, 135, 239, 318; Neeza campus, iv
Rikugo Zasshi, 11
Riverside, California, 298
Robb, Alexander F., 63–64
Robertson, Minnie, 118
Robertson, Norman, 280, 301
Robinson, J. Cooper, 84
Roman Catholics, in Japan, 87–89, 239–240, 256, 284, 313, 318; missionaries, Dominican, 10; Franciscan, 10, Jesuits, 10; German Roman Catholics in Chientao, 59, 63
Roosevelt, President, 234, 340
Ross, A. R., 62
Rural Evangelistic Cooperation Conference, 19
Rusch, Paul, 317
Russia, 62, 216, 235; Orthodox Church in Japan, 316
Russo-Japanese War (1904–05), 12, 15, 82–83, 85, 216–217

Saeki, Yoshiro, Professor, 308, 338
St Luke's Hospital (Tokyo), 151, 153, 198, 317
St Nicholas cathedral (Tokyo), 315
Saito, Makoto, 58, 61
Saito, Soichi, 298
Saito, Takao, 230
Sakata, Paul R, iv
Salvation Army, 5, 211, 233, 237, 241, 245, 260–62, 304, 311, 338
Sandell, Ada, 175
Sasaki, Bishop Shinji, 50, 147, 150, 154, 199, 268–270, 281–284, 287–290, 296, 308–311, 326, 336, 338
Savary, Reg, 287
Schofield, Frank, 5, 7
Scott, William, 98–99, 159, 165–168, 208–209, 276, 303, 314, 319, 322–323, 329–331
Scottish Presbyterians (Manchuria), 82, 97–98, 172, 293
Seinenkai (YMCA), 20, 22, 34;
Seoul, 28, 30, 60, 169
Seven Pillars of Wisdom, 195
Seventh Day Adventists, 314
Severance Union Medical College, 29–30, 174, 319
Shamanism, in Korea, 28
Shanghai, 62, 143, 145, 306; American school in, 145; incident (1932), 39, 210
Shawville (Quebec), 201
Shichi Ichi Zappo, 10
Shikutani, Shigeru, 311
Shimizu, Fumio, 311
Shinkai, Eitaro, 124
Shinkai, Yuroku, 124
Shinkyo, 254
Shintaisei, 263
Shinto, 5, 16, 21, 28, 81–112, 138, 211, 232, 235, 239, 241, 258–259, 284, 305, 330, 338
Shizuoka, 41, 113 119–124, 127, 141, 263–264, 282, 335
Shizuoka Eiwa Jo Gakko, 23, 119–124, 126, 141, 313, 333
Shizuoka Methodist Church, 122
Shizuoka Shimpo, 122
Shrine question, 81–112; crucial issue for Japanese Christians, 5, 81–92, 232; in Korea, 7–8, 92–100, 332; in Taiwan, 100–112, 330–331
Sian incident, 215
Siberia, 28, 30
Simpson, Basil, Bishop, 283, 293
Singapore, 200
Sino-Japanese War (1894–95), 12, 83, 85; (1931–1945), 71, 201, 232, 257, 337
Skelton, O. D., 88
Slum work, in Kameido ward, Tokyo, 26
Snook, V. L., 94, 111, 162, 330
Socialism, Christian, 193; in Japan and Christianity, 13
Social Mass Party, 230
Sous les toits de Paris, 191
South Hamkyung, presbytery, 169; province, 167
South Manchurian Railway, 68
South Tokyo, diocese of, 50, 254, 271, 282, 311
Soviet Union, 139, 215, 224, 231, 300, 340
Spain, 194
Spanish Civil War, 193–194
Spencer, Victor, 49, 148–150, 197–199, 269, 282, 288, 310
Stalin, 224, 234
Staples, Melissa, 118
Start, Dr. Richard K., 151–154, 287, 326
Stone, A. R., 44–45
Stuart, John Leighton, 127
Student Volunteer Movement, 69
Sugai, Todomu, Bishop, 311
Sugamo prison, 311
Sugiyama, Motojiro (Genjiro), 13, 44, 258
Sumida river, 320
Sumire prison, 313
Sumiya, Mikio, iv, 13, 23
Sunday, Billy, 55
Sunday schools, 55
Sungjin, 28, 61, 74, 168–169, 174
Szepingkai, 69, 171–172, 202–203, 292, 324

Tagawa, Daichiro, 246, 249
Tainan Middle School, 103, 110
Taipeh (Taihoku) No. 2 Girls' School, 120
Taisho liberal democracy, 58
Taiwan, 1–3, 27–28, 31–34, 57, 74–82, 85, 100–112, 144, 157, 166, 174,

INDEX 427

178–185, 202–203, 206, 210–211, 235, 252, 272, 291–95, 304, 310, 329, 334; aborigines in and Christianity, 76–78, 180; shrine question, 10, 81–82, 100–112

Taiwanese Christians, 3, 18, 31–34, 57, 81–82, 100–112, 178–185, 210–211, 291–295, 304, 310, 329, 331, 334

Takahashi, Masao, iv

Takata, 148, 195, 200–201, 266–267, 291, 323

Tamsui, 34, 100–111, 202, 210, 333; Girl's School, 102–111; Middle School, 100–111, 331

Tanaka cabinet, 85–86

Tanaka Memorial, 65

Taoism; in Korea, 28

Taonan, 69

Tapson, A. M., 151

Tench, G. R., 145

tennosei, 5, 81, 84, 86, 138

Thomas, Mary, 232

Thunder Over Mexico, 193

Tientsin, 254

tokko keisatsu, 239, 245, 256

Tokyo, 24, 26, 34, 39–42, 47, 52, 82, 113–118, 122, 127, 135, 151, 155, 186, 188, 193, 196, 205, 224, 226, 243, 268, 304, 306, 311–312, 316, 333; diocese of, 283, 306–311

Tokyo First Higher Middle School, 11

Tokyo Imperial University, 16, 39

Tokyo Joshi Daigaku, (Tokyo Woman's Christian College), iv; 24, 125–126, 301, 323, 328, 333

Tokyo Seinenkai (YMCA), 11

Tomita, Mitsuro, 258, 274, 303, 304–306, 318, 320–322, 323

Toronto, 34; missionary authorities in, 7, 50–51, 128, 161, 168, 198, 210, 216, 277, 287, 292, 302–303, 322, 326

Toyama, 314–315; prefecture, 315

Toyo Eiwa Jo Gakko, 23–24, 40, 113–119, 126, 141, 302, 313, 333

Toyohashi, 149

Trinity College School (Port Hope), 143, 198

Trollope, Antony, 201

Tsuda College, 329

Tsuda, Umeko, 329

Tsukada, Osamu, 247

tuberculosis, in Japan, 151–154, 287–288; in Korea, 174

Tumen River, 57, 59

Turner, Dr., 145–146

26 February 1936 incident, 124

Uchimura Kanzo, 11–12, 16, 138, 241, 248

Ukeji, 41

ultranationalism, 212–213

Underwood, Horace, 99

Union Christian College (now Soonjun University), 29

United Church of Canada, 241; missionaries, 1–2, 18, 22, 35–48, 52–53, 55, 57–68, 72–75, 96, 112–146, 153, 157–178, 210–236, 261, 264, 268, 270, 272–291, 312–320, 325–341. *See also* Canadian Methodists, Canadian Presbyterians in Korea

United Nations Association, 319

United States of America, 1, 3, 20, 38, 127, 138–139, 143, 207, 227, 231–232, 234–235, 247, 270, 275, 278, 291, 293, 296–300, 316, 321, 340–341

University of Toronto, 25, 53, 143; Victoria College in, 143

Vancouver, 300

Vories, W. M., 129

Wakatsuki cabinet, 85–86

Waller, John, 49, 151, 198–200, 316–317

Waller, Mrs., 201

Waller, Wilfrid, 201–202

Walton, Murray, 186

Wang, Ching-wei, 231

Washington, 234–235, 340; Conference, 58

Watts, Horace, 195–197, 269–270, 282–285, 288

Watts, Mrs., 195–197

Watts, Ronald, 198

Webster, Senator Lorne, 144

Wesley, John, 253

Western powers, treaties between Japan and, 18
Weston, Walter, 186
Whiting, Melvin, 66–67, 131, 133, 145, 220
Wilkie, Douglas, 77, 179
Williams, C. M., 51
Willson, Eulalie H., 145
Windsor House School, 144–145
Wodehouse, Madeline, 196
Woman's Auxiliary (Canadian Anglican), 52, 146–51, 196–97, 282–83, 288
Women's Christian Temperance Union (WCTU), 18, 43
Woman's Missionary Society (WMS), Canadian Methodist, 22–26, 39, 113; United Church of Canada, 39–41, 113–126, 140, 146, 163, 167, 174, 176, 178, 238, 274, 279, 300–303, 312–314, 332–333
Women's Missionary Society (Western Division)of the Presbyterian Church in Canada (WMSWD), 53–54
Wonsan, 28, 159, 167; Beach, 61, 72, 206; Bible Training School in, 168; Lucy schools in, 167
Wood, John, 286
Woodsworth, H. F., 67, 130, 133, 192
Woodsworth, Captain K. C., 192
World's Student Christian Federation Conference (1907), 17
World Sunday School Association, 17
World War I, 10, 26, 33, 41, 85, 164, 187, 220, 231, 243–244, 313, 323, 337
World War II, 344. *See also* Pacific War
Wright, Dr Robert, 2, 67

Xavier, St Francis, 18

Yamagata Aritomo, 84; cabinet, 83, 85
Yamamoto Hideteru, 20
Yamanashi Eiwa Jo Gakko, 24, 113, 123–126, 141, 333
Yamato damashii, 13, 138
Yanagihara, Sadajiro, Bishop, 268, 283, 308
Yanaihara Tadao, 16, 67, 241, 248; interpretation of *kokutai*, 16, of *Nipponteki Kirisutokyo*, 248

Yashiro, J., Bishop, 268–269, 283, 308, 309–310
Yasui, Sokken, 11, 17
Yasui, Tetsu, 126
Yasukuni shrine, 82, 87
Yates N. P., 33, 75
Yenan, 301
Yenching University (Peking), 127
Yi court, 27-28
Yi, Tai Jun, 165–166
Yokohama, 22, 186, 315; Band, 20, 39; International School in, 145
York, Duke of, 100
Yoshino, Sakuzo, 14–15, 26, 28, 30–31, 67
Young, L L, 53
YMCA, 18, 53, 307; in Japan, 53; in Korea, 161. *See also* Tokyo Seinenkai
YWCA, 34, 117, 122, 126, 307
Yuasa, Hachiro, 90–91, 138, 140, 242, 332

Zenkoku Suiheisha, 13